Writings on International Economics

Writings on
International Economics

Jagdish Bhagwati

Edited by
V.N. Balasubramanyam

DELHI
OXFORD UNIVERSITY PRESS
CALCUTTA   CHENNAI   MUMBAI
1997

Oxford University Press, Walton Street, Oxford OX2 6DP

Oxford   New York
Athens   Auckland   Bangkok   Calcutta
Cape Town   Chennai   Dar es Salaam   Delhi
Florence   Hong Kong   Istanbul   Karachi
Kuala Lumpur   Madrid   Melbourne   Mexico City
Mumbai   Nairobi   Paris   Singapore
Taipei   Tokyo   Toronto
and associates in
Berlin   Ibadan

ISBN 0 19 563985 5

Typeset by Resodyn, New Delhi 110070
Printed in India at Pauls Press, New Delhi 110020
and published by Manzar Khan, Oxford University Press
YMCA Library Building, Jai Singh Road, New Delhi 110001

Contents

Acknowledgements

THE publishers wish to thank the following for permission to reprint articles included in this volume:

Pergamon Press/Elsevier Science Limited for 'Poverty and Public Policy', *World Development*, and 'Socialism and Indian Economic Policy', *World Development*, vol. 3, no. 4, 1957; UNCTAD for 'The Brain Drain, International Resource Flow Accounting, Compensation, Taxation and Related Policy Proposals'; American Economic Association for 'International Factor Mobility: Quid Pro Quo Foreign Investment', *American Economic Review*; Blackwell Publishers for 'Regionalism versus Multilateralism', *World Economy*, vol. 15, no. 5, September 1992, 'Splintering and Disembodiment of Services and Developing Nations', and 'Trade Liberalization and "Fair Trade" Demands: Addressing the Environmental and Labour Standards Issues'; *Financial Times* for 'President Clinton versus Prime Minister Peel: The Obsession with Reciprocity', 31 July 1995; Elseiver Science Limited for 'The Brain Drain, International Integration of Markets for Professionals and Unemployment, *Journal of Development Economics*, 1, 1974; University of Chicago Press for 'Domestic Distortions, Tariffs and the Theory of Optimum Subsidy', *Journal of Political Economy*, February 1963, 'Directly Unproductive Profit-seeking (DUP) Activities', *Journal of Political Economy*, vol. 90, no. 5, 1982, and 'Shifting Comparative Advantage, Protectionist Demands, and Policy Response', in Jagdish Bhagwati (ed.), *Import Competition and Policy Response*, 1982; Royal Economic Society for 'Protection, Real Wages and Real Incomes', *The Economic Journal*, 'Proofs of the Theorems on Comparative Advantage', *The Economic Journal*, March 1967, and 'Why are Services Cheaper in Poor Countries?', *The Economic Journal*, July 1984; Kluwer Academic Publishers for 'Religion as DUP Activity', *Public Choice*, vol. 48, no. 1, 1986; MIT Press for 'Women in Elections', *Studies in Electoral Politics in the Indian States*; Johns Hopkins University Press for 'Democracy and Development: New Thoughts on an Old Question', *Journal of Democracy*, vol. 6, no. 4, October 1995; *Foreign Affairs* for 'The Diminished Giant Syndrome: How Declinism Drives Trade Policy', *Foreign Affairs*; Scientific American Inc. for 'Free Trade and the Environment', *Scientific American*, vol. 269, no. 5, November 1993; Macmillan for 'Quantitative Restrictions and Quotas in International Trade', *International Encyclopaedia of Social Sciences*; World Bank for 'Trade in Services and Multilateral Trade Negotiations', *World Bank Economic Review*, vol. 1, no. 4, 1987; *Indian Economic Review* for 'International Factor Movements and National Advantage', *Indian Economic Review*; George Allen and Unwin for 'The Theory of Immiserizing Growth: Further Applications', Swoboda and Connoly (eds), *International Trade and Money*, London, 1973; American Enterprise Institute for 'Free Trade and Wages of the Unskilled: Is Marx Striking Again?', in Jagdish Bhagwati and Kosters (eds), *Trade and Wages*, Washington, 1994, and *New Republic* for 'Shock Treatment: Poland Jumps to the Market Economy', *New Republic*, 28 March 1994.

1

Introduction

V.N. Balasubramanyam

INDIAN economists are prolific. The establishment of development economics as a sub-discipline of economics in its own right owes much to their contribution. They have written on most aspects of development, including agriculture, poverty and income distribution, and demography. Several of them have written on trade and development issues too, but the name to conjure with in this sphere of development economics is that of Jagdish Bhagwati. His published output, which at the last count amounted to over two hundred articles and forty books, including twenty edited volumes, is still rising.

This vast output covers almost the entire spectrum of trade and development issues. Bhagwati's work has also opened up several new areas for investigation: the economics of brain drain, with which his name is entwined, is but one such example. Indeed, some of his contributions, though they retain the international dimension, range beyond the traditional contours of our discipline to encompass history, politics, and sociology. The trade and development issues he has grappled with over the years are intensely political, and also have sociological and historical dimensions. This should be of little surprise, for much of the theorizing and policy design in the area of trade and development have been conditioned by the reaction of developing countries to their colonial legacy, their suspicion of Western capitalism and its institutions, their belief that international trade and investment inevitably results in unequal exchange and serves to perpetuate their dependence on the developed countries.

We owe the rich literature on trade and development to this

multi-dimensional nature of the subject. Indeed, major intellectual developments in international economics have been inspired by developing country concerns with commercial policy. A selected list of these developments would include political economy perspectives on protection, analysis of the costs of protection, and the more recent work on the interrelationship between trade liberalization and development. It should be added that India's trade and investment policies over the years have provided considerable impetus for work in this area. Bhagwati's work has profoundly influenced the course of this literature, and a brief survey of the major developments in the area of trade and development policy since the decade of the fifties would place his work in perspective.

The Singer–Prebisch Thesis

The origins of the literature on trade and development date back to the 1950s when Hans Singer published his seminal paper on distribution of gains between borrowing and investing countries (Singer 1950). As is well known, Singer's thesis was that the gains from international trade and foreign investment accrued mostly to the developed or countries of the centre rather than the developing countries or the periphery. The thesis has several strands to it: though foreign investment in developing countries undertaken by the developed countries, mostly in export-oriented plantations and minerals, by its very nature generated very little secondary multiplier effects, such activities diverted domestic resources from other areas capable of generating external and internal economies; and in addition there was a secular deterioration in the terms of trade for exports of primary products vis-à-vis manufactures that the developing countries imported. The secular decline in terms of trade thesis was also enunciated by Raul Prebisch, the Latin American economist, and is generally referred to as the Singer–Prebisch thesis.

The theoretical basis for the Singer–Prebisch thesis was that the gains from productivity growth in primary production accrued to the importers of these commodities in the developed countries in the form of lower prices, but the gains from technical change and productivity growth in manufactures was absorbed in the form of increased wages in developed countries, which in turn increased the price of manufactured goods.

The Singer–Prebisch thesis not only spawned a vast literature but has also had a significant impact on trade and investment policies in developing countries. A number of econometric studies have attempted to test the terms of trade hypothesis and reached differing conclusions. The conclusions of these seem to be influenced by the time period to which the tests relate, the category of products and countries included in the statistical samples, and the specific econometric techniques employed (for a review of these studies see Sapsford and Balasubramanyam). As yet there is no consensus on the issue and the thesis continues to be contentious.

Even so, policy-makers in developing countries drew intellectual support from the thesis for the policies designed to promote industrialization through import substitution (IS) in developing countries. Simply put, the argument is that specialization in primary commodities does not pay because of the deteriorating terms of trade. The market left to itself does not function effectively to channel resources away from these activities and therefore industrialization has to be fostered. The best means of doing so would be to provide domestic industry protection from import competition. Such policies were also inspired by Ragnar Nurkse's well known proposition that exports of primary commodities, including food, could not be the engine of growth because of the low income and price elasticities they faced in world markets (Nurkse 1959).

Bhagwati (1988) has referred to these sets of propositions concerning the growth of exports propounded during the post-Second World War years as the First Export Pessimism, which was characterized by the notion that the developing countries could do little about it because it was a phenomenon caused by natural forces. The one course open to policy-makers, as they saw it, was to switch resources away from primary production and exports towards industry and manufacturing. The preferred route to such industrialization was import substitution.

OTHER TRADITIONAL AND NOVEL ARGUMENTS FOR PROTECTION

One of the time-honoured arguments for protection is the infant industry argument. Simply put, the argument is that although certain industries may not be competitive in international markets in the short run, given time they can withstand international competition. This argument for protection, that pins its faith on the ability of industries to become efficient over time, has been variously interpreted. One interpretation is that industries subject to economies of scale need time to exploit them. But if entrepreneurs are aware of the economies of scale they would establish plants of sufficient size to exploit them rather than delay doing so. Another interpretation, blessed by economists, is that industries capable of generating external economies need protection. In the existence of external economies, private rates of return to investment would be lower than social rates of return, a situation unlikely to persuade profit maximizing entrepreneurs to undertake the investments. While the argument is not without its merits, the first best policy in the when external economies exist, is the institution of production subsidies and not tariff protection (Corden 1974; Bhagwati and Ramaswami 1963; Johnson 1971).

MARKET DISTORTIONS AND PROTECTION

Distortions in factor and product markets, in the sense that social and private costs diverge, are yet another justification for intervention in foreign trade. In addition to the existence of external economies discussed above, sectoral immobility of labour and wage rigidity are some of the distortions that intervention in foreign trade through the imposition of tariffs is supposed to rectify (Hagen 1958; Haberler 1950). While Haberler identified many of the fallacies associated with these arguments for protection, it was Bhagwati and Ramaswami (1963) who provided the incontrovertible dictum that a distortion should be appropriately dealt with at its source. Thus, if the distortion is domestic, of the wage rigidity or labour immobility variety, then a labour subsidy rather than a tariff is the appropriate policy that will yield Pareto efficient outcomes. Again, if the distortion relates to foreign trade, such as a monopoly position for the country in external markets, then the appropriate policy is an optimum tariff. The enunciation of this principle concerning appropriate policy interventions in the existence of distortions should rank as the major intellectual development with far-reaching implications for policy, tossed up by the debate on protection. This is a proposition that was elaborated upon by Bhagwati himself (1971) and the late Harry Johnson (1971).

COSTS OF PROTECTION

Traditional analysis of costs of protection is confined to measuring the loss of consumer surplus, the costs of misallocation of resources caused by protection, and the so called dead-weight loss. This sort of a partial equilibrium approach to the analysis of the costs of protection is enshrined in every textbook on international economics and need not detain us here. The IS policies pursued by developing countries, with non-tariff barriers such as quotas forming an important part of the armoury of instruments of protection, however, inspired novel approaches to the analysis of costs of protection and uncovered additional costs of protection.

That non-tariff barriers to imports, such as quotas, generate rents to the quota holders, is well known. Each quota licence carries with it a share of such rents. Quotas are not however the only source of such rents, for rationing and controls over distribution too generate rents. Anne Krueger (1974), who first identified and measured the extent of such rents, estimated that in 1968 in Turkey the rents from import licences alone were a hefty 15 per cent of GNP. In India, for 1964, Krueger estimated that the total amount of rents obtained from public investment, import, and other controls over distribution of commodities amounted to 7.3 per cent of national income. Sizeable though these rents are, it is to be noted that the competition for the acquisition of rent-yielding assets such as quotas diverts scarce resources from other productive activities. Such a diversion of resources lowers welfare, in essence shifting the economy's production possibility frontier inwards. Krueger's analysis of the costs of rent-seeking set in train a number of studies, that extended and built on the foundations of her analysis. The most significant of such extensions is the work by Bhagwati (1982) and Bhagwati and Srinivasan (1980). Bhagwati demonstrated that rent-seeking is but one of the several types of unproductive resource-diverting activities, among others such as lobbying for protection and smuggling, all of which he encompassed under the umbrella of directly unproductive profit-seeking activities (DUP). His seminal essay on the topic is included in this volume and I comment on it later. It is sufficient to note here that it is the pervasive presence of controls over economic activity in developing countries pursuing the IS strategy that inspired this novel analysis of the social costs of protection.

While the analysis of rent-seeking and DUP has attracted much attention because of its novelty, we should not lose sight of the wealth of empirical studies on a variety of other costs associated with protection. These include analysis of the impact of protectionist policies on income distribution, on employment, and on domestic savings in developing countries. The IS strategy, not surprisingly, increased the incomes of entrepreneurs in the protected industries, but it also conferred rents on bureaucrats who administered the various controls over trade and industry in addition to satiating their yen for the exercise of power, and it provided rents for those engaged in the procurement and sale of licences. There is little doubt that the IS strategy increased income inequalities in most developing countries. It should, however, be added that such a shift in income distribution in favour of the upper income groups served to promote savings. Whether or not such savings were channelled into productive investments or expended on luxury consumption goods is hard to say. There is however some evidence to show that in India during the heydays of IS, despite the growth in savings and investment, there was very little growth, for much of the investment proved to be unproductive (Balasubramanyam 1984).

One other consequence of the IS strategy, widely noted in the literature, is its impact on the internal terms of trade between agriculture and manufacturing. In most developing countries pursuing the strategy there was an adverse shift in the terms of trade against agriculture. This shift was mostly a consequence of the tariffs and quotas not only on imports of agricultural equipment and inputs such as fertilizers, but also import restrictions on basic consumer goods purchased by farmers. At the same time, in some developing countries such as India and Pakistan, prices of agricultural products were subject to controls. This policy formed a part of the deliberate strategy of turning the terms of trade against agriculture as a method of funnelling agricultural savings and resources into the manufacturing sector (Mitra 1977). In Pakistan, during the decade of the sixties, farm incomes were estimated to be 11 to 13 per cent lower than they would have been in the absence of import substitution (Little, Scitovsky and Scott 1970). In sum, the strategy served to increase the incomes of the urban rich and lower that of poor farmers.

It is also well documented that the strategy did little for the promotion of employment, for it not only favoured the relatively capital-intensive industries but also promoted capital deepening. In other words, both the choice of techniques and the choice of industries were influenced in a capital-intensive direction by the strategy. This was primarily because of the built in bias of the strategy in favour of industries in competition with imports, which generally tend to be capital intensive. Also, the strategy favoured capital-intensive techniques of production because of the subsidies and other incentives it provided for the use of capital. In India, employment growth in the manufacturing sector barely exceeded 3 per cent per annum during the sixties.

The varied social costs imposed by the IS strategy is now recorded history and has been told and retold (Little, Scott and Scitovsky 1970; Bhagwati and Srinivasan 1976; Little 1982). Yet it took over three decades for some of the developing countries to see the light and renounce the strategy. Standard economic analysis cannot provide a convincing explanation of this zest for the IS strategy. We have to turn to political economy for an explanation.

The Political Economy of Protection

The post-Second World War pessimism concerning exports proved to be unfounded. World trade during the decade of the fifties and

the sixties grew faster than world income, and many of the East
Asian countries that had adopted outward looking strategies of
development shared in this growth. Why then did many developing
countries that had enthusiastically embraced protectionist policies,
adhere to them with tenacity? More to the point, why did they
choose to ignore the mounting evidence that such policies were
unlikely to yield the hoped for benefits and might actually be
counterproductive?

The desire for widespread protection appears to arise not
because of its proven efficacy or because of the demonstrable
validity of various arguments for protection, but because of a
political preference for industrialization (Johnson 1964). Such
political preference for protection is conditioned by the belief
that any other form of economic activity other than industrialization results in a loss of status in the community of nations.
Beyond this is the belief that industrialization, as opposed to
specialization in primary production, generates both pecuniary
and technological externalities and promotes employment and
growth of incomes (for a discussion of these issues, see MacBean
and Balasubramanyam (1978) and Bhagwati (1988)). Even so,
why the pursuit of industrialization through import substitution
rather than through market oriented policies?

The political economy perspective on protection, which provides an insight into the issues raised above, is that it benefits
specific interest groups and such interest groups lobby for protection. Here the analysis is couched in terms of the traditional
analysis of supply and demand for goods. Those who demand
protection are the producers and specific income groups who
wish to maximize the present value of the additional income
streams generated by the reduction in imports. The suppliers
of protection are the elected representatives of the people who
wish to maximize their own welfare — chiefly prospects for
re-election. The model also demonstrates why import protection
is instituted much more easily than the Pareto-efficient free
trade policy, and why a reduction in protection is much more
difficult to achieve, than an increase in protection. As Baldwin
(1982) notes, a Pareto efficient outcome requires redistribution
of income from the gainers to the losers, but such redistribution

rarely occurs; it also requires perfect information. Consumers should realize that the price of a good has risen because of a tariff, but they rarely do; even if they do they may find the costs of registering their opposition to the policy through the political process outweigh the loss of consumer welfare imposed by the protectionist policy. In any case, the costs of protection of a particular industry tend to be so widely spread that the loss to an individual consumer is small. Also, because the con-sumers of a particular good subject to protection are more numerous than the producers, consumer lobbies are difficult to organize. Protection seems to have something for everyone except for the hapless consumer who is either uninformed of the costs imposed on him/her or, even if well informed, power-less to act. As Angus Maddison (1971), commenting on India's IS policies, succinctly put it, the IS strategy,

won support from the bureaucratic establishment because it added to their power, it was supported by politicians because it encouraged their patronage, it met no opposition from established industry because it did not interfere with vested interests, and it was supported by intellectuals who generally identified capitalism with colonialism . . . it aroused no opposition because it conflicts with no vested interests.

Political economy analysis of protection is also rich in insights into the nature of industries that lobby for protection, the role of the bureaucracy in the political process of instituting protection, and the costs and benefits of lobbying. Oligopolistic industries and those geographically concentrated are likely to lobby for protection and benefit most from it (Olson 1965). This is because protection is in the nature of a 'public good', in the sense all of the producers in the protected industry benefit irrespective of their contribution to the lobbying process. In other words, there could be free-riders benefiting from the efforts of a few lobbyists. If the producers in the industry are few in number the free-rider problem can be mitigated. In developing countries such as India it is the big business houses that possess both the resources and the political muscle to lobby for protection. The technologically progressive industries such as steel, chemicals, and pharmaceuti-cals belong to big business houses.

IS IN THEORY AND PRACTICE

IS in practice appears to have been something entirely different from that which the formulators of the philosophy had in mind. Prebisch, one of the proponents of the deteriorating terms of trade thesis, did not advocate widespread protectionist policies; in any case not the sort of import substitution strategy many countries put in place. He believed that the market would react to the adverse terms of trade by moving resources away from primary production into other activities, but his thesis was used by influential policy-makers to justify their embrace of protectionist policies. As Bhagwati argues, the Nurksian thesis with its advocacy of balanced growth may have implied import substitution as also the Prebisch thesis. But the sort of IS strategy they envisaged was a market-oriented one, utilizing optimum export taxes and import tariffs where applicable, rather than widespread controls over trade. The strategy that most developing countries adopted, however, was of the 'slash imports and grow' variety, as Bhagwati (1985) puts it. This variety of IS consigns the notion of economic costs and benefits to the side and concentrates on providing a ready domestic market to entrepreneurs by cutting off imports. What Bhagwati refers to as the 'slash and grow strategy', Lipton and Firn (1960), commenting on India's import substitution policies, christened the 'in principle-principle' — if you can establish an industry in principle, never mind the costs for you get protection from import competition.

It should be emphasized that commentators such as Bhagwati have not ruled IS out of court nor advocated unrestrained free trade grounded in the free market or laissez-faire philosophy. Nor have they advocated export promotion aided by a paraphernalia of subsidies. What they have relentlessly questioned is the adoption of IS policies, or for that matter export promotion policies, that pay little heed to economic costs.

The IS strategy, though beset with problems, was not without its benefits. It endowed countries such as India with a manufacturing sector, perhaps one that is much too diversified and unspecialized, yet a sector with several technologically intensive industries such as chemicals and engineering. Also, it has endowed these countries with a cadre of engineers and technicians, a result of investments in higher education designed to equip the manufacturing sector with the required human capital. It remains to be seen whether or not countries such as India, that have recently liberalized their trade and investment regimes, are able to build upon this legacy of the IS strategy and experience relatively high growth-rates. In any case, the strategy did generate one significant externality: a vast literature with several significant contributions that extended the analysis of international trade and development issues in new directions.

OUTWARD-LOOKING STRATEGY

The saga of IS appears to have lost steam if not come to an end some time around the end of the decade of the eighties, when India finally abandoned its unswerving allegiance to the strategy and inaugurated a fairly extensive set of economic reforms designed to liberalize trade and investment. The compelling reasons for the change of heart on the part of India's policy-makers, and the extent and nature of reforms, have been reviewed elsewhere (Bhagwati 1993; Balasubramanyam 1995) and need not detain us here. It is sufficient to note here that apart from the weight of intellectual opinion in favour of liberalized trade and investment policies, one of the several reasons for the change in direction of economic policies of countries such as Mexico and Brazil in the past, and India recently, is the demonstrated success of the East-Asian countries with outward-looking strategy of development. That is not to say there is consensus in the profession on the virtues of the strategy, its precise mechanics, or its universal applicability. Indeed, examination and analysis of the many facets of the outward-looking strategy constitutes yet another milestone in the history of the sub-discipline of trade and development. The issues here are several, including what precisely an outward looking strategy is and the role of the State in it. Is it specific to the East Asian countries in the sense of its being culture bound, and is its success conditional upon an authoritarian political regime.

DEFINITIONAL AND CONCEPTUAL ISSUES

What is an outward-looking strategy as opposed to the inward-looking IS strategy? The terminology usually used to identify opposing development strategies could cause confusion. The IS strategy is usually referred to as an inward-looking strategy and an export promotion strategy (EP) as an outward-looking strategy. Note that although controls over foreign trade constitute a significant strand of the inward-looking strategy, more often than not it also encompasses a panopoly of controls over domestic investment, regulation of foreign direct investment, public ownership of large segments of industry, and an overvalued exchange rate. An outward-looking strategy does not however imply a conscious policy of export promotion nor the absence of state ownership of industry and state support for economic activity. But unfortunately the notion that an outward-looking strategy is tantamount to laissez-faire has gained common currency. This conception is as erroneous as that which equates the IS philosophy with dirigism. Bhagwati's observation on this issue is worth quoting. In his Ohlin lectures (1988), Bhagwati drawing upon the experience of Far Eastern countries observes that

Far Eastern countries — including Japan — have highly energetic and involved governments, as has long been known to students of trade and payment regimes . . . the key question is not whether there is governmental action in the Far Eastern economies, but rather how these successful economies have managed their intervention and their strategic decision-making better than the unsuccessful economies . . .

And again

an important difference in behaviour of governments toward the private sector seems to be that the Far Eastern governments, by and large, issue prescriptions rather than proscriptions, whereas countries such as India do the opposite. The governments of 'dos' generally produce economic performance superior to that produced by governments of 'donts'.

The outward-looking strategy pursued by the Far Eastern economies such as South Korea, Malaysia, Taiwan, Hong Kong, and Singapore incorporates a significant role for the State in the economic process, but it is designed to support and encourage rather than discourage and hinder enterprise and growth.

Yet another misconception, referred to earlier, is that export promotion and exports at any cost are regarded as an integral part of the outward-looking strategy. Admittedly the East Asian countries that have pursued the outward looking strategy are successful exporters and some may have instituted aggressive export promotion measures. But the advocates of the outward looking strategy do not emphasize export promotion; instead they urge a neutral policy that favours neither the domestic nor the export market.

Again we owe a clarification of this misconception concerning export promotion to Bhagwati (1978). He defines IS and EP in terms of the effective exchange rate for imports (EER_m) and the effective exchange rate for exports (EER_x). Effective exchange rate in this context, is defined as the number of units of local currency actually received or paid for international transactions. Thus, if exports of a particular good were to enjoy a 10 per cent subsidy, the effective exchange rate for exports in local currency would be the nominal rate plus the subsidy. Similarly, if imports of a particular good were subject to a 10 per cent tariff, the effective exchange rate for the good in terms of local currency would be the nominal rate plus the tariff. Now, if the effective exchange rate for imports were to exceed the effective rate for exports, according to Bhagwati's definition, the country would be following an IS strategy, and if the effective exchange rate for exports were to exceed the effective exchange rate for imports the country would be following an ultra-EP strategy. If the $EER_m = EER_x$, the country is said to be following a neutral or an EP strategy.

Several features of Bhagwati's definition of EP and IS are worth noting. It is unfortunate that Bhagwati chose to identify the neutral strategy as EP as it suggests that it has to do with export promotion. But we should not mistakenly identify the strategy with one that provides excessive subsidies for exports. Note that the EP strategy is a neutral one and its policy orientation does not favour production for either the export or the domestic market. Market orientation of production is guided by market forces, factor endowments, and the entrepreneurial and managerial endowments of the country.

The neutral EP strategy also does not preclude IS in particular industries or sectors. It merely requires that there should be no difference between the average EER_m and EER_x. The pursuit of the neutral strategy does not mean that the state has no role to play in the development process. As said earlier, it may have a central role to play as initiator, promoter, and supporter of economic activity.

Bhagwati's classificatory schema has been noted to have its limitations (Singer 1988). The average rates of EER_m and EER_x may conceal large variations in incentives among IS and EP industries. Also, if there are economies of scale in specific activities, they can be best exploited by mixed strategies. Milner and Mckay (1996) note that a model incorporating a non-traded sector along with the two-traded sectors also allows for mixed strategy. The essence of Bhagwati's thesis is, however, that an outward-oriented strategy does not require a bias in policies in favour of the export sector.

THE EVIDENCE

Is there evidence in support of the outward-looking strategy? There is a substantial body of empirical work on the strategy, including the massive seven volume study entitled *Liberalizing Foreign Trade* sponsored by the World Bank (Papageorgiou, Michaely, Choksi 1991). The study examines the experience of seventeen countries with 36 trade liberalization episodes, with liberalization defined as any act that would make the trade regime more neutral — nearer to a trade system free of government intervention. The study, based on individual country studies, comes to favourable conclusions regarding the impact of liberalization on growth. Amongst other things, it finds liberalization is conducive to sustained export growth (it does not lower production and does not inhibit growth), and successful practitioners of liberalization tend to be small, resource poor, politically stable countries. Besides, the study offers some prescriptions concerning the pace and sequencing of liberalization measures.

The study is not however without its methodological and

analytical problems. As Greenaway (1992) in a concise review of the massive study notes, 'the results of the study have to be interpreted with caution, as the claims made for the generality of the results are extravagant'. This sort of a guarded optimism comes through in most other studies on the success of the outward-looking strategies. Greenaway and Nam (1988) in a comparative study of industrialization in developing countries pursuing IS and EP strategies, conclude that both industrialization and macroeconomic performance in outward-looking economies have been superior to that in inward-looking economies. But they add the caveat that this does not necessarily follow that non-intervention by the government and neutrality are the crux of outward orientation, for two of the most outward-oriented economies (Korea and Singapore) have pursued export promotion with some reliance on explicitly interventionist policies. Their further conclusion, that 'whilst the precise determinants of successful industrlization may not be entirely clear, the determinants of unsuccessful industrialization are much clearer', is also worth noting.

It is clear that while we know much about the costs of IS, as practised by most developing countries, we are yet to learn the precise mechanics of EP that generates growth. Some attempts have been made to study the relationship between specific aspects of EP or outward orientation and growth. One such example is the analysis of the relationship between exports and growth (Balassa 1978; Greenaway and Sapsford 1994; Tyler 1981). Most of these studies find a positive association between exports and growth. Greenaway and Sapsford's study unravels some further interesting facts. First, the positive association between exports and growth gets stronger over time, perhaps indicating that exports must reach a threshold before they impact on growth. Second, liberalization of the trade regime usually results in increased exports, but higher export growth does not seem to occur in all liberalization episodes in all countries, or in the case of all liberalization episodes in a particular country. Finally, liberalization has an impact on growth via a change in the rate of growth of exports rather than in a once and for all shift in export share of the country.

The conclusions of these studies provide some sound policy advice: liberalization alone will not get you more exports, it has to be buttressed with sound macro-economic management; liberalization will not shift the economy on to a higher export and growth path, but works its way slowly through increases in the growth-rate of exports; and liberalization does not necessarily mean export expansion. Above all, these studies suggest that the experience of each of the developing countries with liberalization differs from that of the others, and there may be no universally applicable liberalization recipes.

Does all this mean that the outward looking strategy, as opposed to its precise mechanics, is not universally applicable? Is the strategy specific to East Asian countries? And does the implementation of the strategy require authoritarian regimes, and is the strategy specific to small countries?

It is true that some of the developing countries such as Singapore and Korea have had authoritarian political regimes, but others such as Malaysia have democratically elected ones. Available evidence suggests that there is no unique correlation between the type of political regimes in place and economic growth, although there is much to be said in favour of democratic regimes. One of the essays by Bhagwati included in this volume discusses this theme, and I return to it later. Yet another objection to the outward-looking strategy is cast in terms of the 'fallacy of composition'. The argument here is that while a group of developing countries may successfully exploit export markets and grow, an attempt to do so by all of them will simply flood the markets with goods and all of them will experience a decline in the value of exports. There are several problems with this argument. First, it equates the outward-looking strategy with export expansion, but as noted earlier the strategy does not advocate export expansion. In any case, given the currently relatively low shares of developing countries, they have to increase them dramatically before they are able to saturate the world markets. Second, it ignores the fact that every developing country will not specialize in a narrow range of goods, and there is therefore room for diversification and product differentiation. Third, there will be a hierarchy of exporters, with the more successful of the countries exporting the more sophisticated and technology intensive goods and services, and the others specializing in the traditional variety.

Allied to the argument above is that which says that successful export expansion will invite protection from the importing countries; an argument that Bhagwati (1988) refers to as the Second Export Pessimism. The Second Pessimism differs from the First Export Pessimism, discussed earlier, in that while the pessimism of the first was associated with natural causes inhibiting growth of exports, the second attributes it to man-made causes. As Bhagwati argues, while the danger of protectionist measures in the importing countries has to be taken seriously, these are man-made and reversible. His recent work on regionalism, trade, and the environment, and trade and labour standards testify to his concern about the growth in protectionism. Some of his essays on these issues are included in this volume and will be discussed later in this chapter. It is sufficient to note here that such threats of protection can be defused and the newly established World Trade Organization may be a force in doing so. The success of the Uruguay Round Negotiations, though a qualified success, suggests as much. Furthermore, developed countries may find it in their self-interest to lower tariffs on specific goods. Developed countries such as the US seem to be in the market for increased inward foreign direct investment (FDI), largely because of its contribution to job creation. Japanese foreign investment in automobile manufacturing is highly sought after because of its contribution to job creation. Threats of protection may be one method of attracting foreign firms: 'if you are not keen on investing we shall impose tariffs on your exports'. This is a phenomenon referred to by Bhagwati as quid pro quo direct foreign investment, which to an extent defuses protectionist threats. Foreign firms are offered freer access to export markets in return for foreign direct investment. Bhagwati's contribution on quid pro quo FDI is included in this volume and is discussed later in this chapter.

NEW TRADE THEORIES AND TRADE POLICY

The foregoing suggests that the second export pessimism, like the first, may be largely unfounded. But those who continue to favour

interventionist foreign trade policies have found yet another ally
in recent developments in trade theory. The basic tenet of the so
called new theories of trade, which became fashionable during
the eighties, is that once we recognize the existence of increasing
returns, external economies, and oligopolistic and monopolistic
market structures, all of which are either ignored or assumed away
in traditional theories of trade, the classical prescription in favour
of non-intervention in foreign trade is questionable. The argument
that economies of scale can be exploited if protection extends the
size of the domestic market, though valid, is subject to two caveats.
The increased size must be large enough to allow for economies
of scale, and the protected market should not generate X-inefficien-
cies and such other costs.

The new theories suggest though that in certain technologi-
cally-progressive industries the world market may be dominated
by two or three producers, one of whom may be successful
in capturing the market through adroit use of export subsidies
and hence achieve economies of scale in world rather than
domestic markets. Ingenious though the argument is, it too is
subject to qualifications. The first is that trade policy intervention
by one of the producers does not attract retaliation from the
others and, more importantly, that developing countries do possess knowledge of intensive and technologically progressive industries such as aircraft manufacturing. The second of these
assumptions may be much too heroic and we must conclude
that this specific argument for protection based on strategic
grounds may not have much to offer for developing countries
(see Corden (1991) and Greenaway (1991) for a detailed discussion of this issue).

The other strand to the new theories of trade cited in support
of intervention relates to external economies. This is no more
than the infant industry argument discussed earlier and does not
bear repetition.

In sum, the new theories of trade grounded in imperfect competition theory have undoubtedly enriched the discipline of international economics, but they appear to provide little theoretical
support for intervention in foreign trade, especially so in the case
of developing countries.

GETTING PRICES RIGHT

The debate on the inward- and outward-looking strategies of development leaves the impression that we know more about what not to do in trade policy than what we should do. David Greenaway's observation that 'while we may not be entirely clear on the precise determinants of growth, the potential for trade strategy in discouraging growth is, however, rather more apparent', is worth pondering. The outward-looking strategy of development has many more strands to it than the inward-looking one. It is not just a matter of liberalizing the trade regime, but also calls for prudent macro-economic management, investment in education, and state support for the market mechanism. In any case, it most certainly is not just a matter of getting the prices right, nor one of increased investment of capital and labour with little by way of technological and organizational change.

The view that it is all a matter of getting prices right is attributed to the World Bank and that it is all due to increased investment seems to be the view of Paul Krugman (1994), the American economist. Both views relate to the growth performance of the East Asian economies. The World Bank's review of the East Asian experience embodied in a report entitled *The East Asian Miracle* (1993) seems to have provoked these observations. Whether or not the Bank report attributes the success of these economies entirely to 'getting prices right' is arguable, but none of the proponents of the outward-looking strategy can be accused of a blind faith in free-market economics or the power of the invisible hand.

Is the East Asian growth performance to be attributed to increased investment of capital and labour to the exclusion of organizational and technical change, as Paul Krugman (1994) would have us believe? And will the East Asian impressive growth performance peter out as Krugman forecasts? Empirical evidence on Krugman's thesis is as yet sketchy and inconclusive: the evidence relating to Singapore he cites is selective. Krugman's headline-grabbing thesis, labelled by *The* (London) *Economist* as the 'miracle of the sausage makers', serves however to show that we have a lot to learn about the ways and means of implementing the outward-looking strategy and its inner mechanics. Research on these and other issues continues apace.

THE URUGUAY ROUND

A review of trade and development issues would be incomplete without a reference to the recently completed Uruguay Round trade negotiations and its implications for developing countries. The Uruguay Round may not yield spectacular gains to developing countries. Indeed, according to some commentators, much of the gains from trade liberalization may accrue to the developed countries (Nguyen, Perroni and Wigle 1993). The principal sources of gains to developing countries may be confined to those arising from the phasing out of the multifibre agreement (MFA) relating to textiles and clothing, and from reductions in tariffs on agricultural goods.

The Uruguay Round may, however, have far-reaching long-term consequences for the developing countries, primarily because of the inclusion on the agenda of new items for negotiation. These include principally Services, Trade Related Investment Measures (TRIMS), and Trade Related Intellectual Property Rights (TRIPS). The one item that aroused much debate and discussion from the very inception of the Round is Services. The initial opposition of the developing countries, led by India, Brazil, and Egypt, to the inclusion of trade in services for negotiation on the agenda, the compromise solution that resolved the issue, and the institution of a framework for negotiations on services are all now recorded history. The debate on services however tossed up several analytically interesting issues such as whether or not services are different from goods, modes of delivery of services across national borders, the relevance of trade theory for analysis of trade in services, and the reasons for the low cost of services in developing countries.

One development of significance to developing countries, which we owe to Bhagwati, is the demonstration that developing countries, contrary to their own perceptions, possess a comparative advantage in many service activities. This revelation may have muted the opposition of developing countries to negotiations on services as the Round progressed. Three of Bhagwati's seminal contributions to the debate on services are included in this volume of his essays, and I comment on them later in this chapter.

TRIMS and TRIPs, the two other new items on the agenda of the Uruguay Round, are closely associated with FDI in developing countries. TRIMS refer to the various rules and regulations imposed on foreign firms by the host developing countries. These include export obligations, local content requirements and regulations that require employment of local nationals by foreign firms. Various types of incentives offered by developing countries, such as tax holidays and tax concessions, also form a part of TRIMS (for an extended discussion, see Greenaway (1991) and Balasubramanyam (1991)). All such regulations and incentives impinge upon trade flows directly or indirectly, and hence the demand for their inclusion on the agenda of the Uruguay Round by the developed countries.

TRIPS encompass instruments such as patents and copyright designed to protect intellectual property (technology and know-how) from piracy and theft. This too is an aspect which influences trade. The concern here is that in the absence of enforceable property rights, designs and processes can be pirated, and products that embody them can be traded. Admittedly both TRIMS and TRIPS are of significance to developed countries which account for the bulk of FDI.

The initial opposition of developing countries to the inclusion of these items on the agenda may not be entirely unfounded. Amongst several of the objections of developing countries to their inclusion on the agenda, two are worth noting. The first is that TRIMS are essential to regulate and harness FDI to promote development objectives. The second is that TRIPS, which would require developing countries to award patent and copyright protection to products and technological processes owned by foreign firms, may not only result in monopolistic pricing practices by foreign firms, but also deter transfer of technology and know-how. There is much sympathy for these concerns of developing countries on the part of economists (Bhagwati 1991; Maskus 1993; Balasubramanyam 1991). In the event, both TRIMS and TRIPS figured on the agenda and the negotiations resulted in compromise solutions acceptable to developing countries, broadly on the lines suggested by Bhagwati.

I will not elaborate on TRIPS and TRIMS here, and refer the interested reader to the publications cited above. It is however worth noting that both TRIMS and TRIPS bear heavily on various aspects of foreign investment, a branch of international economics on which there is very extensive literature. The endless number of controversial issues relating to foreign investment merits a survey on its own, and I do not attempt it here. The reader of this volume is, however, not entirely deprived of an analysis of some of the issues such as the welfare implications of foreign direct investment and changing attitudes to such investment. Three of Bhagwati's essays on these issues are included in the volume. Yet another issue that is not included in this brief survey relates to international labour migration, principally the migration of professional and talented people from developing countries to the developed countries. As stated earlier, Bhagwati is renowned for his many contributions to the debate on the brain drain phenomenon, and three of his essays on this issue are included in the volume.

The brief foregoing review provides only a flavour of the rich literature on trade and development issues. Justice cannot be done in a short survey either to the wide range of issues or the very extensive literature on the subject. Students can however do no better than read the classic pieces, many of them of enduring value, that have not only enriched the literature but also influenced and shaped economic policy in developing countries. Each of the essays included in this volume, written by one of the foremost exponents of trade theory and policy, has made a major contribution to the subject and many have influenced the course of economic policy. They cover virtually all the issues, briefly discussed in this chapter, and many which are only alluded to. Bhagwati's essays relating to India's economic policy and performance included in this volume are grounded in the major debates on trade development. Some of his essays on trade theory and those covering trade issues from historical and political perspectives included in this volume are an added bonus to the reader. So too the selection of his pieces in the popular press such as

Foreign Affairs, the *New Republic, The Scientific American*, and the *Financial Times*. I now turn to a brief introduction to the essays in the volume.

The 27 essays in this volume, grouped into seven broad categories, reflect the wide range of Jagdish Bhagwati's writings on most of the issues discussed in the foregoing. Most of the essays have been published elsewhere. My choice of the essays for inclusion in the volume has been guided by three considerations: ease of accessibility, impact on policy, and my tastes and preferences. Some of the articles, such as those published in *Foreign Affairs* (Ch. 28) and the *New Republic* (Ch. 27), are not known or easily accessible to the Indian audience. Some others, like vintage wine, have gained in popularity with age, but they originally appeared quite long ago and most librarians would have confined the journals, some dating back to the sixties, to the archives. Almost all the articles included in the volume have had a lasting impact on policy and most have spurred further work by Jagdish Bhagwati's students who are now legion and include celebrities such as Paul Krugman, Gene Grossman, and Robert Feenstra. Many of the recent developments in trade theory and policy, including the analysis of lobbying for protection, the welfare consequences of regionalism, and the controversies surrounding trade and labour standards are inspired by Bhagwati's relentless questioning of the received wisdom on these issues. His work on various aspects of India's economic policy and performance has provoked both controversy and further work.

Section II of the volume consists of three of Bhagwati's early articles on trade theory. The first two extend the traditional Ricardian and Heckscher–Ohlin–Samuelson (HOS) trade theorems in new directions. The article on 'Protection, Real Wages and Real Incomes' (Ch. 3) restates the Stolper–Samuelson with elegance and precision, and generalizes it to include the Metzler paradox. Some of Bhagwati's doubts and dissatisfaction with the original formulation of the theorem surface again in his discussion of the role of trade in the decline in real wages in the rich countries since the early 1980s (see Ch. 23), and in his analysis of the relationship between trade and labour standards.

Chapter 2 on 'Proofs of the Theorems of Comparative Advantage' is, in a manner of speaking, a fallout from Bhagwati's well-known 'Survey of the Pure Theory of International Trade' (1964). The survey alludes to the possible extensions and exceptions to the well-known Ricardian and HOS propositions. Here it is demonstrated that in the context of the traditional $2 \times 2 \times 1$ Ricardian model, trade can take place even if pre-trade price ratios are identical between trading partners. This would be so because of the possibility of multiplicity of production equilibria in the two countries in the presence of identical price ratios. The correct Ricardian corollary, Bhagwati argues, should state that 'where factor prices are identical between countries the volume and direction of trade are indeterminate'. The other side of the coin to this proposition is that even if productivity ratios for the two goods are different between countries, demand conditions may be such that no trade takes place. This article, aside from its interest for the connoisseurs of traditional trade theorems, teaches students the need for precision in the formulation of theoretical propositions. Moreover, it is an excellent example of a master trade theorist at work who can see exceptions to received wisdom.

Bhagwati began his career with a path-breaking article on immiserizing growth (1958), written in 1955 while he was an undergraduate in Cambridge, which attracted the attention of the stalwarts in the profession at the time such as Harry Johnson and Ragnar Nurkse. Growth may immiserize the growing nation because of an adverse change in terms of trade which growth itself may engender. The article on immiserizing growth (Ch. 4), shows that many of the paradoxes noted by Batra and Pattanaik, and Batra, and Scully are but special cases of the more general theory of immiserizing growth developed by Bhagwati in the *Review of Economic Studies* in 1968. These paradoxes refer to cases where both exogenous and growth-induced endogenous changes in the terms of trade reduce welfare in wage distortions of one kind or another.

The article, however, is best known for its demonstration that capital inflows in the presence of a tariff can be immiserizing. The result is arrived at in the context of the $2 \times 2 \times 2$ HOS type of trade model, and incorporates the Rybczynski effect to demonstrate that the tariff jumping variety of capital inflows could be immiserizing. This proposition, which has been developed further by Brecher and Choudhri (1982) and Brecher and Diaz-Alejandro (1977), has far-reaching implications for countries attempting to woo foreign direct investment through the imposition of restrictions on imports. This theoretical proposition also underlies Bhagwati's celebrated dictum that countries pursuing an export promotion (EP) policy are likely to attract both a higher volume of foreign direct investment (FDI) and benefit much more from it than countries pursuing an import-substitution (IS) policy. Both the propositions have been shown to pass rigorous econometric tests in V.N. Balasubramanyam and M.A. Salisu (1991), and V.N. Balasubramanyam, David Sapsford, and M.A. Salisu (1996).

Bhagwati's work is best known for its adroit use of theoretical tools to elucidate propositions for policy. Indeed, his stature as a major scholar of international trade reflects primarily his contributions to the theory of commercial policy. An excellent example of his work, with even greater impact than his work on immiserizing growth, is his analysis of the desirable form of intervention in foreign trade when the economy is characterized by domestic distortions of various kinds. Section III of the book includes the article Bhagwati wrote in 1963 in collaboration with the late V.K. Ramaswami (Ch. 5) on optimum policy intervention in cases of domestic distortions. This article is justly famous for laying the foundations for the modern theory of commercial policy, having been followed by innumerable articles on the subject in the 1960s and 1970s. The well known message of the article is that a subsidy is superior to a tariff in correcting the distortion if the distortion is domestic, as in the case of a wage distortion or an externality, and a tariff is superior to a subsidy if the distortion is in foreign trade. The article also dismisses familiar objections to a subsidy, such as that which argues that a subsidy cannot be raised in a non-distortionary fashion, by noting that a subsidy-cum-tax can overcome this problem. This article was further elaborated by the late Harry Johnson (1965) and generalized by Bhagwati himself (1971).

Section III also includes four other articles, two of which discuss instruments of trade policy, one of which graphically analyses the growing threat of regionalism to free multilateral trade and another the costs and benefits of protection induced profit-seeking activities. The article on 'Shifting Comparative Advantage, Protectionist Demands and Policy Response' (Ch. 6) is unfortunately not as well known as it should be nor is it easily accessible. Most analysts discuss tariffs, quotas, and export of capital and technology as responses to a loss of comparative advantage, but very few consider importation of labour as a possible solution to the loss of competitiveness. This article considers differing policy responses, including importation of labour, on the part of labour and entrepreneurs or owners of capital, to a loss of comparative advantage.

The article, besides discussing the welfare implications of these various options, proceeds to introduce two novel ideas. One of these is the mutual penetration of investment model and the other is the 'biological theory' of international trade in similar products. The former relates to the observed phenomenon of multinationals investing in one another as a method of containing competition and promoting sales. Such mutual penetration of investment results in scale and scope economies in R & D and marketing. The biological theory of trade is an attempt at explaining intra-industry trade in terms of national characteristics that result in the production specific types of products. Both these novel ideas extend traditional explanations of intra-industry trade and FDI in new directions.

Chapter 8 on 'Quantitative Restrictions and Quotas in International Trade', which originally appeared in the *International Encyclopaedia of Social Sciences*, provides a succinct review of the nature of quantitative restrictions, their impact on welfare, and the debate on the equivalence between tariffs and quotas. It should be read alongside Bhagwati's well known analysis of the non-equivalence of tariffs and quotas which has led to the very extensive literature that the chapter in this volume reviews and synthesizes.

The two other articles in Sec. III of the volume (Chs 7 and 9) discuss protection in a wider context and bear witness to Bhagwati's growing interest in the theory of political economy since the 1980s. The usual costs of protection in terms of loss of consumer welfare and misallocation of resources are well known. But, as stated earlier, the costs associated with lobbying for protection, and the time and effort expended in seeking the rents and premia associated with protection, has surfaced in the literature relatively recently. Anne Krueger was the first to identify and estimate such costs in the context of Turkey, which she christened a 'rent-seeking society'. Bhagwati has generalized the phenomenon identified by Krueger to include various sorts of profit-seeking activities that do not in any way contribute to the production of goods and services and rechristened the phenomenon Directly Unproductive Profit-Seeking (DUP), pronounced DUPE. Usually all such profit-seeking activities, which are a resultant of various sorts of trade policy interventions, lower welfare, or contract the availability set open to the economy. They do this by drawing labour and capital from production-oriented activities into the non-production-oriented profit-seeking activities.

A striking feature of Bhagwati's analysis in the article on DUP included in this volume is that, as he noted earlier in a joint article with T.N. Srinivasan, DUP may increase rather than lower welfare. This would be the case if the initial situation prior to DUP is characterized by distortions and conforms to the theory of the second best, which states that in a distortion-ridden situation if you rectify/introduce one or more distortions welfare may increase or decrease.

The last piece in this section on regionalism and unilateralism is of a more recent vintage and provides an example of Bhagwati's ability to challenge received wisdom on a subject. In this instance, he not only provides a succinct review of customs union theory, beginning with the famous Vinerian analysis, but also offers a vividly analytical account of the reasons for the growth of regionalism over the years and a solid defence of multilateralism against the new orthodoxy in favour of regional preferential trade agreements.

Section IV then turns to India. During the early sixties Jagdish Bhagwati was a member of the think tank of Pitamber Pant, the then head of the Perspective Planning Division of India's Planning Commission. Along with Bagicha Singh Minhas and T.N. Srinivasan, Bhagwati contributed to the intense discussions on the planning process and India's economic philosophy that took place at the time. Those were days when development economics was rife with debates on balanced versus unbalanced growth, the binding constraint of foreign exchange on the growth process, and whether or not industrialization should be the prime motor of development. Bhagwati's book on *The Economics of Underdeveloped Countries* (1966), which was translated into several languages, concisely summarizes his thinking on a number of these issues.

At that time he was also an advocate of devaluation of the Indian rupee, for which he led a mini campaign in the pages of the *Economic and Political Weekly*, published from Bombay, a popular outlet then for Indian economists who had anything new to say. These and other articles by Bhagwati published during the sixties, reflect his concern that in the then euphoria for state intervention in economic activity the benefits of the market mechanism were being ignored, with all its attendant consequences for efficiency and equity.

The articles included in Sec. IV reflect this general concern on the part of Bhagwati. In his Vikram Ṣarabhai Lecture on 'Poverty and Public Policy' (Ch. 10), Bhagwati makes the important point that growth is also an indirect poverty-ameliorating policy, reducing poverty by providing gainful employment on a sustained basis, so that in place of the familiar but ill-founded complaints that growth must be sacrificed to direct poverty-amelioration programmes, the true choice confronting planners is how to combine these two alternative methods of optimally attacking poverty. Indeed, without growth, it would even be impossible to maintain the growth of revenues that would finance the direct poverty-elimination programmes.

His impatience with ideological slogans and sound bites that confronted those such as himself who were deeply involved in the planning process in the early 1960s is also manifest in his critical analysis (jointly with Padma Desai) of Socialist thought in India's planning ideas and process. This essay (Ch. 11) shows the range of his interests and his ability to weave broader political and intellectual ideas into his economic analysis to advantage.

Included in this section, to display Bhagwati's ability to traverse new paths, is another joint essay with Padma Desai (Ch. 12), over

two decades old, on 'Women in Indian Elections'. This chapter
may be read along with his well-known article in *World Development* (1973) where he also forcefully raised the issue of gender
and gender discrimination, but in relation to education and nutrition. In each essay, Bhagwati shows how gender works in politics
and economics, raising questions that have now become standard
and fashionable, but which were at the time considered exotic,
bizarre, and unworthy of economists' attention.

These essays have been chosen for this volume because they
show a wholly different dimension of Bhagwati's interests and
achievements — concerns with poverty, with politics and ideas,
with gender — from those often associated with him in India, where
he is primarily known for his contribution to the analysis and
eventual reform of India's trade and industrial policies. These
latter contributions are of course much read in India, starting with
his celebrated 1970 book with Padma Desai on *India: Planning for
Industrialization* and ending most recently with his Radhakrishnan
Lectures at Oxford, *India in Transition*. For an analysis of the
evolution of Bhagwati's ideas on economic reforms, and indeed
more generally, the reader can do no better than read Deena
Khatkhate's (1994) substantial review article on the latter book in
World Development, which documents Bhagwati's role as an independent thinker who fought for economic reforms in the early
years when it was rewarding to an individual's professional
career, in academe and policy circles, to go instead with the
entrenched economic philosophy that superficially looked progressive, but was in reality, badly flawed.

Then again, India more than most other developing countries
has experienced a steady emigration of talented people from her
shores. Bhagwati himself is an illustrious member of this band of
emigrants. Perhaps because he is himself a part of the brain drain,
he is well placed to analyse its causes and welfare implications
in vivid detail. He does not subscribe to the so-called cosmopolitan
model of brain drain, or as he puts it 'the model grounded in the
Hicks–Samuelson value theoretic neo-classical mode'. Contrary to
the conclusions of the cosmopolitan model advocated by Herbert
Grubel, Anthony Scott, and Harry Johnson, Bhagwati detects a
variety of situations in which the phenomenon of brain drain turns

into a brain drain problem and imposes welfare costs on the countries of emigration.

The two articles on the brain drain included in Sec. VI of this volume (Chs 13 and 14), one of them co-authored with the Japanese economist Koichi Hamada, provide not only a superb analysis of the welfare implications of brain drain but also a stout defence of Bhagwati's proposal for a tax on brains. Bhagwati has produced a series of articles and edited several books on the phenomenon of the brain drain, many of which draw upon legal and political aspects. The first of the papers on the subject in the volume, prepared for the UNCTAD, provides an excellent example of Bhagwati's eye for detail and his ability to detect corollaries of a phenomenon, that are easily overlooked.

Although Bhagwati's professional reputation is usually associated with his work on international movements of labour, he has also extended the literature on international capital movements in new directions. The article on international factor movements and comparative advantage, the published version of the V.K. Ramaswami memorial lecture (Ch. 16) is notable for its comparisons of the welfare effects of international capital mobility with those of international labour mobility. Much of the acrimonious debate on the welfare effects of FDI waged during the sixties and the seventies was coloured by ideology, and extreme views and vague generalizations. Bhagwati scrutinizes several of the propositions in the debate and identifies cases where importation of capital may reduce welfare. The article also provides an analysis of the welfare consequences of regional groupings in the context of foreign capital in member countries. The arresting feature of the article is, however, its diagrammatic analysis of the welfare implications of international factor flows, especially so the welfare impact of labour migration.

'Investing Abroad' (Ch. 15) is the published version of the Esmée Fairbairn lecture delivered at Lancaster University. This piece again provides a succinct analysis of the changing attitudes towards FDI, especially so on the part of American politicians and industrialists besieged by Japanese FDI. The essay provides an excellent example of Bhagwati's lecturing style which is laced with anecdotes and apt quotations from the philosophers of yore to the popular press of the day. This lecture also contains a brief introduction to the phenomenon identified and christened by him as quid pro quo FDI: a phenomenon of the mid-eighties, as stated earlier the type of investment that is undertaken to defuse threats of protection. Foreign firms invest abroad even though such investment may not be profitable in order to forestall the subsequent imposition of tariffs and VERs on trade. The gains from trade in subsequent years may outweigh the losses incurred on FDI in the first period. Bhagwati's identification and subsequent modelling of this phenomenon (Ch. 17) is inspired by his intuition and casual observation. In this case the observation refers to US–Japanese commercial relations during the eighties when there was much evidence to show that in several instance Japanese FDI in the US was motivated by the desire to avoid trade friction.

Bhagwati's several contributions to the literature on FDI provide a refreshing change from the ubiquitous theorizing on the origins of the multinational enterprise and the politically charged controversies. The three articles on the subject included in this volume are representative of Bhagwati's contribution to expanding the horizons of the sub-discipline of international economics.

Yet another branch of international economics that gained popularity during the eighties, and gathered intellectual momentum with the inauguration of the Uruguay Round, relates to trade in services. The lively debate on services, encompassing issues such as whether services are different from goods, is the theory of comparative advantage applicable to trade in services, and why services are relatively cheap in poor countries has now produced a substantial body of literature. Bhagwati's imprint on this branch of international economics too is highly visible.

The article on why services are cheaper in poor countries (Ch. 18) is an acknowledged classic in the field. It extends the Kravis–Summers–Heston explanation of the price of (non-traded) services in poor countries in an altogether new direction, and in the process provides several new insights into the economics of services. Simply put, the Kravis–Summers–Heston explanation is that trade equalizes the price of goods across nations but wages are determined by productivity differences. And while productivity in the traded goods sector in poor countries is relatively low, no such sizeable differences in productivity exist in the non-traded service sector. The wage determined in the goods sector, however, applies also to the services sector, and as a consequence the price of services in poor countries tends to be low.

Bhagwati argues that whilst this productivity differences-based line of reasoning is appealing, an alternative explanation that fits more stylized facts can instead be provided by focusing on endowment differences. Utilizing the well known Lerner diagrammatic technique, which relates factor prices to goods prices, Bhagwati demonstrates that in poor countries services are cheap because of their high endowments of labour in relation to capital vis-à-vis the rich countries. This explanation of the price of services in terms of differences in factor endowment ratios between countries also explains the price of goods in relation to services across countries. Typically in countries with high capital–labour ratios, prices of goods tend to be low in relation to those of services in comparison with countries with a low capital–labour ratio. Indeed, available data supports the converse proposition that goods/services price will be much the same in countries with similar per capita incomes. Note here that countries with similar per capita incomes will also have similar factor endowments. All this and more, which will be revealed to the careful reader of the chapter, may seem obvious after reading it, but that which is obvious often requires demonstration, and this Bhagwati does superbly.

A similar experience may be the lot of most readers of Ch. 19 which elegantly demonstrates how services splinter from goods and how in turn goods splinter from services. Also, services can be separated from the provider and embodied in goods as in the case of music tapes and CDs. Services can also be disembodied from the provider without goods coming into the picture, as in the case of transmission of live music performances over the wire. Services can also splinter from goods, as in the case of paint jobs associated with the production of automobiles which are separated and contracted out to specialist paint firms. These and other examples cited by Bhagwati lead one to wonder whether all the ink spilt on drawing distinctions between services and goods and in defining services is worth it.

In any case, the thrust of Bhagwati's graphic exposition is to show that, because of the splintering and disembodiment effects, developing countries may be unwise in opposing liberalization of trade in services. These effects enable them to specialize and enjoy a comparative advantage in various sorts of services. Much more to the point, it may be futile to oppose immigration of labour, for services can be disembodied from the provider and transported across geographical borders. This is, of course, sage advice not only to developing but also developed countries.

The third article on services (Ch. 20) provides a tour de force of the debate on services in all its manifestations. It may be no exaggeration to say that this article, which first appeared in the *World Bank Review*, has had a major impact on policy and may well have influenced the course of the Uruguay Round Negotiations on Services in convincing the key developing countries that they too have a comparative advantage in a range of services, and services are not the sole preserve of the rich countries. Bhagwati's work on services is a natural progression from his work on the brain drain, a progression that appears to have been propelled by the course of events in the world economy.

Consistency is not a virtue economists are credited with, and stories abound about the inconsistent views held: Jagdish Bhagwati, while his thinking does evolve with time, cannot, however, be accused of this. He has for long been an advocate of free trade or rules based trade, both his theoretical work and his popular writings including the media pieces laying bare the fallacies of protectionism and advocating free trade. In recent years the protectionist lobby in the developed countries has found new allies, witting and unwitting, among the environmentalists, human rights activists, and supporters of labour standards.

The three articles in Sec. VII address these issues in diverse ways. *The Scientific American* essay (Ch. 21) addresses environmental standards and clarifies the fact that the optimal way to address environmental issues is not through trade policy but with environment policy. Free trade should be used to maximize the gains from trade; and environment policy, to protect environment efficiently. If, however, there is no environmental policy, it still does not follow that free trade will harm the environment more than protection will. To illustrate this second-best proposition, Bhagwati draws on examples such as the adverse environmental effects of VERs on Japanese cars and the favourable environmental effects of Uruguay Round agricultural liberalization.

Chapter 22 reprints, on the other hand, an essay addressed to the question of the incorporation of environmental and labour standards as prerequisites for free trade at the WTO (which has succeeded the GATT). Delivered at the same Conference, Bhagwati's essay is a response to the plea by Sir Leon Brittan, of the European Union, to incorporate such prerequisites through mechanisms such as a Social Clause. Here too, Bhagwati provides new ways of looking at the problem, while arguing against the amendment of the WTO in this direction.

The final Chapter (Ch. 23) in this section is a much cited article by Bhagwati, with his Columbia student Vivek Dehejia, on the effects of trade on real wages. This has become a big issue in the debate on free trade today, and this article provides a splendid overview of the issues, including a fine review of the Stolper–Samuelson theory as it is used to justify the fears of the OECD countries that trade with the poor countries will immiserize their unskilled workers. The article also provides a lucid statement of a new theory of Bhagwati's that relates the possible immiserization of workers, not to the Stolper–Samuelson argument, but to the globalization process more generally, building on the possible rise of what he calls 'kaleidoscopic comparative advantage', increased labour turnover, and the consequent flattening of the earnings curve of workers who then do not build up skills on the job as they used to. This essay shows Bhagwati's ability to review and synthesize, to use empirical data aptly, and to generate new ideas.

The last section of the volume puts together some samples of Bhagwati's writing that transcend our discipline and foray into history, politics, and sociology. Chapter 24 on Religion as DUP activity (written with T.N. Srinivasan) not only raises more than a chuckle with its wit and humour, but also illustrates the applicability of the tools of trade of the economist to the most unlikely of social phenomena. This obscurely published article, though written with tongue in cheek, should interest India's sociologists and economists.

The other four articles in this section of the volume, have been written with a more serious purpose. The article on democracy and development, Rajiv Gandhi memorial lecture (Ch. 25), is an incisive discussion of the relationship between the choice of political regimes and development. Here Bhagwati argues that the widespread view held until recently that democracy came at a cost, the cost being development, is in need of revision. Readers will be particularly interested in the historical analysis that he provides, linking the Harrod–Domar model into a perceptive and original analysis of the question at hand. Bhagwati concludes that democracy does not hinder development, and in the best circumstances even promotes it. Besides, the best results follow when democracy is combined with markets. Indeed, markets alone may provide development, but democracy without markets is most unlikely to do so: India is an unfortunate example of this proposition. This lecture attests not only to Bhagwati's wide reading but also his familiarity with the work of jurists, political scientists, and philosophers.

Chapter 26 reproduces Bhagwati's trenchant review of Jeffrey Sachs's Robbins Lectures at the London School of Economics on Shock Therapy. The intense debate between the 'gradualists' (led by Padma Desai, now a leading Sovietologist and Harriman Professor of Comparative Economic Systems at Columbia) and the 'shock therapists' (led by Sachs and Andres Aslund), carried on in journals and newspapers such as *The Financial Times*, is well illuminated by Bhagwati's analysis which is replete with apt quotations from Adam Smith and Keynes, and offers an acute critique of the reasons why shock therapy failed in Russia.

Chapter 27 provides a succinct analysis of the reasons for the often observed aggressive pursuit of unilateralism in trade policy on the part of the US and warns against the dangers of regionalism. This brief analysis of contemporary US trade policy draws historical parallels with the experience of Britain during the nineteenth century. The last chapter in this section and in the volume (Ch. 28) is a short piece published in a yet more abbreviated version, in *The Financial Times*. It shows Bhagwati using history effectively to make a contemporary point: It contrasts Prime Minister Peel's decision to make England a unilateral free-trader with President

Clinton's decision to insist on strict reciprocity in reducing trade barriers. He then argues against the latter, asking for 'relaxed reciprocity' in place of the current preoccupation with reciprocity at any cost. Again, this little piece is a good illustration of Bhagwati's ability to make an important point aptly and in an interesting way that makes it immediately accessible to the general public.

This introduction merely provides an overview of the 27 selected articles by Jagdish Bhagwati included in this volume. It does not do justice to Bhagwati's breadth of arguments, theoretical insights, and his carefully thought out economic philosophy developed over nearly three decades of research and teaching. There is no substitute for reading the articles, which themselves may not adequately represent the breadth of Bhagwati's work in the area of trade and development. They are however representative of his philosophy, his wit, his wide reading, his ability to synthesize an immense literature in the space of a few pages, and his seminal contribution to trade theory.

REFERENCES

Balassa, B., 1978: 'Exports and Economic Growth: Further Evidence', *Journal of Development Economics*, vol. 5.

Balasubramanyam, V.N., 1984: *The Economy of India* (Colorado: Westview Press).

——, 1991: 'Putting TRIMS to Good Use', *World Development*, no. 9, vol. 19.

——, 1995: 'India's Trade Policy Review', *World Economy*, in S. Arndt and C. Milner (eds), Special Issue on Global Trade Policy.

Balasubramanyam, V.N. and M.A. Salisu, 1991: 'Export Promotion, Import Substitution and Direct Foreign Investment in Less Developed Countries, *in* A. Koekkoek and L.B.M. Mennes (eds), *International Trade and Global Development* (London: Routledge).

Balasubramanyam, V.N., M.A. Salisu and D. Sapsford, 1996: 'Foreign Direct Investment and Growth in EP and IS Countries', *The Economic Journal*, no. 434, vol. 106, pp. 92–105.

Baldwin, R., 1982: 'The Political Economy of Protectionism', *in* J.N. Bhagwati, *Import Competition and Response* (Chicago: The University of Chicago Press).

Bhagwati, J.N., 1958: 'Immiserizing Growth: A Geometrical Note', *Review of Economic Studies*, 25 (June), pp. 201–5.

——, 1964: 'The Pure Theory of International Trade: A Survey', *Economic Journal*, vol. LXXIV.

——, 1965: 'On the Equivalence of Tariffs and Quotas', *in* R.E. Caves (ed.), *Trade, Growth and the Balance of Payments* (Chicago: Rand–Mcnally).

——, 1966: *The Economics of Underdeveloped Countries* (New York: Mc-Graw–Hill).

——, 1971: 'The Generalized Theory of Distortions and Welfare', *in* J.N. Bhagwati et al. (eds), *Trade, Balance of Payments and Growth* (Amsterdam: North Holland).

——, 1973: 'Education, Class Structure and Income Inequality', *World Development*, vol. 1 (5).

——, 1978: *Anatomy and Consequences of Exchange Control Regimes*, Studies in International Economic Relations (New York: National Bureau of Economic Research), no. 10, vol. 1.

——, 1982: 'Directly Unproductive, Profit Seeking (DUP) Activities', *Journal of Political Economy*, vol. 90.

——, 1984: 'Comment on Raul Prebisch, Five States in My Thinking on Development', *in* G.M. Meier and D. Seers (eds), *Pioneers in Development* (London: Oxford University Press).

——, 1988: 'Export-Promoting Trade Strategy: Issues and Evidence', *World Bank Research Observer*, vol. 3.

——, 1988: *Protectionism* (Cambridge, Mass.: MIT Press).

——, 1993: *India in Transition: Freeing the Economy* (Oxford: Clarendon Press).

Bhagwati, J.N. and P. Desai, 1970: *India: Planning for Industrialization* (London: Oxford).

Bhagwati, J.N. and T.N. Srinivasan, 1976: *Foreign Trade Regimes and Economic Development: India* (London: Macmillan).

——, 1980: 'Revenue Seeking: A Generalization of the Theory of Tariffs', *Journal of Political Economy*, vol. 88.

Bhagwati, J.N. and V.K. Ramaswami, 1963: 'Domestic Distortions, Tariffs, and the Theory of Optimum Subsidy', *Journal of Political Economy*, no. 1, vol. LXXI.

Brecher, R.A. and C.F. Diaz–Alejandro, 1977: 'Tariffs, Foreign Capital and Immiserizing Growth', *Journal of International Economics*, 7 (Nov.), pp. 317–22.

Brecher, R.A. and E.U. Choudhri, 1982: 'Immiserizing Investment from

Abroad: The Singer–Prebisch Thesis Reconsidered', *Quarterly Journal of Economics*, 97 (Feb.), pp. 181–90.

Corden, W.M., 1974: *Trade Policy and Economic Welfare* (Oxford: Oxford University Press).

—, 1991: 'Strategic Trade Policy', *in* D. Greenaway, M. Bleaney and I.M.T. Stewart (eds), *Companion to Contemporary Economic Thought* (London: Routledge).

Greenaway, D., 1991: 'New Trade Theories and Developing Countries', *in* V.N. Balasubramanyam and S. Lall, *Current Issues in Development Economics* (London: Macmillan).

—, 1991: 'Why Are We Negotiating on TRIMS?', *in* D. Greenaway et al. (eds), *Global Protectionism* (London: Macmillan).

—, 1993: 'Liberalising Foreign Trade Through Rose Tinted Glasses', *Economic Journal*, no. 416, vol. 103.

Greenaway, D. and C.H. Nam, 1988: 'Industrialisation and Macroeconomic Performance in the Developing Countries Under Alternative Liberalisation Scenarios', *Kylos*, vol. 41.

Greenaway, D. and D. Sapsford, 1994: 'What Does Liberalisation Do for Exports and Growth?', *Weltwirtschaftliches Archive*, vol. 130.

Haberler, G., 1950: 'Some Problems in the Pure Theory of International Trade', *Economic Journal*, vol. LX.

Hagen, E., 1958: 'An Economic Justification of Protectionism', *Quarterly Journal of Economics*, vol. LXXII.

Johnson, H.G., 1965: 'Optimal Trade Intervention in the Presence of Domestic Distortions', *in* R.E. Baldwin (ed.), *Trade, Growth and the Balance of Payments: Essays in Honour of Gottfried Haberler* (Chicago: Rand–McNally).

—, 1965: 'An Economic Theory of Protectionism, Tariff Bargaining, and the Formation of Customs Unions', *Journal of Political Economy*, vol. LXXIII.

—, 1971: 'Optimal Trade Intervention in the Presence of Domestic Distortions', *in* H.G. Johnson, *Aspects of the Theory of Tariffs*.

Khatkhate, D., 1994: 'Intellectual Origins of Indian Economic Reform: A Review of Jagdish Bhagwati's India in Transition: Freeing the Economy', *World Development*, no. 7, vol. 22.

Krueger, A., 1974: 'The Political Economy of the Rent-Seeking Society', *American Economic Review*, vol. 64.

Krugman, P., 1994: 'The Myth of Asia's Miracle', *Foreign Affairs*, no. 6, vol. 73.

Lipton, M. and J. Firn, 1960: *The Erosion of a Relationship: India and Britain Since 1960* (London: Oxford University Press).

Little, I.M.D., 1982: *Economic Development: Theory, Policy and International Relations* (New York: Basic Books Inc. Publishers).

Little, I.M.D., T. Scitovsky and M. Scott, 1970: *Industry and Trade in Some Developing Countries* (London: Oxford University Press).

MacBean, A.I. and V.N. Balasubramanyam, 1978: *Meeting the Third World Challenge* (London: Macmillan for the Trade Policy Research Centre).

Maddison, A., 1971: *Class Structure and Economic Growth: India and Pakistan Since the Moghuls* (London: George Allen & Unwin).

Maskus, K.E., 1993: 'Trade-Related Intellectual Property Rights', *European Economy*, no. 52.

Milner, C. and A. Mckay, 1996: 'On Neutrality and Export Promotion: Issues and Evidence', *in* V.N. Balasubramanyam and D. Greenaway, *Trade and Development: Issues in Honour of J.N. Bhagwati* (London: Macmillan).

Mitra, A., 1977: *Terms of Trade and Class Relations* (London: Frank Cass).

Nguyen, T., C. Perroni and R. Wigle, 1993: 'An Evaluation of the Draft Final Act of the Uruguay Round', *Economic Journal*, vol. 103.

Nurkse, R., 1959: *Patterns of Trade and Development* (Stockholm: Almqist and Wicksell).

Olson, M., 1965: *The Logic of Collective Action: Public Goods and the Theory of Groups* (Cambridge, Mass.: Harvard University Press).

Papageorgiou, D., M. Michaely and A. Choksi, 1991: *Liberalising Foreign Trade* (Oxford: Blackwell).

Sapsford, D. and V.N. Balasubramanyam, 1994: 'The Long-Run Behavior of the Relative Price of Primary Commodities: Statistical Evidence and Policy Implications', *World Development*, no. 11, vol. 22.

Singer, H.W., 1950: 'The Distribution of Gains Between Investing and Borrowing Countries', *American Economic Review*, Papers and Proceedings.

——, 1988: 'The World Development Report 1987 on the Blessing of Outward Orientation: A Necessary Correction', *Journal of Development Studies*, vol. 24.

Tyler, W., 1981: 'Growth and Export Expansion in Developing Countries: Some Empirical Evidence', *Journal of Development Economics*, vol. 3.

World Bank, 1993: *The East Asian Miracle: Economic Growth and Public Policy, Policy Research Report* (Washington DC: The World Bank).

2

Proofs of the Theorems
on Comparative Advantage

THIS note critically examines the usual statement and proofs of the two principal theories of comparative advantage: (i) Ricardian, and (ii) Heckscher–Ohlin. While none of the analysis offered here is intrinsically novel, it is presented in a way that has fairly important implications for a full understanding — not evident in either the oral or written tradition — of the postulates underlying these theories of comparative advantage. More significantly, it is shown that (contrary to what is thought) certain restrictions on demand conditions have to be specified *even when* the Ricardian theorem and the Heckscher–Ohlin theorem (using the *price* definition of factor abundance) are to be proved.

I

The proofs of the two-country, two-commodity theories of comparative advantage relating to the pattern of trade, whether of the Ricardian or the Heckscher–Ohlin version, depend on two successive arguments.

Argument I

Propositions are proven, relating to the determination of the *pre-trade* commodity price ratio: thus, in the Ricardian model, the pre-trade commodity price ratio is shown to be equal to the labour productivity ratio whereas, in the Heckscher–Ohlin model, it is demonstrated that the relative, pre-trade price of the commodity using the country's abundant factor intensively will be lower than in the other country.

Argument II

(i) It is argued that a country will export that commodity whose relative, pre-trade price is lower than in the other country and will import the other commodity. (ii) *Corollary:* Also usually considered implicit is the proposition that if the pre-trade prices are identical between countries no trade will occur.

The successive Arguments I and II (i) lead to the well-known theorems of comparative advantages: (1) *Ricardian Theorem*, a country will export (import) that commodity in which her comparative factor productivity is higher (lower); and (2) *Heckscher–Ohlin Theorem*, a country will export (import) that commodity which uses her abundant (scarce) factor intensively.[1] Possible corollaries to these theorems, sometimes derived from Arguments I and II (ii), are: (1) *Ricardian Corollary*, where comparative factor productivities are identical between countries, no trade will occur;

[1] That the traditional proofs of both Ricardian and Heckscher–Ohlin propositions rely explicitly on Argument I and implicitly on Argument II (ii) is evident not merely from oral traditions but also from the writings of various theorists.

Thus Ohlin (7, p. 29), for example, in his famous work on *Interregional and International Trade*, leads up, via Argument I, to an assertion of Argument II (ii), and consequently to the Heckscher–Ohlin theorem: 'The first condition of trade is that some goods can be produced more cheaply in one region than in another. In each of them the cheap goods are those containing relatively great quantities of the factors cheaper than in the other regions' (Argument I). 'These cheap goods make up exports, whereas goods which can be more cheaply produced in the other regions are imported' (Argument II (ii)). 'We may say, therefore, that exports are in each region composed of articles into the production of which enter large quantities of cheap factors' (Heckscher–Ohlin theorem, with price definition of factor abundance).

Similarly, a modern author such as Jones (3) on the Heckscher–Ohlin theory terminates his analysis at the point at which Argument I is proven; and implicitly assuming Argument II (ii), proceeds to the Heckscher–Ohlin theorem.

At a more general level, embracing all theories of comparative advantage, Kindleberger (4, p. 88) also assumes Argument II (ii) as valid and proceeds to discuss Argument I substantively by stating that ' . . . the law of comparative costs says that a country exports those products which are comparatively cheap in price at home, and imports those which are comparatively expensive' (Argument II (ii)). 'But economics can say more than this' (Argument I).

These examples could be readily multiplied but hardly need to be.

and (2) *Heckscher–Ohlin Corollary*, where factor endowments are identical between countries, no trade will take place.

In Sec. II, addressed to the Ricardian propositions, it is shown that the Ricardian theorem requires the specification of restrictions (albeit 'reasonable') on demand *in addition* to the postulates always stated. Opportunity is also taken to note that the Ricardian corollary is invalid owing to the familiar multiplicity of production equilibria in the Ricardian model. Finally, in Sec. III, which discuss the Heckscher–Ohlin propositions, it is argued that while the assumption that the consumption pattern be identical between countries regardless of income levels is correctly held to be required only when the *physical* definition of factor abundance (to be discussed later) is used, it is incorrect to maintain that *no* restrictions at all need to be put on demand when the *price* definition is adopted.

II. Ricardian Propositions

(A) *Ricardian Corollary*

The Ricardian corollary, stating that where factor productivity ratios are identical between the two countries no trade will take place, is not logically true. Indeed, not merely can trade take place but, in general, the pattern of trade will also be reversible. This follows immediately from the well-known multiplicity of production equilibria corresponding to the commodity price ratio, which is equated, under perfect competition, with the identical factor productivity ratio in each country.

This is readily illustrated. In Fig. 2.1 (a) the production possibility curves of countries I and II are depicted as $R_I F_I$ and $R_{II} F_{II}$ respectively. Note that these show constant and identical rates of transformation at the margin, because of the one-factor, constant-returns technology and the assumption of identical factor productivity ratios.[2] Argument I holds in this model because the *pre-trade*

---

[2] In the Ricardian model, if labour is the factor of production and x_I and x_{II} the labour productivity ratios in commodity X in countries I and II, respectively, and y_I and y_{II} in commodity Y, then $x_I/y_I = (P_x/P_y)_I$ (the price of X in terms of Y) and $x_{II}/y_{II} = (P_x/P_y)_{II}$ prior to trade. Therefore, any ranking of $(P_x/P_y)_I$ and $(P_x/P_y)_{II}$

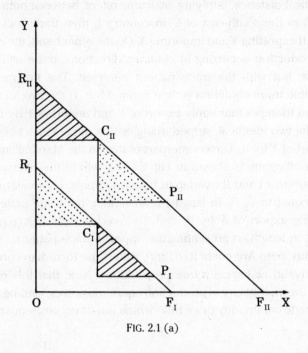

FIG. 2.1 (a)

commodity price ratio in each country will equal the factor productivity ratio. But the factor productivity ratios being identical in the two countries, the pre-trade price ratios in them both will also be equalized. Does Argument II (ii) then necessarily hold, leading to the Ricardian corollary?

It does not. In Fig. 2.1 (a) the contrary possibility is illustrated. Assuming that, at the commodity price ratio $R_{II}F_{II} = R_I F_I$, country II 'chooses' consumption at C_{II} and country I at C_I, the production choice is still wide open for each country. Each country can have production at *any* point on its production possibility frontier. Suppose that the production then is at C_{II} in country II and at C_I in country I; in this case both Argument II (ii) and the Ricardian corollary will prove to be valid. However, suppose that the choice of production is to the north-west of C_{II} in country II and (an

---

prior to trade implies also a corresponding, equivalent ranking of the factor productivity ratios. Therefore, when the factor productivity ratios x_I/y_I and x_{II}/y_{II} are identical, so will be the pre-trade commodity price ratios in the two countries.

identical distance, implying 'matching offers' between both countries) to the south-east of C_I in country I, then trade *will* occur
with II exporting Y and importing X. On the other hand, the choice
of production occurring in contrary directions, trade will again
occur, but with the trade pattern reversed. The full range of
possible trade equilibria is then defined by: (i) the two identical,
dotted triangles that imply export of X and import of Y by II, and
(ii) the two identical, striped triangles that imply export of Y and
import of X by II. The counterpart of this, in the Marshallian offer
curve diagram, is shown in Fig. 2.1 (b), where the offer curves
of countries I and II overlap in both quadrants, the overlap over
OS (equal to $C_{II}P_{II}$ in length) representing the trade pattern involving export of X by II, and the overlap over OQ (equal to
$C_{II}R_{II}$ in length) representing the opposite trade pattern.

Thus, both Argument II (ii) and, with it, the Ricardian corollary
are invalid as logically true propositions. Note that this results
from the multiplicity of production equilibria corresponding to the
pre-trade commodity price ratio which is a direct consequence of

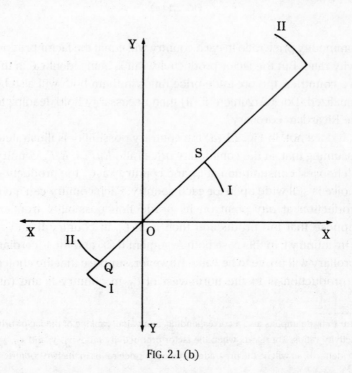

FIG. 2.1 (b)

the Ricardian one-factor, constant returns-to-scale assumption combined with perfect competition. The correct Ricardian corollary therefore is that, where comparative factor productivities are identical between countries, the volume and direction of trade are indeterminate.

(B) *Ricardian Theorem*

However, what about the case where factor productivity ratios are different between countries? In this case again, in view of Argument I retaining its validity, the pre-trade commodity price ratios will differ between the two countries. Does Argument II (i) then necessarily hold, leading to the Ricardian theorem?

It does not. The reason is that demand conditions may be such as to lead to multiple self-sufficiency equilibria. Thus in Fig. 2.2, OQ_IO is the offer curve of country I and $OQ_{II}O$ of country II. Note that, under self-sufficiency, each country has two possible price equilibria: OS_I and OT for country I, OS_{II} and OT for country II. If then the pre-trade equilibrium price ratios are at OS_I and OS_{II}, the equilibrium price ratio will be at OT and no trade will occur, *once*

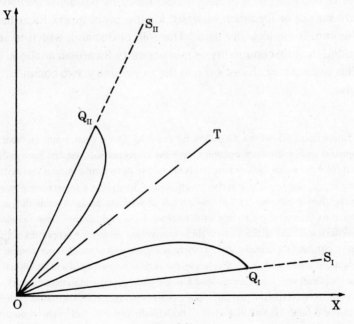

FIG. 2.2

free trade is possible. Argument II (i) thus collapses: although the pre-trade prices are different between the two countries, trade will *not* take place. With Argument II (i), the Ricardian theorem also collapses: the factor productivity ratio in country I equals OS_I, and thus differs from that in country II, which equals OS_{II}, and yet no trade occurs.

Suitable restrictions have to be placed therefore on demand conditions to eliminate this possibility. A sufficient restriction is to assume that societal tastes enjoy the properties of well-ordered individual taste maps — as with Samuelson's social indifference curves.[3] Since, in Ricardo's model, there is only one factor of production and (at points of complete specialization) the marginal product is fixed in terms of the commodity produced, the social demands will be such as to rule out the possibility of a free-trade price equilibrium involving no trade *even when* the taste map of *each* factor-owner is alternatively assumed to be well ordered. Since the latter assumption is quite reasonable, the restriction that needs to be placed on demand conditions in Ricardian analysis is not at all 'significant'. But it is there in any case; and some such restriction must be specified, *in addition to the postulates traditionally set out in Ricardian analysis*, for the proof of the Ricardian theorem to be logically tight.[4] The role of demand, which is admitted in multi-commodity or multi-country Ricardian analysis, is thus not entirely absent even in the two-country, two-commodity case.

[3] Samuelson (10) proves the following theorem: '(*a*) If each group member's demand and indifference contours have the conventional "regular" convexity, and (*b*) if the social welfare function is defined to have similar regular convexity properties, and (*c*) if within the group optimal lump-sum transfers are always made, then it follows: (1) there will result observable demand totals that are functions of market prices and total income alone, and (2) that these demand functions will have all the Slutsky–Hicks or revealed preference properties of any single consumer's demand, and (3) there will exist a set of indifference contours relating to the totals $X, Y, \ldots$ that has all the regular properties of any individual's contours and which we can pretend a single mind is engaged in maximizing.'

[4] As H. Johnson has pointed out to me in correspondence, an alternative restriction could be to assume that some of both goods is demanded in each country at all price ratios.

III. HECKSCHER–OHLIN THEORY

The role that demand conditions can play in undermining the *traditional* proof of the Heckscher–Ohlin theory is rather more significant and not exactly parallel.

However, note first that neither Argument II (ii) nor the Heckscher–Ohlin corollary can be invalidated because of multiple production equilibria in the Heckscher–Ohlin model. This model leads to a non-strictly convex production possibilities set, and hence there is only one production equilibrium corresponding to any commodity price ratio. In *this* respect, therefore, the Heckscher–Ohlin model is at an advantage in comparison to the Ricardian model.

Demand conditions do, however, play a role. To discuss this role with clarity, it is necessary to distinguish between two alternative versions of the Heckscher–Ohlin propositions, stemming from alternative definitions of factor abundance. Under the *physical* definition of factor abundance, if $(K/L)_I > (K/L)_{II}$, where K and L refer to the overall endowments of these two factors, country I is defined as K-abundant or L-scarce. Under the *price* definition, if $(P_K/P_L)_I < (P_K/P_L)_{II}$, where P_K/P_L stands for the price of K in terms of the price of L in the *pre-trade* situation, then I is K-abundant or L-scarce.

Where the *physical* definition is used, the proof of the Heckscher–Ohlin theorem proceeds traditionally by: (1) showing that the K-abundant country I will have, at the *same* commodity price ratio, a higher (X/Y) ratio in production than country II, where X is the K-intensive commodity;[5] (2) assuming that the consumption pattern is identical between the two countries, in the sense that the (X/Y) ratio in consumption, at the *same* commodity price ratio, is identical between the two countries; (3) therewith deducing that, for self-sufficiency, $(P_X/P_Y)_I < (P_X/P_Y)_{II}$, thus completing Argument I, which requires that the K-abundant country will have its pre-trade relative price of the K-intensive commodity cheaper than the L-abundant country, and then (4) arguing, from Argument

---

[5] This proposition is of course valid for incomplete specialization. For proof, see Jones (3).

II (i), that the K-abundant country will export the K-intensive commodity and import the L-intensive commodity.

Where the *price* definition is used, the proof proceeds *directly* to Argument I, avoiding the three specific steps involved in the case of the physical definition. The assumed technology leads to a unique relationship between commodity and factor price ratios,[6] and hence $(P_X/P_Y)_I < (P_X/P_Y)_{II}$ follows immediately from $(P_K/P_L)_I < (P_K/P_L)_{II}$. Beyond that, *only* step (4), involving Argument II (i), is required. Note therefore that, in the case of the price definition, step (3) above does not have to be brought in. In view of this difference, we examine the two proofs, one for each definition, successively. Since the arguments are symmetrical for the theorem and the corollary, only the theorem is considered here to avoid tedious repetition.

(1) *Physical Definition*

Whereas steps (3) and (4) are never explicitly stated and proved, they can be shown to be valid as soon as it is assumed (as in step (2)) that the consumption pattern is identical between countries, at identical commodity prices, regardless of income level. Note that this assumption implies non-intersecting, *homothetic* social market-demand curves, which, in conjunction with the assumption of convexity, rule out any possibility of contradicting steps (3) and (4).

Thus, for example, take step (3). P_s^{II} is the self-sufficiency price-ratio for country II in Fig. 2.3 (a), and the equilibrium consumption and production points C_{II} and P_{II} coincide. C_I and C_{II} then lie on the same ray from the origin because of the assumption in step (2); and P_I lies to the right of P_{II} by virtue of the proposition in step (1). It is then easy to see that the self-sufficiency price-ratio $(P_x/P_y) = P_s^{II}$ for country I will be lower than P_s^{II}. This is because a contradiction, such as shown in Fig. 2.3 (b), requires *intersecting* social market-demand curves, which are ruled out as soon as the assumption in step (2) is made. So also for step (4).

---

[6] This is the proposition well known to trade theorists and first proved by Samuelson (8, 9) for a two-factor, two-commodity model.

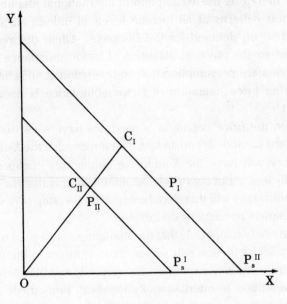

FIG. 2.3 (a)

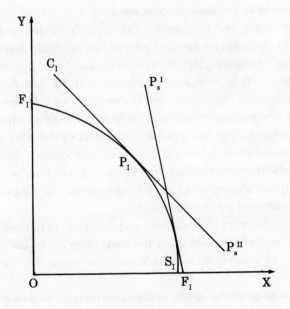

FIG. 2.3 (b)

(2) *Price Definition*

While, therefore, the assumption of international identity of consumption patterns at all income levels is indeed an adequate restriction on demand for the Heckscher–Ohlin theorem to be valid when the physical definition of factor abundance is used, the customary presumption that no restriction at all is necessary when the price definition of factor abundance is used is not correct.

When the price definition is used, we have seen that we bypass steps (2) and (3) and, in fact, infer *directly* that the *K*-abundant economy will have the *K*-intensive commodity cheaper under self-sufficiency. But *before* we can infer from this that the *K*-intensive commodity will therefore be exported (i.e. step (4)), we must again impose restrictions on demand.

What really happens is that the elimination of step (3) by virtue of the price definition still leaves step (4) intact in the chain of argument; and since *each* of the two steps (3) and (4) follows from the assumption of internationally identical, homothetic market-demand curves, *some* assumption with respect to demand continues to be necessary to sustain step (4), even when the price-definition of factor abundance is used.

Once again, the assumption (in step (2)) of internationally identical, homothetic demand curves can be made and will be sufficient to ensure step (4). However, this is an overly-strong assumption. It is sufficient to assume instead that the social market-demand curves, in each country, are well ordered. This is itself a 'significant' restriction on demand because, in view of income-distribution being present in a two-factor model, well-ordered social market-demand curves do not follow immediately from well-ordered individual indifference curves and, as Samuelson (10) has shown, a policy of lump-sum income transfers has to be envisaged for the purpose.[7]

Hence, contrary to customary statements, demand conditions are not entirely irrelevant in the two-country, two-commodity theories of comparative advantage even when the Ricardian

---

[7] Note that the question of stability conditions has not been raised here. Further, the analysis has been confined to one country alone.

model or the Heckscher–Ohlin model (with *price* definition of factor abundance) is being considered.[8]

REFERENCES

Bhagwati, J. and V.K. Ramaswami, 1963: 'Domestic Distortions, Tariffs and the Theory of Optimum Subsidy', *Journal of Political Economy*, vol. 71 (Feb.).

Hagen, E., 1958: 'An Economic Justification of Protectionism', *Quarterly Journal of Economics*, vol. 72 (Nov.).

Jones, R., 1956: 'Factor Proportions and the Heckscher–Ohlin Model', *Review of Economic Studies*, vol. 24 (Oct.).

Kindleberger, C.P., 1955: *International Economics* (Illinois: Richard D. Irwin, Inc.).

Matthews, R.C.O., 1950: 'Reciprocal Demand and Increasing Returns', *Review of Economic Studies*, vol. 17 (Feb.).

Meade, J.E., 1950: *A Geometry of International Trade* (London: Allen & Unwin Ltd.).

[8] The analysis in the text has accepted the framework of the Ricardian and Heckscher–Ohlin models. It is well known, however, that if either the technological or the institutional assumptions are relaxed, Arguments I and II can easily be jeopardized. For example, if increasing returns are assumed, it is known from Meade (6) and Matthews (5) that Argument II (ii) collapses: when the pre-trade prices are different between countries, both patterns of trade may be possible.

Similarly, if there is a wage-differential between the two sectors it is no longer possible to sustain Argument I as logically true. This is because the equality of the commodity price-ratio with the domestic rate of transformation in production (at points of incomplete specialization) disappears (2), so that the required ranking of the pre-trade commodity price ratios in the two countries will not necessarily emerge. On the other hand, if the wage differential operates identically in the two countries, this will be a sufficient condition for sustaining Argument I. As for Argument II (ii), it will continue to hold in the Ricardian case as also in the Heckscher–Ohlin model (with the assumption of internationally identical, homothetic market-demand curves), *despite* the wage-differential and the consequent divergence of the commodity price ratio from the (marginal) domestic rate of transformation in production.

Note finally that, although the assumption of identical wage differentials in the two countries will leave the comparative advantage theorems unscathed, it is *not* correct to argue, as Taussig (11) did, that the terms and volume of trade will also be the same as in the case where there is no wage differential at all.

Ohlin, B., 1952: *Interregional and International Trade* (Cambridge: Harvard University Press).

Samuelson, P.A., 1948: 'International Trade and the Equalisation of Factor Prices', *Economic Journal* (June).

——, 1949: 'International Factor Price Equalisation Once Again', *Economic Journal* (June).

——, 1956: 'Social Indifference Curves', *Quarterly Journal of Economics*, vol. 70 (Feb.).

Taussig, F.W., 1927: *International Trade* (New York: Macmillan Co. Ltd.).

3

Protection, Real Wages,
and Real Incomes[1]

1. IN an article in *The Economic Journal*[2] on 'Protection and Real Wages: A Restatement', Mr Lancaster re-examined the celebrated Stolper–Samuelson theorem and concluded:

This paper does not deny that protection will raise the real wage of one of the factors, but shows that no general statement about which of the factors this will be can be deduced from the relative 'scarcity' of the factors in the Stolper–Samuelson sense.

Although the Stolper–Samuelson theorem 'Protection raises the real wage of the scarce factor' is shown to be an incorrect generalization, a restatement in the form 'Protection raises the real wage of the factor in which the imported good is relatively more intensive' has general validity.

It is proposed in Sec. I of this chapter to systematically review the original Stolper–Samuelson contribution, therewith to advance a critique (distinct from Mr Lancaster's criticism, which is not accepted), of the Stolper–Samuelson formulation of the theorem and then to restate the theorem: this restatement being considered to be the only true and general statement about the effect of protection (prohibitive or otherwise) on real wages of factors in the context of the basic Stolper–Samuelson model. The logical truth of the restated theorem is briefly analysed then in the context of alternative models. Sec. II proceeds to extend the scope of the discussion with the argument that, with a non-prohibitive tariff, a

[1] This chapter comprises the text of a paper read to the Nuffield Economics Society. My thanks are due to Professor Hicks and J. Black for substantial help with its exposition. I am also happy to record my heavy indebtedness to Professor Harry Johnson, who has been generous with suggestions that have led to numerous improvements.
[2] *Economic Journal*, Dec. 1959, pp. 199–210. The following quotation is from p. 199.

sharp distinction must be drawn between the impact on the real wage of a factor and the effect on its real income; some implications of this distinction are then analysed.

I. PROTECTION AND REAL WAGES

2. In the following analysis, I shall take the *basic* Stolper–Samuelson model to mean that the protecting country has two factors, two commodities enjoying different factor intensities, linear and homogeneous production functions subject to diminishing returns (along isoquants), and incomplete specialization in production. Full employment of factors, pure competition, and perfect mobility of factors are also assumed.

Founded on this model, we have three alternative formulations of the theorem concerning the impact of protection on the real wages of factors:

(1) *Restrictive Stolper–Samuelson Theorem*. 'International trade necessarily lowers the real wage of the scarce factor expressed in terms of any good.'[3] This formulation restricts itself to the comparison of the free trade real wage with the self-sufficiency real wage of the scarce factor. The comparison is confined to the case of a prohibitive tariff and excludes non-prohibitive protection. The theorem can be rewritten as follows: prohibitive protection necessarily raises the real wage of the scarce factor.

(2) *General Stolper–Samuelson Theorem*. Protection raises the real wage of the scarce factor.[4] This formulation is clearly intended

---

[3] Stolper and Samuelson, 'Protection and Real Wages', *Readings in the Theory of International Trade* (A.E.A., Blakiston Co., 1949), p. 346.

[4] The actual formulation of the general Stolper–Samuelson theorem is from Lancaster, op. cit., p. 199. While the bulk of their analysis relates explicitly to the restrictive formulation, there are several indications that Stolper and Samuelson also had in mind the general formulation: (1) a large number of quotations they cite from other authors to outline the problem refer to tariffs in general rather than to tariffs of only a prohibitive nature; (2) they feel it necessary to assume that 'the country in question is relatively small and has no influence on the terms of trade. Thus any gain to the country through monopolistic or monopsonistic behaviour is excluded' (op. cit., p. 344); this assumption is quite superfluous, as

be more general and also includes non-prohibitive tariffs. To emphasize this, we may rewrite it thus: protection (prohibitive or otherwise) necessarily raises the real wage of the scarce factor.

(3) *Stolper–Samuelson–Metzler–Lancaster Theorem.* 'Protection [prohibitive or otherwise] raises the real wage of the factor in which the imported good is relatively more intensive.'[5]

In the ensuing analysis any reference to 'the Stolper–Samuelson theorems' should be taken to relate to the initial two formulations alone; reference to the last formulation will always be by its full title.

3. We can begin by setting out the basic elements in the argument leading to the twin formulations of the Stolper–Samuelson theorem:

(1) protection increases the internal relative price of the importable good:

(2) an increase in the relative price of a good increases the real wage of the factor used intensively in its production;

(3) the importable good is intensive in the use of the scarce factor. Therefore,

(4) protection raises the real wage of the scarce factor.

These arguments must each be closely examined.

4. Concerning argument (1), we must distinguish between prohibitive and non-prohibitive protection:

(i) Protection will necessarily raise the relative price of the importable good when the tariff is prohibitive; the free-trade relative price of the importable good is lower than under self-sufficiency.[6]

---

we shall later see, if we wish to sustain only the restrictive formulation of the theorem; and (3) the title chosen for the article is not 'International Trade and Real Wages' but 'Protection and Real Wages'. Lancaster, op. cit., p. 201, also construes the Stolper–Samuelson theorem in its general form; thus witness his argument that 'Protection will cause a movement in the *general direction* $Q'Q$, away from the free-trade point towards the self-sufficiency point' (emphasis mine).

[5] Lancaster, op. cit., p. 199. This theorem has been given its stated name on grounds that are made explicit later.

[6] This is true except in a *limiting* case where the terms of trade will not change

(ii)   Non-prohibitive protection may either raise, leave un-
       changed or lower the internal relative price of the importable
       good. Metzler has demonstrated that this last 'perverse' pos-
       sibility will occur, in the context of my present model, when
       the elasticity of foreign demand for imports (η_x) is less than
       the domestic marginal propensity to consume exportable
       goods (c).[7] It follows, then, that if imports are not inferior
       goods in the protecting country's consumption, this case
       requires inelastic foreign demand; and we can ensure that
       the internal relative price of the importable good always rises
       with the imposition of a tariff by assuming *either* elastic
       foreign demand (sometimes done in the form of assuming a
       small country) *or* a high enough tariff (in the limit, a prohibi-
       tive tariff) for demand to be elastic.

5. Argument (2) follows necessarily from the basic Stolper–Samuelson model. To show this simply, we should recall the technological features of the model employed by Samuelson some years
later in *The Economic Journal*[8] to demonstrate factor-price
equalization: these features are identical with those of the Stolper–Samuelson model in all respects. I propose thus to avoid
altogether the use of the box diagram and work instead with the
unique relationships that Samuelson derived in these later articles

---

with trade. This case can, however, be ruled out, in the context of the model used
here, by assuming that the community indifference curves (used here without
any welfare connotation) are strictly convex. This limiting case will henceforward
be ignored.

[7] Metzler, 'Tariffs, the Terms of Trade and the Distribution of National Income',
Journal of Political Economy, Feb. 1949, pp. 1–29. It should be emphasized that
the Metzler formula for determining the impact of protection on the internal
commodity price-ratio relates to the case where the initial situation is that of free
trade. Where, however, the initial situation itself has a tariff and the impact of
increased protection is the subject of analysis, the 'perverse' possibility mentioned
in the text will occur, as argued in Sec. II, when a slightly altered condition is
fulfilled. The discussion in Sec. I is, however, confined to initial situations of free
trade, as with Stolper and Samuelson, Metzler and Lancaster.

[8] International Trade and the Equalization of Factor Prices', *Economic Journal*,
June 1948, pp. 163–84; and 'International Factor-Price Equalization Once Again',
Economic Journal, June 1949, pp. 181–97.

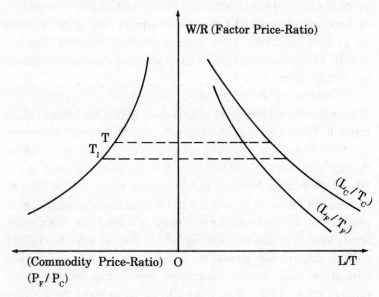

FIG. 3.1

between commodity price-ratios, factor price-ratios and factor propositions in the two industries in a country, from the given assumptions concerning technology alone. These are summarized
in Fig. 3.1, which is reproduced, with slight changes, from Samuelson's 1949 article.[9]

Let L_C and L_F represent the labour employed in producing clothing and food respectively; T_C and T_F being the quantities of land
so employed. W/R represents the ratio of wages to rents; L/T the
factor endowment ratio of the country; and P_F/P_0 the price of food
over the price of clothing. Clothing is the labour-intensive industry,
food the land-intensive industry, at all relevant factor price-ratios.

[9] This diagram is to be found on p. 188 of Samuelson's 1949 *Economic Journal*
article, op. cit. Full exploration of this diagram is to be found in an excellent article
by Professor Johnson, 'Factor Endowments, International Trade and Factor
Prices', *Manchester School*, Sept. 1957, pp. 270–83. Professor Johnson, however,
works with a slightly adapted diagram, to be found in Harrod, 'Factor-price
Relations Under Free Trade', *Economic Journal*, June 1958, pp. 245–55. On grounds
of economy, the discussion of this well-known diagram has been briefly dealt with
in this chapter.

$(L_C/T_C > L_F/T_F$ at all relevant $W/R).$[10] As wages fall in relation to rents, the price of food is shown to rise in relation to that of clothing in a monotonic way. The factor endowment ratio of the country (L/T) fixes the range of the diagram which is relevant. This is a purely technology-determined diagram, and demand conditions are totally absent from it.

T being any given commodity price-ratio (P_F/F_C), change it to T_1 such that the relative price of food rises. With it, the labour-to-land ratios in both food and clothing will rise. The marginal physical product of land in both products will thus rise and of labour fall, so that the real wage of land will be unambiguously increased and of labour decreased. Increase in the relative price of food thus increases the real wage of land, the factor intensively employed in its production; and reduces the real wage of labour, the factor intensively used in producing clothing (whose relative price has fallen).

This argument, it should be noted, rests on the assumption, part of the basic Stolper–Samuelson model, that the rise of the relative price of food does not go so far as to make the country specialize completely on food, in so far as the fall in the real wage of labour is concerned; for, once the country is specialized completely, further increases in the relative price of food will raise the real wage of *both* labour and land, which is destructive of the full validity of argument (2).

Given the basic Stolper–Samuelson model, therefore, an increase (decrease) in the relative price of a good will necessarily increase (decrease) the real wage of the factor intensively used in its production.

6. Argument (3), that the importable good is intensive in the use of the scarce factor, is really the well-known Heckscher–Ohlin theorem. The crucial question that it raises is: does the Heckscher–Ohlin theorem follow from the basic Stolper–Samuelson model? To answer this question, we should first have to define 'factor scarcity'. We may choose from three alternative definitions of factor scarcity:

[10] Although the factor-intensities of the commodities may be reversible, they *cannot* reverse for a country with a *given* factor endowment. At the present stage of my argument, therefore, I do not need to make the strong assumption that factor-intensities are non-reversible at *all* factor price-ratios.

A. *Lancaster Definition.* A country's scarce factor is that which is used more intensively in the production of the importable good. This definition may be described as tautological, since it turns the Heckscher–Ohlin theorem into a valid proposition by *definition*. It may also be described as an internal definition, since it excludes any comparison with the foreign country. It has been suggested by Lancaster.[11]

B. *Heckscher–Ohlin Definition.* A country's scarce factor is that whose relative price is higher than abroad under self-sufficiency. This may also be described as a price definition, since the country's scarce factor is that factor which is more expensive prior to trade than abroad. This definition has been used by Heckscher and Ohlin.[12]

C. *Leontief Definition.* A country's scarce factor is that of which there are fewer physical units per unit of the other factor than abroad. This may also be described as a physical definition, since it defines scarcity with reference to the relative physical quantities of factors.[13]

Using each of these definitions in turn, let us analyse the Heckscher–Ohlin theorem.

A: If the Lancaster definition of factor scarcity is used, then the Heckscher–Ohlin theorem holds by definition.

[11] Lancaster (op. cit., p. 208) argues that 'the only acceptable definition' of a scarce factor is that which defines it as the factor 'which is used more intensively in the good of which more is produced in isolation than in trade'. It is of some interest to note that tariffs designed to influence distribution are probably set with reference to such internal criteria: to raise the real wage of labour, for instance, tariffs are imposed on labour-intensive industries rather than on products of industries using a factor which is scarcer at home than abroad; with the possible exception of the pauper-labour argument for such tariffs.

[12] For a convincing attribution of the authorship of this definition of factor scarcity to Heckscher and Ohlin, see a masterly article by R. Jones, 'Factor Proportions and the Heckscher–Ohlin Theorem', *Review of Economic Studies*, 1956–7, pp. 1–10. The definition may be also illustrated in terms of Fig. 3.1: country A is labour-abundant and country B land-abundant if, under self-sufficiency, $(W/R)_A < (W/R)_B$.

[13] W. Leontief, 'Domestic Production and Foreign Trade: The American Capital Position Re-examined', *Proceedings of the American Philosophical Society*, 28 Sept. 1953; reprinted in *Economia Internazionale*, Feb. 1954. Again, country A is labour-abundant and country B land-abundant if, under self-sufficiency, $(L/T)_A > (L/T)_B$.

B: If the Heckscher–Ohlin definition of factor scarcity is used then the further assumptions of international identity of production functions and non-reversibility of factor-intensities of commodities between the two countries will suffice to ensure the full validity of the Heckscher–Ohlin theorem.[14]

C: If the Leontief definition of factor scarcity is used, then the threefold assumptions of non-reversibilities of factor-intensities of commodities between the trading countries and the international identity of both production functions and tastes will ensure the validity of the Heckscher–Ohlin theorem.[15]

7. We can now sum up on the Stolper–Samuelson formulations as follows:[16]

A.   (1) The restrictive Stolper–Samuelson theorem is logically

[14] This can be readily seen from Fig. 3.1. If $(W/R)_A < (W/R)_B$ and production functions with non-reversible factor-intensities are common between the countries, then we can see that $(P_F/P_C)_A > (P_F/P_C)_B$ under self-sufficiency and the labour-abundant country A will necessarily export the labour-intensive commodity, clothing. We could, of course, specify what appears to be a less restrictive condition than that set out in the text; for instance, we could sustain the Heckscher–Ohlin theorem by assuming merely that, instead of identical production functions between countries, the differences in the production functions are not large enough to outweigh the effect of differences in factor scarcity on the pre-trade commodity price-ratios. I have preferred to use the strong condition (identity of tastes) instead of the weak one on the ground that the use of the latter seems to be bad methodology, amounting to the argument that the Heckscher–Ohlin definition of factor scarcity will suffice to sustain the Heckscher–Ohlin theorem if other factors do not work to invalidate it.

[15] The Heckscher–Ohlin theorem would not hold as a logically true proposition in this case unless we also postulate now international identity of tastes (or the weak postulate that differences in tastes between countries do not affect the issue). This follows from the fact that while, with identical production functions, country A will show a bias towards the production of the labour-intensive commodity, clothing, by virtue of her physical abundance of labour, this bias in production may be more than offset by a bias in A towards the *consumption* of clothing: such that, in self-sufficiency, we find that $(P_F/P_C)_A < (P_F/P_C)_B$ and country A, although physically abundant in labour, would export the land-intensive commodity, food.

[16] The phrase 'logically true' in the following statements is used in the strict mathematical sense: 'A statement that is true in every logically possible case is said to be *logically true*' (Kemeny, Snell and Thompson, *Introduction to Finite Mathematics* (Prentice–Hall, 1957), p. 19).

true if we use: (a) the basic Stolper–Samuelson model, and (b) the Lancaster definition of factor scarcity.

(2) The general Stolper–Samuelson theorem is logically true if we use the further assumption that the elasticity of foreign demand is greater than the marginal propensity to consume exportable goods $(n_x > c)$.

B. (1) The restrictive Stolper–Samuelson theorem is logically true if we use: (a) the basic Stolper–Samuelson model, (b) the Heckscher–Ohlin definition of factor scarcity, (c) the assumption of international identity of production functions, and (d) the assumption of non-reversibility of factor-intensities of commodities between the countries.

(2) The general Stolper–Samuelson theorem is logically true if we use the further assumption that $n_x > c$.

C. (1) The restrictive Stolper–Samuelson theorem is logically true if we use: (a) the basic Stolper–Samuelson model, (b) the Leontief definition of factor scarcity, (c) the assumption of international identity of production functions, (d) the assumption of non-reversibility of factor-intensities of commodities between countries, and (e) the assumption of international identity of tastes.

(2) The general Stolper–Samuelson theorem is logically true if we use the further assumption that $n_x > c$.

A tree diagram, based on this analysis, is presented in Table 3.1.

8. We are now in a position to decide whether Stolper and Samuelson derived their theorems logically. Aside from their basic model:

(1) they adopt, though without complete clarity, the Heckscher–Ohlin definition of factor scarcity and the postulate concerning the non-reversibility of factor-intensities; and, quite explicitly, the assumption of international identity of production functions:[17] this establishes the restrictive Stolper–Samuelson theorem as logically true (B(1));

[17] Stolper and Samuelson, op. cit., pp. 335–40. Some of the argument is, of course, obscure in view of the pioneering nature of the article: a sympathetic interpretation is, therefore, called for. Metzler, op. cit., p. 5, also adopts the Heckscher–Ohlin definition of factor scarcity in discussing the Stolper–Samuelson theorem.

TABLE 3.1

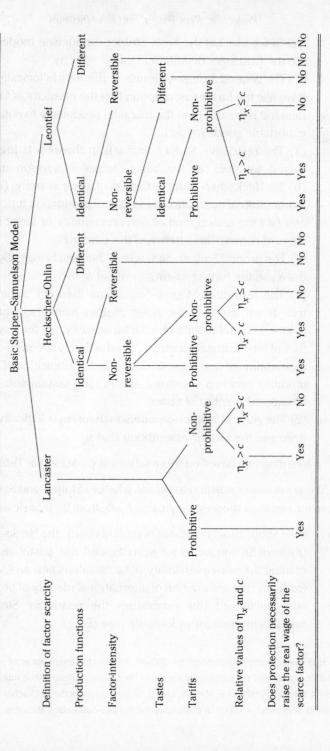

(2)   they further assume that 'the country in question is relatively small and has no influence on the terms of trade';[18] this establishes the general Stolper–Samuelson theorem as logically true (B(2)).

9. No critique of the Stolper–Samuelson formulations can thus be founded on the argument that they are not logically true, given the premises. What we could say, however, is that the theorem should be founded as closely as possible on the *basic* Stolper–Samuelson model alone; and

(1)   that, if we use the Heckscher–Ohlin definition of factor scarcity, the assumptions that we find ourselves making about the international identity of production functions and the non-reversibility of factor-intensities to sustain the twin formulations of the Stolper–Samuelson theorem are, on this criterion, *restrictive*; and

(2)   that, if we use the Leontief definition of factor scarcity (as we should probably want to since it is, in a sense, the most 'objective' we could adopt in this context), we discover ourselves adopting the threefold restrictive assumptions (C(1)) of international identity of production functions and tastes plus the non-reversibility of factor-intensities of commodities, to sustain the Stolper–Samuelson formulations.[19]

10. It will be remembered, however, that these restrictive assumptions were made only because I wished to use argument (3) concerning the validity of the Heckscher–Ohlin theorem.[20] This may also be seen indirectly from the fact that, if we use the Lancaster definition of factor scarcity, no such restrictive assumptions are necessary (A(1)), for the Heckscher–Ohlin theorem has been rendered valid by definition!

The suggestion follows readily from these considerations that

---

[18] Stolper and Samuelson, op. cit., p. 346.

[19] The additional restrictive assumption that $\eta_x > c$ has not been listed here because I wish at this stage to concentrate on only those restrictive assumptions that are made to sustain argument (3).

[20] It is important to remember that these assumptions are restrictive only in so far as we wish to found our theorem exclusively on the basic Stolper–Samuelson model.

we should reformulate our theorem in terms of arguments (1) and (2) alone, while eliminating the use of the troublesome argument (3). This can be readily done; protection (prohibitive or otherwise) raises the real wage of the factor intensively employed in the production of the importable good. This theorem is logically true if we use: (*a*) the basic Stolper–Samuelson model, and (*b*) the assumption that $n_x > c$.

This theorem has been described as the Stolper–Samuelson–Metzler–Lancaster theorem on the following grounds:

(1)   It is *implicit* in the Stolper–Samuelson argument, towards the end of their paper: 'It does not follow that our results stand and fall with the Heckscher–Ohlin theorem. Our analysis neglected the other country completely. If factors of production are not comparable between countries, or if production functions differ, nevertheless, so long as the country has only two factors, international trade would necessarily affect the real wage of a factor in the same direction as its relative remuneration.'[21]

(2)   Metzler *explicitly* states it as 'the Stolper–Samuelson conclusion that tariffs benefit the factors of production which are required in relatively large amounts in the industries competing with imports.'[22]

(3)   Lancaster advances this formulation directly as an *alternative* to the Stolper–Samuelson formulations considered above on the ground that it is more general than the latter.

11. Whereas, however, Lancaster's observation that the Stolper–Samuelson formulations are 'non-universal' (restrictive) is well taken, the argument by which he supports it is erroneous and different from that set out here. Lancaster proceeds by establishing, with the aid of a highly ingenious model, the proposition

---

[21] Stolper and Samuelson, op. cit., pp. 355–6. Homogeneity of factors between countries has not been listed separately as an assumption here because it is believed that this is implicit in both the Heckscher–Ohlin and the Leontief definitions of factor scarcity.

[22] Metzler, op. cit., p. 13. Metzler, of course, does not state it as a rival formulation, but it is abundantly clear that he is aware that this formulation is implicit in the general Stolper–Samuelson theorem.

that, in the context of the basic Stolper–Samuelson model combined with the assumption of a small country facing fixed terms of trade, differences in demand conditions ('which good is the wage-good') will affect the composition of a country's foreign trade. On this proposition he founds the following critique:

The non-universality of the [Stolper–Samuelson] theorem is due to incorrect formulation: if the scarce factor is defined as that which is used more intensively in the good of which more is produced in isolation than in trade (the only acceptable definition), then the previous analysis has shown that different wage-goods may make for different factor scarcities. In this sense, the Stolper–Samuelson formulation is meaningless, since the phrases 'real wages . . . in terms of any good' and 'scarce factor' represent incompatible concepts.[23]

The following comments on Lancaster's critique seem warranted here in view of my preceding analysis.

To begin with, it is difficult to understand what Lancaster means by the statement that 'the previous analysis has shown that different wage-goods may make for different factor scarcities. In this sense, the Stolper–Samuelson formulation is meaningless, since the phrases "real wages . . . in terms of any good" and "scarce factor" represent incompatible concepts'. Which good will be imported into a country will depend in my model on the pre-trade commodity price-ratios in the trading countries; these price-ratios are determined by domestic supply and demand; and domestic demand is affected by 'which good is the wage-good'. If the scarce factor is defined tautologously as that which is used intensively in the importable good, it then follows, from elementary considerations, that 'different wage-goods may make for different factor scarcities'. How does this render the Stolper–Samuelson formulations *meaningless* or make 'real wages . . . in terms of any good' and 'scarce factor' *incompatible* concepts? And, more pertinently, why should this make the Stolper–Samuelson formulation 'non-universal'?

Indeed, if the tautologous definition of factor scarcity is adopted, as Lancaster suggests, then the general Stolper–Samuelson theorem and the Stolper–Samuelson–Metzler–Lancaster theorem

[23] Lancaster, op. cit., p. 208.

are *identical:* the phrases 'scarce factor' and 'factor intensively employed in the importable good' can be used interchangeably. Lancaster cannot, therefore, claim one formulation to be 'non-universal' and the other to be 'universally true': on his own definition of factor scarcity, the two formulations come to the same thing!

To be sure, Lancaster's critique would be valid (though, as I have shown, incomplete) only if the physical, Leontief definition of factor scarcity were proven to have been adopted by Stolper and Samuelson, and were also adopted by Lancaster; as formulated, however, the criticism is merely erroneous.[24] In failing to investigate precisely what Stolper and Samuelson assumed by way of their definition of factor scarcity, Lancaster has further bypassed the only legitimate critique that can be sustained against the actual formulation of the theorem by Stolper and Samuelson: namely, that advanced here.

12. Our task is yet incomplete. Even the Stolper–Samuelson–Metzler–Lancaster formulation does not found the theorem completely and solely on the basic model. We must still make the restrictive assumption that $\eta_x > c$. We should, however, clearly want to go the whole way and remove all restrictive assumptions and restate the theorem to include the entire matrix of possibilities: such that the theorem is logically true, given only the basic Stolper–Samuelson model. This formulation is:[25]

Protection (prohibitive or otherwise) will raise, reduce or leave unchanged the real wage of the factor intensively employed in the production of a good according as protection raises, lowers or leaves unchanged the internal relative price of that good.

This is really the fundamental theorem that Stolper and Samuelson contributed to our knowledge of the properties of the basic

[24] Lancaster has pointed out to me, in private communication, that he really had in mind the physical definition of factor scarcity, despite the printed commitment to the tautologous definition: the tenor of the argument on p. 209 (op. cit.) seems to suggest this, although it follows upon the formulation of the tautologous definition. None of the criticism advanced here should obscure that fact that Lancaster has handled his model with admirable expertise.

[25] This formulation stems directly from argument (2), which is founded exclusively, as the reader will remember, on the basic Stolper–Samuelson model.

model they were using. Given the basic model, my formulation is logically true for all possible cases.

13. It should perhaps be emphasized that the preceding analysis has been centred entirely on the problem of analysing the impact of protection on the real wages of factors in the context of the basic model employed by Stolper and Samuelson. It should be possible, of course, to analyse the problem afresh in terms of models employing alternative assumptions. This, however, would be mostly destructive of the full validity of my theorem.

If we allow for complete specialization with trade, for instance, we can claim only that protection will raise, lower, or leave unchanged the real wage of the factor in which the *exportable* good is postulated to be intensive according as protection raises, lowers, or leaves unchanged the internal relative price of the exportable good. But we cannot extend the theorem to the factor postulated to be used intensively in the production, if any, of the importable good because any increase in the internal relative price of the exportable good after complete specialization must raise the real wage of *both* factors.

However, if we allow the optimum factor-proportions within industries, at given factor price-ratios, to change with scale, my theorem will continue to be logically true and the real wage of the factor intensively employed in a good will rise, fall or remain unchanged according as the internal relative price of that good rises, falls, or is unchanged with the imposition of protection.[26]

On the other hand, if we allow for changing returns to scale in

---

[26] An apparent exception to this proposition may be investigated. Where the optimum factor-ratio changes with scale, at given factor price-ratios, it may happen, for instance, that if the production of labour-intensive importables expands, a higher proportion of labour is released than is needed in import-substitution, even though importables are *on average* more labour-intensive. In this case, increase in the production of importables will lead to a *rise* in the labour-to-land ratios, and hence *reduce* the real wage of labour. This case, however, does not constitute an exception to my theorem, because such technology involves a concave production frontier, so that increase in the production of importables occurs when the price of importables *falls* (and not rises). Hence the logical truth of my proposition, even when we allow for changing optimum factor-ratios with scale.

either or both of the two activities, clearly it becomes impossible to maintain that my theorem will be logically true.

II. Protection and Real Incomes

14. My analysis has so far been concerned with the original Stolper–Samuelson problem of discovering the impact of protection on the *real wage* earned by factors in employment. It seems useful, however, to emphasize that if we are interested in finding out the net change in the *real income* of the factors, it is only in the case of a prohibitive tariff that a complete identity obtains between change in real wage and change in the real income of a factor. Where the tariff is non-prohibitive, the complication arises from the revenue earned by the Government. If this revenue is assumed to be re-distributed to the owners of factors according to some formula, factors will derive incomes *both* from the real wage in employment and from the redistributed proceeds of the tariff-revenue.

Hence arises the interesting possibility that the factor whose real wage has been damaged by protection may still find its real income improved if the formula for the redistribution of the tariff-revenue is heavily biased in its favour. Since this possibility constitutes a qualification to the generally accepted implication of the Stolper–Samuelson analysis, it should be of some interest to delimit the conditions under which it may occur.

To begin with, this possibility of over-compensating the damaged factor *from the tariff-revenue* clearly cannot arise unless the real income of the country as a whole is improved by protection. We know from the preceding analysis that where the real wage of one factor is reduced, that of the other necessarily rises; hence, if protection did not bring some gain to the country as a whole, it should be impossible to overcompensate the factor with the damaged real wage (from tariff-revenues). To rephrase the proposition, then, accrual of gain to the protecting country from the imposition of protection is a necessary, though not sufficient, condition for the possibility of over-compensating the factor with the damaged real wage.[27]

27 That is to say, whereas the country must have gained from protection before

In the following brief analysis I seek to relate this proposition to Metzler's formula for determining the impact of protection on the internal commodity price ratio: partly to establish link with Metzler's pioneering analysis in this field and largely because it enables us to define, and distinguish between, situations in which the factor with the damaged real wage will be export-intensive (intensively used in exportables) and those where it will be import-intensive. The discussion is then briefly extended to the case where the initial situation is that of a tariff instead of free-trade and the effect of an *increase* in protection is the subject of inquiry.

15. In Fig. 3.2 let O_b be the foreign reciprocal demand curve facing country A. F is the free-trade point, OF yielding the corresponding terms of trade. I_a' is the trade-indifference curve of A passing

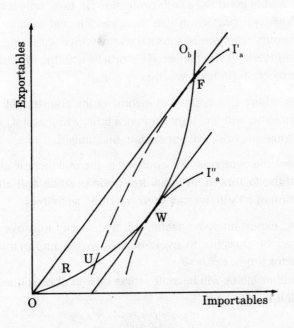

FIG. 3.2

---

the damaged factor can be overcompensated from the tariff-revenues (necessary condition), this gain must be large enough to permit over-compensation (sufficient condition).

through F at a tangent to OF and intersecting O_b at U. Its postulated curvature derives from the assumption of strict convexity of the production frontier and community indifference curves.

(1)   Assume that the tariff-added offer curve of country A intersects Q_b at U. The internal relative price of the importable good is then given by the slope of the trade-indifference curve I_a' at U, which is clearly, by virtue of the postulated curvature of I_a', greater than at F. We can deduce, therefore, that protection can leave the real income of the country unchanged only if the internal relative price of the importable good rises from the free-trade level with the imposition of protection (in turn, only if $\eta_x > c$).

(2)   Similarly, by considering points on O_b to the left of U such as R, we can argue that protection can reduce the real income of the country only if the internal relative price of the importable good rises with protection (in turn, only if $\eta_x > c$).

(3)   However, protection can increase the real income of the country whether the internal relative price of the importable good rises, is unchanged (W), or falls with the imposition of protection (in turn, whether $\eta_x \gtreqless c$).

Thus, where $\eta_x \leq c$, the real income of the country will necessarily improve with the imposition of a tariff; whereas if $\eta_x > c$, the real income may rise, fall, or remain unchanged.

16. Where the comparison is confined to the real income and real wage of the factors in an initial free-trade position and after the imposition of a tariff, we can then conclude as follows:

(1)   the export-intensive factor will necessarily improve and it may be possible to overcompensate the import-intensive factor if $\eta_x < c$;[28]

(2)   neither factor will become worse off and at least one better off if $\eta_x = c$;[29] and

---

[28] When $\eta_x < c$ we know now that: (1) the internal relative price of the importable good falls, thus increasing the real wage of the export-intensive factor and reducing that of the import-intensive factor; and (2) the country must have become better off. Hence the proposition in the text.

[29] Where $\eta_x = c$, we know that: (1) the internal relative price of the importable

(3)   the import-intensive factor will necessarily improve and it
may be possible to overcompensate the export-intensive
factor if two conditions obtain; (i) $\eta_x > c$, and (ii) the tariff is
small enough to yield some gain to the country.

If we assume that importables are not inferior goods in the
protecting country, it is then clear that inelastic foreign demand
($\eta_x < 1$) is a necessary, though not a sufficient, condition for the
emergence of the possibility of overcompensating the import-intensive factor. Where, however, foreign demand is elastic and
importables are not inferior goods, the export-intensive factor will
necessarily find its real wage reduced by protection; and, for the
possibility of overcompensating it to arise, it will be necessary,
though not sufficient, that the tariff be small enough to make the
country better off than under free-trade.

17. If, however, we wish to compare the real incomes and wages
of factors in an initial situation of a tariff and after *increase* in the
tariff, the analysis must be somewhat modified.

To begin with, the Metzler formula must be altered so as to read:
the internal relative price of the importable good will rise, remain
unchanged, or fall according as $\eta_x \gtreqless (1 - c'(1 + t)/(1 - c't))$, where
t is the initial tariff-rate and $c' = (1 - c)$ is the domestic marginal
propensity to consume importables.[30] It will be seen that where

---

good is unchanged, thus leaving unchanged the real wages of both factors; and (2)
the real income of the country must increase. Hence the proposition in the text.

[30] This formula is derived from the following analysis, furnished by Professor
Johnson and replacing my earlier, unsatisfactory attempt.

Symbols: Let p be the *external* terms of trade, measured as the price of the
importable good over the price of the exportable good, t the initial tariff rate, and
$\pi = p(1 + t)$ the *internal* terms of trade. c' is the marginal propensity to consume
importables at the initial terms of trade. C is the initial domestic consumption of
importables, r their production, and $M \equiv C - r$ the initial quantity of imports.
$r_m = (\eta_x - 1) = p/M \cdot \delta Sm/\delta p \, (Sm \equiv M)$ is the elasticity of foreign supply of importables; and $R = tpM$ the tariff revenue.

Analysis: The simplest approach to the problem is to assume the internal terms
of trade to be constant and to investigate the excess demand for importables
when t changes. If the excess demand is positive, the internal terms of trade will
rise to restore equilibrium; if negative, they will fall — assuming, of course, that
we have 'well-behaved' substitution elasticities in production and consumption.

the initial situation is that of free-trade, t will be zero and the formula will reduce to the well-known Metzler formula.

Secondly, the impact on the real income of the country will not bear the same relationship to the shifts in the internal commodity price-ratio as in the previous analysis with the free-trade initial situation. It can be demonstrated, by a geometrical argument analogous to that used earlier, that although the internal relative price of the importable good must still rise for the country to be as well off as prior to the increased tariff, both reduction and increase in the real income of the country are now consistent with any shift in this price.

Thirdly, arguing from the optimum tariff theory, we can claim that the real income of the country will improve with increased protection if two conditions obtain: (i) the pre-increase tariff rate is less than the optimum tariff rate $t < 1/(\eta_x - 1)$; and (ii) *either*

Now, $R = tpM = (t/(1 + t)) \pi \cdot M$. With π constant, we have $dp/dt = -p/(1 + t)$. The shift in the demand for imports due to the change in the tariff is then given by

$$\frac{dC}{dt} = c' \frac{dR}{dt} = c'\pi \left\{ \frac{1}{(1 + t)^2} M + \frac{t}{(1 + t)} \cdot \frac{dM}{dt} \right\}$$

The shift in the supply of imports is given by:

$$\frac{dM}{dp} \cdot \frac{dp}{dt} = \frac{M}{p} \cdot r_m \cdot \frac{dp}{dt} = - \frac{M}{(1 + t)} \cdot r_m$$

The excess demand for importables is then given by:

$$\left(\frac{dC}{dt} - \frac{dM}{dt} \right)$$

$$= \frac{c'\pi}{(1 + t)^2} \cdot M + \left\{ \frac{c'\pi t}{(1 + t)} - 1 \right\} \left\{ \frac{-M}{(1 + t)} \right\} r_m$$

$$= \frac{M}{(1 + t)} \left\{ c'p + (1 - c'pt) \, r_m \right\}$$

Substituting $r_m = \eta_x - 1$, assuming p to be unity initially by choice of units and simplifying, we arrive at the formula that the excess demand for importables will be positive, zero, or negative according as:

$$\eta_x \gtreqless \frac{1 - c'(1 + t)}{1 - c't}$$

It will be seen that this formula reduces to the Metzler formula when t is zero.

the post-increase tariff rate is also less than the optimum tariff rate, *or*, if it exceeds the optimum tariff rate, it is small enough to leave some gain in real income to the country from the increase in tariff.

These considerations lead to the following conclusions:[31]

(1) The export-intensive factor will necessarily become better off and it may be possible to overcompensate the import-intensive factor from *increased* tariff-revenues when three conditions obtain:

(i) $\eta_x < (1 - c'(1 + t)/(1 - c't))$; (ii) $t < (1/(\eta_x - 1))$; and (iii) *either* the post-increase tariff rate is also less than the optimum tariff rate *or*, if it exceeds the optimum tariff, it is still small enough to leave some gain in real income to the country from the increase in the tariff.

(2) The import-intensive factor will necessarily become better off and it may be possible to overcompensate the export-intensive factor from *increased* tariff-revenues when three conditions obtain:

(i) $\eta_x > (1 - c'(1 + t))/(1 - c't)$; (ii) $t < (1/\eta_x - 1)$; and (iii) *either* the post-increase tariff rate is also less than the optimum tariff *or*, if it exceeds the optimum tariff, it is still small enough to leave some gain in real income to the country from the increase in protection.

(3) Where, however, $\eta_x = (1 - c'(1 + t)/1 - c't)$, the real wage of neither factor changes with the increase in protection. It follows, therefore, that the real income of both factors will increase, decrease, or remain unchanged according as the increase in tariff raises, lowers, or leaves unchanged the real income of the country: assuming, of course, that the tariff-revenues are divided among the factors in a given proportion.

---

[31] The first two propositions that follow assume that the factor stated to become necessarily better off continues to receive *at least* the same revenue as in the initial situation; this assumption being made explicit by the use of the phrase 'from *increased* tariff-revenues'. This assumption is needed because otherwise improvement merely in the real wage of a factor due to increased protection could be offset by an accompanying unfavourable distribution of tariff-revenues to the factor after the increase in the tariff.

18. In conclusion, it should be re-emphasized that this brief discussion has been concerned only with the limited task of exploring some of the implications of the proposition that accrual of gain to the protecting country from the imposition of protection is a necessary, though not sufficient, condition for the emergence of the possibility of overcompensating, from tariff-revenues, the factor with the damaged real wage.

4

The Theory of Immiserizing Growth: Further Applications[*]

In this chapter, I consider two applications of the theory of immiserizing growth (Bhagwati 1968).

In Sec. I, I principally examine the paradox of a reduction in the welfare of a 'small' country, with a domestic distortion in production, when its terms of trade improve exogenously. This, and related paradoxes, are seen to be nothing other than special cases of the general theory of immiserizing growth.

In Sec. II, I examine the paradox of a reduction in the welfare of a country following a tariff-induced inflow of capital. This paradox again follows from the theory of immiserizing growth; besides, it is clearly of immediate and direct relevance to policy-making.

I. WAGE DIFFERENTIALS, TERMS OF TRADE IMPROVEMENT, AND IMMISERIZING GROWTH

Batra and Pattanaik (1970) have recently produced the paradoxical proposition that an exogenous improvement in the terms of trade can worsen, rather than improve, welfare if a country has a distortionary wage differential. Batra and Scully (1971) have now added yet another paradox to the theory of trade and welfare in showing that immiserizing growth can occur, *despite endogenous growth-induced improvement in the terms of trade*, if wage differentials are present. It is easy to provide the underlying rationale for these two paradoxes by drawing on recent insights into the theory of immiserizing growth.[1]

* Thanks are due to the National Science Foundation for research support and to Michael Connolly for helpful comments.
[1] The substance of the following argument is now summarized in Batra–Scully (1971).

Batra–Pattanaik Paradox

Let me first examine the Batra–Pattanaik (1970) paradox. It can easily be shown that this paradox is, paradoxically, yet another instance of the generalized theory of immiserizing growth.

This theory (Bhagwati 1968) states that if growth takes place in a country characterized by (a distortion and hence by) a sub-optimal policy, then immiserizing growth can ensue; conversely, growth cannot be immiserizing if optimal policies are pursued (before and after growth). Growth can only improve welfare if optimal policies are pursued; however, if sub-optimal policies are followed before and after growth, immiserizing growth will ensue if the primary gain from growth, measured as the gain which would accrue if optimal policies were followed, is outweighed by the *incremental* loss that could arise from the pursuit instead of sub-optimal policies.

As Batra and Scully have noted, I have used this theory elsewhere (Bhagwati 1968) to show that when there is a wage differential, immiserizing growth can occur for a country with *given* terms of trade and laissez-faire as its economic policy. The reason is that laissez-faire is a sub-optimal policy when there is a distortionary wage-differential, as Hagen (1958) argued in a classic paper.

But I have also noted elsewhere (Bhagwati 1971) that the theory of immiserizing growth can be used to illuminate, and prove, other propositions of trade theory where no growth, in an obvious sense, is involved. Thus, the classic propositions of Gottfried Haberler (1950), which compare free trade (i.e. laissez-faire) with no trade (i.e. autarky) and demonstrate that the two policies cannot be ranked uniquely if production externalities or factor-price rigidities exist, can be readily seen to be examples of the theory of immiserizing growth. This is because, as Baldwin (1948) has shown, the free-trade-situation availability locus lies uniformly outside (except for overlaps) the production possibility curve which is, of course, the no-trade-situation availability locus. Thus, the no-trade and free-trade policies are conceptually the same as pre-growth and post-growth situations. Hence, if there is a distortion in the two situations, so that the two situations are sub-optimal, immiserizing growth can follow: that is to say, free trade can be inferior to no trade.

The Batra–Pattanaik paradox also falls into place in a similar fashion. The exogenous improvement in the terms of trade implies an outward shift of the Baldwin availabilities locus, implying 'growth'; the existence of the distortionary wage differential implies that this 'growth' is occurring in the context of sub-optimal policies. Hence 'immiserizing growth' can occur: that is to say, an exogenous improvement in the terms of trade can worsen welfare.

Batra–Scully Paradox

The Batra–Scully proposition involves a paradox within a world of paradoxes. While it has been shown (Bhagwati 1968) that the existence of wage differentials in a 'small' country can lead to immiserizing growth, they demonstrate that such immiseration can arise even when, for a 'large' country, the terms of trade have *improved* as a result of this growth.

The Batra–Scully paradox is, however, similar to my other demonstration (Bhagwati 1968) of the possibility of immiserizing growth when, for a large country, the pre-growth optimal tariff is kept unchanged after growth and ceases to be optimal in the post-growth situation. In the geometrical illustration (Fig. 4.2, Bhagwati 1968) of this possibility, reproduced here as Fig. 4.1 for convenience, the terms of trade actually improved in the post-growth situation and yet growth was immiserizing;[2] however, the paradoxical phenomenon of improvement in the terms of trade was neither noted nor explained.

And yet this paradox is readily resolved. When the growth occurs and the tariff (which is optimal in the initial, pre-growth situation) is kept unchanged, the tariff ceases in general to be optimal.[3] Hence the loss from this sub-optimal policy can outweigh

[2] Thus, in Fig. 4.1, AB is the pre-growth production possibility curve, B' the post-growth production possibility curve. $QMCR$ the superimposed foreign offer curve facing the country, the post-growth equilibrium shows a lower welfare level implying immiserizing growth ($U > U'$), and the terms of trade have improved after growth (from QC to $QM = Q'C'$).

[3] Note that the foreign offer curve facing the growing country is taken, as always, to be given in the analysis.

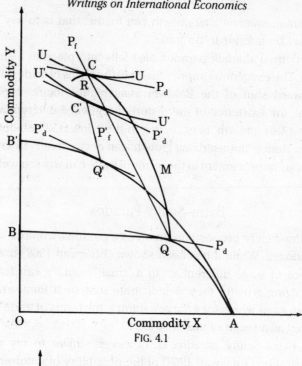

FIG. 4.1

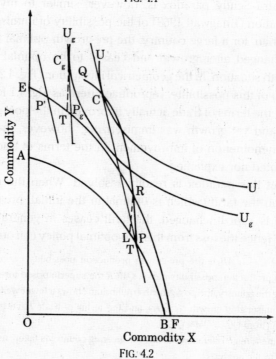

FIG. 4.2

the gain from growth (measured at the point at which an optimal tariff was levied in the post-growth situation too). That this can happen when the terms of trade improve is, in turn, seen as follows. If the growth is heavily biased in favour of the importable good,[4] then the marginal rate of domestic transformation improves in favour of the importable good, thus implying that the optimal tariff should be increased. Since it is not, there is a loss of welfare which outweighs, when large enough, the gain from growth. At the same time, given the foreign offer curve facing the country and the country's unchanged tariff, the growth (which is, in the illustration, ultra-biased in favour of the importable good and hence shrinks the country's own offer curve) will improve the terms of trade. Hence the phenomenon of terms-of-trade improvement can arise simultaneously with the phenomenon of immiserizing growth.

The Batra–Scully paradox is to be explained in similar terms. Their analysis is for a large country with laissez-faire *and* distortionary wage differential: hence they are comparing the pre-growth and the post-growth situations which are both characterized, in general, by sub-optimality arising from *two* distortions: failure to offset the wage differential and failure to pursue a policy designed to exploit the country's largeness (i.e. its monopoly power in trade). Immiserizing growth is therefore possible. At the same time, growth may shrink the country's offer curve, causing the terms of trade to improve. Hence arises the possibility illustrated in Fig. 4.2, where the production possibility curve shifts with growth from AB to EF, the initial terms of trade are PC, the initial welfare level at U, and the new equilibrium is at improved terms of trade $P_g C_g$ but at reduced welfare level U_g, implying immiserizing growth.[5]

---

[4] In Fig. 4.1, the growth is ultra-biased in favour of the importable good so that, at constant commodity prices, growth actually reduces the output of the exportable good.

[5] P' shows the production point after growth if terms of trade were held constant, implying that growth is ultra-biased in favour of the importable commodity Y; and $PRCQ$ is the given foreign offer curve, with $P_g C_g$ parallel and equal in length to PR, implying that the illustrated post-growth equilibrium is consistent with the given foreign offer curve.

II. Tariff-Induced Capital Inflow and Immiseration

The second application of the theory of immiserizing growth arises from Harry Johnson's (1967) demonstration that a 'small' country, growing subject to a constant tariff, can experience immiserizing growth. His analysis clearly points to the possibility of immiseration following from a tariff-induced inflow of capital. However, the analysis cannot be carried over identically and as fully as Tan (1969), in his subsequent examination of the conditions for Johnson's possibility to occur, has implied.[6]

Johnson's analysis relates to a comparison of the pre-growth and post-growth situations, both subject to a given tariff. On the other hand, the analysis of tariff-induced capital inflow and (resulting) immiseration requires a comparison of the free-trade situation with the tariff-inclusive, post-growth (*via* capital influx) situation. I now explore this particular comparison and discuss the conditions under which immiseration will follow.

Johnson's Paradox

In Johnson's paradox, illustrated in Fig. 4.3, the pre-growth tariff-inclusive production is at P_t, the given international price-line is $C_t P_t \parallel C_t' P_t'$, the pre-growth consumption is at C_t and welfare at U_t. With capital accumulation, the production possibility curve shifts from AB to CD, production to P_t', consumption to C_t' and welfare is reduced $U_t' (< U_t)$. It is clear that a necessary and sufficient condition for such immiseration is that the Rybczynski-line $P_t P_t'$ be less steep than the international price-ratio $P_t C_t$; a necessary condition for such immiseration is that the output of the exportable good must fall at constant, tariff-inclusive prices (i.e. growth should be ultra-biased in favour of the importable good).

---

[6] Bertrand and Flatters (1971) also have, subsequent to Tan's work, explored the conditions for Johnson's paradox to occur when capital accumulation is responsible for the growth. Bhagwati (1968) has provided the general theory of immiserizing growth which reduces Johnson's and other earlier (Bhagwati 1958) paradoxes to special cases.

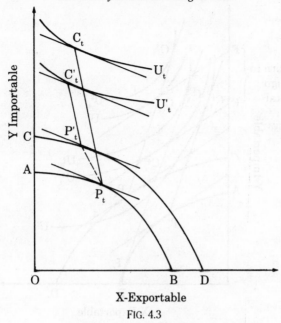

X-Exportable

FIG. 4.3

Tariff-Induced Capital Inflow

When, however, we wish to examine the conditions under which the possibility of immiseration will emerge if we have a tariff-induced capital inflow, we have the following four welfare elements in the transition from an initial free-trade situation to the inclusive tariff and capital inflow situation:

(i) The tariff imposes a production cost by distorting the prices faced by producers.

(ii) The capital influx implies 'growth', at constant tariff-inclusive domestic prices faced by producers, which may imply a welfare gain or a welfare loss.

(iii) The tariff imposes a consumption cost by distorting the prices faced by consumers; and

(iv) The tariff-induced capital influx earns a reward which must be reckoned as a cost, and hence a welfare loss to the tariff-imposing country.

These elements are illustrated in Fig. 4.4. The initial free-trade equilibrium with production possibility curve AB and the fixed

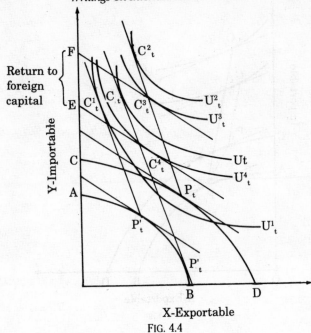

X-Exportable

FIG. 4.4

international price-line $P_t C_t$, is characterized by production at P_t, consumption at C_t, and welfare at U_t. The tariff plus capital influx equilibrium is, with the foreign capital augmented production possibility curve CD, at P_t, C_t^4 and $U_t^4 (< U_t)$, and shows, in consequence, immiseration. The transition from U_t to U_t^4 can be built up through the four elements we have already distinguished:

(i) The tariff shifts production from P_t to P_t' along AB, leading to a decline in welfare from U_t to U_t^1; this is the result of the production distortion.

(ii) The influx of foreign capital shifts production, at tariff-inclusive prices, from P_t' to P_t and therefore welfare from U_t^1 to U_t^2; this welfare shift, *identical* with the one underlying the Johnson paradox (which involves immiserizing growth under a given tariff), may be positive (as in Fig. 4.4) or negative (as in the Johnson paradox).

(iii) Consumption must also be shifted because it will occur at tariff-inclusive prices; this reduces the economy from U_t^2 to U_t^3; and finally

(iv) The return to the foreign capital inflow, measured at *EF* amount of *Y*-goods in domestic prices,[7] will reduce the economy still further to U_t^4.[8]

It is clear, therefore, that the tariff-induced capital inflow immiseration requires far less stringent conditions than the Johnson case. The latter must rely entirely on effect (ii) being negative, this being a necessary and sufficient condition for the immiserizing phenomenon. On the other hand, in the present case, effects (i), (iii), and (iv) being necessarily negative, effect (ii) can be positive and yet be compatible with immiseration, as is indeed depicted in Fig. 4.4. It should be possible to set down formally the necessary and sufficient conditions for immiseration in this case; but this has not been attempted here.

EDITOR'S NOTE

The problem of when a tariff-induced capital inflow will lead to immiserization, raised in Section II has been resolved by R.A. Brecher and C.F. Diaz Alejandro, 'Tariffs, Foreign Capital, and Immiserization', *Journal of International Economics* 7 (1977): 317–22.

REFERENCES

Baldwin, R., 1948: 'Equilibrium in International Trade: A Diagrammatic Analysis', *Quarterly Journal of Economics*, no. 5 (Nov.), vol. 62, pp. 748–62.

Batra, R. and P. Pattanaik, 1970: 'Domestic Distortions and the Gains from Trade', *Economic Journal*, no. 319 (Sept.), vol. 80, pp. 638–49.

[7] While capital will earn the value of its marginal product, the return would have to be modified by phenomena such as corporation taxes. We must therefore take the *net* return into account.

[8] An alternative way to get from U_t to U_t^4 would be to: (i) Go from U_t to U_t^* on the assumption that capital has come in but that we are still in free trade. This would be done by putting the international price-line tangent to *CD* and then tangent, in turn, to U_f^*. This is necessarily a welfare gain. (ii) Go from U_t^* to $U_{t'}^2$ which would be the production loss associated with the tariff, but now taken at *CD*. (iii) Go from U_t^2 to $U_{t'}^3$ which is the consumption loss. (iv) Go finally from U_t^3 to $U_{t'}^4$ which would be the loss from netting out the reward to foreign capital.

Batra, R. and G. Scully, 1971: 'The Theory of Wage Differentials: Welfare and Immiserizing Growth', *Journal of International Economics*, no. 2 (May), vol. 1, pp. 241–7.

Bertrand, T. and F. Flatters, 1971: 'Tariffs, Capital Accumulation and Immiserizing Growth', *Journal of International Economics*, no. 4 (Nov.), vol. 1, pp. 453–60.

Bhagwati, J., 1958: 'Immiserizing Growth: A Geometric Note', *Review of Economic Studies*, no. 68 (June), vol. 25, pp. 201–5.

—, 1968: 'Distortions and Immiserizing Growth: A Generalization', *Review of Economic Studies*, no. 104 (Oct.), vol. 35, pp. 481–5.

Hagen, E., 1958: 'An Economic Justification of Protectionism', *Quarterly Journal of Economics*, no. 4 (Nov.), vol. 72, pp. 496–514.

Johnson, H.G., 1967: 'The Possibility of Income Losses from Increased Efficiency or Factor Accumulation in the Presence of Tariffs', *Economic Journal*, no. 305 (March), vol. 77, pp. 151–4.

Tan, A.H., 1969: 'Immiserizing Tariff-induced Capital Accumulation and Technical Change', *Malayan Economic Review*.

5

Domestic Distortions, Tariffs, and the Theory of Optimum Subsidy[1]

With V.K. Ramaswami

THERE is confusion of varying degrees in the current literature on trade theory concerning the desirable form of intervention in foreign trade when the economy is characterized by domestic distortions (divergences of the commodity price ratios from the corresponding marginal rates of substitution). For instance, the age-old debate over whether tariffs or subsidies should be used to protect an infant industry is still carried on in terms of the respective political and psychological merits of the two forms of protection while their relative economic advantages are assumed not to point in the direction of a definite choice.[2]

Three questions about the use of tariffs, when domestic distortions exist, need to be distinguished here. (1) Is a tariff necessarily superior to free trade (that is, can a tariff rate always be found that yields a welfare position not inferior to that produced by free trade)? (2) Is a tariff policy necessarily superior to any other form of *trade* policy? (3) If the choice can be made from the entire range of policy instruments, which is the optimal economic policy?

[1] An early draft of this chapter was read to seminars at M.I.T., University of Chicago, and Stanford University by one of the authors and subsequently published in the *Journal of Political Economy* in Feb. 1963 with useful suggestions from C.P. Kindleberger and H.G. Johnson.

[2] For instance, C.P. Kindleberger in his *International Economics* (Homewood, Ill.: Richard D. Irwin, Inc., 1958), as does also G. Haberler in his *Theory of International Trade* (Glasgow: William Hodge & Co., 1936), states the economic argument in favour of subsidies and tariffs without stating definitely that one is invariably superior to the other from the economic viewpoint.

In Sec. I we state the general theory that provides the answers to these three questions. In the light of this theory, we examine the propositions advanced in the two central contributions to trade theory in this field: Haberler's justly celebrated 1950 *Economic Journal* paper[3] and Hagen's recent analysis of wage differentials.[4] Sections II and III examine these two analyses. Section IV concludes with some observations concerning the relative advantages of tariffs and subsidies from the practical viewpoint.

I. General Theory

The three questions posed here can be effectively answered by analysing the characteristics of an optimum solution. Thus, for instance, the optimum tariff argument can be stated elegantly in terms of these characteristics. The achievement of an optimum solution is characterized by the equality of the foreign rate of transformation (FRT), the domestic rate of transformation in production (DRT), and the domestic rate of substitution in consumption (DRS). If the country has monopoly power in trade, a competitive free trade solution will be characterized by $DRS = DRT \neq FRT$. By introducing a suitable tariff, a country can achieve $DRS = DRT = FRT$. A subsidy (tax) on the domestic production of importables (exportables) could equalize DRT and FRT but would destroy the quality of DRS with DRT. Hence it is clear that a tax-cum-subsidy on domestic production is necessarily inferior to an optimum tariff. Moreover, it may be impossible in any given empirical situation to devise a tax-cum-subsidy that would yield a solution superior to that arrived at under free trade.

By analogy we can argue that, in the case of domestic distortions, $DRS = FRT \neq DRT$ under free trade. A suitable tariff can equalize FRT and DRT but would destroy the equality between DRS and FRT. Hence it is clear that no tariff may exist that would yield a solution superior to that under free trade. A suitable

[3] G. Haberler, 'Some Problems in the Pure Theory of International Trade', *Economic Journal*, LX (June 1950), pp. 223–40.

[4] E. Hagen, 'An Economic Justification of Protectionism', *Quarterly Journal of Economics*, LXXII (Nov. 1958), pp. 496–514.

tax-cum-subsidy on domestic production would, however, enable the policy-maker to secure $DRS = FRT = DRT$ and hence is necessarily the optimum solution. Hence a tariff policy is also necessarily inferior to an optimum tax-cum-subsidy policy. And the same argument must hold true of trade subsidies also since they too, like tariffs, are directed at *foreign* trade whereas the problem to be tackled is one of *domestic* distortion.

Three propositions, therefore, follow in the case of domestic distortions. (a) A tariff is not necessarily superior to free trade. (b) A tariff is not necessarily superior to an export (or import) subsidy. (c) A policy permitting the attainment of maximum welfare involves a tax-cum-subsidy on domestic production. Just as there exists an optimum tariff policy for a divergence between foreign prices and *FRT*, so there exists an *optimum subsidy* (or an equivalent tax-cum-subsidy) policy for a divergence between domestic prices and *DRT*.

II. HABERLER ON EXTERNAL ECONOMIES

A divergence between the domestic commodity price ratios and the marginal rates of transformation between commodities may arise from what are usually described as 'external economies'. These may take various forms.[5] It is most fashionable at the moment to discuss the external economies arising from the interdependence of investment decisions.[6]

Haberler analyses this problem in terms of the standard

[5] According to Haberler, 'there may be a deviation between social and private cost due to external economies or diseconomies, i.e. due to certain cost-raising or cost-reduction factors which would come into play if one industry expanded and the other contracted — factors which for some reason or other are not, or not sufficiently, allowed for in private cost calculations' ('Some Problems . . . ', op. cit., p. 236).

[6] This has been analysed in the context of international trade by J. Bhagwati, 'The 'The Theory of Comparative Advantage in the Context of Underdevelopment and Growth', *Pakistan Development Review*, II, no. 3 (Autumn 1962), pp. 339–53. See also H. Chenery, 'The Interdependence of Investment Decisions', *in* Moses Abramovitz et al., *The Allocation of Economic Resources* (Stanford, CA: Stanford University Press, 1959).

two-good, two-factor model of trade theory, using geometrical methods. Haberler is aware that a tariff is not necessarily superior to free trade. He is however in error concerning the relative advantages of tariffs and trade subsidies. Further, he does not discuss the optimum economic policy under the circumstances.

Haberler distinguishes between two situations according to whether the domestic production of importables rises or falls (what he calls the direction of 'specialization'). We shall analyse each case separately.

Case I. In the former case, illustrated here in Fig. 5.1a, *AB* is the production possibility curve. The discrepancy between the domestic price ratio and the domestic rate of transformation (*DRT*) leads to self-sufficiency equilibrium at *S*. Free trade, at the *given* international price *PF*, leads to production at *P*, consumption at *F*, export of agricultural goods, and a deterioration in welfare.[7]

The following comments are warranted. First, although Haberler does not state this explicitly, it can be shown that prohibitive protection may make the country worse off (Fig. 5.1b). Second, it follows from Sec. I that *no* tariff may be superior to free trade (this is implicit, we think, in Haberler's statements elsewhere in his paper). Finally, the optimum result could be achieved by a policy of tax-cum-subsidy on domestic production. Such a policy is illustrated in Fig. 5.1c where the tax-cum-subsidy eliminates the divergence between commodity prices and *DRT* and brings production to *P'* and consumption to *F'*.

Case II. Haberler distinguishes the other case by arguing that the self-sufficiency price ratio *RS* may be less steep than the *given* foreign price ratio *PF*. Here the production point is shifted to the right by free trade.[8] In this case, Haberler argues that 'the country

---

[7] Haberler wrongly seems to imply that the country must export agricultural goods in this case. There is no reason why *once there is a domestic distortion*, a country should necessarily export the commodity that is cheaper than abroad in the absence of trade.

[8] This, of course, is erroneous, as noted in n. 7. Haberler implies that under free trade manufactures will now become the exported good. Haberler also describes this case as characterized by specialization in the 'right' direction. He is correct if, by this, he means that the movement of the production point to the right of *S*,

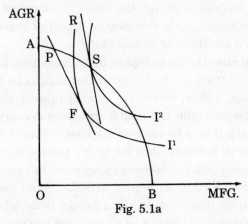

Fig. 5.1a

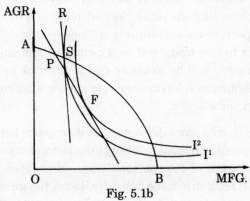

Fig. 5.1b

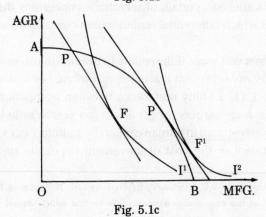

Fig. 5.1c

FIG. 5.1

would specialize in the "right" direction but not sufficiently. *It would after trade be better off than before, but it would not reach the optimum point. . . . In that case an export or import subsidy (rather than a tariff) would be indicated*.[9]

While Haberler is right in arguing that a movement to the right of *S*, when free trade is introduced, will necessarily be beneficial, his conclusion that an export (or import) subsidy is indicated and would be preferable to a tariff is erroneous in every rigorous sense in which it may be understood. First, it cannot be argued that the optimal solution when the policy used is an export (or import) subsidy will be necessarily superior to that when the policy used is a tariff. As argued in Sec. I, both policies are handicapped as they seek to affect *foreign* trade whereas the distortion is *domestic;* there is no reason why one should necessarily be better than the other. Second, nor can it be maintained that an export (or import) subsidy will necessarily exist that will be superior to free trade, just as it cannot be maintained that a tariff necessarily will be available that is superior to free trade. Third, the optimum solution again is to impose a tax-cum-subsidy on domestic production.

Case III. Hagen on wage differentials: A divergence between *DRT* and the domestic price ratio, arising from factor-market imperfections in the form of inter-sectoral wage differentials, has been discussed in relation to trade policy by Hagen. Before we proceed to Hagen's analysis, certain observations concerning the circumstances in which differential remuneration causes a distortion are in order.

The observed wage differentials between the urban and rural sector may *not* represent a genuine distortion. For instance, they may reflect, (1) a utility preference between occupations on the part of the wage-earners, or (2) a rent (on scarce skills), or (3) a return on investment in human capital (by training), or (4) a return on investment in the cost of movement (from the rural to the

---

caused by free trade, will necessarily improve welfare. He is wrong, however, if he means that the commodity exported will be that which would have been exported if the divergence did not exist.

[9] Haberler, 'Some Problems . . . ', op. cit., p. 237. Our italics.

urban sector). There *would* be a distortion, however, where the differential is attributable to, (5) trade-union intervention, or (6) prestige-cum-humanitarian grounds ('I must pay my man a decent wage') that fix wages at varying levels in different sectors. Two other types of explanations may also be discussed: (7) Hagen argues that the differential occurs in manufacture because this is the advancing sector and growing activities inevitably have to pay higher wages to draw labour away from other industries. While this 'dynamic' argument appears to provide support for the distortionary character of the differential, there are difficulties with it. For instance, the fact that a differential has to be maintained to draw labour away may very well be due to the cost of movement.[10] (8) A more substantive argument is that the rural sector affords employment to non-adult members of the family whereas, in the urban sectors, the adult alone gets employment (owing to institutional reasons such as factory acts). Hence, to migrate, an adult would need to be compensated for the loss of employment by the non-adult members of his family.[11] If this is the case, there is certainly a market imperfection (assuming that individual preferences rather than collective preferences, expressed in legislation, are relevant) and hence distortion.[12]

In the following analysis, we shall assume that the wage differential represents a genuine distortion while remaining sceptical about the degree to which such distortions obtain in the actual

[10] Other difficulties also arise when the argument is used in conjunction with a static analysis. These will be discussed later.

[11] This hypothesis was suggested to us by D. Mazumdar.

[12] This 'distortion', unlike the others, involves a contraction of the labour force as labour moves from one sector to another. Hence, the following analysis does not apply and a fresh solution, incorporating a changing labour supply, is necessary. Note here also that the wage differential variety of distortion is quite distinct from the distortion caused when, although the wage is identical between sectors, it differs from the 'shadow' optimal wage. This distinction has been blurred by recent analysts, especially W.A. Lewis, 'Economic Development with Unlimited Supplies of Labor', *Manchester School*, XXII (May 1959) and H. Myint, 'Infant Industry Arguments for Assistance to Industries in the Setting of Dynamic Trade Theory' (paper presented to a conference on 'Trade in a Developing World', International Economic Association (Sept. 1961). Also see Bhagwati, op. cit.

world.[13] We will also adopt Hagen's analytical framework of a
two-commodity, two-factor model and a *constant* wage differential.
The assumption of constancy of the wage differential raises some
difficulties, probably with reasons (3) and (6), but certainly with
reason (7) on which Hagen principally relies. As will be seen
presently, Hagen's analysis involves the *contraction* of manufactures after the introduction of trade; if the wage differential is due
to the fact that manufactures are expanding and drawing labour
away, it should surely reverse itself during the transition from
autarky to free trade. The difficulty is that Hagen, in relying upon
reason (7) while using traditional trade analysis, is illegitimately
superimposing a dynamic argument upon a comparative statics
framework. To analyse the distortion arising from reason (8) an
explicitly dynamic analysis is necessary. Hence, the following
analysis applies, strictly speaking, only to distortions produced
by reasons (5) and (6).

Hagen concludes that a tariff is superior to free trade when the
importable manufacturing activity has to pay the higher wage.

As a result of the wage disparity, manufacturing industry will be undersold by imports when the foreign exchanges are in equilibrium. Protection which permits such industry to exist will increase real income in the
economy. However, a subsidy per unit of labour equal to the wage
differential will increase real income further, and if combined with free
trade will permit attaining an *optimum optimorum*.[14]

Hagen works successively with two models that differ only in
the assumption concerning the number of factors of production.
Since the first model has only one factor and is only a special case
of the second, two-factor model, we shall concentrate here on the
latter. It is assumed that all the standard Paretian conditions obtain
except for the wage differential. We begin with Hagen's analysis
and then comment on it.

---

[13] A. Kafka, 'A New Argument for Protectionism', *Quarterly Journal of Economics*,
LXXVI (Feb. 1962), pp. 163–6.
[14] Op. cit., p. 498. Hagen himself does not state explicitly that he is confining the
analysis to the case where the differential operates against the importable activity.
If the differential were to work in the contrary direction, the results would naturally have to be modified radically.

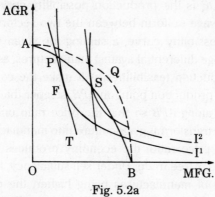

Fig. 5.2a

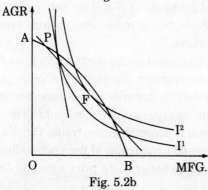

Fig. 5.2b

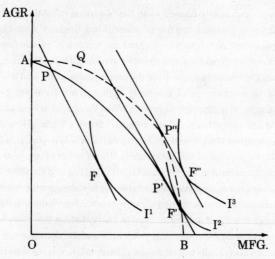

Fig. 5.2c

FIG. 5.2

In Fig. 5.2a, *AQB* is the production possibility curve on the assumption of a wage uniform between the two sectors. *APB* is the production possibility curve, assuming the given wage differential.[15] The wage differential against manufactures, aside from reducing the production feasibilities, will make the commodity price ratio, at any production point on *APB*, steeper than the rate of transformation along *APB* so that the price ratio understates the profitability of transforming agriculture into manufactures. *PT* being the foreign price ratio, the economy produces at *P* and consumes at *F* under free trade. Under self-sufficiency, however, the relative price of manufactures being higher, the economy would produce and consume at *S* and be better off. From this, Hagen concludes: 'Protection of manufacturing from foreign trade will increase real income.'[16]

However, the conclusion must be rectified. First, as illustrated in Fig. 5.2b, where the contrary possibility is shown, prohibitive protection is not necessarily superior to free trade. Second, it may further be impossible, as argued in Sec. I, to find any level of tariff (or trade subsidy) that is superior to free trade. Third, a tax-cum-subsidy on the domestic production of the commodities, which eliminates the divergence between the price ratio and *DRT* (along

[15] The reader can satisfy himself as to the 'shrinking in' of the production possibility curve by manipulating the Edgeworth box diagram. A careful reader of Hagen's paper will note that Hagen draws the 'shrunk-in' production possibility curve so that it is convex (in the mathematical sense). This is, however, a property that does not necessarily follow from the assumptions made, and it is possible to produce counter-examples of concavity, although we have not been able to produce a general mathematical proof. (When this paper was read at Stanford, Paul David drew attention to A. Fishlow and P. David's 'Optimal Resource Allocation in an Imperfect Market Setting', *Journal of Political Economy*, LXIX [Dec. 1961], pp. 529–46, for a proof of this proposition. These writers have also anticipated our criticism concerning Hagen's confusion of statics and dynamics.) We shall use the convex curve, however, as it enables us to state our propositions in terms of equalities and without bothering about second-order conditions; the substance of the propositions *that interest us here* is unaffected by this complication. The divergence between the commodity price ratio and the domestic rate of transformation, which also results from the wage differential, needs rigorous proof, which can be found in Hagen, op. cit., pp. 507–8.

[16] Hagen, op. cit., p. 510.

APB) would necessarily yield a better solution than protection. In Fig. 5.2c, *F'* represents the consumption and *P'* the production reached by the pursuit of such a tax-cum-subsidy policy.[17] Finally, a policy of tax-cum-subsidy on labour use would achieve equilibrium production at *P''* and consumption at *F''* in Fig. 5.2c and produce the 'first-best' result, as recognized by Hagen.

Note that, in contrast to the case of external economies, the optimum tax-cum-subsidy on domestic production, while superior to protection or trade subsidy, does not yield the *optimum optimorum* in the wage-differential case. The reason is straightforward. The wage differential causes *not merely* a domestic distortion but *also* a restriction of the production possibility curve. A tax-cum-subsidy on domestic production measure will, therefore, merely eliminate the domestic distortion but not restore the economy to the Paretian production possibility curve (*AQB*). It will thus achieve the equality of *FRT* and *DRS* with *DRT* along *the restricted production possibility curve* (*APB*) and hence constitute the optimal solution when the wage differential cannot be directly eliminated. Where, however, a direct attack on the wage differential is permitted, the fully optimal, 'first-best' solution can be achieved by a policy of tax-cum-subsidy on factor use.

III. CONCLUSION

We have argued here that an optimum subsidy (or a tax-cum-subsidy equivalent) is necessarily superior to any tariff when the distortion is domestic. It may be questioned, however, whether this advantage would obtain in practice. This question cannot of course be settled purely at the economic level. A fully satisfactory treatment of this issue would necessarily involve disciplines ranging from politics to psychology. However, by way of conclusion,

---

[17] In relation to this point, it is also worth noting that the standard procedure adopted by several tariff commissions, of choosing a tariff rate that just offsets the differential between the average domestic cost at some *arbitrary*, given production of the existing units and the landed (c.i.f.) cost, is not necessarily correct. There is no reason why the tariff rate which just offsets this differential is necessarily the tariff rate which is optimum from the viewpoint of economic policy.

we think it would be useful to consider a few arguments that are relevant to the final, realistic choice of policy:

1. The contention that the payment of subsidies would involve the collection of taxes which in practice cannot be levied in a non-distortionary fashion is fallacious. A tax-cum-subsidy scheme could always be devised that would *both* eliminate the estimated divergence and collect taxes sufficient to pay the subsidies.

2. The estimation problem is also easier with subsidies than with tariffs. The former involves estimating merely the divergence between the commodity price ratio and *DRT* (at the relevant production point). The latter must necessarily extend the exercises to the estimation of the relevant *DRS* (which involves locating both the right level of income *and* the relevant consumption point).

3. The political argument has usually been claimed by free traders to favour the payment of subsidies under external economy arguments like infant industries. It is thought that it would be difficult to pay a subsidy longer than strictly necessary whereas a tariff may be more difficult to abolish. It must be pointed out, however, that this argument also pulls the other way because, precisely for the reasons which make a subsidy difficult to continue, a subsidy is difficult to choose in preference to a tariff.

6

Shifting Comparative
Advantage, Protectionist
Demands, and Policy Response[*]

6.1 INTRODUCTION

ALTHOUGH the threat of 'new protectionism' has arisen with reference to a whole range of industrial activities in the West, and
although there is a tendency to consider all such threats as part
of a general politico–economic phenomenon to be attributed to
factors such as generalized unemployment, increased demands
for job security from the state, etc., it is useful to distinguish
between two extreme, idealized situations.

On the one hand, the pressure of import competition, no matter
how significant, can be seen as being addressed to industries
undergoing a basic shift in comparative advantage, not because of
technological advances arising in different parts of the world that
are not being shared by competing nations, but rather because of
shifts in labour costs or because 'learning by doing' by latecomers
is altering the traditional competitive edge of industries in the West.
These are the 'senescent', 'declining' industries such as textiles,
and shoes and footwear that are labour-intensive and mostly unintensive in skills and R & D, where the newly industrializing
countries of the South are increasingly demonstrating comparative
advantage. Since these industries are characterized by low technical progress — which is perfectly compatible with increasing capital
intensity, of course — Schumpeterian responses in the nature of
induced technical progress à la Weiszacre–Kennedy–Samuelson

* Thanks are due to NSF Grant no. SOC 79–07541 for financial support, to Robert
Feenstra for helpful conversations, and to Robert Baldwin, T. Bayard, Charles
Kindleberger, Gene Grossman, Jean Waelbroeck and John Williamson for valu-
able comments.

are not in evidence. Hence the responses of the entrepreneurs, labour, and communities or townships in which these industries are located, as well as the nature of the governmental policy options and responses, are likely to be quite different from those occurring when the industries are of the type considered immediately below.

This second class of industries is at the other end of the technological scale, being largely characterized by changing comparative advantage because R & D leads to technical change that gives new countries a competitive edge. These industries are at the front end of the dynamic, Schumpeterian capitalist process. The resulting shifts in comparative advantage yield a very different set of responses by the industries losing comparative advantage, and the policy options available to the countries where they are located are also correspondingly different.

In considering these two idealized models, it will be critical to note that the response to shifting comparative advantage will involve differential interaction with international 'factor' mobility. In the former case, a possible and indeed empirically important response (hitherto neglected altogether in the literature) is lobbying for a greater inflow of foreign *labour*. In the latter case, however, among the important responses are a variety of patterns of direct foreign *investment:* for example, the use of threats of protection to induce a reverse flow of foreign investment into the country or mutually penetrating investments in differential but similar products where the different countries have differential advantages.

Moreover, it will be useful to distinguish the following 'actors' among the lobbies seeking governmental response to the shift in comparative advantage: (i) entrepreneurs who may be interested in sales à la Burnham and Galbraith but are generally identified in the formal arguments below with the owners of equity capital in the industry; (ii) labour, distinguished in practice by nationality, skills, and age, but again treated in the formal analysis below as a homogeneous entity; and (iii) the community-cum-township where the affected industry may play a dominant role. The analysis will attempt to identify which policy responses will be sought by one or more of these actors and therefore what political forces the government is likely to confront by choosing one policy response option in preference to another.

6.2 TECHNICALLY UNPROGRESSIVE, 'TRADITIONAL' INDUSTRIES

Since technical change is not important in these industries, the *shift* in their comparative advantage largely reflects changing factor endowments and/or learning in the newly industrializing countries. They are thus also primarily labour-intensive, low-skills industries — in competition with the less developed countries (LDCs). How are these industries in the developed countries likely to react to the adversely shifting comparative advantage?

6.2.1 The Relaxation of Immigration Quotas as a Policy Response Option

As comparative advantage shifts against these unprogressive in-dustries, pressuring them toward a (relative or absolute) contrac-tion of their output, it might appear that all the potential lobbies that were distinguished above — entrepreneurs, labour, and the community — would be seeking relief via only one type of govern-mental response, namely, some sort of protection. This is however plainly not the case, for these unprogressive industries are often at a comparative disadvantage precisely because cost conditions have moved against them, and in labour-intensive industries this is often because labour abroad has become relatively cheaper. Now, introduce into this picture the fact that international mobility of labour is severely regulated by immigration quotas and that the real wages of labour are substantially higher in the West than in many developing countries. It follows immediately that one addi-tional policy response in which entrepreneurs could be interested is for the government to increase the availability of imported labour.

Note that the entrepreneurs' response will typically not include in this case their leaving for the foreign countries where the comparative advantage has shifted. This is due to the fact that these are unprogressive industries where, with no Hymer-like firm-specific know-how to take advantage of, the migration of domestic entrepreneurship is likely to mean merely that the migrant entrepreneurs will have to operate in unfamiliar, relatively riskier foreign situations, without any offsetting technological advantage, and hence at a competitive disadvantage with local producers.[1]

On the other hand, domestic labour should find its own interests better served by a policy of protection rather than by the alternative policy of relaxed immigration quotas. Therefore, while a governmental response in the form of allowing the increased importation of foreign labour will satisfy entrepreneurs, it will not generally satisfy domestic labour. For a rigorous consideration of these issues, turn now to the formal analysis below.

6.2.2 Some Formal Models

Heckscher–Ohlin–Samuelson Model

Take first the $2 \times 2 \times 2$ model of trade theory to rigorously develop the principal implications of our policy-choice problem. Assume two goods X and Y, and two factors K and L, and let Y be L-intensive and the importable good, in conformity with the empirical reality of the problem at hand. I would like to distinguish between the two types of shift in comparative advantage that may affect the L-intensive importable industry Y: (1) that which arises *externally* — either from a shift in the foreign offer curve facing our country

---

[1] The only important exception to this hypothesis (i.e. that in the declining, senescent, unprogressive, labour-intensive industries the typical response would not be for entrepreneurs to move) would appear to come from Japanese experience. However, the shift of some Japanese textiles, for example, to South Korea and other countries in the Far East appears to have been partly a question of 'investment shunting' prompted by GSP. It may also be useful to examine whether the shift has occurred from the technologically more progressive firms among these industries. Again, the few US apparel producers who have gone abroad to take advantage of US tariff provisions under GSP or 806.30–807 (the offshore assembly provision) seem to be the smaller firms with special designing or marketing skills. For a discussion of how Japanese direct investment differs in this respect (i.e. in so far as it occurs also in the 'traditional' labour-intensive industries) from Western direct investment, see Kojima (1978).

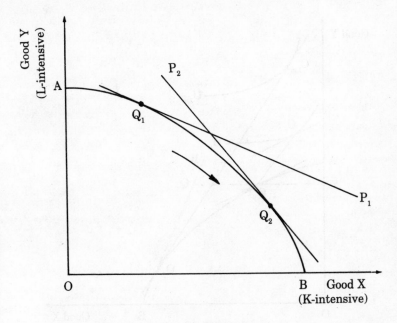

FIG. 6.1

or from a tariff cut by our country, as in the across-the-board tariff cuts of the Kennedy Round; and (2) that which results *internally*, e.g. from capital accumulation or productivity change. In each case, it will also be relevant whether the comparisons between the two policies involve a tariff-free or a tariff-ridden economy when the policy chosen is to import more labour. Throughout, I assume a small country and negligible lobbying costs.

Case I: External shift in comparative advantage, zero initial tariff. Figure 6.1 shows the economy moving from external price ratio P_1 to P_2, adversely affecting production of good Y.

The tariff policy will then restore production of Y to the initial level Y^0 at Q_1 but, as seen in Fig. 6.2, will yield welfare U_t. The alternative policy of restoring Y production to Y^0 by importing labour, on the other hand, will lead to welfare level U_{Lm} as follows. As labour is imported, holding the goods price ratio unaltered at its new free trade position P_2, we can trace the Rybczynski line Q_2R which, at Q_3, yields Y production equal to Y^0. Importation of

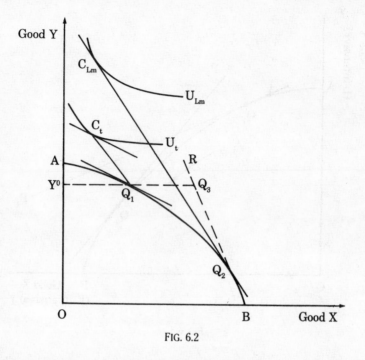

FIG. 6.2

the corresponding amount of labour (*Lm*) would then restore domestic importable output to the initial, pre-shift level. But the *national* welfare level, defined *exclusive* of imported labour's welfare, would be U_{Lm}, with the national budget line $Q_2 C_{Lm}$, since imported labour earns the value of its marginal product which, in turn, equals the increment in output along the Rybczynski line.

A comparison of the two policies, both achieving identical production in the importable industry and thus satisfying entrepreneurs equally in that respect,[2] then shows that the policy of reduced restrictions on the importation of labour dominates that of increasing trade protection in so far as economic welfare is conventionally defined ($U_{Lm} > U_t$), and hence should be the preferred option of an economic welfare-oriented government.[3] At the

---

[2] Indeed, the reward to capital is higher at Q_2 and Q_3 under the labour-importation policy and thus should please entrepreneurs more.

[3] Note that, even if a production subsidy were used for protection, the corresponding welfare (U_{ps}) would, while avoiding the consumption cost of the tariff, still

same time, from the viewpoint of international relations, it should again be a preferred option since relaxing immigration restrictions gives the government good marks whereas increasing trade protection gives it bad marks. On the other hand, at Q_3 and Q_2 under the policy of reduced immigration restrictions, the real wages of labour are less than at Q_1 under the tariff policy, à la the Stolper–Samuelson argument.[4]

The choice between the policy option of reducing immigration restrictions and increasing trade protection in response to an adverse shift in comparative advantage therefore primarily involves the conflicting interests of the *government* (or, more precisely, that part of the government (e.g. in the US, the executive rather than the legislative) which is presumably interested in welfare as defined by conventional economics) and *consumers*, who face lower prices for importables, on the one hand, and *domestic labour*, on the other hand, while leaving the entrepreneurs somewhat indifferent between the two policy options in so far as industry output is concerned but in favour of the policy of importing more foreign labour since this implies greater reward to capital. I shall later amplify other aspects of the conflicting interests involved in the choice between these policies, especially those involved at the community-cum-township level, which cannot be accommodated in the present model. For the present, however, let me go on to show that this basic pattern of conflicts between the different sectors resurrects itself when the external shift is in the presence of a trade restriction, though there are important differences to note, as argued immediately below.

Case II: External shift in comparative advantage, positive initial tariff. The presence of an initial tariff makes a significant difference to the analysis of the effects of different policy responses to an external shift in comparative advantage. This is because the policy of increasing the importation of labour is itself to be judged in the context of a tariff-ridden economy. For the choice now,

---

be inferior to that under the policy of relaxing the immigration restrictions on labour.

[4] Note that the real rewards at Q_2 and Q_3 are identical, since the goods price ratio does not change along a Rybczynski line.

when the external price ratio shifts from P_1 to P_2, is between increasing the tariff to restore production of Y to Y^0 at Q_1 and, instead, increasing the importation of labour to achieve Y^0 while maintaining the tariff at the initial level.

While in Case I, with zero initial tariff, the importation of labour left the national welfare unchanged at the free-trade level (since imported labour earned the value of its marginal product at domestic prices as well as at international prices thanks to free trade), the importation of labour when the labour-intensive importable industry is protected by a tariff is necessarily immiserizing! This result, derived by Uzawa (1969) and Brecher and Alejandro (1977) independently of one another, is seen in Fig. 6.3. There, after the shift of the external price ratio to P_2, the continuing initial tariff makes P_2^D the new tariff-inclusive domestic price ratio. With labour imported, the corresponding Rybczynski line is then Q_2R. Now, if no labour were imported, the equilibrium consumption would be at C_2, which lies on P_2 and on the income-consumption line IC (P_2^D) which is drawn with reference to price ratio P_2^D. If, however, labour is imported and is paid the value of its marginal product

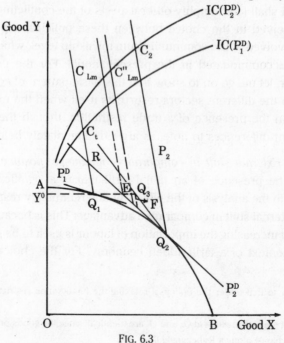

FIG. 6.3

at domestic tariff-inclusive prices, the *national* income at domestic prices will be identical to P_2^D through Q_2. Thus, if labour importation takes production on the Rybczynski line to Q_3, and (for simplicity) we assume that foreign labour consumes entirely in the country of residence, the *national* (net of foreign labour consumption) bundle of production will be along the stretch EF on the national income line P_2^D through Q_2. And, by putting the new international price line P_2 through E and F, and cutting IC (P_2^D), we see that the resulting national consumption will lie in the range of $C'_{Lm} C''_{Lm}$. Evidently therefore importing labour will necessarily be immiserizing.

However, it is equally evident that the alternative policy of resorting to trade protection to restore Y production to Y^0 by shifting back to Q_1, with the new international price ratio P_2, yields consumption at C_t on the income-consumption curve IC (P_1^D) which is drawn with reference to P_1^D (tangent to AB at Q_1). Evidently this is *inferior* to any equilibrium consumption, on $C'_{Lm} C''_{Lm}$, reached under the labour importation policy.

Note therefore that the welfare loss from importing labour is constrained so as to make the labour-importing policy nonetheless a better alternative than the trade protection policy.[5] This means that the basic nature of the conflicting interests of the different actors, as emerging from Case I, survives the complication of an initial tariff while weakening the economic welfare advantage that the government would derive from a policy of importing labour.

Case III: Domestic shift in comparative advantage, zero initial tariff. Nor does a shift in comparative advantage resulting from either domestic factor supply or technical change affect the basic nature of the conflicting interests on the two policy options being considered.

Thus take Fig. 6.4, where a domestic shift of the production

---

[5] This strong ranking would not have followed if the policy comparison had not required identical Y^0 production. Thus it is easy to see in Fig. 6.3 that further shifts up along the Rybczynski line and hence IC (P_2^D) could lead eventually to welfare levels below that at C_t. Note also that the strong ranking might not hold if we were to use a sticky-wage model of either the Brecher (1974a, b), or the Harris and Todaro (1970) variety since that would introduce a domestic distortion in the sense of Bhagwati and Ramaswami (1963); Johnson (1965), and Bhagwati (1971).

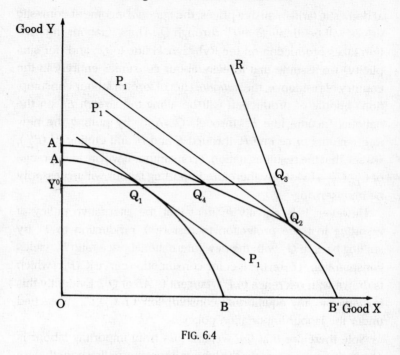

FIG. 6.4

possibility curve from AB to $A'B'$ leads to a strong decline in the 'production advantage' of good Y: at identical goods price ratios, the production of good Y actually declines at Q_2 as compared with Q_1.[6] The international goods price ratio remains unchanged at P_1. It should therefore be manifest that a labour-importing policy will lead to consumption along Q_2P_1 at price ratio P_1, whereas an alternative policy of protection to retain output of Y at Y^0 will lead to production at Q_4 and consumption not merely on the inferior budget line Q_4P_1, but also on a further distorted price ratio tangent at Q_4 to $A'B'$.

Case IV: Domestic shift in comparative advantage, positive initial tariff. The case where the domestic shift in comparative advantage occurs in the presence of a tariff does not need to be spelled

[6] Types of factor accumulation or technological progress which can lead to an increase in the production of the exportable good X and a fall in the production of Y are as follows: an increase in the stock of capital (used intensively in the export industry), and neutral or labour-using technological progress in the export industry (see Findlay and Grubert 1959).

out, since it modifies the argument of Case III in much the same way as Case II modifies Case I: it weakens the economic welfare case for importing labour while leaving it as the preferred option to trade protection.

The analysis in the $2 \times 2 \times 2$ model therefore underlines the robustness of the conclusion that, while entrepreneurs will marginally prefer the importation of more foreign labour to an increase in protection when comparative advantage shifts against their industry, the policy option of increasing the influx of foreign labour will be preferred by consumers and by that branch of the government (if any) that concerns itself with economic welfare conventionally defined, while being considered detrimental to its interests by domestic labour.

However, I might add that Cases III and IV, where the shift is domestically induced, suggests an important difference from Cases I and II, where the shift is externally induced. In the former, if the shift results from capital accumulation leading to a decline in the output of the labour-intensive importable activity (à la Rybczynski), the real wages of labour will be *maintained;* it is just that the 'drawing power' of the importable activity for domestic labour has been reduced as a result of the change in the accumulation. In this case, it is not likely that domestic labour will oppose the import of foreign labour; the labour import will be seen rather as supportive of the output of the labour-intensive industry without coming at the expense of domestic wages. (The protection option will of course *increase* the real wages of labour, but this is unlikely to make the same impression on labour as actually *losing* ground through reduced real wages.) In cases where the shift in comparative advantage is however external, the loss of real wages in the present model is necessarily actual, not just in an opportunity cost sense, when the shift occurs; and therefore the importation of labour as a policy option is likely to be passionately opposed.

Jones–Neary Model

Consider instead the model of Jones (1971) and Neary (1978) in which capital is specific but labour is mobile between the two sectors. This may be considered to be the 'short-run' version of the standard 2×2 model, if labour is assumed to be mobile in the short run but capital is not, an interpretation given by Neary (1978), Mussa (1974), and Mayer (1974).[7] What happens to the choice between labour importation and protection in this model when the terms of trade shift adversely against the labour-intensive importable activity?[8]

The effect of the shift in the terms of trade is now an unambiguous fall in the rental on capital in the labour-intensive importable industry while the return to labour (after reallocation) will rise in terms of the importable but fall in terms of the exportable good. (If the importable sector is 'small', then evidently the real wages of labour are likely to fall, as the weight of the exportable good in consumption will be greater). In this model, therefore, both capitalists and labour are likely to have the incentive to lobby for protection. But capitalists may also settle for increased importation of labour for, as Mayer (1974) has shown, such an increment in labour at a constant goods price ratio will increase the rental unambiguously to capital in both sectors while the real wages fall unambiguously.[9]

In so far as economic welfare is concerned, the choice is again clear-cut in the Jones–Neary model so long as an otherwise free-trade situation without distortions is considered. Thus the protection option implies the standard cost of distorted production and consumption. However, with the real wages declining as labour is imported, the importation of a finite quantity of foreign labour yields a 'surplus' to the host country: labour importation is therefore welfare-improving. Thus that branch of government that responds to an economic-welfare motivation will favour labour importation over instituting a protective tariff.

Industry-specific Foreign Labour Paid a Differential Wage

The preceding two models considered foreign labour to be industry-non-specific and equally assumed that the return to foreign

[7] It is a moot point whether labour is, in fact, always more mobile than capital is malleable!

[8] The analysis of this model and the next could be extended to cases where the shift in comparative advantage is domestically induced, as in Cases III and IV above. This can be readily done by the interested reader.

[9] Note that the output of the importable industry expands under a policy of protection or labour importation.

and domestic labour was equal. However, approximating the West European *gastarbeiter* system more closely, we may assume that foreign labour is imported on an industry-specific contractual basis and can be effectively paid lower wages than domestic labour.

Take this model then and assume a Haberler–Brecher model with Haberler (1950)-type sector-specific factors and Brecher (1974a, b)-type sticky real wages for labour. Let Q_1 be the initial production vector, AQ_1B being the production possibility curve, given the immobility of factors. When the terms of trade shift from P_1 to P_2, turning against the importable, labour-intensive good Y, labour in Y production insists on maintaining its real wages in terms of good X. This leads to workers being laid off in industry Y until the marginal physical product of labour in Y rises sufficiently at Q_2 to restore Y labour's real wages in terms of good X.

In this situation, if the Y capitalists are allowed to import foreign labour to restore their output to Q_1, and foreign labour allows itself to be hired at lower real wages than those that local labour insists on, then part of the incremental output of good Y (this increment being Q_2Q_1) will accrue to the capitalists, as demonstrated in

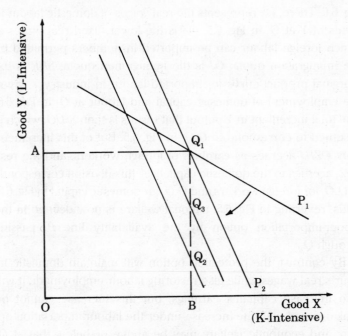

FIG. 6.5

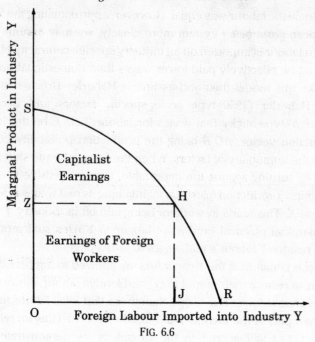

FIG. 6.6

Fig. 6.6. There, *OS* represents the real wages of domestic labour in terms of *Y* at Q_2 in Fig. 6.5; *OZ* is the lower, fixed real wages at which foreign labour can be imported in numbers permitted by the immigration quota; *OJ* is the immigration quota; *SHR* is the marginal product curve for imported labour in industry *Y*, given the employment of domestic capital and labour at Q_2 in Fig. 6.5. The total increment in *Y* output that results is then *SHJO*, which is assumed to correspond to Q_2Q_1 in Fig. 6.5. But of this increment, only *OZHJ* accrues as earnings of foreign workers, and the rest, *SHZ*, accrues to the domestic capitalists; this division corresponds to Q_3Q_1 for foreign workers and Q_2Q_3 for domestic capital in Fig. 6.5. Thus, reverting to Fig. 6.5, national welfare is now defined in the labour-importation option by the availability line P_2 passing through Q_3.

By contrast, the protection option will maintain domestic labour's real wages while also restoring labour employment; it will also increase capitalist earnings, but this increase cannot be rank-ordered with the increase under the labour-importation option; and economic welfare may be above or below that at Q_3 (the labour-importation option) since protection will mean that production will be restored to Q_1 but there will be a consumption-distortion cost which may be large enough to outweigh the production gain vis-à-vis the labour-importation option.[10]

6.2.3 Likely Lobbying Outcomes

What type of lobbying may then be expected in the labour-intensive industries, once we recognize the possibility of using immigration quotas as a policy instrument? Evidently the answer depends critically on the production-cum-trade model that applies to a specific situation; it is also clearly dependent on the precise immigration control system that the country operates. Thus, if we contrast the results of the three models, it is interesting that, in the Heckscher–Ohlin–Samuelson (HOS) model, capitalists would find protection harmful and labour importation of no effect on their earnings, whereas in the other two models *both* options are helpful. Again, labour is actually hurt by labour importation in the Jones–Neary model but is neither hurt nor helped in the other models, whereas protection helps it in all three models. The precise conflicts of interests, reflecting the implications of the two policy options of protection and labour importation, will therefore depend on the specifics of the situation concerning factor-market and immigration-system behaviour. No general conclusions are possible, as indicated by Table 6.1, which categorizes the outcomes.

On the other hand, the models uniformly suggest that entrepreneurs have an interest in getting governments to agree to relax immigration quotas, that governments themselves have a potential interest in the relaxation of immigration quotas since economic welfare is such an important objective, and that labour, in contrast, has a relatively greater interest in the adoption of protectionist measures. I would therefore expect governments to expedite the inflow of foreign labour whenever (a) domestic labour's opposition to this policy option is weak and its lobbying for protection is correspondingly so (as when labour is not effectively organized

---

[10] The production is, of course, identical under both options; i.e. both policies are assumed to take the economy back to Q_1. However, under the labour-importation option, the net-of-remuneration-for-foreign-workers 'production' point is $Q_3 (< Q_1)$.

TABLE 6.1
Effects of Output-restoring Labour-importation and Protectionist Responses to Import Competition in Labour-intensive Industries

Model	Policy Response	Capitalists*	Labour	'Economic Welfare'
Heckscher-Ohlin-Samuelson	Labour importation	Earnings unchanged	Earnings unchanged	Welfare unchanged (Cases I & III)
	Protection	Earnings reduced	Earnings increased (back to preshift level)	Reduces welfare
Jones-Neary	Labour importation	Earnings increased	Earnings lowered	Increases welfare
	Protection	Earnings increased	Earnings increased	Reduces welfare
Haberler-Brecher	Labour importation	Earnings increased	Earnings unchanged	Increases welfare
	Protection	Earnings increased	Earnings increased (via increased employment)	May increase or lower welfare (while increasing domestic employment)

NOTE: The comparison is with the situation where import competition (i.e. shift in comparative advantage) occurs and there is no policy response. The comparison is *not* therefore with the situation *before* import competition.

* The entries here relate, in the Jones-Neary and Haberler-Brecher models, to capitalist earnings in the importable industry.

due, for example, to geographical dispersion of the industry), (b) the government's ability to grant protection is weak (because, for example, of fear of retaliation or respect for GATT Article XIX), and (c) the government's ability to augment immigration is not constrained greatly by the social consequences of increased immigration. More specifically, the following types of hypotheses may well be worth exploring.

1. When the shift in comparative advantage is domestically induced (as in Cases III and IV of the HOS model above), the opposition of domestic labour to the importation of labour is lower, for reasons spelled out earlier. By contrast, when the shift comes from external changes (as in Cases I and II), the opposition of domestic labour to the importation of labour will be the greater. Therefore I would expect that the policy response to a shift in comparative advantage would be, *ceteris paribus*, greater for imported labour when the shift is domestic rather than external.

2. Moreover, where the external shift in comparative advantage is combined with the presence of a native labour force which has low-mobility characteristics (e.g. higher age, residency traditionally in towns or communities in which the roots and ties are strong, which raises the non-pecuniary costs of mobility), the likelihood of protection emerging as the outcome of the lobbying response will be all the greater. For in this case, the option of importing foreign labour will appear particularly unattractive to the low-mobility labour, whose real wages will otherwise face a significant decline. The role of the community or township as a lobbying force in cases where labour has strong historical ties to an area, as in traditional 'textile towns', may also be very important quite independently of the labour force itself. For where such geographical specificity is involved, other jobs are likely to be seen as being dependent not merely on the size of the industry's output but also on traditional spending patterns, and imported labour, with its usual high savings and remittance rates, is unlikely to be quite an adequate replacement in that regard! Moreover, the social cohesion of the community itself may militate against introducing a sizeable foreign labour component into such communities.[11]

---

[11] The project at Sussex University's Centre for European Studies under the direction of Professor Ronald Dore ought to shed more light on these questions.

What type of evidence would indicate that such hypotheses make empirical sense? The foregoing arguments suggest that it is possible to examine episodes such as the response to across-the-board tariff cuts in the Kennedy Round and hypothesize a set of testable propositions.

I would expect, for example, that when across-the-board tariff cuts are made, as after the Kennedy Round, the tariff-cut exemptions (adjusted in so far as they were offset by domestic subsidies — as they often were in varying degree in West Germany according to Riedel (1977) would be generally greater in those traditional industries where the labour force is largely domestic, is geographically concentrated in close-knit communities, or is relatively immobile. In contrast, when quota restrictions are relaxed, I would expect there to be a relatively greater growth of the foreign labour component in those industries in which the labour force already has a significant foreign element, is geographically dispersed, or has a domestic component that is relatively skilled and mobile.

Furthermore, if cross-sectional regressions were run, I would not be surprised if (the subsidy-adjusted) tariff-cut exemptions were inversely related to the initial proportion of foreign labour in the total labour force and to its skill level, and positively related to its average age, as seems to be indicated to some degree in Cheh's (1974) analysis of the US and Riedel's (1977) analysis of West Germany. And this is the important *new* possibility: that the growth rate of foreign labour (absolute or relative to domestic labour) in these industries, reflecting the relaxation of immigration quota restrictions, may be positively related to the initial proportion of foreign labour in the total labour force and to its skill level, and inversely related to its average age. And thus, also, there may then exist an inverse correlation between the tariff-cut exemptions an industry receives and the growth rate of its foreign labour force, in cross-sectional analysis.

6.2.4 Labour Lobbying and the Efficient Tariff: An Aside

Where the labour interest in protection is deep-seated, the foregoing arguments suggest that the governmental response will be to yield to protectionist pressures from the labour lobby; the relaxation of immigration quota restrictions will not be the preferred option.

In such cases, the 'bargaining', between the government and labour may be visualized as being over the degree of protection to be granted to the industry when the comparative advantage has shifted, with labour's primary interest consisting in fully restoring its original economic position and the government's in minimizing the cost of such restoration.

Viewing the conflict in this way, we can develop the notion of an 'efficient tariff', once we recognize that the levy of a tariff will generally raise revenue. Thus, consider for simplicity the $2 \times 2 \times 2$ model where labour's real wage declines with the relative price of the importable good. A shift in comparative advantage improving the terms of trade will hurt labour, triggering the lobbying for a tariff. If then the tariff is used for restoring labour's real wages, there will be an associated loss of welfare to society. However, since the tariff raises revenue, we may consider the following alternative. Suppose that this tariff revenue itself is used to compensate labour through a direct subsidy such that its real income (defined as the *sum* of its real wages in employment and this subsidy, as in Bhagwati 1959) is equivalent to its original real wages. Then the resulting welfare cost to society would generally be lower. Thus a tariff that restores the real *wages* of labour to their original level would generally be inferior to the efficient tariff which is chosen so as to minimize the welfare cost of a tariff that restores labour's real *income* to the original (real wage) level by additionally utilizing the tariff revenue proceeds to subsidize labour's income.[12] This notion of the efficient tariff makes a good deal of sense in so far as the revenue used for redistribution is being generated as a side effect of the protection itself and is *not* being raised *ab initio* for the redistribution![13]

[12] In Ch. 9 of J.N. Bhagwati (ed.) (1982), the analysis considers the lobbying costs of the labour lobby.

[13] If we could raise any amount of revenue as a lump-sum it would of course be trivially true that we could bribe the labour lobby out of any protectionist pressure! The notion of the efficient tariff, on the other hand, is a second best one, and the beauty of it is that the revenue being used for the bribe to labour is generated by the tariff itself. For further discussion, see J.N. Bhagwati (ed.) (1982), Ch. 9.

What this notion of the efficient tariff does therefore is to provide a rationale for a direct subsidy to lobbying labour so long as it is kept within the bounds of the tariff revenue raised from the partial protection granted, when the labour lobby seeking protection is strong and the government feels that there is no political alternative to maintaining the labour lobby's economic position in face of a shift in comparative advantage.

6.2.5 Protectionist Response to Import Competition and the Welfare of the Exporting Country: Some Paradoxes

While the foregoing analysis was addressed to lobbies, policy options, and likely outcomes, focusing exclusively on the country facing import competition, the novel element of foreign labour additionally introduces an interesting, and surely important, element of paradox into the situation regarding protectionist responses to import competition as far as the welfare of the *other* trading countries is concerned.

It is no longer possible to identify the levy of protective tariffs on a country's exports by another as necessarily welfare-worsening — short of standard paradoxes in trade theory — for the simple reason that the protection also redounds to the welfare of foreign labour, which may very well be the country's own emigrant labour. Thus, if the US levies protective tariffs on Mexican textile exports, this will worsen the welfare of the Mexican non-emigrant population but, since some Mexican labour is employed in textiles production in the US, it will also improve the welfare of the Mexican emigrant population. So, depending on what distributional welfare weights are assigned, it can easily be argued that US protection *improves* the welfare of the Mexicans (emigrants *plus* non-emigrants)![14] Interestingly, this paradox is the mirror image of the paradox (analysed in Bhagwati and Tironi, 1980; Bhagwati and Brecher, 1980; and Brecher and Bhagwati 1981) in which the reduction of a tariff in the presence of foreign-owned factors of production may be accompanied by a decline in national welfare

[14] In the standard $2 \times 2 \times 2$ model, it is possible to work out the conditions under which the paradox of welfare-worsening tariff imposition will arise. See Bhagwati and Rivera–Batiz (1980). This paradox was first noted in Bhagwati (1979).

even though the country is small and there are no other domestic distortions.[15]

Another interesting paradox that arises in the presence of foreign labour from LDCs and the DCs (developed countries) is that the country from which the foreign labour comes and the country producing the imports may not coincide. Thus textiles in the US may be using Mexican labour while they face competition from South Korea. Hence there may be inter-LDC conflicts inherent in the decision of the DCs to use or not to use protection in the face of a shift in comparative advantage. For instance, West Germany uses a great deal of Turkish, Yugoslav, and Greek labour in industries that face competition from the less developed newly industrializing countries such as Brazil, Taiwan, South Korea, Hong Kong, and Singapore.

6.3 TECHNICALLY PROGRESSIVE, SCHUMPETERIAN INDUSTRIES

The scenarios concerning lobbying and policy response options discussed in the preceding section change dramatically as attention is shifted to technologically progressive industries. These industries might be described as Schumpeterian since they represent the essence of the dynamic capitalist system that Schumpeter described so beautifully. Technological change, resulting from R & D (whether private or public), is critical to the shifts in comparative advantage in these industries, and this essential fact fundamentally transforms the nature of the lobbying responses and policy options that open up in the face of the ongoing shifts in comparative advantage.

6.3.1 Two Alternative Models of Direct Foreign Investment in Progressive Industries

It will be appropriate to distinguish in the analysis that follows between two models in the direct investment literature, both an

---

[15] Needless to say, varying the tax on foreign capital to its optimal level would eliminate the paradox. This is, however, as removed from reality as differential taxation of foreign labour in the argument in the text and in Bhagwati and Rivera–Batiz (1980).

offshoot of Hymer's (1960) ground-breaking work on direct foreign investment: the 'product cycle' (PC) model of Vernon (1966) and the 'mutual penetration of investment' (MPI) model set forth in my review of Vernon's *Sovereignty at Bay* (Bhagwati 1972) and then amplified in Bhagwati (1978, 1979).

The 'Product Cycle' Model

In the PC model, firms develop R & D-based new products in one country, with a corresponding conferral of comparative advantage of manufacture in that country. As long as the product and its associated processes need to be 'debugged' and simplified, the location of production at home, close to the R & D facilities, is important. With the passing of this stage, the production of the products is freed from this locational requirement and production facilities will shift to wherever wages are cheapest. Thus this model is premised on a shift in comparative advantage in the location of production that reflects a process where R & D-created comparative advantage self-destructs and the process is essentially a result of domestic R & D rather than a result of external changes induced by R & D.

The 'Mutual Penetration of Investment' Model

In contrast, the MPI model is based on the observation that competition occurs among differentiated but similar products, and that increased competition can typically occur in the progressive industries through R & D-induced intensification of the advantages enjoyed by the competitors for their differentiated products. For example, European and Japanese small cars compete with American large cars; and this competition intensifies with time as the Japanese get better at the game (e.g. Toyota started production only after World War II) of R & D in production, marketing, and sales and the Americans get steadily better at producing the 'gas guzzlers'. The MPI thesis then is that the response to such intensified competition could be a mutual investment by the competing firms in one another's R & D-induced advantages. Contrasting the resulting MPI pattern of direct investment and Vernon's PC model, I wrote in 1972:

There is also at least one more dramatic form of international investment which neither Vernon nor other researchers in the MNC field has noted but which may well be the pattern to emerge as a dominant form. In contrast to the case where the MNCs, having developed new products via R & D, export them, and then transit to producing them abroad, there is an alternative 'model' where MNCs in different countries have R & D-induced advantages in producing different types of sub-products (e.g. one MNC in Japan is excellent with small cars and one MNC in US has an edge on large cars; or tyre firms in different types of tyres). In competing in each other's home countries or in third markets in both types of sub-products, it is natural that each MNC would find it difficult to compete effectively with the other in sub-products where it does not have the edge. I would expect that, in this situation, there is likelihood of these MNCs deciding that mutual equity interpenetration, with productionwise accommodation in sub-product specialization according to the advantage possessed, is profitable. Thus, the MNC in US (say, GM) that finds it difficult to compete in the small-car field with the MNC in Japan (say, Toyota) that finds it difficult to compete with the MNC in US in the large-car field, would each decide that the best strategy if you cannot compete with comfort is to follow the policy: 'if you cannot beat them, buy them'. Thus GM would want to buy equity in Toyota for the small car production and Toyota in GM for the large-car production: and GM in US would go off spending resources in producing and improving its own small cars while Toyota in Japan would similarly hold back on its own large-car efforts. One thus gets mutually interpenetrating MNCs within industries, with accompanying division of labour and a novel form of 'cartelization' which goes by sub-products. Linder has made us familiar with trade in commodities between similar countries as consisting of sub-product exchanges: and Hymer and Rowthorn have noted that MNCs from different countries penetrate into each other's countries. My 'model' essentially combines these two and predicts that MNCs with R & D-induced specialization in different types of sub-products within an industry in different countries will interpenetrate.

I then noted that the MPI model was perfectly illustrated by an account in *Forbe's* magazine of 15 November 1970 (p. 22) of the following 'international marriage':

Long the friendliest of competitors. Dunlop and Pirelli neatly complement each other. Dunlop is primarily a manufacturer of conventional cross-ply tyres. Pirelli concentrates on radials. In Europe, Dunlop has perhaps 18 per cent of the market, Pirelli 12 per cent, as against 12 per cent for Michelin, the next largest competitor. In Europe, Pirelli crosses Dunlop's path only in West Germany: Elsewhere, where Dunlop is active, Pirelli stays out; where Pirelli is active, Dunlop stays out. Outside of Europe, Pirelli is active mostly in Latin America. Dunlop in the Commonwealth and North America.

The two companies have even diversified into different areas — Dunlop into sporting goods and precision engineering products, Pirelli into paper, electronics, and cables.

Eventually, of course, both marketing organizations will work as one, with Dunlop pushing Pirelli products where Dunlop is strong, and Pirelli pushing Dunlop products elsewhere. 'The greatest benefits should come from a pooling of R & D, however', explains J. Campbell Fraser, a Dunlop director: 'In the 'seventies and 'eighties, competition will be more and more in terms of innovations. In the UK we have a home base of about 55 million people — that isn't big enough for the kind of R & D we'll need. Pirelli has an even smaller home base, about 45 million. By merging, we'll have a home base of 100 million, enough for the kind of R & D we'll need around the world. . . . . There will not even be any exchange of public shares. Instead each will acquire an interest in the other's operating subsidiaries. The British and Italian companies will operate on their own.

The report went on to note (p. 23) that there will be four companies:

Dunlop Home (the United Kingdom and Europe) with Dunlop owning 51 per cent and Pirelli 49 per cent; Dunlop International (the rest of the world) with Dunlop holding 60 per cent and Pirelli Milan and Pirelli Switzerland 20 per cent each; Pirelli Milan (the Common Market) with Pirelli Milan holding 51 per cent and 49 per cent; and Pirelli Switzerland (all other Pirelli operations) with Dunlop holding 40 per cent, Pirelli Milan 20 per cent, and Pirelli Switzerland 40 per cent.

6.3.2 Shifting Comparative Advantage, Lobbying, and Policy Response Options: Three Patterns

The preceding review of major models of direct foreign investment evidently bears directly on the questions being addressed here, namely, what kind of lobbying responses can be expected, and what options are open for governmental response, when a shift in comparative advantage occurs in technically progressive industries? It is now possible to think of three idealized patterns: (i) the *'product cycle'* scenario, where the shift in comparative advantage occurs from the emergence of cheaper factor costs abroad overtaking the relative cheapness of domestic production due to the proximity to R & D facilities once the new product processes are simplified and debugged; (ii) the *'mutual penetration of investment'* scenario, where international competition is among similar products and technical change intensifies competition among them without conferring a dominant advantage to one class of products (and hence firms and nations) as against another; and (iii) the *'growing dominance of external products'* scenario, where, as in the MPI case, there is international competition among similar products but the technical change (or even a shift in demand, as in the case of the shift in demand away from 'gas guzzlers' toward small cars and hence in favour of non-American car makers who have traditionally specialized in small cars) favours the external producers and represents a growing, adverse shift in comparative advantage.

The first two patterns evidently include, as possible responses to the shift in comparative advantage, the corresponding patterns of direct foreign investment, i.e. the outward migration of entrepreneurs and firms. The last pattern, on the other hand, opens up a more complex set of responses.

The 'Product Cycle' Scenario

In this case, the shift in comparative advantage toward producing abroad and the subsequent transfer of production abroad essentially reflect entrepreneurial decision-making. Besides, the direct foreign investment response is consistent with governmental interest in so far as it represents an economic welfare-improving move (unless domestic or foreign distortions exist).

The lobbying response is therefore to be expected from domestic labour in so far as labour feels that it is 'losing jobs' as a result of this response by the entrepreneurs.[16] Again, therefore, the actors likely to be involved in the lobbying process, in response to the shift of production abroad as comparative advantage shifts abroad, are likely to be labour lobbies.

[16] It is of course easy enough to construct analytical cases where the shift outward of technology-cum-capital, by profit-maximizing entrepreneurs, neither increases domestic unemployment in a Brecher-type model nor lowers the real wages of labour with full employment in the $2 \times 2 \times 2$ model.

However, the policy instruments that the labour lobby can turn to are not identical to those in the case of the 'traditional' industries. Thus, if the market for the product shifts mainly overseas before the production shift overseas takes place, as in some of the PC folklore, then protecting domestic production evidently does not help! Rather, labour would have to seek a subsidy on production or trade, neither of which is likely to appeal very much to the government because of its budgetary implications and because it opens up the possibility of countervailing action under GATT rules. An obvious alternative instrument which labour is likely to seek therefore is the imposition of restrictions on foreign investment — which is indeed what labour unions in the United States have occasionally done. Together with this route, it can also be expected that the unions and labour lobbies will attempt to make such direct foreign investment less attractive by complaining that the practices resulting in cheaper costs abroad are in violation of GATT and other standards, and thus require the imposition of countervailing duties; a procedure that again can help only in so far as the domestic (as against the overseas) market is still of some importance for the product. Again, this option is also occasionally exercised, as in the frequent complaints about the exploitation of child labour abroad in violation of International Labour Organization (ILO) standards, about regional subsidies that aid competing firms abroad, special concessionary treatment of profits made by foreign firms, etc.

Given, therefore, the nature of the shift in comparative advantage to overseas production, the lobbying game reduces in the present instance essentially to one between the government and the entrepreneurs, on one hand, and labour lobbies, on the other. But instead of the lobbying essentially focusing on trade protection, it is likely to focus primarily on the need for controls on investment abroad except in cases where the domestic market still accounts for a major fraction of total sales. Such a situation therefore contrasts with the case of 'traditional' industries, where tariff is a more effective instrument for protecting labour's economic interests. Here, the question of controlling foreign investment by the domestic entrepreneurs is a meaningless option; entrepreneurs in these industries do not seek to respond by out-migration since they do not have Hymer-type know-how that would make it economical to do so, as already noted in Sec. 6.2.

But it *is* pertinent to ask whether the importation of foreign labour is not an option that entrepreneurs would seek as an alternative to investing abroad when the product is standardized and debugged, and cheap foreign labour becomes correspondingly decisive. It must be admitted that the failure to consider this option altogether is a major weakness of the PC doctrine, which has focused wholly on the choice between producing at home with local factors and producing abroad with foreign factors. This omission does make sense when immigration quotas are taken as exogenously specified, but it does not when firms can seek to have the quotas liberalized in response to a shift in comparative advantage. Eschewing formal analysis of a firm's choice between going abroad and seeking more importation of foreign labour, I think it would be fair to assert that, since the wage costs of imported labour are likely to be substantially higher than those of similar labour abroad, the labour importation option will be outweighed by the out-migration of production option unless the industry and the countries involved are such as to make the potential risks and costs of direct foreign investment unduly high. It would appear from casual observation that American entrepreneurs have followed the direct investment route à la Vernon's PC model fairly automatically, whereas West European entrepreneurs in technically progressive industries have followed a mixed strategy, investing in cheap labour countries abroad but also relying on increasing numbers of *gastarbeiters* much as in the 'traditional', labour-intensive industries of Sec. 6.2. It may well be that the greater willingness of West European governments to increase importation of *gastarbeiters* in the 1960s and much of the 1970s, and the relative stringency of US immigration policy in regard to unskilled labour, account for this differential. Whether domestic labour unions would have permitted a shift in US policy in this regard, leading to a shift from the Vernon-style direct investment abroad to importation of cheap labour to the US in the technically progressive industries for their standardized, debugged, labour-intensive operations, is a question that I cannot answer but one that would be interesting to explore. Indeed, it is not at all clear that domestic labour would be worse off under a policy where entrepreneurs out-migrate à la the PC scenario than it would be under a policy where entrepreneurs are allowed to import cheaper foreign labour!

The 'Mutual Penetration of Investment' Scenario

In contrast to the case of PC-type shifts in comparative advantage, I have earlier distinguished shifts in comparative advantage that occur from increased competition from similar products; a state of affairs often brought about by R & D-induced changes in know-how. I have also distinguished between two polar cases: the case in which the intensification of competition does not confer an advantage to one product (and nation) as against another, and that in which the competitive advantage of one product (and nation) increases at the definite expense of the other. Before I proceed to analyse these two cases, however, it is necessary to discuss how trade in similar products comes about.

Alternative Theories of Trade in Similar Products.   Recent analytical work in trade theory by Lancaster (1980), Dixit and Norman (1980), and Krugman (1979) has undertaken formalization of the original notion, inherent in Linder's (1961) pioneering work and in subsequent writings by Balassa (1967) and Grubel and Lloyd (1975), that much of the trade in manufactures among developed countries occurs in what might be called 'similar' products. This formalization has proceeded on the basis of models that assume *identical* know-how among different countries and that specialization in various 'similar' products ensues primarily as a result of scale economies, with basic indeterminacy as to which country produces which of the similar products, and with Linder-like conclusions concerning the *volume* of trade in place of the Heckscher–Ohlin emphasis on predicting the *pattern* of trade. Therefore these theories share the Heckscher–Ohlin assumption of identical know-how but emerge with a contrasting set of outcomes concerning whether the volume or the pattern of trade can be explained.

On the other hand, I find it difficult to accept this type of formalization of trade in similar products among nation-states, neat as it is, and prefer an alternative 'theory', which I will sketch below with a broad brush. Essentially, it seems to me that if we want to introduce the notion of 'similar' products, with different nations trading such products to one another, we really have to give up the Heckscher–Ohlin assumption that all firms, and nations, share identical know-how *ex ante*. I would thus start with the notion that, just as in biological theorizing the 'environment' interacts with 'genetic factors' to produce a phenotype, we can think of an economic process whereby a specific choice of a product type emerges within a nation-society.[17] Thus, think of the income level and the level of R & D in manufacturing as defining the capacity of the society to come up technologically with a given set of characteristic product combinations, e.g. small, medium, and large cars.

The US and Japan share this 'genetic' set of traits; Zaire and Gabon do not. But which phenotype is selected in the market depends on the interaction of this common set of genetic traits with the specific 'environment' of Japan and the US. Thus the land–man ratios, the size and structure of the family, etc., may lead to the evolution of 'gas guzzlers' in the US and of smaller, fuel-economy cars in Japan, as, in fact, has been the case. At the next stage of the argument, then, the successful development of small cars in Japan and of gas guzzlers in the United States gets reinforced by localized technical change in precisely these types of cars with the result that you are now dealing with a situation of *ex ante* differentials in the know-how of producing and selling different types of cars. Next, since 'cars' represent a generic product, representing a certain manner of transportation, the taste for small cars diffuses to the US and for gas guzzlers to Japan as part of the Schumpeterian process of dynamic capitalism, aided by

---

[17] Thus a typical popularized statement of the modern genetic theory is the following: The phenotype is the result of a particular heredity acting on a particular environmental background. Any variation we observe among the members of a related group of organisms living under natural conditions must be phenotypic variation, because it will be the result of different environmental pressures and different genetic histories. Phenotypic variation in a population is the sum of genotypic variation inherent in the combined heredity of the group plus that part of the environmental variation which affects the phenotype.

[Alland, Jr. 1972, p. 9.]

advertising in search of new markets. Thus trade in similar products arises. Scale economies with identical *ex ante* production functions do not of course play any role in this 'theory', and I believe that this scenario may have a greater claim to truth than the recent formal theorizations regarding trade in similar products.

The MPI Scenario. Whether the trade in similar products arises owing to scale economies in the presence of *ex ante* identical production functions or because of an 'ecobiological process' theory like the one I have delineated above, what happens when the competition among similar products intensifies? When it results in a standoff, with the products of neither country's firms gaining dominance through R & D breakthroughs or taste shifts (whether exogenous or advertising-induced), the response of the entrepreneurs is likely to be of the MPI variety if the competition gets tough.[18]

Because no jobs are threatened, this then is an outcome to which unions ought to be indifferent. The entrepreneurs reduce the threat to their profits from import competition by de facto product-wise cartelization, and the government may not be unduly disturbed about the outcome (unless the result is the total elimination of competition in the industry *and* the government has an anti-trust policy which it seeks to implement in this instance).[19] The results are therefore far more sanguine in the MPI scenario than in the PC scenario!

The 'Growing Dominance of External Products' Scenario

However, as soon as the comparative advantage has shifted dramatically in favour of the foreign products so that the domestic and foreign products do not both have a comfortable niche in the market, the picture changes drastically.

In this case, the entrepreneurs will want protection but may settle for greater access to cheaper foreign labour to offset the loss of comparative advantage if they can get the government to

---

[18] Impure forms of the MPI phenomenon may involve a one-way equity purchase in exchange for marketing facilities.

[19] Governments, of course, manage to get worried about direct foreign investments for all sorts of reasons; so perhaps I ought not to be overly optimistic about their benign neglect in this case!

oblige them. While entrepreneurs may be indifferent between protection and greater access to foreign labour, the labour lobby will generally prefer protection to labour importation for reasons which need not be spelled out again. Labour may however be indifferent between a policy of actual protection and one in which they can merely use the *threat* of protection to get the foreign firms in invest where labour is, for the policies will equally secure their jobs. On the other hand, the entrepreneurs will prefer actual protection to the policy that merely uses protectionist threats to draw in foreign firms. For, while the United Auto Workers, for example, does not care whether its members are employed by Datsun or Ford, Ford does!

Thus we have the intriguing response possibility of domestic labour trying to import foreign entrepreneurs (with superior know-how), whereas in the 'traditional' industries (of Sec. 6.2) we had the spectacle of domestic entrepreneurs trying to import foreign labour (implying lower wages)!

As it happens, the protectionist threat resulting from the deteriorating competitive position of the US car industry is a splendid example of the scenarios spelled out above. The American car industry, due largely to the steady erosion of the market for gas guzzlers in recent years, has been turning increasingly to producing small cars for survival, and this has shifted the problem of competition from one where the makers of American and foreign cars each had their own special niche in the market, with MPI (and variants thereof in the form of mutually supportive and profitable arrangements for marketing, joint production, etc.) as the relevant model, to one where the competition is fiercer and over a product type (the small car) where the makers of foreign cars have always had the edge. Indeed, the result has been one of labour unions going abroad and threatening the makers of foreign cars to produce in the US or face protection. The following *New York Times* reports are revealing:

Douglas A. Fraser, head of the United Automobile Workers union, warned Japanese car makers today that they must invest in auto assembly plants in the United States or face the threat of immediate legislation to restrict rising imports of their small fuel-efficient cars.

He told Prime Minister Masayoshi Ohira and Foreign Minister Saburo

Okita at separate meetings today that 220,000 auto workers were un-employed in the United States and that there was a 10.3 per cent un-employment rate in Michigan, his home state and the centre of American auto industry. Japanese auto makers should open operations in the United States to reduce unemployment there, even if only by small amounts, Mr Fraser said. 'You ought to have a sense of urgency', Mr Fraser said he had told the Japanese leaders. He is making a short trip to Japan at the suggestion of Mike Mansfield, the United States Ambassador.

American vehicle imports totalled 2.2 million units in 1979, including about 1.7 million cars, and shipments in 1980 may increase as Americans turn to light, front-wheel-drive Japanese cars. By contrast, Japan imported fewer than 20,000 American cars last year.

The tall, heavily built UAW chief said that Nissan Motor, a leading auto maker here that markets Datsun cars, offered yesterday to build a truck assembly plant in the United States, to avoid a pending 25 per cent import tariff.

'That won't be sufficient', Mr Fraser said.

[*New York Times*, 1980a.]

A stiff Congressional warning went out to Japan today to cut back volun-tarily on automobile exports to the United States or face protectionist quota legislation that would damage the trading interests of both coun-tries.

The chairman of a House trade subcommittee, Charles A. Vanik, Democrat of Ohio, called on the Japanese to roll back their American exports to 1977 levels over a two-year period to avoid what he called the 'last resort' of legislated quotas.

In addition, he said, underscoring recent demands by Douglas A. Fraser, president of the United Automobile Workers, the Japanese must be convinced of the necessity to build important quantities of cars in the United States to avoid protectionist reaction here.

Declining international values for the yen, which make it more profit-able to export from Japan, and the current emphasis on producing competing small cars by the American industry are behind the resistance of the two biggest Japanese producers — Toyota and Nissan — to construct assembly plants in the country. But Honda, a smaller company, has announced plans to manufacture relatively modest numbers of cars in an assembly plant in Ohio.

Mr Vanik's call for voluntary restraint, made at committee hearings crowded today with Japanese reporters, came shortly after two bills were introduced by Michigan legislators to impose quota restraints.

But Congressional analysts believe that sentiment is not yet ready to jell, though it well might if automotive unemployment continues to rise. More than 200,000 auto workers have already been laid off.

At 1977 levels, Japanese sales here would be some 25 per cent below the current rate of 2 million cars a year, which represents well over 20 per cent of all cars sold in the United States.

No other country permits such penetration, Fred G. Secrest, executive vice president of the Ford Motor Company, told the panel.

He reported that, by agreement between British and Japanese producer associations, Japanese imports into Britain were held to about 11 per cent of the market. France, he said, applies an informal but very effective share limit of 3 per cent to Japanese cars. By bilateral agreement, Italy limits Japanese imports to 2,000 cars and trucks, while Spain limits imports of automobiles to a value of $ 500,000 from any exporting country.

Thomas J. Downey, Democrat of Suffolk County, said that American consumers were welcoming Japanese products 'with open arms' and that even during the committee proceedings news photographs were being made by Nikon cameras and voice recordings by Panasonic.

He warned that failure to cut back the flow of Japanese cars would mean 'a wave of protectionism that will sweep across the country and, do irreparable harm to the Japanese economy and ultimately to us'.

[*New York Times*, 1980c]

The reaction to this protectionist lobbying by Japanese car makers is likely to be a response which combines some voluntary export restraints (VERs) and some accommodation to the demands for direct investment in the US either à la Honda in Ohio or in some joint ventures in the US with US car makers, like the proposed deal in Italy between Alfa Romeo, the state-owned car maker, and Nissan, which produces the Datsun, to produce a new medium-sized car at Alfa's plant in Alfasud in Pamigliano, Naples, with Alfa engines and Nissan bodies.[20]

[20] However, the foreign investment response, as already indicated, may not meet with the approval of the entrepreneurs in the Honda type of investment or with that of entrepreneurs other than those going into joint venture in the Alfa–Nissan type of investment. Indeed, as the *New York Times* (1980b) reported on the Alfa–Nissan proposal:

Fiat, not surprisingly, reacted strongly against the proposal, charging that the Nissan deal could become the opening wedge for a Japanese invasion of the Italian automobile market. Fiat, auto industry experts say, is particularly vulnerable to fresh competition because it has been losing some of its market share to other European car makers. . . .

6.4 CONCLUDING REMARKS

The primary emphasis of this chapter has been to examine the strong relationship that exists between the response to intensifying import competition in goods and the nature of international labour and entrepreneurial mobility. In doing this, I have sought to provide a framework to systematize alternative patterns of responses to shifts in comparative advantage, without undertaking a rigorous, theoretical formulation of many of the ideas set forth.

Perhaps the major analytical limitation of this endeavour is the lack of consideration of what political scientists would call the issue of how a nation is governed. Whether, for example, the importation of foreign labour is legal, as in Western Europe, or illegal, as in the US, and whether the unions are successful in their bid for protection instead of permitting a market-oriented adjustment to shifting comparative advantage are issues that require an analysis of how the corporate state works, i.e. how representative democracy interacts with industry and labour. Such a 'political' and public-choice-theoretic analysis would nicely complement my analysis here, essentially by explaining cross-country contrasts in the choices of policy response that have actually occurred as comparative advantage has shifted in recent years.

REFERENCES

Alland, Jr., A., 1972: *The Human Imperative* (New York: Columbia University Press).

Fiat is also beset by sabotage and work stoppages by its workers. The company says that the violence and wildcat strikes caused a 12 per cent decline in production last year and pushed its operating costs up sharply.

To head off the Nissan–Alfa venture, Fiat made a proposal of its own to Alfa early this month, offering to buy 40,000 to 50,000 Alfa engines — the same number that would be involved in the Nissan deal — and mount them on new Fiat models over the next several years. There has also been talk about possible construction of a new Fiat body factory near the Alfasud plant.

Trade unions, if organized by firms, may also then have conflicting interests; and differential location of different firms may also pose questions of conflicting interests, e.g. workers in Alfa Romeo versus workers in Fiat.

Balassa, B., 1967: *Trade Liberalization Among Industrial Countries* (New York: McGraw–Hill).

Bhagwati, J., 1959: 'Protection, Real Wages, and Real Incomes', *Economic Journal* 69, pp. 733–44.

——, 1971: 'The Generalized Theory of Distortions and Welfare', in J. Bhagwati et al. (eds), *Trade, Balance of Payments, and Growth* (Amsteram: North–Holland).

——, 1972: Review of Vernon, 'Sovereignty at Bay', *Journal of International Economics* 2, no. 4, pp. 455–62.

——, 1977: Review of Hymer, *Journal of Development Economics* 4, pp. 391–5.

——, 1978: *Anatomy and Consequences of Exchange Control Regimes* (Cambridge, Mass.: Ballinger).

——, 1979: The Economic Analysis of International Migration, plenary lecture to Nordisk Migrasjonsforskerseminar, Nordic Council of Ministers, Oslo, Norway (Oct.).

—— (ed.), 1982: *Import Competition and Policy Response*.

Bhagwati, J. and R. Brecher, 1980: 'National Welfare in an Open Economy in the Presence of Foreign-owned Factors of Production', *Journal of International Economics* 10 (May), pp. 103–16.

Bhagwati, J. and V.K. Ramaswami, 1963: 'Domestic Distortions, Tariffs, and the Theory of Optimum Subsidy', *Journal of Political Economy* 71, no. 1 (Feb.), pp. 44–50.

Bhagwati, J. and F. Rivera–Batiz, 1980: Protection in the Presence of Immigrant Workers and Sending Country's Welfare: Some Paradoxes, mimeo., May.

Bhagwati, J. and E. Tironi, 1980: 'Tariff Change, Foreign Capital, and Immiserization: A Theoretical Analysis', *Journal of Development Economics* (Feb.), pp. 103–15.

Brecher, R., 1974a: 'Minimum Wage Rates and the Pure Theory of International Trade', *Quarterly Journal of Economics* 88, no. 1, pp. 98–116.

——, 1974b: 'Optimal Commercial Policy for a Minimum-wage Economy', *Journal of International Economics* 4, pp. 139–49.

Brecher, R. and C.D. Alejandro, 1977: 'Tariff, Foreign Capital, and Immiserizing Growth', *Journal of International Economics* 7 (Nov.), pp. 317–22.

Brecher, R. and J. Bhagwati, 1981: 'Foreign Ownership and the Theory of Trade and Welfare', *Journal of Political Economy* 89, no. 3 (June), pp. 497–511.

Cheh, J., 1974: 'United States Concessions in the Kennedy Round and Short-run Labour Adjustment Costs', *Journal of International Economics* 4 (Nov.), pp. 323–40.

Dixit, A. and V. Norman, 1980: *The Theory of International Trade: A Text* (Cambridge: Cambridge University Press).

Findlay, R. and H. Grubert, 1959: 'Factor Intensities, Technological Progress, and the Terms of Trade', *Oxford Economic Papers*, nos 111–21. Also in J.N. Bhagwati (ed.), 1970: *International Trade: Selected Readings* (Harmondsworth, UK: Penguin), pp. 327–40.

Grubel, H. and P. Lloyd, 1975: *Intra-industry Trade* (London: Macmillan).

Haberler, G., 1950: 'Some Problems in the Pure Theory of International Trade', *Economic Journal* 60 (June), pp. 223–40.

Harris, J. and M. Todaro, 1970: 'Migration, Unemployment, and Development: A Two-sector Analysis', *American Economic Review* 60 (March), pp. 126–42.

Hymer, S., 1960: The International Operations of National Firms: A Study of Direct Foreign Investment, dissertation, MIT, published with the same title in 1976 by MIT Press, Cambridge, Mass. (See pp. xxii and 253 of the latter.)

Johnson, H.G., 1965: 'Optimal Trade Intervention in the Presence of Domestic Distortions', in R.E. Caves, P.B. Kenen and H.G. Johnson (eds), *Trade, Growth, and the Balance of Payments* (Amsterdam: North–Holland), pp. 3–34.

Jones, R., 1971: 'A Three Factor Model in Theory, Trade, and History', in J. Bhagwati et al. (eds), *Trade, Balance of Payments, and Growth* (Amsterdam: North–Holland), pp. 3–21.

Kojima, K., 1978: *Direct Foreign Investment* (London: Croom Helm).

Krugman, P., 1979: 'Increasing Returns, Monopolistic Competition, and International Trade', *Journal of International Economics* 9 (Nov.), pp. 469–80.

Lancaster, K., 1980: 'Intra-Industry Trade under Perfect Monopolistic Competition', *Journal of International Economics* 10, pp. 151–76.

Linder, S., 1961: *An Essay on Trade and Transformation* (New York: Wiley).

Mayer, W., 1974: 'Short-run and Long-run Equilibrium for a Small Open Economy', *Journal of Political Economy* 82, pp. 955–68.

Mussa, M., 1974: 'Tariffs and the Distribution of Income: The Importance of Factor Specificity, Substitutability, and Intensity in the Short and Long Run', *Journal of Political Economy* 82, pp. 1191–204.

Neary, J.P., 1978: 'Short-run Capital Specificity and the Pure Theory of International Trade', *Economic Journal* 88 (Sept.), pp. 488–510.

New York Times, 1980a: 'Fraser Bids Japan Build Cars in US', 14 Feb., Sect. D.

—, 1980b: 'Italy Debating Auto Future', 29 Feb., Sect. D.

—, 1980c: Rep. Vanik Warns Japan to Curb Auto Exports, Clyde Farnsworth, 14 Feb., Sect. D.

Riedel, J., 1977: 'Tariff Concessions in the Kennedy Round and the Structure of Protection in West Germany: An Econometric Assessment', *Journal of International Economics* 7, no. 2 (May), pp. 133–44.

Uzawa, H., 1969: 'Shihon jiyuka to kokumin keizai', *Ekonomisuto*, 23 Dec., pp. 106–22.

Vernon, R., 1966: 'International Investment and International Trade in the Product Cycle', *Quarterly Journal of Economics* 80 (May), pp. 190–207.

7

Directly Unproductive, Profit-seeking (DUP) Activities[*]

In recent years, economists have increasingly turned to a theoretical analysis of phenomena such as lobbying for protection, competing for a share of industrial or import licences, including legislatures to enact monopolistic barriers to domestic entry, utilizing resources to evade 'price' or 'command' governmental regulations, etc.

In the area of international trade, theoretical analysis in particular, it would hardly be an exaggeration to say that this has been among the few leading topics of research focus recently. Thus, the theoretical analysis of *tariff evasion*, starting with Bhagwati and Hansen (1973), has witnessed further contributions by Johnson (1972), Bhagwati and Srinivasan (1973), Sheikh (1974), Kemp (1976), Falvey (1978), Ray (1978), and Pitt (1981). The theoretical analysis of activity whereby claimants compete for premium-fetching import licences, and what may therefore be christened *premium seeking*, was begun in a seminal paper by Krueger (1974) and extended by Bhagwati and Srinivasan (1980). The theoretical analysis of *revenue seeking*, where economic agents try to get a slice of the tariff revenue resulting from the adoption of a protectionist tariff, has been initiated by Bhagwati and Srinivasan (1980). The theoretical analysis of *tariff seeking*,

* Thanks are due to the National Science Foundation for grant no. 5–24718 and to the Guggenheim Foundation for partial financial support of the research underlying this chapter. Correspondence with Richard Brecher, Max Corden, and Gordon Tullock has been valuable, and reactions and suggestions from participants at seminars at MIT, Yale, and Princeton, especially Carlos Diaz–Alejandro, T.N. Srinivasan, Susan Rose–Ackerman, Gene Grossman, Richard Brecher, Robert Feenstra, Jonathan Eaton, Avinash Dixit, and two anonymous referees of the *Journal of Political Economy* (1982, vol. 90, no. 51) in which it was first published were extremely useful in revising it.

on the other hand, where lobbies seek protectionist trade tariffs, has been pioneered by Brock and Magee (1978), and has been recently developed by Bhagwati (1980), Feenstra and Bhagwati (1982), and Findlay and Wellisz (1982). At the same time, in non-trade-theoretic literature also, there has been growing concern with lobbying and related phenomena, as in the well-known papers of many distinguished writers, such as Tullock (1967, 1980) and Posner (1975).

In this chapter, I begin in Sec. I by briefly discussing the common, unifying essence of the phenomena so analysed and then arguing why they are best described as directly unproductive, profit-seeking (DUP) activities. Next, I proceed in Sec. II to differentiate analytically among different types of such activities, with a view to classifying them into categories that are analytically meaningful from the viewpoint of their welfare impact. Existing analyses of specific problems, such as tariff seeking and revenue seeking, are then readily identified in Sec. III as belonging to one such category or another, and the welfare consequences demonstrated in these analyses are then shown to be only specific illustrations of a wider class of DUP activities with identical welfare consequences.

I. Directly Unproductive, Profit-seeking (DUP) Activities: The Concept

The essential characteristic of the phenomena whose analysis has recently been undertaken, and many of which have been referenced above, is that they represent ways of making a profit (i.e. income) by undertaking activities that are directly unproductive; that is, they yield pecuniary returns but do not produce goods or services that enter a utility function directly or indirectly via increased production or availability to the economy of goods that enter a utility function. In so far as such activities use real resources, they result in a contraction of the availability set open to the economy. Thus, for example, tariff-seeking lobbying, tariff evasion, and premium seeking for given import licences are all privately profitable activities. However, their direct output is simply zero in terms of the flow of goods and services entering a conventional utility function: for example, tariff seeking yields pecuniary income by changing the tariff and hence factor rewards; evasion of a tariff yields pecuniary income by exploiting the differential price between legal (tariff-bearing) imports and illegal (tariff-evading) imports; and premium seeking yields pecuniary income from the premia on import licences. Thus, these are aptly christened DUP activities. As an acronym, this can be pronounced 'dupe' activities, coming close to the spirit in which economists must view these activities![1]

This distinction between directly unproductive and productive activities is somewhat reminiscent of the Physiocrats and the early Marxists but, in contrast, has, in strictly economic terms, a perfect claim to legitimacy. For example, lobbying to install a distortionary tariff is undoubtedly directly unproductive from an economic viewpoint, though it may possess a political legitimacy and value as constituting an element of a vigorous, pluralistic democracy!

Krueger's (1974) analysis of what she christened 'rent-seeking' activities relates to a subset of the broad class of what are defined here as DUP activities. She is concerned with the lobbying activities which are triggered by different licencing practices of governments. Thus, she lists large numbers of licencing practices leading to lobbying to profit from the securing of such licences. Also, her formal theoretical analysis is concerned with a welfare comparison between import licences/quotas with attendant premium-seeking lobbying activity to earn the premia on these licences vis-à-vis equivalent tariffs that were explicitly assumed not to attract any seeking activity. Thus, her focus is exclusively on licencing/quantity restrictions and the rents thereon,[2] and her

---

[1] The other acronymic alternative, christening them ZOP (zero-output, profit-seeking) activities, is slightly less appealing on that account.

[2] Historians of concepts and phrase making may note that, parallel to Krueger's inspired phrase 'rent seeking' to describe licence-seeking activities, there is also the phrase '*rentier* society', used, e.g. in Bhagwati (1973), to describe much the same kind of phenomenon. In addition, there is also the Leninist (Lenin 1939) use of the phrase '*rentnerstaat*', by which was meant a 'rentier state' or 'usurer state' (1939, pp. 100–1), i.e. a rent-*receiving* society. Marxists, who consider Schumpeterian capitalism to be characterized by Joan Robinson's 'animal spirits', also

rent-seeking activities exclude from their scope other DUP activities, for example, *price*-distortion-triggered DUP activities, or distortion-*triggering* DUP activities.[3]

II. DUP ACTIVITIES: A TAXONOMY

With the general concept of DUP activities spelled out, the analysis can now be addressed directly to the issue of the welfare consequences of DUP activities.

From the viewpoint of the analysis of the welfare consequences of DUP activities, evidently the most fruitful theory-informed taxonomy must build on the distinction between distorted (or suboptimal) and non-distorted (or optimal) situations. Thus, a DUP activity that uses up resources in the context of a distortion may be paradoxically welfare improving, whereas a similar DUP activity that destroys a distortion and achieves a first-best, optimal outcome may be paradoxically welfare worsening.

Noting that when distortions exist almost anything can happen, I hasten to add that the theory and the resulting taxonomy which is built into Table 7.1, and which will be presently explained, presuppose that the world is indeed distortion free except for the distortions with which the DUP activity in question is related in an essential way. Thus, in consideration of premium seeking

---

consider the *rentnerstaat* to be the antithesis of the creative impulses underlying robust capitalism.

[3] Krueger (1974, pp. 301–2) did mention minimum wage legislation, regulation of taxi fares, and capital gains tax treatment in her concluding remarks as also being examples of rent seeking. However, her arguments concerning these are ambiguous, to say the least. Thus, consider the following: 'Capital gains tax treatment results in overbuilding of apartments and uneconomic oil exploration' (p. 302). But this seems to be simply stating the traditional resource-(mis)allocational effects of a tax. At the same time, another concluding paragraph does reiterate the view that her concept and theory of rent seeking are intended to be wholly licences or restriction created: 'Finally, all market economies have some rent-generating restrictions' (p. 302). The precise manner in which Krueger generic class of quota intervention – triggered 'rent-seeking' activities is a subset of the far more general class of DUP activities is set out fully in Bhagwati and Srinivasan (1981). Also, see the extended discussion in Bhagwati (1982).

in Krueger's (1974) analysis, the premium sought by the lobbyists is on distortionary quotas already in place in the model. In her model, therefore, there is an unchanging distortion in place when the directly unproductive premium seeking is introduced, but there are no other distortions.

TABLE 7.1

Examples and Consequences of DUP Activities

		Types of Directly Unproductive Activity	
		1. Initially Distorted and Finally Distorted Situations	
		Legal (1)	*Illegal (2)*
1. Examples of such activity	1. Premium seeking: Krueger (1974); Bhagwati and Srinivasan (1980) 2. Revenue seeking: Bhagwati and Srinivasan (1980)		Tariff evasion or smuggling: Johnson (1972); Bhagwati and Hansen (1973); Bhagwati and Srinivasan (1973); Sheikh (1974); Kemp (1976); Ray (1978); Pitt (1981)
2. Consequences of such activity	Second-best analysis applies; therefore, paradox of beneficial outcome possible (except for pure quantity distortions: Bhagwati and Srinivasan (1981) and Anam (1982))		

		2. Initially Distorted but Finally Distortion-free Situations	
		Legal (3)	*Illegal (4)*
1. Examples of such activity	Tariff-destroying lobbying: Findlay and Wellisz (1982)		Tariff-destroying lobbying with aid of bribes to politicians
2. Consequences of such activity	Second-best analysis applies; therefore, paradox of beneficial outcome possible (except for pure quantity distortions: Bhagwati and Srinivasan (1981) and Anam (1982))		

Table 7.1 (cont.)

		Types of Directly Unproductive Activity	

		3. Initially Distortion-free but Finally Distorted Situations	
		Legal (5)	*Illegal (6)*
1.	Examples of such activity	1. Monopoly seeking: Posner (1975)	Tariff evasion from an optimal tariff situation
		2. Tariff seeking: Brock and Magee (1978); Bhagwati (1980); Feenstra and Bhagwati (1982); Findlay and Wellisz (1982)	
2.	Consequences of such activity	Total outcome necessarily immiserizing. However, subsidiary paradox obtains: distortion imposed without DUP activity may produce lower welfare than when imposed with it.	

		4. Initially Distortion-free and Finally Distortion-free Situations	
		Legal (7)	*Illegal (8)*
1.	Examples of such activity	Zero-tariff-outcome lobbying: Tullock (1967); Findlay and Wellisz (1982)	Theft: Tullock (1967)
2.	Consequences of such activity	Total outcome necessarily immiserizing. No paradoxes obtain.	

Next, I should clarify that the DUP activities considered in the analysis that follows are wholly related to governmental policies: For example, they involve changing these policies or evading them. However, they can in principle be government free or exclusively private. Thus, effort and resources may be (legally) expended in getting a share of the 'going' transfer by an economic agent, what may be described as 'altruism seeking'. Or they may be expended on (illegal) theft, as Tullock (1967) has considered. What I argue here can therefore be simply extended to private activities, even though virtually all examples chosen below concern governmental policy-related DUP activities exclusively.

Furthermore, I make no distinction between activities that utilize real resources directly and those that do not. For, while pure transfers/bribes are often supposed to be resource free, they are not. The direct demand on real resources that a successfully transacted bribe makes may be small, but it is not likely to be negligible.[4]

Finally, I distinguish between legal and illegal activities for two reasons. First, the latter introduce the added element that they constitute an independent element of the social loss in so far as illegality must be considered to be socially disapproved. Besides, it is interesting to note that, except on this dimension, the legal and illegal DUP activities can be shown to belong to analytically equivalent categories of our taxonomy, so that distinguishing between them is only with a view to underlining their analytical similarity in the present context.

With these clarifying remarks, let me then turn to the taxonomy underlying Table 7.1. The taxonomy there, with an eye on welfare analysis, is critically built on the fact that all such DUP activities will involve either a distorted or a distortion-free situation, before and after such activity is undertaken. Thus, four critical classes of DUP activities are distinguished as follows:

Category 1.   Here, the initial and final situations are both distorted.
Category 2.   Here, the initial situation is distorted, but the final situation (thanks to the DUP activity) is distortion free.

---

[4] Krueger (1974, p. 302) makes the interesting point that bribes can get reflected in the expected returns from qualifying to be a civil servant and thus divert resources via that route. However, the question is one of incidence here. If the government keeps civil service salaries low, expecting that the bribes will make up the required difference to attract a given volume of civil servants, the resource-impact analysis of bribes/transfers gets more complex. It would then be necessary to compare the bribe-induced resource diversion with the resource diversion required to collect taxes to pay adequate salaries when lump-sum taxes are unavailable: a unique rank ordering again would not be generally possible.

Category 3. Here, the initial situation is distortion free, but the final situation is distorted.

Category 4. Here, the initial situation is again distortion free as is the final situation (despite the DUP activity).

The fundamental distinction, however, remains that between categories 1 and 2 that relate to initially distorted situations), on the one hand, and categories 3 and 4 (that relate to initially distortion-free situations).

I proceed then to demonstrate that, for DUP activities falling into categories 1 and 2, a beneficial rather than immiserizing outcome is paradoxically feasible, whereas for those falling into categories 3 and 4 it is not.[5] The critical difference is that the former set have initial situations that are distorted, whereas the latter set start with distortion-free initial situations. The existing analyses of DUP activities, detailed above, are then assigned to these four categories, distinguishing further among legal and illegal activities.

III. Welfare Consequences of DUP Activities

The critical analytical point at issue is very simple. The diversion of resources from directly productive to directly unproductive activities, when undertaken in the context of initially distorted situations, is fundamentally different from such diversion occurring in the context of initially distortion-free situations. For, in the latter case, the loss of resources is occurring from a first-best situation and hence must also represent a social loss, whereas in the former case it is occurring in a second-best situation and hence need not represent a social loss but may well be beneficial. Analytically, the

[5] While the focus here is on whether the beneficial DUP activity paradox can arise, it is important to note that, with the second-best nature ignored, the problem in categories 1 and 2 (i.e. where there are initially distorted situations) will lead to other errors, as noted for the case of revenue seeking and premium seeking by Bhagwati and Srinivasan (1980). The taxonomic distinctions drawn here, therefore, are critical even if the analyst is inclined to assert (fallaciously, in my judgment) that the beneficial DUP activity paradox is unimportant in practice. On the question whether such second-best paradoxes are likely to arise in practice, see the discussion in Bhagwati (1980) in the specific context of tariff seeking.

paradox constituted by the welfare improvement following from the undertaking of the directly unproductive activity in a second-best situation is the same as the paradox of immiserizing growth noted by Bhagwati (1958) and Johnson (1967), and generalized in Bhagwati (1968). For, in the former case, withdrawal of resources for unproductive activity and hence 'negative growth' is beneficial, and in the latter case (positive) growth is immiserizing. And, of course, the 'dual' of this is the phenomenon of negative shadow prices of factors noted and analysed in Bhagwati, Srinivasan, and Wan (1978), and in Srinivasan and Bhagwati (1978).

Category 1

In this class of cases, the DUP activities are addressed to initially distortion-ridden situations in an essential fashion. Two legal activities so discussed in the literature are the Krueger (1974) phenomenon of premium seeking and the Bhagwati and Srinivasan (1980) phenomenon of revenue seeking.

Krueger's analysis of premium seeking postulates that, as a result presumably of protectionist demands, import quotas have materialized and characterize the initial situation. The premium-fetching import licences then generate resource-using competition among potential beneficiaries of the licence allocation, and the analysis presupposes that the initial quota level remains unchanged. Therefore, the Krueger analysis of premium seeking is essentially of a legal process of DUP activity undertaken in the context of a distorted situation where the distortion triggering off the DUP activity remains unchanged through the analysis.

The same features characterize the Bhagwati and Srinivasan (1980) analysis of revenue seeking: legal directly unproductive competition for securing a share in the disbursement/transfer of tariff revenue resulting incidentally in the imposition of a tariff thanks to protectionist lobbying, the tariff thus being an exogenously specified, unchanging distortion that triggers off the revenue seeking which is being analysed.

It is easy to demonstrate, as in fact Bhagwati and Srinivasan (1980) have done already, that the lobbying activity being modelled can be paradoxically beneficial despite being directly unproductive, the reason for this paradox being that already outlined above.

This possibility can arise also in the premium-seeking case (unless the quota is defined purely in quantity terms, in which case the second-best possibility of welfare improvement through DUP activity-induced changes in outputs will be prevented by the pure trade constraint from spilling over into the paradoxical outcome).[6]

Next, the existing analyses of illegal trade in the presence of tariffs (and quotas) also fit immediately into the present category 1 of DUP activities. This is because they assume that there is an initially distorting tariff, and the tariff-evading activity is undertaken with this tariff remaining in place through the analysis. In view of the theoretical analysis developed above, it follows immediately that these analyses ought to yield the conclusion that such tariff evasion may be welfare improving (even allowing for the fact that the illegality carries an extra, negative dimension), as they in fact do. Bhagwati and Hansen (1973), for example, show this in a model where the extra real costs of illegality in trade are incurred in the form of the traded goods themselves, this being the 'melting ice' assumption used by Samuelson (1954) to model transportation costs within the confines of the two-by-two model. Smuggling will be beneficial rather than immiserizing in this model, even though it uses up real resources (in the form of produced, tradable goods), since it confers production and consumption gains when the effective tariff is cut by the smuggling. The negative weight attached to the illegality may be considered to be outweighed by the gain noted above, which leaves the net evaluation still a beneficial one. The paradox has repeated itself in the context of illegal trade.

The foregoing examples of Category 1 type DUP activities — premium seeking, revenue seeking, and tariff or *QR* evasion — assume that the specified distortion that triggers off such activity remains exogenous to the activity. It is however easy to imagine phenomena where the distortion may be endogenous to such activity. Thus, revenue seeking may adversely affect the protection implied by the tariff that triggered off the revenue seeking. Bhagwati and Srinivasan (1980) indeed demonstrate in the context of their

[6] General propositions concerning the contrast between DUP activities triggered by price and quantity distortions have been developed in Bhagwati and Srinivasan (1981) and in Anam (1982).

general equilibrium analysis of revenue seeking that the revenue seeking may lead to a Metzler production paradox: The protectionist tariff plus revenue seeking may lead to a lower output of the importable than under free trade! If so, the protectionist lobby may well seek greater protection, thus influencing in principle the original tariff distortion itself, thereby making the eventual tariff level endogenous to revenue seeking. But even this complexity would leave the phenomenon of revenue seeking within the class of DUP activities squarely within Category 1, with its attendant paradox of possible welfare improvement from such activities.

Category 2

In this class of DUP activities, the initial situation that triggers such activities is still distorted, but the outcome turns out to be distortion free.

This category is easily analysed in the light of the foregoing analysis of Category 1. Thus, the overall welfare impact of a DUP activity starting from an initially distorted situation but ending in a distortion-free situation is the sum of two effects:

$$
\left\{
\begin{array}{l}
\text{The welfare impact of a withdrawal} \\
\text{of resources into the directly} \\
\text{unproductive activity, holding the} \\
\text{distortion unchanged (i.e. Category 1} \\
\text{type of analysis)} \\
\qquad +ve \text{ or } -ve
\end{array}
\right\}
+
\left\{
\begin{array}{l}
\text{The welfare impact of} \\
\text{the elimination of the} \\
\text{distortion in the final} \\
\text{situation} \\
\\
\qquad +ve
\end{array}
\right\}
$$

The former effect, as I have argued already, is either positive or negative; the latter, of course, is necessarily positive. The net outcome may therefore be positive or negative. The welfare-improving paradox obtains again, as does the opposite quasi-paradox that a distortion-destroying lobbying activity may lead to immiserization and hence to be only a Pyrrhic victory.[7]

An instance of this, as implied by Findlay and Wellisz (1982) in the context of the analysis of tariff seeking, would be when the resources used up in restoring free trade that is to the lobby's

---

[7] Remember again the caveat concerning pure quantity distortions discussed in Bhagwati and Srinivasan (1981) and Anam (1982).

economic advantage are socially more valuable than the social gains from free trade. An instance of illegal DUP activity of a similar nature would be when the lobbying in the foregoing example was replaced by bribes to congressmen to change their vote to free trade.

Category 3

The paradox of beneficial DUP activities disappears, however, as soon as these activities are undertaken in the context of initially distortion-free situations. Category 3 relates to these when the final situation is the successful creation of a distorted situation.

Two classic examples of such Category 3, legal DUP activities are successful lobbying efforts at creating government-sanctioned monopoly and lobbying for tariff protection: monopoly seeking and tariff seeking. In each such case, the total social loss imposed by the DUP activity in question can be decomposed as the sum of two effects:

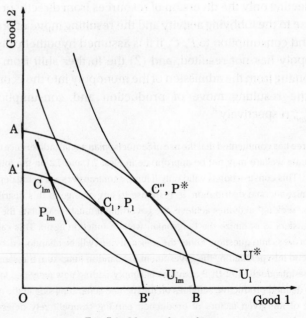

FIG. 7.1 Monopoly seeking

$$
\left.\begin{array}{l}
\text{The welfare effect of the} \\
\text{withdrawal of resources into} \\
\text{the directly unproductive} \\
\text{activity, assuming that no} \\
\text{distortion has resulted} \\
\qquad\qquad -ve
\end{array}\right\}
+
\left\{\begin{array}{l}
\text{The welfare effect of the} \\
\text{imposition of the distortion,} \\
\text{assuming that the resources} \\
\text{have already been diverted} \\
\text{to the directly unproductive} \\
\text{activity} \\
\qquad\qquad -ve
\end{array}\right.
$$

Evidently, there is no source of gain here and hence no room for the paradox of welfare improvement as with Categories 1 and 2 above.

Thus, consider monopoly seeking in Fig. 1. In this small, closed economy which produces at P^* initially, with welfare at U^*, the lobby to secure a monopoly in good I production succeeds. The resources expended-in securing the monopoly shift the production possibility curve down to $A'B'$, whereas the monopoly itself leads to non-tangency of the goods–price ratio with $A'B'$ in equilibrium. Equilibrium production and consumption therefore shift to P_{lm}, C_{lm} and welfare declines to U_{lm} from U^*. The total decline in welfare then can be decomposed into (1) the shift from U^* to U_l reflecting only the diversion of resources from directly productive use to the lobbying activity and the resulting move of production and consumption to P_l, C_l, if it is assumed hypothetically that monopoly has not resulted; and (2) the further shift from U_l to U_{lm} coming from the admission of the monopoly into the economy and the resulting move of production and consumption to P_{lm}, C_{lm}, respectively.[8]

---

[8] A referee has commented that the use of Samuelsonian social indifference curves to evaluate welfare may not be appropriate in Figs. 7.1 and 7.2 on the following ground: 'This construction is valid only if lump-sum transfers are being deployed to optimize income distribution. In response to any change in this distribution that the "seeking" activities achieve, the government must recalculate the lump-sum transfers to optimize the Bergsonian welfare function again. This calls the whole process into question. Either the seek activities will be abandoned, or they will extend into persuading the government to abandon lump-sum transfer. However, the introduction of DUP activities is simply adding new activities to traditionally defined productive activities on the income-generating side in the model, with all of the given factors of production earning competitively determined incomes. In principle, therefore, it is not necessarily implausible to continue the

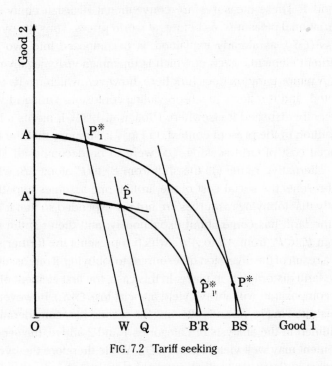

FIG. 7.2 Tariff seeking

Fig. 7.2 illustrates the tariff-seeking case. The protectionist lobby, starting from free trade at P^*, manages in this small economy to spend resources to get a tariff enacted. If we take only the diversion of resources to lobbying into account, at free-trade prices production would shift from P^* to $\hat{P}^*_l$ on the shrunk-in production possibility curve $A'B'$, which represents therefore a loss of RS measured in terms of good 1. Moreover, the tariff resulting from the successful lobbying shifts the production point further to $\hat{P}_l$, which is the final observed equilibrium under tariff seeking; this is tantamount to a further loss of QR in terms of

use of Samuelsonian indifference curves as in the traditional analyses without DUP activities. If this were not so, I would have to agree with the referee that the analysis would then have to 'do without social indifference curves, relying on the usual vague aggregate CV or EV measures' *or* shift to invoking Chipman–Moore type assumptions of identical, homothetic indifference curves for individuals combined with statements that are valid then for potential rather than actual welfare.

good 1. These measures are conventional Hicksian equivalent-variational measures, as before, at world prices. Thus the overall loss (QS), as already explained, is decomposed into two constituent elements, each of which is unambiguously negative.

A minor paradox does lurk here, however, which needs to be noted, and it reflects much prevailing confusion. Though I have recently dispelled it elsewhere (Bhagwati 1980), it merits a brief mention in the present context. In Fig. 7.2, suppose that the total social cost of tariff seeking, QS, were to be decomposed along an alternative route: (1) the shift from P^* to P_l^* along AB, which represents the social cost of the tariff, if one assumes hypothetically that lobbying resources are not yet expended so that it is as if the tariff has come about exogenously; and then (2) the shift from P_l^* to $\hat{P}_l$, from AB to $A'B'$, which represents the further shift as a result of the diversion of resources to lobbying, if one assumes the tariff distortion is in place. In this case, the first element of the decomposition will always yield a social loss (WS); however, as illustrated in Fig. 7.2 and reflecting the second-best considerations outlined in the analysis of Categories 1 and 2 above, the second element may well yield a gain (WQ). While therefore the overall impact of Category 3 activities must be necessarily negative (QS), it would be incorrect to assert or imply that the social cost of a distortion imposed without the aid of directly unproductive activity must be necessarily less than that of the same distortion imposed thanks to such activity; that is, in Fig. 7.2, the shift from P_l^* to $\hat{P}_l$ need not always be a social cost and is, indeed, shown to be a social gain worth WQ.

Finally, these conclusions can be readily extended to examples of illegal activities in Category 3. An instance of this kind would be provided by tariff evasion or smuggling from an optimal, rather than a distortionary, tariff.

Category 4

The final category of DUP activities is provided by those that, starting with an initially distortion-free situation, wind up also with a distortion-free situation despite the resources expended in such activities. A simple but effective example of such an activity is provided by Findlay and Wellisz (1982), and suggested also by

Tullock (1967), where tariff seeking by one lobby is offset by tariff-averting lobbying by another group, and the result is that resources are used up in mutually deterring lobbying that does not affect free trade policy for the small country in the end. Fig. 7.2 would illustrate this case, with a slight reinterpretation. Now, there is evidently a shrinking-in of the production possibility set for goods 1 and 2 from AB to $A'B'$ as resources are diverted to the lobbying activities and therewith a social loss of RS in terms of good 1 since $\hat{P}_l^*$ is now the actual post-lobbying equilibrium, characterized by continuing free trade. The diversion of resources from productive use when the first-best policy (of free trade in this small competitive economy) is in place throughout must obviously be immiserizing.[9] There is no room for paradoxes of any kind here.

Category 4 then is the clearest case of DUP activities, where the simple claims of the early analysts of such activities about their negative impact can be sustained without the slightest qualification. But this is also clearly a very narrow subset of the entire range of activities that have been considered here.

IV. CONCLUDING REMARK

This chapter has then provided a complete theory and taxonomy of the welfare consequences of DUP activities. The existing literature is in consequence synthesized within a general welfare-theoretic framework. The results are summarized in Table 7.1.

REFERENCES

Anam, Mahmudul, 1982: 'Distortion-triggered Lobbying and Welfare: A Contribution to the Theory of Directly-unproductive Profit-seeking Activities', *J. Internal. Econ.*, vol. 12 (Aug.).

[9] An inference of illegal profit-seeking DUP activity in Category 4 would be that of theft which utilizes real resources in attempts at both undertaking and evading it but without creating any distortion (cf. Tullock 1967).

Bhagwati, Jagdish N., 1958: 'immiserizing Growth: A Geometrical Note', *Rev. Econ. Studies* 25 (June), pp. 201–5.

—, 1968: 'Distortions and Immiserizing Growth: A Generalization', *Rev. Econ. Studies* 35 (Oct.), pp. 481–5.

—, 1973: *India in the International Economy: A Policy Framework for a Progressive Society*, Lal Bahadur Shastri Memorial Lectures (Hyderabad, India: Osmania Univ. Press).

Bhagwati, Jagdish N., 1980: 'Lobbying and Welfare', *J. Public Econ.* 14 (Dec.), pp. 355–63.

—, 1982: 'Lobbying and Welfare: A Response to Tullock', *J. Public Econ.*

Bhagwati, Jagdish N. and Bent Hansen, 1973: 'A Theoretical Analysis of Smuggling', *Q.J.E.* 87 (May), pp. 172–87.

Bhagwati, Jagdish N. and T.N. Srinivasan, 1973: 'Smuggling and Trade Policy', *J. Public Econ.* 2 (Nov.), pp. 377–89.

—, 1980: 'Revenue Seeking: A Generalization of the Theory of Tariffs', *J.P.E.* 88, no. 6 (Dec.), pp. 1069–87.

—, 1981: 'The Welfare Consequences of Directly-unproductive Profit-seeking (DUP) Activities: Price *versus* Quantity Distortions', mimeo (New Haven, Conn.: Yale Econ. Growth Center, March).

Bhagwati, Jagdish N., T.N. Srinivasan and Henry Wan, Jr., 1978: 'Value Subtracted, Negative Shadow Prices of Factors in Project Evaluation, and Immiserizing Growth: Three Paradoxes in the Presence of Trade Distortions', *Econ. J.* 88 (March), pp. 121–5.

Brock, William A. and Stephen P. Magee, 1978: 'The Economics of Special Interest Politics: The Case of the Tariff', *A.E.R. Papers and Proc.* 68 (May), pp. 246–50.

Falvey, Rodney E., 1978: 'A Note on Preferential and Illegal Trade under Quantitative Restrictions', *Q.J.E.* 92 (Feb.), pp. 175–8.

Feenstra, Robert and Jagdish N. Bhagwati, 1982: 'Tariff-Seeking and the Efficient Tariff', in *Import Competition and Response*, Jagdish N. Bhagwati (ed.) (Chicago: Univ. Chicago Press (for Nat. Bur. Econ. Res.)).

Findlay, Ronald and Stanislaw Wellisz, 1982: 'Endogenous Tariffs: The Political Economy of Trade Restrictions and Welfare', in *Import Competition and Response*, Jagdish N. Bhagwati (ed.) (Chicago: Univ. Chicago Press (for Nat. Bur. Econ. Res.)).

Johnson, Harry G., 1967: 'The Possibility of Income Losses from Increased Efficiency or Factor Accumulation in the Presence of Tariffs', *Econ. J.* 77 (March), pp. 151–4.

—, 1972: 'Notes on the Economic Theory of Smuggling', *Malayan Econ. Rev.* 17 (April), pp. 1–7. Rpt. in *Illegal Transactions in International*

Trade: Theory and Measurement, Jagdish N. Bhagwati (ed.) (Amsterdam: North–Holland, 1974).

Kemp, Murray C., 1976: 'Smuggling and Optimal Commercial Policy', *J. Public Econ.* 5 (April/May), pp. 381–4.

Krueger, Anne Osborne, 1974: 'The Political Economy of the Rent-seeking Society', *A.E.R.* 64 (June), pp. 291–303.

Lenin, Vladimir I., 1939: *Imperialism: The Highest Stage of Capitalism* (New York: International Publishers).

Pitt, Mark, 1981: 'Smuggling and Price Disparity', *J. Internal. Econ.* 11 (Nov.), pp. 447–58.

Posner, Richard A., 1975: 'The Social Costs of Monopoly and Regulation', *J.P.E.* 83, no. 4 (Aug.), pp. 807–28.

Ray, Alok, 1978: 'Smuggling, Import Objectives, and Optimum Tax Structure', *Q.J.E.* 92 (Aug.), pp. 509–14.

Samuelson, Paul A., 1954: 'The Transfer Problem and Transport Costs, II: Analysis of Effects of Trade Impediments', *Econ. J.* 64 (June), pp. 264–89.

Sheikh, Munir A., 1974: 'Smuggling, Production and Welfare', *J. Internal. Econ.* 4 (Nov.), pp. 355–64.

Srinivasan, T.N. and Jagdish N. Bhagwati, 1978: 'Shadow Prices for Project Selection in the Presence of Distortions: Effective Rates of Protection and Domestic Resource Costs', *J.P.E.* 86, no. 1 (Feb.), pp. 97–116.

Tullock, Gordon, 1967: 'The Welfare Costs of Tariffs, Monopolies, and Theft', *Western Econ. J.* 5 (June), pp. 224–32.

——, 1980: 'Efficient Rent-Seeking', in *Toward a Theory of the Rent-seeking Society*, James M. Buchanan, Robert D. Tollison and Gordon Tullock (eds) (College Station: Texas A&M Univ. Press).

8

Quantitative Restrictions and Quotas in International Trade

QUANTITATIVE restrictions represent one of several policy instruments for dealing with problems of international trade and payments. Other instruments include tariffs on exports and imports, variations in the exchange rate, and monetary and fiscal policies.

In principle, restrictions can be placed on both current and capital transactions between countries. The transfer of capital, for example, can be controlled; this is a typical example of restrictions on capital account. This chapter will, however, focus on quantitative restrictions on *commodity trade* entering a country's current international accounts.

Construed in this way, quantitative restrictions represent the method of controlling foreign trade through quantitative specification of permissible imports (or exports). Hence these restrictions differ from tariff duties, which aim at controlling imports (or exports) by operating directly on the *price* at which commodities are imported (or exported).

Quantitative trade restrictions are imposed, in practice, on both exports and imports. However, those on exports are relatively rare. Examples are the quotas on exports (e.g. of cotton textiles) that Japan applied in the late '60s to avoid the opprobrium of dumping and the quotas on certain agricultural exports (e.g. of oilseeds) that India used to preserve internal supplies.

Import restrictions are imposed in a large number of ways. Where government purchases are involved, imports may be restricted without the need for any explicit licencing procedure. With private sector imports, however, an import licencing system becomes inevitable.

Import licences can take several forms. They may be stated in terms of value or in terms of physical quantity. There may, in addition, be an explicit overall *quota* defining the maximum amount of the commodity permitted to enter the country during a specified period. Alternatively, licences may be issued that specify particular quantities to be imported, without any overall quota for the commodity. Frequently, all commodities are nominally put under import control, but some are permitted in automatically and without limit under a so-called open general licence — as in the United Kingdom and India in the late '60s. In such cases licencing is not at all restrictive.

Import restrictions can be uniformly levied on all imports, or they can be discriminatory. The discrimination can be between different supplying *countries*. Alternatively, it may be between different *commodities*. These distinctions sometimes overlap, as when the discrimination is between two commodities, each of which is exported by a different country. Indeed the practice of assigning quotas (as also tariffs) by detailed commodity categories has been criticized as an underhand method of evading most-favoured-nation and non-discrimination obligations. Import restrictions also discriminate frequently by *currency areas*, rather than by individual countries per se.

Import licences are allocated to domestic importers in various ways, depending on convenience of administration and the economic objectives sought. Two steps are involved in the allocative process. The first is the classification of imports into different categories. Second, procedures have to be devised for allocating the permissible imports within each category to the various claimants.

The classifications vary from country to country. Thus one typical classification, used in India, divides import licences into 'established importers', (EI), 'actual users' (AU), and 'capital goods' (CG). Imports of consumer goods and spare parts require EI licences, allocated to traders. Raw materials are imported through AU licences, allocated to producers using them in their factories. Capital goods are imported through CG licences, allocated to investors with approved projects.

The procedures for the actual allocation to the claimants *within* each category again vary widely. EI licences may be allocated on the basis of previous shares of the traders; AU licences, on the basis of respective production capacities. Allocations on the basis of 'first come, first served' have been practiced, as in the United Kingdom (Hemming et al. 1959). Import licences for raw materials and other goods are sometimes linked to resulting exports, as in India and Pakistan in the late '60s. Allocation by auction has been suggested — on the grounds of economic efficiency and revenue collection (Bhagwati 1962).

History and present use   The use of quantitative trade restrictions in international trade dates back to early times. However, since the original motivation in regulating trade appears to have been the collection of *revenue*, tariff levies on imports and exports preceded the rise of quantitative restrictions. Tariffs came to be supplemented significantly by quantitative trade restrictions when the objective of regulating trade became that of *protecting* domestic industries and improving the balance of payments.

While the use of restrictions diminished between 1750 and 1850, it was revived after World War I and intensified thereafter. Since World War II, however, the General Agreement on Tariffs and Trade (GATT) has attempted to turn the tide. In this, GATT has benefited from the similar objectives of the International Monetary Fund (IMF) with respect to exchange restrictions. (See Tew 1960) for contrasts and parallels between IMF and GATT rules concerning restrictions.) However, GATT's progress toward reduced restrictions has been halting thus far.

There are several reasons for this, most of them recognized by the GATT regulations themselves. Thus, while GATT forbids the use of quantitative restrictions — in article XI — it also explicitly makes provisions, in articles XII and XVIII:B, for their use under certain circumstances. Balance-of-payments difficulties must be cited to invoke either article, and article XVIII:B is applicable only to very low income countries. In addition, under article XVIII:C, the underdeveloped countries have the possibility of using quantitative restrictions to assist developing industries. (Also important in the early post-war years was article XIV, which permitted the use of restrictions against 'scarce-currency' countries and by members going through a 'transitional period'. Today its importance is negligible.)

Needless to say, these articles, especially XII and XVIII:B, have been used continually. Besides, advanced countries have continued to use restrictions to protect domestic agriculture, contrary to GATT obligations. Moreover, non-member countries frequently resort to restrictions.

As of the early 1960s, then, the use of restrictions is still considerable. On the one hand, the advanced countries have agreed to renounce use of restrictions as a regular practice, resorting to them only occasionally to ease severe balance-of-payments strains and more frequently (but with increasing difficulty) to protect domestic agricultural production. On the other hand, the majority of underdeveloped countries, with tight external accounts accompanying their planned developments, have maintained comprehensive import control regimes, and there seems to be no sign of a change in this situation in the foreseeable future.

ECONOMIC EFFECTS

The economic effects of quantitative restrictions have been analysed in two distinct ways. One approach works out the effects of restrictions assuming that the balance of payments is always somehow kept balanced. This is the so-called *real* analysis. It deals with the question of the equivalence of, and differences between, tariffs and quotas, and is basically an extension of tariff analysis, in the 'pure' theory of international trade, to quota restrictions.

The other approach is more important from the practical point of view: it attempts to analyse quantitative restrictions as a policy instrument for handling balance-of-payments difficulties. The typical questions here concern the effectiveness of restrictions in correcting external deficits, both absolutely and in relation to devaluation and deflation. The desirability of *discriminatory* restrictions, which are frowned upon by IMF and GATT, has also been debated.

Real analysis The real analysis is nearly always presented for import tariffs and quotas but applies equally, *mutatis mutandis*, to export tariffs and quotas. The analysis demonstrates that *ad valorem* tariffs and quotas have important similarities and differences.

Traditionally, the question is investigated in the framework of a partial equilibrium model of a perfectly competitive industry. An *ad valorem* tariff will, generally speaking, restrict imports and raise revenue. If the tariff is prohibitively high, it will raise no revenue; if it does not restrict imports at all, it will merely raise revenue. Moreover, it is easily shown that, corresponding to every tariff rate, there is a *quota* that will produce *equivalent* results for the following variables: (1) domestic production of the imported commodity; (2) domestic price; (3) foreign price; (4) domestic consumption; and (5) the quantity of imports. Consistent with this basic equivalence, in the sense defined, there is a well-known difference: a tariff raises revenue, whereas an equivalent quota does not. The revenue accrues as 'monopoly' profit to the quota holders. This difference is clearly of importance.

But the foregoing proposition of equivalence holds only under perfectly competitive conditions in the import industry and breaks down if monopoly elements are introduced. For example, with a monopoly in domestic production, an import quota could well lead to a continuation of the internal monopoly. On the other hand, a tariff would permit imports freely at the tariff-inclusive price and, if the foreign supply is perfectly elastic, the domestic monopolist would eventually find himself in a perfectly competitive situation. Tariffs and quotas could thus lead to radically different market structures, and therefore equivalence of the type obtaining under perfectly competitive assumptions, would not necessarily hold.

These propositions can be inferred from the current literature (e.g. Kindleberger 1953). A more systematic analysis of the equivalence proposition has recently been made, under alternative assumptions with respect to the market structure and allowing monopoly elements to obtain both in domestic production and in quota-holding, which underlines the crucial dependence of the equivalence proposition on the assumption of universally perfect competition (Bhagwati 1965).

Balance-of-payments analysis   The efficacy of quantitative import restrictions in reducing international deficits can be considered either in itself or in contrast to the effectiveness of other instruments of policy.

Quantitative restrictions per se The primary effect of restrictions on imports is to cut imports. But there are secondary effects. The domestic expenditure, diverted from imports, will flow elsewhere. All of it may then cut into exports, leaving the original payments deficit unchanged. Secondary effects must therefore be carefully investigated.

Whether the *net* outcome of the primary and secondary effects can be expected to be favourable, in a specific case, is determined with reference to a proposition that forms the core of the newly developed absorption theory (Alexander 1952; Meade 1951). The proposition asserts that a balance-of-payments deficit reflects an excess of domestic investment over savings and hence any reduction in this deficit requires a reduction in domestic investment and/or an increase in domestic savings.

Thus, unless import restrictions lead to reduced investment or increased domestic savings, they cannot improve the balance of payments, and the secondary effect must necessarily offset the primary improvement. There are various ways in which import quotas may affect domestic savings and investment.

Savings can be affected, for example, in the following ways. (1) The restricted import of a commodity may result in 'forced saving': expenditure may be held off in the expectation of reduction in restrictions in the near future; or there may be no adequate immediate substitute in consumption; or there may be a temporary time lag in shifting to alternative consumption. These arguments are plausible for 'temporary' increases in saving; in the long run, consumption may be expected to readjust itself to the preceding level. (2) Alternatively, import restrictions may cause a shift of income toward profits (accruing to quota-holders). If there is a higher propensity to save by profit-earners than by others, there will be a rise in savings. (3) Counter to this runs the argument that the 'distortion' caused by interference with the pattern of consumption can bring about a fall in real savings (via the fall in real income). (4) Even if none of the preceding possibilities holds and there is diversion of the *entire* expenditure from (prevented) imports to exportables and non-traded goods, additional savings can nonetheless be generated. This may happen, for example, if the indirect tax rates on the exportables, etc., are higher on the average than on the imports, thereby generating a higher tax revenue than previously. (5) Alternatively, if the expenditure is shifted to non-traded goods, raising their prices under full employment, but the mobility of factors between exportable and non-traded goods is low, the (secondary) restrictive effect on the supply of exports would be less than the (primary) restrictive effect on imports. The reduced deficit would be attributable then to the 'forced savings' in the non-traded goods sector. (6) Assume, however, that there is Keynesian underemployment. In this case, a shift in expenditure toward exportables and non-traded goods will have a multiplier effect on incomes, and if the marginal propensity to save is positive, domestic savings will increase, improving the balance of payments by the same amount (ruling out further repercussions through multiplier effects abroad).

Similarly, import restrictions could affect investment. (1) If the deficit is caused by inventory accumulation, quotas on raw material imports can well lead to inventory decline, that is, to reduced investment. (2) Similarly, if capital-goods imports are necessary to domestic investment, restrictions on them could affect domestic fixed investment.

Where, however, no such increase in domestic savings and/or reduction in domestic investment is possible, import restrictions will have to be accompanied by deflation in order to engineer an improvement in the balance of payments under conditions of full employment. Deflation alone will cause unemployment while correcting a deficit. A combination of import restrictions and deflation, on the other hand, will generally bring about both internal and external equilibrium — both full employment and balance in the international accounts. This is only a special case of Tinbergen's principle that n instruments are, in general, necessary to achieve n targets.

Restrictions have been analysed, however, not merely from the viewpoint of their efficacy in reducing external deficits. Two interesting *welfare* questions have also been posed.

One relates to the *optimum* combination of deflation and import restrictions when the objectives are to achieve an assigned improvement in the balance of payments and to maximize the real income of the country, subject to the preceding constraint (Hemming and Corden 1958). Note that here maximization of real income replaces the achievement of full employment as an objective. Since deflation can produce less income (through reduced employment) and restrictions (through 'distortions' in allocation of expenditure among commodities) can offset the income gain from improved terms of trade where relevant, the equilibrium condition naturally involves the equation of these two losses at the margin.

The other welfare question has been posed with respect to the use of *discriminatory* restrictions and relates *not* to national welfare but to *world welfare*. Although both IMF (by discouraging *exchange* restrictions in current accounts) and GATT (through article XIV have set themselves against the use of discriminatory restrictions, theoretical opinion has continued to question this attitude from the viewpoint of world welfare. The classic articles of Frisch (1947; 1948) and Fleming (1951) have argued for discrimination and other writers (e.g. Tew 1960) have supported this case. Fleming's is the most persuasive argument, although based on assumptions of cardinal utility and interpersonal comparisons of welfare, since he formulates his analysis so as to maximize world *real income*, whereas Frisch rests his analysis largely on the debatable objective of maximizing world *trade*.

Restrictions versus devaluation Although restrictions can be contrasted, in principle, with numerous alternative policy instruments, customarily the contrast is made between them and devaluation as methods of improving the balance of payments (Alexander 1951; Hemming and Corden 1958; Johnson 1958, Ch. 6).

When the deficit is generated by 'temporary' factors — such as a decision to shift from cash to inventory accumulation, an essentially 'stock' decision (Johnson 1958) — restrictions and similar measures are naturally preferable to devaluation. Thus, in the example of inventory accumulation, restrictions can be chosen in such a way as to act directly on inventories, whereas a devaluation would start reorienting the economy's production and consumption decisions toward an external surplus. This orientation would then have to be *reversed* when the temporary change was itself reversed. Restrictions thus can avoid the costs of the far-ranging changes that devaluation implies.

On the other hand, when the deficit is of a 'fundamental' nature — arising from a decision to consume more out of given income, an essentially 'flow' decision (Johnson 1958) — the relative desirability of import restrictions or devaluation is more controversial. Most analysts resolve the issue by resorting to the equivalence of restrictions and *ad valorem* tariffs. They cite the optimum tariff argument, which admits tariffs under national monopoly power in trade, and then conclude that devaluation is a superior method of reducing deficits if the country has *already* placed optimum restrictions on trade (Johnson 1958). This view, however, rests on restrictive assumptions — for example, that the equivalence of tariffs and restrictions is universally valid.

Yet other arguments may favour restrictions. Destabilizing speculation, for example, is cited as a reason why devaluation is inferior (Tew 1960): a devaluation may destroy confidence in the currency's stability. On the other hand, the imposition of restrictions also may make speculators expect that a devaluation is on its way, so that devaluation is not necessarily inferior on such grounds. A more persuasive argument is that when a country's currency is being used as an international currency — as are the dollar and the pound sterling — devaluation could imperil the continuation of the system.

Perhaps the chief advantage of restrictions in correcting 'flow' deficits consists in the *speed* with which they can work vis-à-vis devaluation, a difference of great importance to a country with hardpressed reserves. The difference is easily explained. Restrictions immediately curtail imports, while the substitution (and/or multiplier) effects inevitably involve time lags and thus cut into this favourable effect only later. On the other hand, devaluation depends on substitution effects for its effectiveness and hence takes time to improve the balance of payments. No formal models have yet been developed to examine this difference (and this is a serious lacuna in the analytical literature), but it can scarcely be doubted that, in practice, governments are keenly conscious of it in their occasional resort to restrictions.

REFERENCES

Alexander, Sidney S., 1951: Devaluation Versus Import Restrictions as an Instrument for Improving Foreign Trade Balance (International Monetary Fund, *Staff Papers 1*), pp. 379–96.

——, 1952: Effects of a Devaluation on a Trade Balance (International Monetary Fund, *Staff Papers 2*), pp. 263–78.

Bhagwati, Jagdish, 1962: 'Indian Balance of Payments Policy and Exchange Auctions', *Oxford Economic Papers* New Series 14, pp. 51–68.

——, 1965: 'On the Equivalence of Tariffs and Quotas', in *Trade, Growth, and the Balance of Payments: Essays in Honor of Gottfried Haberler*, Richard E. Caves, Harry G. Johnson and Peter B. Kenen (eds) (Amsterdam: North–Holland Publishing; Chicago: Rand McNally) pp. 53–67.

Contracting Parties to the General Agreement on Tariffs and Trade, 1951: *The Use of Quantitative Import Restrictions to Safeguard Balances of Payments: Incorporating the Second Report on the Discriminatory Application of Import Restrictions* (Geneva: The Contracting Parties).

——, 1959: *Review of Import Restrictions Under Articles XII: 4(b) and XVIII: 12(b)* (Geneva: The Contracting Parties).

——, 1964: *The Role of GATT in Relation to Trade and Development* (Geneva: The Contracting Parties).

Corden, W.M., 1958: 'The Control of Imports: A Case Study; the United Kingdom Import Restrictions of 1951–52', *Manchester School of Economic and Social Studies* 26, pp. 181–221.

——, 1960: 'The Geometric Representation of Policies to Attain Internal and External Balance', *Review of Economic Studies* 28, pp. 1–22.

Fleming, J.M., 1951: On Making the Best of Balance of Payments Restrictions on Imports, *Economic Journal* 61, pp. 48–71.

Frisch, Ragnar, 1947: 'On the Need for Forecasting a Multilateral Balance of Payments', *American Economic Review* 37, pp. 535–51.

——, 1948: 'Outline of a System of Multicompensatory Trade', *Review of Economics and Statistics* 30, pp. 265–71.

Hauser, Heinrich, 1939: *Control of International Trade* (London: Routledge).

Hemming, M.F.W. and W.M. Corden, 1958: 'Import Restriction as an Instrument of Balance-of-payments Policy', *Economic Journal* 48, pp. 483–510.

Hemming, M.F.W., C.M. Miles and G.F. Ray, 1959: 'A Statistical Summary of the Extent of Import Control in the United Kingdom Since the War', *Review of Economic Studies* 26, pp. 75–109.

Johnson, Harry G., 1958: *International Trade and Economic Growth: Studies in Pure Theory* (Cambridge, Mass.: Harvard Univ. Press).

Kindleberger, Charles P., 1953; 1963: *International Economics*, rev. 3rd ed. (Homewood, Ill.: Irwin).

Meade, James Edward, 1951: *The Theory of International Economic Policy*, vol. 1: *Balance of Payments* (Oxford Univ. Press).

Nurkse, Ragnar, 1956: 'The Relation Between Home Investment and External Balance in the Light of British Experience: 1945–1955', *Review of Economics and Statistics* 38, pp. 121–54.

Sargent, J.R., 1957: 'Stocks and Quantitative Restrictions', Oxford (University of) Institute of Statistics, *Bulletin* 19, pp. 57–61.

Tew, Brian, 1960: 'The Use of Restrictions to Suppress External Deficits, *Manchester School of Economic and Social Studies* 28, pp. 243–62.

Viner, Jacob, 1934: 'Tariff', in *Encyclopaedia of the Social Sciences* (New York: Macmillan) vol. 14, pp. 514–23.

9

Regionalism versus Multilateralism[*]

1. INTRODUCTION

THE question of 'regionalism', defined broadly as preferential trade
agreements among a subset of nations, is a longstanding one. As
with all great issues, economists have long been divided on the
wisdom of such arrangements. So have policy-makers.

The question of customs unions (CUs) and free trade areas
(FTAs), both permitted under GATT Article XXIV, has long been
a major topic of theoretical research. The focus, however, since
Jacob Viner's (1950) classic treatment of it, distinguishing between
trade diversion and trade creation, has been on showing that
CUs and FTAs were not necessarily welfare-improving, either for
member countries or for world welfare. That is, the case for
preferential trade arrangements was different from the case for
free trade for all. The latter, enshrined in Adam Smith and Ricardo,
and rigorously proven later by Samuelson (1939), Kemp (1972),
and Grandmont and McFadden (1972), is a first-best case. The
former, by contrast, reflects second-best considerations and was
argued by Lipsey and Lancaster (1956–57), Lipsey (1957), Meade
(1956), Johnson (1958a and 1958b) and others.[1]

The recent revival of regionalism, which I describe as the

[*] Thanks are due to Robert Baldwin, James Benedict, Richard Blackhurst, Christopher Bliss, Don Davis, Sunil Gulati, Douglas Irwin, John MacMillan, Arvind
Panagariya, T.N. Srinivasan, and John Walley for helpful conversations and suggestions.
[1] The Vinerian approach to customs union theory has been carried forward by
others, chiefly by Berglas (1979) and Corden (1976). In addition, three alternative
theoretical approaches can be distinguished: by Kemp and Wan (1976); by Cooper
and Massell (1965a and 1965b), Johnson (1965), and Bhagwati (1968); and by
Brecher and Bhagwati (1981). All four approaches are distinguished and discussed
in the graduate textbook by Bhagwati and Srinivasan (1983, Ch. 27) and in Bhagwati (1991a). Each is touched upon later in the text.

Second Regionalism in contrast and because it is a sequel to the First Regionalism of the 1960s, raises anew these old questions about trade diversion. But the historically changed situation which has resurrected regionalism, the context in which it must be analysed, has raised several new issues.

In this chapter, I address these manifold questions, dividing the analysis into a discussion of:

– Article XXIV of the GATT which sanctions CUs and FTAs (Sec. 2);
– the First Regionalism, briefly reviewing the factors that led to it and the reasons why, in the end, it failed (Sec. 3);
– the Second Regionalism, the reasons for its revival and its differential prospects (Sec. 4);
– the key issues that this renewed Regionalism raises, distinguishing among two main questions (Sec. 5);
– the first, relating to the static impact-effect of regional trade blocs (Sec. 6); and
– the second, concerning the dynamic time-path that regionalism offers, in itself and vis-à-vis multilateralism when the objective is to reach (non-discriminatory) free trade for all, so that I ask whether 'multilateralism is the best way to get to multilateralism', distinguishing therefore between 'process-multilateralism' and 'outcome-multilateralism' (Sec. 7).

2. Article XXIV at the GATT: Rationale

The principle of non-discrimination is central to the final conception of the GATT, signed on 30 October 1947 by representatives from 23 countries in Geneva. Article I embodies the strong support for non-discrimination, requiring (unconditional) MFN for all GATT members.

Aside from 'grandfathering' provisions, the only significant exception to MFN is made in Article XXIV which permits CUs and FTAs, and therefore sanctions preferential trade barrier reductions among a subset of GATT members so long as they go all the way to elimination.[2]

---

[2] Two points should be noted. First, there is a difference between intention and

It is an intriguing question why Article XXIV was accepted; and it is a question that also has significance for some of the issues raised by the Second Regionalism. When you think about it, it is a bit odd that an exception to MFN should be allowed so long as it is total (going all the way to 100 per cent) rather than partial (say, 20 per cent preference for favoured friends). Indeed, the post-Vinerian theory of preferential trade areas suggests that 100 per cent preferences are less likely to increase welfare than partial preferences.[3]

The rationale for Article XXIV's inclusion in the GATT therefore must be explained in other ways. Perhaps, there was an inchoate, if strong, feeling that integration with 100 per cent preferences somehow was special and consonant with the objective of multilateralism. Thus, Kenneth Dam (1970, pp. 274–5) quotes the prominent US official Clair Wilcox as follows:

A Custom union (with 100 per cent preferences) creates a wider trading area, removes obstacles to competition, makes possible a more economic allocation of resources and thus operates to increase production and raise planes of living. A preferential system (less than 100 per cent) on the other hand, retains internal barriers, obstructs economy in production, and restrains the growth of income and demand. . . . A customs union is conducive to the expansion of trade on a basis of multilateralism and non-discrimination; a preferential system is not.

Wilcox's statement was little more than assertion, however. But the rationale for inclusion of Article XXIV in the GATT appears to have been threefold, as follows.

–   Full integration on trade, that is, going all the way down to freedom of trade flows among any subset of GATT members,

---

reality: as argued below, the Article XXIV – sanctioned FTAs and CUs have never gone 'all the way'. Second, GATT's MFN is universal only for its members, so it falls short of total universalism. But the important point to remember is that the GATT is open to membership of all who meet the criteria for admission and has generally been inclusive rather than exclusive.

[3] Of course, this theory developed *after* the incorporation of Article XXIV into the GATT, so its inconsistency with Article XXIV, on its own terms, is perhaps only an amusing observation. Note, however, that James Meade was a principal actor in both. The argument is developed in two alternative ways in Lipsey (1960: 507) and in Johnson (1967: 203).

would have to be allowed since it created an important element of single-nation characteristics (such as virtual freedom
of trade and factor movements) among these nations, and
implied that the resulting quasi-national status following from
such integration in trade legitimated the exception to MFN
obligation toward other GATT members.

– The fact that the exception would be permitted only for the
extremely difficult case where all trade barriers would need
to come down, seemed to preclude the possibility that all
kinds of preferential arrangements would break out, returning
the world to the fragmented, discriminatory bilateralism-in-
fested situation of the 1930s.

– Article XXIV could also be viewed as permitting a supplemental, practical route to the universal free trade that GATT
favoured as the ultimate goal, with the general negotiations
during the many Rounds leading to a dismantling of trade
barriers on a GATT-wide basis while deeper integration would
be achieved simultaneously within those areas where politics
permitted faster movement to free trade under a strategy of
full and time-bound commitment. This is an argument that is
now at centre stage: is regionalism truly a building, rather than
a stumbling, bloc towards multilateral free trade for all; in
other words, will it fragment, or integrate, the world economy?

The clear determination of 100 per cent preferences as compatible with multilateralism and non-discrimination, and the equally firm view that anything less was not, meant that when Article
XXIV was drafted, its principal objective was to close all possible
loopholes by which it could degenerate into a justification for
preferential arrangements of less than 100 per cent. Paragraphs 4
through 10 of Article XXIV were written precisely for this purpose.
But, as is now commonly conceded, their inherent ambiguity and
the political pressures for approval of substantial regional groupings of preferences of less than 100 per cent have combined to
frustrate the full import of the original desire to sanction only 100
per cent preferences.

Dam's (1970, p. 290) overall judgement is perhaps too harsh
but it is certainly in the ballpark:

The record is not comforting. . . . Perhaps only one of the more than one dozen regional arrangements that have come before the GATT complied fully with Article XXIV criteria. That was the recent United Kingdom/ Ireland Free Trade Area, and even in that case certain doubts were expressed before the working party. In some cases, the regional arrangements were very wide off the mark. The European Coal and Steel Community, covering only two major product lines, could not even qualify for the special regional arrangement waiver of Article XXIV: 10 but required a general waiver under Article XXV: 5. The New Zealand/ Australia Free Trade Agreement, although not purportedly an example of 'functional integration', provided for the liberlization of an even smaller percentage of inter-member trade. A strong tendency has also been manifested for interim agreements to provide for an even longer transitional period and to contain increasingly fewer detailed commitments for eventual completion of the customs union or free trade area.

3. THE 'FIRST REGIONALISM': FAILURE IN THE 1960s

In any event, it can be correctly asserted (based on the acceptance of Article XXIV into the GATT) that regionalism, in the shape of (100 per cent) customs unions and free trade areas, was not generally considered by the architects of the GATT or by the United States, which was the chief proponent of multilateralism and non-discrimination, as antithetical to the GATT and to these principles.

1. Nonetheless, the United States, long suspicious of discriminatory trade arrangements, restrained itself from resorting to Article XXIV. The formation of the European Community in 1958 marked a partial watershed. The United States put its shoulder to the wheel and saw the Common Market through, negotiating around the different hoops of Article XXIV, emasculating the Article somewhat in order to seek GATT approval of an imperfect union (especially in regard to discriminatory preferences for the eighteen ex-colonies in Africa which the Europeans insisted on retaining, and which required a waiver of GATT rules), all in the cause of what it saw as a *politically* beneficial union of the original six nations that formed the Community. But despite the enthusiasm of many to follow the EC with a North Atlantic Free Trade

Area (NAFTA), and even a Pacific Free Trade Area (PAFTA), centred on the United States, nothing came of it: The United States remained indifferent to such notions.[4]

2. There was an outbreak of FTA proposals in the developing countries as well. While stimulated by the European examples, they were motivated by the altogether different economic rationale formulated by Cooper and Massell (1965a and 1965b), Johnson (1965), and Bhagwati (1968). This was that, given any targeted level of import-substituting industrialization, the developing countries, with their small markets, could reduce the cost of this industrialization by exploiting economies of scale through preferential opening of markets with one another.[5] By the end of the 1960s, however, the attempts at forming regional free trade areas and customs unions along these lines had also collapsed. The problem was that, rather than use trade liberalization and hence prices to guide industry allocation, the developing countries attempting such unions sought to allocate industries by bureaucratic negotiation and tie trade to such allocations, putting the cart before the horse and killing the forward motion.

Thus, while the world was indeed filled in the 1960s with proposals for NAFTA, PAFTA, LAFTA (the Latin American Free Trade Area), and ever more, until one could be forgiven for imagining that a veritable chemical revolution had broken out, regionalism had virtually died by the end of the decade, except for the original European Community and EFTA.

---

[4] Japan indeed probed the possibility of going into such an arrangement with the United States as one of its partners in the 1960s, but to no avail.

[5] The question of 'multilateralism' *versus* 'regionalism' surfaced at a different level even within this preferential trade liberalization among the developing countries. Thus, in the early 1960s, we were discussing whether the Cooper–Massell–Johnson–Bhagwati argument should not be considered on a G-77-wide basis rather than for much smaller groups of developing countries. This was the principal issue before a 1962 UNCTAD Expert Group in New York, of which I was a member, which met over three weeks to draft the recommendation that preferential trade liberalization among the developing countries be 'multilateral', i.e. G-77-wide, rather than narrowly-focused. Unfortunately, the preferential arrangements that were contemplated took the latter, narrower focus.

4. THE 'SECOND REGIONALISM': REVIVAL IN THE 1980s

But regionalism (i.e. preferential trade liberalization) is now back. Those who do not know the history of the First Regionalism are doomed to extrapolate from the current political ferment in favour of FTAs and CUs, and assume uncritically that regionalism is here to stay. Those who know the history may make the reverse mistake of thinking that regionalism will fail again.

I believe that careful analysis of the causes of the resurrection of regionalism suggests that regionalism is likely to endure this time. The principal driving force for regionalism today is the conversion of the United States, hitherto an abstaining party, to Article XXIV. Beginning with the FTA with Israel (a reflection of the special relationship between the two nations and hence of little general value), the FTA with Canada marked a distinct change. Now, the NAFTA is being negotiated with Mexico, and the Enterprise for the Americas Initiative envisages more FTAs with the nations of South America, with Chile at the head of the line.

The conversion of the United States is of major significance. As the key defender of multilateralism through the post-war years, its decision now to travel the regional route (in the geographical *and* the preferential senses simultaneously) tilts the balance of forces away at the margin from multilateralism to regionalism.

This shift has taken place in the context of an anti-multilateralist ethos that has reflected alternative but nonetheless eventually reinforcing views:

– The 'Memorial Drive' school[6] holds that the GATT is dead

---

[6] The MIT economics Department is at 50 Memorial Drive in Cambridge, Massachusetts. I obviously exclude Charles Kindleberger, Paul Samuelson, and the diaspora, including myself! If the views expressed with Dornbusch in a recent *Eastman Kodak* publication (1989) are a guide, Krugman may at times hold one of the positions described above. This pamphlet makes somewhat odd and untenable statements about what the GATT does and does not do. Cf. Michael Finger's (1989) rather blunt analysis of these assertions in *The World Economy* and my own complaints about the confusions following from loose writing on trade policy issues, and the resulting prostitution of an important debate, in Bhagwati (1991b), *The American Enterprise* (Nov.–Dec. 1991). Whether the Memorial Drive school has by now shifted under fire its anti-multilateral stance

(Thurow: Davos) or the GATT should be killed (Dornbusch et al., 1989).[7] Regionalism then is presented in effect as an *alternative* to multilateralism. This school, aptly named in view of its funereal approach to multilateralism, has influence in Democratic circles and plays to the prejudices that one finds in Congressional circles that mistakenly identify multilateralism with America's post-war altruism and regionalism (with its connotation of 'exploiting for ourselves our own markets') with the presumed current necessity to 'look after one's interests finally'.

- An alternative view is that regionalism is a useful *supplement*, not an alternative, to multilateralism. 'We are only walking on two legs' is the popular argument. That we may wind up walking on all fours is ignored.

- It is also often asserted that regionalism will not merely supplement multilateralism. It will also *accelerate* the multilateral process: the threat of going (unilateral and) regional will produce multilateral agreements that may otherwise be held up. (However, this may be an optimistic view since threats that have to be repeatedly implemented, as has been the case with US regionalism, are not efficient ones; and they change external perceptions about what US trade policy priorities are, quite regardless of what the US asserts to be its true intentions. Indeed, the taking of two roads simultaneously can adversely affect the travel down one, as I argue at length below.)

- The panic over the continuing payments deficit has also fed demands for 'quick' results on trade (although the two issues are broadly delinkable: payment surpluses and deficits are macroeconomic phenomena that are not influenced in any predictable way by trade policy changes whose impact on the difference between domestic savings and investment, if any,

---

and joined the more common view that regionalism is a useful supplement, not an alternative, to multilateralism is anyone's guess, given the conflicting reports that are heard of its many oral pronouncements on the lecture circuit from its peripatetic members. But if it truly has abandoned its early vitriolic anti-GATT positions, I would be delighted in its demise.

[7] I rely upon oral presentation at the 1988 annual meeting of the American Enterprise Institute in Washington DC.

can come in different ways that can go in opposed directions). Associated with this has been impatience with the pace of the multilateral trade-negotiating process and the *non sequitur* (examined below) that regionalism necessarily works faster.

– In addition, Europe 1992 and the impending integration of Eastern Europe into the European Community have reinforced the way the formation of the Common Market did with many three decades ago, those in North America who feel that a countervailing bloc must also be formed there. Indeed, the fear that European investments would be diverted to Eastern Europe, once it is integrated with the European Community, was cited by President Salinas of Mexico as a factor decisively pushing him toward the Mexico–US FTA: this would, he felt, enable Mexico to get the necessary investment from America and Japan.

– There are strong non-economic, political and cultural factors also driving Mexico toward a free trade area with its northern neighbour. Just as the Turks since Ataturk have sought to seek a European rather than an Arab identity, the Mexicans now clearly seek an American future rather than one with their southern neighbours. The Hispanic (economic) destiny that many in America fear from illegal immigration and integration with Mexico has its flip side in the American (economic) destiny that Mexico's reforming élite, trained in the top universities in the United States, hopes for.

– The offer in June 1990 by President Bush to get more nations from South America to join the United States in a free trade area, as part of a general package of economic initiatives to assist these nations, is reflective of the compulsions that the debt crisis there imposes on American policy to respond in a regional framework to ensure that this crisis remains manageable and does not engulf the United States, whose banks are principally endangered by it.

– Then again, the response of South American nations to the prospect of FTAs with NAFTA, and in some cases with one another first and then joining up with NAFTA, has been enthusiastic. This time around, the prospects are better than in the 1960s. Quite simply, there is now a marked shift in economic thinking towards trade liberalization and market forces. (The macroeconomic crisis of the 1980s has fed the movement to microeconomic reforms, much as it is currently doing in India.) The changed economic and political attitudes are comforting to those of us who went into the trenches to fight these battles as early as the 1960s. It is also amusing to see those who dismissed our arguments as 'reactionary' or 'ideological' then, now embracing these ideas and policies and the leaders who are implementing them, with no apologies to us and with a façade of independently-obtained wisdom. But frankly, it is good to have them finally on the right side; and it is good to have been in the right.

– Finally, the conjunction of the two dramatic events, Europe 1992 and the US–Canada Free Trade Arrangement, even though fortuitous and prompted by different motivations and historical circumstances, has certainly created a sense elsewhere that regionalism is the order of the day and others must follow suit. In the Far East, for instance, there has been a sense that a Japan-centred regional bloc may be necessary in a bloc-infested world, and Malaysia has actively sought a Japan-centred Asian bloc to rival and confront the US-led Americas' bloc.

5. Regionalism versus Multilateralism: Key Questions

In the light of the above one suspects that the Second Regionalism will endure: it shows many signs of strength and few points of vulnerability. But, if so, those of us who see virtue in a rule-based, open and multilateral trading system must ask searching questions as to its compatibility with such discriminatory trading arrangements. In particular, two major questions must be answered:

– Is the immediate impact-effect of such preferential trade blocs, whether CUs or FTAs, to reduce rather than increase world welfare?

– Regardless of the immediate impact-effect, will regionalism lead to non-discriminatory multilateral free trade for all, through continued expansion of the regional blocs until universal free trade is reached, or will it fragment the world economy? And will, in any event, such a dynamic time path show that regionalism will get us closer to the *goal* of multilateral free trade for all than multilateralism as the *process* of trade negotiation will?

I shall now treat each of these two important, and distinct (if at times analytically interrelated), questions in turn.

6. THE STATIC IMPACT-EFFECT QUESTION

The question of the static impact-effect of preferential trade arrangements such as FTAs and CUs is, quite simply, the question raised by Viner (1950): would not such discriminatory arrangements be trade-diverting rather than trade-creating?[8]

It is important to raise this question because, as Viner taught us, FTAs and CUs are two-faced: they liberalize trade (among members), but they protect (against outsiders). The important issue therefore is: which aspect of an FTA or CU is dominant? Or, to put it in the economist's language: is a particular FTA or CU trade-diverting (that is, taking trade away from efficient outside suppliers and giving it to inefficient member countries) or trade-creating (that is, generating trade from one more-efficient member at the expense of another less efficient member)?

Sadly, one may scan the *op. ed.* articles, the editorials, and the Congressional testimony when the renewal of fast-track authority for the extension of NAFTA to Mexico was being debated in 1991, looking for references to trade diversion — and find scarcely any. Astonishingly, it was not just the politicians and lawyers for Mexico's lobby who equated the FTA with (non-discriminatory) free trade; reputed economists did so too.

What can we say about this issue? In particular, what can we propose to ensure that, if CUs and FTAs are to flourish, they do not become trade-diversionary? Article XXIV's injunction not to

---

[8] Defined in Vinerian fashion, a trade-diverting FTA can still improve a member country's welfare but will generally harm outside countries. The focus below is on the impact on others, as is presumably the intention also of Article XXIV's injunction not to raise the average external tariff.

raise the CU's or FTA's average external tariff can be interpreted as a precaution against trade diversion and harm to countries outside GATT, though (as argued below) this is not a satisfactory way to do it.

In essence, there are three approaches to containing the fallout of trade diversion from CUs and FTAs.

(a) Converting Preferential CUs and FTAs into (Geographically) Regional Blocs

It is occasionally argued that we should encourage geographically proximate countries to form CUs and FTAs, discouraging geographically distant countries from doing so since the latter would be more likely to be trade-diverting. This is a misguided prescription in my view, for several reasons.

To see this, it must be first appreciated that it rests on a syllogism. The first premise is that a CU or FTA is more likely to create trade and thus raise welfare. Given a country's volume of international trade, the higher the proportion of trade with the country's CU or FTA partners and the lower this proportion with the non-member countries. The second premise is that countries sharing borders, or closer geographically to one another, have higher proportions of trade with one another than countries which are further apart.

The first premise is, of course, well known to trade economists from the early post-Vinerian theory, as developed by Lipsey (1958). But Lipsey's argument focuses on the relative sizes of imports from each source vis-à-vis expenditure on domestic goods as the key and decisive factor in determining the size of losses and gains from the preferential cuts in trade barriers.

While the likelihood argument is valid within the Lipsey model, it must be noted that it is only that. Thus, for specific CUs and FTAs, the *actual* welfare effects will depend, not merely on the trade and expenditure shares à la Lipsey, but also on the *substitution* at the margin between commodities. Thus, for instance, the substitution between non-member goods and domestic goods may be very high, so that the costs of discrimination would also tend to be high, *ceteris paribus*. In short, it is important to guess at substitution elasticities among goods *as well as* trade shares, with and between members and non-members of CUs and FTAs, to arrive at a better picture of the likely effects of *specific* CUs and FTAs that may be proposed.

As for the second premise, I have problems with that too, as a policy guideline. If I had access to captive research assistance and funds, I could examine whether, for all conceivable combinations of countries and distances among them, and for several different time periods, the premise is valid. As I do not, I must rely on casual empiricism and a priori arguments. Compare for instance the trade through the 1960s between India and Pakistan with that between India and the UK or the USSR. The former trade has been smaller than the latter. Borders can breed hostility and undermine trade, just as alliances among distant countries with shared causes can promote trade (Gowa and Mansfield 1991). The flag follows trade; and trade equally follows the flag which, at least in the nineteenth century European expansion, was not directly across from the European nations' borders. Again, even if the premise is statistically valid for any set of observations, it may actually be a result of trade diversion: proximity may have led to preferential grant of concessions such as OAP and GSP at the expense of countries elsewhere.

In short, prescriptions to confine CUs and FTAs only to geographically proximate countries are not defensible because both premises have problems: the former is, at best, a likelihood proposition that should not be applied to specific situations where the welfare impact also depends critically on other variables, whereas the latter does not have a firm empirical or conceptual basis.

But possibly the most damaging criticism that can be made of such a prescription is that it concentrates, at best, on the static impact-effect question and ignores the more important dynamic time path question. By prescribing that we must rule out 'distant' country unions, as between the US and Israel or Chile, we would make the CUs and FTAs more exclusive and less open to new members, undercutting the objective of moving speedily towards the shared objective of (non-discriminatory) multilateral free trade for all. That would be tragic indeed.

(b) Designing Disciplines to Minimize Trade Diversion

A different, and my preferred, approach is not to pretend to find rules of thumb to exclude CUs and FTAs 'likely' to be trade-diversionary, but rather to examine the different ways in which trade diversion could arise and then to establish disciplines that would minimize its incidence.

Article XXIV. In a sense, Article XXIV (para. 5) seeks to do this by requiring that CUs, which must have a common external tariff, should ensure that this common tariff 'shall not on the whole by higher or more restrictive than the general incidence of the duties and regulations of commerce applicable . . . prior to the formation of such a union.' For FTAs, the rule is that the 'duties and other regulations of commerce' are not to be 'higher or more restrictive' than those previously in effect.

Evidently, when tariffs change, as in CUs, and some increase and others fall, the scope for skullduggery arises again, since Article XXIV leaves the matter wholly ambiguous. As Dam (1970, p. 217) has noted:

> these ambiguities plagued the review by the CONTRACTING PARTIES to the EEC Treaty of Rome — The Six, having used an arithmetic average, refused to discuss the best method of calculation, because in their view paragraph 5 did not require any special method.

Besides, it is evident to trade economists that maintaining external tariffs unchanged is, in any event, not the same as eliminating trade diversion. What *can* be said is that the lower the external barriers, the less is the scope for diverting efficient foreign supplies to member countries. Thus, a desirable discipline to impose on CUs and FTAs would be to require, for Article XXIV sanction, that one price to be paid must be the simultaneous reduction of the external tariff (implicit and explicit), pro rata to the progressive elimination of internal trade barriers.

Possible ways of ensuring this may be indirect disciplines. One way would be to modify Article XXIV to rule out FTAs with diverse tariffs by members[9] and to permit only CUs with common external

---

[9] In any event, by encouraging rules of origin because the trade barrier walls are not everywhere equally high, FTAs encourage in turn the bureaucratic-cum-

tariffs. With most tariffs bound, this would ensure that for the most part a substantial downward shift in tariffs would be a consequence — that, say, Argentina or Brazil would be lowering her trade barriers, *not* that the United States would be raising hers. Since regionalism is probably going to be a matter of low trade barrier hubs such as the United States and Japan joining with their respective regional spokes, this insistence on CUs could perhaps produce excellent results.

An alternative, surer way would be to insist on CUs but also to write into Article XXIV the requirement that the *lowest* tariff of any union member on an item *before* the union must be part of the common external tariff of the union.

Articles VI and XIX: AD and VERs. But none of this is enough today, for the trade economists who work in a sustained way on the problems of the world trading system are aware that protection today takes the form of unfair capture of fair trade mechanisms such as Anti-Dumping (AD) actions and of Voluntary Export Restraints (VERs). Thus, countries today have access to selective and elastic instruments of protection.[10] Given this reality, even the modification of Article XXIV, to ensure that the external (implicit and explicit) tariff barriers come down as a price for CUs to be allowed under GATT rules, will leave open a big, gaping hole that would be tantamount to an open invitation to trade diversion by these preferential arrangements. Indeed, trade creation can degenerate rapidly into trade diversion, when AD actions and VERs are freely used. Let me explain.

Imagine that the United States begins to eliminate (by outcompeting) an inefficient Mexican industry once the FTA goes into effect. Even though the most-efficient producer is Taiwan, if the next efficient United States outcompetes the least efficient Mexico, that would be desirable trade creation (though the best course would be free trade so that Taiwan would take more of the Mexican market instead).

---

industry capture of the essentially arbitrary 'local content' rules for protectionist purposes.

[10] VERs are evidently selective by countries. AD actions are selective down to the level of the firm, as Brian Hindley has noted.

But what do you suppose the Mexicans would be likely to do? They would probably start anti-dumping actions against Taiwan, which would lead to reduced imports from Taiwan as the imports from the United States increased, leaving the Mexican production relatively unaffected. Trade diversion from Taiwan to the United States would have occurred. Similarly, the effect of Mexican competition against the United States could well be that the United States would start anti-dumping actions and even VERs against Taiwan.

My belief that FTAs will lead to considerable trade diversion (because of modern methods of protection, which are inherently selective and can be captured readily for protectionist purposes), is one that may have been borne out in the EC. It is well known that the EC has profusely used anti-dumping actions and VERs to erect Fortress Europe against the Far East. Cannot much of this be a trade-diversion policy in response to the intensification of internal competition among the member states of the EC?[11]

Two conclusions follow. (1) If inherently discriminatory regionalism is to flourish, as seems likely, then we need greater discipline for AD actions and VERs: Article VI needs reform and Article XIX needs compliance alongside the elimination of VERs (as the Dunkel draft on the MTN recommends). (2) This also implies that regionalism means, not redundancy of the GATT, but the need for its strengthening. Those who think of the two as alternatives are prisoners of defunct modes of thinking, based on the days when protection was a different beast.

(c) Judging Trade Diversion Case by Case

While the foregoing analysis embraces a set of policy framework and incentive-creating reforms to minimize trade diversion, an alternative approach to the problem could be in terms of a case-by-case approach where the approval by the GATT of a proposed

[11] Brian Hindley and Patrick Messerlin are investigating this hypothesis for the GATT Secretariat as part of a set of studies to support the 1992 GATT Annual Report on *Regionalism and Multilateralism*, following the 1991 Annual Report on *Trade and the Environment*.

CU or FTA would depend on the evaluation of its trade-creating and trade-diverting effects, and the requirement that the net anticipated effect be trade-creating.

John McMillan (1991) has argued this in an ingenious paper[12] that proposes a simple test of admissibility: 'does the bloc result in less trade between member countries and outsider countries?' Based on the welfare economics of customs union theory, this is an aggregative test and has therefore some obvious analytical problems. It is also subject to the problem of computing plausible trade outcomes. It is hard enough to apply it *ex post; ex ante*, as a test of admissibility, I see little prospect of its being effectively used to exclude any proposed CU or FTA.

Its principal merit is its apparent simplicity and better grounding in economic theory. Therefore, I endorse the advisability of *some* version of the McMillan test replacing in Article XXIV the current requirement not to raise the average external tariff. But I see it as doing little *in practice* to avoid trade diversion. For this, we will have to rely on changing the incentive structure, including the use of suitable constraints imposed by stricter discipline on selective and elastic targeting of foreign suppliers. The issue of constraining trade-diversion from proliferating preferential groupings is so important that it may not be a bad idea to *combine* the proposals made by me and McMillan, rather than to treat them as alternatives.

7. THE DYNAMIC TIME PATH QUESTION

The question of the dynamic time path is particularly difficult: it is almost virgin territory. Perhaps the theoretical approach to customs union theory that appears to be most relevant to this problem is that of Kemp and Wan (1976). In contrast to the Vinerian approach, Kemp and Wan make the external tariff structure endogenously determined for the CU, such that it improves the CU members' welfare while maintaining the outsiders' welfare unchanged. This restores the pre-Vinerian intuition that a CU

---

[12] This paper has also been commissioned by the GATT Secretariat for its 1992 Annual Report, ibid.

should be welfare-improving. The problem with the operational significance of the Kemp–Wan argument is that it is really an existence argument, without any structure being put on it within the context of a specific model so that we can develop intuition about what the external tariff structure for such a Kemp–Wan CU would be.[13] But, that *any* subset of countries *could* form an unambiguously (world-) welfare-improving union is definitely established by Kemp and Wan.

This also implies that the time path to multilateral free trade for all as the optimum optimorum can be made monotonic.[14] But what it does *not* say is that the union will necessarily expand and, if so, in a monotonically welfare-improving manner. For *that* answer, we must turn to the *incentive structure* that any CU provides to relevant 'groups' for further expansion of the CU.

The incentives in question need not be *economic* incentives. Indeed, it is hard to imagine that the arbitrary groupings of countries that seek FTAs and CUs are dependent on economic arguments as their key determinants. Often, politics seems to drive these choices of partners, as in the case of the EC, and now in the case of FTAs throughout the Americas. This also accounts for the occasional non-regionally proximate choices of partners in such blocs: e.g. US and Israel, and Pakistan, Iran, and Turkey in the early 1960s. But that economic factors contribute to the incentives for such blocs to be formed is not implausible.

Therefore, a meaningful examination of the incentives to form and to expand trade blocs will have to be in the new and growing field of political economy–theoretic analysis. I believe that the models within which we investigate these issues will have to distinguish among at least three kinds of 'agents', which I will detail below with illustrations of the kinds of arguments which we would find relevant:

Governments of member countries. Whether a CU will expand or not will depend partly on the willingness of the CU authorities to

[13] Christopher Bliss (1990) has made a valuable stab at this problem recently.

[14] Such time paths are clearly not unique. Thus, for instance, any number of such paths could be generated by relaxing the requirement that, at each stage, the non-union outside countries be left only as well off as before the new expansion of the CU.

do so. This will be affected by ideas and ideology. Here I worry that CUs will be under pressure *not* to expand because one possible reaction to a CU will be: 'we are already a large market, so what do we really stand to gain by going through the botheration of adding more members?' This is what I call the *Our Market is Large Enough* syndrome. I think, as Martin Wolf has often noted, that large countries tend to be more inward-looking for precisely this type of reason.

In addition, the expansion of the CU to include any specific set of outside countries will imply differential aggregate welfare effects for current members, implying in turn differential incentives for member countries for and against the expansion.[15] In this context, a CU (which generally includes transfers among members) may be more expansionary (à la Kemp–Wan argumentation) than an FTA, though a CU that simultaneously seeks *political* integration may be less willing to expand.

Interest groups in members countries. We need also to consider how interest groups, who lobby for or against CU expansion, will behave. Again, since CUs are a balance of trade-creating and protecting forces, it is possible that the protectionists who profit from the diversion of trade away from efficient suppliers abroad to themselves will line up against CU expansion to include those suppliers. The problem then would be the *These Are Our Markets* syndrome.

It is a sentiment that was tellingly expressed by Signor Agnelli of Fiat: 'The single market must first offer an advantage to European companies. This is a message we must insist on without hesitation.'[16] It is, of course, fine for Signor Agnelli to express such sentiments: after all, Fiat has run for years, not on gas, but on VERs against the Japanese. But should economists also embrace such sentiments?

Interest Groups and Governments of Outside Countries. The third

---

[15] This analysis must use the Brecher–Bhagwati (1981) approach to theorizing about CUs since it relates to analysing the effects of changes in domestic and external policies and parameters on the distribution of income and welfare among member states.

[16] Quoted by Martin Wolf (1989).

set of 'agents' has to be the outside countries. Here, the example of a CU may lead others to emulate and seek entry. Else, the fear of trade diversion may also induce outsiders to seek entry. If so, this acts as an incentive to expand the CU.

This is clearly an uncharted area that is evidently the most interesting for further analysis. I should cite one empirical study by Edward Mansfield (1992) which takes trade data for 1850–1965, and estimates an index of 'power distribution' (reflecting, among other things, trade blocs and economic power distribution). When power was centred in hegemons during periods of British and American hegemony, and when there was 'anarchy', the world economy was relatively liberalized (in the sense that Global Exports/GDP ratio was high); when there were a few middle powers, as could happen with trade blocs, the result was a smaller ratio of trade to GDP.

If Mansfield's analysis is accepted, and if it is considered to be a reasonable approximation to the question whether CUs will have expansionist or protectionist outlooks (mapping perhaps also into their attitudes to CU expansion or stagnation), then the presumption would be that historical experience suggests that trade blocs will fragment the world economy, not go on to unify it. Of course, history does not always repeat itself. But Mansfield's work certainly suggests caution in place of the gung-ho regionalism that has been urged by the Memorial Drive School.

To conclude, consider the following popular assertions by the regionalists:

- regionalism is quicker;
- regionalism is more efficient; and
- regionalism is more certain.

(a) Is Regionalism Quicker?

The regionalists claim that the GATT is the General Agreement to Talk and Talk, whereas regionalism proceeds quicker. But is this really so?

1. Historically, at least, the First Regionalism failed whereas the GATT oversaw the effective dismantling of pre-war tariffs in the

OECD countries and the enlargement of disciplines over NTBs at the Tokyo Round and beyond. A little caution, to say the least, is necessary before celebrating regionalism's quickfootedness.

2. For those who believe that regionalism offers a quick route to effective trade liberalization, Kenneth Dam's analysis quoted above needs renewed attention. There is a world of difference between announcing an FTA or a CU and its implementation; and the comparison is not pleasing if you are in the regional camp.

3. As for speed, even the best example of regionalism, the EC, started over four decades ago (1957) and is now into 1996. The 'transition' has not therefore been instantaneous any more than negotiated reductions of trade barriers under the GATT Rounds. And this despite the enormous political support for a united Europe.

4. Take agriculture. The record of regional trade blocs dealing with agricultural trade liberalization is either non-existent or dismal. The CAP is not exactly the EC's crowning achievement. Indeed, were it not for multilateralism (i.e. the Uruguay Round and the coalition of Cairns Group that crystallized around the MTN), it is difficult to imagine that the process of unravelling the CAP could even have begun.

5. The (actual or potential) exercise of the regional option can also affect the efficacy of the multilateral one. The unwillingness of the EC to start the MTN in 1982 and its largely reactive, rather than leadership, role at the Uruguay Round, are in some degree a reflection of its being less hungry for multilateralism given its internal market size and preoccupations. Then again, is it not evident that, were it not for the EC, the capacity of the French (for whose political predicament there can only be sympathy, much as my deplore its consequence of the willingness to liberalize agriculture) to slow down the reform of the CAP and the liberalization of world agriculture would have been significantly less?

6. Moreover, if regionalism is available as a realistic option, it will encourage exit rather than the seeking of voice and even the manifestation of loyalty to multilateralism.

− This may happen at the level of the bureaucrats who end up preferring small-group negotiations among friends (code

phrase: 'like-minded people') to the intellectually and politically more demanding business of negotiating with and for
the larger community of trading nations.

- Else it may happen that, just as public choice theory à la Olson
tells us in regard to the diffusion of consumer losses and
concentration of producer gains that favour protectionist outcomes, the proponents of regionalism tend to be better focused
and mobilized (they are often regional 'experts' and partisans
who ally themselves with the preferred policy options of the
countries whose FTA cause they support), whereas the support for multilateralism is often more diffused and less politically effective, and therefore takes second place when regionalism
is on the political scene.

- Then again, regionalism may appeal to politicians since it
translates more easily into votes: the wooing of the Hispanic
voters, by urging them to identify with the FTA, was quite
evident during the renewal of the fast-track authority in 1991
for the NAFTA negotiations with Mexico.

- The support of business groups for multilateralism may also
erode with regional alternatives for two different reasons: (i)
If a deal can be regionally obtained, where a 'great deal of
trade' is possible then the multilateral arena may be forgotten.
Thus, if Canada could get the US to agree to a fairer operation
of the unfair trade mechanisms (a matter on which many
Canadians today feel they were mistaken, with Prime Minister
Mulroney and Mr Riesman talking about Americans being
'thugs' or like 'third world dictators'),[17] why bother to fight
the battles at the Uruguay Round where the powerful American manufacturing lobbies, zeroing in with the EC against the
Far East, seek instead to weaken the GATT rules? (ii) Again,
better protectionist, trade-diversionary deals may be obtained
in a preferential arrangement than in the non-discriminatory
world of the GATT: e.g. Mexico's textile interests should benefit in the NAFTA relative to Caribbean and other external

---

[17] Those who think that much of the Japan-bashing is not prejudiced may want to
think about the differential and exaggerated reaction in the US to the bumbling and
far more innocuous remarks of Prime Minister Miyazawa and Speaker Sakarauchi.

competitors in the US market, forthwith weakening Mexican incentive to push for reform in the MFA.

7. Finally, it is true that the free rider problem looks difficult as the number of GATT members increases steadily. Yet, recent theoretical work on GATT-style trade negotiations (Ludema 1990) suggests that the free rider problem may not be an effective barrier to freeing trade. Moreover, as Finger (1982) has pointed out, and as experience of inadequate GSP concessions underlines, developing countries have not been able to free ride as much as their exemption from reciprocity under S&D treatment would imply: the trade concessions on commodities of interest to them have not gone as far as the concessions on commodities of interest to other GATT members without such an exemption. (Unconditional) MFN does not work in practice as well as it should from the free-riders' perspective!

(b) Is Regionalism More Efficient?

Occasionally, the regionalists may be found arguing that regionalism is also more *efficient*: it produces *better* results. A typical argument is that, as part of the NAFTA negotiations, Mexico has accepted virtually all the US demands on intellectual property (IP) protection. A funny story, told in developing country circles, serves to probe this assertion critically:

Ambassador Carla Hills was on a tour of South America, extolling the virtues of Mexico's 'capitulation'. At a dinner in her honour in Caracas, she apparently claimed: 'Mexico now has world class IP legislation.' At this point, President Carlos Peretz supposedly turned to his left and remarked: 'But Mexico does not have a world class parliament.'

The true moral of the story is, however, that, as part of the bilateral quid pro quos in an FTA or CU, weak states may agree to specific demands of strong states,[18] in ways that are not exactly *optimal* from the viewpoint of the economic efficiency of the world trading system. In turn, however, these concessions can distort the outcome of the multilateral negotiations.

[18] In Mexico's case, President Salinas' political stake in getting an FTA with the US is vastly disproportionate to President Bush's.

This may well have happened with TRIPs and TRIMs at the Uruguay Round.[19] As is now widely conceded among economists, the case for TRIPs for instance is *not* similar to the case for free trade: there is no presumption of mutual gain, world welfare itself may be reduced by any or more IP protection, and there is little empirical support for the view that 'inadequate' IP protection significantly impedes the creation of new technical knowledge.[20] Yet, the use of US muscle, unilaterally through Special 301 actions, and the playing the regional card through the NAFTA carrot for Mexico, have put TRIPs squarely and effectively into the MTN.

Again, a distorting impact on the multilateral trade rules from NAFTA negotiations can be feared from the fact that, as a price for the latter to be accepted by the Congress during the delicate renewal of fast-track authority, the US administration had to accept demands for harmonization in environment and labour standards by Mexico with those of the US. This effectively linked in political circles the case for Free Trade with the demands for 'level playing fields' or Fair Trade (extremely widely interpreted),[21] legitimating these demands and weakening the ability of economists and of governments negotiating at the GATT (multilaterally for arm's length Free Trade) to resist this illegitimate constraint on freeing trade.[22]

---

[19] TRIPs are trade-related intellectual property provisions and TRIMs are trade-related investment measures. The weakness of the case for their inclusion in the GATT, at least in the forms canvassed by many lobbies, is discussed in Bhagwati (1991a).

[20] It is not surprising therefore that the spokesmen for TRIPs have shifted from utilitarian methods of argumentation to 'rights': they talk now of 'theft' and 'piracy'.

[21] That the environmental and labour standards negotiations in NAFTA will be 'parallel' rather than 'integrated' is of no consequence, any more than has been running the services negotiations parallel to other negotiations at the Uruguay Round.

[22] The danger posed by the proliferating demands for 'level playing fields' or Fair Trade, chiefly in the US but elsewhere too, is extremely serious. It is analysed, and the theoretical questions raised by it are noted, in Bhagwati (1992b). The environment issue, in particular, has been discussed in this context in the 1991 GATT Annual Report, ibid.

(c) Is Regionalism More Certain?

Much has been made, in the Mexican context, of the argument that the FTA will make trade liberalization irreversible. But something needs to be added here:

– GATT also creates commitments: tariffs are bound. (This does not apply to concessions made under conditionality, of course, by IMF or IBRD.) Mexico *is* a member, if recent, of the GATT.

– Recall Dam (quoted above): Article XXIV is so full of holes in its discipline that almost anything goes. Reductions of trade barriers can be slowed down, as 'circumstances' require, other bindings can be torn up by mutual consent (an easier task when there are only a few members in the bloc but more difficult under the GATT), etc.

– Recall too that regional agreements have failed (LAFTA) and also stagnated (ASEAN). The current mood in Canada over NAFTA is sour and the MTN looks better in consequence.[23] The sense however, that the US has let Canada down and failed to live by the spirit of the FTA agreements will probably not endure. But who knows?

8. CONCLUDING REMARKS

The question of regionalism is thus both a difficult and delicate one. Only time will tell whether the revival of regionalism since the 1980s will have been a sanguine and benign development or a malign force that will serve to undermine the widely-shared objective of multilateral free trade for all. My judgement is that the revival of regionalism is unfortunate. But, given its political appeal and its likely spread, I believe that it is important to contain and shape it in ways sketched here so that it becomes maximally useful and minimally damaging, and consonant with the objectives of arriving at multilateral free trade for all.

---

[23] John Whalley's (1992) splendid paper for this Conference on the US–Canada FTA strongly supports the sceptical views that I have advanced of the Second Regionalism's prospect and wisdom.

REFERENCES

Berglas, E., 1979: 'Preferential Trading Theory: The n Commodity Case', *Journal of Political Economy*, 87, pp. 315–31.

Bhagwati, J.N., 1968: 'Trade Liberalization Among LDCs, Trade Theory and GATT Rules', *in* J.N. Wolfe (ed.), *Value, Capital, and Growth: Papers in Honour of Sir John Hicks* (Edinburgh: University of Edinburgh Press).

——, 1991a: *The World Trading System at Risk* (Princeton: Princeton University Press).

——, 1991b: 'Revealing Talk on Trade', *The American Enterprise*, 2, pp. 72–8.

Bhagwati, J.N. and T.N. Srinivasan, 1983: *Lectures on International Trade* (Cambridge: MIT Press).

Bliss, C., 1990: London: CEPR (mimeo).

Brecher, R. and J.N. Bhagwati, 1981: 'Foreign Ownership and the Theory of Trade and Welfare', *Journal of Political Economy*, 89, pp. 497–512.

Cooper, C.A. and B.F. Massell, 1965a: 'A New Look at Customs Union Theory', *The Economic Journal*, 75, pp. 742–7.

——, 1965b: 'Toward a General Theory of Customs Unions for Developing Countries', *Journal of Political Economy*, 73, pp. 461–76.

Corden, W.M., 1976: 'Customs Union Theory and the Nonuniformity of Tariffs', *Journal of International Economics*, 6, pp. 99–107.

Dam, K., 1970: *The GATT: Law and International Economic Organization* (Chicago: University of Chicago Press).

Dornbusch, R. et al., 1989: *Meeting World Challenges: United States Manufacturing in the 1990s* (Pamphlet issued by Eastman Kodak Company, Rochester, NY).

The Economist, 1991: *Economics Focus* column (July).

Finger, J.M., 1989: 'Picturing America's Future: Kodak's Solution of American Trade Exposure', *The World Economy*, 12, pp. 377–80.

Gowa, J. and E. Mansfield, 1991: 'Allies, Adversaries, and International Trade', paper presented at the American Political Science Association Meetings, Washington, DC (mimeo).

Grandmont, J.M. and D. McFadden, 1972: 'A Technical Note on Classical Gains from Trade', *Journal of International Economics*, pp. 109–25.

Johnson, H.G., 1958a: 'The Gains from Free Trade with Europe: An Estimate', *Manchester School of Economic and Social Studies*, 36, pp. 247–65.

——, 1958b: 'The Economic Gains from Free Trade with Europe', *Three Banks Review*.

Johnson, H.G., 1965: 'An Economic Theory of Protectionism, Tariff Bargaining, and the Formation of Customs Unions', *Journal of Political Economy*, 73, pp. 256-83.

——, 1967: *Economic Policies Toward Less Developed Countries* (Washington: Brookings Institution).

Kemp, M.C., 1972: 'The Gains from International Trade', *Economic Journal*, 72, pp. 803-19.

Kemp, M.C. and H. Wan, 1976: 'An Elementary Proposition Concerning the Formation of Customs Unions', *Journal of International Economics*, 6, pp. 95-8.

Lipsey, R.G., 1957: 'The Theory of Customs Unions: Trade Diversion and Welfare', *Economica*.

——, 1958: 'The Theory of Customs Unions: A General Equilibrium Analysis', Ph.D. Thesis, University of London.

——, 1960: 'The Theory of Customs Unions: A General Survey', *The Economic Journal*, 70, pp. 496-513.

Lipsey, R.G. and K.J. Lancaster, 1956-7: 'The General Theory of Second Best', *Review of Economic Studies*, 24, pp. 33-49.

Ludema, R., 1991: 'International Trade Bargaining and the Most Favoured Nation Clause', *Economics & Politics*, 3, pp. 1-41.

Mansfield, E., 1992: 'The Concentration of Capabilities and International Trade', *International Organization*, forthcoming.

McMillan, J., 1991: 'Do Trade Blocs Foster Open Trade?', University of California at San Diego, (mimeo).

Meade, J.E., 1956: *The Theory of Customs Unions* (New York: North Holland).

Samuelson, P.A., 1939: 'The Gains from International Trade', *Canadian Journal of Economics and Political Science*, 5, pp. 195-205.

Saxonhouse, G., 1992: 'Trading Blocs, Pacific Trade, and the Pricing Strategy of East Asian Firms', Paper Presented to the World Bank Conference on *New Dimension in Regionalism* (2-3 April).

Viner, J., 1950: *The Customs Unions Issue*, Carnegie Endowment for International Peace.

Whalley, J., 1992: 'Regional Trade Arrangements in North America: CUSTA and NAFTA', Paper Presented to the World Bank Conference on *New Dimensions in Regional Integration* (2-3 April).

Wolf, M., 1989: 'European Community 1992: The Lure of the Chasse Gardée', *The World Economy*, 12, pp. 373-6.

10

Poverty and Public Policy[*]

1. INTRODUCTION

THE problem of poverty is particularly acute in India. With 14 per cent of the world's population, we have the misfortune of having almost twice as large a share of the world's poor. Indeed, as I shall presently underline, the question of poverty and its amelioration has been at the centre of our concerns from the beginning of our planning efforts almost four decades ago. Little therefore can be said on it that some distinguished Indian economist has not already said. In some ways, therefore, to talk on the design of public policy for poverty to an Indian audience is to carry coal to Newcastle or, as the old saying goes, to teach your grandmother how to suck eggs. Nonetheless, I hope to provide a fresh perspective by putting the problem into an explicit analytical framework that permits alternative policy designs to be sharply defined and contrasted. I also intend to draw on international experience to put our efforts and problems into both historical and comparative perspectives.

2. ALTERNATIVE POLICY DESIGNS
INDIRECT VERSUS DIRECT ROUTES

It is possible, and perhaps even interesting, to speculate whether poverty would increase or diminish if governments followed a

* This is the text of the 12th Vikram Sarabhai Memorial Lecture delivered in Ahmedabad on 28 August 1987. I have profited greatly from conversation with and comments from Surjit Bhalla. Anil Deolalikar. Atul Kohli, Paul Streeten, T.N. Srinivasan, K. Subbarao, K. Sundaram, Raaj Sah, and Suresh Tendulkar. I have taken the opportunity of drawing extensively on an earlier treatment of some of these issues in my Michigan State University Distinguished Speakers Series Lecture (Bhagwati 1985b) on *Growth and Poverty*, sharpening and extending, however, the analysis presented there and drawing more extensively on Indian experience.

regime of laissez-faire, letting poverty and all else take a natural course. Few will dispute however the proposition that, except in singular circumstances, public policy should assist in accelerating the amelioration of poverty.[1] The key question relates rather to the appropriate design of such public policy.

Economics trains us to think of ends and means, of targets and policy instruments. With the amelioration of poverty as the target, the policy instruments designed to achieve that target can be divided into two principal classes: (i) the *indirect* route, i.e. the use of resources to accelerate growth and thereby impact on the incomes and hence the living standards of the poor; and (ii) the *direct* route, i.e. the public provision of minimum-needs-oriented education, housing, nutritional supplements and health, and transfers to finance private expenditures on these and other components of the living standards of the poor.

The primary distinction between the two approaches is between creating income (and hence consumption) and providing consumption (in kind or through doles). The latter necessarily involves redistribution between different groups unless the financing comes from external resources; the former need have no such component, though complementary policies to bias the creation of income towards the poor, which I discuss below, will often involve redistributive elements. Indeed, within both approaches, the direct and the indirect, we can consider the question of 'biasing' or 'targeting' the policies in favour of the poor. Thus, the indirect growth-oriented route may be supplemented by policies facilitating borrowing and investment by the poor or by redistributive land reform, whereas the direct route may be explicitly targeted towards the poor via means tests or choice of health and nutritional programmes that overwhelmingly benefit the poor.[2]

---

[1] Such a singular circumstance could be a Myrdal-type 'soft' state or a predatory state; the former would preclude effective action whereas the latter would guarantee malign intervention.

[2] There are two principal 'anti-poverty' programmes in India: the Integrated Rural Development Programme (IRDP) and the National Rural Employment Programme (NREP). Both are targeted at the poor and would classify as part of the indirect, growth-based strategy in my typology since they are intended to bias the creation of assets and income in favour of the poor. Thus, for instance, the IRDP aims at

The optimal policy design should generally involve a mix of these two approaches unless the 'productivity' of either in achieving the target substantially dominates that of the other. Thus, for instance, if growth will concentrate increased incomes entirely among the non-poor and there is no upward mobility either, the relevant rate of return to the indirect route is zero. Indeed, if growth can be shown to be immiserizing to the poor, this return would be negative! In such an event, the case for exclusive reliance on the direct route becomes overwhelming, with two critical and compelling provisos: *first*, that it should be shown that the factors, both economic and political, that constrain the effectiveness of the growth process in indirectly reducing poverty do not simultaneously and equally afflict the direct route and prevent it also from effectively providing benefits to the poor; and *second*, that the neglect of the growth process, even if its indirect impact on poverty through increased incomes for the poor is negligible or harmful, would impair in the long run the ability of the state to sustain the expenditures required to finance the more productive direct route, especially in an economy with a growing population.

In economic thinking and in economic policy, the pendulum can swing with astonishing regularity. In the 1950s and 1960s the growth-based indirect route to attacking poverty was the more fashionable, though the direct route was both recognized and far from neglected. By the 1970s, however, nothing but a gloomy

---

targeting the poor in the growth process by providing them with opportunities, in terms of transfer of assets, training etc., for income expansion. The NREP, on the other hand, creates rural employment to build assets such as roads and can therefore be seen as an attempt at biasing the income-expansion process in favour of the poor by promoting labour-intensive technologies and activities, and also, insofar as the assets in turn create income differentially in favour of the poor, via the resulting capital formation. In practice, however, the asset formation, such as road building, may be negligible as when the new roads are immediately washed away, reducing therefore the result in this instance to what it would have been under a transfer payment to the poor via my *direct* route. There is, therefore, an extensive debate in India whether the operation of the IRDP and NREP programmes, while intended as part of the pro-poor-bias indirect (growth) strategy, are not *de facto* reducing to the pro-poor-bias direct (transfer) strategy. On this issue, see the interesting articles by Rath (1985) and Sundaram and Tendulkar (1985). I am indebted to Sundaram and Tendulkar for drawing my attention to these questions.

refrain could be heard that the indirect route of growth was ineffective and, worse still, harmful to the poor, and only the direct route in the shape of a Basic Needs strategy was the answer. By the 1980s, the indirect route was restored to grace and seen in a more favourable light, the alarmist assertions of experience with it were being discredited, and the matching difficulties that attend on travelling the direct route were being increasingly appreciated.

Before I proceed to an analysis of the lessons that we have learnt in consequence of this extensive debate, and what they suggest for Indian public policy on poverty, let me turn to two fallacies that have plagued this debate, making it captive to fractious and misplaced ideological confrontations.

(a) Growth: Target or Instrument?

The first fallacy asserts that growth was a rival target to poverty rather than an instrument to ameliorate it. Indeed, in the 1970s it was commonplace to claim that we had been preoccupied in the 1950s and 1960s with growth, rather than the alleviation of poverty, as our objective. This was the central theme of writings on developmental economics, originating with varying degrees of explicitness from international agencies such as the International Labour Organization (ILO).

Let me confess that this contention may be both true and false. I say this, not in the frolicsome spirit of my good friend, the philosopher Sidney Morgenbesser. On being asked by one of his radical students during the Cultural Revolution whether he thought that Chairman Mao was right in arguing that a proposition could be both true and false, he instantly replied: I do and I don't. Rather, I wish to enter the caveat that developing countries form such a mosaic ranging from city states like Hong Kong to subcontinents such as China, or from democracies like India to dictatorships such as today's Chile and yesterday's Argentina, that almost everything is valid somewhere and almost nothing is true everywhere. I must confess that the enormity of this problem was brought home to me when I, coming from India with its population of over 750 million, recently visited Barbados with a population of 250,000. Asked to talk at the Central Bank, I found myself in the Governor's office on the top floor, only to realize that you could practically look out across the island. There was evidently no sensible distinction here between partial- and general-equilibrium analysis! So, to shield myself, I reminded my audience of the celebrated Mao–Nasser story. On a visit to Peking, Nasser looked unhappy. Concerned, Mao inquired what was wrong. Nasser answered: I am having trouble with my neighbours, the Israelis. How many are there, asked Mao. About two million, Nasser replied. Oh, said Mao, which hotel are they staying at?

I have no doubt that *somewhere* growth became an objective in itself during the early post-war years. Indeed, it may well have in countries where élites identified GNP, and associated size of the national economy, with respectability and strength in the world economy and polity. But, in influential developmental planning circles,[3] GNP was simply regarded as an *instrumental* variable, which would enable planners to impact on the ultimate and *central objective* of reducing poverty.

Indeed, in India, which was the focus of intellectual attention during the 1950s for several reasons, reduction of poverty was explicitly discussed during the late 1950s and early 1960s as the object of our planning efforts. In the Planning Commission, where the great Indian planner Pitambar Pant headed the Perspective Planning Division, work was begun at this time on this precise issue. How could we provide 'minimum incomes' to meet the basic needs of all?

The objective being to provide such minimum incomes, or to ameliorate poverty, rapid growth was decided upon as the principal instrumentality through which this objective could be implemented. Let me explain why we came to focus on growth as the central weapon in our assault on poverty.

I can speak to the issue, as it happens, from the immediacy of

[3] Here, I refer to economists such as myself, B.S. Minhas, K.N. Raj, and T.N. Srinivasan who were actively involved in planning efforts within institutions such as the Indian Planning Commission, and to planners such as Pitambar Pant. That some of the purely academic development economists were preoccupied with models that addressed growth per se, and would discover poverty as an explicit target and as an issue for analysis many years later, is an observation compatible with the fact that some of us at the centre of planning efforts were not so afflicted.

personal experience. For I returned to India during 1961, to join the Indian Statistical Institute which had a small think tank attached to Pant's Division in the Planning Commission. Having been brought in by Pant to work as his chief economist, I turned immediately to the question of strategy for minimum incomes. I assembled such income distribution data as were then available for countries around the world, both functional and personal, to see if anything striking could be inferred about the relationship between the economic and political system, and policies and the share of the bottom three or four deciles. You can imagine the quality of these data then, by looking at their quality now almost a quarter of a century later. Nor did we then have anything systematic on income distribution in the Soviet Union. And we had admittedly nothing on China which was an exotic reality, about to make its historical rendezvous with the Cultural Revolution, but already suggesting to the careful scholar that its economic claims were not to be taken at face value.

The scanning of, and reflection on, the income distribution data suggested that there was no dramatic alternative for raising the poor to minimum incomes except to increase the overall size of the pie. The inter-country differences in the share of the bottom deciles, where poverty was manifestly rampant, just did not seem substantial enough to suggest any alternative path. The strategy of rapid growth was therefore decided upon, in consequence of these considerations, as providing the only reliable way of making a *sustained*, rather than a one-shot, impact on poverty.

I will presently discuss this strategy and its success or failure in some depth.[4] However, let me return to stress the theme that growth was therefore indisputably conceived to be an instrumental variable, not as an objective per se. It is not surprising therefore that the curious assertions to the contrary by institutions and intellectuals who belatedly turned to questions of poverty in the 1970s have provoked many of us who were 'present at the creation' to take the backward glance and then to turn again to stare coldly and with scorn at these non-sensical claims.

[4] I have dealt with the growth strategy at much greater length in my 7th Sir Purshotam Thakurdas Memorial Lecture (Bhagwati 1987) which should therefore be read as a companion piece to this chapter.

Gilbert Etienne, the well-known sociologist-cum-economist, whose heretical and brilliant work on India's Green Revolution I shall soon cite, has exclaimed: 'The claim that development strategies in the 1950s and 1960s overemphasized growth and increases of the GNP at the cost of social progress is a surprising one! . . . Equally peculiar is the so-called discovery of the problem of poverty' (1982: 194, 195). T.N. Srinivasan and B.S. Minhas, both of whom have worked with great distinction on questions of poverty, and who followed me to join Pant's think tank, have been even more critical. I am afraid that I have also been moved to write (1984) in a personal vein: ' . . . on hearing the claim that poverty had only recently been discovered and elevated as a target of development. I fully expected to find that Chapter One of my 1966 volume on *The Economics of Underdeveloped Countries* would be titled Growth; behold my surprise when it turned out to be Poverty and Income Distribution!'

(b) Growth and Ideology: Pull-up versus Trickle-down

The more egregious fallacy, however, has been for several economists and ideologues to assume that the growth-oriented indirect route must necessarily be a conservative option. The more liberal and radical among them have therefore tended to rush to their computers and their pens each time any evidence suggests that the indirect route may be productive of results, seeking to discount and destroy any such inference.

I have never quite understood this phenomenon, for the growth strategy was conceived by us at the start of our planned assault on poverty as an *activist*, interventionist one. The government was to be critically involved in raising internal and external savings, in guiding if not allocating investment, in growing faster so that we could bring gainful employment and increased incomes to more of the poor. Whether the policy framework we worked with in India, of using the indirect growth-based approach, was an appropriate one, and whether this route was efficiently exploited, is a different but critical issue which I will presently address.

Since, therefore, the growth strategy was an activist strategy for impacting on poverty, I have always preferred to call it the *pull-up*, rather than the *trickle-down*, strategy. The trickle-down phrase is reminiscent of 'benign neglect', and its use in the first Reagan administration to accompany efforts at dismantling elements of the welfare state has imparted yet other conservative connotations to it. The pull-up phrase, on the other hand, correctly conveys a more *radical* interventionist image, and the intellectual context in which it emerged was defined by the ethically attractive objective of helping the poor.

Lest it be thought that words do not matter, recall Orwell or the endless battle for the dominant ground between euphemisms and calling a spade a spade. My favourite example from economics is the business schools' preferred use of the word 'multinationals', nudging the subconscious in the direction of multilateralism and hence evoking the image of a benign institution, and the radicals' insistence on calling these international corporations 'transnationals', strongly suggesting transgression.

3. THE INDIRECT, GROWTH-BASED ROUTE: EXPERIENCE AND LESSONS

Let me then turn to the experience with the indirect, growth-based route.

(a) Immiserizing Growth?

It should be conceded immediately that it is easy enough for economists to construct cases where growth will bypass or will even harm the poor. The pious know that affluence can impoverish one's soul; the economist need not be surprised that it can impoverish one's neighbours too. Indeed, in my early scientific work in the late 1950s, I developed a theory of immiserizing growth that established the conditions yielding a yet stronger possibility: growth would immiserize oneself.[5] The precise demonstration concerned an economy where increased productivity led to a sufficiently large deterioration in the terms of trade whose adverse

[5] See Bhagwati (1958). The model used was developed earlier by Johnson (1955) to examine the interactions between growth and trade.

effect outweighed the primary gain from growth. Thus, imagine that extension work leads to farmers raising grain production but this, in turn, lowers the grain price so much that the farmers' income falls instead of rising.

As it happens, the paradox that affluence can immiserize oneself is possible to demonstrate even if the affluence comes from transfer payments. Thus international trade theorists have examined conditions under which the recipient of aid may be immiserized rather than enriched, so that a gift horse turns out to be a Trojan horse instead.[6]

Such self-immiserizing possibilities naturally require more stringent conditions than the possibility that *your* affluence causes *my* misery (even when envy is wholly absent). Thus, consider the scenario where the more affluent farmers adopt the new seeds, grain prices fall, and the marginal farmers who have not adopted the new techniques find their stagnant output yielding less income in consequence. In such a situation, the green revolution immiserizes the poor and, the radicals would hope, may usher in the red revolution.

It is not true that we were unaware of such possibilities, that growth could be a disturbingly uneven process. But the key question was: what should this awareness imply for *policy*? Evidently, you would *first* need to assess both how such unacceptable outcomes would arise in your specific circumstances and the probability of their arising in practice. *Next*, the policy set would have to be augmented to include, in addition to growth, further suitable instruments to prevent these unpleasant outcomes. The former requires judgment, based on empirical assessment; the latter, the possibility of finding suitable and feasible policy instruments.

Let me illustrate by reference to the possibility of immiserizing growth that I cited earlier. In the international context, my 1958 model of immiserizing growth was widely considered relevant, including the distinguished Ragnar Nurkse in his 1959 *Wicksell Lectures*, because of the generally shared empirical assessment that the export markets of the developing countries were extremely tight, implying that the terms of trade would deteriorate sharply

---

[6] Such a paradox may be described as implying an Invisible Shakedown (by the donour). See Bhagwati, Brecher, and Hatta (1984).

as a consequence of growth in the developing countries. But this assessment, not validated by subsequent analysis and events, did *not* imply that growth policy had to be abandoned. Rather, the growth policy had to be supplemented by an appropriate policy of import substitution, so that we would have what Nurkse called 'balanced growth'.[7]

At least in the Indian context, the view taken was that, in the *long haul*, such adverse possibilities could not be the probable, central result of expanding incomes for any sizable group of the poor, but that rather the process would pull up increasing numbers into gainful work.

While, as I have remarked, the limited and sketchy income distribution data revealed little of any consequence on how to improve this pull-up process, there was awareness that the pull-up effect on poverty would improve, *ceteris paribus*, if institutional mechanisms such as special credit facilities for the poor were developed, necessary land reforms were implemented, and the access of the Scheduled and backward classes (which have disproportionate numbers among the poor) to the opportunities provided by a growing economy were enhanced through preferential schemes. *Policy-induced pro-poor bias* was thus to be introduced into the growth process, to offset and outweigh any bias in the opposite direction that the market, interacting with inherited political and social forces, might imply.[8] The concern, therefore, was not with sustained immiserizing outcomes and how to cope with them, but rather with devising policy instruments to bias the growth process towards greater efficacy of the pull-up effects.

There was also a distinct component, in the strategy, of the *direct* route, in the public provision of services such as clean water, sanitation, health services, and education. The primary thrust of the Indian strategy was, however, to rely on the indirect route. This decision reflected the constraints imposed by the

[7] In economic jargon, there is a case for an optimum tariff here. Again, later developments in the theory of immiserizing growth show how it can be ruled out if optimum tariffs are imposed. See Bhagwati (1968, 1986c).

[8] On Indian policies with regard to biasing credit facilities towards the poor, see Tendulkar's (1983) excellent review.

appalling dimensions of India's poverty, and the democratic politics of the country, on our ability to finance a significant reliance
instead on the direct route over a sustained period. Noting the
former constraint on our planning and fiscal efforts, the famous
Polish economist, Michal Kalecki, whose left-wing credentials
were never in doubt, had remarked during his visit to India in
the early 1960s: 'the trouble with India is that there are too few
exploiters and too many exploited'.

(b) The Efficacy of the Growth Strategy

India was the focus of interest and attention in the 1950s; distinguished economists and intellectuals descended on it the way
they do on China today. Our ideas were influential and came to
be widely shared in the efforts by many developing countries to
accelerate their growth-rates. I have argued elsewhere (1984) that
there was a definite optimism during the 1950s and 1960s both
that growth could be rapid and that it would indeed impact on
poverty. But by the early 1970s and later, there were increasing
claims that called the efficacy of this strategy into doubt. The
criticisms took two different forms: (1) that growth was irrelevant
and poverty had increased regardless: a 1977 ILO study (quoted
by Etienne 1982: 198) asserted that 'The number of rural poor in
Asia has increased and in many instances their standard of living
has tended to fall. Perhaps, surprisingly, this has occurred irrespective of whether growth has been rapid or slow or agriculture
has expanded swiftly or sluggishly'; and (ii) that growth had in
fact accentuated poverty: it made the rich richer and the poor
poorer; Ghose and Griffin argued in 1979 that 'It is not lack of
growth but its very occurrence that led to deterioration in the
conditions of the rural poor' (quoted by Etienne 1982: 198).

In assessing these claims of increasing immiserization, or mere
stagnation in living standards, of the poor, it is necessary to examine not just the evidence and its plausibility, but also whether
there was indeed satisfactory growth for the pull-up strategy to
work where it is alleged to have failed. I am persuaded that the
evidence is far less alarming than what it is claimed, that where
growth has been rapid it has impacted on poverty, that in the

Indian case the growth strategy has produced inadequate results because the policy framework for producing growth has produced inadequate growth in the first place, and hence that the Indian experience suggests lessons in favour of superior growth-producing policies rather than lessons against using the growth-based indirect route to affecting poverty.

(i) *International Experience*

Let me first stress that countries such as South Korea and Taiwan, which have grown much faster than us in the post-war period to date, have had a substantial impact on their living standards. To see the force of the argument, that India's poor growth performance has affected its prospects for raising living standards, it is useful to understand the force of compound interest. 'Had India's GDP grown as rapidly from 1960 to 1980 as South Korea's, it would stand at $531 billion today rather than $150 billion — surpassing that of the UK, equal to that of France, and more than twice that of China. India's per capita income would have been $740 instead of $260; even with the benefits of growth inequitably distributed, it is not unreasonable to believe that most of the poor would have been substantially better off.'[9] I shall, therefore, return to the question of our policy framework for promoting growth, especially as the moves towards a New Economic Policy were designed to remedy the deficiencies afflicting that framework.

(ii) *Indian Experience*

But, even with the relatively dismal growth-rate we have had, the evidence is more compelling that some dent has been made on poverty than the doom-and-gloom analysts have often suggested.

The evidence of the National Sample Surveys of consumption is an important source of information here. So are household income and other surveys. Before I sketch what these imply, it is pertinent to remark that many non-economist observers have been

[9] This graphic comparison and scenario come from Myron Weiner's (1986) interesting analysis of the political economy of India's appallingly slow growth-rate, with much of which I am in agreement. I should stress that, in using South Korea's growth-rate to make this comparison compelling, I do *not* mean to imply that we could have improved our economic performance quite that much!

sceptical of the reliability of this type of evidence. Distinguished
social and economic anthropologists such as M.N. Srinivas, Louis
Dumont, and Polly Hill have remarked, with varying degrees of
candidness, on the quality of Indian data on the subject: and, mind
you, these are generally regarded as possibly the best statistics in
the developing world. The concepts are inadequate; the implementation yet poorer. Polly Hill (1984: 495) has written in frustration
and with evident exaggeration that, India's pride, 'the All-India
National Sample survey is perhaps the most remarkable example
of wasted statistical effort in the entire world!' Srinivas has com-
plained of the brilliant mathematical statisticians who devise and
direct the massive questionnaires to be filled out by field investigators that 'This kind of study cannot be left to the hit and run
method of an inferior class of investigators who commute from the
cities to nearby villages'. It is not entirely unreasonable therefore
to rely, at least for an alternative view of the matter, on the results
from the 'naked eye' anthropological-cum-longitudinal approach to
make the required inferences.

   Here, I must confess that I have been much impressed by the
analysis of Gilbert Etienne (1982), who has argued convincingly
from first hand evidence from extended stays in a number of
Indian villages that he surveyed earlier, that poverty has indeed
been impacted on, and that too where agricultural growth has
occurred. Etienne's technique is to do what I call 'doing in India
what you do in China', i.e. disregard the numbers (which in any
case are not available in a reliable fashion for China which has
only recently opened itself to a measured degree of external and
internal scrutiny and independent analysis) and carefully assess
what you see. He has gone back over time to several villages that
he had looked at intensively, often more than a decade earlier.
And he observes, asks, examines, and records: much like Jan
Myrdal (1966) in his celebrated Report from Liu Ling but with
more anthropological, sociological, and economic discipline and
less poetry. The results are what we did expect: growth has indeed
pushed several of the poor on in life. Doubtless, some poor have
been left behind; others have been impoverished even further.
But then, as Arthur Lewis has wisely remarked, it is inherent in
the developmental process that some see the opportunities and

seize them, leaving others behind until they wish to and can follow. Politics and economics can both constrain the capacity of the laggards to follow. Thus, for instance, the green revolution in some instances may well have polarized the distribution of property in the countryside, enriching the farmers with access to credit, fertilizers, and irrigation, and immiserizing those who did not. But, if Etienne is correct, this has not happened in anything like a significant degree in his cross-section of villages in India. Of course, what Etienne observes may be true only for 'his villages'. But his unscientific sample is compensated in some degree by the closer scrutiny and care that the scientific surveys evidently do not possess. What do the latter show?

As it happens, even the statistical evidence from these surveys is corroborative, if not wholly conclusive, of the fact that the proportion of the poor below an accepted poverty line has diminished and strongly suggestive of the hypothesis that growth has been a proximate cause of the reduction in poverty.

The recently published estimates of a team headed by B.S. Minhas, who has distinguished himself for pioneering work on estimating poverty, along with other noted economists such as Dandekar and Rath (1971), are perhaps the most carefully constructed sets of poverty statistics on the subject.[10] They utilize new consumer prices for updating the base-year poverty lines and re-examine the recent calculations of the Planning Commission which had suggested a dramatic decrease in the proportion of the poor in the last decade.[11] It is noteworthy that, while their calculations reduce the degree of improvement estimated by the Planning Commission, they conclude that 'The incidence of poverty in 1983 in terms of proportion of people below the poverty line was substantially lower than the corresponding estimates for the 1970s' (Minhas et al. 1987: 47), though there is no evidence of a fall in the absolute *numbers* below the poverty line and, if anything, there may be a small rise in these numbers, reflecting of course the dual pressure and double squeeze of a low growth rate and a rising population.

[10] Minhas, Jain, Kansal, and Saluja (1987).
[11] These estimates continue to use the definition of poverty line adopted by the Indian Planning Commission in the mid-1970s.

Again, I must note that Minhas's early work (1970, 1971) had drawn attention to the fact that the incidence of poverty goes down in years of good harvests and up in years of bad harvests. This phenomenon is reconfirmed in his recent estimates (Minhas et al. 1987).

My distinguished former student, K. Sundaram of the Delhi School of Economics, who has done notable work with Suresh Tendulkar (1983a, 1983b, 1983c) on the poverty problem, has correctly reminded us (1986) that this relationship requires us to be cautious in inferring any trend in decline of the poverty ratio from the two observations for 1977–8 and 1983 on whose basis we have had to work as far as the estimates based on the NSS Consumer Expenditure Surveys are concerned.[12] The poverty ratio has fluctuated sharply with agricultural production and the time-series evidence suggests that no trend should be inferred unless more data points are available: the two pleasant observations may simply be reflective of good harvests rather than a better trend.

But this very critique or cautious reminder implies that indeed, as Minhas had noted, there *is* some evidence for the favourable impact of growth on poverty, at least in the rural sector.

In fact, Montek Ahluwalia's classic 1978 paper on rural poverty and agricultural performance had analysed all-India time-series data to underline this precise link. This work has also provoked controversy, with the radical response being provided by Saith (1981) who has drawn the opposite conclusions while working with the same data set. Careful analysis of the two papers by Subodh Mathur (1985), examining both the econometrics and the economics of the issue, reaches the conclusion that 'aggregate all-India data support Ahluwalia's contention that agricultural growth reduces poverty'.

However, Srinivasan (1985), who has raised several compelling objections to the econometric procedures and inferences in Saith's analysis, also cautions that Ahluwalia's results, which are only confirmed by inclusion of additional data which have become available since 1978 (Ahluwalia 1985), should not be treated as a decisive test of the pull-up hypothesis. For, the data show

[12] These surveys are available on an annual basis almost continually up to 1973–4 but only for 1977–8 and 1983 thereafter.

that 'there was no upward trend in net domestic product of agriculture per head of rural population – there was very little to trickle-down at the all-India level'. Discussing also the related work by Bardhan (1982), utilizing some state-level data of still less reliability, Srinivasan has concluded that meaningful tests with more and better longitudinal data than have been available are necessary, by regions or areas differentiated by high and low growth-rates, before firm conclusions can be drawn on the issue. But the existing analyses do favour the presumption, for the present, that the effect of growth is to reduce, rather than to bypass or exacerbate, poverty.

Other sources of evidence also suggest that, while poverty remains appalling in its dimensions, it has diminished at least as a proportion of the population. Thus, a careful examination of the estimates of income distribution for India by Bhalla and Vashishtha (1985) concludes that household income surveys (as distinct from NSS surveys-based estimates discussed above) indicate that if households are ranked by per capita incomes, neither the bottom 20 per cent nor the bottom 40 per cent exhibit any significant change in their share of income between 1964-5 and 1975-6. At the same time, of course, per capita income had increased, so that a constant share would imply a higher absolute level, indicating a decline in poverty. Again, however, these surveys suffer from serious difficulties of comparability, arising from differences in definitions and coverage. Comparable data sets relate only to 1970-1 and 1975-6 for the large rural sector: and these again indicate favourable conclusions.

Furthermore, the two recent NCAER longitudinal, nationwide surveys of identical households for 1970-1 and 1981-2 have suggested that, even in the lowest three deciles, there has been a significant rise of households across the poverty line. The proportions who did so are as high as 46 per cent, 41 per cent, and 54 per cent for the lowest, the second-lowest, and the next deciles. The results are indeed remarkable, suggesting both that poverty can be impacted and that it has been. Again, however, trends cannot be inferred from two observations; and there are problems, noted by K. Sundaram (1986: 21-8), with the sample size relating to the poor households and with the fact that there is no way in which it can be inferred whether the households changed their fortunes due to increased productivity and income or due to demographic factors. But, when all this is noted, the fact remains that these surveys yield results that do not provide support for the hypothesis of stagnation or immiserization in the living standards of the poor.

(iii) *Growth and the New Economic Policy*

If then much of this evidence, with all warts duly registered, suggests some success in assaulting poverty, and this too with our only limited success in enhancing growth, the key question becomes: why has our growth been so disappointing?

Our record of growth is admittedly one of acceleration over the pre-Independence period and compares well with that of countries in the nineteenth century. But we need to remember that this is the case with most of the developing countries in the post-war period and that, compared to *them*, we appear as unfortunate laggards.

Indeed, most of us were pleasantly surprised, despite our optimism, at the remarkable growth-rates turned up by the developing countries after World War II. The reasons are probably self-evident. Whereas the pre-Industrial Revolution growth-rates were dependent largely on capital accumulation, they increased in the post-Industrial Revolution period because of unprecedented technical change. The developing countries, by contrast, could combine increasing rates of external and internal savings with influx of off-the-shelf technology and thus grow very rapidly. Many did.

The productivity of the increased rates of investment has, however, varied, depending on the policy framework within which the economy operated. There is sufficient evidence, in my judgment, that our policy framework degenerated by the early 1960s on critical fronts, confining us to a trend growth-rate of roughly 3.5 per cent per annum or about 1.5 per cent per capita growth-rate annually.[13]

[13] Many statistical tests have cast continuing doubt on the question whether our growth-rate has finally accelerated in the decade 1978–88. all plausible ways of splitting the period 1950 to 1984 turn up conclusions that suggest unchanged

Despite an almost three-quarters increase in our fixed invest-ment rate over the period 1950–84, we had little improvement in the growth-rate. If we break the period into 1951 to 1965 (coinciding roughly with the Nehru and pre-wheat-revolution era) and 1968 to 1984 (omitting the two severe drought years of 1965–6 and 1966–7), the trend growth-rate is 3.88 per cent in the former period and 3.75 per cent in the latter, there being no statistically significant difference between the two rates (Bhagwati and Srinivasan 1984). The decadal average percentage growth rate of the 1950s (3.59 per cent), 1960s (3.13 per cent) and 1970s (3.62 per cent) are also similar. Evidently, we got our policy framework wrong.

Economic analysis is often unable to detect unique causes of the phenomena being explained. In this instance also the con-tributory factors are by no means the only two I shall cite; but they are certainly among the most important.[14] The first relates to the excessive and explosive growth of controls over industry and foreign trade until the most recent changes; the second concerns the failure to exploit the advantage of foreign trade.

The growth of controls turned our governmental intervention, so necessary in a developing country, into a counterproductive one. A government of 'don'ts' will stifle initiative; it will also divert entrepreneurial energies into a number of wasteful rent-seeking and other directly unproductive profit-seeking (DUP) activities. By contrast, a government of 'do's', such as that which the suc-cessful countries of the Far East have had, is likely to harness its people's energies more productively, even if its prescriptions are periodically mistaken. It is an increasing appreciation of these questions, and the sense that our Kafkaesque maze of controls could not possibly be sensible, that led me and others during the late 1960s, and recently many others, to call for a progressive dismantling of this monstrous constraint on our economic efforts. I may mention in particular that I.G. Patel, who oversaw our economic policy with distinction for much of this period, recently

---

trends. See Bhagwati and Srinivasan (1984), and Joshi and Little (1986), among other analyses of these trends.

[14] I have discussed these and other explanations at greater length in the 7th Sir Purshotam Thakurdas Memorial Lecture (Bhagwati 1987).

took the occasion of the Kingsley Martin Memorial Lecture to join us, in our corner and ask dramatically for a 'bonfire' of the industrial licencing system.[15]

As for the inability we have exhibited in exploiting the gains from trade in a world economy that grew at unprecedented rates in the 1950s and 1960s, and which still continues to absorb rapidly expanding exports from the developing countries, the explanation lies in what social scientists call the 'self-fulfilling prophecy'. Despite all evidence to the contrary, our planning and policy framework was continually based on what economists call 'export pessimism'. The failure to use the exchange rate actively to encourage exports, as in other countries, the inflexibilities (introduced by the pervasive controls) which must handicap the ability to penetrate and hold fiercely competitive foreign markets, the protection and hence attractiveness of the home market: these policies produced a dismal export performance, while other successful countries expanded their exports rapidly and greatly gained in economic growth.[16] How dismal our export performance has been can be readily understood by noting that our share in world exports was only 0.41 per cent by 1981, having fallen almost continually since 1948 when it was 2.4 per cent. This certainly affected even our industrial sector's growth. For, other countries which began with a much smaller industrial base are not only exporting more manufactures than India but, what is more striking, catching up with India in the absolute size of their manufacturing sector. The size of Korea's manufacturing sector, for example, was less than 25 per cent of India's in 1970 (measured as value-added). By 1981, it was already up to 60 per cent. Korea's manufactured

---

[15] See Patel (1986). He is fully aware, of course, that the elimination of this system is a *goal* whereas the *process* will require extremely careful management. Whether the growth of interests supportive of this system, over its existence in the 1958–88 period will pose insuperable obstacles to its removal is an issue in political economy that I discuss at greater length elsewhere: Bhagwati (1986a, 1986d, 1987).

[16] This is not the place to report yet again on the numerous research projects that showed in the 1960s and 1970s how export pessimism had been unjustified but had led to dismal export, and in turn to dismal economic, performance in many countries. Useful reviews of this research are not available; see Bhagwati (1986b) and Balassa (1986).

exports, negligible in 1962, amounted by 1980 to nearly four times those of India's![17] Simply put, we missed the bus.

I agree that we could not have grown as fast as the Far Eastern economies, the Gang of Four (as I christened them with success many years ago) or the Four Tigers, because we had a much larger agricultural base. Our agriculture, I agree again with Professors Dantwala (1970) and Srinivasan (1982) among others, grew about as fast as could be expected and charges of its neglect are seriously exaggerated.[18] But to infer from this that India could not have grown much faster than it did is to forget again the force of compound arithmetic: non-agricultural growth, in an economy geared to rapidly expanding trade and non-agricultural production, would have provided a growing impetus to the economy, steadily overwhelming the agricultural sector's importance in both value-added and employment.

(iv) *Growth Patterns*

How would such a shift to an export-promoting strategy have affected the pull-up process of creating more gainful employment? The proponents of the import-substituting strategy, on which we continued to place total reliance instead, have suggested that the export-promoting strategy would have been less productive of employment, even if it may have resulted in greater efficiency. Quite aside from the fact that the empirical evidence suggests that the export promoting strategy implies in practice faster growth and impact on poverty, there is yet further evidence that, even in the short run, export promotion has been associated with more labour-intensive investment and production. I refer here to the important findings of Professor Anne Krueger (1983) and her associates in her major three-volume study of this subject. The export-promoting strategy has not merely led to more rapid income growth but also produced greater increase in demand for labour, *ceteris paribus*. A major reason is the labour-intensiveness of export industries in the export-strategy-led countries.

[17] See Bhagwati and Srinivasan (1984).
[18] Ibid.

(v) *Growth and Political Economy Constraints*

Why did these serious deficiencies afflict our planning efforts? The question belongs to the new field of political economy. In particular, my theory of the causes and consequences of proliferation controls is that initially they were the product of ideas and ideology, then they led to the growth of interests, and now as the ideas and ideology have shifted these interests pose a critical obstacle to the desired shift of strategy.

At the outset, few of us realized that controls could proliferate in the way they did. In the early 1950s industrial controls appeared to be sensible instruments, to allocate resources in directions worked out in the Planning Commission. Industrial licencing would eliminate excess capacity by regulating entry; scarce resources would be channelled in optimal directions. Pretty soon, however, the promotional agencies such as the DGTD had largely turned into restrictive and regulatory agencies instead; and in no time we were operating in a regime where an entrepreneur could not even exceed licenced capacity or diversify production lines in any way without retribution. A strait-jacket had evolved from what seemed like a reasonable economic approach to investment allocation.

This economic regime spawned its own interests. The rentier society it yielded, with entrepreneurs enjoying squatters' rights, created a business class that wanted liberalization in the sense of less botheration rather than genuine competition. The bureaucrats, however idealistic at the outset, could not but have noticed that this regime gave them the enormous power that the ability to confer rents generates. The politics of corruption also followed as politicians became addicted to the use of licencing to generate illegal funds for elections, and then for themselves. The iron triangle of businessmen, bureaucrats, and politicians was born around the regime that economists and like-minded ideologues had unwittingly espoused.

As ideas have now changed, through the process of 'learning by undoing', these interests now stand in the way of rapid, if any, change. While the erstwhile partnership of the Prime Minister Rajiv Gandhi and the then Finance Minister Vishwanath Pratap

Singh was apparently determined to take the necessary steps to embark on a programme of removing the strait-jacket on the Indian economy, and their leadership was evidently of great importance in sharply defining a promise of new policies, the hesitations and obstacles from both the intellectuals of the older vintage and the interests of the iron triangle have been manifest, raising acutely the question whether the early momentum for change can be politically maintained.[19]

(vi) *Pro-Poor Bias Policies and Political Economy Constraints*

I am afraid that the pro-poor-bias policies have equally run into difficulties, arising from unequal asset distribution and hence unequal political power at the grass-roots level. The degree of success of policies armed at improving the pull-up effects of the growth process is evidently a function of the extent to which 'countervailing power' is available to the poor through the presence of social action groups and politically viable opposition parties.[20]

Here again, however, I should like to emphasize that, in the longer run, substantial growth itself is a factor generating the necessary countervailing power through the market-place, by raising the demand for labour and increasing its opportunity cost. I hypothesize that the relative success of tenancy reform in Gujerat must have also some relationship to the fact that many of those who 'lost their lands' to it had little incentive to fight and evade the reform in view of the fact that they had already shifted to urban careers and the transaction costs of the efforts at evasion were in consequence just too high.

[19] That the interests followed the ideology and now constrain a shift in the ideology is a thesis different from that of Professor Pranab Bardhan (1985) who differs from me both in starting from the interests and also in relating them wholly to public sector losses and therewith to slow growth. I have discussed the role of public sector savings in India's slow growth at some length in the Sir P.T. Memorial Lecture, again emphasizing the early role of ideas and the *subsequent* role of interests.

[20] Evidence on the relationship of party politics to the successful implementation of anti-poverty programmes have been ably analysed recently by the Princeton political scientist Atul Kohli (1987).

(vii) *Radical Restructuring: Why Not?*

Let me add some remarks about radical restructuring of the asset structure and transition to fuller socialism à la China and Cuba as possible alternatives to our policies for creating a sustained impact on poverty.

I am afraid that the scepticism that marked the enthusiasm for the Chinese experiment appears to have only been reinforced by later developments. In the 1950s it was often thought that if only a Chinese revolution could be ushered into the developing countries, its triumphs in eliminating poverty could be replicated. The scepticism lingered because systematic scrutiny of the Chinese claims was not possible; and there was legitimate cause for wonder whether absolute poverty had truly been reduced and also whether growth could be sustained within the new framework, raising questions about the sustainability of the immediate impact on poverty. Now, after the window has steadily opened wider in the aftermath of the Cultural Revolution and the failures of the Great Leap Forward, we are not sure at all.

We know now that the barefoot doctors generally wore shoes; that their professional competence occasionally exceeded only marginally that of the average grandmother; and that doctors have dragged their feet almost as successfully as elsewhere when assigned to go to the countryside — indeed to the point where Liu-shao-chi's major crimes were declared by the Red Guards and official pronouncements to include sabotage of the campaign to carry doctors to the rural areas. We are further told that the Chinese concept of equality was intra-commune, *not* between communes: the rich communes did not generally share their affluence with those that were destitute. And we are now told by the new regime that over ten per cent of the Chinese population may be below a rather austere poverty line.

These tantalizing glimpses into China's assault on poverty will almost certainly not be allowed to develop into a fuller picture as in other developing countries, since careful and unfettered scholarly scrutiny is unlikely to be possible in the degree necessary. I am afraid therefore that we shall have to reconcile ourselves to the uncomfortable situation where we do not know for certain the extent to which China's ex ante egalitarian methods failed ex post, and whether the failures were due to discordance between their announced and true objectives or due to the limitations of the methods used to achieve the announced objectives.

(viii) *Equitable Asset Distribution*

On the other hand, the proposition that a more equitable distribution of assets at the start of the growth process will generally imply that the new incomes will, in turn, be distributed better is of course quite plausible. In the end, over a longer period, the forces that generate inequality will tend to unequalize the outcomes. But over a generation or two, the net outcomes would be more equal than if we were to start with unequal distribution of assets. The experience of South Korea and Taiwan, where Japanese occupation is largely credited with having brought about the initial asset-ownership equalization, well underlines this near-truism. Also the experience in India, where several micro-level studies have shown the link between asset-ownership and new-income distribution to be a significant factor in a fair number of cases, only underlines the wisdom of supplementing the growth-oriented approach with policy measures that counter this bias (Tendulkar 1983).

A policy of 'redistribution with growth', where the redistribution of assets *precedes* the growth that is designed to impact on poverty, has therefore been advocated by several distinguished economists.[21] If such redistribution can be undertaken politically,

[21] See Adleman and Morris (1973) and Chenery et al. (1974). In this generic class of strategies. I would also include an altogether different kind of proposal that I made for Indian planners to consider in 1973 in the Lal Bahadur Shastri lectures. I argued for a fractional nationalization of land in each village (or similar unit), which could be set apart to form a Chinese-style commune. Those destitute who wished to follow the slow and protracted route offered by the Indian strategy of predominantly relying on growth to impact on poverty, would take their chances there; but those who wished to gain employment and some income right away would have immediate access to the commune à la China. The combination of both strategies, and access to either *by choice*, would mean that the destitute would not be forced into the Indian option of freedom but slow poverty alleviation *or* into the Chinese option of freedom through forced removal to the communes but more rapid and, hopefully, a sustained eradication of abject poverty.

and its implementation is not disruptive economically (as was the case with Soviet collectivization),[22] we can only rejoice.

(ix) *From Income to Consumption*

We also face, even when incomes have reached the poor, a final set of dilemmas.

First, as the sociologists of poverty have long known, the poor may spend their incomes on frills rather than on food. As the Japanese proverb goes: each worm to his taste; some prefer nettles. Perhaps you have heard of the seamen's folklore which recounts the story of the sailor who inherited a fortune, spent a third on women, a third on gin, and 'frittered away' the rest.

Indeed, there is now considerable econometric evidence, reviewed splendidly by Behrman and Deolalikar (1987c), that supports the common-sense view that increases in income do not automatically result in nutritional improvement even for very poor and malnourished populations.[23] Their high income elasticities of expenditure on food reflect a strong demand for the non-nutritive attributes of food (such as taste, aroma, status, and variety), strongly suggesting that income generation will not automatically translate into better nutrition.

For those of us who feel that certain basic needs ought to be satisfied, this tragic assertion of what economists have come to call rather extravagantly 'consumer sovereignty' leaves us confronting a familiar moral–philosophical issue. Should we actively intervene so that the poor are seduced into better fulfilment of what we regard as their basic needs? I do. Indeed, I see great virtue in quasi-paternalistic moves to induce, by supply and taste-shifting policy measures, more nutrient food intake, greater use of clean water, among other things, by the poor. In thus compromising the principle of unimpeded and uninfluenced choice, for the poor and not for others, evidently I adopt the moral–philosophical position that I do not care if the rich are

[22] These are hazards that do not seem to have afflicted China since the elimination of the kulaks seems to have occurred principally during the long civil war itself. See Desai (1975).

[23] For a fine review of India's experience with interventions to fill nutritional gaps at the households level, see Subbarao (1987).

malnourished from feeding on too many cakes but do if the poor are malnourished from buying too little bread, when their incomes can buy them both proper nourishment if only they were to choose to do so. In this, I am in the ethical company of Sofya (Sonia) Marmeladova in Dostoevsky's *Crime and Punishment* who, in turning to prostitution to support her destitute mother, sacrifices virtue for a greater good.

(x) *Whose Consumption: Gender et al.*

Next, in addition to the first, is the other dilemma: that even when households have consumed what is desirable and adequate on a per capita basis, its distribution within the household may be such as to deprive the weaker members, such as females, of an adequate access to the consumption basket. In the 1970s I was somewhat isolated (Bhagwati 1973) as an economist in being seriously interested in the sex-bias that was visible in the statistics on educational enrolments, literacy, infant mortality, and nutritional levels, much of the evidence coming from anthropological findings and other surveys.[24]

Now, almost a decade later, many others have followed and are actively analysing the problem so that we now know more, though not enough, about this key component of our problems in improving living standards. Among the important findings, I should note the Behrman and Deolalikar (1987b) result that the intra-household discrimination may not merely be in the form of lower quantities of food/nutrients allocated to weaker members such as females, but may also occur in the form of greater fluctuations in the quantities allocated to them in response to adverse food price changes.

Additional policy instruments are evidently necessary to offset this bias if the elimination of poverty is to occur more rapidly and equitably. The task here is clearly harder than simply generating more income; and progress in the matter may have to depend on the spread of education in the first place.

---

[24] See, for instance, Sundaram (1973), Rosenzweig, and Schultz (1982), Sen (1984), and Kakwani (1986).

4. The Direct Route: Experience and Lessons

What then have we learnt about the direct route, its efficacy and productivity?

It is important to enter the caveat immediately that the key issue is not whether this route produces results but rather its productivity relative to that of the indirect route. It would be astonishing indeed if greater public health expenditures or direct income transfers did not produce some improvement in the living standards of the poor, even though it is not beyond the ingenuity of economists to produce paradoxes of immiserization in this area too.[25]

(a) Eating Your Cake and Having it Too

At the outset, it is worth noting that there are significant externalities for growth itself from expenditures on publicly provided services. Many of us have been surprised, though pleasantly this time, by the realization that we had exaggerated our early fears about the trade-off between 'consumption' expenditures (such as financing education and health) and investment expenditures aimed at growth and hence ultimate impact on poverty. It is difficult today to appreciate the widespread notion in the 1950s that primary education was simply a 'natural right', whose implementation reflected the availability of resources. That it was possibly an important means for raising productivity and hence growth and therefore reducing poverty, and that it could therefore be justified also on consequentialist ethics, was a later phenomenon. This holds equally for health expenditures which were viewed with inhibited enthusiasm also for fear that they would exacerbate population growth. Only later were they considered to have a possible productivity-enhancing effect on populations that could otherwise be working at impaired efficiency or even to

---

[25] Eg., a successful anti-malaria programme may increase population pressure, reduce real wages, affect nutritional intake of the poor and disproportionately depress their living standards inclusive of their own life expectancy. Economists who like immiserization paradoxes on the indirect route should also look out for them on the direct route.

lead to a lowering of the birth rates if, by reducing infant mortality and increasing survival rates, they enabled parents to produce fewer babies to wind up with their target family size in a steady state.

Much of the currently available indirect or 'macro' evidence on this issue has recently been ably reviewed by Bela Balassa (1983). Thus, for instance, Correa (1970) has argued that improvements in health (proxied by reductions in death rates and in work days lost) and nutrition (measured as increases in calorie intake) added 0.12 to 0.93 percentage points, and improvements in education (measured as the average level of education of the working force) added 0.05 to 0.53 percentage points to the rate of economic growth in nine Latin American countries during 1950–62. Again, Norman Hicks (1980) has estimated that a ten year increase in life expectancy raises per capita GDP growth rates by 1.1 percentage points and a ten percentage point increase in literacy rates by 0.3 percentage points.

But, of course, health and education expenditures affect growth *and* the other way around. Simple regressions can therefore be misleading and simultaneous estimation is necessary. David Wheeler (1980) and Robin Marris (1982) have done precisely this, the former for 88 developing countries for 1960–73 and 1970–3 as well as pooled data for the whole period, the latter for 37 middle-income and 29 low-income countries for 1965–73 and for 1973–8. Wheeler's findings indicate significant impact on growth-rates from increases in calorie intake and literacy rates. Marris's study found that primary education enrolments had a favourable effect on growth-rates of per capita income whereas increased life expectancy and family planning helped through reductions in the rate of growth of population (Balassa 1983: 10–11).

But more compelling is the direct, 'micro' evidence linking health, in particular, to productivity. I should note here the recent econometric work on Indian data by Deolalikar (1988), though there is by now a substantial literature that analyses the issue both theoretically and econometrically.

More is known now, therefore, to wean us away from the fear that such educational and health expenditures are *necessarily* at the expense of growth. What is equally pleasurable is the fact that many of these arguments apply with yet greater force when the expenditures are addressed to the poorer segments of the population. The case for undertaking more such expenditures, with focus on the poor, consistent with being engrossed in the growth strategy, is therefore now seen to be stronger than ever before.[26] I think we have learnt that, within reasonable margins, we may then be able to eat our cake and have it too. Social expenditures could improve the welfare of the poor both directly and indirectly through growth which in turn would impact on poverty. But beyond these margins, the trade-off remains an issue.

(b) Political Economy Constraints

At the same time, as Lakdawala (1986) has recently emphasized, income expansion itself can be a precondition for utilization of the publicly-provided services. For, such income can 'take care of the incidental expenditure incurred in using these facilities' (p. 392).[27]

Indeed, this observation underlines the fact that the political economy factors that have prompted and also constrained the measures to offset the anti-poor biases in the growth-based in-direct route are unlikely to disappear when we turn to the direct route. Thus, nutrition programmes through schools go to those who attend schools and therefore will not seriously impact on the poor whose children do not get to school: a phenomenon already noted by researchers in the 1970s. The successful impar-tation of a pro-poor bias in direct expenditures for improvement of living standards is, in my experience, likely therefore to face difficulties somewhat parallel to those faced in the pursuit of the

---

[26] On the other hand, the difficulties of directing the expenditures on primary education and health effectively to the poorer classes when the élites control the political system need to be recalled. Questions such as the relative priority attached to primary and higher education in state spending and its relationship to the class nature of the state have been discussed at length by economists such as Samuel Bowles and myself. See the extended analysis in my 'Education, Class Structure and Income Equality' (1973a).

[27] This observation is also corroborated by the careful study of the regional variations in the impact of India's Anti-Poverty programmes by Subbarao (1985).

pro-poor-bias policies in the indirect, growth-based route.[28] In the 1970s, when the indirect growth-based route's productivity was being significantly understated in international discussions, as I have already argued, the productivity of the direct route was being overstated by ignoring the politico–economic constraints that also afflict the latter.

(c) Overstated Productivity?

The productivity of the direct route may have been overstated also through an overly-optimistic inference from two allegedly outstanding success stories widely cited in this literature: Sri Lanka and Cost Rica.

As it happens, however, a brilliant analysis of Sri Lanka by Bhalla (1985a, 1985b) and then by Bhalla and Glewwe (1985, 1986) has called this story into question. Apparently, Sri Lanka's claim to attention consisted in substantial direct expenditures and also splendid performance on indices such as literacy, life expectancy, and infant mortality rates which were then assumed to be a result of these direct expenditures. But these indicators were already remarkably high by 1948: a fact that was not allowed for in the argumentation which relied astonishingly on single-time-period cross-country comparisons.[29] When *changes* in these indices are considered for 1960–78, it turns out that Sri Lanka's performance on these criteria shrinks into mediocrity. Of six indicators analysed, for only two — life expectancy and the death rate — does Sri Lanka do better than average; and, if a strict statistical test is used, only the death rate survives to fit this bill.

With this reversal of conclusions based on changes in, rather than on levels of, the performance indicator,[30] the question arises

[28] This is evident also from the important in-depth analysis of the working of the NREP programme in Gujarat State by Indira Hirway (1986a, 1986b).

[29] This argument was advanced by Isenman (1980) and Sen (1981), among others.

[30] The lack of availability of data on changes in levels of direct expenditures prevents us from drawing more compelling inferences here, as noted by Bhalla (1985) himself. Also, such evidence as is available on changes in educational expenditures does not help Bhalla's critics either: See Bhalla and Glewwe (1986) and the later animated comments by Pyatt (1987) and Isenman (1987), and the riposte by Glewwe and Bhalla (1987).

whether the *low* performances of Sri Lanka in this recent post-war period reflects low growth-rates, reinforcing exactly the opposite conclusion to what is presumably being contended! As it happens, estimates of Sri Lanka's per capita income growth show that, during 1960–78, Sri Lanka had a negative annual growth rate of − 1.2 per cent along with only five other countries including Burundi, Benin, and Angola! Can it be that the diversion of expenditures away from growth to ('social') direct expenditures affected growth adversely and hence impacted on the poor more than the direct expenditures helped them? Or were economic policies so bad that growth was adversely affected and impacted on the poor, and increased direct expenditures had to be undertaken to offset the adversity for the poor? In short, the mediocrity of Sri Lanka's in performance on the living standards of the poor may be explainable by hypotheses that only sustain the advisability of assigning primacy to the growth-oriented route to ameliorating poverty.

Of course we can still speculate as to what made Sri Lanka in 1948 such as impressive performer on living standards. Was it high growth-rates or high social expenditures? Was the productivity of the latter high due to specific, manageable problems such as malaria which could be eradicated relatively easily with public health anti-malaria programmes and therefore has little value in inferring general prescriptions? Only detailed historical analysis, carefully sifting among different hypotheses, can throw light on the issue at hand. In the meantime, the ready over-optimism that the early writings on Sri Lanka's post-war experience reflected and spread must be suspended.

5. Concluding Observations

In the end, therefore, I see no quick fix to our immense poverty problem. We can debate whether resources can be moved further at the margin from the indirect, growth-based route to the direct, minimum needs route. But the most important lesson seems to be that, *within* each route, we can and must get significantly more returns than we have to date.

Within the indirect route, the New Economic Policy initiatives point in the right direction and, if successfully brought to fruition, promise a significantly greater impact on poverty in the next two decades than we have had with our inappropriate policy framework and dismal economic performance. Within the direct route, there is continual improvement being sought of course, and an economist has little expertise to offer. Efforts such as integrated, block-level development programmes and the introduction of the village community health workers et al. are the fruit of ongoing processes of learning by experience: they ought to yield results over time.[31]

I have two further thoughts in conclusion. That our low growth rate seems to have reduced our poverty ratio but left the absolute numbers of the poor at an appalling level of over 300 million, suggests not merely that we must doggedly pursue the New Economic Policy initiatives. It also underlines the critical role of a successful population control programme. Derailed by the draconian measures during the Emergency, this programme needs to be pushed vigorously if the fruits of growth are not to be squandered on supporting increasing numbers rather than improving the well-being of fewer people.

At the same time, the political economy constraints on both the indirect and direct routes' ability to reach the poor more effectively, despite governmental attempts at offsetting these biases, underline the overarching importance of the role of voluntary agencies and social action groups. The ex ante intention of the enlightened sectors of our governments will not effectively translate in many instances into ex post outcomes in our assault on poverty without the active association of such agencies.

These social action groups do not merely aid the poor directly but also by acting as watchdogs that assist the poor in securing effective access to the programmes designed by the government for their benefit. This is the lesson, for example, of the Legal Aid Programme in India where the coopting of such agencies has proved to be an essential ingredient in making the programme

---

[31] See the excellent review of these problems and their possible solutions in Lakdawala (1985), based on his tenure as Deputy Chairman of the Planning Commission.

more productive. Indeed, private and public altruism have, therefore, a critically complementary role in creating a shared success
in the assault on poverty.

REFERENCES

Adelman, Irma and Cynthia Taft Morris, 1976: *Economic Growth and Social
    Equity in Developing Countries* (Stanford, CA: Stanford University
    Press, 1973).

Ahluwalia, Montek S., 1976: 'Inequality, Poverty and Development', *Jour-
    nal of Development Economics*, vol. 3.

——, 1978: 'Rural Poverty and Agricultural Performance in India', *Journal
    of Development Studies*, vol. 14.

——, 1985: 'Rural Poverty, Agricultural Production and Prices: A
    Re-examination', *in* John Mellor and Gunvant Desai (eds), *Agricul-
    tural Change and Rural Poverty: Variations on a Theme by Dharam
    Narain* (Baltimore, MD: Johns Hopkins University Press).

Ahluwalia, Montek S., Nicholas G. Carter and Hollis B. Chenery, 1979:
    'Growth and Poverty in Developing Countries', *Journal of Develop-
    ment Economics*, vol. 6.

Balassa, Bela, 1983: 'Public Finance and Social Policy – Explanation of
    Trends and Developments: The Case of Developing Countries',
    DRDERS, World Bank Report No. DRD 65 (Washington, DC: World
    Bank, Nov.).

——, 1986: 'The Importance of Trade for Developing Countries', Paper
    presented to the IBRD–TDRI Conference on 'The MTN and Develop-
    ing Country Interests', Bangkok, Thailand (Oct.–Nov.).

Bardhan, Pranab, 1982: 'Poverty and the Trickle-down in Rural India: A
    Quantitative Analysis' (mimeo.) (Berkeley, CA: University of Califor-
    nia).

——, 1986: *The Political Economy of Development in India* (Oxford: Basil
    Blackwell).

Behrman, Jere R. and Anil B. Deolalikar, 1987a: 'Health and Nutrition', *in*
    Hollis B. Chenery and T.N. Srinivasan (eds), *Handbook on Economic
    Development*, vol. 1 (Amsterdam: North–Holland Publishing Co.),
    ch. 15.

——, 1987b: 'How do Food Prices Affect Individual Nutritional and Health
    Status? A Latent Variable Fixed-effects Analysis' (mimeo.).

——, 1987c: 'Will Developing Country Nutrition Improve with Income? A

Case Study for Rural South India', *Journal of Political Economy*, no. 3, vol. 95.

Bhagwati, Jagdish N.,1958, 1983: 'Immiserizing Growth: A Geometrical Note', *Review of Economic Studies* (June), rpt. *in* Robert Feenstra (ed.), *Essays in International Economic Theory*, vol. 1, *The Theory of Commercial Policy* (Cambridge, MA: MIT Press).

——, 1966: *The Economics of Developing Countries*, World University Library Series (London: Weidenfeld & Nicolson).

——, 1968: 'Distortions and Immiserizing Growth: A Generalization', *Review of Economic Studies*, no. 104, vol. 35 (Oct.).

——, 1973a: 'Education, Class Structure and Income Inequality', *World Development*, no. 5, vol. 1.

——, 1973b, 1985: *India in the International Economy*, Lal Bahadur Shastri Lectures (Hyderabad, India); rpt. *in* J.N. Bhagwati, *Essays in Development Economics*, vol. 1, *Wealth and Poverty* (Oxford: Basil Blackwell), ch. 2.

——, 1984: 'Development Economics: What Have We Learned?', *Asian Development Review*, no. 1, vol. 2.

——, 1985a: 'Gandhi's Break with the Past: Is India's Economic Miracle at Hand?', *The New York Times* (9 June).

——, 1985b: *Growth and Poverty*, Michigan State University Centre for Advanced Study of International Development, Occasional Paper No. 5 (East Lansing: MI: Michigan State University).

——, 1986a: 'Controls must be Liberalized: An Interview with Jagdish Bhagwati', *Frontline* (May–June).

——, 1986b, 1988: 'Export-promoting Trade Strategy: Issues and Evidence', World Bank Policy Issues Paper, VPERS (Washington, DC: World Bank); also in *World Bank Research Observer*.

——, 1986c: 'Immiserizing Growth', *The New Palgrave* (London: Macmillan).

——, 1986d: 'New Economic Policy: Plea for Faster Domestic Liberalization', Interview by P.K. Roy in *The Economic Times* (16 Sept.).

——, 1988: 'Indian Economic Performance and Policy Design', 7th Sir Purshotam Thakurdar Memorial Lecture (Bombay: Indian Institute of Bankers, 21 Dec. 1987).

Bhagwati, Jagdish N., Richard Brecher and Tatsuo Hatta, 1984: 'The Generalized Theory of Transfers and Welfare: Bilateral Transfers in a Multilateral World', *American Economic Review*, no. 4, vol. 73 (Sept.).

Bhagwati, Jagdish N. and T.N. Srinivasan, 1984: 'Indian Growth Strategy: Some Comments', *Economic and Political Weekly* (Dec.).

Bhalla, Surjit S., 1985a: 'Is Sri Lanka an Exception: A Comparative Study of Living Standards', *in* T.N. Srinivasan and Pranab Bardhan (eds), *Rural Poverty in South Asia* (New York: Columbia University Press).

——, 1985b: 'Sri Lankan Achievements: Facts and Fancy', *in* T.N. Srinivasan and Pranab Bardhan (eds), *Rural Poverty in South Asia* (New York: Columbia University Press).

Bhalla, Surjit S. and Paul Glewwe, 1985: 'Living Standards in Sri Lanka in the Seventies: Mirage and Reality' (Washington, DC: World Bank Development Research Department).

——, 1986: 'Growth and Equity in Developing Countries: A Reinterpretation of the Sri Lankan Experience', *World Bank Economic Review*, no. 1, vol. 1 (Sept.).

Bhalla, Surjit S. and P. Vashistha, 1985: 'Income Distribution in India — A Re-examination', *in* T.N. Srinivasan and Pranab Bardhan (eds), *Rural Poverty in South Asia* (New York: Columbia University Press).

Chenery, Hollis B., Montek S. Ahluwalia, C.L.G. Bell, John Duloy and Richard Jolly, 1974: *Redistribution with Growth* (London: Oxford University Press).

Correa, H., 1970: 'Sources of Economic Growth in Latin America', *Southern Economic Journal*, vol. 37.

Dandekar, V.M. and N. Rath, 1971: *Poverty in India* (Bombay: Indian School of Political Economy).

Dantwala, M.L., 1970: 'From Stagnation to Growth', *Indian Economic Journal*, no. 2, vol. 28.

Deolalikar, Anil B., 1988: 'Does Nutrition Determine Labor Productivity in Agriculture? Wage Equation and Farm Production Function Estimates for Rural South India', *Review of Economics and Statistics*, no. 2, vol. 70 (May).

Desai, Padma, 1975: 'China and India: Development During the Last 25 Years', *The American Economic Review*, no. 2, vol. 65.

Dhar, P.N., 1986: 'Indian Economy: Past Performance and Current Issues', Paper presented to the Conference on the Indian Economy, Boston University, Boston, MA.

——, 1987: 'The Political Economy of Development in India', *Indian Economic Review*, no. 1, vol. 32.

Etienne, Gilbert, 1982: *India's Changing Rural Scene, 1963–79* (Oxford: Oxford University Press).

Glewwe, Paul and Surjit S. Bhaila, 1987: 'A Response to Comments by Graham Pyatt and Paul Isenman', *World Bank Economic Review*, no. 3, vol. 1.

Hicks, Norman, 1980: 'Economic Growth and Human Resources', *World Bank Staff Working Paper*, No. 408 (Washington, DC: World Bank).

Hill, Polly, 1984: 'The Poor Quality of Official Socio–economic Statistics Relating to the Rural Tropical World: With Special Reference to South India', *Modern Asian Studies*, no. 3, vol. 18.

Hirway, Indira, 1986a: *Abolition of Poverty in India* (New Delhi: Vikas).

——, 1986b: *Wage Employment Programmes in Rural Development* (New Delhi: Oxford and IBH Publishing House).

Isenman, P., 1980: 'Basic Needs: The Case of Sri Lanka', *World Development*, no. 3, vol. 8.

——, 1987: 'A Comment on "Growth and Equity in Developing Countries: A Reinterpretation of the Sri Lankan Experience" by Bhalla and Glewwe', *World Bank Economic Review*, no. 3, vol. 1.

Johnson, Harry G., 1955: 'Economic Expansion and International Trade', *The Manchester School*, vol. 23 (May).

Joshi, Vijay and I.M.D. Little, 1986: 'Indian Macroeconomic Policies', mimeo. (Oxford: Nuffield College, Oxford University).

Kakwani, Nanak, 1986: 'Is Sex Bias Significant?', *World Institute for Development Economics Research* (Helsinki: Dec.).

Kohli, Atul, 1987: 'Politics of Economic Liberalization in India', mimeo. (Princeton: Department of Political Science, Princeton University).

Kreuger, Anne O., 1987: *Trade and Employment in Developing Countries: Synthesis and Conclusions*, NBER (Chicago: Chicago University Press).

Lakdawala, D.T., 1986: 'Planning for Minimum Needs', Indulal Yagnik Memorial Lecture, *in* T.N. Srinivasan and Pranab Bardhan (eds), *Rural Poverty in South Asia* (New York: Columbia University Press), ch. 12.

Marris, Robin, 1982: 'Economic Growth in Cross Section: Experiments with Real Product Data, Social Indicators, Model Selection Procedures, and Policy Benefit/Cost Analysis', mimeo. (Washington, DC: World Bank).

Mathur, Subodh C., 1985: 'Rural Poverty and Agricultural Performance in India: A Comment', *Journal of Development Studies*.

Minhas, Bagicha S., 1970: 'Rural Poverty, Land Distribution and Development Strategy', *Indian Economic Review*, vol. 5, New Series, pp. 97–126.

——, 1971: 'Rural Poverty and Minimal Level of Living: A Reply', *Indian Economic Review*, vol. 6, New Series, pp. 69–77.

Minhas, B.S., L.R. Jain, S.M. Kansal and M.R. Saluja, 1987: 'On the Appropriate Choice of Consumer Price Indices and Data Sets for Estimating the Incidence of Poverty in India', *Indian Economic Review*, no. 1, vol. 22.

Myrdal, Jan, 1966: *Report from a Chinese Village* (Signet Books edn).

Nurkse, Ragnar, 1959: *Patterns of Trade and Development*, Wicksell Lectures (Stockholm: Almquist & Wicksell).

Patel, I.G., 1986: 'On Taking India into the Twenty-first Century (New Economic Policy in India)', Kingsley Martin Memorial Lecture, *Modern Asian Studies*, no. 2, vol. 21.

Pyatt, Graham, 1987: 'A Comment on "Growth and Equity in Developing Countries: A Reinterpretation of the Sri Lankan Experience" by Bhalla and Glewwe', *World Bank Economic Review*, no. 3, vol. 1.

Rath, N., 1985: 'Garibi Hatao', *Economic and Political Weekly* (9 Feb.).

Rosenzweig, Mark and Paul Schultz, 1982: 'Market Opportunities, Genetic Endowments and Intra-family Resource Distribution: Child Survival in Rural India', *American Economic Review*, no. 4, vol. 72 (Sept.).

Saith, A., 1981: 'Production, Poverty and Prices in Rural India', *Journal of Development Studies*, vol. 17.

Sen, A.K., 1981: 'Public Action and the Quality of Life in Developing Countries', *Oxford Bulletin of Economics and Statistics* (Nov.).

——, 1981: 'Family and Food: Sex Bias in Poverty', *in Resources, Values and Development* (Oxford: Basil Blackwell).

Srinivasan, T.N., 1979: 'Trends in Agriculture in India: 1949–50 and 1977–78', *Economic and Political Weekly*, vol. 15 (30, 31, 32, Special Number, Aug.).

——, 1981, 1982: 'Was Agriculture Neglected in Planning', Paper presented to the Golden Jubilee Seminar of the Indian Statistical Institute (Calcutta: Dec.); revised March.

——, 1985: 'Agricultural Production, Relative Prices, Entitlements and Poverty', *in* John Mellor and Gunvant Desai (eds), *Agricultural Change and Rural Poverty: Variations on a Theme by Dharam Narain* (Baltimore, MD: Johns Hopkins University Press).

Streeten, Paul, 1981: *First Things First: Meeting the Basic Human Needs in Developing Countries* (Oxford: Oxford University Press).

Subbarao, K., 1985: 'Regional Variations in Impact of Anti-Poverty Programmes: A Review of Evidence', *Economic and Political Weekly*, no. 43, vol. 20 (26 Oct.).

——, 1987: 'Interventions to Fulfill Nutrition Gaps at the Household Level:

A Review of India's Experience', Paper prepared for a Workshop on Poverty in India, Queen Elizabeth House, Oxford University.

Sundaram, K., 1973: 'Education, Class Structure and Income Inequality: Further Evidence', *World Development*, no. 6, vol. 1.

——, 1986: 'Growth, Inequality and Poverty: The Indian Experience' (New Delhi: Centre for Policy Research, Chanakyapuri).

Sundaram, K. and S.D. Tendulkar, 1983a: 'Poverty Reduction and Redistribution in Sixth Plan: Population Factor and Rural–Urban Equity', *Economic and Political Weekly*, no. 38, vol. 18 (17 Sept.).

——, 1983b: 'Poverty in the Mid-term Appraisal', *Economic and Political Weekly*, vol. 18 (5–12 Nov.).

——, 1983c: 'Towards an Explanation of Inter-regional Variations in Poverty and Unemployment in Rural India', *in* T.N. Srinivasan and Pranab Bardhan (eds), *Rural Poverty in South Asia* (New York: Columbia University Press).

——, 1985: 'Integrated Rural Development Programme in India: A Case Study of a Poverty Eradication Programme', *in* S. Mukhopadhyay (ed.), *Case Studies on Poverty Programmes in Asia* (Kuala Lumpur, Malaysia: APDC).

Tendulkar, Suresh D., 1983: 'Rural Institutional Credit and Rural Development: A Review Article', *Indian Economic Review*, no. 1, vol. 18.

Weiner, Myron, 1986: 'The Political Economy of Growth in India', *World Politics*, no. 4, vol. 38.

Wheeler, David, 1980: 'Human Resource Development and Economic Growth in Developing Countries: A Simultaneous Model', *World Bank Staff Working Paper*, No. 407 (Washington, DC: World Bank, July).

11

Socialism and
Indian Economic Policy[*]

SOCIALIST ideas have significantly influenced the formulation of the means and objectives of Indian economic policies. This has happened in two distinct ways: via the impact of external, socialist ideologies on the economic and political notions held by élite groups influencing policy-making in India; and via the political constraints imposed on the dominant Congress Party by the relative strength of the left, and the relative weakness of the right, parties in the spectrum of Indian politics. Any serious analysis of the evolution of economic policy instruments and objectives characterizing it, and the nature of the outcome in terms of the fulfilment of frustration of the apparent objectives, must therefore address itself to the interaction of socialist doctrines with it.[1]

1. THE IMPACT OF SOCIALISM ON POLICY FRAMEWORK

Two dominant, socialist influences on serious economic thinking during the period of the struggle for Independence were the example of Soviet communism[2] and the Fabian Society's

[*] Written with Padma Desai.

[1] It should be emphasized that, in turn, the course of economic policy and performance in India has also influenced socialist thinking amongst the intellectuals.

[2] Among the dominant nationalist leaders who articulated extensively on the possibility of adopting a Soviet-type system in India, were Mahatma Gandhi, Nehru, and Tagore. It would seem that, in their evaluation of Marxism–Leninism–Communism, all three categorically rejected the violent means of achieving a socialist system while, in essence, agreeing with its basic objectives.

Thus Gandhi wrote: 'I believe in non-violent . . . communism . . . if communism came without any violence, it would be welcome. For then no property would

deliberations on the nature of the socialist society and the gradualist approach to it,[3] the latter clearly exercising a powerful

---

be held by anybody except on behalf of the people and for the people' (*Harijan*, 13 Feb. 1937: 45). Again: 'What does communism mean in the last analysis? It means a classless society, an ideal that is worth striving for. Only I part company with it when force is called to aid for achieving it' (*Harijan*, 13 March 1937: 152). However, his reaction to the Bolshevik revolution and Soviet achievements was totally negative. Thus: 'India does not want Bolshevism' (*Young India*, 1 May 1920: 18; *Young India*, 24 Nov. 1921: 510). Then again: 'As I took to Russia, where the apotheosis of industrialization has been reached, the life there does not appeal to me. . . . In modern terms, it is beneath human dignity to lose one's individuality and become a mere cog in the machine. I want every individual to become a full-blooded, full-developed member of the society' (*Harijan*, 28 Jan. 1939: 438). It is not surprising that Soviet commentators under Stalin referred to him as a 'Hindu reactionary'.

As for Nehru, his reaction to the Russian revolution, after his visit to the Soviet Union in 1927, was euphoric: ' . . . if the future is full of hope, it is largely because of Soviet Russia and what it has done . . . ' (1946: 64). Later on, there was a slight modification in his euphoria in view of the purge trials. While he believed the trials to be 'bona fide' to the extent that there was a 'definite conspiracy' against the Soviet government, he nonetheless admitted that the trials indicated 'ill health' in the Soviet body politic if it required the employment of such 'violence' as a remedy. (See Nehru 1946: 116).

As for the actual adoption of a Soviet-type system in India, Nehru's attitude was negative both from the point of view of the method of implementing it and, also, its timing. Thus, on the former issue he wrote: 'In regard to the method and approach to this ideal, I may not agree with everything that the orthodox Communists have done. I think that these methods will have to adapt themselves to changing conditions and may vary in different countries . . . ' (as quoted in Bose 1934: 346). On the issue of timing, he was more explicit: 'Much as I wish for the advancement to socialism in this country, I have no desire to force the issue in the Congress and thereby create difficulties in the way of our struggle for independence' (Nehru 1941: app.). Also: ' . . . the Congress stands today for full democracy in India and fights for a democratic state, not for socialism' (ibid.).

[3] In particular, Jawaharlal Nehru, who shaped India's socialist policy after independence, was greatly influenced by Fabian ideas which, in turn, were rooted in the traditions of English utilitarianism, empiricism, and classical economic thought. English socialist tradition, in fact, was reformist from the outset, in contrast to French socialism which was revolutionary. 'The decisive difference lay in the fact that the French Revolution had taught man to think in terms of seizing power' (Lichtheim 1969: 18). The political counterpart of Fabian reformism was the adoption of a parliamentary, constitutional democracy for purposes of

impact through the large numbers of the Indian élite that were processed through the English educational institutions prior to Indian independence in 1947.[4]

Nearly all traditional socialist doctrines lead in the direction of public ownership of the means of production, and (failing total control of the means of production) they equally point in the direction of public ownership of the 'key' sectors of production. The specific shape given to these doctrines in the Indian context was however in the Fabian-type gradualism that characterized the transition to public ownership, *in toto* and of the key sectors. Thus, nationalization of existing capital stock were de facto ruled out. Rather, the government, through successive five-year plans, sought to increase the share of the public sector in total *investment*, expecting at the end of such a sustained effort to raise the government's share of the capital stock to a dominant level: the approach to the Marxist goal of public ownership was thus to be asymptotic.[5] Similarly, on the problem of key sectors, the 'commanding heights' of the economy, defined to include steel and heavy industry, the successive Industrial Policy Resolutions of the government again focused on reservation of these areas to public sector investment rather than

---

socialist legislation: indeed, as Nehru was to conceive of the appropriate political framework for India's transition to socialism.

It may however be noted that the reformist, gradualist political process was reinforced on the Indian scene also by the general rejection (already noted) of violence as a method of political action: this Gandhian preference for peaceful action, in turn, being rooted in Indian religious humanism.

[4] The impact of English *economic* thinking on the Indian élite's attitude to governmental planning should not also be underestimated. At Cambridge (where most of the leading Indian economists were trained until studying in the United States became a viable option), the emphasis was typically on the inadequacy of the Invisible Hand, with little attention to how the Visible Hand system of intervention would operate in practice. Contrast this with the training of the Chicago economists where the failures of actual intervention are continually focused on and, in certain versions of the doctrine, even Benthamite intervention to preserve laissez-faire is considered unnecessary and/or counterproductive.

[5] Thus, in the Second Five-year Plan, the share of the public sector in total investment was estimated at 54.0 per cent and it was planned at 58.6 per cent and 63.7 per cent in the Third and Fourth Plans respectively.

on the takeover of existing private sector concerns (as in the case of the Tata Steel).[6]

While, therefore, the impact of Fabian gradualism, and also the pragmatic sense that the private sector was to be allowed to make a contribution to industrialization in the medium-run while the economy was being transformed into one dominated by the public sector, was evident in the policies just detailed, the impact of the Soviet example was to be manifest in three other areas of economic policy which were to set the stage equally significantly for India's economic performance.[7] First, a policy favouring a shift to heavy industry within the industrialization programme was to characterize the Second Five-year Plan (1956–61), and was to continue into the Third Plan until the shift into the Green Revolution strategy began towards the end of the Third Plan.[8] Next, the industrialization programme was to become subject to targeting for many industries and to detailed industrial licensing, extending to product-level attention and regulation, over the entire, modern, large-scale non-agricultural sector — the key role in elevating this approach to a sacrosanct principle being played by the Industrial Regulation Act of 1961.[9] Finally, the notion that an overview of the economy be taken, and the principal thrust of the economy be defined and given shape within it, led along the Soviet lines to the Five-year Plan formulation: though, here again, the First Plan was a rather loosely-defined exercise, adding

[6] The resulting composition of public sector investment was heavily weighted towards steel, engineering, petroleum, chemicals, and mining and minerals, in that order.

[7] We use the phrase 'Soviet example' quite deliberately. There is, in fact, little evidence that Soviet writings or Soviet political pressure had any significant impact on the thinking of Indian intellectuals or political parties or, more directly, on policy formulation. For a well-argued piece on this point, see Clarkson (1973).

[8] We may speculate that the shift to heavy industry was also reinforced tangentially by Fabian influence. The Fabians had a rationalist faith in industry and science; and Nehru was to share it. His concern with modern technology and science was manifest in areas such as atomic energy and his acceptance of modern, heavy industry as part of India's economic programmes must therefore have been perfectly natural.

[9] Details of this Act, and of the policy of industrial licensing as also target-setting, can be found in Bhagwati and Desai (1970, especially Chs 12–14).

up largely to social-overhead projects and broad fiscal objectives, much along the lines of the Harrod–Domar, flow-model framework, and it was only with the Second Plan that the rather tighter, consistency approach, closer to the Soviet-type planning framework, was adopted and investment allocations were more specifically set out.[10]

It might be noted that these major contours of the Indian economic policy framework, influenced by socialist thinking of the Fabian type and by the Soviet practice of socialism, were reinforced by other factors on the scene and, indeed, in many instances reinforced one another. Thus, the Second Plan was to precipitate a foreign exchange crisis in 1956–7, which led to the view that foreign exchange should be preserved carefully by *administrative* regulation; this, in turn, strengthened the impulse to licence and to target capacity creation and output along Soviet lines. Similarly, the expanded role of heavy industry with the Second Plan reinforced the relative expansion of the public sector share of investment; it was difficult to persuade the private sector to invest in heavy industry and the public sector had to step in, quite aside from ideological reasons, to undertake these investments. To take yet another example, the expansion of the public sector was also seen by many as yielding as economic externality in terms of added savings formation. Tax policy was likely to be constrained by political factors and the public sector concerns could more readily raise the 'revenue' and savings to lead to greater capital formation through a suitable price policy. Again, the industrial and import licensing machinery was not merely directed at the regulation of the composition of industrial production and investment, but was also considered necessary as an

[10] Of these three types of impact of the Soviet example, the Plan-formulation approach was to be enthusiastically received by most commentators and, indeed, to lead to demands on the part of aid agencies for similar efforts by other developing countries. However, the shift to heavy industry was seen as a definite mistake by economic opinion of the Chicago-school variety, reflecting their basic unfamiliarity with the structural models of growth and development planning of the Feldman–Mahalanobis variety — an ignorance that probably still persists. The detailed regulation was not quite noticed at the time, except by conservative commentators whose position was however extreme and precluded governmental planning of industrial investments on *any* scale.

instrument for preventing the concentration of wealth and economic power within a limited number of large industrial houses in the private sector.

Socialist thinking and precept influenced not merely the policy-making élite in the Congress Party that has virtually dominated the political scene since Independence in 1947; it also constrained the flexibility of the Congress Party to move in other directions, because the more doctrinaire left-wing political parties pulled the Congress Party's programmes in the socialist direction, at least at the ex-ante level of party resolutions and declared intentions. Indeed, within the Congress Party itself, the left wing has exerted strong pressure in the direction of socialist programmes, and the party split into the Old and the New Congress, along these lines, with the New Congress of Mrs Indira Gandhi castigating the Old, and now increasingly defunct, Congress as right-wing and reactionary. Indeed, the political ethos of the country has made 'socialism' a good word that wins elections, unlike in the United States where, as Galbraith discovered in the last national election, it is a word that loses elections. Whether, however, the socialist content of the programmes has been real or illusory, and whether the programmes when socialist have been successful or compromised, is a separate issue, undoubtedly of importance, which we defer till later in this chapter.

2. RELATED DIMENSIONS OF POLICY FRAMEWORK

Finally, it is necessary to complete the picture of the economic policy framework in India, as she entered the planning period in 1949–50 and through the decade of the 1950s and much of the 1960s, by sketching in some additional dimensions.

Raising Minimum Incomes Through Growth

It is clear that, from an early stage, Indian policy thinking was dominated by the view that the distribution of income could not be significantly affected by distributive measures of a fiscal type. This view partially reflected the feeling, based on earlier statistical studies, that, short of communist societies, Lorenz-curve type of distribution measures indicated that very little could be changed by way of the distribution of income in different societies. More importantly, this view was reinforced by the view that a long-lasting effect on the incomes of the poor was possible only if the economy was geared to raising incomes, investment, and hence *jobs* for the underemployed as rapidly as possible; the alternative policy of using savings to redistribute consumption immediately, as distinct from investing them, was considered a short-term, myopic policy for a country like India with its staggering problem of poverty, and was to be used only moderately to provide public consumption, as discussed below.

Thus Indian economic policy was essentially set up in the context of a growth model aimed at achieving a rapid rate of growth, reaching increasing levels of domestic saving through appropriate tax effort (as evidenced by the growth of taxes as a percentage of GNP and by the share, of over a quarter during the 1960s, of the public sector in domestic savings formation), and supplementing them during the transition with foreign resources to reach required investment levels.[11] It was optimistically hoped that the economy would then grow to reach self-sustained growth within a perspective of up to 25 years, and that a serious dent would have been made in the problem of ameliorating poverty on a sustained basis.

External Capital

The policy assumption thus, at least by the Second Plan, was that the country *would* utilize foreign assistance,[12] using 'aid to

[11] This is really how foreign aid advocates and agencies often estimated aid requirements. Cf. Bhagwati (1971: Ch. V). For details on Indian planning models, as they evolved through the Plans, consult Bhagwati and Chakravarty (1969).

[12] The decision to utilize foreign aid reflected, not merely the need to supplement the domestic savings effort, but also a number of external factors favourable to the supply of aid to India. Thus, during the late 1950s, the aid climate was generally favourable, faith in India's development effort was running high and, against the background of the Cold War, Nehru's policy of non-alignment was effective in extracting aid from both the Western and Soviet-bloc donors.

end aid'. And, indeed, the utilization of external assistance from all sources, Western and Soviet-bloc, was to run at significant levels from 1956–7 down to the mid-1960s, even though, on a per capita or share of GNP basis, India was among the least-favoured recipients of aid by virtue of its size.[13] As regards private foreign investment, attitudes were coloured by the Indian colonial experience: such investment was closely regulated, directed to specific areas, and left-wing opinion was always critical of it, even though, given India's size, there was no reason to fear that such investment could ever have arrived at levels which would threaten the country with the unenviable status of a banana republic.

Expansion of Public Consumption

Another dimension of the economic programmes, defining the distributional content of the Plans, was provided by educational and health expenditures. These were intended to supplement the growth of private consumption as the growth mechanism led to more jobs and greater incomes for the poor. While, however, these expenditures were built into all Plans, they were not to be the intended focus of a poverty-elimination strategy until the early 1970s.[14]

---

[13] As a proportion of NNP at factor cost, the utilization of external assistance by India was 2.37 in 1957–8, 3.01 in 1960–1, 3.35 in 1963–4, 3.55 in 1964–5, 3.67 in 1965–6, and then fell substantially to 0.69, 0.71, 0.52, and 0.48 during the next four years.

[14] Commenting rather favourably on this aspect of Indian planning, William Lockwood writes: ' . . . Yet it is of great human significance that India, for example, has doubled her food supplies since independence and left behind the great famines of history, that she has tripled the number of children in school until they now approach 100 million, that she has improved health care to the point where life expectancy at birth has risen from 35 to 52, that her factories now provide her people with two million bicycles a year, that her newspaper press, one of the liveliest in the world, now reaches regularly some 20 million readers. . . . ' For details, see Lockwood (1974).

By contrast, K.N. Raj assesses the failures of this aspect of Indian planning in terms of the extent to which the public distribution system (in essential items such as foodgrains) has reached the masses of the people. Thus, at the end of

Land Reform

Perhaps the most-discussed, but the least successful, programmes related to land reform. In a country shot through with a large variety of land tenure systems, there were several dimensions on which land reform could be sought, both on grounds of redistribution and efficiency. *Absentee* landlordism (under the notorious Zamindari system) was made illegal in the north, while security of landholding for the tenant was legislated for in other areas (such as in Gujarat and Maharashtra) with notable success. But efforts at imposing land ceilings and at promoting cooperative farming, two further components of the land reform policy in India, were to fail to take root, as we shall discuss presently.

The resulting Indian policy framework through the 1950s and most of the 1960s can then be characterized, from the standpoint of socialist precept and notions, as having the following dimensions:

(i)   an increasing share of public investments, at over half the share in the total at the outset of the planning process;

(ii) an increasing public share in the capital stock of 'key' industrial sectors such as heavy industry, resulting from a fairly strict (though not total, in practice) reservation of such sectors for public sector investment;

(iii) a definite denial of nationalization of existing capital stock as the means to increasing public ownership;

(iv) the use of substantial targeting, and of far more comprehensive industrial (and import) licensing, to control and direct the level and composition of industrial production and investment at product-level detail;

(v)   the related attempt at using licensing to prevent the concentration of industrial wealth and power within a small number of families and groups;

(vi) a development strategy aimed at raising investments and

December 1972, the population covered by statutory rationing was only 16 million, mainly in the urban and semi-urban areas. Looking at the problem slightly differently, it would seem that whereas at least 20 per cent of the total consumption of foodgrains in the country should be distributed statutorily to low-income groups, this magnitude was in the range of 12 to 13 per cent in the acute drought years of 1966 and 1967. For details, see Raj (1974, especially pt II).

jobs as rapidly as domestic fiscal effort and external assistance would permit, with only moderate use of resources to provide public consumption (health and education, in the main) by way of direct redistribution for ameliorating poverty in the short run;

(vii) an investment-composition strategy that implied both industrialization and, within it, a substantial Soviet-style expansion of heavy industry — turning on its head the traditional, *Western* economic notions that heavy industry should come in the later, rather than the earlier, process of industrialization; and

(viii) an agricultural strategy, whose major components were modest land reforms aimed eventually at, (a) security of tenancy, (b) abolition of absentee landlordism, (c) land ceilings to reduce concentration of landownership, and (d) co-operative farming and marketing, plus land extension, irrigation and community development programmes — *excluding* therefore any radical nationalization of land for state farming or redistribution to landless labourers.

It is perhaps useful also, in the spirit of Indian philosophy, to characterize the socialist dimensions of the Indian policy framework by what they were not. State ownership did not imply workers' control over management or even their significant participation in it: the Yugoslav form of socialism was not an inspiration for Indian socialists on any significant scale. Nor were the socialist arguments of the Lange–Lerner variety, which so greatly dominated the economic debate among the opponents of socialism and the proponents of socialism such as Durbin, of any real import to Indian policy-makers or intellectuals. The Feldman–Mahalanobis-type structuralist arguments on the rational composition of investment that culminated in optimal growth theory were far more influential than the rational price policy implications of the Lange–Lerner variety.

The resulting policy framework was clearly of a mixed economy type, with the modern and growing non-agricultural sectors subject to growing public investments and to extensive licensing and control of private investments and production, while the agricultural sector — still contributing half of the net domestic product — was subject only to comparatively modest attempts at control and/or radical transformation of the prevalent land tenure systems. This policy framework was considered by most observers at the time to be socialist in its main thrust: and indeed it *was* influenced significantly, in its conception, by socialist precepts and example, as we have already noted.

3. Ex-ante Aspirations and Ex-post Performance

Indeed, the combination of an Anglo-Saxon democratic framework and the socialist orientation of India's economic programmes was taken by many Western commentators of liberal persuasion as making the Indian programme an important and desirable enough rival to the Chinese communist model. This favourable perception was to change during the mid-1960s as the socialist elements in the Indian policy framework came increasingly to be contrasted rather with the ideologically more attractive developmental strategies of less neutral countries such as Pakistan and quasi-satellites such as South Korea. Moreover, it was to change also during the early 1970s, but from the opposite perspective as détente with China made Sinology respectable on the mainland United States and as the widespread, uncritical condemnation by armchair Sinologists of the Chinese developmental model was replaced by enthusiastic approbation by jet-setting Sinologists now permitted to peek at the great Chinese experiment.

While, therefore, the Indian policy framework had been oversold earlier, and was later to be undersold, largely as a reflection of Western ideological concerns and intellectual fashions, there is little doubt that its performance during the decades of the sixties and seventies has also raised serious doubts about its efficacy and desirability.

In particular, India's rates of accumulation and growth since the mid-1960s have been disappointing, in relation to her past performance, her plans, as also to the performance of many LDCs of diverse sizes and ideological persuasions. At the same time, an increasing number of studies of income distribution in the country strongly suggest that the bottom deciles have not improved their consumption levels since planning began and may, in fact, have become worse off.[15] The framework of Indian economic policies has therefore been called into question on several dimensions, from the viewpoints of both the capitalist objective of efficiency and the socialist objective of equity. We will however focus our analysis here on the socialist aspects of India's performance.

(1) As the Indian economy has evolved, it has become fairly evident that the above-described mix of policies, addressed to the public and private sectors, has produced essentially a rentier, rather than a socialist (or capitalist) society.

(2) The extent of controls over private production and investment in the modern, large-scale industrial sector, has long exceeded that justified by any economic rationale. It has to be seen rather as a pseudo-socialist policy which, in fact, creates sheltered markets for entrepreneurs who earn rents on their licences and, in the ultimate political analysis, share them increasingly with the party in power. Indeed, the licensing machinery, for distributing imports and scarce materials, has not even succeeded in checking the growth of concentrated economic power by the large industrial houses. At the same time, it has become evident that the price and distributional controls are generally used to buttress non-proletarian interests. For example, of the small number of produced and price-controlled cars, a specific quota goes to government officials who thereby are assigned the high premia that the new cars fetch in the market. The licensing mechanism produces, at best, redistribution essentially *outside* of the poverty sector — from the rich to the not-so-rich — and generates considerable economic inefficiency which, in reducing the productivity of investment, compromises the strategy of rapid growth to provide increasing jobs to the poor.[16]

[15] The evidence has been reviewed well by Pranab Bardhan in 'Redistribution with Growth: Some Country Experience: India', *in* H. Chenery et al. (1974). However, the evidence, in our judgement, is not conclusive and also excludes public consumption.

[16] The detailed evidence in support of this conclusion has been discussed at great length in Bhagwati and Desai, op. cit., and has been further analysed in Bhagwati and Srinivasan (1975). The political and social framework of the policies in this and the next paragraph has been discussed by Rosen (1966).

(3) The expansion of the public sector, in turn, has raised serious questions. The objective of expanding the public sector has actually been adhered to, more or less; indeed, as we shall presently discuss, even nationalizations have been increasingly undertaken, contrary to the early declarations of policy. But the public sector has not generated the expected surpluses for investment and growth. And their management has suffered from the constraints imposed by their bureaucratic structure and the absence of any ultimate penalty for inefficiency — much as the private sector's efficiency has been impaired, though not to the same degree (given the profit motive), by the creation of sheltered markets through the comprehensive licensing system. The Indian system of parliamentary control has also had the effect of further constraining the exercise of initiative, and the consequent ability to survive short-term errors the pursuit of long-term efficiency, on the part of the management which, in any case, was likely to be risk-avoiding owing to its heavily bureaucratic origins.[17]

(4) While therefore the policies in the non-agricultural, modern sector have deployed socialist-type instruments (e.g. strict licensing of the private, and expansion of the public, sectors), the net outcome has been rather to create a rentier society, with its attendant economic inefficiencies, and a political use of these instruments generally to redistribute incomes within groups distinctly above the poverty line and, only fractionally, to groups below that line.

(5) The corresponding lag in pushing land reforms has also been quite notable. It appears that, in the agricultural sector, the land reform legislation has not succeeded in making a significant dent in the concentration of landownership.[18] The benefits of the

[17] Nor have the Indian public sector enterprises been proof from pressures to use them for political purposes, e.g. to take on unsuitable or unnecessary staff; rather there seems to be no evidence that this has been done on a systematic and crippling scale, as in Menderes' Turkey, for example, or significantly more than in the private sector in a society traditionally working on principles of kinship and patronage.

[18] Thus Raj (1964) has argued that:

In the rural sector, land legislation since Independence has not made much difference

Green Revolution again seem to have accrued principally to the larger farmers, with the cheap fertilizers and credit going largely to them rather than to the smaller farmers, and with the landless labour finding its real wages inadequately responsive to the increased productivity of agriculture.[19]

Accumulating evidence, and growing perception, regarding these sharp contrasts between ex-ante aspirations and ex-post realities have naturally raised serious questions among Indian intellectuals about the relationship of the class structure in India to the composition of its political élite and formulation of Indian economic policy, thus raising to the forefront of even neoclassical policy analysis the traditionally neo-Marxist concerns.

The witticism that India's socialist pattern was little more than socialist patter now elicits more than mirth; it is the starting point for serious and systematic reflection on the directions that Indian

---

to concentration in landownership in the rural areas, and has in the main only induced the larger holders of land to either disguise the true position (by partitioning land among members of the same family, reporting tenants as attached labourers, etc.) or, in some cases, to take a more active interest in the cultivation of land in order to prevent the accrual of occupancy rights to others. The available data (such as those provided by the Planning Commission and the National Sample Survey) do not bring out adequately the extent of concentration in landownership (both on account of the definitions of ownership adopted and the various methods of concealment open to owners at the stage of reporting). They also overstate the share of the larger units in 'operated' (as distinguished from 'owned') holdings, since the owners have an interest in reporting themselves as actual cultivators even when they depend really on share-croppers for the cultivation of their land. In reality, therefore, ownership is much more concentrated, and cultivation takes place in much smaller units, than we are led to believe by these statistics. The slow progress of consolidation of plots (except in a few states) makes the actual cultivation units even more fragmented than would otherwise be the case.

[19] However, there *is* some evidence to the contrary. Thus evidence exists that average real farm wages in the Punjab in 1967–9 were significantly above the pre-1966 average. Also, in Kerala and Madras, the two rice-growing states with the highest relative foodgrain acreages of 17 and 14 per cent devoted respectively to the new varieties of rice, real wages of farm labour in 1967–9 rose significantly over the 1954–66 average in comparison to other rice-growing states, where real farm wages declined. For details, see Herdt and Baker (1972). Also, it seems as if the disproportionate share of the larger farmers in cheap credit and fertilizers may partly reflect their greater ability to innovate with risk rather than their political power in the régime.

economic policy and performance can be expected to take. The Indian economist, Raj Krishna, has aptly described the central tendency of Indian policy as 'first-round' socialism: ostensibly socialist measures that wind up being aborted or subverted in execution.

Few intellectuals in India now believe that under the existing political set-up, with a ruling Congress party still heavily dominated by the urban middle class, large-scale entrepreneurs and landed interests, there can be any real moves from a socialist platform to a socialist reality. This is not a political party with a clear ideological commitment like Lenin's Bolsheviks or Mao's communists; and its professed commitment to socialist notions is increasingly seen to be one of political convenience rather than conviction.

Thus, the nationalizations, especially of banking in 1969, were timed so as to assist the (New) Congress party in consolidating its political position rather than out of socialist convictions, the increased trend towards such 'conspicuous' acts of socialism being designed essentially to deflect attention from the lack of genuine progress in distributional and growth objectives in the economy. Paradoxically, therefore, the cosmetics of socialism have been increasingly used, unlike in the Nehru era (when pragmatism largely reflected economic necessity rather than political expediency), as the economic programmes are increasingly seen to lack any real socialist content.

Perhaps such an outcome, from a socialist viewpoint, was inevitable. Unlike the Marxist–communist tradition, which imparts a strong ideological basis for revolutionary struggle and fairly clear objectives to which such a struggle can be addressed, the English socialist tradition (which most Indian intellectuals, including Nehru, inherited) is strictly empirical and non-ideological.[20] Such

---

[20] The English socialist tradition has been empirical–rationalist. Lichtheim notes that 'The British abandoned philosophical speculation in favour of an approach rooted in their non-traditional empiricism: the utilitarian doctrine, with its stress upon practical consequences and the "greatest happiness" of the greatest number' (1969: 12).

By contrast, Marx rejected the utilitarian generalization that reasonable behaviour by individuals results in beneficial outcome for the community. In his

a tradition quite evidently ran the risk, both of degenerating, over time, into socialist patter, without a concrete programme being executed by an ideologically-inspired cadre of socialists, and, indeed, of being captured and turned into an instrument of bourgeois classes pursuing their own interests behind a socialist screen.

Indeed, one might cynically predict that, if the economic difficulties of the present government intensify — as they well might, with the government committed to the rentier framework in the modern, non-agricultural sector for political expediency and with the agricultural expansion thanks to the Green Revolution in jeopardy largely (though not exclusively) due to the exogenous shock of the oil crisis — there could follow a series of acts of apparent socialism to maintain the image of progressivity in the spectrum of ideas on the Indian scene. And, qua policy economists, one might well argue cynically, that the best thing for economists, in this type of set-up, would be to work out a number of such conspicuous acts of socialism which can be pulled out periodically to enable the government to maintain its socialist image, but making sure that they are not economically expensive![21] The policy of bank nationalization in 1969 was precisely

---

judgement, the aggregate does not necessarily equal the sum of its elements, and what is good for the individual could be determined only on the basis of an inquiry into the ultimate truth about history and society, as well as man and nature. The inquiry he undertook was a grand synthesis of philosophy, history and economics. In this fusion, historical reality proceeds from one stage to another in a dynamic but deterministic fashion as a result of continuous interaction between the material base of production and the ideological superstructure relevant to each stage. The ultimate and desirable stage is a classless society via a proletarian revolution. In their attempts at achieving this goal, Lenin and Mao further altered and refined the Marxist framework with endless discussions of what constitutes an objective revolutionary reality and who can be the agents of revolutions, of the distinction between 'spontaneity' and 'consciousness' and tactic and strategy, of the absolute prerequisite of classifying groups in terms of their class allegiance, and so on.

All this, of course, was a far cry from the English socialist tradition which Nehru practised on the Indian scene.

[21] This type of political economy could make a far greater contribution to the economic growth of a country in India's political predicament than any other single piece of economic research!

such a no-loss type of socialist measure that won the Congress party some additional years in office; but the nationalization of wholesale wheat trade in 1973 was an economic disaster and, to its credit, the government decisively backtracked from that decision.[22] Whether the advisers to the present régime will be able to walk this tightrope of bourgeois policies in a socialist framework for much longer, and with minimal damage to the economy, is a question to which there are no obvious answers.

References

Bhagwati, J.N., 1970: *Amount and Sharing of Aid* (Washington, DC: Overseas Development Council).

Bhagwati, J.N. and S. Chakravarty, 1969: 'Contributions to Indian Economic Analysis', *American Economic Review*, 59 (4) Supplement; excerpt reprinted in this volume, ch. 18.

Bhagwati, J.N. and T.N. Srinivasan, 1975: *Foreign Trade Regimes and Economic Development: India* (New York: Columbia University Press, for NBER).

Bose, Subhas C., 1934: *The Indian Struggle, 1920–34* (London: Wishart & Co.).

Chenery, H., M. Ahluwalia, C.L.G. Bell, J. Duloy and R. Jolly, 1974: *Redistribution with Growth* (London: Oxford University Press).

Clarkson, S., 1973: 'The Low Impact of Soviet Writing and Aid on Indian Thinking and Policy', *Survey*, pp. 1–23.

Clarkson, S. and P. Desai, 1970: *India: Planning for Industrialization* (London: Oxford University Press).

Herdt, R.W. and L.A. Baker, 1972: 'Agricultural Wages, Production and High-Yielding Varieties', *Economic and Political Weekly* (Bombay), 7 (13), 25 March.

Lichtheim, George, 1969: *The Origins of Socialism* (New York: Praeger).

Lockwood, W.W., 1974: 'Asian Triangle: China, India, Japan', *Foreign Affairs*, 52 (4), pp. 818–38.

[22] This ability to reverse ill-considered decisions is still one of the major assets of the present Indian régime. Albert Hirschman has argued that the failure to perceive progress may be the chief obstacle to progress. One can improve on this witticism and say rather that the failure to perceive failure may be the chief obstacle to progress.

Nehru, J., 1941: *Toward Freedom, The Autobiography of Jawaharlal Nehru* (New York: The John Day Company).

——, 1946: *in* J.S. Bright (ed.), *Important Speeches, being a Collection of Most Significant Speeches Delivered by Jawaharlal Nehru from 1922–1946* (Lahore).

Raj, K.N., 1964: 'What Does Socialism Imply for Economic Policy in India How?', *Mainstream*, 25 Jan.

——, 1974: *Planning and Prices in India* (Trivandrum: Centre for Development Studies).

Rosen, G., 1966: *Democracy and Economic Change in India* (Berkeley: University of California Press).

12

Women in Indian Elections[*]

ONE of the interesting features of Indian political life is the participation of Indian women. In this respect Indian society is almost certainly less inequitable than the Chinese, Soviet, and the American. Not merely does India have a female prime minister. Women have also succeeded in becoming members of the Lok Sabha and Rajya Sabha; they have been governors and chief ministers of states, ambassadors, members of the cabinet and deputy ministers; and they have held the highest positions in the organizations of the major political parties.

At the same time, the presence of women at the highest political levels coexists with a generally low rate of overall participation in the political life of the country. Thus, in the three elections analysed in this chapter, the number of women candidates was 64, 66, and 237 in the 1962 Lok Sabha, 1967 Lok Sabha, and 1967 legislative assembly elections, respectively. These numbers are more impressive than for other countries, but they must be put against the figures for all candidates, which were 1,985, 2,369, and 16,503, respectively, yielding a participation of women candidates at only percentages of 3.2, 2.8, and 1.4, respectively, for the three elections. Similarly, while the absolute number of women elected to state and national office is quite high (31, 28, and 93 in these elections), the percentage of successful women to the total is, inevitably, quite

* This study (written jointly with Padma Desai) is a byproduct of a more comprehensive and ambitious research undertaking on women in the economic, social, legal, and political structure of contemporary Indian society being conducted by Padma Desai. Thanks are due to Priscilla Battis for making the relevant election reports available to us. Our thanks also go to John Field, whose comments have led to many improvements in this study. Chaiyawat Wibulswasdi computed the regressions. Katherine Laperche Eisenhaure, Mary East, and Marilyn Rash have cheerfully and efficiently typed the tables and the text.

small (only 6.3, 5.4, and 2.7 respectively). These low proportions put into necessary perspective, but cannot dwarf, the fact that women have reached the highest levels of political success and seem to be widely accepted as a 'natural' element of the political scene in India.

This phenomenon raises a number of important and interesting questions that we can pose and answer only very partially and tentatively here, hoping to have them answered later by fuller analysis.

(1) What types of constituencies select and elect women to the central and state legislatures? Are these constituencies characterized by high literacy (as in Kerala), by a tradition of social work (as in Gujarat), by the left-wing orientation of their politics (as in West Bengal), by the impact of the strong Gandhian impetus to female participation in the Congress and the independence movement generally (as in Gujarat, for example)?

(2) How do the political parties compare in selecting women candidates? Are the left-wing parties more egalitarian or is there ground for a Simone de Beauvoir variety of disillusionment in this regard? Are 'communal', 'orthodox' parties such as the Jana Sangh and the Muslim League in Kerala notable for denying nominations to women? To what extent do politically ambitious women choose or find it necessary to run as independent candidates?

(3) Do women tend to succeed more than men in the elections? And if so, what are the reasons? Is it because, owing to built-in discrimination against women, those who get so far as to be selected as candidates must have a special talent which exceeds that required in a man to reach the same stage? Or is it because women tend to attract more votes, in which case one may well ask why even more women are not put up as candidates?

(4) Do women who run for office and those who are elected to the legislatures have any special characteristics? That is, are they unmarried or separated or divorced so that they can pursue their careers, sublimating their family instincts (the female counterpart of Freud's argument for male success in their careers)? Are they very highly educated? Have they been connected by marriage or birth to distinguished *men*, on whose coat-tails they are managing to get the extra edge required to compete with

men in a male-oriented society?[1] Do they come from a back-ground of social work or active participation in the independence movement?

Our analysis to date has been confined to the 1962 and 1967 Lok Sabha and the 1967 legislative assembly elections, and for a more complete picture will clearly have to be extended to other election results (including those produced by the sub-sequent general elections of 1971 and 1972). Furthermore, we are fully aware that inferences from any specific election may be misleading and that a study of active female participation in the political process could well require the simultaneous consideration of local, state, and national elections at any point in time: a task we undertake partially here for 1967 by con-sidering, for some indices, the legislative assembly and Lok Sabha elections together. While the availability of data in the United States and our research capacity (limited to our own extensive resort to calculations, without research assistance) confined us to the results we report below, we hope that profes-sional political scientists, including psephologists, will find our analysis a helpful, pioneering effort and extend it in the directions indicated.

We first consider the question: What are the chances of women being put up as candidates in the elections we have examined? This question may be answered at two levels: (1) Do women tend to be sponsored more in some states than in others: and (2) Do some parties do systematically better in this regard than others? Since the scores produced by ratios, as of women can-didates to the total, are often not very revealing because of the limited number of women involved, we have included the actual numbers and given the resulting ratio values in brackets.

Table 12.1, which lists the Indian states above and below the average ratio of women candidates to the total number of can-didates contesting each election for the country as a whole.

---

[1] This hypothesis is suggested by the background and careers of the two most prominent women politicians in Asia: Mrs Indira Gandhi (daughter of Prime Minister Jawaharlal Nehru) and Mrs Sirimavo Bandaranaike (wife of Prime Min-ister Bandaranaike). One can hardly suppress the thought: will Chiang Ching succeed Mao Tse-tung?

TABLE 12.1

Ranking of States by Ratio of Women Candidates to Total Number of Contesting Candidates

	1962	*1967*		
	Lok Sabha	*Lok Sabha*	*Legislative Assembly*	*Legislative Assembly and Lok Sabha*
Above Average	1. Himachal Pradesh	1. Madhya Pradesh	1. Gujarat	1. Kerala
	2. Gujarat	2. Goa, D & D	2. Andhra Pradesh	2. Gujarat
	3. Assam	3. Kerala	2. Orissa	2. Delhi
	4. Madhya Pradesh	4. Punjab	4. W. Bengal	4. Andhra Pradesh
	5. Rajasthan	5. Madras	4. Kerala	5. Madras
	6. Bihar	6. Bihar	6. Haryana	5. W. Bengal
	6. Andhra Pradesh	7. Uttar Pradesh	7. Assam	5. Orissa
	8. Uttar Pradesh		8. Madras	8. Assam
			9. Maharashtra	8. Bihar
			9. Mysore	8. Madhya Pradesh
			9. Bihar	8. Haryana
				12. Punjab
Below Average	9. Madras	8. Andhra Pradesh	12. Punjab	13. Maharashtra
	10. Kerala	9. Maharashtra	12. Uttar Pradesh	14. Uttar Pradesh
	11. W. Bengal	9. Delhi	14. Madhya Pradesh	15. Mysore
	12. Maharashtra	11. Assam	14. Rajasthan	16. Rajasthan

Table 12.1 (cont.)

	1962		1967	
	Lok Sabha	Lok Sabha	Legislative Assembly	Legislative Assembly and Lok Sabha
Below Average	13. Mysore	11. W. Bengal	16. Tripura	16. Tripura
	14. Orissa	13. Haryana	17. Himachal Pradesh	18. Goa, D & D
	14. Punjab	13. Orissa	18. J & K	19. Himachal Pradesh
	14. Delhi	15. Gujarat	19. Goa, D & D	20. J & K
	14. Manipur	16. Rajasthan	20. Manipur	21. Nagaland
		17. J & K		21. And. & Nic.
		17. Mysore		21. Chandigarh
		17. Nagaland		21. Dadra & NH
		17. Himachal Pradesh		21. Laccadive
		17. Laccadive, et al.		21. Manipur
		17. Pondicherry		21. Pondicherry
		17. Tripura		
		17 Manipur		
		17. And. & Nic.		
		17. Dadra & NH		
		17. Chandigarh		

NOTE: The indicated numbers give the rank ordering. Union Territories are included.

SOURCE: Calculated from col. (2) in Apps 12.1–3.

Table 12.1 divides the states accordingly for the three elections under review and also for the 'sum' of the two 1967 elections.[2]

The order of magnitude of differences among the states is not very great; nor is it negligible either. Thus in the 1962 Lok Sabha elections Gujarat had a high ratio of .088 (that is, one in eleven parliamentary candidates was a woman, or 6 of 68 overall), whereas Orissa and Punjab had no female candidates. And the 1967 assembly results show a high in Gujarat of .023 with lows of .005 for Jammu & Kashmir and .011 for Madhya Pradesh and Rajasthan.

The range of women candidates can thus spread from zero to nearly 9 per cent among the states but is usually much smaller. At the same time, there is an inevitable criss-crossing, between elections, in the rank ordering of the states, and also some problems raised by changing territorial groupings. We may virtually conclude, therefore, that no striking differences seem to emerge as a persistent pattern among the states and union territories: a negative conclusion of some interest in itself.

And yet, a closer look at the results, provides *some* confirmation of our conjectures and equally some paradoxes seem to emerge as strong possibilities. Thus, we are surprised that West Bengal, which was among the first Indian provinces to experience the modernizing 'renaissance', and which encouraged female participation in the independence struggle, is generally a below-average performer: less than 2 per cent of the candidates (25 out of 1,310) contesting the elections under review in West Bengal were women. On the other hand, Gujarat, which has a long tradition of social work and consciousness, and which was touched very greatly by the independence movement, shows (unsurprisingly)

---

[2] The reader may wonder about the rationale of combining the Lok Sabha and legislative assembly election results for 1967. We think that such a procedure is sensible if we consider women politicians within a state to form a pool, and if we further assume that the women within the pool are assigned to one level or the other by the party nomination process. Of course, if such an assumption or an alternative sufficiency restriction is not made, it would not be meaningful to look at the two election results together. The reader may well find it revealing even to *contrast* the 1967 Lok Sabha and legislative assembly elections — a task we have not attempted.

a better performance than most other states: 21 out of 760, or 2.8 per cent of the candidates there were women.

West Bengal's relatively poor performance is particularly noteworthy given the egalitarian views of many of its intellectuals, and suggests the question, now increasingly raised outside India, whether socialist regimes and/or intellectuals systematically tend to perform disappointingly in the matter of promoting women's rights and participation in public life.[3] The disillusionment on this score ranges from intellectuals such as Simone de Beauvoir to activists such as Jane Alpert, the Weatherman who wrote distressingly from underground on the subject of male chauvinism among her revolutionary associates (including her husband).[4] It is also remarkable that major intellectual and influential writings on women's rights have come primarily from such figures as the utilitarian John Stuart Mill and India's own Mahatma Gandhi, and not in a comparable degree from the tradition of Marx. Here is a paradox to ponder.

This also leads us to our next observations, which emerges quite dramatically from the statistical results: (1) The Congress Party is by far the best performer on selecting women candidates, and (2) the Communists are no better in this regard than right-wing parties such as Swatantra and the Jana Sangh.

Were it not for the Congress party, whose traditions in the matter of feminine participation were heavily influenced by Mahatma Gandhi, female participation in electoral contests would have been more than halved at the assembly level in 1967, whereas the total candidates fielded would have been reduced by only a fifth; and female participation would have been reduced by between 50 and

---

[3] Note, however, that Kerala is not quite as disappointing as West Bengal. But then note also that the Bengali Communists, who are reputed to be more intellectual than their counterparts in Kerala, often consider the latter as unsophisticated and 'impure', a Brahmanical attitude that often cuts across Indian political parties and other secular institutions!

[4] It is true, of course, that women in the Soviet Union are actively involved in economic life, thanks largely to the tragic depletion of manpower in the World War II. But this does not seem to carry over into their holding, in substantial numbers, the better-paid and more prestigious jobs in Soviet society any more than is true of China and the United States, for example.

60 per cent and the total by less than 25 per cent in both the 1962 and 1967 Lok Sabha elections.

If we regress the ratio of women to total candidates on the proportion of Congress to total candidates in each state (leaving out union territories) in each election (the data are summarized in Table 12.2), we get the following estimated equations for the three elections under review,

(1)	1962 Lok Sabha Elections	x =	.050	$-.062Y$ $(R^2 = 0.016)$
			(.038)	(.139)
			((1.322))	((.444))
(2)	1967 Lok Sabha Elections	x =	.016	$+.035Y$ $(R^2 = 0.023)$
			(.014)	(.058)
			((1.108))	((.600))
(3)	1967 Legislative Assembly Elections	x =	.009	$+.027Y$ $(R^2 = 0.248)$
			(.005)	(.020)
			((1.849))	((1.352))

where x is the ratio of women to total candidates and Y the proportion of Congress to total candidates in each state. The bracketed numbers are standard errors and the double-bracketed numbers are 't' values. Equations (1) and (2) do not show any significant fits; but equation (3) does (at level of significance .02), indicating a *positive* relationship between the two variables, in consonance with out hypothesis. Moreover, the Spearman Rank Correlation coefficients for the three pairs of data are –.121, +.085, and +.491 respectively; again, the last figure of .491, for the 1967 legislative assembly data, is the strongest and positive. Thus, statistical tests on the election results strongly suggest (for 1967 data) that the ratio of women to total candidates rises with the proportion of Congress to total candidates, underlining our thesis that the Congress Party's policy of nominating relatively more women candidates is a principal factor in increasing the overall incidence of women as electoral nominees.

We may next ask if our results would change if we took as our index of female participation, *not* the ratio of women to total candidates, but rather the proportion of seats contested by women.

TABLE 12.2

Ratios of Congress to Total Candidates and Women to Total
Candidates, by State, in the 1962 and 1967 Elections

State	1962 Lok Sabha		1967 Lok Sabha		1967 Legislative Assembly	
	Ratio of women to total candidates	Ratio of Congress to total candidates	Ratio of women to total candidates	Ratio of Congress to total candidates	Ratio of women to total candidates	Ratio of Congress to total candidates
Andhra Pradesh	.034	.292	.024	.244	.020	.267
Assam	.073	.293	.021	.276	.016	.238
Bihar	.034	.227	.038	.168	.014	.157
Gujarat	.088	.323	.012	.168	.023	.273
Haryana	–	–	.015	.134	.017	.172
Jammu & Kashmir	–	–	0	.267	.005	.257
Kerala	.020	.280	.049	.311	.019	.314
Madhya Pradesh	.069	.220	.069	.213	.011	.190
Madras	.026	.263	.039	.307	.015	.301
Maharashtra	.012	.262	.022	.243	.014	.216
Mysore	.011	.295	0	.270	.014	.294
Nagaland	–	–	0	0	–	–
Orissa	0	.388	.015	.308	.020	.232
Punjab	0	.206	.040	.173	.013	.166
Rajasthan	.054	.189	.009	.190	.011	.204
Uttar Pradesh	.032	.192	.026	.168	.013	.141
West Bengal	.018	.321	.021	.286	.019	.265

Table 12.2 ranks the states by this index, also dividing them,
as in Table 12.1, into two groups separated by the mean of the
index. Our conclusions based on Table 12.1 are again broadly
confirmed: there is criss-crossing of the states between elections
in their rank ordering; there are no clear patterns that are readily

discerned; and Gujarat seems to do well and West Bengal comparatively poorly.

Furthermore, the overwhelming role of the Congress party in sponsoring women candidates is again evident from an examination of the proportion of female candidates in each election coming from the Congress. Table 12.2 presents these proportions in each state for the three elections. The percentage highs go up to 70 for Mysore, 71 for Andhra Pradesh, and 80 for Gujarat in the 1967 legislative assembly elections; to 80 for Andhra Pradesh, and 100 for West Bengal, Assam, Mysore, and Kerala in the 1962 Lok Sabha elections; and to 75 for Andhra Pradesh, 80 for Madras, and 100 for Assam, Gujarat, and Haryana in the 1967 Lok Sabha elections. In all, Congress has put up at least half of the women running for office in 31 of the 47 state elections shown.

The relatively low number of independent women candidates, absolutely and in relation to the total number of women candidates, also underlines the critical importance of more active exploration by the political parties themselves of the need to promote the accelerated selection of women candidates in a more egalitarian and progressive spirit. Indeed, if only all the non-Congress parties had increased their women-selection ratios to that of the Congress party, this alone would have practically doubled the number of women candidates during the 1967 assembly elections (from 174 for all the major parties to 323) — while, of course, still keeping the ratio of women to total candidates very much lower than the ratio of women to men among the registered voters.

Notwithstanding the still limited participation of women in competitive politics as candidates, one of the more remarkable phenomena revealed by our analysis of the election results is the high rate of success that women candidates seem to enjoy in getting *elected*. While the possibility of being nominated by a political party is slender for a woman, as is the likelihood of her becoming an independent candidate, the astonishing thing is that she has a phenomenal chance of 'making it' once she is on the ballot. Moreover, this chance greatly outweighs the 'average' chance of 'making it' (defined by the ratio of all candidates to all constituencies).

This conclusion is practically true for all parties, for all states, for all the elections we have looked at![5] Thus, to take ex-post probabilities of women being elected, these are .484 for the 1962 Lok Sabha, .431 for the 1967 Lok Sabha, and .392 for the 1967 legislative assembly elections! And, as always, they are equally impressive for the Congress party at .788 for the 1962 Lok Sabha, .500 for the 1967 Lok Sabha, and .592 for the 1967 legislative assembly elections. Congress party 'performance' again dominates that of the other political parties in this area, as in the other areas discussed in this chapter.

What do we make of this remarkable fact? The high success rate most probably reflects the fact that, given the discrimination against women, a woman has to have exceptional ability as a candidate to be nominated in the first place and that, as a result, women candidates are likely to be more 'gifted' and hence are more likely to win than men candidates. At the same time, it is improbable that the electorate 'prefers' women to men candidates; for were that the case, we would not be likely to observe the very low participation rate in elections by women.

In conclusion, we may re-emphasize the exploratory nature of our inquiry and the inferences drawn from it; and we reiterate the need to extend the analysis to other elections, while also systematically probing several of the questions listed in the beginning of this study — questions that can only be answered by further fieldwork on women candidates and on constituency characteristics. We hope that some of our propositions and hypotheses in this review of basic patterns will stimulate further research by political scientists working on India.

---

[5] Thus the winning record of women is *not* to be explained solely by the fact that women tend to run disproportionately as Congress candidates and that Congress candidates, in turn, win disproportionately.

13

The Brain Drain:
International Resource Flow
Accounting, Compensation, Taxation
and Related Policy Proposals[*]

1. INTRODUCTION

THIS chapter is addressed principally to analysing several major issues relating to the phenomenon of international migration of skilled people from the developing countries (LDCs) to the developed countries (DCs), popularly described as the 'brain drain'.

Section 2 places such migration into perspective vis-à-vis migrations that occur among LDCs and among DCs, this analysis serving to highlight the special characteristics of the brain drain from LDCs into DCs that must be borne in mind when we turn to the policy-oriented conceptual and measurement analyses of the later sections. Towards that end, the principal dimensions and patterns of the brain drain are also sketched with extreme brevity, for certain policy suggestions in regard to taxing the brain drain, for example, have inter-LDC *distributional* consequences which should reflect the shares of the LDCs in the overall brain drain into DCs.

Section 3 then discusses the possible arguments and modalities for extension of the present international resource accounting framework to include the flows implied by the brain drain.

Section 4 develops the analysis in the direction of examining the reasons why the brain drain 'phenomenon' may also then

---

* Prepared for the Division on Transfer of Technology, UNCTAD, in July 1977. Minor editorial changes have been made. *Author's Note*: Since this chapter was written, my views on the feasible and optimal format of an income tax by LDCs on their nationals abroad have evolved, as explicitly spelled out in chapter 14, esp. pp. 352–9.

imply a brain drain 'problem' and, in the light of that, developing the concept of 'loss to the LDCs' from the brain drain — a concept that must be sharply separated from the concept of the 'capital flow' from LDCs to DCs implicit in the brain drain.

Section 5 then discusses the alternative policy proposals that have been advanced in relation to the brain drain, either to mitigate such losses to LDCs or, *more generally*, to tax the brain drain to raise resources for LDCs of origin or LDCs en bloc.

Section 6 then focuses directly on alternative proposals to tax the brain drain: distinguishing particularly among the suggestions to tax the DCs for the benefit of the LDCs of emigration to institutionalize an 'international compensation mechanism' and the suggestion to tax the incomes of the migrants themselves. The rationales of such taxes, and the possible objections that may be levelled against them and their possible rebuttal, will be the subject matter of our discussion here.

Section 7 summarizes the major conclusions and recommendations.

2. PATTERNS AND SPECIAL FEATURES OF LDC-TO-DC BRAIN DRAIN

Since the focus of this chapter is exclusively on *analytical* issues arising from policy proposals advanced in regard to the brain drain from LDCs into DCs, this is not the occasion to analyse the available statistical information on such flows. However, a few salient points must be noted, if only because the policy discussions need to take these carefully into account.[1]

First, the impact of the post-Second World War shift in the

---

[1] The statistical discussions are greatly handicapped by lack of systematic and comprehensive information for most DCs of immigration, as also by the lack of comparability of such data across most countries owing to different definitions and coverages. Nonetheless, all is not lost and the interested reader can refer to the recent contributions by Balacs and Gordon (for the UK), Maki and DeVoretz (for Canada) and Lucas, Dellalfar, Pelcovits, etc. (on the USA) in Bhagwati and Partington (1976) and Bhagwati (1976a). Valuable information is also contained in US House of Representatives (1974).

immigration policies of major DCs, away from the earlier racial-origin quotas to more equal access by all nationalities, was to significantly increase the share of the LDCs in the immigration into DCs. Combined with this, of course, was the considerable increase in the share of PTK immigrants — the PTK being the category of professional, technical, and kindred workers in the US Immigration and Naturalization Service classification that corresponds generally to the groups of migrants who are considered to constitute the 'brain drain' — in the overall immigration into the United States, in particular, and also into Canada and the UK.[2]

Second, the pattern of PTK immigration from LDCs to DCs is not necessarily bilateral but will often proceed multilaterally. Indian doctors transit to the UK and then to the USA; Pakistani PhDs in the USA migrate to Canada until they qualify for an entry on immigration visas into the USA; Sri Lanka doctors go to the UK while UK doctors emigrate to the USA, and so on. This implies that, in analysing the statistics, as also the impact of different policy measures, it is necessary to take into account a complex pattern of effects. Thus, decline in Canadian PTK immigration followed from the relaxation of the US immigration policies: it was no longer necessary to 'wait' in Canada as much as before. Similarly, tightening entry into one country may not reduce the brain drain but merely 'divert' it into another DC.[3]

Third, casual empiricism plus recent statistical exercises lead to the important distinction between 'gross' and 'net' brain drain: many migrants seem to return to LDCs or, at least, to shift back and forth. Thus, the policy analysis must take into account the complications from 'to-and-fro' and 'reverse' migrations instead of considering the problem as one of 'permanent' or 'once-and-for-all' migration.[4]

Fourth, a significant portion of the gross immigration consists

[2] For more details, see Bhagwati (1976b).

[3] Thus, it is possible to distinguish, as in international trade theory on customs unions, between 'brain drain creation' and 'brain drain diversion' as a result of policy changes.

[4] Recent statistical exercises suggest that outflow may be as much as 30 per cent of gross immigration of LDC PTKs into DCs. See Balacs and Gordon on the UK, for example, in Bhagwati and Partington (1976).

of 'stay-on' LDC students in DCs. The proportion varies by profession, being clearly negligible in the case of doctors and high for engineers.[5] This fact is critical, for example, to our later discussion of the conventions to be adopted in imputing capital flows to the brain drain since DC-education, in so far as it represents DC-incurred expenditures, may be therefore netted out from the imputation.

Fifth, in anticipating possible LDC interest in several tax and other proposals, the LDC-composition in, and overall size of, the brain drain will be relevant. Here, it is necessary to note that the overall PTK flow into DCs is likely to be almost exclusively a function of the restrictiveness of the DC policies (though these in turn may slightly accommodate to the so-called 'push' factors). On the other hand, the share of the LDCs en bloc into this total, as also their *individual* shares of this, will reflect (given ran-domized access to the immigration queue) the internal labour market situation vis-à-vis the external economic prospects and relevant economic magnitudes.[6] This does mean that these levels and patterns are difficult to forecast with accuracy. Thus, for example, recent US legislation has practically shut off immigration of foreign doctors into the US as of early 1977: this could not have been forecast even in 1975! The virtual demise of the huge US space programmes earlier had similarly dealt an unanticipated blow to immigration of scientists, principally from other DCs, to the point where the European DCs had felt their brain drain problem to be eased sufficiently to have the OECD cease working on a now obsolete problem.[7] Again, the effect on the LDC-to-DC brain drain of the OPEC countries' enormous demands for PTK manpower imports, while difficult to analyse, could not have been foreseen as late as 1971.[8]

---

[5] For the statistics, see Table 4 in Bhagwati (1976b), which gives the proportions of different types of immigrants admitted by change of visa status: the conversion of student status being of course only a subset of the latter.

[6] The role of economic factors in explaining migration patterns in numerous econometric studies has been reviewed at length by Krugman and Bhagwati in Bhagwati (1976).

[7] On the latter, see Grubel and Scott (1977: ch. 1).

[8] For speculation on these effects, see Bhagwati (1976a: 8); also see below.

Sixth, it is useful to place the LDC-to-DC type of 'brain drain' migration into perspective vis-à-vis other types of migrations. In particular, two sets of contrasts may be distinguished. On the one hand, the LDC-to-DC migration may be contrasted with the LDC-to-LDC and the DC-to-DC migrations of PTK manpower. On the other hand, the 'brain drain' migration may be contrasted with the 'expulsion', 'exit-from-socialism', and 'flight-from-authoritarianism' type of migrations.

(1) Thus, consider the first contrast. The LDC-to-LDC migration of PTK manpower used to be relatively unimportant in the past, being confined largely to UN-sponsored technical assistance that deployed LDC experts in other LDCs. However, with the success of OPEC, this type of intra-LDC migration has become extremely important. Its contrast to the LDC-to-DC migration, however, consists in the fact that the OPEC countries have wealth and income but not the developmental attributes that usually go with these: so that while the LDC emigration to the DCs has a great inducement to stay on in the DCs with their 'modern' forms of culture and democratic ways of life, these amenities and advantages of modernization are hardly available in any of the OPEC countries, and certainly not in the more traditional societies such as Saudi Arabia and Kuwait. Thus, the Egyptian and other high-level PTK migrants to these countries are far more likely to be 'reverse' migrants: and therefore this migration needs to be regarded, from a policy point of view, as being quite different to the LDC-to-DC migration of PTK personnel. This argument is only reinforced from the 'demand' side: few of the oil-rich Middle East countries, with their abundant oil and scarce manpower, are likely to want permanent immigration of 'superior' personnel from any one area. Aside from the resentments that are bound to breed from the inherent strains arising from the intellectual superiority of the immigrant and the financial dominance of the native population that hires him, the natives are likely to fear 'reverse assimilation' and loss of identity, thus wanting to have an immigrant PTK workforce that is very definitely *temporary* and variable in terms of its national and cultural composition.[9]

[9] This a priori observation would seem to be confirmed by the recent success of the South Koreans in garnering construction contracts in the Middle East. They

On the other hand, the DC-to-DC PTK migration would seem to contrast identically with the LDC-to-DC migration — i.e. to be subject to greater reverse migration — but for a totally different reason: namely, that the differences in economic conditions and rewards between LDC and DCs are far more substantial than those among DCs, so that relatively minor relative changes in labour market conditions, for example, may induce reverse migration in the former, but not in the latter, case. This difference also accounts, in large part, for the complacency with which DC-origin economists tend to reject arguments about the disruptive effects of the brain drain on LDC institution-building (which has frequently to be done from a primitive level), on domestic salary levels (which come under great strain because of the impossibility of matching the tremendously higher DC levels), etc., whereas the LDC-origin economists accept them readily from the immediacy of their LDC experience.

(2) Next, the 'brain drain', which by and large reflects economic and quasi-economic considerations, must be contrasted with three other types of PTK emigration from LDCs: (i) the 'expulsion' type of migration, as with the expulsion of Asian professionals (among others) from Uganda; (ii) the 'exit-from-socialism' type of migration, as with the emigration of PTK 'bourgeoisie' from Tanzania and Chile (under President Allende),[10] where the spread of egalitarianism in the shape of greatly reduced salary and wealth differentials prompts the exit; and (iii) the 'flight-from-authoritarianism' type of migration, where the PTK personnel flee political repression under military or other forms of dictatorships.[11]

These are, of course, 'polar types', and specific PTK migrations may have shades of more than one of these classes of migration.

---

are reputed to import Korean labour at all levels, keep it strictly under control and segregated from the local populations, and to remove it as soon as the contract is completed.

[10] Perhaps the emigration of doctors from socialized medicine and high taxes, the twin features of a 'socialist' welfare state in the UK, also falls under this rubric.

[11] Examples of this are the flight from Portugal to Brazil under the Salazar regime and from Spain to Latin America generally under the Franco regime. Recent examples would include reverse flights from some countries in Latin America to Portugal and Spain, as the latter have shifted to democratic regimes and the flouting of human rights in the former has increased.

The distinctions are useful, however, in the asymmetries of behaviour that they imply for economic analysis of PTK migration. Thus, for example, remittances may be confidently expected from the 'brain drain' migrants, but less so from the 'exit' and 'flight' types and none from the expulsion type where whole families tend to be uprooted. This applies also to flow of externalities in the form of return visits by professionals to LDCs of origin. Again, the brain drain outflow is likely to be smoother and smaller than the 'exit' or 'flight' variety, and therefore less damaging in its immediate impact on the LDCs.

However, from the viewpoint of policy-making, such as the adoption of the brain-drain-related taxes analysed below, these different types of LDC PTK migration into DCs are not likely to be operationally distinguishable and will have to be disregarded, with the exception of possible exemption of those in the 'flight' category who are admitted explicitly as 'political refugees' (an admittedly delimited and small category in any event).

3. ON MODIFYING INTERNATIONAL RESOURCE ACCOUNTING TO INCORPORATE THE BRAIN DRAIN FLOWS

The salient facts about skilled international migration from LDCs to DCs, presented above have a direct bearing (as we shall presently see) on the questions to which we now turn: (i) should the flow of skilled manpower be incorporated into international accounting on the flows between LDCs and DCs of capital; and (ii) if so, how should this be done?

The international accounting of *capital flows* currently includes only the nominal capital flows that occur at both private and official levels. These also include, of course, flows that are sometimes 'imputed', as in the case of valuation of second-hand machinery imported by multinationals as part of their equity investment in the LDCs. Needless to say, the bulk of these flows run *from the DCs to the LDCs*.

Moreover, it will be recalled that it was customary for many years to regard private and official capital flows as both providing capital 'assistance' to the LDCs, as if the private flows were also some form of aid; and it took much effort to separate aid from private capital flows and to relate the targets at UNCTAD to aid proper.[12] Nonetheless, the fact remains that an overall balance sheet of international *capital* flows (as distinct from *aid* flows) will include private and official flows alike.

Given this situation, it is well worth investigating whether the migration of skilled manpower from the LDCs to the DCs should not be capitalized and then included in such a balance sheet of 'capital flows', with the concept of capital therefore being broadened but in a thoroughly appropriate manner. The advantage of such a balance sheet of LDC–DC 'capital' flows would be that it would bring into better perspective the overall capital flow situation, and particularly assist in deflating the exaggerated notion still held by many DC observers of the 'assistance' provided by DCs to LDCs through capital flows. Indeed, from the viewpoint of capital-flow accounting in LDC–DC economic relations, it would be ideal to separate three distinct elements: the official flows, the nominal capital flows, and the imputed capital flows implicit in (and representing the capitalized equivalent of) the flows of skilled manpower.[13]

How is such capitalization of the brain drain flow to be done? Fundamentally, there are two approaches that may be taken, with profoundly different implications. First, the *'historic cost'* approach may be taken, under which the educational costs embedded historically in the migrant may be added up to their present worth. Second, the hypothetical question may be asked: if the migrant's services were buyable in a free market, what would his present worth be as an asset? This present worth is clearly given by the *'present discounted value'* of the migrant's marginal product over his expected lifetime.[14]

The two measures will have different implications. Thus, for

---

[12] This is not to deny that private capital flows may also be beneficial to LDCs. But then so is trade with LDCs beneficial to DCs, and that is not regarded as aid from LDCs to DCs!

[13] It may be noted, with some amusement, that Marxist economists may instead wish to decompose the nominal capital flows into their 'labour equivalent' and to draw up a balance sheet of overall labour transfers among DCs and LDCs! It is difficult to imagine, however, what use such a balance sheet could be put to, if any.

[14] For full analysis, see below.

example, in the case of an unskilled migrant, his educational expenditures are negligible and the imputed capital flow on a historic-cost basis would be negligible. On the other hand, the present discounted value of such a migrant is clearly positive as long as he is employable in the DC of immigration and there would be no decisive reason to exclude his inclusion from a balance sheet of capital flows that would include imputed capital flows.

Next, it is pertinent to note that the educational expenditures embodied in the migrant are not necessarily to be regarded, under either type of imputation procedure, as productive of 'human capital' (in the sense of *socially* productive investment). Thus modern economists are familiar with two other, novel and relevant theories of education which suggest that the higher education embodied in a migrant may instead be a screening device (to enable employers to distinguish the brighter from the duller prospective employees) or an instrument of job competition. In either case, no 'human capital' is involved and education is only *privately* productive of higher incomes to the educated.[15]

Note further that neither measure has affinity to the totally distinct measures of the 'gains to DCs' or the 'losses to LDCs' that are also often discussed in regard to the brain drain.[16] Indeed, much confusion follows from an inadequate appreciation of this distinction. The distinction should be readily grasped however once an analogy is drawn between the present distinction and the obvious and familiar distinction between a measure of (nominal) capital flows and measures of their welfare effects on the host and the investing countries.

Moreover, it must be noted that the process of imputation is complicated by the presence of two alternative sets of relevant prices: those that pertain to DCs and those that obtain in LDCs. Since these are *segmented* markets, owing to lack of free migration, and since the commodity prices required for the imputation relate in part to non-traded goods and in part to traded goods whose

[15] For the screening theory of education, see Arrow (1973) and Spence (1973). For job competition theory see Bhagwati (1973), Fields (1974), and Bhagwati and Srinivasan (1977).

[16] Nor should any of these measures, in turn, be confused with the measure of the gain in welfare accruing to the migrants themselves.

prices are not equalized across DCs and LDCs because of artificial and natural obstacles, we are faced with the necessity of developing estimates based alternatively on DC and LDC prices.

Furthermore, the process of imputation is bedevilled by the fact that PTK migration is often 'to-and-fro' rather than of a once-and-for-all variety, and by the additional fact that part of the educational expenditure of many migrants is incurred in the DC of immigration. Thus, if we take historic cost measures, an LDC PTK migrant who has completed some education in the LDC will be evaluated, say, at LDC prices when he migrates; then he acquires additional education in the DC which is, of course, incurred in DC prices; when he returns to the LDC, the reverse flow of capital will then include historic cost measured partly in LDC prices and partly in DC prices, so that a convention may be evolved with regard to which prices should be *consistently* used.[17]

Having then noted some of the principal difficulties that the process of imputation will raise, we should also add that such problems are inevitable when imputation of prices is involved: a fact that is fully familiar to national income statisticians who have had to deal with imputing incomes in the non-market sector in LDCs and are now to address themselves to the task of imputing incomes to women's household work. Thus, nothing should be considered insuperable with regard to implementing the suggestion to impute a 'capital' figure to the brain drain flow. It is useful therefore to proceed with defining in greater depth the two principal types of measures of imputed capital flows that we have distinguished above, focussing first on the simpler once-and-for-all migration case and next on the 'to-and-fro' and 'reverse' migration case.[18]

Once-and-for-all Migration

Using the suffixes 'e' and 'i' to refer to the LDC of emigration and DC of immigration, we may now set out the two sets of concepts and their possible variants.

[17] In addition, as I discuss below, the fact that the DC invests in an LDC national's education prior to his formal migration creates obvious problems for estimating the LDC to DC flow of imputed capital in this instance.

[18] The following discussion is based largely on Bhagwati (1976a: 12–19).

(1) *Historic cost measures.* Here, we can define HC_e as the measure of the direct and indirect educational costs embodied in the migrant at the time of the emigration to the DC.

Simple as this procedure sounds, especially to those familiar with the now standard techniques for estimating educational costs, note that the estimated costs would be at domestic prices and would have to be converted into 'standard dollar' values or some such *agreed-upon* (now that exchange rates are no longer stable) equivalent, common standard.

But, more important, there is the difficult problem that arises because the formal act of migration of an LDC national to a DC may follow his acquisition of *some* education in the DC. Should we then estimate his historic cost imputed flow as the cost of LDC-education alone? Since our focus is on estimating the LDC to DC capital flows, this may seem to be more appropriate than leaving the DC-incurred costs in the estimate (though, if we were to count them in, we would still be faced with the problem of choosing between estimating these costs at DC or at LDC prices, the latter being necessary if we wish to make the estimate at *one* set of prices).[19] On the other hand, it can equally soundly be argued that what is being measured is the historic cost of education embodied in the LDC national *as and when he migrates to the DC*, so that the question of where that investment came from is not relevant to this particular exercise (though it could well be pertinent to an exercise, for example, aimed at estimating the 'saving in investment costs' to the DCs from having the PTK immigrants from the LDCs). The latter convention is, in fact, the simpler and proper one: and it is the one that ought to be adopted for historic cost measures. It does require, of course, for the *overall*

---

[19] Even if we wish to leave out DC-incurred educational costs, it may still be inappropriate to calculate the historic cost as above since it implies that the act of migration is being notionally shifted to the point in time at which the LDC national arrived in the DC for education. Migration may still be considered to have taken place at the actual time of occurrence and then a figure put on the LDC-education that the migrant might *alternatively* have undertaken prior to actual migration. This 'notional' imputation would then amount to evaluating the migrant's historic cost at his *total* DC + LDC educational expenditures, all these being estimated at LDC prices.

capital-flow accounting between LDCs and DCs, that the DCs be allowed then to include their domestic expenditures on educating LDC students as part of the capital flows from DCs to LDCs. Indeed, in so far as foreign aid is utilized for educational expenditures in LDCs, such accounting is already being done; and extending this practice to DC domestic expenditures on LDC students would both complete this accounting and also be a neater alternative than trying to separate, in the LDC PTK immigrants, the contributions made by DCs and LDCs to their educational costs.[20]

Identically, then, we may also value the historic cost measure, with the above qualifications and explanations again applicable, at the prices relevant to the DC of immigration: denoting this as the HC_i measure. It is evident that, given the normal excess of DC over LDC educational costs, we should expect HC_i to exceed HC_e.

(2) *Present discounted value measures.* Here, we are faced with a number of alternatives. Basically, the valuation procedure involves pricing the immigrant as an asset that yields a certain income: so that if there were indeed a market for this asset, this would be the valuation that it would command in the market. The alternatives then arise simply from the fact that the market for such an asset may be envisaged in different ways. In particular, we may distinguish among three basic types of concepts: (i) PDV^{PMP} where we assume that the prospective employer takes into account the private marginal product in employment of the immigrant over his lifetime and then bids for the asset; (ii) PDV^{wage} where we assume instead that there may be monopsonistic hiring by employers so that the asset will be valued at capitalized wages which are below the private marginal product; and finally (iii) PDV^{SMP} where we may envisage a situation with the bidding reflecting also the social, rather than the private, marginal product of the immigrant in the DC. These different measures may then be discussed below.

PDV_e^{PMP}. This is the present discounted value in the LDC of

[20] It may be noted that if the DC-incurred educational expenses on LDC students in DCs are to be computed as part of DC capital flows to LDCs, they will be recorded at DC prices. For consistency, therefore we would want to compute the historic cost measures also, such that the DC-incurred educational measures are recorded at these same prices: recording them at LDC prices, for example, would then bias the accounting in favour of DCs!

emigration, taking the private marginal product of the emigrant. In this measure, we take the present discounted value of the PTK emigrant, as it would emerge in a capital market, from bidding so as to exploit the services of this 'asset'. From the point of view of prospective employers in a decentralized system, the relevant parameters in the calculation are clearly the familiar discount rate, the time-span over which the emigrant would be producing the services, and the estimated private marginal product of the emigrant over this time-span.

PDV_e^{wage}. This is the present discounted value in the LDC of emigration, taking the wage of the emigrant. This measure would diverge from PDV_e^{PMP} if the wage diverged from the private marginal product. This would happen if wage were less than PMP because the employer was monopsonistic (e.g. the state has monopolized the activity, as with medicine). In this case, we can argue that the wage ($<$ PMP) would get discounted back to its present value for capitalizing the PTK income: an interpretation that makes sense if we think of this monopsonist as offering a capitalized, current value to the worker for the latter's services over his lifetime.[21] Therefore $PDV_e^{\text{wage}} \leq PDV_e^{\text{PMP}}$ according as wage $\leq$ PMP.

$PDV_e^{\text{SMP(1)}}$. This is the present discounted value in the LDC of emigration, taking the total, social marginal product of the emigrant. This measure would include in the income stream the entire marginal product attributable to the emigrant. This makes sense if we hypothesize a capital market where *countries* are willing to bid for the asset in equation: an LDC would then bid so as to impute the *total*, social marginal product to the emigrant and hence the capitalization would reflect this. Naturally, in the presence of externalities, $PDV_e^{\text{SMP(1)}} > PDV_e^{\text{PMP}}$.

$PDV_e^{\text{SMP(2)}}$. This is also a present discounted value in LDC of emigration, taking the total, social marginal product but *subtracting out* the remuneration (wage) of the immigrant in the LDC. The rationale for this measure would be that, if an LDC were bidding for this migrant asset, it would probably take into

[21] Note however that, in practice, it is extremely unlikely that the estimate of PDV would be undertaken except by reference to the wage earned, so that the distinction between *PMP* and the wage may not be empirically easy to implement.

account the 'net' benefit that the LDC derives from the immigrant's presence: and this would then imply subtracting out his domestic remuneration (wage) from his social contribution (SMP) at home. If this is done, as would seem rational for the LDC, then clearly $PDV_e^{SMP(2)} < PDV_e^{SMP(1)}$, but $PDV_e^{SMP(2)}$ may be less *or* greater than PDV_e^{PMP}.[22]

Next, note that these measures can again be computed from the DC data: and here it is not just a question of using different DC 'prices' but also there can be parametric differences such as in the span of working life used in the calculation. Thus, we have:

PDV_i^{PMP}. This is the present discounted value of the immigrant in the DC of immigration. This is the counterpart of PDV_e^{PMP} and discounts back the income stream, defined by the private marginal product, in the country of immigration. The two measures will diverge in so far as the PMPs, at parity conversion, are unlikely to be equal, the discount rates should generally be different, and even the working lifespans are not identical between DCs and LDCs.

PDV_i^{wage}. This is the present discounted value, using the wage, of the immigrant in the DC of immigration. This is then the counterpart of PDV_e^{wage}.

$PDV_i^{SMP(1)}$. This is the present discounted value of the immigrant in the DC of immigration, taking the social marginal product in the DC. This measure is the counterpart of $PDV_e^{SMP(1)}$ and, for reasons of the kind already spelled out, the two will not generally be identical.

$PDV_i^{SMP(2)}$. This is the present discounted value of the immigrant in the DC of immigration, subtracting out the DC wage from the SMP in the DC, and clearly corresponds to $PDV_e^{SMP(2)}$

'Reverse', 'Net' versus 'Gross', 'To-and-fro' Migrations

Our discussion of the several possible measures above indicates the difficulties that arise from handling the imputation problems of

[22] The $PDV_e^{SMP(2)}$ measure is also describable as a 'slavery-equivalent' measure: an employer buying a slave would be taking the 'net' contribution that a slave will make on the plantation and equating that to the notional 'wage' of the slave; and capitalization of the lifetime stream of such 'wages' will then represent the present discounted value price of the slave.

permanent, once-and-for-all migrations. As we have already noted, however, the PTK immigrants from LDCs do occasionally happen to return to their countries of origin, or to other LDCs, constituting a 'reverse' flow requiring us to distinguish between 'net' and 'gross' flows. They also, most unfortunately for statisticians and economists, do not seem to make up their minds even then and seem sometimes to swing to and fro between DCs and LDCs. This phenomenon raises problems for our computed imputations of capital flows, to which I address myself briefly at this point.

Two critical points need to be noted at the outset. (1) From the viewpoint of measurement, it is clear that relatively unambiguous criteria are necessary at each stage of measurement. Thus, since ex ante intentions of migrants are generally *not* reliable, we should stick to ex post migrations. Hence, quite regardless of whether a migrant intends to return to his LDC, he should be classified as a migrant as long as he takes an immigrant visa, much in the way short-term capital is regarded as such even if the intention may be to hold an asset for ever. A set of simple and feasible conventions could surely be evolved, to classify immigrants as having 'effectively' migrated from one country to another, taking ex post into account movements according to well-defined categories. The problems here are no greater than those encountered in allocating financial flows to categories such as short-term and long-term movements. (2) Next, since we have already seen that the presence of two countries involves differential valuations, on any one concept, the question naturally arises about possible consistency in measures at different points of migration of the same person. Thus, if historic cost valuation is adopted, we could evaluate the emigrant from LDC, at initial migration, at LDC valuation. When he returns, we could add to this value the incremental cost of education in the DC at DC valuation *or* evaluate the same at equivalent LDC costs. There seems to be no compelling reason to choose among these alternatives except that we may well put some premium on being consistent and evaluate *all* costs at LDC-equivalent values, whether incurred in LDCs or DCs.[23]

---

[23] Note, however, that if such a convention is followed, the *overall* capital-flows accounting between LDCs and DCs must evaluate an item *identically* everywhere: thus recall our analysis of the historic cost measures in this regard.

(1) *Historic cost measures*. Take the complex case where the emigrant is educated in the LDC, acquires further education as a non-immigrant student in the DC, works in the DC as an immigrant, and then returns to the LDC.

(i) Taking *consistent* HC_e valuation, at costs in the LDC, we could measure the imputed flow of capital to the DC as the historic costs incurred up to the point of emigration: hence, the educational costs (direct and indirect) of the DC education would be evaluated at the value of such educational costs if incurred in the LDC, since emigration is not considered to have taken place in the example until *after* the DC education is complete. The reverse flow should then also be measured at the same LDC-equivalent historic cost, HC_e.

(ii) Alternatively, the valuation could be carried through, at each point of cross-over, in terms of DC-equivalent historic costs, HC_i.

(iii) On the other hand, we could take historic values, *as incurred*, evaluating them at the values in the countries where they were incurred, even though this involves adding together values at different 'prices'. Thus, the LDC-educational costs would be recorded at LDC values, HC_e, and the DC-educational costs at DC values, HC_i. Their sum, in our example, would be recorded initially as the flow of imputed capital to the DC and later as the return flow to the LDC.

(2) *Present discounted value measures*. These of course raise particularly serious computational difficulties, as the valuations must be made (if we stick to the consistency requirement, in the sense of the preceding subsection) entirely with reference to the discount rate, the time-span of remaining working life, and the 'income' (i.e. PMP, wage or SMP) as relevant to either the LDC or the DC. Thus, with LDC valuations, we would need to compute the imputed flow from the LDC to the DC in the foregoing example at the value of the fully trained immigrant; and the return flow to the LDC would measure the same value at 'income' over the working timespan remaining to the immigrant at the point of the reverse migration. And the same, with DC valuations, would hold for PDV_i measures, taken consistently.

My analysis therefore indicates the kinds of issues and problems that will arise in developing a set of imputed capital flow estimates of the brain drain flow. To emphasize, none of the difficulties attendant on such an exercise is insuperable. Indeed, the difficulties are no more substantial than those that statisticians in a number of areas, chiefly national income accounting, have already been successfully addressing for numerous years and which are, in fact, already subjected to solution by international agreement on conventions for the purpose of standardized national income accounting. And, I might note, professional economists have actually engaged in making statistical estimates of imputed capital, in some form or the other, in relation to the brain drain itself, though not with the precise definitions and objectives I have addressed in this chapter.[24]

4. BRAIN DRAIN PHENOMENON VERSUS BRAIN DRAIN ROBLEM: ON DEFINING LDC LOSSES FROM THE BRAIN DRAIN

I may shift now to the alternative, and quite distinct, concept of 'LDC losses' from the brain drain. (There is also, of course, the related concept of the 'DC gains'.) Whereas the imputed capital flow concept, discussed in the preceding section, has absolutely no welfare significance in itself, the concept of LDC losses is obviously a welfare concept and, as such, raises long-familiar issues.

Before we turn to these, note that it is also the concept which is appropriate to the notion of 'compensation': for compensation to LDCs implies some welfare loss which has to be compensated, whereas the use of the imputed flow of capital concept can only

---

[24] See, for example, Grubel and Scott (1977, chs 10 and 11). Their computations are addressed to the US–Canadian exchange of professional manpower. The arguments produced in this pioneering work against proposals to tax the brain drain are, however, not particularly cogent and do not consider the now-popular version of this proposal in which the LDCs would simply extend their income tax jurisdiction over their nationals working abroad, as do the United States and the Philippines. See, in particular, the Symposium on this question in the *Journal of Public Economics*, August 1982, and especially my introduction to it.

be the more limited one, suggested earlier, of preparing a more balanced picture of capital flows between DCs and LDCs.

Note also that, while several LDCs undoubtedly have a brain drain 'phenomenon', we should not jump to the conclusion that they also have a brain drain 'problem': in the sense of a welfare-reducing outflow of PTK personnel. Indeed, much of the debate among economists rests on this precise issue: with DC-based economists often somewhat complacent in this regard and LDC-based economists usually biased in the other direction.

How do we approach the problems of defining the loss of welfare to LDCs from the brain drain? As it happens, the analytical issues involved in an economic evaluation of the consequences of the brain drain for the countries of emigration (and immigration) have been technically discussed by me elsewhere (Bhagwati and Rodriguez 1976). Here, it should suffice to state in non-technical language the principal contours that such an analysis should take and what, in fact, can be reasonably presumed to be the consequences of the brain drain for the LDCs.[25]

Conventional Economic Analysis

Defining the LDCs for this purpose as 'those left behind by the emigrants', and further defining the welfare impact with reference merely to overall income (or social utility) — with no weights attached to income-distribution and unemployment rates, for example, for the present — we can cite the basic proposition that an economist would begin his analysis with:[26]

As long as the emigration is characterized by: Wage = PMP = SMP, there will be no welfare impact (adverse or beneficial) on those left behind.

This 'basic' proposition, attributable to Grubel and Scott (1966),

[25] The following analysis is borrowed from my extended treatment of the issues in 'The Brain Drain', prepared for the 1976 ILO Tripartite World Conference on Employment, Income Distribution and Social Progress and the International Division of Labour.

[26] PMP stands for private marginal product, i.e. the contribution to output, attributable to the gainful activity of the emigrant, in the activity itself; SMP stands for PMP plus (or minus) gains (or losses) in output, so attributable, but outside the activity itself.

merely states that the *claim* that the emigrant makes on the LDC of emigration is the wage he earns (for that is what enables him, by that amount, to partake of the national income); on the other hand, the *contribution* that he makes to national income is the total (social) marginal product, which is clearly SMP, and which may of course exceed or fall short of his immediate contribution to output in his painful employment, i.e. his PMP (the private, marginal product).

Now, if we assume that the LDC economy is perfectly competitive, so that each person earns a wage that equals his PMP, and further that the LDC is not characterized by any distortions or imperfections in the market system so that the PMP and SMP are also then equal, then it follows that wage = PMP = SMP, and that, therefore, the emigrant's claim on the national income will have just been offset by his contribution to it, so that the net result will be neither to harm nor help those who are left behind with his emigration.

But as soon as this basic proposition is formulated, it becomes evident how departures from it can arise in practice and, in fact, will in the realities that characterize the LDCs. Three polar types of such departures from the case for no-impact from the brain drain may be distinguished:

Case I: Wage $\neq$ PMP = SMP
Case II: Wage = PMP $\neq$ SMP
Case III: Wage = SMP $\neq$ PMP

Note that Case III is listed only for completeness' sake; it is not easy to think of a realistic counterpart for it. Besides, the world may be characterized by a combination of two or all the three cases distinguished. I now proceed to discuss in some depth Cases I and II which happen to encompass all the principal arguments that can be advanced to illuminate the adverse (and, for that matter, also the beneficial) effects of the brain drain on LDCs of origin.

Case I: wage = PMP $\neq$ SMP. Three classic arguments on how the brain drain can harm the people left behind in the LDCs of emigration relate to Case I by stating conditions under which the emigrant's wage will be *below* the SMP, so that his emigration will deprive the LDC (excluding the emigrant) of the implied net benefit that his presence was contributing.

(1) The first argument relates to a simple point, that the emigration of (a *finite* number of) emigrants will, by altering the proportions in which different factors of production are employed, affect their remuneration. Hence, if emigration implies that the reward of the emigrating labour is increased, it also follows that the emigrants were getting paid *less* than their PMP (over a finite range, considered together).[27] In other words, there was a surplus of the average wage of the emigrants *as a group* over their average addition to output (i.e. $w < PMP$), which accrued to the LDC of emigration (excluding the emigrants), and which is now lost with the emigration.[28]

The magnitude of this loss depends, of course, on the extent to which the emigrant class of professionals can be substituted for by the country of emigration; and these losses can well be high if the emigrant professionals are not easily replaced or substituted for.

(2) The second argument relates to the emigrant's wage being below his PMP (= SMP) because of monopsonistic pricing of the emigrant professionals. This may be taken to be the case, for example, with the pricing of medical personnel in a nationalized health service of the British variety. Alternatively, it may be the case with any class of professionals where the employer is monolithic (as in some LDCs) and hence the labour market for the profession in question is not competitive but rather is monopsonistic.

(3) The third argument concerns the fact of taxation which can reduce the (net) remuneration of the emigrant class of professionals below their PMP (= SMP). This is very likely to be the

---

[27] To put it another way, the emigrants were driving down their own reward below their marginal product: their increased numbers meant that, while the last member of the labour force did earn *his* PMP in a competitive market, this was not true for the earlier members whose PMP had been higher and whose wage would also have been correspondingly higher if only additional members had not been added to the labour force and had therefore not driven down the wage paid to each.

[28] This point was made by Berry and Soligo in a famous article, 'Some Welfare Aspects of International Migration', *Journal of Political Economy*, 77 (1969).

case with professionals who, in countries with progressive tax systems, are likely to be net contributors to, rather than net beneficiaries from, the rest of the system.

Case II: wage = PMP ≠ SMP. Here again, a number of different examples can be distinguished.

(1) There is first the simple case of 'externality' where the market does not capture for the professional his true worth to society. An important example is probably the case of doctors in many LDCs: their worth cannot really be measured by their earnings, as the mere presence of a doctor in an area, deprived of such services earlier, could be almost priceless.

(2) Then, there is the example of what economists call 'increasing returns to scale': a group of professionals may be worth much more than a subset of them and the wages paid to each member of the group may not reflect this *extra* productivity. This problem is what is referred to in discussions of the 'institution-building' roles of talented emigrants, especially research scientists and professors.

(3) Yet another instance is provided by the fact of educational subsidization of professional training in LDCs, as indeed in most DCs as well. The emigration of the educated, in this situation, could imply no real loss *if* one assumed that the returns to the subsidized-investment-in-education would have accrued to the emigrant anyway (and not to those left behind) *and* that the emigration does not result in an increase in the number of people educated. However, if one postulates an economy in which this emigration leads to other natives being educated by way of replacement, partially or fully, then indeed there is an overall expansion of subsidized education, with increased losses from the subsidization programme, *ceteris paribus*. This is then clearly a case where, thanks to the government subsidy to education, the remuneration enjoyed by the emigrant equals his PMP but his emigration will inflict an *additional* loss such that one must classify this as an instance where wage = PMP < SMP, and therefore the brain drain is harmful.

(4) Yet another, equally important, example that is of interest in the discussion of the brain drain, where a domestic distortion can lead to divergence between the remuneration and the SMP

of emigrants, concerns the presence of sticky wages and consequent unemployment. In fact, it is frequently argued, especially in relation to Filippino doctors and Indian engineers (both constituting rather substantial fractions of recent flows of skilled manpower from the LDCs), that there is unemployment in these professions in the LDCs of emigration and that therefore there is not a brain drain problem, but just skilled emigration which is better described as a 'spillover', 'safety valve', 'overflow' phenomenon, with no harm for the LDC of emigration since the SMP of such emigrants is zero.[29]

If this interpretation is assumed to be correct, then clearly we have a situation where wage = PMP = SMP (= 0). However, we have decided to include this phenomenon of emigration from the unemployed into the class of Case II examples because it can be argued, quite plausibly, that such emigration is *not* one with zero SMP but rather leads to harmful effects and that therefore wage(= 0) = PMP < SMP. Thus it can be shown (as Hamada and Bhagwati (1975) have formally done) that the outflow abroad of doctors from the overcrowded urban areas with unemployment could inhibit the gradual spillover of such doctors into the rural areas with high social productivity: the (external) brain drain thus slows down the beneficial 'internal diffusion' process which, in a capitalist framework, is an imperfect but real substitute for the Maoist policy of sending doctors to the countryside.

Similarly, it could be argued that the emigration from a pool of currently unemployed professionals could, in the long run, raise the number educated by raising expected returns from such professional training and thus increase educational costs without increasing output, thus *reducing* national income (net of educational costs).[30] Here again we then have wage (= 0) < SMP (as the emigration reduces SMP and hence the lack of emigration must be construed to increase SMP).

---

[29] In fact, if the emigrant was receiving a State dole, or subsisting from resources other than his savings while unemployed, it could be argued that the emigration actually improves the welfare of those left behind because his claim on national income (by the amount of his subsistence) exceeded his contribution (which was zero).

[30] For a formal modelling of this point, see Bhagwati and Hamada (1974).

Finally, it should be noted that if the emigration accentuates the sticky wage distortion by raising the wage level of the emigrant class of professionals through the emulation effect, this will generally accentuate the loss from the emigration noted in the previous paragraph (Bhagwati and Hamada 1974).

While the preceding examples concern cases where the emigration leads to a loss because the wage is below SMP, it is possible to think of externalities which lead to wage (= PMP) > SMP, so that the brain drain is welfare-improving for the LDC of emigration. Two examples may be noted, both relating to the fact that the emigrant's income or output abroad may accrue to the LDC in some fashion.

(5) One example relates to the fact that the output of the emigrant may have the nature of a public good and hence may also be available to the LDC. This may be the case with professors and research scientists. Besides, their output may be greater because of better facilities and environment in the DCs. On the other hand, the orientation of this output may be towards DC rather than LDC needs. Whether the net effect is positive for LDCs would then depend on the relative strengths of these offsetting effects.

(6) Another example relates to the notion that distinguished emigrants do not need to be at home but can inspire students and researchers from afar; that, in fact, by working with greater distinction (owing to better facilities leading to superior performance) abroad, they can inspire better. But this argument must be set off against the possibility that the LDC students and researchers may be demoralized into thinking that only work abroad can lead to distinction and success, thus inhibiting the growth of domestic confidence and capability in scientific achievements: a phenomenon that anyone who has tried to build up institutions in LDCs is likely to be acquainted with.

Additional Welfare-impact Considerations

The discussion so far has assumed that: (A) the effect of the brain drain on the flow of goods and services, or national income, is an adequate indicator of the consequence of the brain drain on LDC welfare; and (B) the emigration is, in effect, permanent and there are no 'feedback' effects of any kind. Neither of these assumptions is, however, valid and hence they must now be relaxed, each in turn.

(A) *Additional indicators of welfare impact.*   Three aspects of the problem of defining welfare consequences more adequately will now be discussed.

(1) *Unemployment.*   Note first that our analysis did not attach any significance to unemployment per se.[31] However, the increase or reduction in unemployment, consequent upon the brain drain, is of interest in itself.

The precise effect of the brain drain on unemployment, not merely in the class of professionals emigrating but (indirectly) in other occupations too, will clearly depend on what kinds of labour markets and other related characteristics of the country are postulated. Suffice it here to note, however, that the general argument that, in conditions of unemployment (as at any point of time), emigration will reduce unemployment presupposes that the supply of such professionals does not increase so as to offset this outflow. But this is not at all evident as migration will raise the *expected* wage of such professionals by both *initially* reducing the unemployment pool and because emigration brings into the expected wage the substantially higher foreign salaries. The increased incentive to secure this professional training therefore may well increase the supply of such professionals beyond the level which would offset the outflow, thus *adding* to unemployment, rather than diminishing it.[32] Furthermore, if the emulation effect operates such that the emigration, via implied furthering of the integration of the international markets for professionals, leads to an increase in the *actual* salary levels of the class of emigrating professionals (airline pilots presumably being a good example of this 'emulation effect'), then the probability of unemployment level (and rate) increasing (rather than reducing)

---

[31] Unemployment was considered only in so far as it affected the outcome for national income (or utility), the latter being the only focus of analysis.

[32] For a model where the conditions that would generate this possibility are rigorously spelled out, see Bhagwati and Hamada (1974). Another modified model is presented by McCulloch and Yellen (1975).

with the emigration, is increased. And if we visualize a 'leap-frogging' process of secondary wage increases, triggered off by such migration-plus-emulation-induced primary salary increases, unemployment in other labour markets could also increase.[33]

(2) *Income distribution and inequality.* The effect of the brain drain on income distribution and on inequality also needs to be spelled out. But, in doing this, we need to distinguish among alternative ways of defining these distributional concepts.

Now, if we regards as an egalitarian objective, not merely equality of access but also equality of success,[34] then a reduction of wage differentials is *prima facie* a virtue. In such an event, if the brain drain leads, via the emulation effect, to an increase in the professional salary level, it is (in egalitarian terms) an adverse impact. This is in fact precisely what bothers social and economic planners who worry about the effect that the possibility of emigration has on the domestic ability to maintain desired salary structures: either they can erect emigration restrictions à la communist countries so as to eliminate the emulation effect but at the cost of humane values, *or* they must sacrifice their egalitarian objectives.[35] Note that this argument also exposes the shallowness of the assertion, often made by opponents of concern over the brain drain, that the brain drain is a result of 'inadequate' LDC policies such as 'failure' to remunerate their professionals well: it implicitly superimposes on these LDCs their value judgment that they must alter their salary structures in an inegalitarian direction.

An alternative way to look at the inegalitarian impact of the brain drain would be in terms of access: i.e. we could examine whether it permits those at the lower half of the income distribution in an

[33] Again, for formal analysis of such possibilities in a fully-specified model, see Bhagwati and Hamada (1974).

[34] This distinction might also be described as one between opportunity and outcome. See Bhagwati (1973).

[35] Indeed, thanks to the possibility of evasion of emigration barriers, few Communist countries can also escape the consequences of the coexistence with countries with greater inequality in rewards for the skilled and talented. Thus, Frederick Pryor's data on East European salary differentials suggest that the East German differentials are larger than others and the explanation seems to lie in the *comparative* ease with which native professionals can slip across to (West Germany in) the outside world (Pryor 1968).

economy to transit to the unequal-and-higher rewards permitted by emigration. Indeed, the classic nineteenth-century immigration into the United States from the highly stratified European countries probably fits into this egalitarian version of the consequences of emigration. However, the brain drain from the LDCs hardly fits this description: enough is known about the inegalitarian access to educational facilities in many LDCs[36] to suggest strongly that the access to professional emigration, in consequence, must be regarded as principally available to the better-endowed among the LDC population.

Finally, we could examine the purely income-distributional consequences of the brain drain in terms of either the functional or personal income distribution. Nothing can be stated categorically one way or the other, however, in regard to either of these: everything depends on the model used to depict the reality in LDCs *and* the precise definition of income distribution chosen; and no 'presumption' would seem to be plausible, at least to me. Thus, take a model where emigration leads to a replacement of the educated emigrant by one more educated person, and if it is assumed that sticky wages imply that no more new employment is created, then total output will not change, whereas one unemployed person will have become educated and hence employed. Then, if we take the share of wages in national income, this is unchanged. If we take the national income *excluding* the increased cost of education (since one more person is being educated), the share of wages has gone up. If we take the ratio of wages to educated and uneducated workers, this has remained unchanged. If we take the ratio of *average* wages to the educated to *average* income of the uneducated *plus* unemployed, then this has fallen (since unemployment is reduced). And so on. Indeed, the income distributional consequences have been noted, for the brain drain problem, increasingly of late, by general-equilibrium economic theorists (e.g. Bhagwati and Hamada 1974; McCulloch and Yellen 1975): and the reader can readily adapt these, and other, analyses to their own preferred indicator of income distribution in the LDC of emigration.

---

[36] For a discussion of this evidence, primarily in the Indian context, see Bhagwati (1973).

(3) *GNP*. It is not immediately obvious that the welfare of 'those left behind' will not depend, both directly *and* indirectly, on the effect of the brain drain on GNP. Thus, it is possible that a society derives satisfaction from being 'big' in its economic size: an economic counterpart of what is politically the well-known phenomenon of 'big power chauvinism'. But, more respectably, it is clear that a larger economic size could, in turn, produce larger economic gains. Thus, for example, it could lead to better bargaining abilities on economic issues with others in the world economy and hence an enhanced share in the gains from trade, investment, etc. Thus, in so far as the brain drain reduces LDC GNP, as it surely must (except in singular circumstances) in the long run, it could prima facie have an adverse impact on the LDCs.

(4) *Technical labour force*. Finally, the sheer availability of a technical labour force, with attendant scientific attitudes, may be critical in determining the pace of modernization. As the 1974 US House *Report* on the brain drain put it rather well:

An educated élite plays a primary role in society, and the social loss to the LDCs from this drain can have adverse effects far beyond the impact of specialized disciplines. In general, highly skilled manpower is part of the larger infrastructure of a social élite that is necessary for development. Beyond their specialized areas the scientist, engineer and physician contribute to a nation's political, social, and cultural development. They help set the tone of society, and establish national values and goals. . . . In a profound sense, medical and other scientifically trained persons occupy pivotal positions in that they help change values, a necessary condition for changing institutions. . . . Developing countries need not only specific skills but also leadership and organizing ability. A continuing drain of highly trained people can over the long run add to a sense of national frustration, generate a contagious movement, lower the sense of worth of those who remain [that is, the 'left-behind' syndrome], reduce further the small group of potential political and administrative leaders, and reduce the cadre of technically trained people who must be at hand when the process of development gathers momentum.[37]

(B) *To-and-fro migration and 'feedback' effects*. In conclusion, we must note also that the welfare analysis of the brain drain must

[37] *Report*, pp. 138–9; quotation marks and footnotes from the original have been omitted.

be modified to take into account the fact that professional migration is no longer a 'permanent' affair, but is rather characterized by reverse or even 'to-and-fro' movements by the migrant professionals.

For this analysis, such a phenomenon points to three major qualifications to the contention that the brain drain implies a loss to the LDCs of emigration.

(1) The professionals, returning off and on to their LDCs of origin, can contribute net income to these LDCs in a number of ways. Thus, for example, typically professors and research scientists tend to visit LDC institutions on DC Foundation grants.

(2) Secondly, since the brain can appreciate from better environment, the returning professional might be able to generate *greater* externality to his LDC than when the initial emigration occurred. Thus, for example, recall the fact that the Chinese achievements in atomic capability came from Chinese scientists who had resided and matured in the United States.

(3) And finally, while the inflow of remittances from the emigrants is not conditional on the return or to-and-fro character of the migration, it would seem appropriate to assume that the continued (personal) linkage with the LDC of origin should strengthen, rather than weaken, the impulse to remit (or take savings home on permanent return).

It is not probable that these offsetting factors can be sufficiently large to eliminate the adverse effects of the brain drain on many LDCs of emigration, though it is likely that some LDCs have a brain drain phenomenon but not a brain drain problem.

5. Alternative Policy Proposals in Regard to the Brain Drain: Compensation, Taxation, etc.

There are several alternative proposals which have been advanced by economists and policy-makers in regard to the brain drain. However, they often have different objectives that are insufficiently distinguished from one another. Nor are their differential requirements in terms of the kinds of actions that need to be taken in order to implement them adequately sketched in the documents that contain them. Our first task must therefore be to sort out analytically the different proposals and their rationales.

Thus, we may first note that there are basically the following quite different types of proposals in the literature on the brain drain:

(i)   proposals aimed at reducing the brain drain: dividing, in turn, into 'restrictive' policies and 'incentive' policies;

(ii)   proposals that are aimed at 'compensating' the LDCs for the losses alleged to have been suffered by the LDCs from their PTK emigration: these proposals then being directed not at reducing the brain drain, but rather at offsetting its ill-effects on the LDCs; these proposals, in turn, dividing into compensation being paid by the DCs *or* by the PTK migrants themselves;

(iii)   proposals that are aimed at taxation (of PTK immigrants) to achieve global allocative efficiency, i.e. to maximize 'world welfare';

(iv)   proposals that are aimed at *some* form of brain drain related taxation in order, frankly, to raise developmental resources for LDCs, *either* by taxing DCs for this purpose on the ground that DCs *benefit* from such PTK immigration and should share these gains with LDCs, *or* by taxing the PTK migrants themselves on the ground that they enjoy DC-quota-restrictions-generated *rents* that can be taxed without ill-effects for developmental spending;

(v)   proposals that would tax LDC PTK migrants for LDC developmental spending as an 'inducement', through example of self-help, for the DCs to undertake enhanced aid programmes; this constituting therefore an *externality* argument for the proposed tax; and

(vi)   proposals that would tax LDC PTK migrants for achievement of efficiency-cum-equity in the LDCs and/or for preventing deleterious effects in the LDCs: this constituting an *LDC-welfare-based* rationale, as against, the *global-efficiency* rationale underlying (iii) above.

Note that (ii)–(vi) above will all raise *some* revenue, in general, for LDCs. However, the *objectives* of the proposals under each are different; and the implied tax bases (i.e. who pays the tax) are not necessarily identical either. Note additionally that the different proposals differ also according to whether: (i) they require only LDC implementation; (ii) they require only DC action; or (iii) cooperative action by LDCs and DCs is required, which in turn is distinguished by whether bilateral or multilateral action is appropriate or necessary.

Policy Proposals to Reduce the Brain Drain

The policy proposals addressed to reducing the brain drain are the more fashionable in most discussions of the subject, and divide into 'restrictive' and 'incentive' policy suggestions.

Restrictive policies. The restrictive policy actions are, of course, the LDC counterpart of DC immigration restrictions; the latter already restrict the overall PTK inflow to desired levels while the proposed LDC restrictions can shift the breakdown of their total between LDC and DC sources of emigration. These restrictions can take the form of denial of passports for exiting professionals, requirements of periods of domestic service for newly graduated professionals (as with medical graduates in many countries), or making exit more difficult in other ways (as when the holding of the American Medical Association's ECFMG examination for foreign doctors is forbidden in India). Few of these restrictions can really be applied to those students who 'stay on' abroad after their studies, though even here the government of Sri Lanka had experimented with making the renewal of passports conditional on transmission of funds, etc., and could well have made the renewal impossible so as to attempt forcing the return of the emigrés.

Typically, however, these kinds of restrictions are both likely to be nuisances and surmountable inequitably by the powerful or the ingenious and to be resented at large by the very professionals who are sought to be held back, with possibly adverse effects on their efficiency and commitment to their societies. Hence, these restrictions are invoked only infrequently and are occasionally cancelled (as in Sri Lanka) in response to effective protests by the professionals.

A DC policy action addressed to reducing the PTK inflow from LDCs (though not necessarily from LDCs plus DCs), was the now-defunct United States policy ruling that required exchange visitors from LDCs, in PTK categories, to return to their home country or another LDC for a period of two years before they could re-enter the US as immigrants. A later example was the US legislative action making the immigration of foreign medical graduates virtually impossible and to rely instead on expanding domestic training facilities.

Incentive policies. As for the incentive policy suggestions, these are generally LDC-focused, and designed to make emigration less attractive. Thus, salary increases, improved research facilities, etc., are typically advocated. But while a number of institutional features of professional life in LDCs could be improved, the basic difficulty lies in the impossibility of significantly narrowing the gap in professional facilities on a wide scale when the DCs and LDCs are so widely separated in their resource situation in the first place. Besides, prescriptions to raise professional salaries yet further towards international levels have inegalitarian and wel-fare-reducing consequences which LDCs surely cannot ignore. Thus, even if these policies were to be implemented somehow on a significant scale, and were then to reduce the outflow of profes-sional manpower, they would have to be carefully weighed for their other deleterious effects on the LDCs adopting them.

Mention also needs to be made here again of the occasional argument that several LDCs have over-expanded their education-al facilities and that their PTK emigration is a direct result of such over-expansion and consequent unemployment. Now, in regard to this argument, it is certainly likely that if the scale of educational facilities could be reduced in any country experiencing emigra-tion, it would *ceteris paribus* (regardless of unemployment levels) tend to lower emigration to higher-wage DCs by raising, under 'normal' assumptions, the domestic return to education. How-ever, the desirability of such a policy would depend on the precise conditions in the labour market for these professionals and the social objectives of the LDC question. Thus, if the *net* domestic availability (i.e. domestic supply *minus* emigration) of the professionals falls as their total output is restricted, this could well be considered a serious negative effect of the policy. Even if the labour market situation is one characterized by a temporary 'surplus', given the current sticky wage level, it is perfectly conceivable that the reduced domestic availability (including the present surplus) inhibits the diffusion of this kind of professional (e.g. doctors) into the countryside where the social returns to their professional presence is highly valued. However, as already noted in Sec. 4 above, the desirability of restricting educational facilities for the production of the emigrating class of professionals, even when there is current 'unemployment' or 'surplus', is by no means to be taken for granted. Furthermore, it is extremely improbable that a policy of restricting educational facilities for professionals, even if evaluated to be desirable, can be politically implemented, especially when emigration possibilities have made the returns from such educational attainment even more attractive.

Turning next to the incentive policies that the DCs can adopt to reduce the inflow of professionals from LDCs into the DCs, two major types can be distinguished. First, the attraction of permanent emigration can be reduced, *ceteris paribus*, by enabling temporary access to DC facilities by LDC professionals in a number of ways. Thus, in regard to research-oriented professionals, the major Foundations in the DCs have initiated programmes to finance recurrent and protracted visits by LDC professionals to DC universities and institutes: this permits flirting to be an effective substitute for marriage! Such programmes enable LDC professionals to retain their domicile in the LDCs where they can proceed with institution-building, etc., at the substantially lower LDC salaries, while enjoying both an increased average income level and intellectual stimulus from the foreign visits. The counterpart of these programmes is the financing of visits by DC scientists to LDC institutions. In both cases, of course, the results can be deleterious if the programmes are ill-administered: thus, if the LDCs manage them such that the foreign visits are controlled and allocated on a patronage basis, the programme will even generate diversion of professional energy into patronage cultivation; and the use of funds to bring in low-grade but highly paid DC scientists may well generate resentment from the indigenous professional community.

Second, a DC policy that could, *ceteris paribus*, reduce the brain drain would be a surtax on the LDC professionals' income in the DCs of immigration: the tax proposal that has been advocated (on several rationales) by me in 1973 and later (Bhagwati and Partington 1976). Econometric analysis of the brain drain into the United States suggests that a reduction in the (net of tax) relative wage of the DC and the LDC has a negative, though small, effect on immigration flows. Essentially, such a tax on the brain drain could at the margin be deflecting (in a small way) the DC-restricted immigration away from the LDCs (whose nationals would have to pay the tax) to the DCs (whose emigrating nationals would not have to pay the tax).

Policy Proposals to Compensate the LDCs for Losses Caused by the Brain Drain

Next, we have what are essentially compensatory-financing proposals. These involve *either* compensation schemes to be financed by the *DC of immigration* to compensate for the losses inflicted on the LDCs by the brain drain *or* compensation schemes to be financed by the *emigrants* themselves for these LDC losses.[38]

The *moral* rationale for these two alternative methods of compensation may be stated as follows. (1) In the case of compensation paid by the DCs, the moral appeal may rest on the arguments that the coexistence of the prosperous DCs and the poor LDCs

---

[38] In addition, we could include here the notion that DCs ought to 'replace', through technical assistance, the professionals that they 'take' from the LDCs: in fact, balance sheets of loss and gain of professional manpower through the brain drain and the technical assistance programmes are occasionally drawn up. Quite aside from the fact that the notion of replacement is tricky, given the quality differences implicit in the professional categories being considered, the two sets of movements have asymmetries of great importance: the emulation effect (considered in Sec. 4) can follow from the emigration and may be only reinforced, rather than offset, by the technical-assistance-sponsored inflow; the LDC may well, and often will, attach significance to having its own stock of professional manpower rather than being dependent on technical assistance that may suddenly vanish; and so on.

leads to this PTK emigration from LDCs and therefore it is fair to expect that the DCs should assist the LDCs in coping with such losses; that, by so doing, the DCs would also be helping to prevent the LDCs from self-protecting, quantitative emigration restrictions that offend against the kind of humane international order that DCs often argue as their ideal; and that if DCs, in turn, are likely to have also *gained* from such PTK immigration (as would seem to be the general presumption in light of immigration policies that are closely geared to national interest), then the moral obligation to assist the poor LDCs to cope with their losses is correspondingly greater. (2) The moral case for making the PTK emigrants pay compensation to the LDCs, on the other hand, is simply that their *considerable* improvement of income, obtained by LDC-permitted emigration that inflicts losses on 'those left behind', imposes a moral obligation on them to partially share their gains with these groups.[39]

Next, it should be noted in regard to the compensatory-financing proposals, whether they relate to the DCs of immigration or the emigrants themselves as assesses, that the essential problem with them is that they presuppose a commonly agreed upon methodology and procedures for defining the LDC losses that are to be compensated. It is difficult to see, given the wide differences that can sometimes obtain on these issues (as I have noted in Sec. 4), how such an agreement can be readily obtained. But even if it were, it is certain that the losses would fluctuate annually, causing equivalent fluctuations in the compensatory finance that would be forthcoming (and, if the tax were collected on emigrants, the tax rate would also, in general, fluctuate). Working with LDC losses as the basis for the transfer of funds (revenue) to LDCs experiencing the brain drain phenomenon is therefore a rather impractical procedure − *unless* it is taken as a general rationale rather than as also providing a firm base for calculating the revenue to be raised for the LDCs.

Note moreover that two principal types of taxes on the professional migrants might be distinguished when the LDC-losses are

---

[39] Note that a moral, as also an efficiency, case for taxing such emigrants, *even if there were no losses imposed on LDCs by the brain drain*, can be developed, as set out below.

the rationale for the tax: (1) the Soviet-style exit tax; and (2) a surtax on post-immigration incomes. The now-defunct Soviet exit tax was rationalized on the assumption that the USSR would be reimbursing itself for the educational costs incurred on the emigrant.[40] The surtax on the post-immigration income of the emigrant could also be calculated and assessed so as to equal the estimated loss to the LDC of emigration; but this would cause practical difficulties in levying the surtax rates so that it is again best to regard the LDC-losses as providing only a general rationale, and *not* a tax-revenue target, if the option of a surtax on post-immigration incomes is chosen as the alternative on the basis of this rationale.

Policy Proposal for Taxing the Brain Drain to Achieve Global (Allocative) Efficiency

While, however, the proposals for compensation considered above are primarily based on *moral* considerations and therefore cannot be expected to command universal acceptance, it is interesting to note that a case can also be made for taxing LDC PTK immigrants' incomes in DCs (in a manner to be detailed presently) on grounds of *global allocative efficiency*.

This argument is basically a simple and persuasive one. Thus, if the DC and the LDC are characterized by income taxes, the tax rate in the LDC is higher than in the DC, the PTK migration is to the DC, then it will be readily appreciated that the optimal allocation of total DC-plus-LDC PTK labour between the two regions requires that the LDC-origin PTK worker be taxed identically regardless of his residence and work location. This argument implies that the PTK immigrant into the DC be taxed at the *higher* LDC rate, with of course double-taxation relief for DC taxes. And the difference between the (lower) DC tax rate and the (higher) LDC tax rate constitutes therefore a tax on the brain drain, levied de facto in the form of supplementary taxation of the DC incomes of

---

[40] The differences between the exit tax and the tax on incomes in the country of immigration, even if the objectives are identical, are quite profound and favour the latter. See, for argumentation, J. Bhagwati and W. Dellalfar, in Bhagwati and Partington (1976).

TABLE 13.1

Income Tax Rates in Selected DCs and LDCs

	US Federal tax		Canada Federal tax		UK
	tax	(a)	tax	(b)	
US $ 5000					(£ 2000)
S	$ 491 (9.8)		$ 444.84 (8.90)	$ 611.02 (12.22)	$ 1053.75 (21.08)
M	322 (6.4)		152.24 (3.04)	229.17 (4.58)	918.75 (18.38)
M + 2C	98 (2.0)		32.18 (0.64)	72.49 (1.45)	618.75* (12.38)
US $ 10,000					(£ 4000)
S	1530 (15.30)	$ 1984 (19.84)	1559.22 (15.59)	2065.28 (20.65)	2553.75 (25.54)
M	1190 (11.90)	1519 (15.19)	1204.42 (12.04)	1602.27 (16.02)	2418.75 (24.19)
M + 2C	905 (9.05)	1148 (11.48)	1057.22 (10.57)	1410.17 (14.10)	2118.75* (21.19)
US $ 20,000					(£ 8000)
S	4255 (23.8)	5456 (27.28)	4470.45 (22.35)	5905.70 (29.53)	6381.25 (31.91)
M	3400 (17.0)	4455 (22.28)	3974.36 (19.87)	5250.34 (26.25)	6156.25 (30.78)
M + 2C	3010 (15.11)	3918 (19.59)	3761.56 (18.81)	4969.22 (24.85)	5677.88* (28.39)
Rate of exchange			US $ 1 = $ 1 CDN		£ 1 = US $ 2.5

All data pertain to 1974. Figures in parentheses represent percentages.

S: single; M: married; M + 2C: married with two children.

* Assuming that both children are under 11 years old.

(a) This column includes the federal income tax, the New York State tax and the New York City tax. Deductions for the federal income

Table 13.1 (cont.)

tax are assumed at 15 per cent of the total remuneration. For the New York State and City taxes standard deductions have been used.

(b) This column includes the federal income tax and the provincial income tax at the minimum rate of 30.5 per cent of the federal income taxes before the special federal 5 per cent tax reduction.

	Argentina	Colombia	Mexico
US $ 5000	$a 25,000	112,500 pesos	62,450 pesos
S	$ 325.8 (6.52)	$ 1238.44 (24.77)	$ 357.82 (7.16)
M	257.4 (5.15)	1197.33 (23.95)	357.82 (7.16)
M + 2C	135 (2.7)	1164.44 (23.29)	357.82 (7.16)
US $ 10,000	$a 50,000	225,000 pesos	124,900 pesos
S	1629.8 (16.30)	3130.67 (31.31)	1094.26 (10.94)
M	1514.6 (15.15)	3087.33 (30.87)	1094.26 (10.94)
M + 2C	1291.4 (12.91)	3052.67 (30.53)	1094.26 (10.94)
US $ 20,000	$a 100,000	450,000 pesos	249,800 pesos
S	5478.6 (27.39)	7205.11 (36.03)	4074.04 (20.37)
M	5325 (26.63)	7158.44 (35.79)	3923.44 (19.62)
M + 2C	5037 (25.19)	7121.11 (35.61)	3772.84 (18.86)
Rate of exchange	US $ 1 = $ 5.00 (official rate)	US $ 1 = 22.50 pesos	US $ 1 = 12.49 pesos

All data pertain to 1974, except for Argentina and Colombia, where data pertain to 1972.

S: single; M: married; M + 2C: married with two children. Figures in parentheses represent percentages.

Table 13.1 (cont.)

Taiwan	Hong Kong	India[+]	Korea	Philippines
NT $ 190,000	HK $ 28,250	Rs 39,550	2,400,000 won	P34,500
$ 397.37 (7.95)	$ 248.89 (4.98)	$ 1566.53 (31.33)	$ 752.5 (15.05)	$ 807.6 (16.15)
345.26 (6.91)	122.79 (2.46)	1566.53 (31.33)	677.5 (13.55)	750.2 (15.0)
275.79 (5.52)	69.69 (1.39)	1566.53 (31.33)	602.5 (12.05)	663.0 (13.26)
NT $ 380,000	HK $ 56,500	Rs 79,100	4,800,000 won	P69,000
1398.42 (13.98)	1194.69 (11.95)	5287.67 (52.88)	2615 (26.15)	2813.9 (28.14)
1295.79 (12.96)	896.02 (8.96)	5287.67 (52.88)	2515 (25.15)	2730.4 (27.30)
1145.26 (11.45)	743.36 (7.43)	5287.67 (52.88)	2415 (24.15)	2591.3 (25.91)
NT $ 760,000	HK $ 113,000	Rs 158,200	9,600,000 won	P138,000
4672.63 (23.36)	3000 (15.0)	14,329.20 (71.65)	7290 (36.45)	8416.2 (42.08)
4518.68 (22.59)	3000 (15.0)	14,329.20 (71.65)	7165 (35.83)	8310.1 (41.55)
4292.89 (21.46)	3000 (15.0)	14,329.20 (71.65)	7040 (35.2)	8136.2 (40.68)
US $ 1 = NT $ 38	US $ 1 = HK $ 5.65	US $ 1 = Rs 7.91	US $ 1 = 480 won	US $ 1 = P6.90

[+] Surcharge included. Figures in parentheses represent percentages.

SOURCE: Hamada (1977).

LDC PTK immigrants.[41] While, further, the global efficiency argument does not require that the supplementary tax revenues accrue to LDCs, actually granting them to LDCs would also constitute a source of revenue for them.

Are LDC tax rates, in fact, generally higher than DC ones? Table 13.1 certainly suggests that they are, although we should bear in mind that evasion is probably larger in LDCs and also that the LDC rates could not possibly be extended to DC incomes without adjustment for differential cost of living. Nonetheless, the basic argument that LDC tax rates are higher remains valid.

Proposals Addressed to Raising Developmental Resources for LDCs

An altogether different objective of some tax proposals related to the brain drain has been frankly raising developmental resources for LDCs: this being the direct and principal objective, as distinct from being an incidental (and favourably regarded) outcome of policies addressed to other objectives.

In this class of tax proposals we must distinguish again between the proposal for DCs to transfer (normal) tax revenues to LDCs on the ground that they enjoy gains from the brain drain and should therefore share these gains for a larger purpose such as developmental spending in the LDCs — note that this argument does *not* require that the LDCs experience any losses from the brain drain, as discussed earlier — and the distinct proposal to tax the *immigrants' incomes* in the DCs instead, the argument in this latter instance being that the immigrants enjoy rents generated by the DC immigration quotas and that these rents should be partially taxed in order to use the proceeds for a larger social purpose such as developmental spending in the LDCs. The simplest analogy to these notions is the scheme, already implemented, whereby the proceeds from the sale of IMF gold at market prices are being used for assisting the LDCs.

---

[41] This version of the proposal by me to tax DC incomes of the PTK LDC immigrants was suggested by Professors Oldman and Pomp in Bhagwati and Partington (1976).

Proposals to Utilize 'Externality' to Generate Greater Resources for LDCs

Related to the preceding arguments is the important point made by Professor Jan Tinbergen that a tax on the brain drain, in the form of taxing their DC incomes for developmental spending in the LDCs, could have the 'externality' effect of persuading public opinion in the DCs (through demonstration of self-help by LDC-origin nationals) to vote for greater transfers of resources by DCs.[42] Presumably, the DC nationals would not feel, as they often seem to do, that LDCs like to exhort DCs to tax their citizens for aid to LDCs while doing little of it themselves, and that a demonstration of willingness to tax their own successfully emigrated nationals would help to counter this feeling.

In a somewhat similar vein, Professor Saul Mendlovitz has argued also that the taxation of PTK LDC immigrants in the DCs could be the first step towards the ultimate adoption of the more broad-based proposals such as a 1 per cent tax on individual incomes in all countries, for raising developmental resources for LDCs.[43]

Note that these arguments also run counter to the assertion sometimes made that all brain-drain-related 'link' proposals to transfer resources to DCs would cut into 'normal' aid flows: that such transfers would substitute for other aid, leaving no increment in the total. Besides, it should be noted that there is absolutely no reason to regard supplementary taxation of LDC PTK immigrants' incomes for transfer to LDCs as a DC contribution of resources (even though the DCs would have to assist in the collection of the revenue, as argued below in section 6). Any legislator who would seek to argue that this was a DC contribution of resources is on exceptionally weak ground and should be readily disabused of such a self-serving notion, so that it should be easy to argue against any attempts to cut down normal aid flows because of revenues from the brain drain tax on LDC PTK immigrants' incomes.

---

[42] Cf. his endorsement of my proposal to tax the brain drain in this form: 'It is my hope that this tax might also help to convince public opinion in the rich countries that more has to be done in the field of development cooperation', in Bhagwati and Partington (1976).

[43] Cf. his Preface in Bhagwati and Partington (1976).

Proposals Aimed at Providing Tax Policy Instrument to Achieve Efficiency-cum-Equity in LDCs

Finally, we should consider two particular arguments for taxing LDC PTK immigrants' incomes in DCs, which are designed *not to compensate* the LDCs for losses inflicted by the brain drain, but rather to provide a policy instrument which, if available, would *prevent* the LDCs of emigration from suffering efficiency-cum-equity losses.

The straightforward argument, based on the emulation effect, is that the deleterious effect of the brain drain comes about not merely through emigration per se but rather through the effect it has of underlining vastly higher incomes in the DCs, and then through its effect in raising domestic salary levels through emulation. In this case, the domestic 'distortion' in the salary structure is accentuated by the possibility of emigration for these higher salaries, possibly resulting in income losses through additional unemployment, etc. Furthermore, income inequality would be accentuated also, since the PTK salaries would rise whereas the average wage of the non-emigrant non-PTK workers is unlikely to: so that the salary structure gets skewed. Therefore, both in terms of efficiency and equity, the possibility of emigration to DCs with their significantly higher salary levels creates problems for the LDCs of emigration. In this scenario, the imposition of a brain drain tax on PTK migrants' earnings in DCs would reduce their 'net-of-tax' salaries and thus help to moderate these adverse effects on the LDCs (quite aside, of course, from raising some revenue which could be routed to LDCs).

A somewhat more complex form of argument has, however, been developed by economic theorists working in the theory of public finance. This argument demonstrates the following: in an economy that is using income taxation to achieve equality of incomes, there is a trade-off between equality and efficiency since the income tax inhibits effort and/or investment in education; the resulting per capita income will, however, be lower for LDC nationals if PTK (educated) emigrants can leave and not be taxed on their foreign incomes; the introduction of a tax on foreign earnings of the PTK emigrants will then enable an improvement in per capital income of LDC nationals; and that, if an educational subsidy *and* the extension of the income tax to foreign earnings are both introduced into the model (where the income tax distorts the choice of the length of education), these will enable the LDC to achieve the optimal solution in terms of equity-cum-efficiency, equality being achieved with maximum feasible per capita incomes.

Having surveyed the major types of policy proposals, their major features and rationales, I now turn to a more direct focus on the tax proposals, now organizing the different arguments by each type of tax proposal rather than by specific objectives of the different proposals, and also examining some of the practical feasibility aspects of these proposals.

6. MORE ON ALTERNATIVE TAX PROPOSALS

We may distinguish between tax proposals that require DCs to bear the (immediate) tax burden and those that require taxing the incomes of the PTK immigrants' incomes in the DCs of immigration. Of these two major types of tax proposals, the former have received political attention from LDC spokesmen so far, but negligible attention from professional economists and scientists, whereas the latter have received little political attention to date but have instead been the subject of considerable analytical scrutiny from distinguished lawyers and economists, while also receiving attention in documentation on the subject of the brain drain in international organizations such as the ILO and the UNCTAD, and in professional legal and economic journals in different countries.

DCS Paying the Tax

Taking the former kind of proposal first, we can immediately state the possible rationale therefore as *either* that the DCs ought to *compensate* the LDCs for the losses that the brain drain into the former imposes on the latter, *or* that the DCs gain from the brain drain and therefore, regardless of whether there is any loss to the

LDCs, they ought to share these gains (based on inflow of LDC nationals) with the LDCs who need developmental resources.

Of these two notions, the former (suggesting compensation for LDCs) would appear to be the principal motivating force behind recent pronouncements of LDC spokesmen calling for a brain-drain-related transfer of resources/revenues by DCs. Thus, witness the following two sample statements:

I would also like to propose the establishment of an International Labour Compensatory Facility (ILCF). It could be elaborated along the lines of the Trust Fund for Compensatory Facilities of the International Monetary Fund. The proposed Facility would draw its resources principally from labour importing countries, but in a spirit of solidarity and goodwill, other ILO members may contribute to it. The accumulated resources will be diverted to developing labour-exporting countries in proportions relative to *the estimated cost incurred due to the loss of labour.*[44]

The Commission on Development recommends that, in order to *compensate* for the reverse transfer of technology, resulting from such exodus, amounting to several billions of dollars for the last decade, special arrangements including the possibility of establishing special funds, should be made to provide the necessary resources for strengthening the technological capabilities of the developing countries.[45]

However, given the controversy that surrounds the question as to the magnitude, if not the existence, of losses to LDCs in a meaningful and measurable sense, it would appear to be pertinent to rest the case for a brain-drain-related transfer of funds from DCs to LDCs *also* on the former moral rationale: namely, the gains by DCs from the influx of such a brain drain. That such a gain exists is generally conceded, national immigration policies on levels *and* composition having generally been dictated by national interest (except in the case of political refugees: a problem that must be kept distinct from the present problem of the brain drain).[46]

---

[44] Cf. Address by the Crown Prince Hassan bin Talal of Jordan to the 63rd Meeting of the ILO, Geneva, 10 June 1977, p. 8, emphasis added. Note the emphasis on 'compensation' and the notion of losses suffered by loss of manpower.

[45] Cf. *Report* of the Contact Group on Industrialization and Transfer of Technology, CIEC, Paris, 14 May 1977; emphasis added.

[46] The presumption that DCs gain from PTK immigration has recently been challenged by Dan Usher (1977), on the ground that the immigrants receive more

Whether such a DC contribution to LDCs would add to total transfers, or be a mere substitute for other aid flows, is a question that might be posed. It would seem that the substitution of one form of revenue transfer for another has been exaggerated. The presumption of LDC difficulties and DC gains is persuasive, and the moral case for DC revenue transfers based on these two presumptions is one that may find a sympathetic chord in the DCs; in this event, the substitution for other forms of aid may be correspondingly less probable since the moral (or other) case for different forms of resource transfers is surely not identical. It may also be noted that if the proposed tax on DCs is *coupled* with a tax to be borne by the PTK immigrants themselves — as *their* contribution to LDC developmental spending — the acceptability of the former and reduction in the substitutability of both together for other forms of resource transfers to LDCs may be increased.[47]

Taxing LDC PTK Immigrants' Incomes in DCs

The proposal to tax LDC PTK immigrants' incomes in DCs, as distinct from the proposal to get DCs to transfer resources (from general tax revenues) to LDCs, was originally suggested in 1972 by me (Bhagwati 1972). It has subsequently been explored in depth in several writings by distinguished lawyers and economists, so that its rationales, revenue dimensions, legal and administrative implications, and political-cum-human rights aspects have been laid bare by intensive scrutiny.[48]

---

from their share in public expenditures than they give up by way of taxes. However, his calculations are not persuasive and do not, in my judgement, undermine the plausible presumption that PTK immigrants, belonging generally to the DC groups that are subject to progressive taxation in DCs, are likely to be making a net contribution to, rather than a net claim on, the DCs through the tax system; and hence the presumption of DC gain from PTK immigration can only be reinforced on this account.

[47] This coupling has been suggested in Bhagwati and Partington (1976), and will be noted again below.

[48] Cf. the numerous papers in Bhagwati and Partington (1976), Bhagwati (1976), Hamada (1977) and Balacs (1976), to mention some of the major writings on this proposal.

The different rationales, and associated implications for the format of the proposed tax, are therefore relatively easy to state. There are basically four different types of arguments in justification of such a tax (all mentioned in my earlier analysis but now brought together with additional comments).

Rationale 1. One rationale is that the PTK immigrants ought to be taxed in order to compensate the LDCs for the losses that their migration entails, so that a fraction of their certain economic gains from the migration to DCs is utilized for this purpose.[49] If the tax rate were to be chosen with reference to the losses, the LDC losses would have to be quantified and then divided up among the emigrants and, strictly speaking, since the losses will generally vary by the kinds of professionals being considering, the tax rate would presumably be different by each such class of PTK migrants. However, there is clearly no reason to go in for such 'fine tuning' here any more than with other classes of tax policies already in place in different countries; and it would seem perfectly appropriate to treat the rationale as leading to a general case for such a brain drain tax, with the tax rate actually chosen (at some single figure or schedule) on grounds of practicality and administrative convenience.

Rationale 2. A related, but distinct, rationale on moral principles may be that, even if there is no LDC loss involved, the migration makes these LDC nationals significantly better off and that the LDC tax network should enable the LDCs to tax these incremental incomes, on broadly progressive lines, for LDC social purposes. This moral argument does involve an extension of the progressive tax principle, normally applied to domestically based nationals, to nationals in other countries: and it should be noted that it does not run contrary to 'acceptable' norms of tax behaviour.[50]

Rationale 3. Leaving 'moral obligations' aside, there is also the 'purely economic' argument that the extension of the LDC tax

[49] Note again that the 'losses' go well beyond the 'educational costs' that are referred to in the popular writings on the brain drain.

[50] Thus, see the paper of Oldman and Pomp in Bhagwati and Partington (1976). They do note, however, that for a number of reasons the countries that extend their taxation to incomes earned by nationals residing abroad is very small.

schedule to PTK emigrants' earnings in DCs would achieve global efficiency in the sense of permitting optimal allocation of the world supply of PTK manpower. While this argument (already stated earlier) does imply that different LDC emigrants should pay *differential* (own LDC-related) taxes in DCs, again it could be considered for administrative convenience that the actual implementation be undertaken with *identical* supplementary tax rates being applied to all LDC PTK immigrants.

Rationale 4. Then again, another rationale runs in terms of the proposed tax providing the LDC with a policy instrument that enables the LDC to achieve greater efficiency and/or equity in where the PTK emigration occurs. These arguments were considered in section 4. Note that they also imply that the tax rates levied could differ by PTKs of different classes and different LDC nationalities. However, on grounds of administrative convenience again, the tax rates could be standardized across all categories of the brain drain.

Rationale 5. Finally, recall the argument that the imposition of such a tax on the PTK immigrants to supplement LDC developmental spending could have the 'externality' effect of stimulating additional DC transfers of resources to the LDCs, by demonstrating that LDCs were willing to tax the incomes of their own professionals for development in a self-help fashion rather than merely by exhorting DC nationals to undertake the tax burden of financing LDC development through increasing aid flows.

If any or all of these rationales were indeed to be accepted in order to tax LDC PTK immigrants' incomes in DCs, what order of magnitude would the resulting revenues be, and what legal, administrative and other issues might be raised?

Revenue implications. As it happens, the revenue question has been treated at some length for the USA, UK, and Canada, and estimates made on the basis of fairly careful calculations. Table 13.2 sets out the resulting estimate of US $500 million per annum in 1976 on the following assumptions: (i) the tax would be levied at the rate of 10 per cent on net-of-DC-tax incomes for a period of up to 10 years only after formal migration; (ii) the US categorization of

TABLE 13.2

Estimates for US, Canada, and UK, and for all DCs[a, b]

Item	US	Canada	UK
Period over which the stock of professional LDC immigrants is considered. (Tax estimates relates to the terminal year of the period)	1961–71 (11 years)	1963–72 (10 years)	1964–72 (9 years)
Total stock of PTK immigrants in the terminal year of the relevant period[a]	208,309	37,653 (+ 18,315, if certain other professional and technical occupations are not excluded)	60,759 (New Commonwealth and alien LDCs)
Average, after-(DC)-tax, of annual incomes of different categories of immigrants	Physicians, dentists and surgeons $ 23,807 Scientists (natural) $ 11,415 Nurses $ 5987 Engineers $ 12,550	Physicians and dentists $ 20,734 Nurses, medical and dental technicians $ 5692	Doctors and dentists £2,280 Nurses £1,025 Scientists (natural and social) £2,050

Table 13.2 (cont.)

Item	US	Canada	UK
	Technicians $ 7807	Scientists (natural) $ 13,438 Teachers $ 7582 Engineers $ 13,794	Teachers £1,823 Engineers £2,054
Estimated total revenue from a 10 per cent tax on disposable incomes of professional LDC immigrants	$ 231.7 million (1971)	$ 52.0 million (1972) (of which $ 13.6 million from certain excluded professions)	£10.8 million (1972) (8.6 million New Commonwealth + 2.2 million alien)
Total revenue (1972):[b] Sum of US, Canada, and UK		≥) $ 300 million	
Total revenue (estimating additional 25 per cent revenue from EEC, Australia, and other DCs)		(≥) $ 375 million	
Total UN receipts[c] (total revenue + equal matching contributions by DCs from general revenues)		(≥) $ 750 million	

Table 13.2 (cont.)

Item	US	Canada	UK
Total UN receipts (1976) (additionally allowing for taxation of international civil servants and inflation during the 1970s)		(≥) $ 1 billion	

NOTES: The definitions of LDCs in the three studies is broadly comparable, except for negligible differences. However, the definitions of PTK or professional manpower are probably not that close. For Canada, the *detailed* estimates refer only to a subset. However, the *revenue* estimate has been calculated also for the full PTK set, and this is the $ 52.0 million figure (of which $ 13.6 million represents the professions omitted by the authors from their detailed calculations, these professions being listed in their Table 1). For definitions of professional immigrants used in the Balacs and Gordon paper for the UK, given the data availability there, see their paper.

a   Numbers in the original surveys by Bhagwati and Pelcovits on the US, by DeVortez and Maki on Canada, and by Balacs and Gordon on the UK.

b   An exchange rate of $ 2.5 to £1.00 has been used. The Canadian dollar has been simply treated as identical with the US dollar.

c   Estimates of the total receipts that the UN would get if the tax proceeds were matched by an equal contribution by DCs from their general revenues.

SOURCES: Bhagwati and Pelcovits, app. to Bhagwati and Dellalfar, for US; Balacs and Gordon, for UK; DeVoretz and Maki, for Canada, all from Bhagwati and Partington (1976).

PTK migrants would be (more or less) followed; and (iii) international civil servants would also be included in the coverage.

The figure rises to US $1 billion *if* a *matching* DC contribution of revenue (à la first tax proposal, discussed above) is made. Note also that the revenue would be both untied (by source or project or commodity) and fully grant-equivalent, and hence worth about 2 to 3 times as much as an 'average' aid flow of the same nominal magnitude.

Legal and administrative problems. The tax proposal has been extensively explored by lawyers. It would appear that, for it to be constitutionally feasible in the USA, it will have to be a tax imposed by LDCs and collected by DCs, the same being enshrined in a multilateral treaty.[51] There is presumably no constitutional barrier in the UK but the tax, if it is to be acceptable, may have to be imposed by all DCs of immigration so that the constitutional requirements of the US would automatically define the requirements of implementing the tax altogether.

The administrative problems of collection by DCs need not be particularly great. The treaty would make the collection legally enforceable by DC courts whereas the cost of collection need not be large if the existing tax forms can be negligibly amended to identify the immigrants who are eligible and to allow for their supplemental contribution (though the investigative costs to avoid evasion would have to be added separately).

Political problems. Three political problems have been identified. In the UK, a problem with the tax may be that it might be popularly regarded as discriminatory by race since the LDC immigrants would be predominantly from the 'coloured' races.[52] A multilateral treaty, and the fact that the LDCs themselves would be active in seeking such a treaty, ought however to counter this notion. Identically, it might be feared that such a tax would alienate the professionals from their own LDCs if they resent having to pay the tax. Again, the fact that the payment would not be identified with the action of any particular LDC, but would be part of a

---

[51] See the Oldman and Pomp analysis in Bhagwati and Partington (1976), and also the summary by Partington.

[52] Cf. Partington's piece on the UK in Bhagwati and Partington (1976).

multilateral treaty and conventions, ought to deflect this possible resentment away from 'source-of-origin' LDCs.

Finally, in the DCs generally, the tax may be regarded as being in violation of 'human rights'. In this regard three rebuttals are necessary. First, the tax (unless exceptionally steep rates are being considered that are obviously not going to be acceptable) surely is *not* a quantitative restriction and would actually only cut into some of the very definitely large economic gains made by the migrants. It is, quite definitely, *not* a violation of any fundamental human rights any more than the DC taxation of such migrants is, which also reduces their incentive to immigrate. Second, the truly *effective* restriction on the free migration of human beings from LDCs to DCs is *not* any LDC policy, present or proposed, but the enormously restrictive *immigration* quotas practised by the DCs themselves. Hence, I might be excused for regarding with some amusement, if not derision, the notion that DCs ought to find such a tax unacceptable on human rights grounds! And a cynic may well regard such complaints, coming from DC intellectuals and policy-makers, as self-serving and better addressed to the immigration authorities of their own governments. Finally, Professor Frank Newman has examined the 'law' at the United Nations on human rights and would appear to argue that a multilateral treaty embodying the proposed brain drain tax could be found consistent with the existing conventions and understandings.[53]

Optimal format of the tax.   It would appear that the optimal format of the proposed tax would have to be one where it is levied by LDCs, collected by DCs, and preferably the proceeds routed through a United Nations agency (such as the UNDP) to the LDCs for developmental spending. The recipients among the LDCs ought to reflect, to a predominant extent, the LDC-nationality composition of the PTK migrants (or else these LDCs would not have interest in supporting the tax, especially as it would cut inward remittances to some extent) while at the same time *not* being tied *completely* into it (or else one would run into opposition from DCs that object strongly to certain LDCs politically and would not wish to be a party to collecting revenues for them).

---

[53] Cf. his contribution in Bhagwati and Partington (1976).

This is, in fact, the format in which the tax has finally been proposed for adoption by the international community in recent writings by its proponents.[54]

These dimensions of the optimal format of the proposed tax can hardly be overemphasized, for the Pakistan government's attempt in January 1976 to tax the foreign earnings of its nationals 'migrating' to the Middle East, à la the proposal to tax the brain drain, had to be hurriedly withdrawn. It created great resentment against the government, was seen to be unenforceable, and cut into remittances because the potential assesses felt that the remittances might provide a clue to their foreign incomes. Clearly, none of these difficulties would attend a tax where the DCs would collect and enforce the tax that was levied under a collective treaty by DCs and LDCs.

Other Alternatives

Finally, two alternative tax and quasi-tax proposals may be listed here, neither of which need to be confined to PTK immigrants.

First, it may be suggested that the United States' practice of tax-exempting contributions to approved charities be extended to contributions made by LDC immigrants to LDCs. Thus, a considerably more lenient ruling for eligibility may apply for contributions by these immigrants to LDC-based developmental and charitable organizations or to international agencies for spending in LDCs.[55] This would seem like a splendid idea and need not be considered to be an alternative to the tax proposals just discussed. This proposal does imply, of course, that there is a small dent being made in the DC revenues by granting such exemptions: therefore, this would appear to be a proposal that mixes private initiative with DC tax revenue contributions.

Second, following the recent US practice of taxpayers being allowed to earmark part of their taxes to finance Presidential elections, it might be suggested that LDC immigrants in DCs be allowed, in the same way, to earmark (up to, say, 30 per cent of

[54] Cf. ch. 1 in Bhagwati and Partington (1976); and Bhagwati (1976c, d, e).
[55] This suggestion is made in the paper by Oldman and Pomp in Bhagwati and Partington (1976: 182).

their) taxes for routing to a designated UN agency for developmental spending.

7. MAJOR CONCLUSIONS AND RECOMMENDATIONS

The preceding analytical review of the principal policy-oriented issues related to the brain drain leads to several conclusions of which the few major ones may now be sketched here.

(1) It is possible to measure the imputed capital flows implicit in the flow of PTK manpower from LDCs to DCs. The task of imputation is by no means insuperable and can indeed be undertaken by international agreement on a set of conventions on several procedures and concepts that are no more 'strange' or difficult than those that statisticians and economists continually deal with in arriving at, for example, national income accounts on a standardized basis.

(2) Such a measure of imputed capital flows is useful in providing a balanced picture of the capital flows currently taking place between DCs and LDCs, by deflating appropriately the otherwise inflated figure of DC capital flows to LDCs that are often cited as evidence of the benefits derived by LDCs from DCs.

(3) The appropriate measure for any international compensation mechanism, on the other hand, must relate to LDC losses from the brain drain. These can be defined only with complexity and are likely to be only broadly convertible into monetary figures. They can however form the basis for compensatory tax revenues collected from *either* DCs (from their general tax revenues) *or* the LDC PTK immigrants themselves (as a supplementary tax on their DC incomes).

(4) Rationales can be developed, however, for both these types of taxes (i.e. on DCs *and* on the immigrants) *without* reference to LDC losses.

(5) The rationales for the supplementary tax on LDC PTK immigrants' incomes in DCs, moreover, rest not merely on moral arguments but also on grounds of global allocative efficiency *and* on grounds of LDC equity and efficiency goals. Besides, the revenue implications of such a tax are substantial. Such a tax is

therefore worth considering seriously as part of the overall reform of the international economic order under way with the *NIEO* negotiations.

(6) Such taxation can usefully be combined with matching contributions by DCs from their general revenues.

(7) Moreover, it can be supplemented by two DC tax policy changes: greatly liberalized permission to PTK LDC immigrants to make tax-deductible contributions to LDC-based charitable organizations *and* to international agencies for developmental and social spending in LDCs; *and* permission to PTK LDC immigrants to designate up to a large fraction of their DC tax payments for routing to LDCs via a specially designated international agency such as the UNDP.

REFERENCES

Arrow, K.J., 1973: 'Higher Education as a Filter', *Journal of Public Economics*, 2.

Balacs, P., 1976: *The Brain Drain and Reverse Transfer of Technology* (Geneva: UNCTAD).

Berry, A. and R. Soligo, 1969: 'Some Welfare Aspects of International Migration', *Journal of Political Economy*, Sept.–Oct.

Bhagwati, J.N., 1972: 'The United States in the Nixon Era: The End of Innocence', *Daedalus*, 101 (4), pp. 25–48.

——, 1973: 'Education, Class Structure and Income Equality', *World Development*, 1, pp. 1–36; rptd in vol. 1, ch. 11.

——, 1976a (ed.): *The Brain Drain and Taxation: Theory and Empirical Analysis* (Amsterdam: North-Holland), vol. II.

——, 1976b: 'The Brain Drain', *International Social Science Journal*, 28 (4), pp. 694–712.

——, 1976c: 'Taxing the Brain Drain', *Challenge* (July/Aug.).

——, 1976d: 'Brain Drain', *Zeitschrift der Österreichen Forschungsstiftung für Entwicklungshilfe*, 2.

——, 1976e: 'L'Exode des Cerveaux', *International Social Science Journal* (UNESCO), 18 (4).

Bhagwati, J.N. and K. Hamada, 1974: 'The Brain Drain, International Integration of Markets for Professionals and Unemployment: A

Theoretical Analysis', *Journal of Development Economics*, 1 (1); rptd in *EIET*, ch. 47, vol. 2.

Bhagwati, J.N. and M. Partington, 1976 (eds): *Taxing the Brain Drain: A Proposal* (Amsterdam: North-Holland), vol. I.

Bhagwati, J.N. and C. Rodriguez, 1976: 'Welfare-theoretical Analyses of the Brain Drain', *in* Bhagwati (1976a); rptd in *EIET*, ch. 46, vol. 2.

Bhagwati, J.N. and T.N. Srinivasan, 1977: 'Education in a "Job-Ladder" Model and the Fairness-in-Hiring Rule', *Journal of Public Economics*, 7; rptd in *EIET*, ch. 49, vol. 2.

Fields, G., 1974: 'The Private Demand for Education in Relation to Labour Market Conditions in Less-developed Countries', *Economic Journal*.

Grubel, H. and A. Scott, 1966: 'The International Flow of Human Capital', *American Economic Review* (May).

——, 1977: *The Brain Drain* (Ontario: Wilfrid Laurier University Press).

Hamada, K., 1977: 'Taxing the Brain Drain: A Global Point of View', *in* J. Bhagwati (ed.), *The New International Economic Order: The North–South Debate* (Cambridge, Mass.: MIT Press).

Hamada, K. and J. Bhagwati, 1975: 'Domestic Distortions, Imperfect Information and the Brain Drain', *Journal of Development Economics*, 2 (3), rptd *in* Bhagwati (1976a) and *EIET*, ch. 48, vol. 2.

McCulloch, B. and J. Yellen, 1975: 'Consequences of a Tax on the Brain Drain for Unemployment and Income Inequality in Less Developed Countries', *Journal of Development Economics*, 2 (3); rptd *in* Bhagwati (1976a).

Pryor, F., 1968: *Public Expenditures in Communist and Capitalist Nations* (London: Allen & Unwin).

Spence, M., 1973: 'Job Market Signalling', *Quarterly Journal of Economics*, 87.

US House of Representatives, 1974: *Brain Drain: a Study of the Persistent Issue of International Scientific Mobility*, Subcommittee on National Security Policy and Scientific Development of the Committee on Foreign Affairs, Sept. (Washington, DC: Government Printing Office).

Usher, D., 1977: 'Public Property and the Effects of Migration Upon Other Residents of the Migrants' Countries of Origin and Destination', *Journal of Political Economy*, 85 (5), pp. 1001–21.

14

The Brain Drain, International Integration of Markets for Professionals and Unemployment[*]

1. INTRODUCTION

NEARLY the entire *theoretical* literature on the effects of the 'brain drain' from the less developed countries on their welfare has been undertaken in the framework of neoclassical models of the Hicks–Samuelson value-theoretic variety.[1]

While the analysts in this genre have greatly clarified certain issues such as the nature of the objective function to be specified, their analysis and prescriptions have been constrained by the theoretical model which they work with. The central result of their analysis, attributable to Grubel and Scott (1966), that brain drain should not prima facie be a cause for concern as the drained person will only take away the value of his marginal product which he himself earns anyway, can be rather obviously shown to be subject to the limitations that, (i) for finite, rather than infinitesimal, shift of labour, there would still be a loss to those left behind;[2] (ii) if the social marginal product exceeds the private marginal product, thanks to strong externalities, as would seem to be the case with doctors and exceptionally gifted academics about whose

* With Koichi Hamada. Thanks are due to the National Science Foundation for financial support of the research underlying this chapter. It was originally written while K. Hamada (University of Tokyo, Bunkyoku, Tokyo) was visiting M.I.T. on a Fellowship from the American Council of Learned Societies. Helpful comments on it were received from T.N. Srinivasan, Robert Solow, Herbert Grubel, and an anonymous referee.

[1] See, in particular, Grubel and Scott (1966) and Johnson (1972).

[2] On the other hand, depending on the size of the emigration and the nature of the production function, this loss may still be very small.

emigration typically the underdeveloped countries seem to worry, then again there *is* a loss to those left behind;[3] and, (iii) if the state has financed the education that is embodied in the skilled worker who migrates, *and* if it is assumed that the state would have taxed this skilled worker — a realistic assumption when there is progressive taxation — partially or wholly to 'recover' the return on this investment, then his emigration does deprive those left behind of this return and thus worsens their welfare.

These are useful insights into the problem of the 'brain drain'. However, admittedly, the analysis is overly simple and could be extended in many directions. An obvious growth-theoretic extension would be to bring in savings behaviour and maximization of welfare over time for those left behind. Or, within the confines of the Hicks–Samuelson model, the analysis could be enriched to allow for remittances from the emigrated people: an argument that qualifies the conclusions in favour of permitting the brain drain. The neoclassical model could further be extended *fully* in the direction of trade-theoretic models with factor movements: the effect of the labour migration on the commodity terms of trade of the labour-losing country could be readily analysed along the lines of the recent Jones (1967) and Kemp (1966) contributions to the welfare theory of international capital movements.[4]

But few of these extensions of the Hicks–Samuelson value-theoretic model are anything but analytic modifications that admit into the model the kinds of complexities which the model itself, rather than reality, suggests. It is necessary therefore to see

---

[3] On the other hand, things could be greatly stretched and it be argued that, for some emigrants, their contribution to social product still continues to accrue to the home country: e.g. an Indian scientist's achievements abroad 'inspire' his countrymen at home; and that this happens *without* their earning their private product from the home country's GNP and also that their social product may even *increase* if their achievements improve in a more efficient and productive environment than that existing in their home country.

[4] Johnson (1967) has extended the analysis of the problem in a yet different direction, by assuming that migration of skilled labour reduces *both* the labour and the capital stock of the emigrating country. However, his analysis is limited by his assumption that human capital and physical capital are perfect substitutes — an assumption that would naturally provide a downward bias to the damaging effects of brain drain.

whether an alternative value-theoretic model can be devised which comes closer to reality as observed in certain under-developed countries.

In particular, certain important aspects of the educated man-power problem in underdeveloped countries have been noted by the non-theorists:

(1) The existence of international income inequality implies that, for the educated élite which is better informed about the developed world, and more integrated with it regarding notions of a 'good life' and related values, the salary levels demanded *and* fixed by the élite groups themselves tend to reflect the salary levels of comparable groups in the more developed countries. René Dumont (1969) has argued for French Africa:

During the last phase of colonialism, the policy was to equalize salaries of Africans and Europeans in similar jobs, a defensible position only in the framework of 'assimilation'. The native civil servant, in addition to his regular salary, received a colonial supplement. This has been reduced in some cases, but not abolished. At independence, this pseudoequality has led to flagrant disparity with the rest of the population, whose stand-ard of living is often a fifteenth of the French.

Massive departure of the French resulted in a high rate of promotion of subordinate African civil servants, who thus earn even more now than before, for the same qualifications. The student returning from France is appointed director if he is the only African technician or graduate in his field [p. 80].

Indeed, this phenomenon has been noted by Osvaldo Sunkel (1971) for Latin America and by Dudley Seers and Richard Jolly (1972) for a wider group of countries. Thus, we can postulate a socio–economic situation in which the real wage levels of the educated élites are set by fiat, legislation, unionization, etc., at levels that reflect the degree of response to the international élite integration effect just outlined.

(2) This phenomenon of educated élite wages, 'way out of line with the average per capita income of the underdeveloped coun-tries', is next regarded as often leading to a 'leap-frogging' process under which the lowest wages tend to get pulled up by the highest: hence the phenomenon of such institutionally defined wages tends to run through the entire labour market.

(3) With these institutionally defined wages, it is inevitable that the labour market must work so as to have open unemployment of labour (except in singular cases); and this too is an observed phenomenon: educated and also uneducated people are often unemployed in the developed countries.

(4) At the same time, the phenomenon of high wages accruing to the (employed) educated élite, creates a political demand for education. René Dumont (1969) has again described the French African situation vividly:

Present Education Obstructs Progress

This statement may appear paradoxical to many readers, particularly coming from the pen of a professor, since education was the essential foundation of development in Europe, America, Japan, the Soviet Union, and China. In Africa it has a certain utility, but this is greatly curtailed by the social milieu on to which the educational system was grafted. For most African children, in town and country alike, school represents above all a means of entering the élite class. Even in the most backward areas of the bush everyone has grasped the fact that the official with clean hands earns more and works much less.

Pushed by his parents, a peasant child realizes that he can never go very far in agriculture; the only way to get ahead is to get out. He goes to school and works very hard, to this end, sometimes at the price of incredible sacrifices. I have heard of a child in Chad who walks twice a day the twenty kilometres separating his house from school.

. . . Before long, these young people end up in the shanty-towns of the capitals and become social parasites. Their days are spent writing requests for jobs; requests that pile up in all the administrations. Some of them, in Douala for example, join the underground [pp. 88–89].

But this is a situation which is to be found in a large number of underdeveloped countries, indeed.

(5) And the demand for education is translated into educational expenditures by the state, in these underdeveloped countries, with visible alacrity. In India, for example, the number of colleges expands, with little time lag, to accommodate the students who qualify with 'pass marks' from the high schools: and the standards in the latter have, in turn, fallen to accommodate the larger flows of students seeking educational qualifications.

A value-theoretic model that accounts for these phenomena is clearly more relevant for analysis of the questions pertaining to the labour market, such as the welfare effect of the brain drain in several underdeveloped countries than the neoclassical model (which assumes fully flexible wages, for example).

We proceed therefore to the construction of precisely such a model in Sec. 2 and then analyse the phenomena of brain drain and increasing international integration of élite groups in its framework in Sec. 3. In Sec. 4, we discuss a number of variants of this basic model. In Sec. 5, we draw together the welfare implications of emigration in the framework of our model and its variants, also examining the effects of taxing emigrants — a policy that has sometimes been advocated in the literature.[5] In particular, since our model allows for the existence of unemployment for both educated and uneducated labour, our discussion of welfare will involve examination not merely of the (conventional) impact on the domestic availability of goods and services for final use but also of the effect of each policy measure on the level and degree of unemployment, if any, of each class of labour.[6]

2. THE BASIC MODEL

The simplest general equilibrium model, incorporating the features described above, which can be constructed for our analysis, is set out below.

Assume two commodities m_1 and m_2. Let their outputs M_1 and M_2 be related to the inputs by the following production functions that possess the standard properties including twice differentiability and linear homogeneity,

---

[5] See, for example, Bhagwati and Dellalfar (1973).

[6] We might as well note explicitly that the kind of model we build and analyse here is not universally valid, even on casual empiricism. Thus, for example, in Japan, the (relative) wage level of intellectuals in Japan has managed to remain virtually unaffected by the significantly higher level of remuneration for their counterparts in the West. This may be one of the many respects in which Japan has apparently differed from the other 'latecomers' in the process of industrialization and integration with the world economy and polity, exhibiting a remarkable ability to adhere to an 'inner-directed' posture in her political and cultural methods.

$$M_1 = F_1(L_1), \tag{1}$$

$$M_2 = F_2(L_2), \tag{2}$$

where L_1 is the quantity of skilled/educated labour employed in producing m_1, and L_2 is the quantity of unskilled/uneducated labour employed in producing m_2. Note that educated labour enters only m_1-production and uneducated labour enters only m_2-production. Diminishing returns to L_1 and L_2 are postulated, implying implicit, specific 'non-labour' factors. We further assume a 'small' country, in Samuelson's sense, so that the commodity price ratio $p_1/p_2 = \pi$ is exogenously fixed and commodity m_2 is the numeraire.

We next assume that the real wage of educated labour is fixed, by international emulation and associated union determination or wage legislation, at level $\bar{w}_1$ in m_2-units. Note that this automatically defines $(\partial F_1/\partial L_1)\pi$ and hence L_1 and M_1. Similarly, assume that the 'leap-frogging' process fixed the minimum wages of unskilled labour L_2 at $\bar{w}_2$ ($= \partial F_2/\partial L_2$), and hence also L_2 and M_2. Thus we can write the following two factor market equations:

$$\partial F_1/\partial L_1 = \bar{w}_1/\pi, \quad \text{or } L_1 = g_1(\bar{w}_1/\pi), \tag{3}$$

$$\partial F_2/\partial L_2 = \bar{w}_2, \quad \text{or } L_2 = g_2(\bar{w}_2). \tag{4}$$

Then with U_1 and U_2 denoting the unemployed, educated, and uneducated labour respectively, N_1 and N_2 denoting educated and uneducated labour supply respectively, and $\bar{N}$ representing the total fixed labour supply, we have three balance equations:[7]

[7] Bhagwati and Srinivasan (1972) have analysed an alternative adjustment mechanism for the labour market, where the unemployment of skilled labour is not permitted as long as there are enough jobs in the unskilled labour market. Under this theory, the available supply of skilled labour first gets absorbed in the skilled labour market, and the spillover then takes the available jobs in the unskilled labour market (where the two kinds of labour are equally productive but the employers have a sociological preference to giving jobs to skilled over unskilled applicants). The Bhagwati–Srinivasan model is designed to study the phenomenon of 'overqualification', whereby the educated seem to get into the uneducated-level jobs over time: a phenomenon which has sometimes also been called the 'upgradation' of jobs.

$$L_1 + U_1 = N_1, \tag{5}$$

$$L_2 + U_2 = N_2, \tag{6}$$

$$N_1 + N_2 = \bar{N}. \tag{7}$$

But we next need to know how the available labour supply will divide between N_1 and N_2. To do this, we need to introduce equations to determine the supply of educated labour N_1. We shall assume that there will be a positive inducement to get educated as long as the expected wage for educated labour exceeds the expected wage for uneducated labour.

Let the expected wage for educated labour Ew_1 then be the *average* wage for it, namely,

$$Ew_1 = \bar{w}_1 \, (L_1/N_1), \tag{8}$$

and the expected wage for uneducated labour Ew_2 be the *average* wage for it:

$$Ew_2 = \bar{w}_2 \, (L_2/N_2), \tag{9}$$

and the equilibrium condition then is:

$$Ew_1 = Ew_2. \tag{10}$$

Note that this equilibrium condition makes sense in so far as we are assuming that the State undertake the cost of education, and not labour itself. It is assumed therefore that as long as $Ew_1 > Ew_2$, there will be a politically effective excess demand for State-financed educational facilities to be opened up, for N_2 to be turned into N_1 until $Ew_1 = Ew_2$. However, to analyse the effect of this assumption on the level of national income, we may simply subtract the cost of this education from national production of m_1 and m_2 to arrive at the national income available for consumption:

$$Y = (\pi M_1 + M_2) - kN_1, \tag{11}$$

where k is the fixed educational cost, in m_2-units, per person; this cost being subtracted from total output of M_1 and M_2 to arrive at the net output available for consumption Y.[8] It follows that increasing Y is tantamount to increasing the value of a conventional social welfare function defined in terms of goods and services available for domestic consumption.

This basic model thus has eleven equations and eleven unknowns: M_1, M_2, L_1, L_2, U_1, U_2, N_1, N_2, Ew_1, Ew_2, and Y. It is also a model in terms of which we can meaningfully analyse a number of questions relating to the brain drain problem and the phenomenon of international integration of the educated labour markets.

3. BRAIN DRAIN AND INTERNATIONAL INTEGRATION OF MARKET FOR PROFESSIONALS

This basic model can be easily contrasted with the case where both wages are flexible and labour pays for the cost of education. Note first that we have here *three* sources of economic inefficiency: the two sticky wages plus the free education. In the absence of these three inefficiencies, the economy would have reached the standard Pareto-optimal equilibrium with the following first-order conditions:

$$w_1 - k = (\partial F_1 / \partial L_1) - k = (\partial F_2 / \partial L_2) = w_2, \qquad (12)$$

with full employment of labour. In analysing the model with the three inefficiencies which we have noted, we now proceed through successive possibilities, analysing the effects on unemployment and national income in four alternative cases:

Case I. Our-Joneses-keeping-up-with-their-Joneses: This is a case where the country's educated/skilled labour, on integrating with the outside-world's educated/skilled labour, demands and achieves an increment in its salary level: this is therefore the case where there is primary increase in w_1.

Case II. Keeping-up-with-our-Joneses: This is a case where we have

---

[8] To ensure proper dimensionality in the analysis that follows, this educational cost must be regarded as the 'annual' flow equivalent of the educational cost incurred to train a man. Also, to simplify the analysis, we do not introduce private educational expenditure until Sec. 4.

the well-observed 'leap-frogging' process, so that the rise in w_1 (the wage of skilled labour) leads to a sympathetic rise in w_2 (the wage of unskilled labour).

Case III. Emigration-of-our-Joneses: This is a case where the emigration of skilled labour to higher-wage areas abroad leads to higher expected wage to skilled labour: *either* via mere reduction in unemployment of skilled labour at home and consequent increased assurance of the domestic wage $(\bar{w}_1)$ *or* via pushing up the expected wage because the wage rate abroad is higher than the domestic wage.

Case IV. The general case of emigration and rise of wages: This is a general case where the emigration of skilled labour is also accompanied by a sympathetic rise in the domestic wage $(\bar{w}_1)$: which is plausible because greater emigration could imply greater integration of the professional markets for skilled labour internationally. This general case therefore considers the totality of effects from Case II and Case III: the emigration effect of Case III being combined with the dual wage-increase effect of Case II.

We now analyse these cases in turn. The following analysis is carried out on the assumption that a marginal change in wages or emigration still leaves some unemployment in each sector; otherwise, neoclassical competitive analysis would become applicable.

Case I. Our Joneses keeping up with their Joneses

This is the case where the educated labour force is getting culturally integrated internationally, and the effect is to exercise an upward pull on its domestic salary level. This phenomenon of 'our-Joneses-keeping-up-with-their-Joneses' can be analysed simply then by analysing the effect of a shift in w_1.

We can see the effect of the increase in $\bar{w}_1$ on employment by differentiating (3) and (4):

$$dL_1/d\bar{w}_1 = (1/\pi)\, g_1'\, (\bar{w}_1/\pi) < 0,$$
$$\text{because } g_1'\, (\bar{w}_1/\pi) = (\partial^2 F_1/\partial L_1^2)^{-1} < 0, \tag{13}$$

$$dL_2/d\bar{w}_1 = 0. \tag{14}$$

The employment in m_1-sector will decrease in response to the rise in wages in its own sector and the employment in m_2-sector remains the same.

However, unemployment in both sectors depends on how labour divides into the two types of labour. We can readily see the effect of the wage increase in m_1-sector on the division of labour supply into the two types, by deriving:

$$dN_1/d\bar{w}_1 = (1 - \eta_1) N_2 L_1 / (\bar{w}_1 L_1 + \bar{w}_2 L_2), \qquad (15)$$

where $\eta_1 \equiv (\bar{w}_1/L_1) (dL_1/d\bar{w}_1)$ is the elasticity of the demand for labour in m_1-industry. Further, (15) simplifies to:

$$dN_1/d\bar{w}_1 = (1 - \eta_1) N_1 N_2 / (\bar{N}\bar{w}_1), \qquad (16)$$

or, in elasticity terms,

$$(\bar{w}_1/N_1) (dN_1/d\bar{w}_1) = (1 - \eta_1) N_2/\bar{N}. \qquad (17)$$

Thus the supply of educated labour increases or decreases, depending on whether the elasticity of demand for labour in m_1-industry, is less or more than unity. This result is easy to understand, of course, because the outcome regarding the supply of educated labour depends on the impact effect of the wage change in m_1 on the expected wage (Ew_1) in that sector: and the expected wage will rise in so far as the actual wage rises but fall in so far as (educated) labour is laid off by profit-maximizing entrepreneurs in m_1 in consequence. The net outcome is determined by whether the elasticity of demand for labour in m_1 is higher or lower than unity: in the former case, the net effect is to lower the expected wage Ew_1; in the latter, the net effect is to increase it.[9]

---

[9] At the same time, it is easy to see that the elasticity of demand for labour, η_1, is the ratio of the elasticity of substitution of the production function, σ_1, and the capital share, α_1:

$$\eta_1 = -\frac{\bar{w}_1}{L_1} \frac{dL_1}{d\bar{w}_1} = -\frac{F_L^1}{L_1 F_{LL}^1} = \frac{F_L^1}{\bar{K}_1 F_{LL}^1} = \frac{F_L^1 F_K^1}{F^1 \cdot F_{KL}^1} \cdot \frac{F^1}{F_K^1 \bar{K}_1} = \frac{\sigma_1}{\alpha_1}.$$

We may therefore restate the above proposition: the supply of educated labour increases or decreases depending on whether the elasticity of substitution in m_1-industry is smaller or larger than the capital share in m_1-industry.

We can now analyse the effect on absolute the relative unemployment of each sector.

(a) *Absolute Level of Unemployment of Educated Labour*

$$(d/d\bar{w}_1)(N_1 - L_1) = (1 - \eta_1) N_1 N_2 / (\bar{w}_1 N) + \eta_1 L_1 / \bar{w}_1. \quad (18)$$

Thus if the elasticity of demand for educated labour is less than unity, the absolute level of unemployment increases because the supply of educated labour increases while the demand decreases. However, even if the elasticity of demand for educated labour is greater than unity, so that the supply of educated labour is reduced (owing to reduced expected wage Ew_1), the absolute unemployment of educated labour would increase if the demand for such labour reduces even further; this would be the case if:[10]

$$L_1/N_1 \geq N_2/\bar{N}, \quad (19)$$

or

$$L_1/N_1 < N_2/\bar{N}, \quad \text{but} \quad \eta_1 < [1 - (L_1/N_1)/(N_2/\bar{N})]^{-1}. \quad (20)$$

In developing countries the elasticity of substitution in industrial sectors seems to be low, so that it is likely that the elasticity of demand for labour in m_1-sector is less than unity. Moreover, (22) is quite likely to be satisfied unless the unemployment rate in m_1-industry is extremely high. We can therefore conclude that the absolute unemployment in educated labour will most probably increase if the wage of educated labour increases.

(b) *Relative Unemployment of Educated Labour*

Similarly, from (14) and (17), we can derive:

$$\frac{N_1}{L_1} \frac{d}{d\bar{w}_1} \left(\frac{L_1}{N_1} \right) = -\frac{N_2}{\bar{N}} \frac{1}{\bar{w}_1} \left\{ \left(\frac{\bar{N}}{N_2} - 1 \right) \eta_1 + 1 \right\} < 0. \quad (21)$$

Thus the relative unemployment of educated labour will always increase when the wage in m_1-industry increases.

[10] This can be seen by rewriting eq. (18) as:

$$(d/dw_1)(N_1 - L_1) = \{ 1 - \eta_1 + \eta_1 (L_1 \bar{N}/N_1 N_2) \} N_1 N_2 / (\bar{w}_1 \bar{N}).$$

(c) *Unemployment of Uneducated Labour*

Since the employment of uneducated labour depends on its unchanged wage, it will clearly not change. However, the *unemployment* of uneducated labour will increase or decrease, depending on whether its supply increases or decreases. Thus if $\eta_1 < 1$, so that the resulting improvement in Ew_1 has led to increase in educated labour, the stock of uneducated labour (N_2) will have been reduced and hence also the unemployment of uneducated labour. Similarly, if $\eta_1 > 1$, the unemployment of uneducated labour will have increased.

(d) *National Income*

Next, it is easy to see that:

$$dY/d\bar{w}_1 = - L_1\eta_1 - k (1 - \eta_1) (N_1 N_2 / \bar{N} \bar{w}_1). \tag{22}$$

National income will therefore change when $\bar{w}_1$ rises, because of two effects: (i) the decline in employment of (educated) labour will diminish output of m_1 without any offset from increment in output in m_2 where the employment has not changed; and (ii) the cost of educating labour will change, depending on whether the supply of educated labour increases or decreases. Clearly, therefore, when $\eta_1 < 1$, the increase in the supply of educated labour will work to accentuate the reduction in income from the first effect: thus the result must be to unambiguously reduce national income, as is evident from (22). Moreover, even if we take the other case where $\eta_1 > 1$, provided that condition (19) or (20) is satisfied *and* $k < \bar{w}_1$, the *net* effect will be to reduce national income, which is again evident from (22). The only case when income will increase is where k is large, η_1 is extremely large, and the initial unemployment rate of educated labour is large and violates eq. (19). The results in this case are summarized under the column (Effect I) in Table 14.1.

Case II. *Keeping up with our Joneses*

The next question we ask is what happens if the rise in $\bar{w}_1$ leads, in turn, to a sympathetic rise in $\bar{w}_2$ via the well-observed 'leapfrogging' process: this may be called the 'keeping-up-with-our-own-

TABLE 14.1
Effects of Rise in Wages

Impact on:	Symbol	Effect I Our-Joneses-keeping-up-with-their-Joneses	Effect II Keeping-up-with-our-Joneses $\theta \equiv dw_2/dw_1$
Educated labour	$\dfrac{dN_1}{d\bar{w}_1}\left(=-\dfrac{dN_2}{d\bar{w}_1}\right)$	$(1-\eta_1)\,N_1N_2/(\bar{w}_1\bar{N})$	$-\theta(1-\eta_2)\,N_1N_2/(\bar{w}_2\bar{N})$
Unemployment of educated labour	$\dfrac{d}{d\bar{w}_1}(N_1-L_1)$	$(1-\eta_1)\,N_1N_2/(\bar{w}_1\bar{N})+\eta_1 L_1/\bar{w}_1$	$-\theta(1-\eta_2)\,N_1N_2/(\bar{w}_2\bar{N})$
Rate of employment of educated labour	$\dfrac{N_1}{L_1}\dfrac{d}{d\bar{w}_1}\left(\dfrac{L_1}{N_1}\right)$	$-\eta_1/\bar{w}_1-(1-\eta_1)\,N_2/(\bar{w}_1\bar{N})$	$\theta(1-\eta_2)\,N_2/(\bar{w}_1\bar{N})$
Unemployment of uneducated labour	$\dfrac{d}{d\bar{w}_1}(N_2-L_2)$	$-(1-\eta_1)\,N_1N_2/(\bar{w}_1\bar{N})$	$\theta[\,(1-\eta_2)\,N_1N_2/\bar{w}_2\bar{N}+\eta_2 L\bar{w}_2/_2]$
Rate of employment of uneducated labour	$\dfrac{N_2}{L_2}\dfrac{d}{d\bar{w}_1}\left(\dfrac{L_2}{N_2}\right)$	$(1-\eta_1)\,N_1/(\bar{w}_1\bar{N})$	$\theta[\,-\eta_2/\bar{w}_2-(1-\eta_2)\,N_1/(\bar{w}_2\bar{N})]$
National income	$\dfrac{dY}{d\bar{w}_1}$	$-\eta_1 L_1-k\,(1-\eta_1)\,N_1N_2/(\bar{w}_1\bar{N})$	$\theta[\,-\eta_2 L_2+k\,(1-\eta_2)\,N_1N_2/(\bar{w}_2\bar{N})]$

Joneses' phenomenon. We can indeed explore all the questions considered for Case I, for the case where *both* $\bar{w}_1$ and $\bar{w}_2$ rise.

The effect on employment in m_1-sector naturally remains the same as above; but there is now an additional negative effect on employment in m_2-sector, thanks to the induced rise in w_2. Instead of (14) we have

$$dL_2/d\bar{w}_1 = g_2'(\bar{w}_2)(d\bar{w}_2/d\bar{w}_1) < 0. \tag{23}$$

Thus, defining $d\bar{w}_2/d\bar{w}_1 \equiv \theta(\theta > 0)$ and $\eta_2 \equiv -(\bar{w}_2/L_2)(dL_2/d\bar{w}_2)$, we get the results tabulated in Table 14.1.

In addition to the effect through the rise in w_1 (Effect I), the effect through the rise in w_2 (Effect II) is superimposed.

Note that, in contrast to Case I, the directions of the impacts are ambiguous because the induced rise in $\bar{w}_2$ can offset the effects of the primary increase in $\bar{w}_1$. Take, for example, the impact of the increase in $\bar{w}_1$ on the level of the educated labour force (N_1). For Effect I, the level of N_1 will rise if $\eta_1 < 1$; however, for Effect II, the induced rise in $\bar{w}_2$, implying $\theta > 0$, will work to reduce N_1 if $\eta_2 < 1$, thus making the direction of the combined effect indeterminate. An interesting implication of the impact on national income in the last row of Table 14.1 is that it is more difficult to exclude the possibility of increased income from the process of wage-increases. For example, take the extreme case where $\eta_1 = \eta_2 = 0$, and $d\bar{w}_1 = d\bar{w}_2$, i.e. $\theta = 1$. Then

$$dY/d\bar{w}_1 = k(\bar{w}_1 - \bar{w}_2)N_1N_2/(\bar{w}_1\bar{w}_2\bar{N}) > 0.$$

In this special case where the elasticities are zero, and where the factor intensities are consequently fixed, the simultaneous wage rise will increase national income because less people will get educated, thus reducing the cost of education, while employment in each sector is kept constant.

Case III. Emigration of our Joneses

We can now turn to the issue of actual emigration of educated labour. We can set up the problem by assuming an exogenous emigration of educated labour, Z, which does not *in itself* lead to a simultaneous rise in the (actual) wage $\bar{w}_1$ for educated labour;

only in Case IV will be consider the fully general case where the emigration causes rise in $\bar{w}_1$ as also an induced rise in $\bar{w}_2$ in accordance with Case II.

Eq. (5) must then be rewritten as:

$$L_1 + U_1 + Z = N_1, \tag{24}$$

so that the total educated labour is now the sum of the domestically employed and unemployed plus emigrated labour.[11]

There are alternative ways in which we can now explore the impact of such emigration on the system, but all of them must operate through the primary impact on expected wage in the educated labour market. Let us take three possibilities.

(I): We may assume that the migration of a new educated members of the working force does not have any impact on the expected wage, as the migration is not wage-induced and does not lead to similar expectations. Then, in this singular case, *as long as* the migration of labour still leaves *some* unemployment of educated labour, the division of labour into the two types of labour is unaffected, so that the only effect is a reduction in the unemployment of educated labour. Clearly, moreover, production and national income are unchanged. However, since per-capita income and the relative employment rate of educated labour are increased, social welfare should be increased by the 'brain drain' for any reasonable social welfare function. If, therefore, the migration is welfare-improving for the migrants — an assumption that seems reasonable if they are pursuing self-interest — the emigration is a 'good' event, causing welfare improvement for both the migrants and those left behind.

(II): But this 'well-behaved' result will no longer carry through if we assume that the expected wage to educated labour will improve with the migration. This may happen in at least two plausible ways. *Either* the emigration may be treated as reducing the unemployment in the market for educated labour, so that the

[11] We should note here the delicate problem of the timing of education and emigration. There would be little difficulty of interpretation, however, if we regard this analysis as the comparison of two stationary states with and without migration, or more precisely one with some migration and the other with marginal increase in migration.

emigration is treated as raising the wage merely by increasing the number employed, without taking into consideration the incremental wage accruing to those employed abroad as distinct from those employed at home: this may be called the *incremental-employment-effect* variant of the model. *Alternatively*, we may assume that the fact that the emigrants earn a differentially higher wage also affects the expected wage: this may be called the *incremental-employment-and-differential-wage* variant. We examine the former variant first.

For the *incremental-employment* variant, the effect of the emigration is to change the equation for the expected wage in m_1 as

$$Ew_1 = \bar{w}_1 (L_1 + Z)/N_1. \tag{25}$$

Thus the division of total labour between the two groups (educated and uneducated) is determined now by:

$$\bar{w}_1 (L_1 + Z)/N_1 = \bar{w}_2 L_2/N_2. \tag{26}$$

Noting that the employment of labour in neither sector is affected by dZ, we can next show that

$$dN_1/dZ = N_1 N_2/\{ (L_1 + Z) \bar{N} \}. \tag{27}$$

We thus see, from (27), that the increase of educated labour supply will be less than the amount of migration of educated labour if $(L_1 + Z)/N_1 > N_2/\bar{N}$ (which is a relation very similar to (19) earlier). Thus, under the above inequality, the unemployment of educated labour increases, and the unemployment of uneducated labour decreases, due to the effect of an increase in N_1.[12]

The effect on *national income* is quite simply:

$$dY/dZ = - k (dN_1/dZ). \tag{28}$$

[12] If the unemployment is defined as $U_1/N_1 = 1 - (L_1 + Z)/N_1$, we can show that

$$\frac{d}{dZ}\left(\frac{U_1}{N_1}\right) < 0, \text{ because: } \frac{d}{dZ}\left(\frac{L_1 + Z}{N_1}\right) = \frac{1}{N_1}\left(1 - \frac{(L_1 + Z)}{N_1} \frac{N_1 N_2}{(L_1 + Z) N}\right)$$

$$= \frac{1}{N_1}\left(1 - \frac{N_2}{\bar{N}}\right) > 0.$$

National income is seen, from (28), to diminish unambiguously because of the cost of educating the increment in educated labour.

But we may well ask what happens to *per capita income*, as the total amount of labour in the system is diminished too. Now, clearly:

$$\frac{d}{dZ}\left(\frac{Y}{\bar{N}-Z}\right) = \frac{kN_2}{(\bar{N}-Z)^2}\left(-\frac{(\bar{N}-Z)}{\bar{N}}\frac{N_1}{L_1+Z} + \frac{Y}{kN_2}\right).$$

Hence, if $kN_2/Y < (L_1+Z)N_1$, for example, the average income will increase with the emigration. That is, if the ratio of the hypothetical educational cost of training all uneducated labour to national income is smaller than the employment rate of educated labour, the national income per labourer will increase. Another way of looking at it is to see that $d(Y/(\bar{N}-Z))/dZ > 0$ if $k\,(dN_1/dZ) < Y/(\bar{N}-Z)$, i.e. the per capita income would increase if the increase in the educational cost is less than the per-capita income.

(III): We may finally explore the *incremental-employment-and-differential-wage* variant. We thus assume now that the labour force will indeed take into account the foreign wage level at which the emigrants get hired. If we then denote the foreign wage as $\bar{w}_f$, we can write the expected wage in m_1 as:

$$Ew_1 = (\bar{w}_1 L_1 + \bar{w}_f Z)/N_1. \tag{29}$$

In this case, we now can derive the following modified results:

$$dN_1/dZ = \bar{w}_f N_2/(\bar{w}_1 L_1 + \bar{w}_2 L_2 + w_f Z) = \bar{w}_f N_1 N_2/\{N(\bar{w}_1 N_1 + \bar{w}_f Z)\}, \tag{30}$$

$$dY/dZ = -k\,(dN_1/dZ) = -k\bar{w}_f N_1 N_2/\{N(\bar{w}_1 L_1 + \bar{w}_f Z)\}. \tag{31}$$

It is then easy to see that the change in the level of the educated labour force (N_1) in the new equilibrium will readily exceed the emigration if $\bar{w}_f$ is large enough relative to $\bar{w}_1$. Therefore in the case when the high wage rate in foreign countries is taken into account in assessing the expected wage rate, it is quite probable that unemployment in educated sector increases in both an absolute and relative sense.

In addition, as is evident from (31), national income will fall; and it is easy to see that the possibility of decreasing per capita income also is more likely than before.[13] Therefore in the society whose welfare function depends on per capita income and unemployment rates, national welfare will quite possibly fall unless the evaluation of reducing unemployment rate in the m_2-sector more than offsets the loss due to decreasing per capita income and increasing unemployment in the m_1-sector.

Case IV. The General Case of Emigration and Rise of Wages

If the wage of educated labour is rigidly fixed because it reflects the salary levels of comparable groups in the more developed countries, it is quite conceivable that $\bar{w}_1$ itself is affected by the amount of migration of educated labour. The more migration there is, the more then could be the upward pull from the internationalization of this educated élite to domestic wage fixation. This rise in $\bar{w}_1$ may in turn trigger additional wage rise in $\bar{w}_2$, as analysed in Case II.

Thus the effects of migration on employment, supply of educated labour, and national income in this fully general case can now be decomposed as the sum of (1) the *direct* effect of migration keeping wage levels constant and (2) the *indirect* effect of the resulting wage increases. The latter component is in turn decomposed into (1) the effect of the wage increase in the m_1-sector and (2) the effect of a wage increase in the m_2-sector that it induces. Thus taking the *incremental-employment-and-differential-wage* variant, and evaluating for simplicity the expression for the initial impact, namely, at the point where $Z = 0$, we may summarize the expressions for the total effect of emigration as in Table 14.2.

The following observations, based on these results, are relevant

---

[13] This is readily seen as follows. For a unit of emigration, population decreases by $1/(N-Z)$ per cent. On the other hand, national income decreases by $k\bar{w}_f N_1 N_2 / \{N(\bar{w}_1 L_1 + \bar{w}_f Z) Y\}$. The fact that the latter may exceed the former can then be readily seen as follows. Let us take the special case of the impact of initiating emigration, that is, $Z = 0$. If the following, quite possible, relationship holds:

$$\bar{w}_f / \bar{w}_1 > (L_1/N_1)\,(Y/kN_2),$$

then the relative rate of decrease in national income is larger than that of decrease in population, thus leading to the reduction of per capita income.

Table 14.2
Total Effects of Migration

Impact on:	Symbol	Direct effects of migration	Effect I	Effect II
			Indirect effects through:	
			Rise in $\bar{w}_1$	Rise in $\bar{w}_2$
Educated labour	$\dfrac{dN_1}{dZ}\left(=-\dfrac{dN_2}{dZ}\right)$	$\dfrac{\bar{w}_f}{\bar{w}_1}\dfrac{N_1N_2}{NL_1}$	$\dfrac{(1-\eta_1)\,N_1N_2}{\bar{w}_1\bar{N}}\,\theta\,\dfrac{d\bar{w}_1}{dZ}$	$-\dfrac{(1-\eta_2)\,N_1N_2}{\bar{w}_2\bar{N}}\,\theta\,\dfrac{d\bar{w}_2}{dZ}$
Employment of educated labour	$\dfrac{dL_1}{dZ}$	0	$-\eta_1\dfrac{L_1}{\bar{w}_1}\dfrac{d\bar{w}_1}{dZ}$	0
Unemployment of educated labour	$\dfrac{d}{dZ}(N_1-L_1)$	$\dfrac{\bar{w}_f}{\bar{w}_1}\dfrac{N_1N_2}{NL_1}$	$\dfrac{(1-\eta_1)\,N_1N_2}{\bar{w}_1\bar{N}}+\eta_1\dfrac{L_1}{\bar{w}_1}\dfrac{d\bar{w}_1}{dZ}$	$-\dfrac{(1-\eta_2)\,N_1N_2}{\bar{w}_2\bar{N}}\,\theta\,\dfrac{d\bar{w}_2}{dZ}$
Employment of uneducated labour	$\dfrac{d}{dZ}(N_2-L_2)$	0	0	$-\eta_2\dfrac{L_2}{\bar{w}_2}\,\theta\,\dfrac{d\bar{w}_2}{dZ}$
Unemployment of uneducated labour	$\dfrac{d}{dZ}(N_2-L_2)$	$-\dfrac{\bar{w}_f}{\bar{w}_1}\dfrac{N_1N_2}{NL_1}$	$-\dfrac{(1-\eta_1)\,N_1N_2}{\bar{w}_1\bar{N}}\dfrac{d\bar{w}_1}{dZ}$	$\left\{\dfrac{(1-\eta_2)\,N_1N_2}{\bar{w}_2\bar{N}}+\eta_2\dfrac{L_2}{\bar{w}_2}\right\}\theta\,\dfrac{d\bar{w}_2}{dZ}$
National income	$\dfrac{dY}{dZ}$	$-k\dfrac{\bar{w}_f}{\bar{w}_1}\dfrac{N_1N_2}{NL_1}$	$-\left\{\eta_1L_1+\dfrac{k(1-\eta_1)\,N_1N_2}{\bar{w}_1\bar{N}}\right\}\dfrac{d\bar{w}_1}{dZ}$	$\left\{-\eta_2L_2+\dfrac{k(1-\eta_2)\,N_1N_2}{\bar{w}_2\bar{N}}\right\}\theta\,\dfrac{d\bar{w}_2}{dZ}$

concerning the effects of emigration of educated labour in our model.

(1) Note that the *direct* effect of emigration on employment in either sector is nil. However, if the foreign wage level is taken into account in calculating the expected wage (Ew_1), this increases the supply of educated labour (N_1) and will reduce national income by the incremental educational cost. If the foreign wage level ($\bar{w}_f$) is high enough, we could also have increased unemployment of educated labour and reduced per capita income.

(2) The induced wage-increase of educated labour, if any, will work to reduce the employment of educated labour. If the elasticity of demand for educated labour (η_1) is below unity, the supply of educated labour will increase, thus increasing unemployment of the educated, both absolutely and relatively; further, national income will also be likely to fall.

(3) Finally, if we have the leap-frogging process, such that $\bar{w}_2$ also rises in response to the rise in $\bar{w}_1$, the effect of this will be towards reducing the employment of uneducated labour. This effect would thus work to increase the expected wage (Ew_2) in this sector (if $\eta_2 < 1$) and thus to mitigate the increase in the supply of educated labour (when $\eta_1 < 1$): the net result could even be to reduce, the supply of educated labour in the new equilibrium. The loss of national income would also be reduced in so far as the supply of educated labour is reduced; however, unless the effect of reducing the cost of education is large, it is unlikely that it will offset the loss in national income caused through the contraction of output of m_1 and m_2 resulting from the rise in $\bar{w}_1$ and $\bar{w}_2$, respectively.

Thus, in our model, even without invoking the presence of 'externalities' (leading to differences between the private and social marginal product of the emigrants), we see that the emigration of educated labour can easily lead to unfavourable effects on national income, per capita income, and on the unemployment (absolute and relative) of educated and uneducated labour through the effect of the migration on expected-wage formation in the market for educated labour, the upward pull on the (actual) wage of educated labour, and the leap-frogging upward pull on the (actual) wage of uneducated labour. And, as we proceed now to discuss in greater detail in Sec. 4, the internalization of the cost of education will not necessarily reduce the income cost of the migration. Nor will the payment by the foreign country of the cost of education of the immigrants eliminate the adverse effect of the migration.

4. ALTERNATIVE ASSUMPTIONS

Before we proceed to an explicit welfare analysis of the effects of brain drain in Sec. 5, we now sketch briefly the effects of varying some of the assumptions in the model of Secs 2 and 3.[14]

4.1 Internalizing the Cost of Education

The reader may well ask what happens if we let people pay for their own education, so that the educational cost is 'internalized'. In this case, instead of (10), we will have:

$$Ew_1 - k^* = Ew_2, \tag{10'}$$

where k^* is the amount of educational cost that is internalized $(k^* \leq k)$.

Since employment depends on the *actual* wage, however, the employment effects in the model are unchanged whereas the allocation of the labour force between the two groups (educated and uneducated) will be directly affected. In consequence, we now have:

$$dN_1/d\bar{w}_1 = (1 - \eta_1) N_2 L_1 / [\bar{w}_1 L_1 + \bar{w}_2 L_2 - k^* (N_1 - N_2)]. \tag{15'}$$

---

[14] Incidentally, none of our quantitative conclusions depend on the assumption of allowing only two sectors. In fact, even in the presence of many sectors, we still obtain:

$$(\bar{w}_1/N_1) (dN_1/d\bar{w}_1) = [(\bar{N} - N_1)/\bar{N}] (1 - \eta_1)$$

and

$$w_1/N_j) (dN_j/d\bar{w}_1) = -(N_1/\bar{N}) (1 - \eta_1),$$

where

$$\bar{N} \equiv \sum_{j=1}^{n} N_j, \quad \text{for } n \geq 2.$$

Since it is easy to show that the denominator is positive,[15] the behaviour of N_1 continues, as in the earlier case of free education, to depend on the elasticity of demand for labour.

The resulting impact on the other comparative-statics results established for the case of free education can be readily worked out by the reader. It may be noted, however, that, contrary to general intuition, the internalization of the educational cost does not necessarily reduce the undesirable impact effect of the brain drain in our model: the welfare impact of an increment in $\bar{w}_1$ under free education ($k^* = 0$) is given by (22) for Case I, and under internalized cost by:

$$dY/d\bar{w}_1 = - L_1\eta_1 - k\,(1 - \eta_2)\,N_2L_1/[\bar{w}_1L_1 + \bar{w}_2L_2 - k\,(N_1 - N_2)], \quad (22')$$

and, in general, when a welfare cost is involved (as when $\eta_1 < 1$), the two costs cannot be uniquely ranked.

Similarly, for Case III, we may note again that the adverse effect of emigration on employment and income is not necessarily reduced if the cost of education is internalized as in (10'). Thus, for example, (27) is modified in the case of internalized educational cost ($k^* = k$) to:

$$dN_1/dZ = \bar{w}_fN_2/\{\bar{w}_1L_1 + \bar{w}_2L_2 + \bar{w}_fZ - k\,(N_1 - N_2)\}, \quad (27')$$

and it is clear that the new, additional term $- k\,(N_1 - N_2)$ could, in principle, work in either direction. Also, eq. (31) for impact on national income would modify to:

$$dY/dZ = - k\bar{w}_fN_2/\{\bar{w}_1L_1 + \bar{w}_2L_2 + \bar{w}_fZ - k\,(N_1 - N_2)\}. \quad (31')$$

And this means that the effect of internalizing the cost of education could well be to *increase*, rather than diminish, the cost in national income from the emigration in our model: this being yet another instance of second-best theory.

All this, of course, is not to deny that, for any *given* levels of $\bar{w}_1$, $\bar{w}_2$, and Z, the *progressive* internalization of the cost of education will be employment-and-income-*improving*. We can show that the increased internalization of the cost of education will, while

[15] By (10'), we have: $\bar{w}_1L_1 + \bar{w}_2L_2 - k^*(N_1 - N_2) = \bar{w}_2\,(L_2/N_2)\,\bar{N} + k^*N_2$.

leaving unchanged the employment in each sector, reduce the supply of educated labour (N_1) and hence its (total) cost (kN_1):

$$dN_1/dk^* = - N_1 N_2 / \{w_2 (L_2/N_2) N + K^* N_2\} < 0. \qquad (32)$$

Therefore, as long as unemployment in educated labour exists, increasing the education cost borne by labour itself will save the education cost by $- k dN_1$. Note further that, even if the cost paid by labour (i.e. k^*) approaches the 'true value' of k, the unemployment of educated labour may still exist.[16] In such a case, the imposition of higher cost ($k^* > k$) for education may prove to be optimal in this second-best problem with wage rigidities![17]

4.2 Irreversibility of Education

We may next address ourselves to the question of what happens in the 'short run' when the educated labour force cannot be reduced. The effect of this clearly is to accentuate — by eliminating the possibility of reducing the educated labour supply, N_1, and thus saving on its cost, kN_1 — the loss possibilities in the model. There is thus no relief for the 'let-us-not-worry-about-brain-drain' economists from shifting to the short run!

4.3 The Case where the Labour Market in m_2-Sector is Competitive

Next, what happens if the 'uneducated-labour' sector is 'competitive', so that the sticky-wage assumption applies only to educated labour? In this case, instead of (10) we will now have:

$$(L_1/N_1) \cdot \bar{w}_1 = w_2, \qquad (10'')$$

and

$$N_2 = L_2.$$

[16] Suppose $\bar{w}_1$ and $\bar{w}_2$ are fixed higher than the equilibrium full employment wage rate indicated by (12). Then the phenomenon discussed in the text could readily occur.

[17] Note again that the saving in educational costs, which we have been discussing, applies only in the 'long run', for comparison of two stationary states in our model.

Further, since w_2 is no longer fixed, it will now be determined by:

$$w_2 = g(L_2), \quad g' < 0.$$

Finally, we will have the total labour supply constraint as:

$$N_1 + N_2 = \bar{N}.$$

Solving these four equations, we would then get:

$$dN_1/d\bar{w}_1 = L_1(1 - \eta_1)/(w_2 - N_1 g'), \tag{33}$$

and it is easy to see that (33) has the same qualitative property as (16) in our basic model in Secs 2 and 3.[18]

4.4 Cost of Education Paid by Country of Immigration

It is sometimes asserted that if the host country pays the cost of education, brain drain would cease to be harmful. In our model, this is of course easily allowed for by assuming that the country of emigration recovers (kdZ) worth of transfer income from the country of immigration. It is again easy to see, as already noted in sect. 3, that all this does is to modify the last row of Table 14.2 by the addition of the term (kdZ) and that the net effect on income, and the effects on unemployment, can still be adverse.

5. WELFARE EFFECTS OF BRAIN DRAIN AND INTEGRATION OF MARKETS FOR PROFESSIONALS

We may now draw together the principal analytical results of Sec. 3 to derive welfare conclusions. To do this, however, we need to explicitly specify the social welfare function.

It is our contention that the traditional trade-theoretic analysis of the Grubel–Scott–Johnson variety yields conclusions more

---

[18] It may be interesting to note, however, that the change in $\bar{w}_1$ will now endogenously change w_2. And, in the case where $\eta_1 < 1$, $dw_2/d\bar{w}_1 = -g'(dN_1/dw_1) > 0$, since $dN_2 = -dN_1$, so that a rise in $\bar{w}_1$ leads to a rise in w_2. This is, of course, not the same as the 'leap-frogging' in our Case II; a phenomenon that is ruled out by the 'competitive' assumption for section m_2.

favourable to the phenomenon of brain drain and integration of markets for professionals, not merely because the model used for analysis is simplistic. It is also because the social welfare function used for analysis is really limited in confining itself to arguments that rule out many relevant variables.

In fact, we think that it could make much sense to define a social welfare function which has at least the following arguments:

(1) *National income:* The sense of security, bargaining power in trade and economic negotiations, the need for defence, and a number of political and economic variables of importance could depend, not just on per capita income, but on national income as an aggregate.

(2) *Level of emigration:* Those who have lived in the less developed countries know that the emigration of skilled manpower in certain occupations, such as scientific research in particular, creates a sense of inadequacy, which may stifle creative endeavour in domestic environment.

(3) *Level of educated/professional manpower:* The technological ability of the population may matter much to the independence and creativity of the population; hence a fall in the (short run and long run) level of the educated labour force due to the phenomena being discussed by us could cause as adverse effect on social welfare.

(4) *Unemployment:* Unemployment, whether absolute or its rate, is also of importance to social welfare. More directly, it affects political stability and social cohesion, if nothing else, and is of immediate concern to the developing countries. In this regard, the unemployment among the educated may be even more explosive than among the uneducated, as is evident from the fact that the leadership of the revolutionary movements in Calcutta, for example, has derived from unemployed, educated students.

(5) *Income distribution:* In the absence of fiscal ability to redistribute incomes, the direct income distributional impact of the phenomena under discussion will also often be the final effect. And it should clearly enter the social welfare function. In the

context of our model, we could thus include in the arguments of the social welfare function, for example, the relative share of wage income in total national income: $(\bar{w}_1 L_1 + \bar{w}_2 L_2)/Y$.[19]

Thus, a realistic social welfare function should probably read as follows:

$$U = U\{Y, Y/N, Z, N_1, L_1/N_1, L_2/N_2, (\bar{w}_1 L_1 + \bar{w}_2 L_2)/Y\}. \quad (34)$$

We forego a taxonomic exercise, exploring the outcomes on welfare and possible trade-offs among alternative arguments in this welfare function, for different parametric combinations of the elasticities η_1, η_2 and other parameters such as θ and k appearing in the expressions in Table 14.2. The reader can readily do this for himself; and we have already discussed briefly in Sec. 3 some of the possible outcomes with regard to national income, per capita income, supply of educated labour, and the level and rates of unemployment in both classes of labour.[20]

Emigration Tax

Rather, we may sketch here the answer to the question as to what would happen if the country of emigration were to impose a tax on emigration. To analyse this policy, assume that a recurring poll tax (that would be paid annually by the migrant) is levied on each emigrant.[21] Restricting our analysis to the effect on the income of

[19] Alternatively, we could use as an argument the weighted sum of per capita utilities: e.g. where $U(w_1)$ is the per capita utility in labour class i with $U' > 0$ and $U'' < 0$, the social welfare function could have the argument: $\sum_i U_i(w_i) L_i$.

[20] The only effects, which we have not worked out in Sec. 3, relate to income distribution. This, however, can be readily worked out. Thus, for the general Case IV, we can write:

$$\frac{Y}{\bar{w}_1 L_1 + \bar{w}_2 L_2} \frac{d\{(\bar{w}_1 L_1 + \bar{w}_2 L_2)/Y\}}{dZ} = \frac{1}{\bar{w}_1 L_1 + \bar{w}_2 L_2} \left(L_1(1 - \eta_1) + L_2(1 - \eta_2)\,\theta\,\frac{d\bar{w}_1}{dZ} \right)$$

$$+ \frac{k\bar{w}_f N_1 N_2}{Y\bar{N}\bar{w}_1 L_1} + \frac{1}{Y} \left\{ \eta_1 L_1 + \frac{k(1 - \eta_1) N_1 N_2}{\bar{w}_1 \bar{N}} \right\} \frac{d\bar{w}_1}{dZ}$$

$$+ \frac{\theta}{Y} \left[\eta_2 L_2 - \frac{k(1 - \eta_1) N_1 N_2}{\bar{w}_1 \bar{N}} \right] \frac{d\bar{w}_1}{dZ}.$$

[21] The effect of the usual poll tax would be of a once-for-all nature. However, in order to conform to our analysis in terms of flows, it would be useful to conceive

those left behind (for reasons of space), we should expect a two-fold effect: (i) the direct effect of the tax on revenue, which may then be treated as income redistributed to those left behind; and (ii) the indirect effect on unemployment levels, income, etc., which would operate through the effects on expected and actual wage levels.

(i) If we take T as the (recurring) poll tax paid by the emigrants (Z), the tax revenue will be TZ. As T is changed, this revenue will change by:

$$Z(1 - \eta_f^T), \tag{35}$$

where η_f^T is the elasticity of emigration with respect to the poll tax (i.e. $-T/Z \cdot dZ/dT$). Clearly, this *revenue effect* will be positive or negative, depending on the elasticity of emigration with respect to taxation.

(ii) As for the 'indirect' effect, this can be indicated via the simplified Case III assumption of the *incremental-employment-and-differential-wage* variant, i.e. by assuming that (only) the expected wage is modified downwards by the tax. Thus, we must rewrite (29) as follows:

$$Ew_1 = [\bar{w}_1 L_1 + (\bar{w}_f - T)Z]/N_1. \tag{29'}$$

Substituting (29′) into (10) and differentiating with regard to T, we obtain

$$\frac{dN_1}{dT} = -\frac{N_2 Z - N_2(\bar{w}_f - T)(dZ/dT)}{\bar{w}_1 L_1 + \bar{w}_2 L_2 + (\bar{w}_f - T)Z},$$

which can be written as

$$\frac{dN_1}{dT} = -\frac{N_2 Z(1 + \varepsilon_f)}{\bar{w}_1 L_1 + \bar{w}_2 L_2 + (\bar{w}_f - T)Z} < 0, \tag{36}$$

where ε_f is the elasticity of emigration with regard to effective foreign wages $(w_f - T)$.[22] Thus an increase in T will in the long run

of a recurring poll tax along the lines of the Bhagwati–Dellalfar (1973) proposal (which relates to an income tax related to the income of the emigrant, an unimportant difference if we assume a unique $\bar{w}_f$).

[22] Note that $(\bar{w}_f - T/T)\eta_f^T = \varepsilon_f$.

always decrease the supply of educated labour, and this effect is strengthened if the emigrant is responsive to the recurring poll tax. As before, the income change is then:

$$\frac{dY}{dT} = -k \frac{dN_1}{dT} = \frac{kN_2 Z (1 + \varepsilon_f)}{\bar{w}_1 L_1 + \bar{w}_2 L_2 + (\bar{w}_f - T) Z} > 0. \qquad (37)$$

Thus, the net impact on the income of those left behind will be given by the sum of these two, direct and indirect, effects (36) and (37):

$$Z (1 - \eta_f^T) + \frac{kN_2 Z (1 + \varepsilon_f)}{\bar{w}_1 L_1 + \bar{w}_2 L_2 + (\bar{w}_f - T) Z}. \qquad (38)$$

A sufficient (but not necessary) condition for the per capita income of those left behind to improve due to the emigration tax would, therefore, be that $\eta_f^T < 1$.[23]

The reader could readily extend the analysis of the poll tax on emigration to examine the impact on the other arguments in the social welfare function; considerations of space prevent us from undertaking this task ourselves.

6. Concluding Remarks

It is clear, of course, that our results are in contrast with those of the traditional, fully neoclassical model because of the assumptions of 'rigid' wages and resulting unemployment. Under the conventional assumptions of flexible wages and absence of unemployment, the results of emigration are both simpler and easily stated: (i) for internalized cost of education ($k^* = k$), the emigration will reduce national income but, in increasing the average product of labour, will also raise per capita income under the 'normal' assumption of diminishing marginal productivity of labour;[24] and

---

[23] Note that the 'indirect' effect works only in the long run. Furthermore, we have ruled out the more general case where the emigration may also affect the *actual* wage. If this were allowed, then the emigration tax might well reduce the *actual* wage in the m_1, and possibly m_2, sectors, and hence moderate the income loss on that account.

[24] The *apparent* contradiction between this statement and the earlier Grubel–Scott

(ii) for free education ($k^* = 0$), the other polar case, and no compensation for educational costs by the country of immigration, it is possible (though not inevitable) that the average product of labour, and hence per capita income, falls as a result of emigration of educated labour.

Our results are both more complex and less comforting than these. They are also more realistic. They should suffice to raise doubts about the complacency concerning the brain drain phenomenon resulting from the analysis in the existing literature.[25]

---

argument that emigration leaves unchanged the welfare of those left behind is easily resolved. The Grubel–Scott result is based on the fact that the emigré was earning w (the wage) and thus everyone other than him was getting $(Y - w)$, whereas his departure reduces Y itself by w: hence the result for those left behind is the sum of the reduction in income due to emigration $(dY/dL = -w)$ and the increment in available income as the emigrant loses his claim on income defined by his wage $(+w)$, which means no-impact. On the other hand, $d(Y/L)/dL = (1/L)[w - (Y/L)] > 0$ as the wage, which equals the marginal product, will be below the average product: hence emigration will *raise* per capita income, i.e. *improve* the welfare of those left behind. This contradiction is easily resolved, however, once it is seen that the Grubel–Scott argument assumes that the income accruing to the emigré prior to emigration is w, the wage, whereas the per capita-income argument in effect assumes it to be Y/L ($> w$): the former assumption thus yields no impact whereas the latter yields improvement for those left behind. In this chapter we have examined the impact on *both* income and per capita income; results under the Grubel–Scott assumption can however be readily derived by taking the impact on income and adding to it the consumption of the emigrant, defined as his wage rate $\bar{w}_1$), on the assumption that the emigrant was employed prior to emigration, or possibly a lower sum if we assume that he was unemployed and was subsisting on someone else's income.

[25] We have not modelled here, as an anonymous referee has pointed out, some of the real-world complexities that arise on a different dimension from those (e.g. sticky wages and unemployment) considered here: for example, the effects of the quality and content of higher education and professional training in the advanced countries on the phenomenon of brain drain. Thus, it is well known that the brain drain occurs in part via the settling down abroad of LDC students who have been receiving higher education abroad. To some extent, this phenomenon results from the fact that the type of training received abroad makes these students somewhat ill-suited at times to any useful work at home and, if they do return, makes them conduits of disequilibrating disturbances in the domestic economy. We would however need a different model to study these kinds of relationships and effects: to admit everything into one model would be to make it too complex.

REFERENCES

Bhagwati, J. and T.N. Srinivasan, 1972: Overqualification, Education and Welfare: A Theoretical Analysis, mimeo. (Cambridge, Mass.: MIT Press).

Bhagwati, J. and W. Dellalfar, 1973: 'The Brain Drain and Income Taxation: A Proposal', World Development 1, no. 1.

Dumont, R., 1969: *False Start in Africa* (New York: Praeger).

Grubel, H. and A. Scott, 1966: 'The International Flow of Human Capital', *American Economic Review* (May).

Johnson, H.G., 1967: 'Some Economic Aspects of Brain Drain', *Pakistan Development Review* 3.

——, 1972: 'Labour Mobility and the Brain Drain', *in* G. Ranis (ed.), *The Gap Between Rich and Poor Nations*, Proceedings of the 1970 IEA Conference at Bled, Yugoslavia (New York: Macmillan).

Jolly, R. and D. Seers, 1972: 'The Brain Drain and the Development Process', *in* G. Ranis (ed.), op. cit.

Jones, R., 1967: 'International Capital Movements and the Theory of Tariffs and Trade', *Quarterly Journal of Economics* (Feb.).

Kemp, M., 1966: 'Gains from International Trade and Investment', *American Economic Review* (Sept.).

Sunkel, O., 1971: 'Latin American Underdevelopment in the Year 2000', *in* J. Bhagwati (ed.), *Economics and World Order: From the 1970s to the 1990s* (New York: Macmillan).

15

Investing Abroad

DIRECT foreign investment, or DFI as I shall call it today, has grown energetically in the post-war period. The net direct investment outflow from the OECD countries rose fourfold to over $13 billion annually between 1965 and 1980. The stock of DFI abroad, on the other hand, had increased nearly threefold within a decade to over $300 billion by 1980.

DFI has also diversified in its sectoral composition over this period, away from the historical preponderance of raw materials and extractive industries, to manufactures, and then again, in recent years, to services. The sectoral shifts are manifest particularly in the estimates of the stock of US DFI in the developing countries: in 1976, only 18 per cent of this total was in extractive industries whereas the share of services had risen to 43 per cent.

The flows have further diversified into a veritable web. Developed countries invest in developing countries and into each other, while developing countries also seek global outreach in other countries. Even the socialist countries have turned increasingly to DFI from the capitalist West, with the Coke–Pepsi market wars played out vicariously in Sino–Soviet rivalries as Mr Brezhnev embraced Pepsi and Mr Deng naturally then turned to Coke!

The resulting 'globalization' of economic activity has emerged as an important new reality. It reflects the interplay of 'natural' market forces with policy changes, both in developing and developed countries, during the post-war period. Recently, new forces have emerged that serve to invigorate and strengthen these trends towards more DFI and globalization. Important consequences for economic analysis and policy-making are also becoming manifest. These causes and consequences of DFI, in their major outline, are what I propose to address here.

I. The Post-war Interplay of Market Forces and Policies

(a) Market Forces

The market forces that have fuelled the post-war growth of DFI have attracted the intellectual attention of both conventional economists and, quite naturally, also the Marxists among us.

(i) *Hymer, Vernon et al.*

The mainstream history of DFI analysis is now universally regarded as the handiwork of the late Stephen Hymer, with whom I was privileged to study at MIT during the mid-1950s. As always, there are antecedents. But the credit inevitably will go, not to those who had insights and no system, but to those who design the architecture. Here, Hymer broke through the unproductive equation of DFI with international capital flow analysis and its emphasis therefore on interest rate differentials and arbitrate as the explanatory variables. In its place, he emphasized the rents that a firm could earn from setting up its own production elsewhere, using special advantages such as *knowhow* in its possession. Today, we distinguish between *firm-specific* and *country-specific advantages*. And the question of 'appropriability' of these rents through DFI as against simply sale of technology at arm's length has been fruitfully analysed. But the central Hymer insight has remained at the core of these important analytical developments.[1]

The most popular and justifiably celebrated progeny of the Hymer Revolution was the *Product Cycle* theory of Professor Raymond Vernon. Starting with home-based R & D and innovation generating a new product, the firm would produce at home and then extend sales abroad. Next, however, as the production process got simplified, debugged and transplantable to where factor costs were lower, the foreign sales would yield to DFI and production elsewhere. As such shift in production to foreign locales via DFI occurred, reverse sales to the home market would also follow

---

[1] See in particular, Magee (1977) and the recent modelling by Markusen (1984) and Helpman (1984). See also Dunning (1981) and Caves (1982) for fine, recent reviews of many contributions to DFI analysis.

in the last stage, closing the circle. The story could have been told by simply substituting DFI with sale of the simplified technology at arm's length to foreign producers *instead*. DFI however comes in, bringing in Hymer critically, since it generates greater returns to the firm's specific advantages than arm's length sale of know-how would.

Many DFIs fit this mould, of course. It is noticeable however that the product cycle story essentially involves the shift of investment location in response to factor proportions advantage, without involving the question of competition and market structure in any essential way. The DFI could be, for instance, by a single secure monopolist. But a great number of DFIs are undertaken essentially in the context of *import competition*, where DFI is a *response* to a situation of intensifying competitive threat from foreign producers of similar products. A shift in location, admittedly still founded on Hymer-type specific advantages, so as to reduce costs by exploiting foreign factor costs and thus increase survivability in a competitive struggle, is the scenario that better fits many DFIs. Not exploiting the factor costs that give your competitors abroad a competitive edge is to look at the Darwinian process from the vantage point of a loser.

But if you recycle the Hymer–Vernon theory thus, it becomes evident that DFI may be inhibited by other, alternative responses to such intensification of competition, or that DFIs of other variety may appear if the source of the international competitive pressure is other than simply factor costs. Let me elaborate.

(ii) *Alternative Responses: Labour Importation*

Perhaps the most interesting alternative response in the post-war period has been the importation of foreign labour, as under the *Gastarbeiter* programme of the European countries such as Germany and Switzerland, until the early 1970s when the policy fell victim to the economic slowdown in the aftermath of the OPEC successes.

The irony is that the 'big thinkers' such as Marx and Lenin failed to predict this response, assuming that the capitalists would reach out for the proletariat but not that the proletariat would move to the capitalists. The irony is even more compelling when you think of the asymmetry in their thoughts between the *internal* process where the proletariat indeed moved to the capitalists (as when the rural Enclosures were argued to create and supply to the urban areas the necessary proletariat) and the *external* process where the movement was supposed to be exactly the other way around.

If then DFI takes the firm out to cheap labour, whereas the *Gastarbeiter* policy brings the cheap labour to the firm, the two phenomena could be regarded as *substitutes* in the economist's sense. But are they necessarily so? I suspect that the importation of labour did dampen the outflow of DFI from Western Europe during the 1960s. Perhaps the outflow of DFI might even have accelerated during the 1970s, as the *Gastarbeiter* programmes were abruptly frozen, had it not been for the slowdown of investment generally as part of the depressed world economy that had triggered the termination of the *Gastarbeiter* programme in the first place.

But I should add that DFI and labour importation across nation states may also turn out to be complements in a different sense and context. Thus, in the recent policy discussions concerning how the country of immigration may reduce the numbers seeking to come in and hence, given the enforcement expenditures, diminish in turn those who immigrate illegally, it has been assumed that DFI (and indeed foreign aid too) can stem the tide by creating more jobs in the countries of emigration and by reducing the wage gap that must influence the decision to seek illegal entry. Thus, the US–Mexico problem of illegal immigration is widely regarded as amenable to a partial solution along these lines. In this sense, DFI and illegal immigration are again seen as substitutes: one impacts negatively on the other.

But it is not evident that the argument is valid, even if plausible. For, *ceteris paribus*, any reduction in wage differentials and in expected income improvements from migration ought to reduce the incentive to migrate. However, as always, paradoxes can surface: (a) Immigrants may be those who can afford to migrate in the face of imperfect capital markets. If so, the capacity to migrate may be the constraint on migration rather than the incentive to do so. Foreign investment or aid, in raising incomes of the proletariat, may then bring more migrants over the border, rather than less. (b) Again, the networking aspect of migration means that Multinational Corporations (MNCs) may serve to provide conduits whereby migration may increase. Thus, the Mexican employees of Coca-Cola in Mexico City may establish contacts with their US fellow-managers and workers, get these US friends to procure jobs and labour certification required for immigration, and manage to get further down the road on to immigration into the US than they otherwise would have done. (c) Then, again, in an interesting recent contribution, the socio-logist Sassen–Koob (1984) has argued that foreign investment and immigration are complementary rather than substitutes because DFI itself creates a proletariat in the host countries, leading in turn to eventual outmigration.

Among the arguments advanced by Sassen–Koob in support of this contention are the following: (i) export-oriented MNCs use female labour which, in turn, creates a female proletariat that is itself integrated ideologically into a non-traditional set of values that are a precondition to outmigration to the capitalist centre; (ii) often, the female workers experience rapid turnover, creating female unemployment that also fuels outmigration; (iii) the spread of the proletarian ideology goes beyond the female workers to their families and other members of the workforce so that out-migration of others also is encouraged; and (iv) the city centres such as New York, in turn, are now the source of low level jobs even in high-tech modern industries where this emerging pro-letariat can find jobs. These arguments are imaginative but the evidence in support of them is, I am afraid not compelling.

I might add that the possibility of complementarity between immigration and investment can arise also because the former leads instead to the latter. Thus, German firms may get used to working with Turkish labour in Germany, and this itself may encourage them to take up profitable opportunities to invest in Anatolia. Again, the returning Turkish *Gastarbeiter* may have spread seeds of modernization and proletarian values that serve to accelerate the formation of the type of labour that German MNCs would like to employ, thus facilitating their investment in Turkey. Again, networking may imply that the immigrant groups in a developed host country may serve as conduits for facilitating the perception of investment opportunities, may promote joint ventures between themselves and MNCs in their countries of origin, and so on. Thus, even if it were to be observed that, at least at first glance, DFI and immigration were positively rather than inversely related, the relationship could move from immigration to DFI rather than the other way.

I might finally observe that, from the 'grand' Marxist perspective, the theme that outward DFI from the capitalist centre may itself prompt inward immigration of the (DFI-created) proletariat from the periphery with abundant labour is most satisfying (even though the evidence for it is unconvincing). For, it represents an intriguing new twist, a novel and fitting finale, to the evolutionary, historic stages through which capitalism evolves as a 'world system' in the Immanuel Wallerstein sense.[2] It restores therefore the phenomenon of immigration of the proletariat abroad, as against taking of DFI to this proletariat, from its contrapuntal position vis-à-vis Marxist prediction to a more organic, consistent position within the unfolding drama of the world capitalist system.

(iii) *Alternative DFIs: Cross-investments a la MPI*

Let me now turn to the issue, not of responses to import competition that constitute an alternative to DFI, but rather of DFI responses other than outward DFI to exploit lower factor costs.

I have long argued that, where the source of import competition is technical change in progressive, Schumpeterian industries, causing competition among similar products, the response of the producers of similar import-competing products (none dominant) cannot logically be outward DFI since lower factor costs abroad are not what is driving the foreign competition. Rather, it may be the *mutual penetration of investment* (MPI) response, yielding mutual DFI by international competitors into one another. Thus, in 1972, reviewing Professor Vernon's (1971) important volume on *Sovereignty at Bay*, I wrote:

---

[2] For an illuminating and comprehensive review of Marxist, dependency and world-system views on the development process and hence tangentially on the role of DFI therein, see Blomstrom and Hettne (1984).

There is also at least one more dramatic form of international investment which neither Vernon nor other researchers in the MNC field has noted but which may well be the pattern to emerge as a dominant form. In contrast to the case where the MNCs, having developed new products via R & D, export them and then transit to producing them abroad, there is an alternative 'model' where MNCs in different countries have R & D-induced advantages in producing different types of sub-products (e.g. one MNC in Japan is excellent with small cars and one MNC in US has an edge on large cars; or tyre firms in different countries have acquired an edge in producing and competing effectively in different types of tyres). In competing in each other's home countries or in third markets in both types of sub-products, it is natural that each MNC would find it difficult to compete effectively with the other in sub-products where it does not have the edge. I would expect that, in this situation, there is likelihood of these MNCs deciding that mutual equity interpenetration, with production-wise accommodation in sub-product specialization according to the advantage possessed, is profitable. Thus, the MNC in US (say, GM) that finds it difficult to compete with the MNC in the small-car field, with the MNC in Japan (say, Toyota) that finds it difficult to compete with the MNC in US in the large car field, would each decide that the best strategy if you cannot compete with comfort is to follow the policy: 'if you cannot beat them, buy them'. Thus GM would want to buy equity in Toyota for the small car production and Toyota in GM for the large car production; and GM in US would go off spending resources in producing and improving its own small cars while Toyota in Japan would similarly hold back on its own large car efforts. One thus gets mutually interpenetrating MNCs within industries, with accompanying division of labour and a novel form of 'cartelization' which goes by sub-products. Linder has made us familiar with trade in commodities between similar countries as consisting of sub-product exchanges; and Hymer and Rowthorn have noted that MNCs from different countries penetrate into each other's countries. My 'model' essentially combines these two and predicts that MNCs with R & D-induced specialization in different types of sub-products within an industry in different countries will interpenetrate.

This model is almost ideally illustrated by the following example which Martin Zimmerman has unearthed for me. *Forbes* of 15 November 1970 (p. 22) notes the following 'international marriage':

Long the friendliest of competitors, Dunlop and Pirelli neatly complement each other. Dunlop is primarily a manufacturer of conventional cross-ply tyres, Pirelli concentrates on radials. In Europe, Dunlop has perhaps 18%

of the market, Pirelli 12%, as against 12% for Michelin, the next largest competitor. In Europe, Pirelli crosses Dunlop's path only in West Germany: Elsewhere, where Dunlop is active, Pirelli stays out; where Pirelli is active, Dunlop stays out. Outside of Europe, Pirelli is active, Dunlop stays out. Outside of Europe, Pirelli is active mostly in Latin America, Dunlop in the Commonwealth and North America.

The two companies even diversified into different areas — Dunlop into sporting goods and precision engineering products, Pirelli into paper, electronics and cables.

Eventually, of course, both marketing organizations will work as one, with Dunlop pushing Pirelli products where Dunlop is strong, and Pirelli pushing Dunlop products elsewhere. 'The greatest benefits should come from a pooling of R & D, however', explains J. Campell Fraser, A Dunlop director: 'In the seventies and eighties, competition will be more and more in terms of innovations. In the UK we have a home base of about 55 million people — that isn't big enough for the kind of R & D we'll need. Pirelli has an even smaller home base, about 45 million. By merging, we'll have a home base of 100 million, enough for the kind of R & D we'll need around the world. . . . There will not even be any exchange of public shares. Instead each will acquire an interest in the other's operating subsidiaries. The British and Italian companies will operate on their own.'

The report goes on to note (p. 23) that there will be four companies: Dunlop Home (UK and Europe) with Dunlop owning 51% and Pirelli 49%; Dunlop International (rest of the world) with Dunlop holding 60% and Pirelli, Milan and Switzerland, 20% each; Pirelli Milan (Common Market) with Pirelli Milan holding 51% and 49% and Pirelli Switzerland (all other Pirelli operations) with Dunlop holding 40%, Pirelli Milan 20% and Pirelli Switzerland 40%.

I must yield to the temptation to quote the further remark, that:

But interpenetration among MNCs with competing R & D induced specialization in different sub-products may not be the only important new form of international MNC investments to emerge. Alternative possibilities are one-way penetrations by MNCs. Thus, it is entirely possible for GM to expect to buy its way into profitable Japanese small car production, for example, by merely offering its distributive outlets, access to funds and/or R & D facilities, and perhaps the political offer of not clamouring for quota protection. Indeed, the recent political pressures on MITI in Japan to open up Japan to US investment in several areas has been so considerable that it seems entirely probable that the model of one-way penetration is about as relevant as the model of interpenetrations.

I should warn you, however, that despite my prescient resort to the hypothetical General Motors — Toyota DFI outcomes, you should not lay the fact of their later realization at my door but rather attribute it to the importance of the forces whose consequences for novel DFI outcomes I was noting.[3]

The MPI variety of DFI, in fact, can be regarded also as a fascinating sub-species of the phenomenon of 'cross-investment' that Hymer and Rowthorn (1970) had noted in response to Servan Schreiber's hysterical alarm over the American DFI invasion of Europe. They were concerned with noting that the investments into each other's country were a growing reality. But what they addressed were principally mutual DFI in wholly different industries: e.g. German DFI in USA automobiles and American DFI in Germany in tractors. But it is easy to see that cross-investments may occur in a more interesting form, within the same industry: as when MNCs invest in each other's country in office equipment manufacture, a phenomenon that Hymer was no stranger to. But the MPI variety of cross-investment is far the most dramatic: it occurs across and mutually within the firms in the industry. Hence the three varieties of cross-investments I have distinguished may be christened: national-level, industry-level and firm-level cross-investments.

While the formal modelling of the national-level cross-investments can readily reflect the product-cycle scenario, and can be therefore placed in the context of conventional competitive models,[4] the latter two require resort to the new theories of competition and hence of trade in similar products. My former student, Professor Elias Dinopoulos (1985b), has done precisely this: modelling the MPI theory of DFI in the context of the Lancaster–Helpman theory of trade in similar products, but in

[3] I have discussed the MPI and related DFI scenarios further in Ch. 6 of this volume. I am indebted to Professor Vernon for reminding me that the MPI type of cross-investment *may* be fragile, perhaps more so than the product-cycle variety and others, and that the Dunlop–Pirelli MPIs did not survive long. We have too little experience to date, however, to offer informed guesses on the issue of fragility or stability of the different types of DFI.

[4] See the recent model by Jones, Neary, and Ruane (1983) which generates such cross-investment by using the sector-specific factor model.

a major variant thereof which reflects a formalization in turn of the taste-difference-generated, 'biological' model of trade in similar products that I have proposed recently [Bhagwati (1982); Dinopoulos (1985a)].

(b) Policy Factors

While therefore these *market* forces have propelled DFIs into a growing role in the world economy, the role of *policy* measures, in the broadest sense, has also been significant.

(i) The factor-proportions variety of DFI, seeking lower costs of production abroad, has been attracted by developing countries following the Export-promoting (EP) strategy, with export processing zones, tax concessions et al. In turn, the developed countries have occasionally enacted tariff concessions on off-shore assembly, again encouraging assembly-type DFI abroad. (ii) By contrast, the majority of the developing countries, following the Import-substituting (IS) strategy, have used tariffs and quota restrictions to protect domestic markets and therewith to induce 'tariff-jumping' DFI. (iii) Again, in a significant and growing variant on this strategy, recently the *threat* of protection has been used to induce foreign firms, who are crowding out domestic production through exports, into undertaking DFI so as to defuse that threat. (iv) Finally, the governments of the developed countries, and their multinationals, have increasingly accommodated to the notion, somewhat inflammatory at the outset of the post-war period, that the host country regulations and 'performance requirements' have come to stay, thus creating the adaptive and consensual ethos that has permitted DFI to grow in the post-war period to date. Let me address these diverse pro-DFI factors, in turn.

(i) *EP-oriented Interventions*

The host country incentives, such as tax holidays, to attract DFI of the EP variety are commonplace enough. Among the EP-strategy countries, however, the major incentive has been simply the conjunction of cheaper costs and the EP orientation.

The interesting phenomenon is rather the emergence of Duty

Free Zones in many of the IS-oriented economies, designed to attract EP-type DFI. This flirtation with free trade, in arm's length enclaves, while continuing the policy of protection on the mainland, reminds me of the remark of Professor Paul Rosenstein–Rodan, the great pioneer of development economics who never gave up his Austrian ways: 'promiscuity is easier than marriage'. But if such zones are easier to embrace than the EP-strategy, DFI attracted by them may equally be counterproductive in terms of your welfare. Here we have yet another example of the caveat that Professor Jacob Viner made us familiar with by drawing attention to the possibility of trade-diverting customs unions: that a move *towards* free trade is not the same as a move *to* free trade; the former may immiserize you even though the latter will generally be beneficial.[5]

But if EP-oriented DFIs have been attracted thus by host-country policies, a contribution has also been made by policies of the countries from which DFI originates. Principal among these policies have been the 'offshore assembly' incentives that have been enacted by several developed countries. Thus, for example, Joseph Greenwald and Kenneth Flam (1985) at the Brookings Institution, who have recently produced an important work on this subject, note that the United States under Tariff items 806.30 and 807.00 permits the duty-free entry of US components sent abroad for processing or assembly, whereas the countries of the European Economic Community also have similar 'outward processing' provisions: all encouraging foreign assembly, often via DFI in adjacent countries with cheap labour. Thus, more than half of US sales of certain products in textiles and electronics are now assembled abroad, whereas the imports of such products currently constitute a sixth of total US imports of manufactures. No estimates are offered by these authors of how much offshore-assembly DFI would have occurred through market forces alone, and how much therefore should be attributed to these tariff-concession incentives. But there is little doubt that the incentives have played a contributory role.

[5] See the analysis by Hamada (1974), Hamilton and Svensson (1982) and Wong (1986) of Duty Free Zones and their welfare effects.

(ii) *IS-oriented Interventions*

In the end, however, the market forces have basically driven the EP-type DFI, with the policy factors playing a modest role. By contrast, the IS-type DFI has been almost wholly policy-driven. The IS strategy, on both domestic investments and DFI, has been cut from the same cloth: 'Protect your market and attract home-based investments to serve that market.' Popularly, this is also known as the strategy for attracting 'tariff-jumping' DFI, though the developing countries pursuing this strategy often resorted to quota restrictions rather than tariffs as their policy instruments.

Two major questions have been raised concerning the IS-oriented DFI. The major object of attention has been the issue of the benefits that such DFI confers on the host country. The most dramatic analytical insight has been provided by several international trade theorists who have considered the serious possibility that such DFI may actually be harmful, not just less productive than it appears to the naked eye. The complicating factor, producing the paradox, is of course that the influx of DFI is being induced by a distorting protectionist policy. It is then evident, as the theory of immiserizing growth implies and I noted (Ch. 4), that the returns to DFI *may* exceed its social marginal product. Professor Hirofumi Uzawa, and subsequently other Japanese economists such as Professors Noburo Minabe and Koichi Hamada, arrived at the stronger proposition that, in a conventional neoclassical 2×2 model with the importable good, capital-intensive, protection-induced capital inflow would *necessarily* immiserize. Independently, and insightfully, this proposition was developed and integrated into both the theory of capital mobility and the theory of immiserizing growth by Professors Richard Brecher and Carlos Diaz–Alejandro (1977). I have argued (Bhagwati 1978) that this analytical finding may well be a significant element in the explanation of the observed failure of IS-addicted countries to perform as well as the EP-oriented countries.[6]

---

[6] Frobel, Heinrichs and Kreye (1980), writing from a Marxist perspective, and focusing implicitly on EP-oriented DFIs have argued for the ill-effects of such investments too. Considering them to be part of 'worldwide economic inter-penetration' (p. 8), they are led to argue that such DFIs contribute to 'the economic

I have also suggested (Bhagwati 1978: Ch. 8) that, over the long haul, the magnitude of IS-oriented DFI cannot be as striking as with EP-oriented DFI, for the simple reason that it is limited by the host-country market which induces it in the first place. Professor Balasubramanyam (1984), who is distinguished for his work on DFI in the developing countries, has examined this hypothesis and his preliminary analysis has led him to conclude that:

The lack of detailed time series data on inflows of FDI into LDCs with different types of foreign trade regimes prevents a full scale statistical test of this hypothesis. However, the data that could be readily assembled lend some support to the first facet of the hypothesis concerning the relative magnitude of FDI under the IS and EP strategies of development (Table 2). In order to take account of the differences in market size, data on the total stock of FDI for selected LDCs are expressed as a proportion of their population and GNP. These indicators relate to the years 1967 and 1978.

For the year 1978 FDI as a percentage of GNP was high in countries pursuing the EP strategy (Singapore, Hong Kong, Taiwan, Malaysia, and Kenya) compared to that in countries pursuing the IS strategy in the recent past (India, Brazil, Ghana, Argentina). Much more significant is the fact that in the case of most countries pursuing the EP strategy the stock of FDI as a percentage of GNP increased substantially over the period 1967–1978. In a majority of the countries pursuing the IS strategy, however, this ratio of FDI to GNP declined appreciably.

[Balasubramanyam 1984: 125–6.][7]

(iii) *Quid Pro Quo (or Protection-threat-induced) DFI*

Let me now turn to drawing attention to a novel class of policy-induced DFI currently arising amongst the developed countries, that I like to call Quid Pro Quo DFI [Bhagwati (1985a)]. Increasingly,

---

dependency of the developing countries on the industrialized countries'. Again, 'after decades and centuries of the underdevelopment of the so-called developing countries the recent export-oriented industrialization of these countries offers but faint hope that [sic] living standards and conditions of the mass of their populations will undergo any substantial improvements in the foreseeable future' (p. 7). I am afraid I find neither of these contentions to be persuasive, and the latter is certainly inconsistent with the facts of the EP-strategy's results.

[7] He is currently engaged in the necessary statistical tests which currently suggest that this conclusion is robust.

the *threat* of protection has been used to stimulate DFI from foreign competitors in an industry. The quid pro quo for the investing firms is in the reduced threat of protection that follows from such DFI (as I explain below) and hence in less impaired access to the market of the host country.

Of course, the use of protection to attract DFI was a well known tactic of the import-substituting developing countries, as I have already discussed, and led to 'protection-induced' (or, in common parlance, 'tariff-jumping') DFI. By contrast, the quid pro quo investments that are emerging are 'protection-threat-induced' DFI.

Why does the threat of protection attract DFI? I do not have in mind a trivial variation on the theme of tariff-jumping investment, i.e. that DFI occurs in anticipation of a closing market. Rather, the argument is that DFI may be aimed at *defusing* the protectionist threat which, in fact, may have been designed precisely with a view to stimulating such DFI in the first place. I will presently discuss why such a 'defusing effect' may follow. But, assuming that it does operate, the rationale of the quid pro quo DFI can be readily spelled out. Essentially, from the viewpoint of the exporting country, if DFI can help it to reduce the potential threat of protection, the losses (or reduced profits) from producing partially in the host country via DFI rather than at home are offset by the profits gained through keeping access to host country markets open. Individual firms making the DFI will of course undertake such DFI, perceiving this effect on their own profitability. But there would also be an incentive for governments to encourage such DFI if the effect is one of defusing the protectionist threat more generally, constituting an externality to the individual firm.[8]

[8] Bhagwati, Brecher, Dinopoulos, and Srinivasan (1986) have recently modelled Quid Pro Quo DFI in a competitive framework, where capital flows occur in a world with atomistic firms, utilizing and augmenting the analytical framework in the earlier analysis of Bhagwati and Srinivasan (1978) which had shown that, if the first-period export level can affect the probability of market-disruption-induced quotas being invoked in the second period, an optimal tariff argument exists for restraining exports in the first period below the myopic one-period-maximization level. Dinopoulos and Bhagwati (1986) models Quid Pro Quo DFI, on the other hand, in a market-structure context where individual firms undertake DFI in a two-period context, taking into account the non-myopic interaction between DFI and protection.

DFI can reduce the probability of the host country invoking protection by favourably influencing the Congresses and the Parliaments where the protectionist lobbies operate; it can also co-opt these lobbies themselves into softening their protectionist efforts. Let me address each route, in turn.

DFI from the exporting country is often seen as a thoughtful gesture that contributes to employment in and the well-being of the importing country. It can thus help defuse protectionist threats quite generally in the legislatures where the lobbyists of the exporting country can cite the benefits accruing from such investments to soften the hostile attitudes and threats directed at the exporting country. The most dramatic example of such a linkage is in the case of Japanese DFI in the US.

There are, indeed, as everywhere, alarmist voices raised by American politicians at the social implications of DFI. My favourite examples includes Governor Lamm of Colorado, worried about 'economic colonialism', declaring that: 'It seems so clear that, when the Japanese are buying our productive resources, it has serious long-term implications. The United States invented the video recorder and now they'll be made by the Japanese. The long-term implication is that our children will be working for the Japanese.' (*New York Times*, 16 Sept. 1985.) Then again, Representative Jim Wright, majority whip in the US Congress, wrote in the *Wall Street Journal* (3 Oct. 1985) that:

We ought to be exporting computers, not shares of IBM. We should seek to sell more, not sell out.

To accept the de-industrialization of America while exulting in the growth of foreign ownership and influence in our domestic institutions could be an unwitting prescription for slowly becoming an economic colony again.

But these viewpoints are very much a fringe phenomenon. There is little doubt that Japanese DFI in the United States is viewed as a positive contribution, as 'a way to keep American factories open and workers employed'. (*New York Times*, 26 July 1985.)

The protection-threat-defusing effect can equally operate through co-opting the agents, firms, and unions that agitate for protection. By offering technology and profits through joint ventures, the firms can be converted to freer trade; by offering jobs, DFI can turn unions equally away from protection. In fact, I might venture to suggest that whether Quid Pro Quo DFI, so inspired, will be in the form of wholly owned subsidiaries or joint ventures with host-country producers may reflect factors such as the relative lobbying strength of labour and capitalists in the industry. Toyota teamed up with General Motors, to produce a small car under the umbrella of New United Motor Manufacturing, presumably reflecting the clout that General Motors carries with the Administration. Quite appropriately, it was rewarded when the automobile Voluntary Export Restraints (VERS) came up for renewal in 1984: of all the car-makers, General Motors was the one that broke ranks and lobbied against new VERs. But wholly owned subsidiaries, where the foreign investor continues competing with local firms instead of joining them, may also make sense if the labour unions are strong and also the more effective protection-threatening lobby. By offering contracts and jobs to these unions, the incoming DFI can co-opt these unions into accepting continuing imports.

How significant is Quid Pro Quo DFI today? Qualitatively, it is easy to recognize its importance on the US–Japan scene. Indeed, quite aside from Japanese firms' own statements, it is manifest that the Japanese government is acutely aware that DFI generates positive externalities for Japan, and that it therefore encourages such DFI and seeks to profit from it through lobbying in the US.

Thus, the Japanese Economic Institute, which is associated with the Japanese government, issues regular bulletins from its Washington headquarters on Japan's expanding DFI in the United States. Arguing that 'Japanese-affiliated manufacturing companies have become an important source of jobs for American workers, both directly and indirectly through their purchases of goods and services' (*JEI Report* No. 15A, p. 4), these handouts explicitly describe DFI from Japan as being protectionism-related. A recent report observes:

Although Japanese exporters have always regarded onshore manufacturing as a way to bolster their sales in the United States, many companies with a significant stake in the US market did not decide to invest here until they were faced with actual or potential import restrictions.

In what has become the best known example of the correlation, Mitsubishi Electric Corp., Sharp Corp., Toshiba Corp., and Hitachi Ltd., began to supply the US colour television market primarily from domestic production facilities after an orderly marketing agreement with Japan went into effect in 1977, thereby joining Sony Corp., Matsushita Electric Industrial Co. Ltd., and Sanyo Electric Co. Ltd., which already has US colour television plants. Japan's top bearing makers – Nippon Seiko K.K., NTN Toyo Bearing Co. Ltd., Nachifujikoshi Corp., and Nippon Miniature Bearing Co. Ltd. – also built or acquired plants in the United States to avoid trade barriers.

For other Japanese manufacturers, the threat of US trade restrictions tipped the scales in favour of US production. Microwave ovens, which were the subject of an antidumping investigation, are made in the United States by four Japanese producers – Matsushita Electric, Sanyo Electric, Sharp and Toshiba. Japan's leading semiconductor manufacturers – Fujitsu Ltd., Nippon Electric Co. Ltd., Hitachi and Toshiba – also invested in American production facilities in the late 1970s, prompted in part by mounting complaints about their market inroads from domestic producers. [*JEI*, 1982: 2.]

I should caution, of course, that some of this Japanese DFI may simply be protection-induced, as with the conventional tariff-jumping investments. That, however, a fair fraction of its is undertaken to *defuse*, rather than *circumvent*, protection and hence qualifies as Quid Pro Quo DFI is evident from the GM–Toyota and other examples. Sorting out the relative role of these two model-types is a task awaiting further research.

I might add that the beneficial Quid Pro Quo linkage applies to DFI and not really to portfolio investments. Indeed, it is arguable that the enormous increase in Japanese portfolio investments in the United States has produced not goodwill but rather illwill towards Japan. By raising the price of the US dollar, such inflows have created the Dutch Disease phenomenon: creating the current account deficit as its counterpart, bringing enormous pressure on the export industries of the US, and fuelling greatly the demands for protection against Japan. Forgotten in the arithmetic are the jobs that are created by the inflow of the portfolio capital in the first place! This remarkable asymmetry in the linkage effects of portfolio capital inflow and DFI is somewhat reminiscent of the contrast that developmental economists have long noted between project aid and general-purpose or programme aid. The former has always been preferred by donors who correctly observe that projects are visible and readily create goodwill for the donors, whereas programme aid is invariably lost into oblivion since no one can readily identify its often considerable benefits.

I should also observe that, whatever mechanisms by which the quid pro quo of reduced protection threat is obtained, whether through goodwill in the legislatures or through reduced protectionist lobbying by consequently co-opted capitalists or labour unions in the host country, this type of DFI reflects artificial pressures, rather than market forces. It thus shares with protection-induced DFI the demerits of being fundamentally inefficient: it distorts the allocation of economic activity among nations. But the parallel terminates there. For, the protection is actually *in place* and serves to create the artificial profits that crystallize the DFI in the *protection*-induced latter case. However, with the *threat*-induced former case, the objective of the DFI is precisely to reduce, and possibly eliminate, the probability of protection being enacted at all! Again, the implications for the lobbying positions of the foreign investors are dramatically different under the two DFIs. In the latter case, since the protection serves to make the host country market profitable for the DFI in the first place, the DFI is likely to become party to the lobbies seeking to keep the protection intact. However, the DFI that responds to the threat of protection, seeking therewith to moderate that threat, will join in lobbying against protection instead.

(iv) *Adaptive Attitudes and Policies*

I should be remiss if I did not also note the steady accommodation in the attitudes of the developed country multinationals undertaking DFI and their governments towards the control-oriented policy shifts by the developing countries in the post-war period, progressively reducing the early tensions that Professor Raymond Vernon (1977) described as *Storm Over Multinationals* and facilitating the growth of DFI that I have sketched.

The political scientists, Professors Charles Lipson (1985) and Stephen Krasner (1978) (1985, ch. 7), in brilliant studies of the evolution of the international regime pertaining to DFI, have noted how multinationals have accommodated to the domestic control-oriented aspirations and policies of host countries. Lacking co-operation for tougher postures from the allies in Europe and Japan, and faced by internal 'corporate fractionalization and divergent self-interest' that equally undermine the feasibility of hard line positions, even the hegemonic US government has had no option but to adopt 'adaptive strategies' that work generally within the guidelines set by the host developing countries themselves. Greater tolerance for host-country policies, such as those well-analysed by Professor Charles Kindleberger (1973), including insistence on joint ventures and performance requirements relating to the hiring of indigenous labour and exporting a target fraction of output, has become commonplace.[9] Even expropriation, steadily diminishing as a phenomenon, has been sought to be handled by investment guarantees rather than by gunboat diplomacy, with the occasional flexing of muscle in the Congress tantamount to little more than ritualistic reflex action.

As Professor Isaiah Frank (1980) has persuasively documented through extensive interviews, the multinationals have come to accept this new, implicit regime, cooling the 'high noon' atmospherics of conflict between national sovereignty and multinations 'beyond control' that seemed at one time certain to afflict foreign investment in the developing countries.[10]

---

[9] See, for instance, the article by Robert Gibson (1985) in the *Los Angeles Times*, documenting the increasing willingness of US multinationals to entertain joint ventures abroad. Export performance requirements have however come under critical scrutiny from the US government as part of its increasing preoccupation with the question of 'fair trade'.

[10] Lipson has graphically analysed how the interplay of 'corporate preferences' and state interests has brought this about, so also the role played by the efforts at legitimation of the new regime by developing countries on the international stage. Krasner (1985: 195) is also perceptive and worth quoting on the remarkable nature of this outcome, in comparison with other issues dividing the developing and the developed countries:

Developing countries have altered principles, norms, rules, and decision-making procedures related to direct foreign investment. National regulations are increasing. The sanctity of contrasts can no longer be adequately defended. The proposition that under the old regime MNCs possessed unfair bargaining power has been widely accepted. Particularly in raw material exploitation there has been a fundamental shift in effective

The growing sophistication of several developing countries in dealing with DFI, by policy rather than by inflammatory rhetoric, has also assisted in the process, pulling DFI back into the mutual gain arena of commerce and economics, and away from the zero-sum presumptions of politics.

II. New 'Systemic' Factors Favouring DFI

As it happens, this mutually adaptive process has been reinforced by new 'systemic' factors that have recently emerged, favouring the growth of DFI. Among these, three are notable.

(a) Shifting Ideological Attitudes: China and India

First, there is a shift of ideological attitudes in some important developing countries that returns DFI to a warm embrace by them today.

China under Mr Deng is of course a supreme example. It is interesting to recall Lenin's window to the capitalist West under the New Economic Policy (NEP) from 1921. Lenin then extensively sought and secured Western trade and credits. But the ideological rationalization then was that this was the way to build Communism by exploiting capitalist greed, the faster to eventually destroy the very capitalist systems abroad. As Kamenev put it pointedly in 1921, justifying the Anglo–Soviet Trade Agreement:

. . . the foreign capitalists, who will be obliged to work on the terms that we offer them, will dig their own grave. . . . Foreign capital will fulfil the role Marx predicted of it. [Quoted by Kennan (1962: 178).]

George Kennan's imagined Politburo proclamation piquantly captures this cynical ideological affirmation, even as the capitalists are embraced:

---

control in favour of host countries. Multinationals have been compelled to alter their behaviour. Simply by being sovereign states, by utilizing the constitutive principle of the international system, developing countries have been able to change the rules of the game for direct foreign investment. In other issue areas, where domestic action alone has more limited impact, the Third World has had a more difficult time.

We despise you. We consider that you should be swept from the earth as governments and physically destroyed as individuals. . . . But since we are not strong enough to destroy you today — since an interval must unfortunately elapse before we can give you the *coup de grace* — we want you during this interval to trade with us, we want you to finance us. . . .

An outrageous demand perhaps. But you will accept it nonetheless. You will accept it because you are not free agents, because you are slaves to your own capitalist appetites, because when profit is involved, you have no pride, no principle, no honour. [Kennan 1962: 176.]

Little of this ideological militancy can be detected in Mr Deng's China. The 'open door' policy towards capital, techniques and knowhow from the capitalist West is not simply a tactical manoeuvre: it is very much part of an end of Communist ideology and the rise of the capitalist mentality.[11] The external policy changes in support of DFI et al. have been firmly embedded in a policy shift that exhibits cascading reforms aimed at dismantling the Maoist legacy also in internal economic organization.

I find it fascinating, and an intellectual puzzle, that these external and internal policy changes have been accompanied by astonishing Chinese claims as to their anticipated impact on China's economic performance. Growth-rates up to 2,000 AD of nearly 10 per cent annually have been projected. Even sophisticated visitors such as Leonard Silk (1985b) of the *New York Times* have written of growth-rates during the last few years of nearly 11 per cent and subsequently of 18 per cent! These claims must sound utterly implausible to development economists who know that, with 80 per cent of its labour force in agriculture where long-sustained growth-rates of output of even 4 per cent are a supreme achievement, you would need a Confucian miracle for such manna to fall from the capitalist skies. It would appear that the Chinese leaders have moved from one Great Leap Forward to another. Chairman Mao's was to be taken by Marx's altruistic,

---

[11] The internal war against Maoist remnants is not entirely over yet, however. See, for example, Leonard Silk's (1985a) recent report on China's infighting on ideology, filed from Canton. Inevitably, the revisionist supporters of Mr Deng's new ways invoke tactically the numerous writings of Lenin during NEP in support of supping with the capitalist devil even if one was ideologically a committed Marxist. See, for example, Li Huajie and Zhang Hanyang (1982).

complete man; Mr Deng's is to be taken by Adam Smith's selfish, economic man! We can only hope that, when ex post realities fall well below ex ante promises, Adam Smith's wisdom will not fall by the wayside, returning China to its old ways.

As of now, however, Mr Deng's China is actively embracing DFI in its four *special Economic Zones*, all located along the South China coast. Aimed initially at overseas Chinese, these zones have been made increasingly attractive to all others with the usual enticements: tax holidays, guarantees on repatriation, increased access to the mainland markets, and tax-free imports. In April 1984, China went further and announced the creation of 14 'open cities' along its long coastline where DFI would enjoy somewhat similar privileges (Sit 1985).

India, the other 'sleeping giant' of Asia, has also witnessed a similar, if more measured and less frenetic, shift towards a more welcoming role for DFI. The Indian shift has also resulted from a change in regime, from Mrs Gandhi's to Mr Rajiv Gandhi's stewardship. Fabian socialism has given way to pragmatism and a willingness to shift the economy out of a constricting bureaucratic stranglehold and an excessively inward-oriented posture. The young Prime Minister's desire to absorb high-tech knowhow rapidly accelerated a more tolerant attitude to DFI.

(b) Debts and Conditionality: South America

While the new warmth of China and India towards DFI is to be attributed largely to the decline of ideology, the door to DFI is being slowly opened also in the countries of South America through sheer economic necessity. The acute economic difficulties in these debt-ridden countries, and their hopelessly precarious foreign exchange situation, have shifted the margin in favour of accommodating to the inflow of DFI when its costs and benefits are assessed. The door to DFI is being slowly opened wider, under these economic compulsions, almost as predicted by the left wing critics of debt-led growth in the 1970s who claimed that such a strategy of financial integration into the capitalist centre would inevitably pave the way to facilitated entry into the periphery of monopoly capital – i.e. in bourgeois language, of DFI.

This aspect of the current situation makes the impatient attitude of the more ideologically inclined members of the US administration somewhat dangerous and counterproductive. It is not uncommon to encounter declarations of resentment at the continuing host-country regulations on DFI when foreign exchange is so evidently scarce and relief is desired on debts. The itch to kick open the slowly-opening door to DFI has thus been very evident in the US in recent years. But, in kicking the door open, it may well be swung it back shut; for the leaders of these developing countries walk on a political tightrope where they must protect their left flanks even as they turn to capitalist DFI.

The ideological compulsions and the special-interest lobbying from DFI-seekers have even found their way into the Baker Plan, unveiled in October 1985 at the Seoul meeting of the International Monetary Fund (IMF) and the World Bank to tackle the deteriorating debt situation. After years of focusing on the IMF, hard conditionality and deflation as a way of restoring the credit-worthiness of the debtor developing countries, the US government saw its IMF-centred strategy imperilled by the threatened spread of de facto defaults and unilateral actions such as President Garcia's announcement that repayments would not exceed 10 per cent of annual Peruvian exchange earnings. The fact that little new, *net* lending was forthcoming despite great austerity à la IMF-programmes meant that the intended return of the debtor countries via trial and tribulation to creditworthiness had been simply too optimistic.

Increasingly, therefore, the debtor countries saw the choice facing them to be between, on the one hand, the IMF programme solution of the pre-Baker Plan variety that produced deflation and distress but no net funds, and alternatively saying: 'we will go alone, at our own pace'. In the latter case there would be no conditionalities, and the fund inflow situation would be *no worse* since the Western banks would simply have to lend the accruing amortization and interest liabilities or involuntarily face a de jure default that would also force a major crisis upon them. Thus seen, the IMF–US programme to deal with the debt crisis was in evident peril. A few weeks before the Seoul meeting, President de la Madrid of Mexico virtually stated that unless the scales were tipped by international measures to increase the net inflow of funds, his and other debtor governments would be sorely tempted to move in favour of the latter option, following in Peruvian footsteps.

In consequence, the Baker Plan, put together to forestall these untoward possibilities, has shifted focus from the IMF to the World Bank, with emphasis on generating new, net inflows and on growth rather than deflation in the debtor countries. Ideas which only three years earlier were ideologically reprehensible have thus been embraced as the second Reagan Administration has shifted, from the first Administration's view that a strong does of necessary deflation would be followed by the market forces generating new flows, to necessary intervention to generate the necessary flows through multilateral measures.

But the quickstep is still in ideological shoes. For, the World Bank funds, in turn, are predicated on conditionalities that includes micro-incentives reflecting market forces *and*, pertinent to this theme, warming moves towards DFI. Mr Baker may himself be an ideologue; or he may be simply sugarcoating for Senator Jesse Helms and his friends the compelling shift to the World-Bank-centred, liberal-sounding strategy. Either way, the desire to push DFI heavy-handedly past the governments of the debtor countries, as they seek the funds under the Baker Plan, is manifest and will have to be prudently restrained lest, in the volatile political climate of the debtor countries, it proves destabilizing and hence counterproductive.

(c) Multilateral Trade Concerns

Finally, there is a set of interesting and powerful trade-related factors that has emerged, forcing DFI onto our multilateral concerns and certainly promising to favour its future growth. Two related arguments may be distinguished.

(i) *DFI-requiring, Effective Access to Markets*

First, trade itself may be inhibited, and hence the promised access to foreign markets may be compromised, if critically related DFI is not permitted. This concern surfaced during the term of the US Treasury Secretary Connolly who felt that the access to Japanese markets was de facto reduced for United States' exporters of goods because Japanese distributors raised the effective cost of handling US goods through a variety of practices that could be interpreted as implying an invisible tariff surcharge. Presumably, such implicitly collusive Japanese behaviour could raise the 'true' tariff facing US (and other foreign) exporters over and above the much-touted, low visibility Japanese tariff. The way to circumvent this phenomenon therefore was via DFI that would, by establishing local distributive outlets, acquire access to Japanese consumers at the visible tariff. Such 'tariff-reducing' DFI, of course poses an interesting analytical possibility: an otherwise harmful DFI by an exporting country may become beneficial because of the gains from trade accruing from the reduction in the invisible tariff.[12] Whether, in fact, Japan's import performance can indeed be correctly regarded thus as an act of inscrutable Oriental tariff-making by implicit social consensus that requires the antidote of Occidental DFI is another matter. On that, my view is sceptical, based on the econometric work of the Japanologist Gary Saxonhouse which suggests that, by disaggregated Standard International Trade Classification (SITC) categories, Japan's import shares are well within the range predicted by several explanatory variables on cross-country data, leaving no room for an inadequacy to be explained by invisible tariff-making. But this would not be the first time that an interesting theory has no empirical basis but has nonetheless impacted on policy.

(ii) *Trade in Services and DFI*

The other interesting but realistic argument for DFI has emerged in the context of the recent focus on trade in services. Services are to be distinguished from goods by the characteristic that they are generally non-storable, being provided to the user as they are produced. As a result, interaction between provider and user is essential. Such interaction may however be possible at long distance, as when services are provided on the wire. But haircuts cannot still be had at long distance. User-provider *physical proximity* is thus a key characteristic of many service transactions even

---

[12] I have analysed this possibility further in my 1982 Yxtaholm IEA conference paper (1985b).

though technical change may be turning more of them into long-distance services where such proximity becomes unnecessary.

The argument has been forcefully advanced by the banking and telematics sectors recently that proximity to their users has become increasingly necessary for effective transaction of their services.[13] They, and increasingly other service sectors such as insurance companies, accounting and legal firms, and providers of other business services such as advertising, have therefore, lobbied to have the 'right to establish', i.e. the right of making DFI, granted and embodied in an international compact on service trade that would complement the General Agreement on Tariffs and Trade (GATT) which, by original protocol and subsequent practice, governs only trade in goods.

DFI, in the shape of the right to establish, is thus seen by many as an essential component of the *trade* compact that would have to be negotiated to bring services, now estimated at over a quarter of world commerce, into the discipline of a facilitating international framework. Indeed, it is presently an important component of the negotiating strategy at the forthcoming trade talks by the US, the leading proponent of a services compact. That DFI is also a key ingredient, as I have argued, of the current US Administration's economic ideology that only serves to accentuate the US trade negotiators' position on this issue. Both factors in turn combine to constitute a significant DFI-supporting role by the US, still the *force majeure* in the world economy.

III. POLICY AND ANALYTICAL
CONSEQUENCES OF GROWING DFI

As these systemic forces foster DFI, and the world economy gets more globalized and integrated in consequence, both in manufactures and increasingly in services, there follow serious consequences for economic policy and analysis which we must recognize if we are to continue being relevant. I should like, in

---

[13] See the extended conceptual analysis, as also the discussion of its consequences for the forthcoming trade talks, in my Xth Annual Lecture of the Geneva Association (Bhagwati 1985c).

conclusion, to focus on three such consequences which I find particularly compelling.

(a) Tariff-making at Bay

A remarkable implication of the DFI process has been that the world economy now has fairly influential actors who have a commitment to free trade.

A fairly common complaint on the part of analysts of political economy has been the asymmetry of pressure groups in the tariff-making process: the beneficiaries of protection are often concentrated while its victims tend to be either diffused as are end consumers or are unable to see the losses to themselves as when protection indirectly affects exports and hence those engaged in producing exportables adversely.

DFI and the growing maze of globalized production have changed this equation perceptibly. When DFI is undertaken, not for tariff-jumping of locally-selected markets, but for exports to home country or to third markets, as is increasingly the case, protectionism clearly threatens the investments so made and tends to galvanize these influential multinationals into lobbying to keep markets open.

Thus, for example, it was noticeable that when the US semiconductor suppliers recently gathered to discuss anti-dumping legal action against Japanese producers of memory microchips known as EPROMS (or erasable programmable read-only memories), noticeably absent were Motorola Inc. and Texas Instruments Inc. who produce semiconductors in Japan and expect to be shipping some back to US.[14]

Indeed, I should imagine that a principal reason why US protectionism has not translated into a disastrous Smoot–Hawley scenario, despite high unemployment levels and the seriously 'overvalued' dollar (in the Dutch Disease sense), is that few Congressmen have constituencies where DFI has not created such pro-trade, anti-protectionist presence, muddying waters where otherwise protectionists would have sailed with great ease. The 'spider's web' or 'spaghetti-bowl' phenomenon resulting from DFI

[14] See the report by Miller (1985) in the *Wall Street Journal*.

that crisscrosses the world economy has thus been a stabilizing force in favour of holding the protectionists at bay.

While I have detailed here the consequences of DFI already *in place*,[15] it should be remembered that the *possibility* of understanding DFI when faced with import competition *also* provides an alternative to a protectionist response. Since this is the capitalist response, rather than that of labour which would 'lose jobs abroad', the defusion of protectionist threat that is implied here works by breaking and hence weakening the customary alliance between both pressure groups within in industry in their protectionist lobbying with which Professor Steve Magee has made us long familiar.

Interestingly, in the context of the *Quid Pro Quo* DFI that I discussed earlier, labour unions can themselves use DFI as an alternative response to protection, by using the protectionist threat to induce the foreign competitive firms to invest rather than export, to 'create' rather than 'destroy' jobs.

In short, both actual DFI (through the 'spaghetti-bowl' effect) and potential DFI (outward by domestic capital and quid pro quo inward by foreign capital) are powerful forces that are influencing the political economy of tariff-making in favour of an open economy.

(b) Inferring Competitive Efficiency et al.

Yet another significant consequence of DFI expansion has been the growing irrelevance of concepts such as competitive efficiency, comparative productivity growth etc., when applied, as traditionally, to domestically situated activities alone.

If many industries today are establishing DFI abroad, producing and exporting from these 'offshore' facilities, how can it make sense to focus wholly on 'mainland' activity and its characteristics

---

[15] These are in fact well known from the important work of Professor Gerald Helleiner (1977) and others. These authors have shown that MNCs have become active agents exercising political pressure in favour of free trade, especially in products they produce. See also the interesting econometric analysis of US MNCs and their effect on the structure of US trade barriers, by Lavergne and Helleiner (1985). Their work however does not extend to the *potential* DFI effects in favour of freer trade that I discuss above.

to make inferences about the competitive position of a country or its industries? Indeed, since DFI is undertaken by the more progressive, Schumpeterian industries that respond to import competition by going abroad, there would be a systematic downside bias in confining attention to progressivity in the mainland activities! And yet, prominent economists, including Professor Lester Thurow recently, have been doing precisely this, and drawing alarmist conclusions about the decline of American industry and its competitiveness![16]

While I drew attention earlier to the importance of DFI and hence of offshore production and exports in overall sales and exports of multinationals, this phenomenon needs to be underlined in the present context. Professor Silvio Borner (1985) of Basle, in his work appropriately entitled *Die Sechste Schweiz*, Switzerland's sixth canton constituted by Swiss production abroad, has focused our minds clearly on the issue I am raising here. His analysis of 15 of the largest Swiss industrial multinationals showed, for instance, that they expanded their foreign employment dramatically until, in 1980, only 25 per cent of their employees were located in Switzerland'. The share of investment on mainland too has declined to 32.4 per cent, and production to 25.6 per cent. As much 38 per cent of R & D expenditures are now incurred abroad.

As for the US, the conclusions are equally startling in magnitude. Professors Magnus Blomstrom and Robert Lipsey, who are currently engaged on an extensive statistical analysis of Swedish and American DFI abroad, have preliminary findings that show that the proportion of manufacturing exports by US affiliates abroad (excluding sales to the US) to the total exports by US multinationals and their affiliates in manufactures is as high as 52 per cent, and that this share has steadily grown between 1965 and 1978. Again, the commonly cited figure that the US share of world exports of manufactures has fallen steadily in two decades from 21.3 per cent in 1957 to 12.3 per cent in 1977 proves to be wholly midleading. When the exports of US affiliates offshore are added, the 1977 share of the US in world exports of

[16] See my review of Thurow's *The Zero-sum Solution*, in *The New Leader* (Bhagwati 1985d) where I raise some of these questions.

manufactures climbs again well over 20 per cent! No more need be said to draw attention to the perils of drawing inferences in disregard of these remarkable facts.

(c) Policy Effects

Finally, the interdependence that the growth in DFI represents has affected policy-making in critical ways. Professor Richard Cooper, the pioneer in exploring such effects, has noted how such effects can include the erosion of policy effectiveness and also the reversal of the expected consequences of traditional policy instruments.

On the *policy-erosion* phenomenon, let Professor Cooper (1985) speak for himself:

. . . structural changes in the world economy [i.e. greater openness and internationalization of markets] . . . [are leading] to an erosion of our government's capacity to do things the way it used to. The United States occasionally responds to this erosion by lashing out and extending its jurisdiction to the rest of the world, leading to international friction. I see extraterritoriality, as it is called, as a natural, although not necessarily a desirable, response to the erosion of our capacity to control our own environment. So when we find Canadian securities traded in the US over-the-counter market, the Securities and Exchange Commission (SEC), which is charged with protecting the American public from securities fraud, sends letters to Canadian companies instructing them to comply with SEC regulations. Well, the Canadians are outraged; the SEC does not have any jurisdiction over them, according to them. But the SEC is doing its job the only way it considers workable. When the US government embargoes trade to Cuba or to Vietnam, as it did many years ago, and the US firms operating out of France, Belgium, Spain or Canada sell US-designed products made by US owned firms to Cuba or Vietnam, the US Treasury responds by imposing asset controls on US firms operating abroad. The Belgians are outraged. They argue that while the company is owned by an American firm, it is legally a Belgian entity, subject to Belgian, not US, law. In 1982 the Reagan administration felt very strongly about preventing a new gas pipeline from the Soviet Union to Europe. In its frustration with its inability to persuade foreigners to its view, the US government simply slapped both export and asset controls on the US and foreign firms that had the technology for the pipeline (and it thereby gave the Soviet Union a foreign policy coup in Europe that in its wildest imagination Moscow could not have gotten on its own). Even Britain, our firmest ally, was most outraged by the extension of American jurisdiction of British firms.

The *policy-altering* effect of DFI is evident, on the other hand, in the recent theoretical analyses of Professor Richard Brecher and myself[17] where we have explored how traditional conclusions, such as the optimality of free trade, may be reversed if foreign factors of production are present in the economy. For, the distribution of income implied by a policy, otherwise optimal, may lead to a welfare loss that outweighs the gains traditionally calculated for economies without DFI in their midst. Heuristically, shifting from autarchy to free trade will yield gains from trade, as Adam Smith and Paul Samuelson have shown, but these gains may be outweighed by a redistribution of income away from domestic to foreign-owned factors in your midst. While I would not consider these particular reversals of our traditional policy conclusions important enough to worry about in general, they do alert us to possibilities that may well be important in specific parametric cases, as when the proportion of DFI in total investment may be sizable.

It is evident therefore that economists and policy-makers alike have to be increasingly alert to the significant consequences that the increased globalization of the world economy through DFI entails. Stephen Hymer was wrong when he predicted that the multinational corporation, or DFI, would overwhelm the nation state and render it impotent or obsolete. But his instincts were uncannily correct: DFI would grow into a phenomenon that we simply could not ignore.

REFERENCES

Balasubramanyam, V.N., 1984: 'Incentives and Disincentives for Foreign Direct Investment in Less Developed Countries', *Weltwirtschaftliches Archiv*, Band 120 Heft 4, pp. 720–35.

Bhagwati, Jagdish, 1972: 'Review of Vernon: Sovereignty at Bay', *Journal of International Economics*, 2, pp. 455–62.

[17] See Bhagwati and Brecher (1980) and Brecher and Bhagwati (1981), and also the earlier analysis by Bhagwati and Tironi (1980).

Bhagwati, Jagdish, 1973: 'The Theory of Immiserizing Growth — Further Applications', *in* Michael Connolly and Alexander Swoboda (eds), *International Trade and Money* (London: Allen & Unwin Ltd.), pp. 45–54.

——, 1977a: 'Review of Hymer', *Journal of Development Economics*, 4, pp. 391–5.

—— (ed.), 1977b: *The New International Economic Order: The North-South Debate* (Cambridge, MA: MIT Press).

——, 1978: *Anatomy and Consequences of Exchange Control Regimes*, NBER (Cambridge, MA: Ballinger Co.).

——, 1979: 'International Factor Movements and National Advantage', *Indian Economic Review*, 14(2), pp. 73–100; 9th V.K. Ramaswami Memorial Lecture; rptd in Bhagwati (1983), ch. 42.

—— (ed.), 1982a: *Import Competition and Response*, NBER (Chicago: Chicago University Press).

——, 1982b: 'Shifting Comparative Advantage, Protectionist Demands and Policy Responses', *in* Bhagwati (1982a), pp. 153–84.

——, 1983: *Essays in International Economic Theory*, vols 1 and 2, Robert Feestra (ed.) (Cambridge: MIT Press).

——, 1984: 'Incentives and Disincentives: International Migration', *Weltwirtschaftliches Archiv*, Band 120 Heft 4, pp. 678–701.

——, 1985a: 'Protectionism: Old Wine in New Bottles', *Journal of Policy Modelling*, 7(1), pp. 23–33.

——, 1985b: 'Structural Adjustment and International Factor Mobility: Some Issues', *in* Karl Jungenfelt and Douglas Hague (eds), *Structural Adjustment in Developed Open Economies*, Proceedings of a Conference of the International Economic Association held at Yxtaholm, Sweden (London: Macmillan Ltd.).

——, 1985c: *Trade in Services and Developing Countries*, Xth Annual Lecture of the Geneva Association, delivered at London School of Economics, 28 Nov.

——, 1985d: ' "Pull-up" Not "Trickle-Down" ', *The New Leader*, 16–30 Dec., New York.

Bhagwati, Jagdish and Ernesto Tironi, 1980: 'Tariff Change, Foreign Capital and Immiserization: A Theoretical Analysis', *Journal of Development Economics*, 7 March, pp. 71–83.

Bhagwati, Jagdish and Richard Brecher, 1980: 'National Welfare in an Open Economy in the Presence of Foreign Owned Factors of Production', *Journal of International Economics*, 10 Feb., pp. 103–15.

Bhagwati, Jagdish and John Ruggie (eds), 1984: *Power, Passions and*

Purpose: Prospects for North-South Negotiations (Cambridge, MA: MIT Press).

Bhagwati, Jagdish, Richard Brecher, Elias Dinopoulos, and T.N. Srinivasan, 1986: '*Quid Pro Quo* Foreign Investment and Optimal Policy Intervention' (revised) Feb., mimeo., Columbia University.

Blomstrom, Magnus and Bjorne Hettne, 1984: *Development Theory in Transition* (London: Zed Books).

Brecher, Richard and Jagdish Bhagwati, 1981: 'Foreign Ownership and the Theory of Trade and Welfare', *Journal of Political Economy*, 89(3) (June), pp. 497–511.

Brecher, Richard and Carlos Diaz–Alejandro, 1977: 'Tariffs, Foreign Capital and Immiserizing Growth', *Journal of International Economics*, 7, pp. 317–22.

Caves, R.E., 1982: *Multinational Enterprise and Economic Analysis* (Cambridge: Cambridge University Press).

Cooper, Richard, 1985: 'International Economic Cooperation: Is it Desirable? Is it Likely?', *Bulletin of the American Academy of Arts and Sciences*, 39(2) (Nov.), pp. 11–35.

Dinopoulos, Elias, 1985a: 'A Formulation of the "Biological" Model of Trade in Similar Products', Jan., Columbia University International Economics Research Center Working Paper No. 60; forthcoming in *Journal of International Economics*, 1986.

——, 1985b: 'Mutually-penetrating, Intra-industry Cross-investment: A Theoretical Analysis' (revised), Oct., mimeo., Michigan State University.

Dinopoulos, Elias and Jagdish Bhagwati, 1986: '*Quid Pro Quo* DFI and Market Structure', Feb., mimeo., Columbia University.

Dunning, John, 1981: *International Production and the Multinational Enterprise* (London: Allen & Unwin).

Frank, Isiah, 1980: *Foreign Enterprise in Developing Countries* (Baltimore: Johns Hopkins University Press).

Frobel, Folker, Jurgen Heinrichs and Otto Kreye, 1980: *The New International Division of Labour* (Cambridge: Cambridge University Press).

Gibson, Robert W., 1985: 'Firms Warming to Joint Ventures Abroad', *Los Angeles Times*, 9 June.

Grunwald, Joseph and Kenneth Flamm, 1985: *The Global Factory: Foreign Assembly in International Trade* (Washington DC: Brookings Institution).

Hamada, Koichi, 1974: 'An Economic Analysis of Duty-Free Zones', *Journal of International Economics*, 4, pp. 225–41.

Hamilton, Carl and Lars Svennson, 1982: 'On the Welfare Effects of a Duty-Free Zone', *Journal of International Economics*, 12, pp. 45–64.

Helleiner, G., 1977: 'Transnational Enterprises and the New Political Economy of United States Trade Policy', *Oxford Economic Papers* (March).

Helpman, Elhanan, 1984: 'A Simple Theory of International Trade with Multinational Corporations', *Journal of Political Economy*, 92, pp. 451–71.

Hymer, Stephen, 1960: 'The International Operations of National Firms', Ph.D. dissertation, Massachusetts Institute of Technology, Cambridge, MA.

Hymer, Stephen and Robert Rowthorn, 1970: *in* C.P. Kindleberger (ed.), *The International Corporation* (Cambridge, MA: MIT Press).

Japan Economic Institute, 1982: Report No. 15A, Washington DC.

Jones, R.W., J.P. Neary and F. Ruane, 1983: 'Two-way Capital Flows: Cross-hauling in a Model of Foreign Investment', *Journal of International Economics*, 13, pp. 357–66.

Kennan, George F., 1960: *Russia and the West* (New York: Mentor Books).

Kindleberger, Charles P. (ed.), 1970: *The International Corporation* (Cambridge, MA: MIT Press).

——, 1973: 'Restrictions on Direct Foreign Investment in LDCs', *in* J. Bhagwati and R.S. Eckaus (eds), *Development and Planning* (Cambridge, MA: MIT Press).

Krasner, Stephen, 1978: *Defending the National Interest: Raw Material Investments and US Foreign Policy* (Princeton: Princeton University Press).

——, 1985: *Structural Conflict: The Third World Against Global Liberalism* (Berkeley: University of California Press).

La Huajie and Zhang Hanyang, 1982: 'Xue xi Liening guanyu zurangzhi de lilun' (Learn from Lenin's Theory Regarding the Leasing System), *Gang-Au jingji* (Guangdong), 4.

Lavergne, Real and G. Helleiner, 1985: 'United States Transnational Corporations and the Structure of United States Trade Barriers: An Empirical Investigation', mimeo.

Lipson, Charles, 1985: *Standing Guard* (Berkeley: University of California Press).

Magee, Steve, 1977: 'Information and the Multinational Corporation: An Appropmability Theory of Direct Foreign Investment', *in* Bhagwati (1977).

Markusen, James, 1984: 'Multinationals, Multi-Plant Economies, and the Gains from Trade', *Journal of International Economics*, 16, pp. 205–26.

Miller, Michael, 1985: 'Big US Semiconductor Markers Expected to Sue Over "Dumping" of Japanese Chips', *Wall Street Journal*, 1 Oct.

New York Times, 1985: 'Foreign Investment in US Up Sharply', 16 Sept.

Sassen–Koob, Saskia, 1984: *The Foreign Investment Connection: Rethinking Migration*, mimeo., New York.

Silk, Leonard, 1985a: 'China's Fight Over Ideology', *The New York Times*, 2 Oct.

——, 1985b: 'China Hits its Stride', *The New York Times*, 27 Oct.

Sit, Victor S.F., 1985: 'The Special Economic Zones of China', *The Developing Economies*, 23(1), pp. 69–87.

Vernon, Raymond, 1966: 'International Investment and International Trade in the Product Cycle', *Quarterly Journal of Economics*, 80 (May), pp. 190–207.

——, 1971: *Sovereignty at Bay* (New York: Basic Books).

——, 1977: *Storm Over the Multinationals: The Real Issues*, (London: MacMillan).

Wong, Kar-yiu, 1986: 'International Factor Movements, Repatriation and Welfare', *Journal of International Economics*, vol. 21, pp. 71–83.

Wright, James, 1985: 'Letter to the Editor', *Wall Street Journal*, 3 Oct.

16

International Factor Movements and National Advantage[*]

I AM particularly touched by the invitation to give the V.K. Ramaswami Lecture this year. We were close personally and our friendship was enriched by a considerable body of joint theoretical work that was conceived and executed during his visits to Oxford and mine to Delhi over a period of many years.

Ramaswami's distinction lay, not in creating dazzling but irrelevant logical constructs, but rather in the uncanny instinct with which he sensed an interesting analytical problem in issues of practical policy. Thus many of his most interesting trade-theoretic papers had a direct policy relevance, in the best tradition of economic science. And, despite the many claims on his time — it is remarkable that he was an overworked bureaucrat — he found the energy and the inclination to turn his analytical gifts on a wide range of problems.

For example, he wrote two seminal papers on subjects that have been at the centre of active trade-theoretic research subsequently: the celebrated [1963] paper on distortions that stimulated and defined the framework of the recent, voluminous literature on the theory of policy intervention in an open economy; and his famous [1971] construction of an example designed to show the impossibility of devising an effective-rate-of-protection (ERP) index in the presence of generalized substitution, which was to generate sufficient controversy to provide the impetus for other theorists to analyse the ERP index in general-equilibrium models.

He wrote much else. Indeed, the subject-matter of this lecture

* Thanks are due to National Science Foundation Grant No. SOC77–07188 for financial support of the research underlying the 9th V.K. Ramaswami Memorial Lecture, 1979, that forms the basis of this chapter. Pranab Bardhan, Koichi Hamada and T.N. Srinivasan made helpful suggestions on an earlier draft of the lecture.

was immediately evident to me when, in the course of recently formulating the analytical problems raised by the international movements of labour, I thought of a new policy-suggested problem only to have my memory jogged that Ramaswami probably had formulated the same problem many years ago. On consulting his posthumously collected *Essays*, I was delighted to find that my memory had served me right. Indeed, here was a beautiful little piece, of five terse and economical paragraphs so characteristic of Ramaswami, on the very same problem of international factor mobility and national advantage! As I shall argue presently, this neglected piece poses an interesting problem of considerable originality: and one that has some relevance today.

Nothing would be more appropriate, therefore, than the present occasion to rescue this contribution of Ramaswami's from oblivion. And, in doing this, I have decided to set it in the perspective of the modern policy-related, welfare theory of international factor flows.

I. Asymmetries and Philosophical Contrasts

I shall proceed initially to analyse international capital mobility, focusing on its interaction with national advantage, and will consider labour mobility across countries only later.[1] It should suffice to say here that consideration of international labour mobility can be treated symmetrically with the analysis of capital mobility, except for two critical questions: *first*, the simultaneous consideration of mobility by both factors opens up, as will be evident below, policy and analytical questions that consideration of only one of them precludes; and *second*, there *is* a fundamental asymmetry between the two types of factor mobility across countries, when considering the impact of such mobility on 'national' advantage.

This fundamental asymmetry in the treatment of international mobility of capital and of labour is to be traced to the fact that, in the latter case, there is an ambiguous definition of the population over which welfare is to be defined.

[1] I shall abstain from discussing recent analytical work on international transfer of technology, including that which is pertinent to discussing *direct* foreign investment. My analysis is primarily focused on capital and labour flows.

Thus, the investment of capital abroad does not affect, in principle, the group over which 'national' welfare will be defined. By contrast, the 'migration' of human beings raises the question: are the migrants part of this group? There is no universal answer to this question. Migrants who are temporary, because of explicit rules in that regard, as with *gastarbeiters* in Western Europe and imported workers in the oil-rich Middle East, will evidently classify as part of the 'national' population. But what of permanently emigrating nationals? If they do 'go away' for good, as with emigration from Soviet Russia, there is a convincing case for treating 'national' welfare as defined only over 'those left behind'.[2] On the other hand, with a large fraction of the highly skilled migration from the LDCs to the DCs as seems to be the case today, if this migrant population is characterized by retention of ethnic ties to the country of origin, a high frequency of visits and even continuation of citizenship status in many cases, the fact of permanent migration (embodied in the holding of immigrant visas) is thoroughly compatible with the analyst including such migrants in the definition of 'national' welfare for the country of origin.

The critical nature of this issue will become apparent from a single example. Suppose that the migration leaves those left behind marginally impoverished, while the migrants improve their condition (as would be the presumption with voluntary migration). If the immigration is to be treated as justifying the definition of national welfare only over those left behind, migration evidently has worsened national welfare. However, if the migrants are to be treated as a part of the national population, social welfare functions could easily be imagined that would enable the migration to be demand welfare-improving.

With this cautionary note against unwarranted parallels between the analyses of capital and labour mobility, let me now draw attention to a sharp distinction between two different questions that may be raised to advantage in the welfare-theoretic analysis of international factor mobility.

These two questions may be posed, while formulating my analysis (without loss of generality) from the viewpoint of a capital-importing rather than capital-exporting country. The classic

[2] These issues have been raised in Bhagwati and Rodriguez (1975).

question is whether capital inflow, *left to itself*, is to national advantage; and the companion question relates to the nature of *policy intervention* to regulate the inflow to secure national advantage.

The former question has traditionally divided economists into two major ideological camps which I have described elsewhere (Bhagwati 1976) as the 'benign neglect' and the 'malign neglect' schools. The 'benign neglect' school is where the liberal economists have traditionally gravitated, since it ties in with their customary tendency to look for the positive sum game (i.e. every party to a transaction gains) aspects of an economic transaction; the Invisible Hand caresses each and all. By contrast, economists in the 'malign neglect' school have focused rather on the zero (or even negative) sum game dimensions of such transactions: the Invisible Hand strokes some and strangulates others. These diverse viewpoints are nowhere more pronounced than in the ever-expanding literature on the impact of foreign investments on national advantage.

Related, but not identical, philosophical differences divide economists on the related question of optimal policy intervention. Thus, most economists are inclined to proceed by assuming that, since the foreign investment inflow possibility necessarily augments the set of opportunities available to a country, optimal policy intervention can only improve welfare. However, this view implicitly disregards the possibility, central to writings from the Chicago school as also predictably from the other end of the political spectrum, that governments do not function so as to pursue the public interest but are rather the creatures of special interests, so that the politically *feasible* outcomes when foreign investment was available may well be dominated by those obtaining in its absence. The greatest contrast, therefore, follows between those who, focusing on optimal interventions by host governments, unconsciously transit to the extreme view that foreign capital inflow will occur in the presence of welfare-maximizing policies, and those who, following after a fashion in the Marxist tradition, go to the other extreme and consider the inflow to be occurring in the context of local policies designed to serve the interests of domestic élite groups (often sharing the spoils with the foreign élites in darker versions where the bourgeoisie of the world unites).

II. The Welfare Impact of Capital Inflow

It will serve us well to keep these politico–philosophical contrasts in view as I proceed with, and frankly concentrate on, the more technical analysis of the issues at hand. I proceed immediately, however, to the *first* of the two questions that I posed above: namely, the impact of foreign capital inflow, left to itself, on national advantage.

(a) Basic Proposition: No Impact

The simplest and most insightful way to address this question is to build the analysis around the central proposition that, in the absence of distortions, a 'small' inflow of foreign capital will neither harm nor benefit the recipient nation. For, the rental on such capital (γ) will then equal the value of its private marginal product *(PMP)* which, in turn, will equal the social marginal product *(SMP)*:

$$\gamma = PMP = SMP$$

The rental represents the cost, and the social marginal product the gross gain, to the recipient country: and their equality ensures the absence of gain or loss.

(b) Gain from 'Large' Inflow

This paradoxical outcome, that the inflow of capital or its absence is a matter of indifference to the recipient country, reflects of course the assumption that the influx is small. When it is 'large', diminishing returns and the ensuing decline in the rental on foreign capital leaves the economy with a surplus: the rental equals the private marginal product for the marginal inflow, but the total return to all capital is less than its contribution to national product, the difference accruing to the economy as a gain in income and hence in welfare. This is readily seen for a one-sector economy where the standard measure of the gain to the economy from a large inflow of foreign capital is the area under the marginal product curve net of the return to the capital. This is the striped

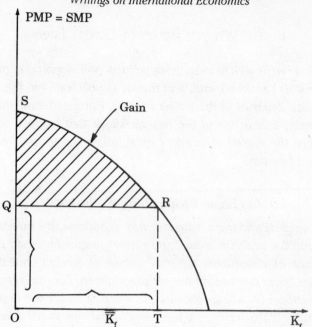

FIG. 16.1: K_f is the amount of foreign capital. Rental (γ) is OQ and total return to foreign capital is $OQRT$. SR is the marginal product curve. SQR is therefore the measure of the gain to the economy from the capital inflow.

area in Fig. 16.1 where $\bar{K}_f$ is the magnitude of the inflow, γ is its competitive rental, $OSRT$ is the total increase in product from the capital inflow, and $OQRT$ is the total return to foreign capital, with SR being the marginal product curve as foreign capital inflow is varied.[3]

The role of diminishing returns in this welfare-improving outcome is critical, for it is evident that if the capital inflow can be absorbed *without* diminishing returns, the no-impact proposition will resurrect itself even though the inflow is not small. Thus, consider a typical 2×2 model. With given commodity prices, it follows that factor prices and therefore factor proportions in the two commodities will remain unchanged, provided complete specialization or factor intensity reversal does not occur. The inflow

[3] For an extension of this argument to a dynamic framework of a growing economy, see Bardhan (1970) and Hamada (1966).

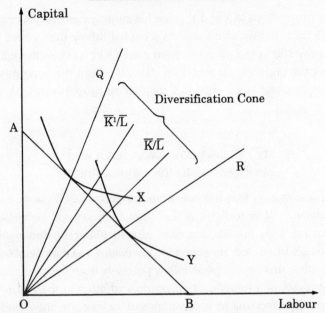

FIG. 16.2: *OQ* and *OR* are the factor proportions in *X* and *Y* respectively. *QOR* is the diversification cone. As long as the overall endowment ratio lies in this cone, diversification will obtain at factor price-ratio *AB*. A shift in endowment, for example from $\bar{K}/\bar{L}$ to $\bar{K}'/\bar{L}$, will *not* change factor prices and factor proportions. Diminishing returns are therefore frustrated within the cone *QOR*.

and the resulting change in the factor endowment ratio will then produce a change only in relative outputs of the two commodities, with the relative and absolute output of the labour-intensive commodity falling and of the capital-intensive commodity rising (à la Rybczynski 1955). The capital inflow therefore will *not* cause a decline in the reward to capital: diminishing returns will have been frustrated. More generally, as along as the economy remains within the McKenzie–Chipman diversification cone, defined on the pre-inflow factor prices, rewards to factors will *not* change, *no matter how large the capital inflow is:* and correspondingly the no-impact proposition will hold. This is illustrated in Fig. 16.2. At the pre-inflow factor price-ratio *AB*, the factor propositions in *X* and *Y* production are given by *OQ* and *OR*, respectively. The overall factor endowment ratio $\bar{K}/\bar{L}$ is only a weighted sum of the factor proportions in X and Y, given full employment. Any increase in the total endowment ratio via a capital inflow that leaves the economy still in the diversification cone QOR, as does the inflow raising the endowment ratio to $\bar{K}'/\bar{L}$, will permit the economy to remain at factor price–ratio AB, with factor proportions in X and Y unchanged.

(c) Distortions: Exogenous and Endogenous to the Capital Inflow

The presumption that follows, from the postulates of large flows and absence of distortions, is that capital inflows will be welfare-improving, with the limiting case of zero impact if diminishing returns are frustrated. However, the interesting and important qualifications to this presumption follow precisely from the recognition and analysis of a number of distortions, whether in the nature of market imperfections or policy-imposed. In essence, they lead to an inequality between private and social marginal products to foreign capital, so that the situation is characterized by:

$$\gamma = PMP \neq SMP$$

Analytically, it is useful to distinguish here between cases where the capital inflow occurs subject to a given *exogenous* distortion and where the distortion is *endogenous* to, and therefore varies with, the capital inflow. I shall therefore develop initially a number of policy-relevant general-equilibrium arguments based on given, exogenous distortions and then discuss a model of a distortion-changing capital inflow that captures an oft-discussed implication of foreign investment.

(i) *Exogenous Distortions*

(a) The simplest example of a distortion-caused inequality between private and social marginal products in general-equilibrium analysis, which reinforces the presumption of gain from such inflow, is provided by the factor market distortion à la Arthur Lewis (1954). Here, labour is available in elastic supply at a constant real wage. If we graft this argument on to a two-factor, one-commodity model, it is easy to see that a pre-specified real

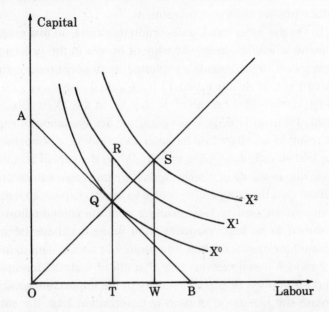

FIG. 16.3: In this one-sector, Lewis type model, the pre-specified real wage pre-fixes technique along OQS. Augmenting capital from QT to RT increases output, *not* to X^1 but, to X^2 since TW amount of additional labour will be forthcoming. Therefore, for a small augmentation of capital, the rental to capital will be $(X^1 - X^0)$ but the contribution to national income will be larger: $(X^2 - X^0)$.

wage pre-fixes the choice of technique, and the incremental capital resulting from the capital inflow leads to incremental employment and hence to incremental national product that *exceeds* the private marginal product to capital. Thus, in Fig. 16.3, let the fixed real wage lead to fixed choice of capital–labour ratio along OQS. As capital flows in from initial equilibrium at Q, in amount QR, the increment in national output for given labour OT will be $(X^1 - X^0)$ and will accrue, for a small inflow, to the foreign capital. However, the actual increment in output will be $(X^2 - X^0) > (X^1 - X^0)$, since labour employment will *also* increase from OT to OW, given the assumption of elastic labour supply at the given real wage. Therefore, $SMP > PMP$ for the capital inflow. The Lewis model, should you think that it captures the essence of the economy, leads therefore to an optimistic assessment of the welfare impact of foreign investment.

(b) On the other hand, a distortion that *can* lead to a contrary outcome is where foreign investment occurs in the presence of unexploited, or inadequately exploited, monopoly power in trade: a situation that results in what I have called elsewhere (1971) a foreign distortion. As some of us showed in the 1950s (Bhagwati [1958], Johnson [1955]), even domestic accumulation of capital can result in a welfare loss for such an economy: a phenomenon now known as immiserizing growth. When the capital accumulation is due to inflow of foreign capital, we must also subtract from national gain the competitive return to foreign capital, so that the conditions for welfare loss resulting from the capital inflow can be shown to be less restrictive than those that have been established for immiserization from domestic accumulation. In the 2×2 model, it still remains true that either inelastic foreign demand for imports or capital-intensity of the importable good will increase the likelihood of such immiserization from the capital inflow; however, these conditions are no longer critical to such a paradoxical outcome in view of the added source of loss from the earnings of foreign capital and the fact that the capital inflow implies a capital outflow from the rest of the world which, in turn, *could* contract the external offer curve, faced by the recipient country, and thus be an external source of welfare loss.

(c) Finally, let me draw on yet another, still more policy-relevant, matter of the manner in which the influx of capital may immiserize the recipient country. Suppose that the capital inflow occurs in the presence of a tariff. This may occur due to a deliberate policy of the government aiming at inducing a tariff-jumping investment, and indeed the analysis I present here has relevance in determining the desirability of such a policy. But the postulated inflow may occur *exogenously* to the tariff. Assume then that, in the 2×2 model, foreign capital is introduced into a small economy with a tariff in place. With other distortions assumed away, the tariff is then the only (policy-imposed) distortion in the system and entails a loss for this small economy for *any* level of factor endowments. A small inflow can then be shown to be *necessarily* immiserizing when the importable is capital-intensive and necessarily welfare-improving when it is labour-intensive: in the former case, $\gamma = PMP < SMP$ and in the latter case, $\gamma = PMP > SMP$.

This *is* a strong conclusion, for, what we know from the theory of immiserizing growth is that, in a tariff-distorted small economy, domestic capital accumulation *can* be, but is *not* necessarily, immiserizing when the importable is capital intensive. When capital accumulates through influx of foreign capital, however, the competitive return to foreign capital is an added source of national loss and makes immiserization a *necessary* outcome.[4]

While this is true for small inflows, the effect of large flows is somewhat more complex. As the flow increases, the fact that factor proportions are fixed due to given commodity (and hence factor) prices ensures that what happens for a small inflow will hold for large inflows, the economy's welfare will continue to decline. However, the production of capital-intensive importables will continue to increase in relation to their consumption with increasing capital inflow, thus eventually resulting in autarky. Further inflow will therefore begin reducing the relative price of the importable below its tariff-inclusive price, while keeping it above the external price. This reduction in the relative price of the capital-intensive importable will then be a source of welfare gain since it will successively reduce the rental on foreign capital à la the celebrated Stolper–Samuelson (1941) analysis. Therefore, beyond autarky, successive capital inflows will improve welfare until the process is halted by the domestic relative price of the importable falling so far below the tariff-inclusive price as to equal the external price. This restores the free trade situation and correspondingly the free-trade welfare level: this being the familiar Mundell (1957) result. As more capital flows in, it is absorbed by a relative and absolute decline in the importable output: the economy is operating in the diversification cone and welfare remains unchanged. Eventually, the economy reaches complete specialization on the importable good and then classical diminishing returns set in as more capital comes in, resulting again therefore in welfare improvement à la MacDougall (1960)

---

[4] This remarkable conclusion has been arrived at by Brecher and Diaz–Alejandro (1978), building on the earlier work of Johnson (1967) and Bhagwati (1973), and independently by Hamada (1974) and Minabe (1974) who built on an earlier piece in Japanese by Uzawa (1969).

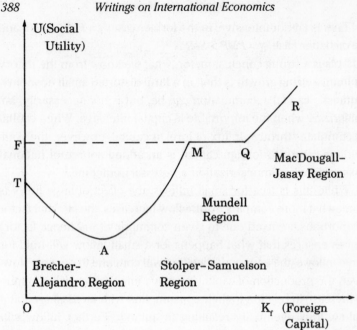

FIG. 16.4: For a small economy without domestic distortions, a tariff will bring social utility down to *T* from *F* (at free trade). Influx of capital, in this economy with importable capital-intensive, will successively reduce welfare down till autarky obtains at *A*. Thereafter, utility will increase due to Stolper–Samuelson effect until the free trade goods price-ratio is reached at *M*. At *M*, and as long as diversification obtains along *MQ*, the utility will therefore be at the free trade level. At *Q*, complete specialization will occur on the importable. Diminishing returns thereafter will bring gains along *QR*.

and Jasay (1960). These successive outcomes are illustrated in Fig. 16.4. The decline in utility as the economy imposes a tariff is from *F* to *T*. The inflow of capital, K_f leads to successive decline in social utility down to *A* where autarky is reached. Utility then increases monotonically until the free trade level is reached and the Mundell equilibrium is established at M. Utility stays constant thereafter until *Q*, when complete specialization in production of the importable is reached. Further inflows of capital then lead to increasing welfare, along *QR*, owing to classical diminishing returns in the importable industry.

This analysis has direct relevance to the important issues that have been raised recently by trade and developmental economists concerning the appropriate foreign trade strategy for developing countries. It is now indisputable that countries that have pursued an export promoting strategy have done remarkably better than those that have persisted with an inward-looking, import-substituting one. Among the reasons for this superior performance, we must surely reckon the social efficiency of foreign investment in the export promoting countries and its inefficiency in the import replacing ones. The latter group of countries would appear to be characterized by the conditions favourable to immiserizing capital inflow that I have already sketched: protective policies combined with capital intensity of the importable activities. On the other hand, the foreign investments in the export promoting countries, far from being of the tariff-jumping, local market-oriented variety, have been essentially to exploit local cost conditions à la the Heckscher–Ohlin model, thus coming much closer to the welfare-improving set of conditions sketched by me earlier.[5] The distortionary policies that reduce the productivity of domestic investments in the import-substituting regimes thus also adversely affect the gains from foreign investments, suggesting strongly therefore the wisdom of Ian Little's observation that foreign investment is as good or bad for you as your own policies.

(ii) *Endogenous Distortions*

My analysis so far related to the welfare impact of foreign capital inflow in the presence of *given* distortions in general equilibrium, and I drew on three such distortions of interest: the Lewis-type factor market distortion, the foreign distortion represented by unexploited monopoly power in trade, and the foreign distortion constituted by a tariff in a small economy.

But distortions can themselves be endogenous to the policy or parametric change being considered. Those familiar with the theory of distortions and commercial policy will recall that a production distortion resulting from monopoly in production is

[5] For a detailed empirically-based analysis of these issues, see Bhagwati (1978, Ch. 8).

not invariant to commercial policy: the introduction of free trade by a small country eliminates the distortion by destroying the domestic monopoly. Hence free trade continues to be the optimal policy in this case, whereas a production distortion resulting alternatively from an externality which is invariant to commercial policy requires a production tax-cum-subsidy to achieve optimality! We do not have to go far to find analyses of the welfare impact of foreign investment that reflect analogously its effect on the distortions existing in the recipient economy.

An apt illustration of such a distortion-changing analysis of foreign investment is readily built on the empirical observation that foreign firms typically tend to become islands of high wages which then tend to spread to local firms in a leapfrogging process. The consequences of the influx of foreign firms can then be analysed, where this wage-augmenting effect operates, in terms of the sticky-wage model of the Harris–Todaro (1970) type wherein the inflow both adds to the availability of capital in the modern sector and raises the sticky wage with in it. The effect of the influx of capital in such a sticky-wage model would generally lead to an inequality between private and social marginal products in any event because the sticky wage is evidently distortionary: the outcome is however influenced also by the fact that the level of the sticky wage is itself endogenous to the inflow of capital. The divergence between private and social marginal products arises simply because the model will generally yield a solution characterized by unemployment in the modern sector, so that the influx of capital, with the added wage raising effect in the modern sector, may well reduce welfare below the pre-inflow level.[6] This possibility, which can be readily demonstrated, is evidently of relevance to policies of host governments that often impose on foreign firms, on grounds of equity and indigenization, the obligation to pay to nationals the high salaries that foreigners earn in similar jobs: such policies may well be a source of welfare loss as modelled above.

On the other hand, the impact of the foreign firms may well be benign in influencing domestic distortions: as when unduly low

[6] A formal, general-equilibrium analysis of brain drain along similar lines is deployed by Bhagwati and Hamada (1974).

salaries set by governmental fiat may be pulled up to desirable levels as a result of the stress arising from the entry of foreign firms with higher salary levels.

(d) Two Distortion-Related Arguments in Developmental Policy

I should like to turn next to an analysis of two distortion-related arguments concerning foreign investment that are standard fare in developmental policy discussions and which, while influential, are somewhat less tractable to formal analysis than the neat arguments developed by me so far. They relate to the impact of foreign investments in the 'grey' areas of entrepreneurship and of domestic and foreign savings.

(i) *Entrepreneurship*

Among the more persistent worries relating to foreign investment has been the fear that its entry would deter the domestic growth of entrepreneurship. For those who consider the growth of such entrepreneurship to be the key to sustained development, the deterrent effect could be a serious source of inequality between the private and social marginal products of foreign investment.

There is no systematic analytical work, to my knowledge, that establishes this deterrent effect, though its existence cannot be ruled out. It stands, of course, in contrast to the generally favourable effect on efficiency that the presence of competitive firms is supposed to have in more traditional arguments.

The remedies suggested or practised to minimize this deterrent effect have been diverse. They include the celebrated but unimplemented Hirschman (1969) suggestion that a special institution be set up to buy up foreign firms at fair prices at future dates so that foreign investment in certain sectors, when introduced owing to necessity, would self-destruct on schedule. The policy of forced joint ventures, such that foreign firms must seek local equity participation, is yet another, rather common policy. However, if the domestic environment is protective and conducive to the creation of a rentier rather than a Schumpeterian situation, then the result is going to be the sharing of the rents between local groups and the foreign firms, and the creation of a rentier rather than a genuine entrepreneurial class.

It is worth remarking that these entrepreneurial concerns do suggest selective restriction of foreign investment rather than generalized restriction of the kind I will presently discuss. Moreover, mention needs to be made of the role of capital market imperfections in the general area. Thus, one of the important arguments produced in favour of selective restriction is that often local firms in the poor countries, owing to inadequate access to short-term liquidity, may be taken over by foreign firms for a pittance – the foreign firms being able to do this because they have much better access to funds – and therefore the government ought to prevent such takeovers (Kindleberger 1973). This contention implicitly assumes of course that competition among foreign firms will not impute the correct social valuation to the local firms being taken over *and* that the local government will be able to identify such a situation with reasonable accuracy.

A related argument for selective control over foreign investment, based rather on imperfections arising from governmental policy, is that if *QR*s, licensing, and other such barriers to competition create rents in specific activities, foreign investment should be barred from such activities as its *PMP* will exceed its *SMP*, *ceteris paribus*, by the amount of the rents.

(ii) *Savings: Domestic and Foreign*

Yet another source of distortion in the host economy may follow from the induced impact of the foreign inflow on domestic savings and on *other* foreign inflows.

A clearly distortionary situation can, for example, be identified if MNCs are a lobby against foreign aid and hence reduce the free resources available to the economy. On the other hand, as always with such arguments, we must also reckon with the reverse, more agreeable distortion: i.e. once MNCs are *in* the country, they often champion the local causes, including the aid-seeking efforts of their host countries.

The adverse impact on domestic savings from foreign capital inflows is statistically well established in innumerable works.[7] But

[7] These have been reviewed extensively in Bhagwati (1978, ch. 6).

the evidence remains essentially anchored on simple regressions, with minor exceptions, and alternative formulations of this substitution hypothesis (e.g. that the adverse effect would be expected to register itself in the public sector, rather than overall savings, as in Bhagwati and Srinivasan (1977, pp. 234–5) are not exactly supportive of the hypothesis.

The contention that such an adverse effect on domestic savings, if any, necessitates restriction of such foreign capital inflows, however, presupposes that this adjustment in the domestic savings effort is not a Fisherian response to augmented resources and that we are dealing with an inherently distorted situation with a suboptimal savings decision process.

(e) Arguments Involving Inapplicability of Social Utility Function

There are also influential arguments, often raised against the free inflow (or outflow) of foreign capital, which essentially involve the inapplicability of analysis based on a well-defined social utility function. I will deal with two major types of argumentation here: (1) taste formation and income distribution; and (2) political objectives.

(i) *Taste Formation and Income Distribution*

An important argument advanced against MNCs has been the contention in Latin American circles that the post-war MNCs in these countries have been responsible for 'distorting' domestic tastes in favour of élitist consumption, shifting resource allocation to industries providing such consumption, and producing a distorted development that is income-distributionally undesirable.

Fundamentally, this objection to MNCs departs from the distortionary arguments predicated on a social utility function in raising the issue of changing values in a fashion that is considered to be undesirable. At the same time, I think that it confuses cause with effect. The highly unequal income distribution predates the arrival of modern MNCs; the tastes for modern goods are formed as these new goods arrive on the DC stage and spread through the world economy, *quite independently* of local investment by the MNCs;

and it is because these goods were imported, thanks to such income distribution and taste formation, that the process of import substitution inevitably implied the induced entry of MNCs to produce these goods. The local presence of MNCs is therefore a consequence, *not* a cause, of the unequal income distributional structures and the diffusion of consumption pattern from the DC to LDC élites.

That the foreign élites and the local élites *then* transit to a symbiotic relationship that reinforces such taste distortion and constrains the policy options towards the support of undesirable political and economic policies is a different issue: but it is also an issue that dominates the thinking of many intellectuals concerned with MNCs. While the argument just analysed interweaves the issue of taste formation with the issue of income distribution, the effect of foreign investment per se on either has also been raised in the policy literature.

MNCs have been criticized, for instance, for influencing tastes of consumers in products, and of producers in technological choice, in 'undesirable' directions. In regard to consumer taste in products, one needs to distinguish between arguments that are built on the intransitive notion that my tastes are better than yours and those that reflect *disexternalities* from specific new products. That tastes do get conditioned to *some* degree by producers of differentiated products in a dynamic, capitalist economy is evident, though the Galbraithian vulgarization that they are entirely so determined will impress only the illiterate. But I can see no philosophically convincing way of resolving disputes based on conflicting assertions of desirable tastes. The fact does remain that, for economies emerging from the Ricardian world of basic needs, perhaps the important economico–philosophical problem *is* one that we economists cannot resolve: whether to let tastes, and therefore consumption and availabilities, develop in response to market forces or whether any intervention in this process can be justified on deeper grounds than those based on the evident belief that a particular lifestyle is so fetching that it must be forced on others who are unable to see its advantages.

The argument about disexternalities from new products is, however more tractable though, in practice, extremely difficult to assess. A classic example is provided by the widespread condemnation of Nestlé for propagating formula food for babies in the less developed countries (LDCs): the charge being that this had bamboozled mothers into giving up nutritious breastfeeding and resulting in malnutrition, additionally because LDC mothers often failed to use boiled water and sterilized utensils for formula preparation. If the few empirical studies on these issues were not extremely tenuous, while also being conceptually confused, the argument against Nestlé would appear decisive. This is however not the case. For example, how do we reckon with a mother — and of these there are many, if not most — who uses formula during the day so that she can go out to work rather than be confined to the home to breastfeed her child? How do we assess the externality of such 'freeing' of the women for greater participation in economic life against the alleged disexternality of malnutrition? Thus, even with the question of externalities from the introduction of new products for old needs, the contentions can rapidly descend into the grey region where the dictates of individual prejudices and preferences are to be pitted against those of his opponents.

As for income distributional implications, perhaps the politically most potent criticism of MNCs has come from the *outflow* end, with DC trade unions charging that MNCs were transferring jobs abroad and/or worsening labour's share in national income.

These concerns of trade unions can be formalized in models that build in distortionary sticky wages associated with unemployment; and the effects of international capital mobility can be readily grafted onto a traditional trade-theoretic model with sticky wages as in Brecher (1974a, 1974b) and Lefeber (1971). This type of model would create a wedge between *SMP* and *PMP*, thanks to the sticky wage distortion, quite regardless of income distributional issues, of course.

Alternatively, we could choose to work with a non-distortionary, flexible-wage, full-employment model of the standard trade-theoretic variety, in which case the effects on factor shares follow from the effects of the capital flows on resource allocation and hence on factor rewards. The simulations by Thurow (1976) of the effects of capital outflow on US labour incomes, built on a one-product economy, are only the simplest version of the kind of analysis that opens up in this area; whereas the familiar Stolper–Samuelson analysis of the income distributional impact of alternative trade policies can be obviously extended to the analysis of income distributional implications of alternative levels of capital in the economy, as in Thurow and White (1976).[8]

(ii) *Political Objectives*

Next, there are numerous arguments that are really based on the introduction of 'non-economic' objectives into the social utility function. Thus, the total volume of foreign investment inflows is often sought to be restrained so as to avoid 'dependence'. Similarly, foreign investment in specific sectors is occasionally ruled out or regulated because they are considered politically 'sensitive' and hence in the exclusive domain of domestic financing and control. The activities of MNCs in local politics, ranging from the financing of politicians or parties favourable to their interests to encouraging and fomenting foreign subversion à la ITT in Chile to the virtual military involvement of the Union Meuniere in Katanga, are all possibilities which cannot be taken lightly, and suggest that the host country concerns with the domestic consequences of foreign firms are not exactly the results of a deranged imagination.

But there are also arguments that reduce in essence to a simple divergence between *PMP* and *SMP* because of political factors leading to economic externalities. A good illustration is provided by the exercise of political muscle by the US on its MNCs to implement economic embargoes against Cuba and Vietnam. This led to Canadian subsidiaries of US MNCs also being subjected to this arbitrary restriction of Canadian trading opportunities purely in US, rather than Canadian, interests.

III. Optimal Policy Intervention

Having indicated the nature of these arguments concerning the welfare impact of capital inflow, let me now turn to the problem

[8] For a dynamic analysis of the income distributional consequences of capital inflow combined with influx of capital-intensive technology, see Bardhan and Lapan (1973).

of optimal policy intervention: the second of the two welfare-theoretic questions that I distinguished at the outset.

I will briefly advance three formal arguments, straying back now to the formal models where my comparative advantage lies.

(1) For a one-product economy, as portrayed in Fig. 16.1, assume that capital flows in at a fixed rental: i.e. *QR* in Fig. 16.1 is the supply curve of foreign capital. It is also then the marginal cost curve for foreign capital and the free trade inflow *OT* is evidently optimal. No intervention is necessary.

(2) Where, however, the foreign supply of capital is subject to a rising cost, it is plain that the host country will profit from restricting the inflow. In Fig. 16.5, unrestricted inflow, given the rising supply price of foreign capital, will overshoot to *OT* whereas the optimal level of inflow is *OS*, given by the intersection of the

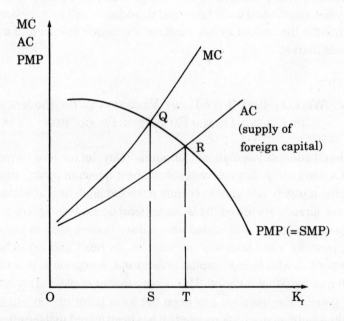

FIG. 16.5: This variation on Fig. 16.1 draws in the supply curve of foreign capital *(AC)* and the marginal curve to it *(MC)*. Free inflow of capital will imply inflow of *OT* capital. Optimal inflow however is *OS* where the marginal cost of capital and its *PMP* (= *SMP*) are equal. *ST* is the amount of restriction required: by a suitable tax on capital inflow that takes the tax-inclusive *AC* curve through *Q*.

marginal product and the marginal cost curves at Q. Optimal restriction then requires that the inflow be reduced by amount ST by imposing a tax that takes the tax-inclusive average curve through Q.

(3) Kemp (1966) and Jones (1967), in two classic articles, have generalized this analysis to the 2×2 model where capital mobility cannot be interfered with without also influencing the goods market. Their analysis thus integrates two diametrically opposed problems: the levy of an optimal goods tariff when factors do not move and the levy of an optimal factor tax-cum-subsidy when the traded goods aspect does not obtain (as in a one-product model). As you would expect, either from Tinbergen (1952) and Meade (1951), or from the theory of distortions and commercial policy à la Bhagwati and Ramaswami (1963) and Johnson (1965), the Jones–Kemp analysis shows that generally two policy instruments — capital and trade taxes and subsidies — will be necessary to handle the impact in two markets: the factor market and the goods market.

IV. Welfare Impact on Tariff Variation in the Presence of Foreign-Owned Factors of Production

Before I address international labour mobility, let me now turn to yet a different, policy-relevant second-best question arising from capital mobility which has recently attracted analytical attention. I have already reviewed the welfare-theoretic analysis where foreign capital inflow was varied with a distortionary tariff in place. Suppose we now turn this question on its head and ask what happens if, with foreign capital present in the economy, it is the external *tariff* that is varied. This is not a matter of playing analytical games: the question has been the focal point of concern in Latin American discussions where it has been feared that the effect of regional trade liberalization, as with the now defunct Andean Common Market, would be to benefit multinationals and to leave the member countries with little gain and possibly even a welfare loss.

This novel and important problem lends itself to analysis fairly readily and it is easy to show (Bhagwati and Tironi 1978) that trade liberalization may be welfare-worsening in the presence of foreign-owned factors in the economy even though it would be welfare-improving in their absence. This can be demonstrated with a simple example. Thus, take the case of a small economy with none of the customary distortions. For such an economy, with all factors domestically-owned, free trade is the optimal policy and *any* tariff reduction is welfare-improving. However, assume now that, in a 2×2 model, all capital is foreign-owned and all labour domestically-owned. Let Y be the importable good and X the exportable good, the former being labour-intensive and the latter capital-intensive. To avoid tariff revenue problems, let me then compare free trade with autarky in such an economy. Clearly then, starting from autarky, the move to free trade will reduce the relative price of the labour-intensive importable good Y and hence result in a decline in the real wage of labour and a rise in the real rental of capital. Since labour is in fixed supply, it is clear that it is unambiguously hurt, and, since all capital is foreign-owned, this is tantamount to net welfare for the country having declined.

This paradoxical demonstration of immiserization following a tariff reduction builds on the simplifying assumptions of absence of tariff revenue and the exclusive identification of each factor as either foreign owned or nationally owned. These simplifications can of course be readily relaxed.

Thus the analysis of tariff change has been extended to incorporate the more general case where each factor set embraces both foreign-owned and national factors of production (Bhagwati and Brecher 1978). Moreover, as regards tariff revenue effects, note that what evidently underlies the paradox is the redistribution of income towards foreign factors that occurs with the relative goods price change that follows upon the tariff change.[9] It follows therefore that the paradox may arise equally from the redistributive effect operating via tariff revenue distribution.

This is neatly demonstrated by Bhagwati and Tironi (1978) in their analysis of a trade diverting customs union in the Viner–

---

[9] See, however, Bhagwati and Brecher (1978) where it is noted that a *differential trade pattern* between the national and the foreign-owned factors is essential if such redistribution is to result in immiserization of the national factors.

Lipsey model of complete domestic specialization on the production of the exportable, which therefore altogether rules out any redistributive effect from production change. This model clearly has a tariff revenue effect since the tariff revenue is lost as imports are switched from the non-union country before the union to the partner country after the union. If the tariff revenue was entirely distributed by the government to domestic labour, and capital is wholly foreign, we then can get a redistributive effect *against* domestic factors. Thus, even a 'large' consumption gain and 'small' terms of trade loss may be compatible with welfare loss if this 'redistributive' effect from the tariff revenue is large enough in a pure trade diverting union. And if we were to assume that some or all revenue goes to foreign factors, then clearly a trade diverting union, with no substitution in consumption and hence no consumption gain, may still result in improved welfare because of the 'redistributive' effect related to the tariff revenue: creating another paradox vis-à-vis the traditional conclusion that a trade diverting union, in the absence of a consumption gain, must necessarily be harmful!

Fig. 16.6 illustrates the case where such improvement in welfare takes place in a pure trade diverting union with zero consumption gain. Assume there that consumption takes place in the fixed proportion along the ray $OC_1C_2C_3$. Let Q be the endowment of Y-goods, with these being divided between foreign capital and domestic labour in the ratio QQ_L/Q_LO. Prior to the customs union, trade takes place from Q to C_3 at the non-union country's foreign price ratio QM and the domestic price ratio is RS. The tariff revenue generated is QR and is redistributed to foreign capital. The tariff revenue inclusive of income of *foreign capital* is therefore Q_LR (QQ_L of earnings plus QR of revenue), while the income of *labour* is Q_LO. With consumption of each factor group lying along the same ray $OC_1C_2C_3$, the pre-union consumption point for labour is C_1 on its budget line Q_LS_L, while the difference between C_3 and C_1 constitutes the bundle consumed by foreign capital. The union then eliminates trade with the outside country and diverts it to the partner country at its price line Q_LS_L'. Since Q_LS_L' is steeper than QM, the country's terms of trade have deteriorated: as necessary for a trade diverting union. However,

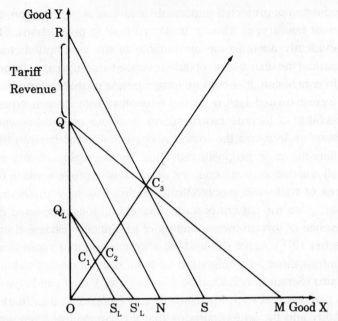

FIG. 16.6: This illustrates a welfare-improving trade diverting union in the Viner–Lipsey model. The gain arises entirely through the 'redistribution effect', related to tariff revenue redistribution, arising in the presence of foreign-owned factors of production in the economy. All labour is assumed domestic and all capital is foreign-owned. Tariff revenue is redistributed to capital. QM is pre-union terms of trade and $Q_L S_L'$ the after-union terms of trade. Before union, labour share of income is OQ_L since tariff revenue QR accrues entirely to capital. $Q_L S_L'$ dominates $Q_L S_L$. Consumption is along $OC_1 C_2 C_3$, with fixed coefficients, so that consumption gain cannot arise. The gain to labour, and hence improvement in national welfare, follows *despite* the deterioration in terms of trade following on the trade-diverting shift to partner-country imports and without any consumption gain.

the loss and more is absorbed by foreign capital; and domestic labour improves its welfare because its new budget line is $Q_L S_L'$ and therefore, the shift from C_1 to C_2 implies a corresponding *improvement* in national welfare. The trade diverting union has therefore clearly been beneficial even though there is no consumption gain (nor production gain, i.e. decline in domestic production of protected importable in favour of imports from the partner country, or Viner's 'trade creation' in production). This is evidently an outcome attributable to the assumption made regarding the distribution of tariff revenue to foreign capital alone.

In conclusion, it should no longer puzzle us that the presence of foreign-owned factors in the economy, with its consequent possibility of income redistribution in favour of foreign-owned factors, undermines the logical necessity of a number of other welfare-theoretic propositions. Thus, for example, while for a small non-distortionary country, exogenous improvements in the terms of trade will monotonically improve welfare under free trade, given the pattern of trade, this will no longer be so in the presence of foreign-owned factors of production (Bhagwati and Brecher 1978). Again, the traditional conclusion that a transferee country cannot be immiserized by the transfer if market stability obtains (Samuelson 1952, 1954; Mundell 1960) must yield now to the paradox that such immiserization is compatible with market stability and the added paradox that it is compatible even with the transferee country's terms of trade improving (Brecher and Bhagwati 1979).

V. INTERNATIONAL LABOUR MOBILITY

Finally, let me turn to a consideration of international labour mobility. This introduces in the analysis certain asymmetries vis-à-vis the analysis of international capital mobility. At the same time, it enables us to consider analytical problems that arise from the simultaneous presence of *both* capital and labour mobility across countries. I will address each of these aspects, in turn.

(a) Asymmetries

Labour mobility across countries has indeed many parallels to capital mobility. Thus, the fundamental proposition that a small capital inflow in an economy without distortions will not harm or help the host country resurrects itself in the well-known argument in the theory of the brain drain that a limited degree of emigration will not harm or help those left behind because the emigrant will have been earning his social marginal product and therefore his departure will reduce his contribution to national product and his own earned share in it by identical amounts.

The rather elementary, though not unimportant, asymmetries arise of course in so far as some of the distortions that are relevant to the analysis of international labour mobility are likely to be different from those pertinent to questions of international capital mobility. Thus, for example, an important argument in the brain drain literature relates to how the wage earned by the emigrant may be less than his *PMP* (= *SMP*) because of monopsonistic hiring: as with doctors in the UK under socialized medicine, so that the emigration prima facie imposes a loss on those left behind. Evidently this argument has no plausible relevance to capital flows.[10]

But the more fundamental asymmetries arise from the fact that the migration raises the question, as I noted earlier in my introductory marks, regarding the appropriate manner in which we are to consider national welfare, i.e. how the migrants are to be treated in considering national advantage.

Let me illustrate the differences between international capital mobility and labour mobility that arise from this fundamental question by borrowing from Koichi Hamada (1977) a brilliant argument based on the familiar analysis of factor flows in a single-product model. Take Fig. 16.7, which portrays a factor flow occurring from an LDC to a DC, the world endowment of the factor being O_1O_2 and the marginal product schedule of the factor for the DC being measured from O_1 and that for the LDC from O_2. Assume away all distortions so that one can legitimately concentrate on gains and losses within the framework of Fig. 16.7.

Let O_1A and AO_2 then be the national endowments of the factor in the DC and the LDC, respectively, *before* migration. Assume now that the factor in question is labour. When migration is allowed, an amount, AB, of labour will migrate from the LDC to the DC. Therefore, the domestic product of the LDC will reduce by the area $QRAB$, and the income received by those left behind will diminish by the area of the triangle QRT, reflecting the 'large' flow

---

[10] The only weak parallel is provided by the possibility of artificially low interest rates maintained for lending by governments.

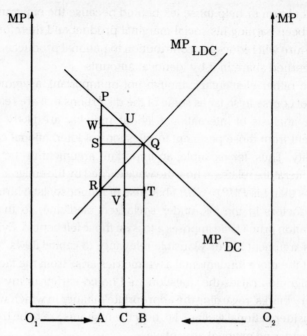

FIG. 16.7: Q_1Q_2 is the world supply of the factor. LDC and DC marginal product schedules are sketched. O_1A and O_2A are the initial endowments for the DC and LDC respectively. Introduction of migration leads to outmigration from the LDC of AB.

For Capital:	Total Gain	=	PRQ
	LDC Gain	=	SRQ
	DC Gain	=	PSQ
For Labour:	Total Gain	=	PRQ
	Emigrants' Gain	=	$SRTQ$
	LDC (excluding emigrants) Loss	=	RTQ
	DC (excluding immigrants) Gain	=	PSQ

effect which I already discussed in relation to capital mobility. The domestic product of the DC will increase by $PABQ$, and the income received by those originally living in the DC will increase by PSQ. The gain obtained by the emigrants themselves is clearly equal to $SRTQ$.

Now, if we were instead considering capital on the horizontal axis, then the welfare gain due to the movement of capital, amounting to the triangle *PQR*, would be distributed to the two countries in amounts *PSQ* and *SRQ*. Thus *both* countries gain by the free movement of capital. On the other hand, in the case of labour migration, not only is this total gain *PQR* distributed to the pre-migration population of the DC and the migrants who constitute the new residents there, but there is actually a *loss* of an amount equal to the area *QRT* suffered by the non-migrants in the LDC.

Thus we have an asymmetry between the case of foreign capital outflow and that of labour emigration, arising obviously from the fact that the income earned on capital invested abroad is part of national income while we are assuming here that the migrant labour, and its income, falls outside the definition of LDC income. In brief, the total world gain *PRQ* decomposes into an LDC gain of *SRQ* and DC gain of *PSQ* in the case of capital outflow and into emigrants' gain of *SRTQ*, an LDC (net of emigrants) *loss* of *RTQ* and a DC (net of immigrants) gain of *PSQ* for the case of labour outflow.

On the other hand, this asymmetry would disappear if the migrants were to be treated as part of the population over which national welfare was defined, though we could still be left with unavoidable income-distributional issues since the migrants benefit and the non-migrants lose.

I might add that this income distributional implication of out-migration of labour, when present, provides a rationale for proposals to extend the domestic tax jurisdiction to incomes earned abroad by nationals. Quite simply, on grounds of the familiar compensation principle alone, a policy of free outmigration of labour would need in these circumstances to be accompanied by a policy that taxes the welfare-improving migrants to compensate those left behind. Of course, this argument for taxing the migrants presupposes that the non-migrants in the country of emigration suffer a loss, as built into the model of Fig. 16.7. However, a number of alternative rationales have been provided for such taxation: e.g. that the migrants, especially the highly skilled, enjoy windfall gains due to severe immigration restrictions and hence these rents should be taxed for spending on socially agreeable purposes; and that equity demands that nationals who work abroad should not altogether escape the domestic tax net, i.e. that the US practice of taxing its citizens no matter where they reside, under Internal Revenue Code Section 911 ought to be adopted since there should be no 'representation without taxation'.[11]

(b) Optimal Choice Between Capital and Labour Mobility

In conclusion, let me turn to the problem that Ramaswami had addressed nearly two decades ago and which, as I remarked earlier, has become pertinent today. The problem is best illustrated with regard to the migration of labour to the United States. As is widely known, the US has an enormous inflow of illegal migrants who come in principally from Latin America and, in particular from Mexico. The immigration barriers have not been successful in stemming this inflow which is variously estimated as having led to a stock of close to 10 million illegal immigrants. In response to this inflow, and as a result of the growing and effective trade union pressures, the Carter administration had to take cognizance of the problem in its social, legal, and economic dimensions. In this context, it has occasionally been suggested that the US ought to encourage the flow of funds, both private and public, in order to create greater prosperity in Mexico in order to reduce the economic disparities that fuel the illegal exodus.

With regard to the deployment of public funds, in the form of foreign assistance, towards this end, it is of course possible to think of this as a bribe to the countries of illegal emigration to use *their* control machinery more effectively to stem the flood. For, democracies such as the United States, with their strong civil-libertarian and liberal lobbies, are not in a position to start shooting happily at the illegal migrants and the effectiveness of controls on migration may be enhanced from the emigration end by offering suitable incentives to these countries of emigration. But, even if this is true, the fact remains that the principal motivation behind such a policy remains the creation of more job

[11] For a comprehensive statement of these rationales, and the economic and ethical arguments involved, see Bhagwati (1979) and the earlier studies of Bhagwati and Partington (1976).

opportunities and improved standards of living in the poorer countries of emigration.

This however immediately suggests a related and interesting question. Suppose that we have a capital-rich country, the United States, and a capital-poor country, Mexico. Assume that the United States can unilaterally decide on two alternative courses of action, *both* assumed to be feasible: i.e. it allows its capital to migrate to Mexico, while *effectively* closing the border to immigration; or, *alternatively*, that it prohibits *capital* outflow but permits immigration of Mexican labour. If then the United States can *also* choose optimal taxes and subsidies on such factor flows, so that we wind up comparing *optimal* ways of choosing between the two forms of mobility, which would be to greater national advantage?

As it happens, this is precisely the analytical problem to which Ramaswami (1968) provided a neat solution in a one-sector model. Starting from a position where the United States has no prohibitions, it is evident that if capital mobility is considered, the United States will maximize its welfare by imposing an optimal tax on capital outflow, for diminishing returns abroad to the capital inflow creates a divergence between average and marginal return to United States capital abroad, and since the market equates only the average rental abroad to domestic rental, laissez-faire leads to excessive investment in Mexico. Ramaswami then showed very neatly that the United States would do yet better if it permitted immigration of Mexican labour instead, while levying an optimal tax on its earnings. Thus, consider the notional argument that the United States, having invested optimally abroad, withdraws its capital and permits immigration of the Mexican workers who are using United States capital in Mexico. As the per capita capital stock in Mexico is left unchanged by this notional withdrawal, the Mexican immigrants need only be paid the wage they received hitherto; and if they continued to work with the same amount of capital per head as was previously employed in Mexico, the United States population is no better or worse off. However, this situation implies two unequal sets of capital–labour ratios in the United States, and evidently the adoption of a *uniform* capital–labour ratio for all production will improve income and enable the United States to increase welfare if it taxes the earnings of immigrants so as to keep their net wages constant at the Mexican level and distributes the tax proceeds to the United States population. Thus, *some* tax rate on immigrant earnings obviously exists that secures higher welfare for the United States than would be achieved under the alternative policy of optimal restriction of foreign investment.

An elegant way of understanding this outcome is to see that it implies that optimal taxation of the import of the scare factor is preferable to optimal restriction of the export of the abundant factor. In either case, of course, the optimal restriction ensures equality of the foreign marginal cost or return from the country's viewpoint with the domestic return or cost. When a country exports its abundant factor, however, it ends up using that factor more intensively abroad than at home; and import of the scarce factor eliminates the loss on that account.

It is easy to imagine interesting extensions of this strand of argumentation. Evidently, the 2×2 Jones–Kemp analysis of the optimal combination of taxes and subsidies on trade and capital mobility could be extended to gain insight into the conditions under which a capital-rich country may find it profitable to permit the mobility of one factor rather than another. That this and other extensions will follow is beyond doubt, and they will constitute yet fresh evidence of the originality and strength of Ramaswami's theoretical contributions to international economics.

REFERENCES

Bardhan, Pranab, 1970: *Economic Growth, Development and Foreign Trade* (USA: John Wiley and Sons).

Bardhan, Pranab and Harvey Lapan, 1973: 'Localized Technical Progress and Transfer of Technology and Economic Development', *Journal of Economic Theory* (Dec.).

Bhagwati, Jagdish, 1958: 'Immiserizing Growth: A Geometrical Note', *Review of Economic Studies* (June).

——, 1971: 'The Generalized Theory of Distortions and Welfare', *in* J. Bhagwati et al. (eds), *Trade Balance of Payments and Growth*, Kindleberger Festschrift (Amsterdam: North–Holland).

Bhagwati, Jagdish, 1973: 'The Theory of Immiserizing Growth: Further Applications', *in* M. Connolly and A. Swoboda (eds), *International Trade and Money* (London: George Allen and Unwin).

—— (ed.), 1976: *The Brain Drain and Taxation: Theory and Empirical Analysis* (Amsterdam: North–Holland).

——, 1976: 'The Developing Countries', in *A Symposium in the World Economy* in *The Great Ideas Today* (Chicago: Encyclopaedia Britannica, Inc.).

—— (ed.), 1977: *The New International Economic Order: The North-South Debate* (Cambridge, Massachusetts: MIT Press).

——, 1978: *The Anatomy and Consequences of Exchange Control Regimes*, N.B.E.R. (Cambridge, Massachusetts: Ballinger Co.).

——, 1978: 'International Migration of the Highly Skilled: Economics, Ethics and Tax Arrangements', *Third World Quarterly* (June).

Bhagwati, Jagdish and V.K. Ramaswami, 1963: 'Domestic Distortions, Tariffs and the Theory of Optimum Subsidy', *Journal of Political Economy* (Feb.).

Bhagwati Jagdish, Ronald Jones, Robert Mundell and Jaroslav Vanek (eds), 1971: *Trade, Balance of Payments and Growth* (Amsterdam: North–Holland).

Bhagwati, Jagdish and Koichi Hamada, 1974: 'The Brain Drain, International Integration of Markets for Professionals and Unemployment', *Journal of Development Economics*, vol. 1(1).

Bhagwati, Jagdish and Carlos Rodriguez, 1975: 'Welfare–Theoretical Analyses of the Brain Drain', *Journal of Development Economics*, vol. 2(3).

Bhagwati, Jagdish and Martin Partington (eds), 1976: *Taxing the Brain Drain: A Proposal* (Amsterdam: North–Holland).

Bhagwati, Jagdish and T.N. Srinivasan, 1977: *Foreign Trade Regimes and Economic Development: India*, N.B.E.R. (Cambridge, Massachusetts: Ballinger Co.).

Bhagwati, Jagdish and Ernesto Tironi, 1980: 'Tariff Change, Foreign Capital and Immiserization: A Theoretical Analysis', *Journal of Development Economics*, vol. 7, pp. 71–83.

Bhagwati, Jagdish and Richard Brecher, 1978: 'National Welfare in an Open Economy in the Presence of Foreign-Owned Factors of Production', *MIT Working Paper No. 224* (Oct.).

Brecher, Richard, 1974a: 'Minimum Wage Rates and the Pure Theory of International Trade', *Quarterly Journal of Economics* (Feb.).

Brecher, Richard, 1974b: 'Optimum Commercial Policy for a Minimum Wage Economy', *Journal of International Economics* (May).

Brecher, Richard and Carlos Diaz Alejandro, 1977: 'Tariffs, Foreign Capital and Immiserizing Growth', *Journal of International Economics* (Nov.).

Brecher, Richard and Jagdish Bhagwati, 1979: 'Foreign Ownership and the Theory of Trade and Welfare', MIT, mimeo., March; and *Carleton Economic Papers*.

Hamada, Koichi, 1966: 'Economic Growth and Long-Term Capital Movements', *Yale Economic Essays*, vol. 6, Spring.

——, 1974: 'An Economic Analysis of the Duty Free Zone', *Journal of International Economics* (Nov.).

——, 1977: 'Taxing the Brain Drain: A Global Point of View', *in* Bhagwati (ed.), *The New International Economic Order* (Cambridge, Massachusetts: MIT Press).

Harris, John and Michael Todaro, 1970: 'Migration, Unemployment and Development: A Two-Sector Analysis', *American Economic Review* (March).

Hirschman, Albert, 1969: *How to Divest in Latin America and Why*, Princeton Essays in International Finance, no. 76 (Nov.).

Jasay, Anthony, 1960: 'The Choice Between Home and Foreign Investment', *Economic Journal* (March).

Johnson, Harry, 1955: 'Economic Expansion and International Trade', *Manchester School* (May).

——, 1965: 'Optimal Trade Intervention in the Presence of Domestic Distortions', *in* R.E. Caves et al. (eds), *Trade, Growth and the Balance of Payments* (New York: Rand–McNally).

——, 1967: 'The Possibility of Income Losses from Increased Efficiency or Factor Accumulation in the Presence of Tariffs', *Economic Journal* (March).

Jones, R.W., 1967: 'International Capital Movements and the Theory of Tariffs and Trade', *Quarterly Journal of Economics* (Feb.).

Kemp, Murray, 1966: 'The Gain from International Trade and Investment: A Neo-Heckscher–Ohlin Approach', *American Economic Review* (Sept.).

Kindleberger, Charles, 1973: 'Restrictions on Direct Foreign Investment in LDCs', *in* J. Bhagwati and R.S. Eckaus (eds), *Development and Planning* (Cambridge, Massachusetts: MIT Press).

Lefeber, Louis, 1971: 'Trade and Minimum Wage Rates', *in* Bhagwati et al. (eds), *Trade, Balance of Payments and Growth* (Amsterdam: North–Holland).

W. Arthur, Lewis, 1954: 'Economic Development with Unlimited Supplies of Labour', *Manchester School*, vol. 22, pp. 139–91.

MacDougall, G. Donald A., 1960: 'The Benefits and Costs of Private Investment from Abroad: A Theoretical Approach', *Economic Record*, vol. 36, pp. 13–35.

Meade, James, 1951: *The Balance of Payments* (London: Oxford University Press, R.I.I.A.).

Minabe, Noburo, 1974: 'Capital and Technology Movements and Economic Welfare', *American Economic Review* (Dec.).

Mundell, Robert, 1957: 'International Trade and Factor Mobility', *American Economic Review*, vol. 47, pp. 321–35.

——, 1960: 'The Pure Theory of International Trade', *American Economic Review* (March).

Ramaswami, V.K., 1968: 'International Factor Movements and the National Advantage', *Economica* (Aug.).

——, 1970: 'International Factor Movements and the National Advantage: Reply', *Economica* (Feb.).

——, 1971: *Trade and Development: Essays in Economics*, in J. Bhagwati, H.G. Johnson and T.N. Srinivasan (eds) (London: Allen Unwin).

Ramaswami, V.K. and T.N. Srinivasan, 1971: 'Tariff Structure and Resource Allocation in the Presence of Factor Substitution', *in* Bhagwati et al. (eds), *Trade, Balance of Payments and Growth* (Amsterdam: North–Holland).

Rybczynski, T.N., 1955: 'Factor Endowment and Relative Commodity Prices', *Economica* (Nov.).

Samuelson, Paul, 1952: 'The Transfer Problem and Transport Costs', *Economic Journal* (June).

——, 1954: 'The Transfer Problem and Transport Costs', *Economic Journal* (June).

Stolper, Wolfgang and Paul Samuelson, 1941: 'Protection and Real Wages', *Review of Economic Studies* (Nov.).

Thurow, Lester, 1976: 'International Factor Movements and the American Distribution of Income', *Intermountain Economic Review*, Spring.

Thurow, Lester and Halbert White, 1976: 'Optimum Trade Restrictions and their Consequences', *Econometrica* (July).

Tinbergen, Jan, 1952: *On the Theory of Economic Policy*, Contributions to Economic Analysis Series (Amsterdam: North–Holland).

17

International Factor Mobility: Quid Pro Quo Foreign Investment[*]

THE theory of international trade took off in two major directions in the 1980s. First, while the 1950s through the 1970s had witnessed major developments in the theoretical analysis of *factor* market imperfections, the 1980s were marked by the theoretical exploration of *product* market imperfections. The latter effectively implemented, in the sphere of trade, the agenda that the classic works of Edward Chamberlin and Joan Robinson on monopolistic competition and imperfect competition had more generally set before the profession in the 1930s.

Second, trade theorists participated in pioneering the revolutionary shift in economic theorizing that has brought political processes explicitly into the analysis of economic phenomena and policy. Among the important early theoretical developments were the analysis of directly unproductive profit-seeking (DUP) and rent-seeking activities by Anne O. Krueger (1974), Bhagwati (1982), and a variety of endogenous tariff models.[1]

The political-economy-theoretic reformulation and explanation of the classic questions of international economics continue to grow apace. This is manifest also in the theory of direct foreign investment (DFI), which has recently been refocused so as to include explicitly the fact that the policy framework in the host country can be endogenous to the direct foreign investment in ways that needed to be formally incorporated in the positive and normative analysis of DFI.

In particular, it is possible to identify a novel form of DFI in which it occurs at a loss in period 1 (from the viewpoint of myopic one-period profit maximization), with a view to (endogenously)

---

[*] Written with Dinopoulos, Elias and Kar-yiu Wong.

[1] For an analytical synthesis of the volumous literature, see Bhagwati et al. (1984).

defusing the threat of protection in period 2, therefore maximizing the two-period payoff from the interlinked decisions on trade and investment. In Bhagwati (1985), where this possibility was identified, the phenomenon was christened 'quid pro quo DFI' because the quid pro quo for a DFI incurring a first-period loss is the improvement in the expected second-period payoff from the increased probability of keeping the export market open in period 2.

I. Alternative Possibilities

The classic case of tariff-induced DFI occurs when the tariff (or quota) is exogenously specified and tariff-jumping investment occurs. Quid pro quo DFI, by contrast, occurs as an attempt to reduce the probability of protection being successfully imposed: it is tariff-defusing. How does such defusion of the threat of protection arise?

Casual empiricism readily suggests alternative possibilities. Consider the following economic agents in the home country (Japan) and the host country (United States):

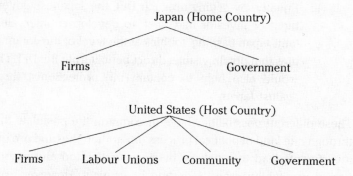

With DFI from Japan into the United States at issue and the threat of protection (say, voluntary export restraints [VERs]) in the United States against Japan in response to Japanese export success a perceived danger, quid pro quo DFI can arise in several ways. Consider for instance the following.

1. The Japanese government may encourage DFI in the United States with a view to buying goodwill from the US government and reducing the probability that it will grant protection

to the lobbies seeking it. This route therefore operates through the 'supply of protection' in the United States.

2. In oligopolistic industries where the quid pro quo in terms of the enhanced probability of maintaining market access will accrue to the firms themselves, the incentive to undertake such quid pro quo DFI obtains at the firm-level itself.

3. Again, in both cases, the quid pro quo may operate, not through affecting the supply of protection in the United States, but through affecting the 'demand for protection' by the economic agents in the United States:

    (i)   The quid pro quo DFI may co-opt the US firms that seek to lobby for protection against Japanese rivals. For example, the Toyota–General Motors joint venture in 1984 was followed by General Motors breaking ranks in 1985 when the rest of the auto industry sought renewal of the VER restraint on Japanese autos.

    (ii) Alternatively, the quid pro quo DFI may coopt the labour unions and weaken their incentive to lobby for protection to 'save jobs'.[2]

    (iii) Equally, by setting up such DFI, the Japanese government or investor may seek to develop countervailing 'anti-Japan-bashing' lobbies at the level of the communities that obtain visible, direct benefit from the DFI. This would also help to contain the protectionist threat against Japan.

These different possibilities have in common the postulate that, through one kind of political process or another, the quid pro quo investments lead to a linkage between first-period and second-period profitability from trade and investment. However, each possibility generates its own model.

From an analytical point of view, the models can be divided into three categories: (i) those that use perfectly competitive market structures and those that use oligopolistic market structures; (ii) those that model the (Japanese) government as the agent deciding on the investment and those that focus on the

---

[2] Given the insider–outsider problem, this type of quid pro quo DFI is likely to arise only when the beneficiaries are members of the same union as those threatened with layoffs due to the protectionist threat.

(Japanese) firm's decision instead; and (iii) those that treat the probability of the (US) government imposing protection as specified exogenously as simply a function of the DFI and those that determine it endogenously from the utility-maximizing behaviour of the lobbying agents (in the United States).

Evidently, the choice of assumptions within each of these three categories can entail compatible choices in others. Thus, if the analyst uses the perfectly competitive model, the agents deciding on the quid pro quo DFI cannot be atomistic firms, which do not behave strategically; however, the protectionist threat could be modelled either exogenously or endogenously.

The existing theoretical analyses of quid pro quo DFI exhibit a considerable diversity of approaches. They not only develop the positive (i.e. explanatory) theory of quid pro quo DFI; they also examine its welfare implications. However, while the focus of the tariff-jumping welfare-theoretic analyses has been on the impact on the host country (since the analysis was motivated by tariff policies in developing countries designed to attract such tariff-jumping investments), the welfare-theoretic analysis of the tariff-defusing quid pro quo models began with the impact on the home country (Bhagwati et al. 1987) and have only subsequently been extended to the impact on the host country (Dinopoulos and Wong 1991).

The formal analysis of quid pro quo DFI was first undertaken by Bhagwati et al. (1987), using the general equilibrium $2 \times 2 \times 2$ model of trade theory. This model had been utilized earlier by Bhagwati and T.N. Srinivasan (1976) to analyse the optimal policy for a country in regard to its current trade if the proposed policy affects the probability of trade restrictions being invoked later by the other country. In a generalization of that analysis. Bhagwati et al. (1987) analysed the optimal policy in regard to trade and DFI abroad if exports and DFI now were *both* to affect the probability of trade restrictions being invoked by the other country later.

Their analysis therefore produced an argument for intervention to encourage quid pro quo capital outflow, while the firm-level outflows were determined entirely by atomistic, myopic firms. The model reflected, though in a deeper way, the presumed encouragement being provided by the Japanese government to firms to invest abroad.

The oligopolistic case in which a firm itself will undertake quid pro quo DFI 'overinvesting' in period 1, so as to maximize two-period profits by defusing the threat of protection, was analysed in Dinopoulos and Bhagwati (1986), and Dinopoulos (1989).[3] Dinopoulos also considered the free-rider problem (as when Toyota undertakes DFI in the US and the quid pro quo benefits accrue equally to Nissan, which does not), showing that the quid pro quo DFI level varies inversely with the number of firms in the investing country.

Despite the key differences noted above, the Bhagwati et al. (1987) analysis and the analyses of Dinopoulos and Bhagwati (1986) and Dinopoulos (1989) shared one critical assumption: the protectionist threat was specified as a function of the first-period, DFI, exogenous to any specific 'lobbying' activity.[4] The view was that the mere act of DFI would serve to reduce the threat by earning goodwill. A grateful community in the area of investment might perhaps provide the political counterweight to protectionism via their Congressmen.

However, the active lobbying is often by firms and labour under the threat of import competition. To model that, it is necessary to 'endogenize' the threat function. Wong (1989a) proceeded to do that by introducing unemployment (assuming a minimum wage) and a labour union that would lobby for protection from imports. Given the fixed wage, for any level of DFI, protection will raise the product price and hence reduce unemployment. The union is then assumed to lobby for the full-employment-generating protection, and the probability of obtaining protection increases with lobbying resources spent. Thus, the expected level of protection becomes a function of lobbying and DFI.[5] As with previous analyses, the host-country government behaviour is not explicitly modelled (this restriction being removed in subsequent analysis

---

[3] Dinopoulos (1989) did not consider optimal policy intervention, but it is evident that the oligopolistic firm-determined quid pro quo investment will not generally be welfare-maximizing for the home or the host country.

[4] Thus, Bhagwati et al. (1987) worked with the probability (of a quota being invoked) function $G = G(E^1, K^1)$, where $G_1 > 0$ and $G_2 < 0$, with E^1 being the period–1 exports and K^1 being the period–1 DFI by the home country.

[5] In a later paper, Laixun Zhao (1991) also endogenizes the wage.

by Dinopoulos (1992), who models bargaining among the foreign firm undertaking the DFI, the home-country union, and the home-country government). It is then easy to see that quid pro quo DFI can arise in this model.

The welfare economics of quid pro quo DFI in Wong's model have been analysed in Dinopoulos and Wong (1991). Following the generalized theory of distortions and policy intervention, and focusing primarily on host country welfare rather than on home country welfare (as in Bhagwati et al. 1987) the authors argue that the fixed-wage distortion can be removed at the source as the first-best policy for the host country (assuming, of course, that there are no other distortions to be remedied). It is then shown that, as a second-best policy, a production subsidy does better than restrictions on DFI inflow or 'counterlobbying' by the host government.

II. THE EVIDENCE FOR QUID PRO QUO DFI

Economic theorizing often proceeds from casual empiricism. The theorizing of the quid pro quo DFI phenomenon is no exception (Bhagwati 1990). There is however some plausible, more-than-anecdotal evidence that the acceleration in Japanese DFI in the US in the early 1980s was due to a mix of 'political' reasons: some partly in anticipation of the imposition of protection, and others partly to defuse its threat. Thus, in a survey of Japanese firms undertaking foreign investment between 1980 and 1986, the ministry of International Trade and Investment (MITI) found that the overwhelming majority of firms cited 'avoiding trade friction' as their principal motivation (Bhagwati 1990; see also Wong 1989b).

Of course, the calculation of the quid pro quo investors may prove to be invalid. Thus, the DFI may create ill will rather than goodwill. In the case of Japanese DFI in the United States, there has been some backlash, and it is now perceived by some as also being a threat. Then again, there have been demands (by Lee Iacocca, for instance) to add the Japanese DFI production to the Japanese exports in enforcing VER limits. If this is done, it would of course tend to frustrate the quid pro quo investors' intention to invest so as to maintain export market access.

III. Other Political–Economy–Theoretic DFI Possibilities

The distinguishing feature of quid pro quo DFI is the economic exploitation of the political linkage between the investment and the formulation of trade policy; but then other such linkages can be found. Thus, in 1981, MITI allocated over 70 per cent of the US VER to Toyota, Nissan and Honda, allocating the rest to Mitsubishi, Mazda, Fuji, Isuzu and Suzuki (H. Shibata 1990). Subsequently, American manufacturers invested in these suppliers (e.g. Ford acquired 24.41 per cent of Mazda's stock, and General Motors acquired 5 per cent of Suzuki's stock. By pressurizing MITI to increase these firms' quotas (i.e. by therefore endogenously determining their quota allocations in Japan), these American manufacturers appear to have made their DFI profitable. James G. Benedict (1992) has therefore proposed that a rent-extracting VER-induced DFI could occur in the VER-restrained country whenever the firms in the VER-imposing country have the clout in the VER-restrained country to lobby for a greater share (of the quota) to be allotted to their partners.

In the future, the theory of DFI will be extended to this and other possibilities, in addition to further developments in the theory of quid pro quo DFI, supplementing the conventional politics-free approaches to the theory of DFI.

References

Benedict, James G., 1992: 'VERs: An Empirical Analysis of Selectivity in International Trade', Ph.D. dissertation, Columbia University.

Bhagwati, Jagdish N., 1982: 'Directly Unproductive Profit-Seeking Activities', *Journal of Political Economy*, Oct., pp. 90, 988–1002.

——, 1985, 1991: 'Investing Abroad', Esmee Fairbain Lecture, University of Lancaster, UK, Nov.; reprinted in Douglas Irwin (ed.), *J.N. Bhagwati: Political Economy and International Trade* (Cambridge, MA: MIT Press), pp. 309–39.

——, 1990: 'The Theory of Political Economy, Economic Policy and Foreign

Investment', *in* M. Scott and D. Lal (eds), *Public Policy and Economic Development* (Oxford: Clarendon), pp. 27–54.

Bhagwati, Jagdish N., Brecher, Richard A., Elias Dinopoulos and T.N. Srinivasan, 1976: 'Optimal Trade Policy and Compensation Under Endogenous Uncertainty: The Phenomenon of Market Disruption', *Journal of International Economics*, Nov., pp. 6, 317–36.

——, 1984: 'DUP Activities and Economic Theory', *in* David Colander (ed.), *Neoclassical Political Economy* (Cambridge: Ballinger), pp. 17–32.

——, 1987: 'Quid Pro Quo Foreign Investment and Welfare: A Political–Economy–Theoretic Model', *Journal of Development Economics*, Oct., pp. 27, 127–38.

Dinopoulos, Elias, 1989: 'Quid Pro Quo Foreign Investment', *Economics and Politics*, 1 (2), pp. 145–60.

——, 1992: 'Quid Pro Quo Foreign Investment and VERs: A Nash Bargaining Approach', *Economics and Politics*, March, 2, pp. 43–60.

Dinopoulos, Elias and Jagdish, N. Bhagwati, 1986: 'Quid Pro Quo Foreign Investment and Market Structure', unpublished manuscript presented at the 61st Annual Western Economic Association International Conference, San Francisco, July.

Dinopoulos, Elias and Kar-yiu Wong, 1991: 'Quid Pro Quo Foreign Investment and Policy Intervention', *in* K.A. Koekkoek and C.B.M. Mennes (eds), *International Trade and Global Development: Essays in Honour of Jagdish Bhagwati* (London: Routledge), pp. 162–90.

Krueger, Anne O., 1974: 'The Political Economy of the Rent-Seeking Society, *American Economic Review*, June, 64, pp. 291–303.

Shibata, H., 1990: Impact of Voluntary Export Control on the Exporter's Economy: A Theory and the Case of the Japanese Automobile Industry, unpublished manuscript presented at the International Political Economy of Export-Restraint Arrangements, Washington, DC, 5–8 June.

Wong, Kar-yiu, 1989a: 'Optimal Threat of Trade Restriction and Quid Pro Quo Foreign Investment', *Economics and Politics*, Nov., 1, pp. 277–300.

——, 1989b: 'The Japanese Challenge: Japanese Direct Investment in the United States', *in* Kozo Yamamura (ed.), *Japanese Investment in the United States: Should We Be Concerned?* (Seattle: Society for Japanese Studies), pp. 63–96.

Zhao, Laixun, 1991: Endogenous Protection and Direct Foreign Investment, unpublished manuscript presented at the Third Annual Southeastern Conference on Economic Theory and International Trade, Nashville.

18

Why are Services
Cheaper in Poor Countries?[*]

I. The Empirical Phenomenon

In their important work on international comparisons of national incomes and of comparative price structure, Kravis, Heston and Summers (1982: 8) have noted that 'services are much cheaper in the relative price structure of a typical poor country than in that of a rich country'.

This phenomenon has now been fairly systematically documented by the data, gathered under their supervision, of the United Nations International Comparison (ICP) which covers 34 countries. Table 18.1 reproduced from their work (1982), and Fig. 18.1 based on rows 3 and 11–13, indeed show this tendency for the relationship between relative service prices and real per capita GDP in this Kravis–Heston–Summers 34-country 6-group sample. The tendency is strongly evident except for the intermediate groups III and IV.

II. The Kravis–Heston–Summers Explanation: International Productivity Differences

An explanation of this phenomenon was provided by Kravis–Heston–Summers as follows:

As a first approximation it may be assumed for purposes of explaining the model that the prices of traded goods, mainly commodities, are the

* Thanks are due to the National Science Foundation for partial support of the research underlying this chapter which was first published in *The Economic Journal*, July 1984. Alan Deardorff, Robert Feenstra, Irving Kravis, Paul Samuelson, Kar-yiu Wong, an anonymous referee and the Editor made useful suggestions.

Table 18.1
Nominal and Real Per Capita Absorption of GDP in the Form of Services and Commodities, and Price Indexes, by Real Per Capita GDP Group, 1975

	Income group					
	I	II	III	IV	V	VI
1. Number of countries	8	6	6	4	9	1
Real GDP per capita (US = 100)						
2. Range	0–14.9	15–29.9	30–44.9	45–59.9	60–89.9	90 and over
3. Mean	9.01	23.1	37.3	52.4	76.0	100.0
Per capita expenditures converted at exchange rate						
4. GDP (US = 100)	3.7	12.1	24.2	38.7	82.3	100.0
5. Commodities (US = 100)	5.0	15.2	31.1	50.6	92.7	100.0
6. Services (US = 100)	2.0	8.1	15.5	23.4	69.1	100.0
7. Share of services	22.2	28.4	27.4	25.6	36.8	43.9
Per capita quantity indexes (based on PPP-conversion of expenditures)						
8. Commodities (US = 100)	8.8	23.4	37.5	53.8	77.4	100.0
9. Services (US = 100)	9.4	22.7	37.0	49.2	73.0	100.0
10. Share of services	33.8	31.7	31.8	30.3	31.2	32.3

Table 18.1 (cont.)

			Income group			
	I	II	III	IV	V	VI
Price indexes (US = 100)						
11. GDP	40.6	51.7	64.7	73.5	107.5	100.0
12. Commodities	57.2	65.9	83.1	94.0	119.0	100.0
13. Services	20.7	34.1	41.2	46.3	94.6	100.0
14. 13/12	0.36	0.52	0.49	0.49	0.79	1.00

Line 2 $\dfrac{\text{(expenditure in domestic currency/population)} \div \text{purchasing power parity}}{\text{GDP in US/US population}} \times 100.$

Line 3   Simple average of values within each income class.

Line 4 $\dfrac{\text{(expenditures in domestic currency/population)} \div \text{exchange rate}}{\text{GDP in US/US population}} \times 100.$

Lines 6, 7, 9, 10 and 13 include public consumption as well as household expenditures.

Lines 11–13 purchasing power parity ÷ exchange rate × 100.

SOURCE: Kravis–Heston–Summers (1982).

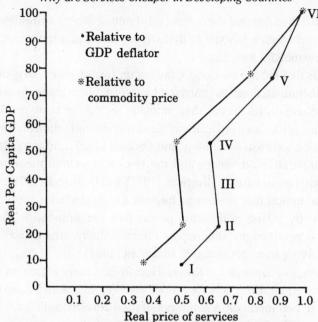

FIG. 18.1   Relative price of services and per capita GDP
for six country groups, 1975.

same in different countries. With similar prices for traded goods in all
countries, wages in the industries producing traded goods will differ from
country to country according to differences in productivity — a standard
conclusion of Ricardian trade theory. In each country the wage level
established in the traded goods industries will determine wages in the
industries producing nontraded goods, mainly services. Because international productivity differences are smaller for such industries, the low
wages established in poor countries in the low-productivity traded goods
industries will apply also to the not-so-low productivity service and other
nontraded goods industries. The consequences will be low prices in
low-income countries for services and other nontraded goods. [1982,
p. 21.]

This is an interesting explanation and indeed is to be found also
in Balassa (1964) and Samuelson (1964) and, as Kravis has pointed
out to me, in a splendid early analysis in Harrod (1933, Ch. IV).
Kravis et al. explore it further and insightfully. But it does raise,
within the parameters of its own approach, the question whether
we cannot formalize it in general equilibrium, also extending the

formalization beyond the excessively limiting Ricardian framework of a single factor, labour, so that we get closer to a more realistic and meaningful formulation.

This can indeed be done, drawing on two elements of general equilibrium analysis as practised by international trade theorists: (i) the use of the Lerner diagrammatic technique relating goods to factor prices, as used to advantage in analysing technical change in the 2-good case by Findlay and Grubert (1959) and the pattern of comparative advantage and the Heckscher–Ohlin theorem in the many-good case by Bhagwati (1972) and Deardorff (1979); and (ii) the notion that we can go beyond the single-factor Ricardian theory by taking multifactor production functions with Hicks-neutral productivity differences internationally, this generalization having been proposed in Bhagwati (1964).[1]

Then, to formalize the Kravis–Heston–Summers argument in a general equilibrium, 2-factor model, take Fig. 18.2. X and Y are two 'traded' commodities; S is the non-traded service. Suffixes R and P refer to the Rich and Poor countries, respectively. Assume the standard restrictions on constant-returns-to-scale production functions in each activity. Putting a wage-rental price line, ω, tangent to the corresponding isoquants then defines, as shown by Lerner, the corresponding goods price vector. Evidently, $\bar{X}_R$ will exchange for $\bar{Y}_R$ and each, in turn, for $\bar{S}_R$, in the Rich country.[2]

The Kravis–Heston–Summers argument assumes that in the Poor country, if the same traded goods' prices prevail due to free trade and productivity is indeed lower by λ in the traded sector, $\lambda\bar{X}_P$ exchanges for $\lambda\bar{Y}_P$ yielding, of course, the same $X : Y$ price ratio. But the service sector is equally productive as in the Rich country. Hence, $\lambda\bar{X}_P$ exchanges for $\lambda\bar{Y}_P$ but for $\bar{S}_P$. Hence, trade

---

[1] Thus, if I and II are countries, and X and Y are two activities using factors K and L, let

$$X^{\mathrm{I}} = \phi^{\mathrm{I}}(K_X, L_X) \text{ and } X^{\mathrm{II}} = \lambda\phi^{\mathrm{I}}(K_X, L_X).$$

If $\lambda > I$, country II has Ricardian-style neutral productivity advantage in producing good X. The Ricardian theory of comparative advantage is then reformulated in Bhagwati (1964) in terms of comparative λ differences across trading countries.

[2] Evidently, since they are tangent to the same factor price line, $P_x\bar{X}_R = P_y\bar{Y}_R = P_S\bar{S}_R$ ($= \omega OQ$ worth of wages). Therefore $p_x/p_y = \bar{Y}_R/\bar{X}_R$, etc.

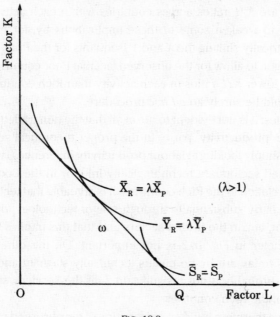

FIG. 18.2

will link the Rich and the Poor countries but lead to $\bar{S}_R = \lambda \bar{S}_P$ ($\lambda > 1$), yielding therefore the observed phenomenon that the relative price of the service sector is lower in the Poor country.

This theoretical, general-equilibrium[3] formulation of the Kravis–Heston–Summers argument is based on a more satisfactory notion of 'productivity' advantage than simply labour productivity and is fully rigorous. But it does also imply at least two other unrealistic

[3] A conventional demand side can be readily added to the model to close it. Evidently, the configuration of demand and factor endowments must be such that, within each country, the wage–rental ratio is the same, as in the argument formalized via Fig. 18.1. With presumably the relative endowment of labour higher in the poor countries, this implies that the argument permits demand there to be skewed more in favour of services. Line 10 in Table 18.1, and private conversation with Kravis, suggest however that the share of services in total expenditure is not differentially greater in the poor countries. Demand differences have been discussed also by Samuelson (1964) in the context of the purchasing power parity doctrine.

consequences: that the wage–rental ratio, ω, is equal across countries as are K/L ratios across countries within each activity. It is *possible* to weaken some of these implications by, for example, parametrically shifting the $\bar{X}$ and $\bar{Y}$ isoquants for the Poor country to the right, to allow for the observed fact that Poor countries seem to have lower K/L ratios in each activity than Rich countries. But that would be surely an *ad hoc* procedure.

Besides, it is not evident to me at all that the non-traded sectors do have 'productivity' parity in the proper theoretical sense (as against simply looking at labour productivity differences) whereas the traded sectors are technologically inferior in the Poor countries in relation to the Rich countries. It is arguable that technology diffuses fairly substantially through sale of technology, direct investment, etc. in the traded sectors and that this implies that the λ parameter in Fig. 18.2 is not important. On the other hand, services today are by no means technically stagnant and hence there is probably a not insignificant λ in the services sector in favour of the Rich countries.

Can we therefore build an explanation of the observed phenomenon of real price of services being lower in Poor countries *without* resorting to a particular specification of comparative productivity ranking between countries in their traded (commodity) and non-traded (services) sectors, while *also* explaining the *labour*-productivity rankings? I believe it is indeed possible to do so, as shown immediately below. In fact, I propose to develop an explanation which, while altogether ignoring differential ('true') productivity differences across sectors between countries, manages to 'explain' simultaneously a number of related empirical observations in Kravis, Heston, and Summers (1982), as also the fact that groups III and IV in Table 18.1 do not conform to the central phenomenon being discussed here.

III. An Alternative Explanation

Consider then the same basic model as in Fig. 18.1. But now assume, as in Fig. 18.3, that the Rich and Poor countries have identical production functions in each sector: 'productivity' differences are

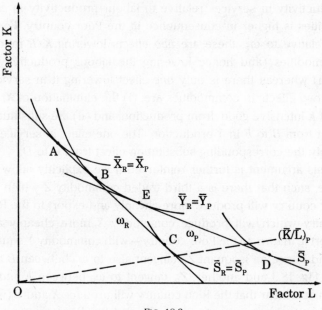

FIG. 18.3

thus assumed to be nonexistent. Let ω_R be the wage–rental ratio obtaining in the Rich country, implying that $\bar{X}_R$ exchanges for $\bar{Y}_R$ for $\bar{S}_R$.

If, however, the Poor country were to have this wage–rental ratio, its overall endowment ratio $(\bar{K}/\bar{L})_P$ for all employment would have to be spanned by OA and OC, with AOC (not drawn) constituting the McKenzie–Chipman diversification cone. But if, as in Fig. 18.3, $(\bar{K}/\bar{L})_P$ lies outside this diversification cone, ω_R is not feasible and the Poor country, being so abundantly endowed with labour, would have to have a *lower* wage–rental ratio such as ω_P. The consequence is that production of X is no longer possible at the goods price ratio $\bar{X}_R = \bar{Y}_R$ given from the Rich country, whereas $\bar{Y}_P$ will now exchange, *not* for $\bar{S}_P$ but for $\tilde{S}_P$, the choice of K/L ratios being OE and OD, respectively, in the Poor country. The new diversification cone defined by EOD, of course, spans $(\bar{K}/\bar{L})_P$. This immediately means that the relative price of services is cheaper in the Poor country since $\tilde{S}_P > \bar{S}_P$.

But, aside from yielding the central phenomenon to be explained, my construct also shows that it may be found that labour productivity in services relative to labour productivity in commodities is higher in consequence in the Poor country. For, at ω_P relative to ω_R, these are *two* effects lowering K/L ratio in commodities (and hence lowering the labour productivity in them) whereas there is only *one* effect lowering it in services. The two effects in commodities are: (i) the elimination of X, the most K-intensive good, from production; and (ii) the substitution effect from B to E in Y-production. The one effect in services is simply the corresponding substitution effect from C to D.[4]

This argument is further reinforced if we explicitly allow for trade, such that there is a third traded commodity Z which the Poor country will produce more cheaply and export to the Rich country which will produce commodity X more cheaply and export it, in turn, to the Poor country — with commodity Y equally Z, and hence an isoquant $\bar{Z}_R$ tangent also to ω_R between B and C in Fig. 18.3 and another, $\bar{Z}_P$, tangent to ω_P between E and D. Then, it is clear that the Rich country will produce X and Y (with Z being too expensive to produce) and the Poor country will produce Y and Z (with X being too expensive to produce), while each country will of course be producing its own non-traded Services. The Rich country will thus necessarily export X and the Poor country will necessarily export Z, if each country consumes some of each good. Hence, the Rich country alone will be producing commodity X which is the most K-intensive good whereas the Poor country alone will be producing commodity Z

---

[4] Yet another reinforcing explanation, resting on inter-activity technological differences, could be that the elasticity of substitution in (traded) commodities is higher than in (non-traded) services. Theoretically, it might be argued that technical change, which is faster historically in commodities, tends also to be capital-using and hence may be simultaneously imparting greater flexibility in choice of techniques and hence may imply a higher elasticity of substitution. Recent empirical evidence does not however seem prima facie to support this. Thus, Dale Jorgenson tells me that his 1978 work on post-war US data shows that manufacturing, services–trade–communications, transportation, and agriculture–mining–construction have substitution elasticities between capital and labour of 1.1, 1.09, 0.17, and 0.35, respectively. Careful splicing of this work to the Kravis–Heston–Summers classifications *may* however prove to be consistent with the hypothesis advanced in this footnote; so may other econometric evidence for other countries and periods.

which is the least K-intensive traded good: thus only reinforcing further the effect (i) distinguished earlier in the preceding paragraph.[5]

It is, indeed, remarkable that this is precisely what Kravis, Heston, and Summers (1982) report:

Kuznets' own work relating first to 1950 and later to 1960 and the independent work of Chenery and Syrquin (1975) summarizing the period 1950–70 show clearly that the productivity of the service sector relative to the commodity sector tends to be inversely related to the income level of the country. This finding is confirmed when sectoral productivity indexes, circa 1975 are regressed against real per capita GDP for the 20 ICP Phase III countries for which data for such indices were available. In the following regression, productivity in the service industries *(SP)* relative to productivity in the commodity industries (CP) of each country is taken as the dependent variable and the ICP estimate of 1975 real per capita GDP *(r)* is the independent variable (standard errors are shown in parenthesis):

$$\ln (SP/CP) = 7.3988 - 0.3100 \ln r \qquad \bar{R}^2 = 0.618$$
$$(0.4349) \; (0.0550) \qquad \text{S.E.E.} = 0.198$$
$$n = 20$$

The coefficient of r is negative and highly significant. The higher the country's per capita income, the lower its service sector productivity relative to its commodity sector productivity.

My explanation also implies that, as $\bar{K}/\bar{L}$ endowment ratio rises, and therefore GDP per capita increases, the wage–rental ratio would tend to rise and hence for K/L ratios in each sector to rise. I.e. in Fig. 18.3, the (K/L) ratio at OE in the Poor country is exceeded by those at OB and OA in the Rich country; also, that at OD is exceeded by that at OC. This again is observed statistically by Kravis, Heston, and Summers (Table 18.2).

Finally, it is clear that these effects, both the central phenomenon of the relative service decline with GDP per capita and

---

[5] By introducing a range of traded commodities and allowing the wage–rental ratio to vary downwards, the argument in the text can be extended to successive pairs of countries without difficulty. Note also that, while Fig. 18.3 shows only one commodity (Y) to be produced in common by the Rich and Poor countries, this is not a necessary outcome. The number of such commonly produced commodities can be expanded as greatly as desired.

TABLE 18.2

Capital–Labour Ratios[*]

Income group	Commodities	Services
I	4.39	2.48
II	9.24	5.16
III	5.64	6.21
IV	6.91	6.32
V	16.27	9.44
VI	21.94	10.96

[*] $ 1000 worth of capital per man-year.

the associated comparative labour productivity observations between sectors and within sectors across countries, depend in my construct on the fact that, for the pair of countries being compared, their comparative factor endowments are sufficiently apart so as not to permit them to be at the same wage–rental ratio and hence to be in the same diversification cone. If therefore two countries or groups of countries are close together in GDP per capita, we would expect that the several correlative phenomena explained in this chapter would also be correspondingly weak.

And this seems more or less to be so. Thus, if we examine Table 18.2, it is evident that the capital–labour ratios in the two 'sectors' (commodities and services) are not substantially changed between country groups II–IV. This would suggest that these lie more or less within the same diversification cone and hence we would not expect to observe substantial change in the relative price of services within the range of per capita GDP variation defined by these groups. It is therefore somewhat remarkable that, as Table 18.1 and Fig. 18.1 show, the relative price of services is indeed fairly constant over groups II–IV! My explanation, therefore, seems even more compelling.[6]

[6] Kravis has kindly drawn my attention to Kravis and Lipsey (1983) where a 'factor proportions' explanation, consonant with that advanced in this chapter, is stated.

IV. CONCLUDING REMARK

This chapter has therefore formulated in general equilibrium the Kravis–Heston–Summers explanation of the observed phenomenon that services are cheaper in the poor countries. It has also provided another, alternative general-equilibrium explanation that altogether abstracts from the Kravis–Heston–Summers focus on comparative productivity differences among sectors across countries and focuses instead on comparative endowments. This alternative explanation is also demonstrated to fit in addition other associated phenomena noted by these distinguished authors.[7]

The explanations provided are 'stylistic' rather than in the form of econometric estimations. In this, they conform to the explanations provided in Bhagwati (1977), again drawing on general-equilibrium production theory in international economics, of the well-known statistical observation by Chenery (1960) and other authors that the share of manufactures in national income generally rises with *per capita* income.

REFERENCES

Balassa, B., 1964: 'The Purchasing-Power Parity Doctrine: A Reappraisal', *Journal of Political Economy*, vol. 72 (Dec.), pp. 584–96.

Bhagwati, J.N., 1964: 'The Pure Theory of International Trade: A Survey', *Economic Journal*, vol. 74 (March), pp. 1–84.

——, 1972: 'The Heckscher–Ohlin Theorem in the Multi-Commodity Case', *Journal of Political Economy*, vol. 80 (Sept.–Oct.), pp. 1052–5.

——, 1977: 'Comment on: Transitional Growth and World Industrialization

[7] My Fig. 18.3 paradigm rationalizes the relative cheapness in poor countries of labour services and of non-tradeables that are of especially high labour intensity. If all non-tradeables, taken as a whole, were of average or higher-than-average capital intensity, my paradigm would not also rationalize the principal Kravis–Heston–Summers finding — namely that national income comparisons based on crude exchange rate calculations exaggerate twofold the superiority of per capita real incomes in the affluent regions in comparison to the poor regions. I kill two birds with one stone if it is realistic to expect that being of high labour intensity predisposes a good to be relatively immobile in international trade.

by Hollis B. Chenery', *in* B. Ohlin, P. Hesselborn and P. Wijkman, *The International Allocation of Economic Activity* (London: Macmillan).

Chenery, H., 1960: 'Patterns of Industrial Growth', *American Economic Review*, vol. 50 (Sept.), pp. 624–54.

Chenery, H. and M. Syrquin, 1975: *Patterns of Development 1950-1970* (London: Oxford University Press).

Deardorff, A., 1979: 'Weak Links in the Chain of Comparative Advantage', *Journal of International Economics*, vol. 9 (May), pp. 197–209.

Findlay, R. and H. Grubert, 1959: 'Factor Intensities, Technological Progress and the Terms of Trade', *Oxford Economic Papers*, vol. 11 (March), pp. 111–21.

Harrod, R.F., 1933: *International Economics*, Cambridge Economic Handbooks (London: Nisbet & Cambridge University Press).

Kravis, I., A. Heston and R. Summers, 1982: 'The Share of Services in Economic Growth' (mimeo.), in *Global Econometrics: Essays in Honor of Lawrence R. Klein*, F.G. Adams and Bert Hickman (eds) (Cambridge: MIT Press).

Kravis, I. and R. Lipsey, 1983: 'Toward an Explanation of National Price Levels', Princeton Studies in International Finance, no. 52.

Samuelson, P.A., 1964: 'Theoretical Notes on Trade Problems', *The Review of Economics and Statistics*, vol. 46 (May), pp. 145–54.

19

Splintering and Disembodiment of Services and Developing Nations

SERVICES have long attracted the attention of economists. The classical economists, from Adam Smith down to Karl Marx, were interested in them, as distinct from goods, for the purpose of defining productive labour. The Marxist prescription, and faithful Communist practice, to omit them from national income accounts is a direct consequence of this interest.[1]

More recently, services have attracted attention from other perspectives. Following on the work of P.J. Verdoorn,[2] elevated to the Verdoorn Law, Nicholas Kaldor argued forcefully that manufactures (goods) were characterized by greater technical progress than services[3] and in the United Kingdom he successfully seduced a Chancellor of the Exchequer, James Callaghan, into adopting the Selective Employment Tax in 1966 (abolished in 1973). The notion that services are generally unprogressive has also been the basis of less dramatic, but influential, explanations by other economists of the phenomena, such as haircuts are cheaper in the poor countries, among whom are Bela Balassa,[4] Paul Samuelson,[5] Irving

[1] I thank Alan Deardorff, Eli Ginzberg, Helena Stalson, Irving Kravis and Gene Grossman for helpful conversations or for reading an earlier draft of this chapter which was first published in *The World Economy*, June 1984 and subsequently in *Essays in Development Economics*, Gene Grossman (ed.) (Oxford: Basil Blackwell; Cambridge, MA: MIT Press, 1985).

[2] P.J. Verdoorn, 'Fattori che regolano lo sviluppo della produttivita del lavoro', *L'Industria*, no. 1, 1949, pp. 3–11.

[3] Nicholas Kaldor, *Causes of the Slow Economic Growth of the United Kingdom* (Cambridge: Cambridge University Press, 1966) and Kaldor, 'Economic Growth and the Verdoorn Law: A Comment on Mr Rowthorn's Article', *Economic Journal*, Dec. 1975, pp. 891–6.

[4] Bela Balassa, 'The Purchasing Power Parity Doctrine: A Reappraisal, *Journal of Political Economy*, Dec. 1964, pp. 584–96.

[5] Paul Samuelson, 'Theoretical Notes on Trade Problems', *Review of Economics*

Kravis, Alan Heston, and Robert Summers,[6] with an alternative 'factor-endowments' explanation that I recently proposed which altogether abstracts from the approach based on progressivity.[7]

Then again, concerns have been raised by some that the shift to a 'service economy' in the rich countries imperils jobs by displacing labour through technical change: a contention that sits ill at ease with the concern of Professor Kaldor and others that services are generally unprogressive. But both contentions equally seek to propel policy in the direction of promoting 'reindustrialization'.

Finally, services have come to the forefront in recent discussions on the reform of the General Agreement on Tariffs and Trade (GATT) since the US Administration has been seeking to extend the scope of the GATT, traditionally confined to trade in goods, to trade in services. While the principal lobby behind these efforts is constituted by the financial and 'high-tech' communication industries, and the conventional definition of services in balance-of-payments accounting evidently does not correspond to that in nation-income industry-of-origin accounts, the American position has prompted a negative response from the developing countries, in part because many of them assume that they must have a comparative disadvantage in services.[8]

That services have become a major focus of attention is beyond doubt. Equally, it is clear that services are a nebulous concept,

and Statistics, May 1964, pp. 145–54.

[6] Irving B. Kravis, Alan Heston and Robert Summers, *International Comparisons of Real Product and Purchasing Power* (Baltimore: Johns Hopkins Press, for the World Bank, 1978).

[7] Jagdish N. Bhagwati, 'Why are Services Cheaper in the Poor Countries?', *Economic Journal*, June 1984.

[8] Some observers have remarked that the negative response of developing countries has been prompted by a conviction that if GATT discussions focus on trade in services, many issues of deep concern to them, to do with trade in goods, will continue to be brushed aside by the major trading powers. See, for example, Hugh Corbet, 'Obstacles to Liberalizing Trade in Services', in *Dawn of a New Global Economy: the World through 2000* (Bala Cynwyd, Pennsylvania: Chase Econometrics, 1984). For a discussion of how the question of liberalizing trade in services was taken up in the United States, see Corbet, 'Prospect of Negotiations on International Trade in Services', *Pacific Community*, Tokyo, April 1977.

frequently embracing activities with differential and opposed characteristics, for instance in regard to their technical progressivity and labour intensity. A closer look at what constitutes services, at their relationship to goods and at the dynamic process that defines and governs this relationship, and hence the characteristics of services, is therefore necessary.

In this chapter, I propose to argue that, given the (appropriate) way in which we distinguish goods from services, technical and structural change defines a continuous process during which services splinter off from goods and goods, in turn, splinter off from services. Furthermore, this 'splintering process', in so far as goods emerge from services, is associated with a 'disembodiment effect' such that the services, initially embodied in the person providing them (for example, Placido Domingo singing at the Metropolitan), and requiring the physical presence of the provider of the services at the time of use, are disembodied as a result of technical change and encapsulated into what we call goods (such as the invention which brings Placido Domingo via records — that is, goods — into our homes). I shall further argue that the services-from-goods splintering process generally yields service activities that are technically progressive and possibly capital intensive, whereas the goods-from-services splintering process, reflecting the disembodiment effect, generally leaves behind a residue of service activities that are technically unprogressive and generally labour intensive.

Moreover, I will propose that the disembodiment effect applies equally to services becoming available over distances without the physical presence of the provider of these services where used, *even though no transition in consequence to goods is involved*. Thus, while records and books represent the disembodiment effect resulting in goods where earlier we had services of theatrical performances and lectures, the practice of transmitting engineering services over the wire from Houston to Paris and medical diagnoses over the computer from New York to the Adirondacks represents the disembodiment effect which leaves the services sector intact. I shall argue, however, that this intra-service sector disembodiment effect has important implications, (i) for comparative advantage, (ii) for the question of extending the GATT to trade in services and, (iii) for immigration restrictions.

What are services? And how should they be distinguished from goods? These questions, as T.P. Hill remarked in a perceptive article on the subject,[9] preoccupied classical economists, including Adam Smith[10] and John Stuart Mill.[11]

SERVICES VERSUS GOODS

At one level, all value added in an economy comes from services; that is, from factor services. What is produced, and carries an explicit or implicit valuation, is automatically a return to some factor for its services. But this truism is not what concerns us here.

What concerns us here is the attempt at distinguishing services from goods from the viewpoint of either *production* or *consumption*. The former is customarily described as the breakdown by industry of origin; the latter is often christened the breakdown by share of final-demand services in national expenditure. The two approaches naturally do not yield identical coverage since, as is evident, the latter refers only to final-demand services and would exclude services, however defined, which are produced for intermediate use.

While the definitions of services in practice are nebulous — and are allowed to embrace at times even governmental enterprises, which may be producing anything but services, simply because governmental outlays are automatically included as service expenditures — an attempt can be made to identify certain principles that underlie the distinction between services and goods.

As Professor Kravis has noted,[12] these principles, inferred from

[9] T.P. Hill, 'On Goods and Services', *Review of Income and Wealth*, Dec. 1977.

[10] Adam Smith, *The Wealth of Nations* (London: Strahan & Cadell, 1776) Bk I, ch. 3, my edition having been the one, with an introduction by Max Lerner, published in 1937 by Random House, New York, in its Modern Library series.

[11] John Stuart Mill, *Principles of Political Economy* (London: John W. Parker, 1848), the 1909 edition, with an introduction by Sir William Ashley, being reprinted in 1961 by Augustus M. Kelly, New York; and Mill, *Essays on Some Unsettled Questions of Political Economy* (London: John W. Parker, 1844), Essay III.

[12] Kravis, *Services in the Domestic Economy and in World Transactions*, Working

received practice, suggest that the working definition of services is that they are generally non-storable. As Professor Hill has argued:

the fact that services must be acquired by consumers as they are produced means that they cannot be put into stock by producers. Because the only goods which cannot be put into stock are highly perishable goods, the impression has been formed that services must also be perishable, but this analogy is totally false. The inability to stock services has nothing whatsoever to do with their physical characteristics: it is a logical impossibility because a stock of changes is a contradiction in terms.[13]

At the same time, Professor Kravis notes that yet another criterion often used to identify services is that their production involves a:

relatively low value of commodities embodied in them as intermediate inputs. Starting with almost any plausible definition of services, it will be found that the proportion of value added to gross output is high in services and that the proportion of intermediate inputs in the form of services is high relative to commodity inputs. Commodities to a much greater degree involve the further processing of physical things, so that commodity inputs loom large in value added and even larger among intermediate inputs relative to service inputs.[14]

Still another characteristic of services, as defined from the standpoint of industry of origin, is that they must be transacted between separate units. Professor Hill goes so far as to argue that 'a service may be defined as a change in the condition of a person, or of a good belonging to some economic unit, which is brought about as the result of the activity of some other economic unit, with the prior agreement of the former person or economic

---

Paper No. 1124 (Cambridge, Massachusetts: National Bureau of Economic Research, 1983).

[13] Hill, loc. cit., p. 337.

[14] Kravis, op. cit., pp. 5–6. Professor Kravis notes that all these definitions run into problems. For example, messages taken by telephone-answering firms are storable and yet they are classified as a service activity. Again, retail and wholesale trade can hardly be called unintensive in the use of goods as intermediates unless we arbitrarily dismiss the goods distributed from appropriate categorization as intermediates in the trade activity.

unit'.[15] Whether we accept the qualification about the voluntariness of the transaction,[16] it is evident that the normal practice,
indeed, is to classify services as such only if they take place
between different economic agents. As I note below, following
on Professor Kravis's interesting observations, this means that
industry-of-origin breakdowns between services and goods can
change simply because of intra-unit transactions changing to inter-
unit transactions, with no real change in the overall structure of
the economy having taken place.

All these characteristics, in one form or another, have definitely
influenced the way national-income and related statisticians have
been classifying services. To see more clearly what the services
are that we customarily talk about, note that a typical classification
on the share of services in final expenditures on gross domestic
product (GDP) breaks them down into: housing, medical care,
education, hotels and restaurants, public transport, communication, recreation, barber and beauty shops, and government. On
the industry-of-origin side, a typical classification, though, shows
services to be: electricity, gas and water, trade, transport, storage
and communication, finance, insurance and real estate, personal
services, and governmental services.[17]

We have here, therefore, in spite of the relative simplicity of
the various criteria used to distinguish services from goods, a
complex of activities that fall conventionally under the rubric of
services. What I propose to do now is to consider how the
dynamics of technical and structural change keeps shifting this
kaleidoscope and to gather some insights from this into orthodox
questions relating to the progressivity of services and comparative advantage in them.

[15] Hill, loc. cit., p. 318.

[16] We would have to treat governmental services, including collective services,
as having been generated by some form of implicit social contract to make them
compatible with the suggestion of Professor Hill about voluntariness (ibid.).
Professor Hill does discuss collective services separately.

[17] But the 'service' categories in the balance-of-payments accounts, and hence
also to some extent in the discussions on the extension of the GATT to trade in
services, are very different. For an excellent discussion of these other concepts,
see Kravis, *Services*

'SPLINTERING PROCESS' AND 'DISEMBODIMENT EFFECT'

As economies grow or change their structure, technical change and economies of scale interact to splinter services from goods and goods from services.

Services from Goods

A principal reason why services splinter from goods is simply a consequence of the way industry-of-origin services are identified. Any intra-firm transactions, even when they partake of the nature of services otherwise so defined, are automatically classified as part of that firm's output. If the firm is producing goods, then such transactions are classified as part of the value added in the goods sector. For instance, if a car factory has a paint job done on the premises using its own labour and capital, that is a part of car production. If the paint job is, however, farmed out to another firm, then it is classified as a service. This is seen even more dramatically when considering transport or accounting within and outside the firm. Within a firm producing goods it would all go into goods production, whereas when purchased from outside the value added from these activities would classify as services.

Thus we get the remarkable phenomenon that as specialization emerges owing to economies of scale, and service activities are taken out of the firm and become part of inter-firm transactions, there will be a shift in the relative proportions in the production of goods and services in favour of the latter. Two consequences immediately follow.

First, since specialization will reflect economies of scale, these services will tend to be seen as technically progressive — unless, of course, the economies of scale that prompted specialization outside the user-firms simply stop at the stage at which such specialization ensues! Hence, I should expect that the services that emerge from this type of splintering process from goods will tend to be progressive rather than technically stagnant; they are part of the dynamic process of change in the economic system.

Second, since this source of the growth of services simply reflects specialization outside firms of activities that were already a part of goods production, it is independent of any *demand* influence such as, say, the growth of services reflecting a high income elasticity of demand for services. Thus, in explaining why services grow relative to goods, this explanation will work if we are looking at the industry-of-origin shares; it will not work if we are looking at final-use shares. Professor Kravis has used this distinction precisely to reconcile his findings that 'the "real" share of spending on aggregate services is not very different between poor and rich countries'[18] and that, at the same time, the share of service industries in production and GDP is significantly higher in the rich than in the poor countries.

Goods from Services

But if services splinter off from goods in the way described above, goods typically splinter off from services. In this instance, though, they leave behind a residue of unprogressive services.

Consider, then, the example of Luciano Pavarotti. When the gramophone was invented, there was in fact a tremendously sharp technical change in the service activity called 'musical services'. But what happened in the classification of goods and services? Gramophones and records are 'goods' and the technical change simply resulted in a new industry that falls under the goods sector. Thus we have been left with the ex post observation that the 'musical services' industry is technically unprogressive and also highly labour intensive in general. If technical progress in traditional service industries, such as music, lecturing, et cetera (mostly final-use services), indeed takes the form where the service is 'disembodied' from the physical presence of the provider and embodies those services in goods that can then be bought in the market place, then we have a splintering process where technical change simply creates new goods that tend to displace the services from which they grew and where technical change therefore leaves behind, in the services sector, the labour-intensive and 'unprogressive' component of the pre-technical-change sector.

The disembodiment effect that characterizes technical change creating goods from services is accordingly responsible for a class

[18] Ibid., p. 8.

of services where progressivity is generally considered to be low. We then have this paradox: that technical progress in these sectors itself creates the outcome that, given the way these sectors are defined, wind up technically stagnant!

Moreover, the two different splintering processes tend to divide services into two classes as far as progressivity is concerned: the services-from-goods process tends to create progressive service industries, whereas the goods-from-services process tends to create (a residue of) unprogressive service industries.

Other Arguments

I should also add that the traditional British notion that services are unprogressive appears to have been fuelled not just by the Verdoorn statistics but also by casual empiricism. Contrary to the philosopher of science Thomas Kuhn, I believe that many theories can be, and occasionally are, a reaction based on serendipity and casual observation rather than a result of growing crisis as 'contradictory' facts accumulate and embarrass the existing paradigm. This certainly seems to have been true of Newton's Law of Gravity and of Einstein's Theory of Relativity (where I side with the views of another celebrated philosopher of science, Gerald Holton). And it holds, in the present instance, I think for British economists such as Professor Kaldor. It is not hard to believe that they were influenced by the fact that, as they stepped out of an Oxford or Cambridge college in the early 1950s, they ran into the little post office and the little shop often run by aged folk and selling Cadbury's chocolates for sixpence: both supremely impressive examples to the naked eye of low productivity and absence of technical change. It was no wonder that these casual, but continuously reinforced, impressions would produce the view that employment must be shifted out of services into the modern and progressive goods industries, if need be by a tax on employment in services. The astonishing thing, but not altogether surprising to those who know Britain, is that this viewpoint got translated into the Selective Employment Tax, with exemptions of course for the High Table services provided to 'Oxbridge' dons!

As it happens, governmental services, presumably because of incentives related to the bureaucratic and political aspects of these services (and, indeed, also of governmental activities producing goods in many instances), do seem to be subject to unprogressivity. Kenneth Galbraith's colourful admonition against 'Post Office Socialism', to spur India's massive public sector into greater efficiency and profits, gets to the heart of the problem here.

But the retail sector raises different issues. Here, the fact that retailing has gone from the small shops and scale to innovative organizations, as represented by Sears Roebuck for instance, itself suggests the obsolete nature of thinking based on the early observations of the British scene. The same observation applies in yet greater degree to transport, where even the nineteenth century witnessed tremendous technical advances which had a profound impact on world commerce and income, with trade coming to be seen as the 'engine of growth'. Again, similar technical advances have continued in varying but impressive degrees in the modern communication industries, and also in related service industries such as finance and banking. In these service industries, the rates of technical change cannot on average have been less dramatic, than those in the goods industries.[19]

DISEMBODIMENT EFFECT: CONSEQUENCIES FOR COMPARATIVE ADVANTAGE AND GATT EXTENSION TO SERVICES

Let me return, however, to the theme of the disembodiment effect, for this idea can be pushed in yet another pertinent direction. With rapid technical change occurring in the information and communication networks, it seems increasingly clear now that the performance of a number of services, which would have required the physical presence of the provider of the services where they are used, is no longer critically dependent on physical presence. Traditionally, as just argued, technical change in services has

[19] For a useful statistical analysis of differential progressivity among different service industries, see William Baumol, Sue Anne Blackman and Edward Wolff, 'Unbalanced Growth Revisited: Asymptotic Stagnancy and New Evidence', mimeo., Jan. 1984.

occasionally taken the form where this 'disembodiment' has taken the shape of the services in turn becoming embodied in goods, with consequences that have just been analysed. But we must increasingly contend with the fact that the disembodiment now takes place in a manner where services are simply 'transmitted over the wire' to the users. This was brought home very clearly in the celebrated case of Dresser Industries which got into the middle of the conflict between the opposed policies of the Mitterand Government of the French Republic and the Reagan Administration in the United States in regard to sanctions aimed at the construction of the Soviet pipeline to Western Europe. Dresser's Paris branch ground to a halt simply because the Reagan Administration ordered the group's headquarters in the United States to terminate engineering and other service and information flows from Dallas! Thus, on 'trade wars over data', an article in the *New York Times* in March 1983 read:

Each day, from offices and construction sites in 100 countries, employees of Dresser Industries tap into the company's central computers in the United States. Through a complex network of terminals and satellites, the database spews forth a torrent of up-to-the-minute design information, financial data, personnel files, and inventory listings — all crucial to operations of the giant oil and gas equipment maker.

But for a few weeks of corporate agony last August, President Reagan cut Dresser's computer lifeline. To enforce his sanctions against companies building the Soviet Union's trans-Siberian pipeline across Western Europe, Mr Reagan ordered the Dallas-based company to end all technical communications with its French subsidiary, which was manufacturing compressors for the project.

'We had no choice', recalled Edward R. Luter, senior vice president for finance. 'Somebody in Pittsburgh', where Dresser's database was then situated, 'flipped the switch and suddenly Dresser–France was cut off.' Almost immediately, an Australian company terminated a $ 3 million order with Dresser–France, realizing that without access to the central database the company was virtually paralyzed.[20]

Evidently, technical revolution in the information and communication industries, which seems to be the cutting edge of high-tech industries today, implies that what I have christened the

[20] David Sanger, 'A Trade War over Data', *New York Times*, 13 March 1983, p. F1.

'disembodiment effect' is an increasingly important phenomenon. But, if this is indeed so, then we must look in a fresh light at the whole issue raised by the US of extending the GATT to trade in services. The lobbying for this extension has come from financial circles, with American-based multinational enterprises interested in sales of services (including supportive services on durables) through establishments abroad also playing a major role. The result has been that many developing countries have looked upon the position of the United States, as possibly American negotiators themselves have, as being primarily to support American interests. And, since trade negotiations are unfortunately conducted on the perverse assumption that tariff reductions made are a loss rather than a gain, developing countries have felt it necessary to protect themselves by objecting to the effort of the United States. I should add that this position has not been universal among the developing countries; ones such as Singapore and Hong Kong, which have relatively open doors for multinational enterprises in areas such as finance and insurance, feel that they too can compete effectively in these activities and would not mind if the GATT was extended to trade in services.

But it is realized that services will increasingly be disembodied in the manner discussed here, then it is possible to argue that the more advanced developing countries, the newly industrializing countries, which are abundantly endowed with skills, may well find a new comparative advantage opening up in the over-the-wire transmission of their skilled services! This has already happened with regard to software. It could happen, à la Dresser engineering services, with data being transmitted to users in overseas locations for engineering, medical, and a host of other skilled services. Thus the newly industrializing countries may well find that there is something for them too in the GATT being extended to trade in services — provided that the extension is truly to services of all kinds.[21]

The implication of such technical developments, already on their way, is fascinating also for immigration policy. Hitherto, it has always been possible to restrict the inflow of skills by regulating

---

[21] If the disembodiment effect occurs via embodiment in goods, however, the present GATT provisions would cover that.

the relative composition of skilled and unskilled labour. At least, ex ante, such a composition is sought to be regulated, although illegal immigration often blurs the outcome. If skilled immigrants are competitive with domestic skilled and middle-class labour, then the latter can be protected by reducing the skilled immigration. But if the services of skilled foreigners can come in over the wire, without their personal presence being strictly necessary, then you have a real problem on your hands, especially if the GATT is revised to say that services must flow as freely as goods! The disembodiment effect is thus potentially of tremendous significance for trade and immigration questions, opening up possibilities that are truly revolutionary in the way we must begin to think about these questions in the already-foreseeable future.

Incidently, the implication I have drawn for immigration policy, in the context of the demand to extend the GATT to trade in services, is very different from the relationship with immigration policies which has been drawn by many critics of the American position in the GATT deliberations. The position of the US has been regarded as self-serving and hence untenable because immigration restrictions prevent developing countries from exporting their manpower to the developed countries, so that the services of these people are, in a real sense, not subject to free trade. To open up the GATT to trade in services that interest the US is therefore unfair and the American position therefore somewhat 'hypocritical' in a world regime of immigration restrictions.[22] I feel now that this position, which was explicitly adopted in argumentation by some spokesmen for developing countries at the GATT ministerial meeting in November 1982, is inappropriate.

Basically, we must draw a distinction between services as embodied in the supplier of the services and requiring their physical presence where the user happens to be and services that can be disembodied from the supplier and provided without a physical

---

[22] This is the position that has been propounded orally by many commentators, including me, as a first reaction to American efforts on services. For a statement of similar sentiments, see, in particular, Carlos F. Diaz–Alejandro and Gerald K. Helleiner, *Handmaiden in Distress: World Trade in the 1980s* (Ottawa: North-South Institute, 1982; Washington: Overseas Development Council, 1982; and London: Overseas Development Institute, 1982).

presence being necessary. I would, indeed, like to see a freer flow of services embodied in people; that is, an easing, preferably even a dismantling, of immigration restrictions.

Unfortunately no country in the world, *including* developing countries, will contemplate a world without immigration restrictions. This is certainly one of the unfortunate concomitants of national sovereignty, as seen in the twentieth century, which witnessed the rise of national immigration legislations. It seems to me, therefore, to be the wrong kind of tactic to invoke immigration quotas in the context of the demand for freeing (disembodied) services from restrictions: immigration restrictions apply rather to embodied services and, in any event, developing countries would not dismantle them. Besides, as I have said, the developing countries will tend to gain from such freeing of the restrictions on trade in (disembodied) services, not merely from the fact that they will be able to import such services more cheaply, but also in the sense that they, too, should have some comparative advantage in certain types of services which may have a potential for very rapid growth as the information revolution intensifies.

20

Trade in Services and
the Multilateral Trade Negotiations[*]

THE question of inclusion of services in the Uruguay Round was a principal source of discord between the Group of Ten (G10), led by Brazil and India, and the developed countries, led by the United States in the negotiations prior to the Punta del Este meeting.[1] In between these two 'hard-line' groups[2] were doubtless other developing countries sharing G10-type concerns. Nonetheless, they felt sufficiently pressured by the ballooning protectionist threat in the United States and the energetic and relentless diplomacy of its negotiators, to become with the European Community (EEC) the 'moderate' brokers of a compromise solution at Punta del Este.

But the compromise merely clears the way for the trade talks to be launched despite the discordant views on services. The compromise relates to procedures on which the contending parties fought because, as I shall explain below, they symbolized

* Thanks are due to Brian Hindley, Ambassadors Shukla and Batista at the GATT, and Ambassador Muchkund Dubey for helpful conversations. The comments of Harvey Bale, Narongchai Akrasanee, David Lee, Tony Lane, Paul Leuten, Martin Wolf, and others at the Bangkok conference where the paper underlying this chapter was first presented, have also led to necessary revisions.

[1] The G10 was the group of developing countries consisting of Argentina, Brazil, Cuba, the Arabic Republic of Egypt, India, Nigeria, Peru, Tanzania, Vietnam and Yugoslavia.

[2] It has become customary in some sections of the press to describe the G10 as 'hard-line' developing countries and the G48 as being led by 'moderate' developing countries and 'medium-sized' developed countries, when equally accurately the latter could be described as the 'medium-sized' developing countries and the 'moderate' developed countries. The dialogue between the two sides with opposed viewpoints is difficult enough to manage without the addition of such pejorative characterizations of the principles.

substantive differences. These differences are serious and they raise both broad conceptual questions and narrow negotiating issues. This chapter seeks to address these issues and to define the possible agenda that the developing countries may seek in the service negotiations that are now to begin.

I. The Question of Tracks: Form and Substance

The procedural issues that divided the US from the G10, if we may confine ourselves to the principals, related to two questions:

1. Would the General Agreement on Tariffs and Trade (GATT) be augmented to handle a service compact, or would there be a separate institution or agreement to oversee and regulate world commerce in services?
2. Would the negotiations for arriving at such a compact be conducted under GATT auspices or independently; by contracting parties or by a different group; and parallel to the next round of talks on goods or disjoint from that?

The US position at the outset was to augment the GATT to include services, leaving the form of such an augmentation to the negotiations themselves. That shape may, as a witticism went, be simply to add to the GATT Articles the two words 'and services' wherever the word 'goods' appeared, or alternatively, taking the cue from the conventional *Oxford English Dictionary*, in which 'man' embraces 'woman', to declare that 'goods' imply 'services' in the Agreement. But, as often, good wit is bad economics; and services raise issues that go well beyond the scope of the GATT as it currently stands.

It followed equally that the US wanted the new round of trade talks to include the negotiation of the services compact. The so-called single track was therefore the preferred US option. By contrast, Brazil and India, and the G10 as a whole, wished to delink the GATT from a potential services agreement and derive comfort rather than suffer embarrassment from the fact that the acronym for the General Agreement on Services would be GAS. In turn, therefore, it was reasonable for them to seek a neat separation in the negotiating procedures for goods and for services: this was the dual-track procedure proposed by Brazil in June 1985.

The negotiations, according to this formula, would be distinct for services, would be undertaken by governments rather than GATT contracting parties, need not be parallel to those in goods, would not be under GATT auspices, and would lead to a services compact outside the GATT.

What transpired at Punta del Este was a compromise between these two opposed procedural designs. The dual track was preserved in that the 'contracting parties' would negotiate on goods but would change their hats to 'governments' when they negotiated on services. But the G10 yielded to the extent that both groups would operate under the aegis of the Trade Negotiating Committee, to which they would take their recommendations; and the question of whether the GATT would be augmented or bypassed via a separate services compact was deliberately avoided.

Why all this fuss? Was it really a 'farce', as US ambassador Yeutter is reported to have remarked? As it happens, it was not. Underlying these procedural issues is a key, substantive source of discord. The US, and lately the EC, have given the impression that they would trade concessions on their imports of goods, for concessions on their exports of services. Recent US Section 301 actions (which are trade actions directed at what are deemed unfair practices adversely affecting US exports) have even explicitly followed this type of linkage with a degree of energy that leaves little doubt of US earnestness in the matter. The linkage has been formulated not merely in terms of 'rollbacks' of barriers against developing countries' exports of goods in exchange for access to developing country markets in services. More seriously, the linkage has been made in terms of denying 'standstills' and hence *added* protection being threatened, for developing country exports of goods if they did not offer 'reverse' market access on services.

Opposed to this approach has been the position of the G10 that most 'rollbacks' and 'standstills' on goods merely require the contracting parties to conform to explicit GATT rules. The demands of the developed countries such as the US that goods and services should be linked are seen as offering conformity to GATT rules on goods as an exchange for developing countries opening up new areas such as services to market access. This is considered to be unfair and wrong. In short, the US position is construed as a demand for an *unrequited* concession by developing countries on services masquerading as a quid pro quo trade of concessions by developing and developed countries.

The single-track and dual-track modalities are therefore not superficial phenomena but reflect the desires of their respective proponents to choose bargaining procedures that reflect and hence enhance these substantive positions. Single-track negotiations do underline linkage; dual-track negotiations do not.

II. SERVICES VERSUS GOODS: CONCEPTS AND CONSEQUENCES

It is important, at the outset, to recall the conceptual advances that international economists, following as usual in the footsteps of activist policy-makers, have now made in the matter of defining services. This conceptualization should provide the underpinnings for the positions that governments must consider in formulating the general principles of a services compact, just as the theory of trade and welfare provides the underpinnings for the general principles that underlie GATT and for the impulse to trade liberalization that informs current World Bank conditionality.

How, then, are services to be defined? Or how are they different from goods? Adam Smith, John Stuart Mill, and many others raised these questions, but perhaps the earliest answer to them was attempted by T.P. Hill (1977) only relatively recently. Hill focused on the fact that producers cannot accumulate a stock or inventory of services, stressing that services must be consumed as they are produced. This key element will not characterize all items that we customarily define as services: for example, 'answering services' do store messages. But such exceptions do not detract from the usefulness of a definition of services that characterizes them as non-storable because they require the simultaneously of provision and use.[3]

[3] Another characteristic of services which is necessary is that services occur *between* different economic agents or otherwise all activities and value added would collapse into the service sector. An implication of this characteristic is that

Services Requiring Physical
Proximity versus 'Long-Distance' Services

If services must be used as they are produced, then there must of necessity be *interaction* between the user and the provider of the service. A producer of goods, by contrast, can produce but store, and generally transact with users at any subsequent time. But this interaction, in turn, implies that we can contemplate two essential categories of services: first, those that necessarily require the physical proximity of the user and the provider; and second, those that do not, though such physical proximity may be useful. As I have noted in the preceding chapter:

Basically we have to draw a distinction between services as embodied in the supplier of the services and requiring their physical presence where the user happens to be and services which can be disembodied from the supplier and provided without a physical presence being necessary.[4]

Physical proximity essential.   The class of services where physical proximity is essential is usefully thought of as consisting of three categories based on the mobility of the provider and user of the services.

The first category is *mobile provider, immobile user*. This class of services *requires* that the provider go to the user, while the reverse mobility is physically infeasible. If an Indian or Korean firm had won the bid for construction of the Connecticut Turnpike,

---

the definition of services reflects economic organization or 'market structure'. If Mr Smith paints a car on the assembly line inside your auto plant as your worker, then his wages are part of goods production and value added. But if he does the same job from his own establishment, his wages or income are part of service production and value added. For a detailed discussion of this question, see Bhagwati (1987a and ch. 19).

[4] In ch. 19, I focused on the latter class of services (which I now call 'long-distance' services) discussing how the 'disembodiment' effect can frustrate the intention of immigration restrictions on skilled labour. Conversely, Gary Sampson and Richard Snape (1985) have drawn on this twofold distinction to explore further the *former* class of services, where physical proximity of the provider and the user is involved, with a valuable classification of such services which I use, with some simplification, below.

unskilled Indian or Korean labour services could have been provided only by moving them to Connecticut. Supplies of brute, Ricardian-style labour services must be relocated to the user's locale, as we have seen in the Middle East since the 1970s.

The second category is *mobile user, immobile provider*. This is another important class of services in which the user must move to the provider. Open-heart surgery cannot currently be done in Zaire because, even though Dr Cooley can go from Houston to Kinshasa, there is no way the necessary support services and hospital care can be duplicated there. In this class of services, some key elements are simply not geographically transferable to the user's location.

The third category is *mobile user, mobile provider*. For this range of services, mobility is symmetrically possible. Haircuts, tailored suits, and lectures are the type of services which are in principle transmittable between user and provider in either's location, the only difference being the cost of so doing.

The generic class of services, where the provider must move to the user, as a sheer physical necessity (as in the first category above) or because of overwhelming economic advantage in so doing relative to alternative means of effecting the service transaction at long distance (as discussed immediately below), I call 'temporary-factor-relocation-requiring' services.

Physical proximity inessential: the 'long-distance' services. In the second broad class, which I call 'long-distance' services, physical proximity between providers and users may be useful, but it is not necessary. Live music concerts and data transmission 'over the wire' are obvious examples. Traditional banking and insurance services fall into this category, in principle, since loans could be secured by mail or phone, and insurance policies are often so purchased. The scope for long-distance service transactions will increase with the advance of technology (see Ch. 19). This has important implications for broader issues such as the trend effect of immigration restrictions on the relative wages of skilled and unskilled labour since skilled services may increasingly be transacted 'long-distance' whereas the latter cannot.

Physical proximity between provider and user in many services (especially in banking) does involve substantially greater efficiency, however, and at times may allow a wider range of possible transactions even when long-distance or arm's-length transaction is feasible. Technical change that has opened up product diversification in banking, for instance, has reinforced this aspect. In legal services, continuous interaction between local client and overseas lawyers is deemed essential for efficient service and has fuelled lobbying efforts by multinational legal firms to secure ways of establishing physical proximity to their clients abroad.

The vast majority of service providers are likely to require and therefore press for physical proximity. The question of devising a service compact, whether as part of an augmented GATT or outside the GATT, is thus inextricably bound up with the question of provider-mobility across national borders.

The negotiations on services must therefore somehow come to terms with the implications of this essential connection, in many services, between international factor mobility and international trade. While we have accepted the distinction between these two phenomena since the founding of both economics and the GATT, it vanishes for these, indeed the preponderant class of, services. Factor mobility and trade are simply two integral aspects of the service transaction. For this reason, I prefer to talk of service *transactions* rather than service *trade*, so that we do not lose sight of this dual nature of the services that do not fall into the 'long-distance' mould.

This essential connection of services with international factor mobility has critical implications for government restrictions on service transactions. If services require factor mobility, then the ability of governments to exclude or impede service transactions does not depend altogether on restrictive border measures on trade. Restrictions on factor inflow can suffice for this purpose.

Hence arises the immediate and compelling need to go beyond the conventional focus on border trade measures such as tariffs or non-tariff barriers (NTBs) for services. This fuels the demands for the 'right to establish' domestic outlets.[5]

---

[5] At the time of US treasury secretary Connolly's efforts to 'open up Japan', the 'right to establish' question applied to *goods* trade. It was then believed that, unless Japan permitted US goods exporters to set up their own retail outlets,

But the phrase 'right to establish' conceals a continuum of factor-mobility phenomena that embrace both capital and labour mobility. It can cover the right of an American bank to establish a branch in Bombay, implying foreign investment, and the right to employ foreign personnel locally, implying skilled and semi-skilled importation of labour. It can extend to a Korean firm's right to construct a road or a harbour by importing skilled and unskilled labour, *both* constituting (according to sound economic theory as spelled out above) an integral component of the service transaction in that sector.

Equally, it can extend to an English multinational legal firm setting up an office in Tokyo, with local personnel but with English barristers or American lawyers who fly in and out to work with multinational Tokyo-based and other local clients. It could include hospital management contracts with short-term inflows of managerial personnel.

In short, factor mobility can be complex, not fitting into any particular mould. What *is* certain however is that the concept of the 'right to establish' cannot meaningfully or justifiably be circumscribed to exclude the inward mobility of foreign labour and its services. And the problem that this raises cannot be dismissed simply by saying, 'Oh, we cannot dismantle immigration restrictions and have free mobility of labour across national borders'. For, as I have argued earlier (Bhagwati 1987a), the concept that we can work with is that of *temporary-factor-relocation-requiring'* services and hence of temporary residence by foreign labour to execute service transactions. For example, Korean construction firms would bring in workers to build a turnpike; when the task was completed, the workers would return to Seoul. Or an Indian legal firm would have lawyers come from New Delhi for specific assignments or predetermined periods, the firm then rotating the personnel as necessary to avoid permanent residence (for example, immigration) of specific individuals.

Conceptual clarification of the nature of service transactions therefore has led to a keen awareness that freeing trade in services and the associated 'right to establish' question, will also raise

---

market access to Japan could not be effective. The economic implications of this issue have been discussed and modelled in Bhagwati (1982a).

serious questions relating to labour relocation. As long as the 'right to establish' was regarded as simply a question of US banks, insurance companies, and multinational professional firms setting up branches in Bangkok, Dar-es-Salaam, and Tokyo, there was at times a certain sense of patronizing disdain for the hesitations of the countries that found the factor-mobility aspects worrisome.

As Hindley (1987) shrewdly remarks, however, a certain ambivalence has apparently crept into the US negotiating attitudes, now that the labour-mobility issue suggests that openness to foreign services may create immigration problems for it. On the one hand, the impression has sometimes been given by US officials that the overall services compact should confine itself to long-distance and arm's-length transactions, ruling out 'right-to-establish' questions and hence the corresponding enormous range of services that require such establishment.

On the other hand, since the powerful US lobbies from the service sector continue to clamour for the 'right to establish', some official spokesmen have instead tended to opt in favour of an emasculated (and conveniently self-serving) notion of the 'right of presence' or 'right of market access', euphemisms that are designed to artfully ensure that the labour-mobility aspects of the 'right to establish' questions will be soft-pedalled.[6]

Exclusion of services that require significant temporary relocation of labour, however, would rule out of the compact a range of services in which some of the principal developing countries that have been sceptical about or opposed to negotiating services happen to have sufficient skills and endowments to consider developing exports of such services.[7] Apart from a handful of developing countries such as Singapore and Hong Kong, which entertain offshore banking and insurance establishments without hesitation, 'such a definition of "services" . . . excludes any substantial *export* interest on the part of developing countries' (Hindley 1987, p. 4). It would also necessarily reinforce the position of those developed countries that seek concessions on services from developing countries in exchange for their (real or

[6] Compare with Hindley's (1986a) penetrating discussion of this issue.

[7] This implication was noted earlier in Bhagwati (1987a, 1985a, 1985b) and has been further discussed by Hindley (1987), among others.

apparent) concessions on goods to the developing countries. The question therefore is pertinent to the issues that divide the G10 and the US.

Regulation

Another aspect of the difference between services and goods is the much more pervasive application of regulation to services than to goods, and the rare harmonization of regulatory provisions across national boundaries.

The *critical* difference, however, arises from the fact that these regulations often apply to the *provider* of the services while their intent is to protect the *user* of the services, whereas with goods the regulations apply to the *product itself*. Thus, with trade in goods, it is possible for foreign suppliers to meet national regulations by manufacturing to necessary standards. While it is not uncommon to hear complaints about how different health, safety, and human rights traditions and standards result in 'unfair' competition, it is conventional with goods not to be bothered by the behind-the-trade-scene regulations as they differentially affect rival *producers* in competing countries. With services, this detachment is often impossible. The regulations imposed on the provider can critically affect the service transaction, as for instance with reserve requirements that an insurance company has to meet before it is allowed to even begin to attract any customers.

This regulatory difference between services and goods implies that, while local establishment by a foreign provider to supply a service will permit the fulfilment of local regulatory criteria, sale of such services from a base abroad where the regulatory criteria are less strict, will not. This difficulty with regulation arises with 'long-distance' or arm's-length transactions, whereas the difficulty (identified earlier) with service transactions requiring physical proximity between provider and user arose where such long-distance transactions were infeasible or significantly inefficient.

The lack of harmonization amongst regulatory systems has led to major difficulties with service trade liberalization in the EEC (Hindley 1986a). The EEC does not lack the 'right to establish'. But the incapacity to sell services from a base abroad, where the regulatory regimes are dissimilar, has been a major obstacle to liberalization and accounts for the minuscule progress so far witnessed.

A gung-ho reaction to this issue would be to permit regulatory systems to 'compete through their outputs'. A less demanding or restrictive system would then prosper at the expense of those that restrict or regulate more. In their present deregulatory mood, US officials may then see a triumph of the more efficient resulting over the less efficient. It is unlikely that others will see the matter this way, however, any more than the US would if the boot were on the other leg. Within the EEC freer service trade has not been permitted to transpire; and successful efforts have not been made to harmonize the service trade regimes. It is unlikely that the developing countries, where regulation sometimes tends to be stiffer, will be enthusiastic about these matters either.

Between the hesitations over the 'right to establish' and the desire to emasculate it to developed country advantage, on the one hand, and the hesitations over the indirect competition between unharmonized regulatory regimes that the developing countries with greater attention to the role of the state must fear when services are transacted without the benefit of local establishment, on the other, it seems as if progress toward the general principles underlying a service compact is likely to be slow.

Infrastructure, National Security and Other Constraints on Liberalization

Overlaying these difficulties is the fact that some of the service sectors (for example, banking) are regarded by the hesitant developing countries to be part of their infrastructure which they feel they must control for political reasons, much as, say, the US restricts ownership by foreign nationals in its media (services) sector. Again, trans-border data flows and the information sector are regarded as sensitive areas that raise issues bordering closely on 'national security' for the 'middle powers' such as Argentina, Brazil, and India.

In these areas it is therefore difficult to urge the developing countries to discard such notions altogether, especially when these types of asymmetrical views about some services and many goods are held by many influential citizens within the developed countries themselves. (As I argue later, however, their fears and concerns are greatly exaggerated and need to be carefully evaluated in their own interest.) Consider the following impassioned pronouncement:

We ought to be exporting computers, not shares of IBM. We should seek to sell more, not sell out.

To accept the de-industrialization of [our nation] while exulting in the growth of foreign ownership and influence in our domestic institutions could be an unwitting prescription for slowly becoming an economic colony again.

It came not from Prime Minister Rajiv Gandhi or from President Alfonsin. The author was US Representative Jim Wright, majority whip in the US Congress, writing in the *Wall Street Journal* (3 Oct. 1985).

III. COMPARATIVE ADVANTAGE IN SERVICES, COST OF PROTECTION, AND POLICY-MIX SOLUTIONS

The foregoing analysis highlights the difficulties that emerge for the impending service negotiations, especially as they reflect the special characteristics that serve to set services apart from goods. But before I turn to the prospects for different solutions to these difficulties, it is necessary to speculate on where the comparative advantage in service transactions may lie, especially between the developing and the developed countries. Several observations on that issue are in order.

First, while the trade data for services are extremely unreliable, Sapir's (1985) careful analysis of what is available strongly underlines what common sense would suggest: many traded services tend to be intensive in the use of technology and of capital, whether human or physical. This should give the developed countries the competitive edge since they are abundantly endowed with human and physical capital. It is suggestive that when Sapir (p. 37) looks at the balance of trade in services, it is the advanced newly industrializing economies such as the Republic of Korea,

Singapore, and Taiwan that come out with small positive or negative balances rather than the large deficit of many developing countries.[8]

It would however be totally wrong to infer that developing countries simply cannot find traded services that they can export successfully. Table 20.1, compiled by Sapir, gives an aggregated and very rough picture of service trade among the two groups of industrialized and developing countries for 1980. The data can be read two ways. On the one hand, they show that the service exports of developing countries are a substantially smaller fraction of their total exports than is the case with industrialized countries' share of service to total exports. On the other hand,

TABLE 20.1

Trade between the Industrialized
and Developing Countries, 1980

(billions of dollars[a])

Category of merchandise and services	Industrialized-country exports to developing countries	Developing-country exports to industrialized countries
Merchandise trade, of which:	277	385
Fuels	6	258
Other primary products	44	67
Manufactures	227	60
Service trade, of which:	72	30
Transport	35	10
Travel	14	12
Other private services	23	8

[a] Billion is 1,000 million.

SOURCE: Sapir (1985, Table 2); data for merchandise trade are based on GATT (1983); and for service trade, on own estimates.

[8] In itself, however, the trade balance would of course, be an inconclusive piece of evidence on the issue.

the developing countries' service exports are by no means negligible, as recorded, and appear to reflect earnings not only from
tourism and transport but also from 'other private services' (that
include professional, design, construction, and related services).

TABLE 20.2

Market Share of International Construction
Measured by New Contracts Awarded to the Top
Two-hundred and Fifty International Contractors, 1980–4

(billions of dollars)

Country	1980	1981	1982	1983	1984
United States	48.3	48.8	44.9	29.4	30.1
	(45)	(36)	(36)	(31)	(38)
France	8.1	12.1	11.4	10.0	5.4
	(7)	(9)	(9)	(11)	(7)
Germany, Fed. Rep.	8.6	9.9	9.5	5.4	4.8
	(8)	(7)	(8)	(6)	(6)
Italy	6.2	9.3	7.8	7.2	7.8
	(6)	(7)	(6)	(8)	(8)
United Kingdom	4.9	8.7	7.5	6.4	5.7
	(5)	(6)	(6)	(7)	(7)
Other European	9.2	12.6	10.3	9.1	7.2
	(8)	(9)	(8)	(10)	(9)
Japan	4.1	8.6	9.3	8.7	7.3
	(4)	(6)	(8)	(9)	(9)
Korea, Rep.	9.5	13.9	13.8	10.4	6.8
	(9)	(10)	(11)	(11)	(8)
All other	9.4	10.5	8.6	7.0	5.9
	(9)	(8)	(7)	(7)	(7)
Total	108.3	134.4	123.1	93.6	80.5

NOTE: Figures in parentheses represent percentages.

SOURCE: Various issues of *Engineering News Record;* from ongoing studies by
U.S. Office of Technology Assessment.

Second, detailed studies further underline the export possibilities that the energetic, outward-oriented newly industrializing
economies have in services. Thus, for example, Table 20.2

TABLE 20.3

Cumulative Foreign Awards of Top
International Contractors by Economy, 1978–83

(billions of dollars)

Economy	Awards
All countries, of which:	566.6
All developing countries, of which:	99.2
Korea, Rep.	56.2
Turkey	10.0
Yugoslavia	7.4
Brazil	5.8
India	3.9
Taiwan	3.4
Philippines	3.2
Argentina	3.0
Lebanon	1.4
Pakistan	1.3
Kuwait	0.7
Singapore	0.6
Malaysia	0.5
Panama	0.4
Mexico	0.2
Thailand	0.2
United Arab Emirates	0.2
Colombia	0.1
Indonesia	0.1

NOTE: Countries are ranked according to the foreign contract values of their top firms. Until 1980, the top 200 firms were surveyed; since then, this number was raised to 250.

SOURCE: Compiled by Sapir (1986, Table 2) from *Engineering News*, various issues.

suggests that the earlier US domination of the world market for international *construction* may have diminished with the medium-level developed countries and a newly industrializing economy such as Korea taking significant shares in the 1980s. A non-negligible share of the developing countries is evident from Table 20.3. In the more complex field of international design contracts, the data again shows a sizable share of contracts being awarded to firms from Brazil, India, Korea, Lebanon, and Taiwan (Sapir 1986, Table 3).

Third, there is little doubt that the broader group of newly industrializing economies, not just the super exporting economies like Korea, but also the traditionally inward-looking ones like India, have the skills to develop export advantages, not merely in computer software (a good, not a service) and in an increasing range of 'on-the-wire' services that new technologies make possible, but also in the services that imply temporary relocation of skilled labour. I would expect that legal and professional services, with right of establishment, exhibit a *mutual* rather than one-sided export advantage for developing and developed countries. The developing countries must not be misled into thinking otherwise simply because the initiative to include such trade in a services compact comes almost wholly from multinational firms in the developed countries. Why?

The reason is that such services are not homogeneous. It is necessary to think of 'dualistic' structures here (Bhagwati 1986d). The advantage in tendering services at the multinational level is likely to inhere in developed countries: indeed, these multinationals are piggybacking on their multinational clients in other sectors that have operations abroad. Only as the developing countries expand their own multinationals in non-service sectors, as is beginning to happen, will they begin to develop some 'linked' advantage in professional services.

At the other end of the spectrum, however, the advantage must belong to lawyers, doctors, and accountants in the developing countries because, while they are equally competent, they can work more cheaply and offer a range of services where price competition is decisive.[9] If they are allowed to enter under

---

[9] The question of whether they would be allowed to indulge in price competition is critical. Attempts by professional associations to regulate minimum prices would then be in restraint of trade.

'temporary-factor-relocation' visas to make service transactions possible, I see no reason why they cannot increasingly take a sizable fraction of the market at that level.[10]

Such a 'dualistic' view is quite consonant with mutual trade in 'similar products'. A product is a vector of characteristics, and different countries can have advantage in some and not in others. In service transactions, physical proximity accentuates such differential elements and can lead to mutual comparative advantage within a sector for suppliers from different countries.

Fourth, the export possibilities become even more compelling for developing countries if the issue of unskilled labour mobility in the execution of specific short-term contracts (as in the Middle East), is resolved in favour of its inclusion in the 'right to establish'. It is already within the realm of probability, thanks to the widespread use of such unskilled labour, including that by US international contracting firms, during the 1970s and 1980s. It also has legitimacy in the practice of Western Europe in its post-war 'guest-worker' systems and in the latest US legislation permitting over 300,000 workers to be imported for specific types of short-term work (that is, in US agriculture).[11]

Fifth, it is important for developing countries to recognize that a great number of traded services are intermediates. Protecting the banking and insurance sectors for example, increases the domestic prices of these services. As they are inputs into other goods, this can raise prices of export goods and undermine export prospects.

The effects of protecting intermediate services are similar to those that result from increasing the cost of intermediate goods such as steel.[12] But the adverse effects on exports of goods are

[10] It is important not to confuse the 'brain drain' question with the issue of temporary relocation of labour. I have discussed the contrasts in Bhagwati (1985c).

[11] In the spirit of the US service sectors' demands, the developing countries may well ask for equal access to these jobs instead of having them de facto assigned to applicants south of the Rio Grande.

[12] The successful outward-oriented regimes have succeeded in ensuring that internationally traded intermediate goods are available to domestic producers at world prices. Similar logic should also apply to internationally traded intermediate services.

more serious in the present instance because, in denying the domestic exporters of goods access to efficient banking services, the protective policies succeed in denying access to more than cheaper credit. More important, exporters are denied access to the entire vector of services that modern international banks can provide to facilitate international commerce. The protection of intermediate services, in the interest of goals such as political control, therefore has costs that are not negligible and have presumably not been properly assessed by the developing countries.

Finally, it is important to recognize that policies such as the protection of locally produced computer hardware in the telematics and information sectors may represent an unnecessarily expensive way of securing a country's objectives. If the objective is to build up national technological know-how through 'learning by doing' (rather than developing the industry itself), then the cost of such a policy is to spread computer illiteracy amongst the population and high costs to producers who must make do without lower-cost access to modern information technology in the production process.[13]

A country such as India (and possibly Argentina and Brazil as well) has the possibility of using an alternative policy instrument to achieve the desired mastery of know-how without these costs. Remember that a country's know-how is embodied in its citizens. Looking at the composition by national origin of scientists in only the artificial intelligence, robotics, and computer science labs and institutes in the US, it is possible to find numerous Indian mathematicians and scientists even in leadership positions. These Indians embody know-how in these fields at the very cutting edge of technology.

Since the sociology of international migration of professional

---

[13] In India, import-substitution in computer hardware has led to higher costs, unavailability, and enormous lags in the use of computers in tourism, the judiciary and schools. The import-substitution policy has had the effect of distancing greatly even a highly educated population and skills-endowed economy such as India from the modern world outside. It also inhibits the rapid adoption of modern information technology-based processes that are essential to absorbing high-productivity economically efficient advances in the manufacturing sector.

classes increasingly permits immigrants to retain ethnic ties to their countries of origin — and therefore the 'diaspora' model has increasingly come into its own — the Indian government has the option of utilizing this US-based resource any time it wishes to do so.[14] Going the protectionist route will yield a lower level of embodied technology in resident nationals (who may also leave anyway) *and* will sacrifice computer literacy and efficiency in production. Permitting cheap imports at world prices avoids these costs, and utilizing the superior know-how embodied in a country's nationals abroad also secures know-how at its best and cheapest.[15]

To put it differently, the *two objectives* of (i) spreading computer literacy and encouraging adoption of efficient production processes, and (ii) building up technical know-how among the country's nationals are impossible to achieve with one policy instrument, namely, protection. They are achievable, and are in effect Pareto-dominated in outcome, by the use of *two policy instruments:* (i) world price imports of computers and related technology; and (ii) an open door policy on emigration combined with a policy of utilizing the know-how embodied in the country's nationals abroad.

Such a policy mix breaks from the protectionist mould and requires an imaginative and simultaneous use of policies from what are generally considered to be unrelated areas of governmental intervention. But they do offer the prospect of a superior approach for those countries such as India which have the talents and the skills in the field of information to make such an approach feasible.

[14] When a people are geographically dispersed but ethnically linked, this new reality has several important implications for a variety of other policy issues such as the appropriate exercise of income tax jurisdiction on a country's nationals when they are internationally mobile. See Bhagwati (1982a) and Bhagwati and Wilson (1987).

[15] Although I talk of 'nationals', there is little doubt that even those who change nationalities today often have attachment to their countries of origin. Nonetheless, this distinction in turn raises the issue whether developing countries ought not to consider permitting their nationals to hold dual nationality as part of the policy option that I advocate above.

IV. Developing Countries:
Bargaining Options and Strategies

What positive approaches emerge that the developing countries may take in the forthcoming negotiations on services?

Developing countries cannot be expected to opt en bloc for any one approach on services, any more than we can expect them to have identical positions on agricultural liberalization or the developed countries to agree on the optimal redesign of safeguard procedures. Thus, Hong Kong and Singapore can be expected to be agreeable to the more 'hard-line' developed country positions on services. Brazil and India can be expected to oppose them. They, and also the developing countries that initiated the Uruguay Round under the G48 umbrella, will have to decide what kind of game they want to play now that the players are coming onto the field.

The options that they must consider are best determined by the demands that the developed countries, especially the United States, have been making.[16] These options will have to be defined in terms of the *responses* that the developing countries make to these demands or negotiating positions, as they have been indicated so far. Let me begin with what are generally understood to be the broad outlines of the current US positions, however negotiable they may prove to be in the course of the Uruguay Round itself.

Generally Perceived US Positions

Inclusion of services in the Uruguay Round, and indeed of other 'new' sectors and areas such as intellectual property and trade-related investment rules, is considered to be part of a 'grand

---

[16] While the discussion below focuses on the US, it is clear that, unlike in the 1982 GATT Ministerial meeting, the EEC also perceives export competitiveness for itself in services and hence is closer than before to the US positions on it. See, for example, the recent statements of Willy de Clercq (1986) to this effect. Table 20.4 on the US (below) therefore could be readily modified to one for the EEC, with agriculture being considered as a 'loss' instead of a 'gain'. Japan, with its enormous surplus, also sees clear comparative advantage in the financial services area.

trade-off' where these new areas benefit the United States. *In return*, the United States is willing to consider rollbacks and stand-stills (consistent with the exercise of trade-affecting, GATT-compatible actions such as countervailing duties, anti-dumping, and Section 301 actions) on goods (see also, however, the discussion below).

The 'grand trade-off' is seen in terms of both cosmopolitan interest (that is, what international economists describe as 'world welfare') as well as US interest (that is, what international economists describe as 'national welfare'). The former position emphasizes that an efficient world allocation of resources requires that 'everything be put on the table': the outmoded GATT must be redesigned, augmented in scope, and brought up to date to embrace new realities. The latter position is developed in terms of US comparative advantage having shifted to the new areas so that, if the US is to yield on goods, it is fair for it to ask others to yield on services and new issues. A brief tabular arrangement of US–perceived losses and gains in relation to those of the developing countries in terms of the mercantilist logic of trade barriers bargaining is set out in Table 20.4.

A third argument in the US in favour of this grand trade-off is that the current presidential administration is too beleaguered to hold protectionists at bay in Congress unless the advanced developing countries (and, of course, Japan and the EEC) open up their markets to US exports of services as a quid pro quo.[17] These countries are faced with what could be construed as a rather difficult situation: trade concessions appear to be demanded of them as a way of ensuring that market access for their exports is continued.

But this, in turn, reflects a substantial shift in US positions in trade negotiations from what I have called GATT-style 'first-difference' reciprocity to 'full' reciprocity.[18] The US has increasingly looked at, not the balance of advantages from *changes* in

[17] The US government has encouraged such export-seeking lobbies as a political countervailing force to the trade-threatening protectionist lobbies.

[18] I note with pleasure that Brian Hindley (1987a) has embraced this terminology. The use of the phrase 'aggressive reciprocity' to denote full reciprocity is inappropriate: full reciprocity could equally be pursued in a tranquil way.

trade barriers, but the balance of advantages from the trading system in toto.

TABLE 20.4

Perceived US Benefits and Losses in
Relation to those of Developing Countries from the
Prospective Liberalization of Trade in the Uruguay Round

US 'Benefits'	US 'Losses'
1. Services	1. Rollback of the Multifibre Arrangement (MFA) and other voluntary export restraints (VER) and Organized Marketing Arrangements (OMA) on goods
2. Intellectual property	
3. Trade-related investments	
4 Reverse market access to developing countries	2. Standstill on VERs, OMAs on goods
	3. More stringent use of safeguards and tighter rules to prevent abuse of countervailing-duty and anti-dumping actions
5. Agriculture[a]	
	4. Improved structural adjustment

a   Agriculture is included as a benefit because agricultural liberalization in cereals is expected to favour US exports, mostly at the expense of the EEC and Japan but, depending on the final package, even at the expense of some developing countries.

Doubtless this attitude stems from the macroeconomic difficulties that the overvalued US dollar entails and the resulting substantial adjustments forced on the traded sector. It also stems from the 'diminished giant syndrome' that has afflicted the US as its effortless post-war hegemony in the world economy has been threatened by the relentless advent of the Pacific Century.[19] But overlaying these two factors has been the fundamental fact that the GATT's basic conception, and indeed that of the US as its leading founder, was always based on contractual and (fully) reciprocal rights, with member states enjoying symmetrical rights and obligations. The US, which emerged as the *force majeure* in

[19] On this, see Bhagwati and Irwin (1986) on the parallels between late nineteenth-century Britain and the present-day US in the rise of 'fair trade' movements.

the 1940s, permitted Western Europe to effectively get away with non-reciprocity while it worked through the 1950s to achieve current account convertibility, and agreed to special and differential treatment for developing countries until now.

The current US insistence on full reciprocity can then be seen as an inevitable return to the original symmetrical conception of the world trading order. Hence, it is *not* a position that the developing countries (or Japan, which is alleged, rightly or wrongly, to offer less than symmetrical access to its own markets) are likely to be able to challenge with success, much as they consider it to be unfair from the perspective of first-difference reciprocity. My judgement therefore is that the developing countries must proceed from the unhappy premise that the US, especially its Congress, cannot be expected to trade access to its markets any longer without significant elements of reciprocity from the developing countries, even if the balance-of-trade deficits are somehow eliminated.

The Developing Country Options

From the viewpoint of the hesitant developing countries, the US position presents one major difficulty even if they are prepared to accept the reality of full reciprocity and yield on their sense hitherto that the so-called bargain being offered to them simply is not one. It is unclear what the US and the EEC can offer by way of standstills and rollbacks on goods if these developing countries offer concessions on services. I quote one influential commentator, who was a member of the US administration:

The issue for the United States is whether a meaningful standstill and rollback commitment would apply to existing US restrictions in sugar, meat imports, textiles, steel, automobiles, etc. as well as the use of future 301 actions in both goods and services trade. Ideally, the United States would like this commitment to apply only to new measures, not existing restrictions or extensions of existing programmes (such as another VRA [voluntary restraint agreement] in steel or tightening sugar quotas under the existing programmes). According to US interests, it would not apply at all to trade legislation consistent with GATT (201, CVD [countervailing duty], and AD [anti-dumping] provisions and national security), and it would mean submitting 301 cases to GATT but only in goods. In new areas — services, etc. — the United States would remain free to retaliate under 301, including retaliation in goods areas, without submitting to GATT rules. [Nau 1986, pp. 22–3.]

This has been the sense of the remarks reported in the US press by Ambassador Yeutter on his return from Punta del Este. It is also consonant with the substances of Martin Wolf's 'Europessimistic' argumentation on special and differential treatment presented in *The World Bank Economic Review* (vol. 7, no. 4, Sept. 1987): few meaningful concessions on rollbacks and standstills on goods can really be expected and the developing countries ought to yield on reverse market access largely because it is good for them to liberalize as suggested by the export-promoting strategy.[20] Doubtless, as I have already emphasized in Sec. III, even unilateral trade liberalization in intermediate services should have big payoffs for the developing countries. But if only we could persuade trading nations to accept such compelling arguments, we would not have to worry about rollbacks and standstills either. The developing countries cannot realistically be expected to be less mercantilist than those who preach free trade but practice mercantilism themselves. This is a pity, but also a reality.

This reinforces, in my judgement, a suggestion I made earlier (Bhagwati 1985c), that the developing countries ought to participate actively in the service negotiations instead of rejecting them on grounds of first-difference reciprocity unfairness. They should then seek quid pro quo (in terms of export possibilities) within the service sector itself.

Not merely is it risky to establish linkage between goods and services when the goods 'benefit' is less likely than the services 'loss', it is also silly to let the developed countries define the service compact all by themselves in a way that can then be fully expected to serve their own narrower, export interests rather than reflecting more fairly and adequately the general principles as set out in recent analyses and recapitulated in Sec. II above.[21] The latter would also serve the interests of developing country exporters.

[20] On the merits of this strategy, see the extended review in Bhagwati (forthcoming)
[21] It seems probable that the failure of the developing countries to be actively involved in the Tokyo Round negotiations on the subsidies code, for example,

As I argued in Sec. III, quid pro quo within the service sector certainly exists for the skill-abundant, newly industrializing countries, and especially so if the temporary-factor relocation-requiring labour and skilled labour-intensive services are not omitted in the formulation of a services agreement.[22]

The difficulties that I detailed in Sec. II that plague rapid progress in service liberalization also imply that the Uruguay round is unlikely to yield anything more concrete than a code or an agreement of principles. It is importable that actual service liberalization under the code will emerge during the course of the Round itself.

This prospect also underlines the wisdom of a strategy in which the developing countries offer to discuss services, thus assuaging the desire to begin bringing them under trade discipline and hence helping to head off protectionist pressures on goods trade. At the same time, they can utilize the opportunity to ensure that their export prospects are adequately reflected in the service code.

My suspicion is that, while this multilateral 'constitution making' on the principles of a services Agreement will go on, the US will continue to use bilateral approaches with the aid of Section 301 to pry open selected service sectors in selected countries. This is probably unavoidable, given the immense Congressional and lobbying pressures to produce quick results.

To some extent, the US Trade Representative (USTR) can be

until fairly late may have caused the code to be written against their interests (for example, in the blanket restrictions on export subsidies) and hence have led to widespread refusal by the developing countries to sign it..

[22] Feketekuty's (1986) extended analysis and documentation of US visa practices in regard to domestic entry for *temporary* business purposes needs to be read by the sceptical among the developing countries. Evidently, there is far more room for active diplomacy and negotiations here than is commonly believed. Also, the reader should consult the entire issue of the *Chicago Legal Forum* (1986, vol. 1, no. 1), which deals with the question of trade in legal services across nation states and which contains the Feketekuty (1986) and Bhagwati (1986) papers, especially those by Barton, Cone, Noyelle, and Rossi. Needless to say, the negotiators will have to address complex issues which get even worse in dealing with unskilled labour mobility. For example, while firms can bring in professionals of different nationalities under the temporary visas, could a US firm bring in Bangladeshi construction labour to Düsseldorf?

expected to ensure that these bilateral approaches are adopted to 'set useful precedents' for the wider, multilateral code. At the same time, there is some cause for apprehension that the sectoral lobbying pressures to produce results may lead to 'quantity' rather than 'rule' outcomes (as strongly suggested in an insightful study by Cho (1986) of the US–Korea 301 episode on the opening of the Korean insurance market).[23] This tendency to substitute 'quantity' outcomes in favour of US export sectors rather than to secure rule-oriented liberalization abroad is a peril that has not been easy to avoid. This was evident in the case of beef quotas in Japan in which the United States reportedly wanted a larger share rather than genuine Japanese liberalization which would have allowed Australian beef to triumph over that both from the US and Japan. Similarly, in negotiations on trade in semiconductor chips, an assured market share in Japan for US *firms* was actively urged and, while not finally in the pact, is still the basis by which Japanese 'performance' on the pact has been judged to be in-adequate and hence to require the retaliatory tariffs imposed by President Reagan in April 1987. This is such an interesting in-novation in trade policy that I have (Bhagwati 1987b) christened it as VIEs (voluntary import expansions).[24]

There is little that the developing countries targeted for bilateral negotiations will be able to do since it is evidently a case where the strong prevail over the weak. This is the oldest argument in the book for resort to multilateralism, which has been regarded as the only shield of the weak. Evidently, as such bilateral targeting and quantity targets multiply, the wisdom of the developing coun-tries joining in devising a multilateral compact will become in-creasingly evident.[25]

---

[23] Thus, one of Cho's central conclusions is that 'both governments approached the case with the perception that the main issue of negotiation is the *sharing of profit* [rents] in Korea's insurance market. In the process of negotiation, both governments (especially the US) basically represented the interests of their in-surance industries. The effect of the results of the negotiation on other sectors and efficiency of the economy as a whole has not been an important con-sideration'. (1986, p. 17).

[24] See also the discussion of this issue in Bhagwati and Irwin (1987) in the context of recent US trade policy.

[25] For those in the US who believe therefore that such bilateralism, or

Yet another compelling reason for the developing countries to join in writing the multilateral rules is that rules, written between 'equals', will tend to underplay the problems that 'unequals' face in service liberalization. An individual would have to be deranged to imagine the largest American banks taking over wholly from the largest five British banks in the UK if banking were fully liberalized. Yet such fears are routine in New Delhi and Dar-es-Salaam. The 'political control' issues take on an added significance in the context of such fears. I spend a fair amount of time arguing with the risk-averse that such scenarios do not make much sense for New Delhi either, that it would be an act of insanity for a large American bank to open branches in India's vast hinterland, that its clientele and operations would most likely be in international transactions.

But it is evident that the unequals have fear; and, as the Russian proverb goes, fear has big eyes. So, we will need to incorporate, at least for developing countries, some quantity safeguards, just as we have GATT Article XIX as a safeguard on goods. These would have to be more generous for the developing countries, subject to eventual and negotiated erosion with 'graduation', perhaps even slower-paced than as now discussed for goods. In essence, therefore, we should contemplate freer, not free, trade in services, and, contrary to the conventional rules of the strange English language where 'freer' should mean more free than 'free', the developing countries should remember that it is just the other way around. But these explicit safeguards to assuage their fears will not arrive like manna from heaven. The developing countries will have to argue for this; they cannot do it if they do not actively participate in the rule-making.

Everything therefore points to one simple piece of advice for the hesitant developing countries: get into the negotiations on the code and exercise a voice; to exit is certainly the inferior alternative.

'plurilateralism' — what a lovely euphemism for 'regionalism' and other non-multilateral arrangements — is only a tactical device to get rapidly towards multilateralism, it would be wise to remember that such arrangements create vested interests *against* new entry, no matter what you write into the rules!

REFERENCES

Bhagwati, Jagdish, 1982a: 'Structural Adjustment and International Factor Mobility: Some Issues', *in* Karl Jungenfelt (ed.), *Structural Adjustment in the World Economy* (London: Macmillan).

——, 1982b: 'Taxation and International Migration', *in* Barry Chiswick (ed.), *The Gateway: U.S. Immigration Issues and Policies* (Washington, DC: American Enterprise Institute).

——, 1984: 'Splintering and Disembodiment of Services and Developing Nations', *The World Economy* 7, no. 2 (June), pp. 133–43.

——, 1985a: 'GATT and Trade in Services: How we can Resolve the North-South Debate', *Financial Times*, 27 Nov.

——, 1985b: *Opening up Trade in Services: U.S. Should Heed Third World Demands*, New York Times, 10 Nov.

——, 1985c: 'Trade in Services: How to Change Indian Strategy', *Economic Times* (India), 2 Dec.

——, 1986: 'Economic Perspectives on Trade in Professional Services', *Chicago Legal Forum* 1, no. 1 (March), pp. 45–56.

——, 1987a: 'International Trade in Services and its Relevance for Economic Development', *in* Orio Giarini (ed.), *The Emerging Service Economy*, Services World Economy Series 1 (New York: Pergamon Press).

——, 1987b: 'VERs, Quid Pro Quo DFI and VIEs: Political-Economy-Theoretic Analyses', *International Economic Journal* (Seoul) 1(1) Spring, pp. 1–15.

——, Forthcoming: 'Export Promoting Trade Strategy: Issues and Evidence', *World Bank Research Observer*.

Bhagwati, Jagdish and Douglas Irwin, 1986: 'Lessons from Nineteenth Century Britain: Fair Trade Could Trap the Democrats', *New York Times*, 22 June.

——, 1987: 'The Return of the Reciprocitarians: U.S. Trade Policy Today', *The World Economy* 10, no. 2 (June), pp. 109–30.

Bhagwati, Jagdish and John Wilson (eds), 1987: *Income Taxation and International Personal Mobility* (Amsterdam: North-Holland).

Cho, Yoon Je, 1986: 'U.S.-Korea Disputes on the Opening of Korean Insurance Market: Some Implications' (Washington, DC: World Bank Development Research Department).

de Clercq, Willy, 1986: 'The European Community and GATT Negotiations on Trade in Services', Speech at Lugano Economic and Financial Symposium, 27 May.

Feketekuty, Geza, 1986: 'Trade in Professional Services. An Overview', *Chicago Legal Forum* 1, no. 1 (March).

GATT, 1983: *International Trade 1982–83* (Geneva: GATT Secretariat).

Hill, T.P., 1977: 'On Goods and Services', *Review of Income and Wealth* 23, no. 4 (Dec.).

Hindley, Brian, 1986a: 'Introducing Services into GATT', Paper prepared for the European meeting on the position of the European Community in the New GATT Round convened by the Spanish Ministry of Finance and the Economy and the Trade Policy Research Centre, Residencia Fuente Pizarro, Collado–Villalba, Spain, 2–4 Oct.

——, 1986b: 'Liberalization of Service Transactions' (Washington, DC: World Bank Development Research Department).

——, 1987: 'A Comment on Jagdish Bhagwati's Geneva Association Lecture', in *The Emerging Service Economy*, Services World Economy Series 1, Orio Giarini (ed.) (New York: Pergamon Press).

Nau, Henry, 1986: 'Bargaining in the New Round: The NICs and the United States', Georgetown University Paper for the Quadrangular Forum Meeting, Vermont, 18–20 July.

Sampson, Gary and Richard Snape, 1985: 'Identifying the Issues in Trade in Services', *The World Economy* 8, no. 2 (June), pp. 171–82.

Sapir, André, 1985: 'North–South Issues in Trade in Services', *The World Economy* 8, no. 1 (March), pp. 27–41.

——, 1986: 'Trade in Investment-Related Technological Services', *World Development* 14, no. 5, pp. 605–22.

21

Free Trade and the Environment

ECONOMISTS are reconciled to the conflict of absolutes: that is why they invented the concept of trade-offs. It should not surprise them, therefore, that the objective of environmental protection should at times run afoul of the goal of seeking maximum gains from trade. Indeed, economists would be suspicious of any claims, such as those made by soothsaying politicians, that both causes would be only mutually beneficial. They are rightly disconcerted, however, by the passion and the ferocity, and hence often the lack of logic or facts, with which environmental groups have recently assailed both free trade and the General Agreement on Tariffs and Trade (GATT), the institution that oversees the world trading system.

The environmentalists' antipathy to trade is perhaps inevitable. Trade has been central to economic thinking since Adam Smith discovered the virtues of specialization and of the markets that naturally sustain it. Because markets do not normally exist for the pursuit of environmental protection, they must be specially created. Trade therefore suggests abstention from governmental intervention, whereas environmentalism suggests its necessity. Then again, trade is exploited and its virtues extolled by corporate and multinational interests, whereas environmental objectives are embraced typically by non-profit organizations, which are generally wary of these interests. Trade is an ancient occupation, and its nurture is the objective of institutions crafted over many years of experience and reflection. Protection of the environment, on the other hand, is a recent preoccupation of national and international institutions that are nascent and still evolving.

Last year the environmentalists' hostility to trade exploded in outrage when an impartial GATT Dispute Settlement Panel ruled in favour of Mexico and free trade, and against the US and the welfare of the dolphin. The US had placed an embargo on the import of Mexican tuna on the grounds that the fish had been caught in purse-seine nets, which kill dolphins cruelly and in greater numbers than US law permits. The GATT panel ruled, in effect, that the US could not suspend Mexico's trading rights by unilaterally proscribing the methods by which that country harvested tuna.

This decision spurred the conservationists' subsequent campaigns against free trade and the GATT. The GATT has no shortage of detractors, of course. Indeed, some of its recent critics have feared its impotence and declared it 'dead', referring to it as the General Agreement to Talk and Talk. But the environmentalist attacks, which presume instead GATT's omnipotence, are something else again.

An advertisement by a coalition of environmental groups in the *New York Times* on 20 April 1992, set a new standard for alarmist, even scurrilous, writing, calculated to appeal to the instincts rather than the intellect. It talks of 'faceless GATT bureaucrats' mounting a 'sneak attack on democracy'. This veiled reference to Pearl Harbour provides an example of a common tactic in trade controversy: Japan-bashing. The innuendos have continued unabated and are manifest in the endless battles in Congress over the supplemental environmental accords for the North American Free Trade Agreement (NAFTA). The hostility is also intruding on the conclusion of the Uruguay Round of the GATT talks initiated in 1986, with the environmentalists opposing the establishment of the new Multilateral Trade Organization, which is meant to provide effective discipline and a necessary institutional structure for GATT.

It is surely tragic that the proponents of two of the great causes of the 1990s, trade and the environment, should be locked in combat. The conflict is largely gratuitous. There are at times philosophical differences between the two that cannot be reconciled, as when some environmentalists assert nature's autonomy, whereas most economists see nature as a handmaiden to humankind. For the most part, however, the differences derive from misconceptions. It is necessary to dissect and dismiss the more egregious of these fallacies before addressing the genuine problems.

The fear is widespread among environmentalists that free trade increases economic growth and that growth harms the environment. That fear is misplaced. Growth enables governments to tax and to raise resources for a variety of objectives, including the abatement of pollution and the general protection of the environment. Without such revenues, little can be achieved, no matter how pure the underlying motives may be.

How do societies actually spend these additional revenues? It depends on how getting rich affects the desire for a better environment. Rich countries today have more groups worrying about environmental causes than do poor countries. Efficient policies, such as freer trade, should generally help environmentalism, not harm it.

If it was sought to predict what growth would do to the environment, however, it would also be necessary to would consider how it affect the production of pollution. Growth affects not only the demand for a good environment but also the supply of the pollution associated with growth. The net effect on the environment will therefore depend on the kind of economic growth. Gene M. Grossman and Alan B. Krueger of Princeton University found that in cities around the world sulphur dioxide pollution fell as per capita income rose. The only exception was in countries whose per capita incomes fell below $ 5,000. In short, environmentalists are in error when they fear that trade, through growth, will necessarily increase pollution.

Economic effects besides those attributable to rising incomes also help in protecting the environment. For example, freer trade enables pollution-fighting technologies available elsewhere to be imported. Thus, trade in low-sulphur-content coal will enable the users of local high-sulphur-content coal to shift from the latter to the former.

Free trade can also lead to better environmental outcomes from a shift in the composition of production. An excellent example is provided by Robert C. Feenstra of the University of California at Davis. He has shown how the imposition of restraints on Japanese automobile exports to the US during the 1980s shifted the composition of those exports from small to large cars, as the Japanese attempted to increase their revenues without increasing the number of units they sold. Yet the large cars were fuel inefficient. Thus, protective efforts by the US effectively increased the average amount of pollution produced by imported cars, making it more likely that pollution from cars would increase rather than diminish in the US.

Although these erroneous objections to free trade are readily dismissed (but not so easily eliminated from public discourse), there are genuine conflicts between trade and the environment. To understand and solve them, economists draw a distinction between two kinds of environmental problems: those that are intrinsically domestic and those that are intrinsically transnational.

Should Brazil pollute a lake lying wholly within its borders, the problem would be intrinsically domestic. Should it pollute a river that flows into Argentina, the matter would take on an intrinsically transnational character. Perhaps the most important examples of transnational pollution are acid rain, created when sulphur dioxide emissions in one country precipitate into rain in another, and greenhouse gases, such as carbon dioxide, which contribute to global warming wherever they are emitted.

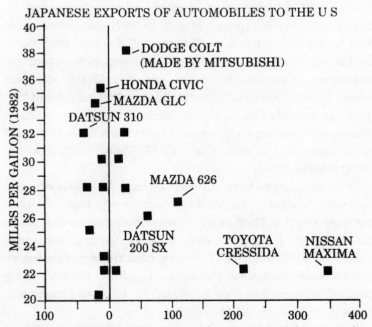

JAPANESE EXPORTS OF AUTOMOBILES TO THE U S

FIG. 21.1: Change in Quantity of Cars Exported, 1979–82 (percentage)
SOURCE: Robert C. Feenstra, University of California, Davis.

Why do intrinsically domestic environmental questions create international concern? The principal reason is the belief that diversity in environmental standards may affect competitiveness. Businesses and labour unions worry that their rivals in other countries may gain an edge if their governments impose lower standards of environmental protection. They decry such differences as unfair. To level the playing field, these lobbies insist that foreign countries raise their standards up to domestic ones. In turn, environmental groups worry that if such 'harmonization up' is not undertaken prior to freeing trade, pressures from uncompetitive businesses at home will force down domestic standards, reversing their hard-won victories. Finally, there is the fear, dramatized by H. Ross Perot in his criticisms of NAFTA, that factories will relocate to the countries whose environmental standards are the lowest.

But if the competitiveness issue makes the environmentalists, the businesses, and the unions into allies, the environmentalists are on their own in other ways. Two problem areas can be distinguished. First, some environmentalists are keen to impose their own ethical preferences on others, using trade sanctions to induce or coerce acceptance of such preferences. For instance, tuna fishing with purse-seine nets that kill dolphins is opposed by US environmental groups, which consequently favour restraints on the importation of such tuna from Mexico and elsewhere. Second, other environmentalists fear that the rules of free trade, as embodied in GATT and strengthened in the Uruguay Round, will constrain their freedom to pursue even purely domestic environmental objectives, with GATT tribunals outlawing disputed regulation.

Environmentalists have cause for concern. Not all concerns are legitimate, however, and not all the solutions to legitimate concerns are sensible. Concern over competitiveness has thus led to the illegitimate demand that environmental standards abroad be treated as 'social dumping'. Offending countries are regarded as unfairly subsidizing their exporters through lax environmental requirements. Such implicit subsidies, the reasoning continues, ought to be offset by import duties.

Yet international differences in environmental standards are perfectly natural. Even if two countries share the same environmental objectives, the *specific* pollutions they would attack, and hence the industries they would hinder, will generally not be identical. Mexico has a greater social incentive than does the US to spend an extra dollar preventing dysentery rather than reducing lead in gasoline.

Equally, a certain environmental good might be valued more highly by a poor country than by a rich one. Contrast, for instance, the value assigned to a lake with the cost of cleaning up effluents discharged into it by a pharmaceutical company. In India such a lake's water might be drunk by a malnourished population whose mortality would increase sharply with the rise in pollution. In the US the water might be consumed by few people, all of whom have the means to protect themselves with privately purchased water filters. In this example, India would be the more likely to prefer clean water to the pharmaceutical company's profits.

The consequences of differing standards are clear: each country will have less of the industry whose pollution it fears relatively more than other countries do. Indeed, even if there were no international trade, we would be shrinking industries whose pollution we deter. This result follows from the policy of forcing polluters of all stripes to pay for the harm they cause. To object, then, to the effects our negative valuation of pollution have on a given industry is to be in contradiction: we would be refusing to face the consequences of our environmental preferences.

Nevertheless, there is sentiment in favour of enacting legislation against social dumping. Senator David L. Boren of Oklahoma, the proponent of the International Pollution Deterrence Act of 1991, demanded import duties on the ground that 'some US manufacturers, such as the US carbon and steel alloy industry, spend as much as 250 per cent more on environmental controls as a percentage of gross domestic product than do other countries . . . I see the unfair advantage enjoyed by other nations exploiting the environment and public health for economic gain when I look at many industries important to my own state.' Similarly, Vice President Al Gore wrote in *Earth in the Balance: Ecology and the Human Spirit* that 'just as government subsidies of a particular industry are sometimes considered unfair under the trade laws, weak and ineffectual enforcement of pollution control measures should also be included in the definition of unfair trading practices.'

These demands betray lack of economic logic, and also ignore political reality. Remember that the so-called subsidy to foreign producers through lower standards is not given but only implied. According to Senator Boren, the subsidy would be calculated as 'the cost that would have to be incurred by the manufacturer or producer of the foreign articles of merchandise to comply with environmental standards imposed on US producers of the same class of merchandise.' Anyone familiar with the way dumping calculations are made knows that the Environmental Protection Agency could come up with virtually any estimates it cared to produce. Cynical politics would inevitably dictate the calculations.

Still, there may be political good sense in assuaging environmentalists' concerns about the relocation of factories to countries with lower standards. The governments of countries with higher standards could do so without encumbering free trade by insisting that their businesses accede to the higher standards when they go abroad. Such a policy lies entirely within the jurisdictional powers of a country with higher standards. Moreover, the governments of countries with lower standards would be most unlikely to object to such an act of good citizenship by the foreign investors.

Environmentalists oppose free trade for yet another reason: they wish to use trade policy to impose their values on other communities and countries. Many environmentalists want to suspend the trading rights of countries that sanction the use of purse-seine nets in tuna fishing and of leg-hold traps in trapping. Such punishments seem however to be an inappropriate use of state power. The values in question such as human rights, are not widely accepted but idiosyncratic. It is a question of wonder when the opponents of purse-seine nets put the interests of the dolphin ahead of those of Mexico's people, who could prosper through more productive fishing. To borrow the campaign manifesto of President Bill Clinton: Should we not put people first?

Moreover, once such values intrude on free trade, the way is opened for an endless succession of demands. Environmentalists favour dolphins; Indians have their sacred cows. Animal-rights activists, who do not prefer one species over another, will object to our slaughter houses.

The moral militancy of environmentalists in the industrialized world has begun to disillusion their closest counterparts in the undeveloped countries. These local environmentalists accuse the rich countries of 'eco-imperialism', and they deny that the Western nations have a monopoly on virtue. The most radical of today's pro-environment magazines in India, *Down to Earth*, editorialized recently:

In the current world reality trade is used as an instrument entirely by Northern countries to discipline environmentally errant nations. Surely, if India or Kenya were to threaten to stop trade with the US, it would hardly affect the latter. But the fact of the matter is that it is the Northern countries that have the greatest [adverse] impact on the world's environment.

If many countries were to play this game, then repeated suspensions of trading rights would begin to undermine the openness of the trading system and the predictability and stability of international markets. Some environmentalists assert that each country should be free to insist on the production methods of its trading partners. Yet these environmentalists ignore the certain consequence of their policy: a Pandora's box of protectionism would open up. Rarely are production methods in an industry identical in different countries.

There are certainly better ways to indulge the environmentalists' propensity to export their ethical preferences. The US environmental organizations can lobby in Mexico to persuade its government to adopt their views. Private boycotts can also be undertaken. Indeed, boycotts can carry much clout in rich countries with big markets, on which the targeted poor countries often depend. The frequent and enormously expensive advertisements by environmental groups against the GATT show also that their resources far exceed those of the cash-strapped countries whose policies they oppose.

Cost–benefit analysis leads to the conclusion that unilateral governmental suspension of others' trading rights is not an appropriate way to promote lesser ethical preferences. Such sanctions can, on the other hand, appropriately be invoked multilaterally to defend universal moral values. In such cases — as in the censure of apartheid, as practiced until recently in South Africa — it is possible to secure widespread agreement for sanctions. With a large majority converted to the cause, the GATT's waiver procedure can be used to suspend the offending country's trading rights.

Environmentalists are also worried about the obstacles that the current and prospective GATT rules pose for environmental regulations aimed entirely at domestic production and consumption. In principle, the GATT lets a country enforce any regulation that does not discriminate against or among foreign suppliers. We can, for example, require airbags in cars, provided that the rule applies to all automobile markets. The GATT even permits rules that discriminate against trade for the purpose of safety and health.

The GATT, however, recognizes three ways in which regulations may be set in gratuitous restraint of trade; in following procedures aimed at avoiding such outcomes, the GATT upsets the environmentalists. First, the true intention — and effect — of a regulation may be to protect not the environment but local business. Second, a country may impose more restrictions than necessary to achieve its stated environmental objective. Third, it may set standards that have no scientific basis.

The issue of intentions is illustrated by the recently settled 'beer war' between Ontario and the US. Five years ago the Canadian province imposed a 10-cents-a-can tax on beer, ostensibly to discourage littering. The US argued that the law in fact intended to discriminate against its beer suppliers, who used aluminum cans, whereas local beer companies used bottles. Ontario had omitted to tax the use of cans for juices and soups, a step that would have affected Ontario producers.

The second problem is generally tougher because it is impossible to find alternative restrictions that accomplish exactly the same environmental results as the original policy at lower cost. An adjudicating panel is then forced to evaluate, implicitly or explicitly, the trade-offs between the cost in trade disruption and the cost in lesser fulfillment of the environmental objective. It is therefore likely that environmentalists and trade experts will differ on which weights the panel should assign to these divergent interests.

Environmentalists tend to be fearful about the use of scientific tests to determine whether trade in a product can be proscribed. The need to prove their case is always an unwelcome burden to those who have the political power to take unilateral action. Yet the trade experts have the better of the argument. Imagine that US growers sprayed apples with the pesticide Alar, whereas European growers did not, and that European consumers began to agitate against Alar as harmful. Should the European Community be allowed to end the importation of the US apples without meeting *some* scientific test of its health concerns? Admittedly, even hard science is often not hard enough — different studies may reach different conclusions. But without the restraining hand of science, the itch to indulge unnecessary fears — and to play on the fears of others — would be irresistible.

In all cases, the moderate environmentalists would like to see the GATT adopt more transparent procedures for adjudicating disputes. They also desire greater legal standing to file briefs when environmental regulations are at issue. These goals seem both reasonable and feasible.

Not all environmental problems are local; some are truly global, such as the greenhouse effect and the depletion of the stratospheric ozone. They raise more issues that require cooperative, multilateral solutions. Such solutions must be both efficient and equitable. Still, it is easy to see that rich countries might use their economic power to reach protocols that maximize efficiency at the expense of poorer countries.

For instance, imagine that the drafters of a protocol were to ask Brazil to refrain from cutting down its rain forests while allowing industrialized countries to continue emitting carbon dioxide. They might justify this demand on the grounds that it costs Brazil less to keep a tree alive, absorbing a unit of carbon dioxide every year, than it would cost the US or Germany to save a unit by burning less oil. Such a trade-off would indeed be economically efficient. Yet if Brazil, a poorer country, were then left with the bill, the solution would assuredly be inequitable.

Before any group of countries imposes trade sanctions on a country that has not joined a multilateral protocol, it would be important to judge whether the protocol is indeed fair. Non-members targeted for trade sanctions should have the right to an impartial hearing of their objections, requiring the strong to defend their actions even when they appear to be entirely virtuous.

The simultaneous pursuit of the two causes of free trade and a protected environment often raises problems, to be sure. But none of these conflicts is beyond resolution with goodwill and by imaginative institutional innovation. The aversion to free trade and the GATT that many environmentalists display is unfounded, and it is time for them to shed it. Their admirable moral passion and certain intellectual vigour are better devoted to building bridges between the causes of trade and environment.

REFERENCES

Bhagwati, Jagdish, 1993: 'American Rules, Mexican Jobs', *New York Times*, 24 March, Sec. A, col. 1, p. 21.

Bhagwati, Jagdish and T.N. Srinivasan, 1993: 'Trade and Environment: Does Environmental Diversity Detract from the Case for Free Trade?' (mimeo), Yale University.

Grossman, Gene M. and Alan B. Krueger, 1993: 'American Free Trade Agreement', *in* Peter M. Garber (ed.), *The Mexico-US Free Trade Agreement* (Cambridge, Mass.: MIT Press).

Hudec, Robert E., 1993: ' "Circumventing" Democracy: The Political Morality of Trade Negotiations', *New York University Journal of International Law and Politics*, Sept.–Oct., no. 2, vol. 25, pp. 401–12.

22

Trade Liberalization and 'Fair Trade' Demands: Addressing the Environmental and Labour Standards Issues*

1. INTRODUCTION

I PROPOSE here to argue why many of the demands, emanating principally from the rich countries, to impose 'higher' environmental and labour standards on the poor countries as preconditions for trade liberalization, ought to be rejected. Since practical policy-making cannot ignore political realities while statesmanship simultaneously requires that these realities be confronted creatively and in a principled way, I suggest alternative ways in which these demands, which are politically salient can be channelled into policy proposals that are better crafted and more consonant with the principles of free trade.

2. WHY HAVE DEMANDS FOR FAIR TRADE ARISEN?

The demands for imposing environmental and labour standards on the poor countries reflect several factors. Let me mention just a few of the more compelling ones that bear on the environmental and labour standards questions,[1] while addressing their merits later.

* In this chapter I have drawn liberally on my 1994 Wincoot Lecture delivered in London.

[1] I have dealt with these factors systematically in my extended analysis in 'Demands to Reduce Domestic Diversity Among Trading Nations', which is ch. 1 of vol. 1 of the 2-volume set of studies in Jagdish Bhagwati and Robert Hudec (eds),

First, the fierce competition as the world economy gets increasingly globalized has led to increased sensitivity to any domestic policy or institution abroad that seems to give foreign rivals an extra edge. If then a country's producers have lower environmental and labour regulatory burdens, that is objected to as 'unfair'.

Second, protectionists see great value in invoking 'unfairness' of trade as an argument for getting protection: it is likely to be more successful than simply claiming that you cannot hack it and therefore need protection. This has made the diversity of burdens for an industry among different countries appear illegitimate, making demands to reduce it look like a reasonable alternative to overt protectionism.

Third, some in the environmental and labour movements worry about the effect that competition with 'lower'-standards countries will have on their own standards. If trade shifts activity to where the costs are lower because of lower standards, and if additionally capital and jobs move away to exploit lower standards abroad, then the countries with higher standards may be forced to lower their own.

Fourth, aside from these 'economic' and political concerns focused on their own society, the environmental and, especially, labour lobbies have moral concerns. They feel a sense of transborder moral obligation to human beings abroad: they would like child labour to cease abroad because they worry about children abroad; they do not want Mexicans to suffer from lower environmental standards; and so on.

These arguments cover a broad spectrum and are typically jumbled together in the popular and in political discourse. But they must be kept sharply distinct in our reflections and analysis if we are to arrive at proper policy judgments, as I hope to do now. Let me begin with environmental questions and then turn to labour issues, bearing in mind the proposals that are currently in the political arena.

Fair Trade and Harmonization: Prerequisites for Free Trade?, MIT Press, 1996. Volume 1 is on *Economic Analysis* and vol. 2 is on *Legal Analysis*, and both are the product of a substantial Ford Foundation-financed project under the auspices of the American Society of International Law, Washington DC.

3. THE QUESTION OF ENVIRONMENTAL STANDARDS

Let me first distinguish between 'domestic' environmental problems, as when a country pollutes a lake which is entirely within its own frontiers, and 'global' environmental problems, when there are trans-border externalities, as with the acid rain, global warming and ozone-layer problems.

I shall consider the domestic problems initially, observing at the outset that normally an economist would not expect to object to different environmental standards in the same industry in different countries (i.e. to what I will call Cross-country Intra-industry, CCII, differences in standards, typically in the shape of pollution tax rates).

(a) Indefensible Demands for Eco-dumping

The diversity of CCII standards will follow from differences in trade-offs between aggregate pollution and income at different levels of income, as when richer Americans prefer to save dolphins from purse-seine nets whereas poorer Mexicans prefer to put people first and want to raise the productivity of fishing and hence accelerate the amelioration of Mexican poverty by using such nets. Again, countries will have natural differences in the priorities attached to which kind of pollution to attack, arising from differences of historical and other circumstance: Mexicans will want to worry more about clean water, as dysentery is a greater problem, than Americans who will want to attach greater priority to spending pollution dollars on clean air. Differences in technological know-how and in endowments can also lead to CCII diversity in pollution tax rates.

The notion therefore that the diversity of CCII pollution standards/taxes is illegitimate and constitutes 'unfair trade' or 'unfair competition', to be eliminated or countervailed by eco-dumping duties, is itself illegitimate. It is incorrect, indeed illogical, to assert that competing with foreign firms that do not bear equal pollution tax burdens is unfair.[2] I would add two more observations:

[2] This conclusion is derived and extensively defended in Bhagwati and Srinivasan (1996).

– We should recognize that if we lose competitive advantage because we put a larger negative value on a certain kind of pollution whereas others do not is simply the flip side of the differential valuations. To object to that implication of the differential valuation is to object to the differential valuation itself, and hence to our own larger negative valuation. To see this clearly, think of a closed economy without trade. If we were to tax pollution by an industry in such an economy, its implication would be precisely that this industry would shrink: it would lose competitive advantage vis-à-vis other industries in our own country. To object to that shrinking is to object to the negative valuation being put on the pollution. There is therefore nothing 'unfair' from this perspective, if our industry shrinks because we impose Higher Standards (i.e. pollution taxes) on our industry while others, who value that pollution less, choose Lower Standards (i.e. pollution taxes).

– Besides, it is worth noting that the attribution of competitive disadvantage to differential pollution tax burdens in the fashion of CCII comparisons for individual industries confuses absolute with comparative advantage. Thus, for instance, in a two-industry world, if both industries abroad have lower pollution tax rates than at home, both will not contract at home. Rather, the industry with the *comparatively* higher tax rate will. The noise that each industry makes on basis of CCII comparisons, aggregated to total noise by all industries, is then likely to seriously exaggerate the effect of different environmental valuations and CCII differences on the competitiveness of industries in Higher Standards nations.

Yet another concern needs to be laid at rest if the demands for upward harmonization of standards or eco-dumping duties in lieu thereof are to be effectively dismissed. This is the concern I noted at the outset: that free trade with countries with Lower Standards will force down one's Higher Standards. The most potent of these concerns arises from the fear that 'capital and jobs' will move to countries with Lower Standards, triggering a *race to the bottom* (or more accurately a race towards the bottom), where countries lower their standards in an inter-jurisdictional contest, below what some or all would like, in order to attract capital and jobs.[3] So, the solution would lie then in coordinating the standards-setting among the nations engaged in freer trade and investment. In turn, this *may* (but is most unlikely to) require harmonization among countries to the Higher Standards (though, even then, not necessarily at those in place) or perhaps there might be improvement in welfare from simply setting minimum floors to the standards.

This is undoubtedly a theoretically valid argument. The key question for policy, however, is whether the empirical evidence shows, as required by the argument, that: (1) capital is in fact responsive to the differences in environmental standards, and (2), different countries/jurisdictions actually play the game then of competitive lowering of standards to attract capital. Without both these phenomena holding in a significant fashion in reality, the 'race to the bottom' would be a theoretical curiosity.

As it happens, systematic evidence is available for the former proposition alone, but the finding is that the proposition is not supported by the studies to date: there is very weak evidence, at best, in favour of interjurisdictional mobility in response to CCII differences in environmental standards.[4] There are in fact many ways to explain this lack of responsiveness: (1) the differences in standards may not be significant and are outweighed by other factors that affect locational decisions; (2) exploiting differences in standards may not be a good strategy relative to not exploiting them; and (3) lower standards may paradoxically even repel, instead of attracting, DFI.[5]

While we do not have similar evidence on the latter proposition, it is hardly likely that, as a systematic tendency, countries would be actually lowering environmental standards in order to attract capital. As it happens, countries, and even state governments in federal countries (e.g. President Bill Clinton, when Governor of Arkansas), typically play the game of attracting capital to their jurisdictions: but this game is almost universally played, not

---

[3] Wilson (1996) demonstrates that there can be a 'race to the top'. This possibility is disregarded in the analysis above, as in the public discourse.

[4] The evidence has been systematically reviewed and assessed by Levinson (1996).

[5] These factors are analysed in Bhagwati and Srinivasan (1996).

by inviting firms to pollute freely, but instead through tax breaks and holidays, land grants at throwaway prices, etc., resulting most likely in a 'race to the bottom' on business tax rates which wind up below their optimal levels! It is therefore not surprising that there is little systematic evidence of governments lowering environmental standards in order to attract scarce capital. Contrary to the fears of the environmental groups, the race to the bottom on environmental standards appears therefore to be an unlikely phenomenon in the real world.

I would conclude that both the 'unfair trade' and the 'race to the bottom' arguments for harmonizing CCII standards or else legalizing eco-dumping duties at the WTO are therefore lacking in rationale: the former is theoretically illogical and the latter is empirically unsupported. In addition, such WTO-legalization of eco-dumping will without doubt facilitate protectionism. Anti-dumping processes have become the favoured tool of protectionists today. Is there any doubt that their extension to eco-dumping (and equally to social dumping), where the 'implied subsidy' through lower standards must be inevitably 'constructed' by national agencies such as the Environmental Protection Agency in the same jurisdiction as the complainant industry, will lead to the same results, even more surely?

The 'fixing' of the WTO for environmental issues therefore should not proceed along the lines of legitimating eco-dumping.[6] However, the political salience of such demands remains a major problem. It may then well be asked: are there any 'second-best' approaches, short of the eco-dumping and CCII harmonization

---

[6] There are other issues. One principal class relates to the current GATT restrictions, as reflected in recent GATT Panel findings as in the two Dolphin–Tuna cases involving the US on 'values'-inspired restrictions on imports of products using processes that are unacceptable, which will have to be clarified and will be the subject of new negotiations. My own views on the best solution to this class of problems, as also to the other principal class of problems raised by environmentalists who fear that it is too easy for countries to challenge the Higher Standards which they have enacted in their own countries (an issue that was at the heart of the latest GATT Panel finding, mostly in US favour, in the EU–US case on differentially punitive US taxes and standards on higher gasoline using cars) are developed at length in Bhagwati and Srinivasan (1996); unfortunately, I have no space to address them here.

proposals, that may address some of the political concerns at least economic cost?

(b) Extension of Domestic Standards in High Standards Countries to their Firms in Low Standards Countries

The political salience of the harmful demands for eco-dumping duties and CCII harmonization is greatest when plants are closed by a country's own multinationals and shifted to other countries. The actual shifting of location, and the associated loss of jobs in that plant, magnify greatly the fear of the 'race to the bottom' and of the 'impossibility' of competing against Low Standards countries. Similarly, when investment by a country's own firms is seen to go to specific countries that happen to have lower standards, the resentment gets readily focused against those countries and their standards. However, when jobs are lost simply because of *trade* competition, it is much harder to locate resentment and fear on one specific foreign country and its policies as a source of unfair competition.[7] Hence, a second-best proposal could well be to address this particular fear, however unfounded and often illogical, of outmigration of plants and investment by the country's firms abroad to Low Standard countries.

The proposal is to adapt the so-called Sullivan Principles approach to the problem at hand. Under Sullivan, US firms in South Africa were urged to adopt US practices, not the South African apartheid ways, in their operations. If this principle that the US firms in Mexico be subject to US environmental policies (choosing the desired ones from the many that obtain across different states in this federal country) were adopted by US legislation, that would automatically remove whatever incentive there was to move because of differences in the environmental burden.[8]

This proposal that a country's firms abroad behave as if they were at home — do in Rome as you do in New York, not as the Romans do — can be either legislated unilaterally by any High Standard country or by a multilateral binding Treaty among

---

[7] This, of course, does not apply equally to trade in highly differentiated products like automobiles where we can get fixated on specific countries, e.g. Japan.

[8] See Bhagwati (1993).

different High Standards countries. Again, it may be reduced to an exhortation, just as Sullivan Principles were, by single countries in isolation or by several, as through a non-binding but ethos-defining and policy-encouraging OECD Code.

The disadvantage of this proposal, of course, is that it does violate the diversity-is-legitimate rule (whose desirability was discussed by me). Investment flows, like investment of a country's own funds and production and trade from this, should reflect this diversity. It reduces, therefore, the efficiency of gains from a freer flow of cross-country investments today. But if environmental tax burden differences are not all that different, or do not figure prominently in firms' locational decisions, as the empirical literature (just cited) seems to stress, the efficiency costs of this proposal could also be minimal while gains in allaying fears and therefore moderating the demand for bad proposals could be very large indeed.

Yet another objection may focus on intra-OECD differences in High Standards. Since there are differences among the OECD countries in CCII environmental tax burdens in specific industries for specific pollution, this Proposal would lead to 'horizontal inequity' among the OECD firms in third countries. If the British burden is higher than the French, British firms would face a bigger burden in Mexico than French firms. But such differences already exist among firms abroad since tax practices among the OECD countries on taxation of firms abroad are not harmonized in several respects. Interestingly, the problem of horizontal equity has come up in relation to the demands of the poor countries (that often find it difficult to enforce import restrictions effectively) that the domestic restrictions on hazardous products be automatically extended to exports by every country. That would put firms in the countries with greater restrictions at an economic disadvantage. But agreement has now been reached to disregard the problem.

Other problems may arise: (i) monitoring of a country's firms in a foreign country may be difficult; and (ii) the countries with Lower Standards may object on grounds of 'national sovereignty'. Neither argument seems compelling. It is unlikely that a developing country would object to foreign firms doing better by its citizens in regard to environmental standards (that it itself cannot afford to impose, given its own priorities, on its own firms). Equally, it would then assist in monitoring the foreign firms.

(c) Trans-border Externalities:
Global Pollution and WTO

The preceding analysis considered the trade issues that arise between countries even when the environmental problems are purely domestic in their scope. They can arise, of course, even when these problems involve trans-border spillovers or externalities. However, the latter are generally more complex. Let me consider only the problems that arise when the problem is not just *bilateral* (as with, say acid rain, where the US and Canada were involved) or regional, but truly *global*.

The chief policy questions concerning trade policy when global pollution problems are involved instead, as with ozone layer depletion and global warming, relate to the cooperation-solution-oriented multilateral treaties that are sought to address them. They are essentially ties into noncompliance ('defection') by members and 'free riding' by non-members. Because any action by a member of a treaty relates to targeted actions (such as reducing CFCs or CO_2 emissions) that are a public good (in particular, that the benefits are non-excludable, so that if I incur the cost and do something, I cannot exclude you from benefiting from it), the use of trade sanctions to secure and automatically enforce compliance turns up on the agenda.

At the same time, the problem is compounded because the agreement itself has to be *legitimate* in the eyes of those accused of free-riding. Before those pejorative epithets are applied and punishment prescribed in the form of trade sanctions legitimated at the WTO, these nations have to be satisfied that the agreement being pressed on them is efficient and, especially, that it is equitable in burden-sharing. Otherwise, nothing prevents the politically powerful (i.e. the rich nations) from devising a treaty that puts an inequitable burden on the politically weak (i.e. the poor nations) and then using the cloak of a 'multilateral' agreement and a new WTO, legitimacy to impose that burden with the aid of trade sanctions with a clear conscience.

This is why the policy demand, often made, to alter the WTO to legitimate trade sanctions on members who remain outside of a treaty, whenever a plurilateral treaty on global environmental problem dictates it, is unlikely to be accepted by the poor nations without safeguards to prevent unjust impositions. The spokesmen of the poor countries have been more or less explicit on this issue, with justification. These concerns have been recognized by the rich nations.

Thus, at the Rio Conference in 1992, the *Framework Convention on Climate Change* set explicit goals under which several rich nations agreed to emission level-reduction targets (returning, more or less, to 1990 levels), whereas the commitments of the poor countries were contingent on the rich nations footing the bill.

Ultimately, burden-sharing by different formulas related to past emissions, current income, current population, etc. are inherently arbitrary; they also distribute burdens without regard to efficiency. Economists will argue for burden-sharing dictated by cost-minimization across countries, for the earth as a whole: if Brazilian rain forests must be saved to minimize the cost of a targeted reduction in CO_2 emissions in the world, while the US keeps guzzling gas because it is too expensive to cut that down, then so be it. But then this efficient 'cooperative' solution must not leave Brazil footing the bill. Efficient solutions, with compensation and equitable distribution of the gains from the efficient solution, make economic sense.

A step towards them is the idea of having a market in permits at the world level: no country may emit CO_2 without having bought the necessary permit from a worldwide quota. That would ensure efficiency,[9] whereas the distribution of the proceeds from the sold permits would require a decision reflecting some multilaterally-agreed ethical or equity criteria (e.g. the proceeds may be used for refugee resettlement, UN peacekeeping operations, aid dispensed to poor nations by UNDP, WHO fight against AIDS, etc.). This type of agreement would have the legitimacy that could then in turn provide the legitimacy for a WTO rule that permits the use of trade sanctions against free-riders.

[9] This efficiency is only in the sense of cost minimization. The number of permits may, however, be too small or too large, and getting it right by letting non-users also bid (and then destroy permits) is bedevilled by free-rider problems.

3. THE QUESTION OF LABOUR STANDARDS
AND THE SOCIAL CLAUSE

The question of labour standards, and making them into prerequisites for market access by introducing a Social Clause in the WTO, has parallels and contrasts to the environmental questions that I have just discussed.

The contrast is that labour standards have nothing equivalent to *trans-border* environmental externalities. A country is labour standards are purely *domestic* in scope: in that regard, the demands for 'social dumping' for lower labour standards that parallel the demands for eco-dumping have the same rationale and hence must be rejected for the same reasons.

But a different aspect to the whole question results from the fact that labour standards, unlike most environmental standards, are seen in moral terms. Thus, for example, central to American thinking on the question of the Social Clause is the notion that competitive advantage can sometimes be morally 'illegitimate'. In particular, it is argued that if labour standards elsewhere are different and unacceptable morally, then the resulting competition is morally illegitimate and 'unfair'.

Now, when this argument is made about a practice such as slavery (defined strictly as the practice of owning and transacting in human beings, as for centuries before the Abolitionists triumphed), there will be nearly universal agreement that if slavery produces competitive advantage, that advantage is illegitimate and ought to be rejected.

Thus, we have here a 'values'-related argument for suspending another country's trading rights or access to our markets, in a sense similar to (but far more compelling than) the case when the US sought to suspend Mexico's tuna-trading rights because of its use of purse-seine nets.[10] The insertion of a Social Clause for Labour Standards into the WTO can then be seen as a way legitimating an exception to the perfectly sensible GATT rule that

---

[10] I talk of the US suspending Mexico's trade rights since the GATT Panel in the Dolphin-Tuna case upheld these rights for Mexico. If it had not, I should be talking simply of the US denying market access to Mexico

prohibits the suspension of a contracting party's trading rights concerning a product simply on the ground that, for reasons of morality asserted by another contracting party, the process by which that product is produced is considered immoral and therefore illegitimate.

The real problem with the argument, however, is that universally-condemned practices such as slavery are rare indeed. True, the ILO has many Conventions that many nations have signed. But many have been signed simply because, in effect, they are not binding. Equally, the US has itself not signed more than a tiny fraction of these conventions. The question whether a substantive consensus on anything except well-meaning and broad principles without consequences for trade access in case of non-compliance can be obtained is therefore highly dubious.

Indeed, the reality is that diversity of labour practice and standards is widespread in practice and reflects, not necessarily venality and wickedness, but rather, diversity of cultural values, economic conditions, and analytical beliefs and theories concerning the economic (and therefore moral) consequences of specific labour standards. The notion that labour standards can be universalized, like human rights such as liberty and habeas corpus, simply by calling the 'labour rights' ignores the fact that this easy equation between culture-specific labour standards and universal human rights will have a difficult time surviving deeper scrutiny.

Take the US itself (since it is a principal proponent of the Social Clause) and it is immediately evident that its labour standards are 'advanced' and that it is only providing 'moral leadership' on the question vis-à-vis developing countries, is hard to sustain and that the US logic on the question can lead the US itself into a widespread and sustained suspension of its own trading rights if there was an impartial tribunal and standing to file complaints was given to concerned citizens and NGOs rather than to governments that would be intimidated from taking it to court by the power of the US.

Thus, for instance, worker participation in decision-making on the plant, a measure of true economic democracy much more pertinent than the unionization of labour, is far more widespread in Europe than in North America: would we then condemn North

America to denial of trading rights by the Europeans? Migrant labour is ill-treated to the level of brutality and slavery in US agriculture due to grossly inadequate and corrupt enforcement, if investigative shows on US television are a guide: does this mean that other nations should prohibit the import of US agricultural products? Sweatshops exploiting female immigrants in textiles with long hours and below-minimum wages are endemic in the textile industry, as amply documented by several civil-liberties groups: should the right of the US to export textiles then be suspended by other countries as much as the US seeks to suspend the imports of textiles made by exploited child labour?

Even the right to organize trade unions may be considered to be inadequate in the US if we go by 'results', as the US favours in judging Japan: only about 12 per cent of the US labour force in the private sector is unionized. Indeed, it is no secret, except to those who prefer to think that labour standards are inadequate only in developing countries, that unions are actively discouraged in several ways in the US. Strikes are also circumscribed. Indeed, in essential industries they are restricted: but the definition of such industries also reflects economic structure and political realities, making each country's definition only culture-specific and hence open to objection by others. Should other countries have then suspended US flights because President Reagan had broken the Air Traffic Controllers' strike?

Lest it is thought that the question of child labour is an easy one, it is necessary to remember that even this raises complex questions, as was indeed recognized by the ILO, though not in many of the arguments heard in the US today. The use of child labour, as such, is surely not the issue. Few children grow up even in the US without working as babysitters or delivering news-papers; many are even paid by parents for housework in the home. The pertinent social question, familiar to anyone with even a nodding acquaintance with Chadwick, Engels and Dickens, and the appalling conditions afflicting children at work in England's factories in the early Industrial Revolution, is rather whether children at work are protected from hazardous and oppressive working conditions.

Whether child labour should be altogether prohibited in a poor country is a matter on which views legitimately differ. Many feel that children's work is unavoidable in the face of poverty, and that the alternative to it is starvation which is a greater calamity, and that eliminating child labour would then be like voting to eliminate abortion without worrying about the needs of the children that are then born.

Then again, insisting on the 'positive-rights'-related right to unionize to demand higher wages, for instance, as against the 'negative-rights'-related right of freedom to associate for political activity, for example, can also be morally obtuse. In practice, such a right could imply higher wages for the 'insiders' who have jobs, at the expense of the unemployed 'outsiders'. Besides, the unions in developing countries with large populations and much poverty are likely to be in the urban–industrial activities, with the industrial proletariat among the better-off sections of the population, whereas the real poverty is among the non-unionized landless labour. Raising the wages of the former will generally hurt, in the opinion of many developing country economists, the prospects of rapid accumulation and growth which alone can eventually pull more of the landless labour into gainful employment. If so, the imposition of the culture-specific developed-country-union views on poor countries about the rights of unions to push for higher wages will resolve current equity and inter-generational equity problems in ways that are normally unacceptable to these countries, and correctly so.

(a) The Social Clause: A Bad Idea

We are then led to conclude that the idea of the Social Clause in the WTO is rooted generally in an ill-considered rejection of the general legitimacy of diversity of labour standards and practices across countries. The alleged claim for the universality of labour standards is (except for a few rare cases such as slavery) generally unpersuasive.

The developing countries cannot then be blamed for worrying that the recent escalation of support for such a Clause in the WTO in major OECD countries derives instead from the desire of labour unions to protect their jobs by protecting the industries that face competition from the poor countries. They fear that moral arguments are produced to justify restrictions on such trade since they are so effective in the public domain. In short, the 'white man's burden' is being exploited to secure the 'white man's gain'. Or, to use another metaphor, 'blue protectionism' is breaking out, masked behind a moral face.

Indeed, this fearful conclusion is reinforced by the fact that none of the major OECD countries pushing for such a Social Clause expect to be the defendants rather than plaintiffs in Social Clause-generated trade-access cases. On the one hand, the standards (such as prohibition of child labour) to be included in the Social Clause to date are invariably presented as those that the developing countries are guilty of violating, even when some transgressions of these are to be found in the developed countries themselves. Thus, according to a report in *The Financial Times*, a standard example used by the labour movement to garner support for better safety standards is a disastrous fire in a toy factory in Thailand where many died because exits were shut and unusable. Yet, when I read this report, I recalled a similar example (but far more disconcerting when you noted that the fatalities occurred in the richest country in the world) about a chicken plant in North Carolina where also the exits were closed for the same reason. Yet the focus was on the poor, not the rich, country.

At the same time, the choice of standards chosen for attention and sanctions at the WTO is also clearly biased against the poor countries in the sense that none of the problems where many of the developed countries would be found in significant violation — such as worker participation in management, union rights, rights of migrants and immigrants — are meant to be included in the Social Clause. Symmetry of obligations simply does not exist in the Social Clause, as contemplated currently, in terms of the coverage of the standards.

The stones are thus to be thrown at the poor countries' glass houses by rich countries that build fortresses around their own. Indeed, the salience which the Social Clause crusade has acquired in the US and Europe, and its specific contents, owe much to the widespread fear, evident during the NAFTA debate in the US, that trade with the poor countries (with abundant unskilled labour) will produce unemployment and reductions in the real rages of the unskilled in the rich countries. The Social Clause is, in this perspective, a way in which the fearful unions seek to raise the costs of production in the poor countries as free trade with them threatens their jobs and wages.

(b) If not Social Clause, What Else?

If this analysis is correct, then the idea of a Social Clause in the WTO is not appealing; and the developing countries' opposition to its enactment is justified. We would not be justified then in condemning their objections and unwillingness to go along with our demands as depravity and 'rejectionism'.

But if a Social Clause does not make good sense, is everything lost for those in both developed and developing countries who genuinely wish to advance their own views of what are 'good' labour standards? Evidently not.

It is surely open to them to use other instrumentalities such as non-governmental organization (NGO)-led educational activities to secure a consensus in favour of their positions. Indeed, if your ideas are good, they should spread without coercion. The Spanish Inquisition should not be necessary to spread Christianity; indeed, the Pope has no troops. Mahatma Gandhi's splendid idea of non-violent agitation spread, and was picked up by Martin Luther King, not because he worked on the Indian government to threaten retribution against others otherwise; it just happened to be morally compelling.

I would add that there is also the possibility of recourse to private boycotts, available under national and international law; they are an occasionally effective instrument. They constitute a well-recognized method of protest and consensus-creation in favour of particular moral positions.

With the assistance of such methods of suasion, a multilateral consensus must be achieved on the moral and economic legitimacy of carefully-defined labour standard (and formally agreed to at the ILO today in light of modern thinking in economics and of the accumulated experience of developmental and labour issues to date, and with the clear understanding that we are not just passing resolutions but that serious consequences may follow for follow-through by the signatory nations). The ILO is clearly the institution that is best equipped to create such a consensus, not the GATT/WTO, just as multilateral trade negotiations are conducted at the GATT, not at the ILO.

In turn, the annual ILO monitoring of compliance with ILO conventions is an impartial and multilateral process, undertaken with the aid of eminent jurists across the world. Such a process, with changes for standing and for transparency, should be the appropriate forum for the annual review of compliance by nation states of such newly-clarified and multilaterally-agreed standards. Such monitoring, the opprobrium of public exposure, and the effective strengthening therewith of NGOs in the offending countries (many of which are now democratic and permissive of NGO activity) will often be large enough forces to prod these countries into corrective action.

In extraordinary cases where the violations are such that the moral sense of the world community is outraged, the existing international processes are available to undertake even coercive, corrective multilateral sanctions against specific countries to suspend their entire trading rights.

Thus, for instance, under UN embargo procedures, which take precedence over the GATT and other treaties, South Africa's GATT membership proved no barrier to the embargo against it precisely because the world was virtually united in its opposition to apartheid. Even outside of the UN, the GATT waiver procedure has permitted two–thirds of the Contracting Parties to suspend any GATT member's trading rights, altogether or for specific goods (and now, services).

I must add one final thought to assure those who feel their own moral view must be respected at any cost, even if others cannot be persuaded to see things that way. Even they need not worry under current international procedures. Thus, suppose that (say) American or French public opinion on an issue (as in the Tuna–Dolphin case for the former and the Beef–Hormone case for the latter) forces the government to undertake a unilateral suspension of another GATT member's trading rights, there is nothing in the GATT nor will there be anything in the WTO, which will then compel the overturning of such unilateral action. The offending contracting party (i.e. the one undertaking the unilateral action) can persist in a violation while making a compensatory offer of an alternative trade concession or the offended party can retaliate by withdrawing an equivalent trade concession. Thus, unless there is resentment against having to pay for virtue (since the claim is that 'our labour standard is morally superior'), this is a perfectly sensible solution even to politically unavoidable unilateralism: do not import glass bangles made with child labour in Pakistan or India, but make some other compensatory trade concession. And remember that the grant of an alternative trade concession (or tariff retaliation) makes some other activity than the offending one more attractive, thus helping one to shrink the offending activity: that surely should be a matter for approbation rather than knee-jerk dismissal.

•

REFERENCES

Bhagwati, J., 1993: 'American Rules, Mexican Jobs', *The New York Times* (24 March).

Bhagwati, J. and R. Hudec (eds), 1996: *Fair Trade and Harmonization: Prerequisites for Free Trade?* (Cambridge, Mass.: MIT Press).

Bhagwati, J. and T.N. Srinivasan, 1996: 'Trade and the Environment: Does Environmental Diversity Detract from the Case for Free Trade?', *in* J. Bhagwati and R. Hudec (eds), *Fair Trade and Harmonization: Prerequisites for Free Trade?* (Cambridge, Mass.: MIT Press), ch. 4, vol. 1.

Levinson, A., 1996: 'Environmental Regulations and Industry Location: International and Domestic Evidence', *in* J. Bhagwati and R. Hudec (eds), *Fair Trade and Harmonization: Prerequisites for Free Trade?* (Cambridge, Mass.: MIT Press), ch. 11, vol. 1.

Wilson, J., 1996: 'Capital Mobility and Environmental Standards: Is There a Theoretical Basis for a Race to the Bottom?', *in* J. Bhagwati and R. Hudec (eds), *Fair Trade and Harmonization: Prerequisites for Free Trade?* (Cambridge, Mass.: MIT Press), ch. 10, vol. 1.

23

Free Trade and Wages of the Unskilled — Is Marx Striking Again?[*]

WHERE does the threat to free trade come from today? Not from the developments in the theory of imperfect competition in product markets that defined the scientific revolution in trade theory in the 1980s. That revolution is now absorbed, and its major figures have returned to the fold of free trade, as leaders of other such revolutions have done before them (Bhagwati 1992). Instead, there are now, in our judgement, two new threats, each posing great danger.

The first threat comes from the proliferation of demands for fair trade or level playing fields as preconditions for free trade. Where conventionally such demands were confined to foreign subsidies and predatory dumping, they have now multiplied to a variety of domestic policies and institutions, including environmental and labour standards and technology policy. The presumption today

* Written with Vivek H. Dehejia. This chapter was prepared for the Workshop on Trade and Wages at the American Enterprise Institute, 10 Sept. 1993. It draws, and builds, on earlier work by Bhagwati (1991a) done at the Russell Sage Foundation, whose financial support in 1990 and 1991 is gratefully acknowledged. In that work, the contention that trade was depressing the real wages of the unskilled was first challenged by using the general equilibrium (Stolper–Samuelson) argumentation of trade theory to analyse the claims to that effect in the emerging labour-economists' studies of the question. An alternative explanation of a possible adverse impact of trade on wages was also advanced, in terms of the effect of an increased randomization of comparative advantage in different manufactures leading to more rapid turnover among them by the unskilled, resulting in the reduction of incremental rewards due to staying on the job longer. The chapter also draws on work by Dehejia (1992b), who models the alternative approach just described. In revising this work, we have profited from the comments of the workshop participants, especially of Susan Collins. Conversations with Douglas Irwin, Paul Samuelson, T.N. Srinivasan, Arvind Panagariya, and Martin Wolf were helpful.

is that diversity among countries in these domestic policies is harmful to the case for free trade and that free trade with such diversity, instead of being mutually beneficial, will lead to predation at individual expense. The difficulty of achieving harmonization of these several domestic policies (even in the European Community, where political congruence is far greater than among nations trading at arm's length), and the ease with which such demands can be multiplied to new areas of diversity by protectionists make the task of liberalizing trade or maintaining open markets that much more difficult.[1] The problems that the North American Free Trade Agreement (NAFTA) has run into with the environmentalists and the labour unions in the US because of different and lower environmental and labour standards in Mexico; the strong opposition to the General Agreement on Tariffs and Trade (GATT), and to the Uruguay Round's completion around the Dunkel Draft by the environmental non-governmental organizations (NGOs); the Clinton administration's capture by the Japan-fixated revisionists; and the surrender of key administration economists to demands for managed trade because Japan's domestic institutions are 'different', and allegedly lead to a lack of level playing fields for market access, are a reminder of the grave importance the question of fair trade has acquired today.

But the other issue that imperils free trade is the fear that has grown in the US and in western Europe that the freeing of trade with the poor countries of the South will hurt the real wages of the unskilled. The Russian proverb warns, Fear has big eyes. But the fear in this instance is prompted by the stagnation of US proletarian wages in the 1980s and the substantial increase in

---

[1] Bhagwati (1991c), in the Harry Johnson Lecture on *The World Trading System at Risk*, identified this as one of the major problems confronting the world trading system today. Subsequently, the Ford Foundation has supported a major project on the subject of Fairness Claims and Gains from Trade, addressed precisely to the question of the virtues and vices of diversity (in domestic policies and institutions among trading nations), directed by him and Professor Robert Hudec of Minnesota Law School. Nearly thirty international and other economic theorists, international lawyers, and political scientists wrote analytically oriented papers with policy implications. The findings were presented at a June 1994 conference in Washington, DC, organized by the American Society for International Law.

European unemployment, which has presumably substituted for the fall in wages, during the same period. There is real cause for worry. At a time when the capacity of the Western states to maintain, leave aside raise, social expenditures to countervail the market-determined declines in real wages has been crippled (as witness the fate of the original Clinton budget proposals), and when the declinist rhetoric of the election campaign reinforced pessimism about the American economy's future, it is not surprising that workers have become fearful of real wage stagnation or decline and, with it, of trade which they believe (but without good cause, as we will suggest) is an important, if not the principal cause of this baleful phenomenon. While Karl Marx's prediction of the immiseration of the proletariat was proven wrong by history, will he strike again now through the integration of the North with the South in freer trade?[2]

Indeed, it is curious that there has been a reversal of attitudes between the countries of the North and those of the South when trade between them is appraised. During the 1950s and 1960s, much of the South regarded trade with the North as a threat, not as an opportunity, was fearful that without protection it could not industrialize, and turned to import substitution while the North was opening to the South (as to itself) through extensive liberalization. Today, starting with the 1980s, there have been fearful voices in the North, dreading trade with the poor South as a recipe for descent into the wages and working conditions of these impoverished nations. Many in the South, conversely, see trade with the North as an opportunity, not a peril. The contrast between Mexico's and the US Congress's reaction to NAFTA is a stark example of this role reversal.[3]

[2] Scholars of Marx are, of course, divided over the question whether, in addition to his prediction of a falling rate of profit, Marx did indeed predict a falling real wage for the proletariat. But enough scholars, and much of the public, believe that he did, justifying our allusion above.

[3] We speak in aggregate terms of fears and opinions, fully aware that there are exceptions to the fears of trade in the North (indeed, also in the US Congress on NAFTA) and to the embrace of trade as an opportunity in the South (as among leftist political parties in India). Nonetheless, the central thrust of intellectual and policy-making opinion has changed favourably in much of the South, and the fears have grown, though not yet overturning policy, in much of the North.

In this chapter, we want to address this fear, prevalent in the North. There is little prospect that we can get much farther toward free trade if this issue is not addressed clearly and persuasively. Here we will not present original empirical work, but instead will clarify the issues from the viewpoint of international trade theory and relate the arguments to empirical evidence available from others' studies. Directions for future research should emerge from our analysis.

FACTOR PRICE EQUALIZATION: A THEORETICAL *CURIOSUM* OR INESCAPABLE DESTINY?

Interestingly, the major theoretical construct that, implicitly or explicitly, has provided the intellectual support, and lent the air of plausibility, to the fears in the North of immiseration of the unskilled from freer trade with the South has been the celebrated factor price equalization (FPE) theorem (and the Stolper–Samuelson (SS) theorem which shows the adverse impact of free trade on the factor of production that is scarce in the country relative to that overseas in the country's trading partners — that is, presumably unskilled labour in the North vis-à-vis unskilled labour in the South, in relation to other factors of production such as capital).[4]

It is interesting, of course, that when Paul Samuelson wrote his celebrated twin articles on the FPE theorem in the *Economic Journal* in 1948 and 1949, the theorem was considered at first to be implausible[5] and hence possibly wrong,[6] and then to be

[4] In the symmetric n × n case, the FPE theorem implies the SS theorem (as stated above), but the SS theorem does not imply the FPE theorem. In principle, it is enough to have the SS theorem to generate the fears that, if importing labour-intensive goods from the poor, labour-abundant South, free trade will harm the real wage of labour.

[5] Paul Samuelson wrote the second article because the first one met with scepticism and the *Economic Journal* had to destroy in proof two articles, including one by the celebrated Cambridge economist Pigou, questioning the FPE theorem after Samuelson's first article appeared. Pigou remained sceptical and asked Richard Kahn if Samuelson had consulted a mathematician for his univalence proof. Informed that Samuelson was one himself, Pigou reportedly replied: I mean a British mathematician.

[6] Gunnar Myrdal, and others, also found the FPE theorem implausible, because

little more than a theoretical *curiosum*. At the same time, when Wassily Leontief (1953) came up with his startling finding that the US was exporting labour-intensive exports, the search for explanations that was set off primarily focused on the reasons why the FPE theorem, building on the Heckscher–Ohlin–Samuelson model, would *not* hold in the real world because one or more of the sufficiency conditions (such as the absence of factor-intensity reversals) were unrealistic. In short, the approach to the FPE theorem was not that it defined reality; rather it was that the theorem provided the researcher with the necessary clues as to why it did not.

By contrast, economists have generally tended to regard FPE today as an inescapable destiny, with the unskilled proletariat facing inevitable immiseration or, at a minimum, a heavy drag on the rise of its real wages. Two examples should suffice.

The first occurred at a Williamsburg retreat for freshmen congressmen organized by the American Enterprise Institute and the Brookings Institution following the 1992 election. One of the authors, Jagdish Bhagwati, and Lester Thurow were joint panelists. In speaking about NAFTA, Thurow, an influential Democrat, reminded his audience of the economists' FPE theorem and its implications – drawing not protectionist conclusions but the prescription to raise the skills of our labour force.

For the second example, let us quote the celebrated author of FPE, Paul Samuelson himself, in a speech in Italy in 1992, with the caveat that was is not meant to be a scholarly analysis of the matter at hand:[7]

First, any top-notch jobs that used to pay well have *not* disappeared from the face of the globe. They have merely migrated from Europe and North

---

they equated the equalization of real wages in the theorem with per capita real income equalization. Obviously, the latter would still be different in the Heckscher–Ohlin–Samuelson world of identical technologies but different capital–labour endowment ratios.

[7] Besides, the quote is only an excerpt of a speech that contains several shrewd observations on the relevance of free trade at the end of the twentieth century. See Paul Samuelson (1992).

America to Japan, Korea, Taiwan, Singapore, Hong Kong, Malaysia, and elsewhere. (The tennis racket I play with comes from Korea. My partner plays with one made in Taiwan. These words are written on a word-processor from Japan. So it goes.)

Have the jobs migrated permanently? Or will they come back? Can good governmental policies bring them back?

Last December when I attended a Nobel Jubilee, I was being driven to the Stockholm airport. Along the road we passed many of Sweden's best factories. They seemed to the tourist's eye to have lost some of their bright glitter and busyness. 'No wonder', I thought, 'that the miracle of the progressive Swedish welfare state has petered out since 1970. Now there is nothing that these factories can do which cannot be done almost as well in the Pacific Basin — and often with Asian labour at real wage rates only half that prevailing in Sweden. And surely much the same can be said about factories in Turin, Brussels, Birmingham, and Chicago. As Madrid and Barcelona begin to enjoy higher living standards, surely they too will begin to encounter effective competition from the developing nations that now master modern routines and have access to up-to-date technical knowledge'.

Let me not exaggerate. Of course, the most resourceful Swedish and American operations can survive at some positive level. But all of us cannot be above average. As the billions of people who live in East Asia and Latin America qualify for good, modern jobs, the half billion Europeans and North Americans who used to tower over the rest of the world will find their upward progress in living standards encountering tough resistance.

But if economists find the FPE argumentation inherently plausible, as defining an inevitable pressure on the real wages of the unskilled in today's developed countries, with their presumed freer trade and further freeing of trade with the poor countries, we must not forget two countervailing arguments, one theoretical and one empirical.

The theoretical, which we develop more systematically below, simply resurrects the earlier view, albeit with greater sophistication and evidence that FPE's heavy hand is far more frail than currently imagined.

The empirical, at the gut level, is simply that the phenomenon of the drag on real wages of the unskilled appeared in the 1980s when the US and the European Community were turning to protectionism instead of opening their markets extensively to the developing countries, as during the 1950s and 1960s. The same is true for the inflow of foreign investment into the US, whether direct foreign investment (DFI) or the flip side of our current account deficit. Both show a net *increase* in augmentation of US capital from foreign sources in the 1980s, both absolutely and in relation to the 1950s and 1960s (Lipsey 1992). Thus, casual empiricism suggests exactly the opposite of what is generally believed! If these facts on trade barriers and foreign investment are confirmed by careful analysis, we have a paradox on our hands from the viewpoint of those who think otherwise: a paradox that could be resolved along the lines developed by us below.

But it is not just the FPE theory's seeming plausibility that has dammed foreign trade with the South as a significant cause of the immiseration of the unskilled. The early presumption to that effect was also fed by notable empirical studies by leading labour economists. The study most cited, both in academic circles and in the media (see Passell 1992), was the 1990 study by George Borjas, Richard Freeman, and Lawrence Katz (1992), which concluded that the 1980s had indeed seen trade adversely affect US unskilled wages. While this study seemed to draw on trade-theoretic concepts (arguing that the trade had led to an effective, relative augmentation of unskilled labour supply in the US and thus depressed its real wage), we argue below that it really did not and that their argument was insufficient for the conclusions reached.[8]

We will consider why the FPE theorem and the SS theorem generally implied by it are not quite an adequate guide to thinking about the problem at hand. We then consider in depth why the Borjas–Freeman–Katz (1992) and Kevin Murphy–Finis Welch (1991) studies, which alerted us to the adverse impact of trade on US real wages, were not well grounded in general-equilibrium theory of the type that underlies the FPE and SS theorems, and indeed much of conventional trade theory, thus leaving unproven their case (which implicitly drew on such reasoning).

---

[8] In doing so, we will draw primarily on Bhagwati (1991a) (1991b). Recently, Lawrence and Slaughter (1993) have endorsed this critique in their analysis of the problem of trade and wages. Their empirical analysis provides additional evidence, supplementing that in Bhagwati and calling even more compellingly into doubt the Stolper–Samuelson argumentation.

WHY FPE AND SS THEOREMS
ARE INADEQUATE GUIDES TO REALITY

If we look at the assumptions that underlie the FPE theorem, it becomes immediately obvious that they are extraordinary demanding. Few would find the theorem compelling as a guide to thinking about the real world if only they were familiar with these assumptions — without which the iron hand of the FPE theorem on real wages of the US unskilled cannot be taken seriously.

Thus, the FPE theorem requires that technology (as also tastes) be identical across trading countries. But then, despite identical know-how, South and North can de facto be operating in different technological worlds if the production functions, while identically shared, are characterized by possible factor intensity reversals (such that the same good, at the same goods prices, is intensive in its use of factors differently in South and North); and if the relative factor endowments are such that South and North are actually characterized by such reversals. Production functions that can lead to such reversals of factor intensity include constant elasticity of substitution (CES), where different constant elasticities of factor substitution between sectors are sufficient to create such reversals.[9] Much empirical work done after the Leontief paradox alluded to above underlines the distinct possibility that such reversals, both potential and actual, are not theoretical *curiosa* at all.[10] When such reversals arise, evidently both South and North can have rising real wages of unskilled labour thanks to free trade.

Differences in technological know-how itself can of course lead to a similar outcome. The spread of multinationals and the rapid

[9] This was first noted by Minhas (1962) in a classic paper, based on his Stanford dissertation. In trade theorists' language, factor intensity reversal possibility means that the capital–labour ratios in the two goods will cross over at some wage–rental ratio. If factor endowments are such that the two trading groups, South and North, are on opposite sides of the cross-over, then the same good will be capital-intensive in the South and labour-intensive in the North in trade. That is, technology will de facto be different in equilibrium, even though technological know-how is identical in North and South.

[10] See, for instance, the extended review of such work in the early survey of trade theory in Bhagwati (1964).

diffusion of technology have narrowed this possibility, but primarily among the developed countries, where convergence of know-how has been documented by Baumol et al. (1989). Know-how manifestly differs across North and South. It can thus be readily shown again that the possibility that free trade will increase the real wages of unskilled labour in both South and North.

Yet another way in which technology can differ across trading countries in equilibrium is, of course, when scale effects operate. Scale economies, whether modelled in the old way to allow for perfect competition or in the new way where they lead to imperfect competition, will also enable real wages to rise in both North and South from free trade. And few would deny that scale economies are relevant.

Thus, for many reasons, the presumption that real wages in the North and the South will converge as a result of free trade can be considered unrealistic. We will develop here only three, which we consider to be particularly pertinent, and relate them to the SS theorem, assuming that the rich country is importing unskilled labour-intensive goods and exporting human and physical capital-intensive goods, and that the terms of trade improve when trade is freed. In this (2×2) version of the theorem, which is consonant with the FPE theorem, the real wage of unskilled labour falls.[11]

Scale Economies

We have already indicated that scale economies can invalidate the SS theorem, causing both factors' real wages to rise. The reason is obvious: the redistributive effect that militates against the real wage of unskilled labour can be outweighed by the 'lifting-all-boats' effect of scale economies on the marginal products and hence on the real wages of both factors.

The first theoretical demonstration of this phenomenon was

---

[11] Thus, instead of focusing on whether there is convergence of real wages in South and North, we focus directly on the question on centre stage: will cheaper labour-intensive imports from the South under freer trade cause our real wages of the unskilled to fall? In principle, of course, it is theoretically possible for the latter to occur while FPE fails: for example, the factors that militate against SS, detailed above, may hold in the South and not in the North.

made by Arvind Panagariya (1980), who modelled scale economies in the old way where they were external to the firm but internal to the industry. Thus we are able to work with models of perfect competition.

Elhanan Helpman and Paul Krugman (1985) established the same conclusion in the context of scale economies internal to the firm, and hence under imperfect competition. Their analysis was, however, restricted to the special case where the output per firm did not rise with trade. Thus the added gains from trade were caused by variety rather than reduced cost due to scale. Drusilla Brown, Alan Deardorff, and Robert Stern (1993) have now produced a more general and illuminating analysis allowing for these and other effects.[12]

Diversification

The SS theorem (as also the FPE theorem) depends on the equilibriums under autarky and free trade lying in the diversification cone − that is, trade should not lead to complete specialization. When it does, the unique relationship between goods and factor prices breaks down. Although the factor prices are unique at complete specialization on a good, goods prices are manifestly not unique, because rising prices for the good will be compatible with continued specialization on it.[13]

Equally, while the SS redistributive effect operates so long as trade shifts production toward a good without causing complete specialization, once specialization is achieved it follows that any further rise in that good's (relative) price will mean that both factors will gain from it: the lifting-all-boats effect from this improvement in the terms of trade (implied by the rise in the relative price of the specialized good where, and in terms of which, their reward is fixed at specialization) will ensue. The net effect could be to leave both factors better off under free trade than under autarky.[14]

---

[12] Their Michigan CGE model, applied to Mexico, and incorporating imperfect competition due to scale economies, also predicts a rising real wage for the US from NAFTA.

[13] We are working here with the 2×2 version of the SS and FPE theorems. For higher dimensionality, see Ethier's (1984) fine review.

[14] We deliberately compare autarky with free trade because, when either of the

But this lifting-all-boats effect will of course help each factor proportionately to how much it consumes of the cheaper imported goods. Hence it is pertinent to observe, as the work of William Cline (1990, pp. 201–6, especially Table 8.3) on textiles shows and as casual empiricism suggests for other imported goods such as low-quality footwear, the groups at the bottom of the income distribution (which must include the unskilled) disproportionately spend their incomes on imported goods whose prices are heavily influenced by protection (such as the voluntary export restraints (VERs) on footwear and the Multifiber Agreement (MFA) on textiles). Deardorff and Haveman (1991) have made the complementary observation that the invoking of administered protection has been typically for industries which are *not* intensive in the incidence of poverty in their workforce, suggesting that protection so given is, in its direct effect, to the (relative) disadvantage of the industries that are, and hence of the poor.

Trade and Competition

The lifting-all-boats effect can also arise if trade means greater competition and discipline, causing X-efficiency effects which may be captured analytically as Hicks-neutral technical change. If we do this, and if we assume that the effect operates throughout the economy, in both traded sectors, then clearly both factors get their real wages improving from this, countervailing and possibly reversing the fall in the real wage of the SS-impacted factor.

But, even if we were to assume that the production function improvement arises differentially more in the import-competing sectors, then we can see immediately from the early work on the general-equilibrium income-elasticities of supply under technical

---

equilibriums being compared has tariff revenues being generated, we must make assumptions about how the revenue is disposed of. Where it is assumed to be redistributed to the factors qua consumers, we must distinguish between the effect of the trade policy in question on real *wages* and real *incomes* (inclusive of revenue transfers), as in Bhagwati (1959) and subsequent analyses of the SS theorem. This distinction is clearly important in policy discussions, as noted earlier. The adverse effect on real wages of trade, if any, could be offset by fiscal policy in principle, especially if trade leads to greater income and hence greater tax capabilities.

change[15] that, ceteris paribus, the effect will be to raise the real wage of the factor intensively used in these sectors: that is, of unskilled labour in our instance.

The econometric evidence on this hypothesis is hard to find. However, Jim Levinsohn's (1993) work on the imports-as-competition hypothesis, while not exactly specified in the manner suggested here, is successful in testing that hypothesis with the use of Turkish industry data under near-controlled-experiment conditions. This work suggests that our specification of the effects of trade on technical change via competition may also be borne out. As in many areas we discuss in this chapter, we must confess that ideas and hypotheses outrun plausible econometric evidence, suggesting more questions than answers for empirical research.

Convergence – To Whose Real Wage?

Even though we do not consider the FPE theorem (and the SS theorem) to be compelling, for the aforementioned reasons, suppose that convergence of real wages of the unskilled will occur as a result of trade between poor and rich nations. Will that then mean, as Ross Perot and Pat Choate (1993) have argued in their anti-NAFTA tract (1993) that (say) NAFTA 'will pit American and Mexican workers in a race to the bottom'? In short, will convergence get US real wages down to the Mexican levels prior to NAFTA, or will it raise the latter up to American levels prior to NAFTA? Where will the real wages settle in each country?

In the context of NAFTA, given the relative sizes of the US and Mexico, we would guess that goods prices will gravitate toward US prices: so, then, will factor prices. For freer trade in the world economy, between South and North, a gut answer is harder to give. We need to investigate the question analytically before we can give an informed answer; to our knowledge, no such analysis currently exists. But it is clear that the widespread presumption that, in case of convergence (which we have argued need not be expected anyway), the real wages in the rich countries will gravitate down toward the levels in the South appears to be based on panic rather than logic.

[15] See also the excellent paper by Findlay and Grubert (1959).

Early Labour Studies

Should we nonetheless have changed our minds in light of the early labour-economists' studies, especially by Borjas–Freeman–Katz (1992) and by Murphy and Welch (1991), which attributed a definite role to international trade in explaining the unhappy behaviour of the real wages of the unskilled in the 1980s?

Excellent as these studies are, our major source of dissatisfaction with them, and hence our inability to admit them as evidence in favour of the thesis they support, is that nowhere do they build on the essential fact that trade should affect goods prices in the desired direction before anything can be inferred concerning the trade-induced effects on factor rewards.[16] We will consider this by examining the Borjas–Freeman–Katz study that was available by mid-1990. It has been much cited by economists and in the media (Passell 1992, in the *New York Times*), and it has provided intellectual support to those fearful of the effects of trade on real wages of the unskilled.[17]

Borjas, Freeman, and Katz essentially compute the unskilled labour embodied in American imports (using the observed coefficients of labour use in domestic import-competing industries) and in American exports, treating the former as notional additions to and the latter as subtractions from the stock of such labour. Since

---

[16] This is, of course, at the heart of the FPE and SS theorems. Indeed, it is a central part of the general equilibrium theory of international trade.

[17] Deardorff and Hakura (1993), in ch. 3 of Bhagwati and M. Kosters (eds) (1994), suggest alternative questions. For instance, if technical change saving on unskilled labour happens exogenously, would the real wages of the unskilled fall more or less if the economy were in free trade rather than in autarky? Alternatively, we could ask whether exogenous shifts in the trade offers of foreign nations in trade with us will help or harm unskilled wages — a question that can be fitted more readily into the analysis in the text, since factor prices again would change only in so far as goods prices change because of this exogenous shift in the foreign offer curve.

We should stress that, in the following critique, we define the question of the impact of trade on wages in the following policy-relevant sense is integration into the world economy through the reduction of trade barriers the cause of decline in the real wage of the unskilled? That is also clearly the intent of the labour economists' studies, although the ones we call 'early' studies do not specify a clear question and a model that can analytically deal with it.

imports use more unskilled labour per dollar of gross value than exports, and since the trade deficit means that imports exceed exports, this exercise yields a substantial 'addition' to America's unskilled labour, thanks to its trade. Furthermore, since in view of expanding trade deficits during the 1980s, this addition to the unskilled labour stock would have been accentuated, it would seem logical to conclude that trade must have contributed pari passu to the observed decline in the real wage of unskilled labour.[18]

This logic is indeed plausible. However, it runs into a problem. The only way that real wages can be affected is if, at constant (relative) factor prices, productivity increases or, with productivity change ruled out, through a change in factor prices. Since the burden of the explanation advanced is through exogenous trade changes, the analysis must presume a change in factor prices that is unrelated to productivity change or other domestic factors. But such a change in factor prices must reflect a trade-induced change in goods prices. Borjas, Freeman, and Katz should have investigated the change in goods prices, establishing that, during the period that real wages of unskilled labour fell, the (relative) price of unskilled labour-intensive import-competing goods fell too. Else, their argument is incomplete and cannot be accepted.

Alan Deardorff and Robert Staiger (1988) have shown that, under certain conditions, a positive correlation will exist between relative changes in factor prices and relative changes in the factor content of trade. But their model still requires associated changes in goods prices. Our objection is simply that if these changes in goods prices do not conform to what is required, and observed correlation between changes in factor prices and factor content must be dismissed as spurious. As noted below, both the earlier Bhagwati (1991a) and the later Robert Lawrence–Matthew Slaughter (1993) studies show that goods prices have changed in the *opposite* direction to that required for the SS explanation. Indeed, it is easy to see that the Borjas–Freeman–Katz technique will indicate that real wages have fallen because of trade even when they have not changed. Thus, consider the following simple analytics.

---

[18] Presumably they have in mind, then, an aggregate production function with diminishing returns. See however the section below on aggregate production function.

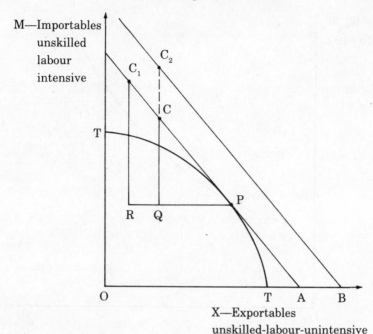

FIG. 23.1: Change in Trade as Trade Deficit Changes
SOURCE: Authors.

Consider Fig. 23.1 where, for the US economy, the set of production possibilities defined on the (only) two goods M and X is OTT, with TT as the 'frontier'. The goods–price ratio $(P_M P_E)$, which is the relative price of the two goods, is given internationally; at the outset, it is CP. Then, an efficient market economy will produce (at the tangency of the price-line with TT) at P; consumption will be at C; and balanced trade will occur with QC of imports being exchanged for PQ of exports.

In turn, the goods–price ratio will determine the factor-price ratio, as shown in Fig. 23.2. Assume two factors of production, high school (HS) and college (C) graduates: the former are unskilled and the latter skilled. The importable industry is HS-intensive in the sense that it uses, at any factor prices W_{HS}/W_C, a higher proportion of HS to C in production than does X, the exportable industry. This is quite intuitive: if the industry M using HS intensively suffers a reduced price, the (relative) reward of HS could be expected to fall. This relationship is, of course, at the heart of the SS theorem.

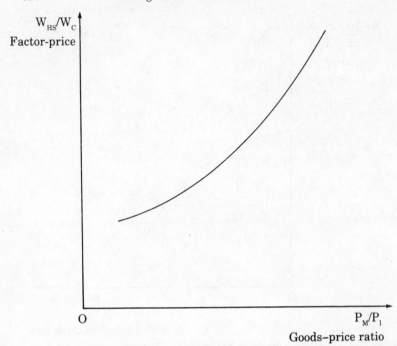

FIG. 23.2:   Relationship Between Goods-Price and Factor-Price Ratios
SOURCE: Authors.

Now, return to Fig. 23.1. Assume that trade increases at constant goods prices (that is, without intensifying import competition), because of C shifting to C_1.[19] Imports and exports increase to C_1R and PR, respectively. The Borjas–Freeman–Katz calculation would now show an increase in the notional addition to the American stock of HS. But nothing would have happened to W_{HS}/W_C and to the real wage of HS, since the goods–price ratio has not changed.

Similarly, assume instead that the US now runs a trade deficit so that it can spend AB more than its national income OA, measured in terms of good X. National expenditure then takes place along BC_2 instead of along the income-determined national budget line AC. Let the consumption bundle chosen then be C_2, implying that the deficit is associated with an equivalent increase in imports and leaves exports unchanged. The Borjas–Freeman–Katz calculation will then again show that the endowment of HS has risen

[19] This could happen, for example, by a shift in tastes.

notionally, since *HS*-intensive imports exceed *HS*-unintensive exports by the amount of the new deficit.[20] But nothing again would have happened to W_{HS}/W_C and to the real wages of *HS* in the US economy.

Thus, we cannot conclude with Borjas, Freeman, and Katz that trade in the 1980s depressed the real wages of the unskilled: their methodology can create invalid inferences to that effect. More important, they do not show that the domestic prices of the unskilled labour-intensive import-competing goods fell relatively during the 1980s: without that, they cannot invoke the SS or the FPE variety of argumentation to 'explain' the decline in unskilled-labour wages. Indeed, there seems to be no evidence to suggest that the external terms of trade improved significantly in the 1980s for the US, although this may have as much to do with the lack of exogenous improvement as to the increased adoption of voluntary export restraints that generally transfer rents to exporters and thus offset the improvement in terms of trade.

At minimum, as noted by Bhagwati (1991a), if we look at the import and export price indexes for manufactured goods (which exceed 90 per cent in weight in the total indexes) in Fig. 23.3, the evidence points the other way: import prices *rise* in relation to export prices.[21] A subsequent empirical study by Lawrence and Slaughter (1993) has reinforced the Bhagwati critique. The authors find a rise in the relative price of non-production labour (skilled labour)-intensive goods as against production labour (unskilled labour)-intensive goods at the 2- and 3-digit SIC classification levels. This more disaggregated analysis confirms the impression that our highly aggregated figure 2–3 conveys, since both show that the relative prices have moved in the 'wrong' direction as far as the FPE–SS explanation is concerned.

A further critical piece of evidence presented by Lawrence and Slaughter is that most sectors (again, at the 2- and 3-digit levels) have become *more* intensive in their use of non-production labour as compared with production labour in the 1980s. This fact is at

[20] Even if we were to assume homothetic preferences, so that the consumption of both goods increases in the same proportion, exports will still fall, imports will still rise, and once again the notional endowment of *HS* will rise.

[21] See Bhagwati 1991a, 1991b.

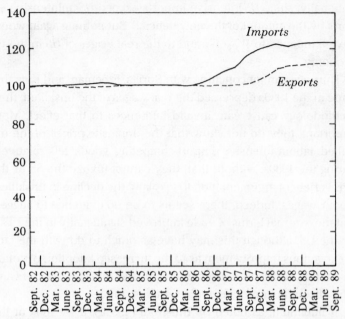

FIG. 23.3: Import and Export Prices of Manufactures for the United States (Sept. 1982–Sept. 1989)

SOURCE: Bureau of Labour Statistics, US Department of Labour.Relationship Between Goods-Price and Factor-Price Ratios.

variance with the FPE–SS approach, since a key implication of the FPE–SS hypothesis is that firms in all sectors will economize on the more expensive factor, skilled labour, and hence will become more intensive in their use of unskilled labour.

This second piece of evidence, in conjunction with the first, effectively kills the FPE–SS hypothesis as a tenable explanation of the phenomenon of the rising wage differential and falling wages of the unskilled. The Borjas–Freeman–Katz conclusion that trade has adversely affected wages may well be right, but their analysis does not show this, and we can be quite confident that the FPE–SS explanation has been a red herring in the story.[22]

[22] It is worth noting that several partial-equilibrium studies of the effect of trade on wages, which unlike Borjas–Freeman–Katz do use prices rather than quantities, most notably Grossman (1986, 1987) and Revenga (1992), also fail to find a significant effect of trade on wages in most of the industries studied.

Technical Change — A Trade-Independent Explanation

Contrary to the Borjas–Freeman–Katz conclusion, both casual empiricism and the work of Mincer (1991), Davis and Haltiwanger (1991), and Bound and Johnson (1992) strongly suggest that skills-based technical change is the key culprit in the 1980s story and in the unfolding scenario for the 1990s and beyond.[23]

These labour economists cite the prototypical example of the computer revolution, a whole spectrum of technological innovations that inherently require their users to have skills easier for a college graduate than for a high school graduate to acquire today. To put it in another way, a computer with a single skilled operator can replace half a dozen unskilled typists — a phenomenon that we see in our own departmental offices and in the publishing houses that publish our books. Indeed, the work of Mincer (1991) is extremely suggestive in this regard. Looking at research and development expenditures per worker, Fig. 23.4, panel A, and deploying a simple model, he is able to predict remarkably well (Fig. 23.4, panel B) the college graduates' wage premiums over the wages of high school graduates.

If, as in the section below on aggregate production function, we consider an *aggregate* production function approach, we can see readily that unskilled labour-saving technical change (in a two-factor framework with skilled and unskilled labour) will reduce the wage differential and can depress the real wage of unskilled labour if the factor-substitution effect of the technical change is outweighed by the total productivity effect.[24]

---

[23] The decline of unions, as discussed by Freeman (1991), the erosion of the real value of the minimum wage, as discussed in Blackburn, Bloom, and Freeman (1990), and changes in pay norms, as discussed by Mitchell (1989) are factors that, if taken into account, would imply that the pressure on real wages has been institutionally allowed to translate into actual decline in them. Conversely, in the different, more 'sheltering' type of EC institutional setting, this pressure presumably causes a relatively lower decline in wages and greater increase in unemployment. For a recent comprehensive survey of alternative explanations, see Levy and Murnane (1992).

[24] Diagrammatically, the latter relates to the upward rescaling of the isoquants, whereas the former concerns their being twisted so that, at any factor-price ratio, the ratio of skilled to unskilled labour chosen rises as is consistent with the evidence (see the FPE section above).

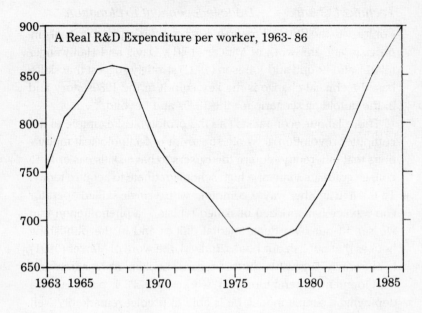

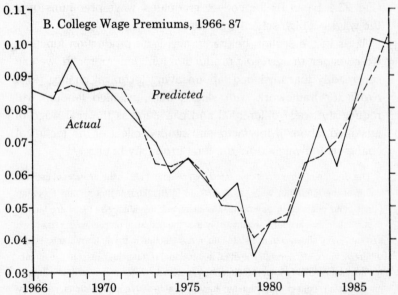

FIG. 23.4:   Wage Premiums of College Graduates Relative to High School
Graduates, with Respect to R & D Expenditures per Worker, 1963–87

SOURCE: Jacob Mincer, *Studies in Human Capital: Collected Essays of Jacob Mincer*, vol. 1 (Hampshire, England: Edward Elgar, 1993).

The analysis gets more complex when we disaggregate the economy, as in the trade-theoretic models, into two sectors with different factor intensities. The effect on the wage differential and the real wage of the unskilled will depend then on the total rate of change: how biased it is against unskilled labour and its relative incidence in the two sectors.

Thus, if the change is uniformly spread in both sectors, and the economy remains diversified in the new equilibrium at the old goods– and factor–price ratios, the result will be to maintain the wage differential. The factor–price ratio corresponding to the goods–price ratio will not change after the uniform technical change, whether Hicks-neutral or biased.[25] Although the real wage of unskilled labour will surely rise with Hicks-neutral technical change, it may not if the technical change is (pro-)skills-biased, and the bias effect outweighs the total productivity effect.

We would then argue that the disaggregated-sectors model suggests that the happy experience of the 1950s and 1960s may have been due to technical change that was substantial, was more uniformly spread among exportables and importables, and was more neutral than biased whereas, in the 1980s, it has probably been slower (perhaps due to slowed investment and hence slower absorption of new technology), has been more focused on skills-intensive exportables, and has also been more skills-biased. Taken in conjunction, these three factors would tend to widen the wage differential while putting downward pressure simultaneously on the real wages of the unskilled.[26] These ideas must of course be tested empirically.

But the preceding analysis takes technical change to be exogenous to trade. Larry Mishel has rightly raised the question: if trade competition *induces* technical change, could we not then relate the effects on real wages back again to trade? Our judgement, however, is that this would work against, not in favour of,

---

[25] The goods–price ratio can itself change if the country's terms of trade are variable: demand conditions then would also have to be considered to determine the new equilibrium goods– and hence factor–price ratios.

[26] These ideas were explored in the context of a general-equilibrium model of two tradeable goods and two factors plus a non-trades services sector, using the Komiya model, in Bhagwati (1991a, 1991b).

those who think that trade is adversely affecting the real wages of the unskilled. For if we proceed along the assumption that trade competition induces neutral technical change in the import-competing unskilled; labour-intensive industries, this should raise, not lower, the real wage of the unskilled. Again, if we assume instead that trade exerts a little downward pressure on the real wages of the unskilled and that the search for technical innovation is biased in favour of economizing the use of the factors of production whose wages are rising instead, the effect again will be to reinforce the conclusion that trade-induced technical change helps, not hurts, the real wages of the unskilled.[27]

KALEIDOSCOPIC COMPARATIVE ADVANTAGE:
FOOTLOOSE INDUSTRIES AND LABOUR TURNOVER

The technical change-based explanation, of course, takes us away from trade as a cause of the phenomenon of depressed real wages of the unskilled. Indeed, it was the difficulty we had with the FPE-cum-SS-theoretic approach to this conundrum that helped focus on this alternative explanation.

But if the obvious FPE–SS-type trade explanation is not compelling, all is not lost. It is possible to develop an alternative trade-based explanation (Bhagwati 1991a; 1991b) that departs altogether from the FPE–SS approach. We doubt that this alternative explanation can carry the weight that the technical change (and technological) explanation probably does, but it could well be a contributory factor of some, perhaps also growing, importance.

The new hypothesis comes from the observation that the world economy is now increasingly integrated and that the convergence of technology among the Organization for Economic Cooperation and Development (OECD) countries and the spread of global multinational corporations around the world have brought many modern industries within the grasp of countries. Many more industries therefore are 'footloose' now than before: small shifts in costs can cause comparative advantage to shift suddenly from one

[27] See the discussion of the Kennedy–Weizsacker theory of induced technical change in Samuelson (1965).

country to another.[28] Thus, we suspect that comparative advantage has, over time, become kaleidoscopic: one country may have comparative advantage in X and another in Y today, and tomorrow it may suddenly go the other way. This volatility in comparative advantage will have two serious consequences.

The first consequence will be far greater sensitivity to notions of fair trade. Firms will be looking over one another's shoulders to see if that lethal epsilon advantage enjoyed by the other firm is attributable to some unfair domestic institution or policy on its home turf. Demands for 'level playing fields' will multiply. They have already done so, as we noted in the first section of this chapter.

The second consequence is that the volatility in comparative advantage will generally imply, ceteris paribus, more labour turnover. Thus the frictional or 'natural' unemployment should rise, as it appears to have in the 1980s. But the added turnover, in turn, could mean that the growth curve of earnings may become flatter, because a more mobile labour force could be accumulating less skills. As one of the authors, Bhagwati, has written elsewhere (Bhagwati 1991a and 1991b), 'a rolling stone gathers no moss and a moving worker gathers no skills'. As it happens, a forthcoming study by the OECD, reported on by *The Economist* (1993) in the Economics Focus column entitled 'Musical Chairs', confirms this conjecture:

So the OECD concludes that there is a clear link between employment stability and skill training. But which causes which? Most likely the two are mutually reinforcing: too high a rate of labour turnover discourages investment in workplace skills; and workers who get no training are likely to show less commitment to their current employer and so may change jobs more often. A vicious circle develops as higher labour turnover produces a less trained and hence a less loyal workforce.

Then, we get a trade-dependent explanation as to why increased labour turnover reduces, ceteris paribus, the real wage of unskilled labour. But what about the wage *differential* between

[28] This is also the view implicit in the imperfect-competition worlds of symmetric firms, although the analysis often goes in the direction of arguing how footloose industries land in one rather than another country as economies of scale are exploited.

unskilled and skilled labour? Our argument seems to apply symmetrically to all labour. Therefore, to produce an explanation also
of increased wage differential, we would have to introduce some
source of asymmetry that relatively shields the skilled from the
rolling stone gathers no moss effect.

Such an asymmetry may accrue from the greater transferability
of workplace-acquired skills by the skilled. An accountant handling IBM, for example, can shift his acquired know-how readily
to a new job at Caterpillar or Chrysler, but working better on the
assembly line for automobiles at Ford may not transfer to working
at a blast furnace in Pittsburgh, or for that matter to flipping
hamburgers at MacDonalds.

Again, the fallow, search-period spells between jobs are probably used by college graduates (the skilled) to retool and acquire
added and more suitable skills — having learned once, an individual can and will learn again. High school graduates and
dropouts (the unskilled) are less likely to do so, having not learned
in the first place. We can only speculate about this; empirical
knowledge is hard to come by on this particular hypothesis. Jacob
Mincer and Yoshio Higuchi's 1988 study attempts to link labour
turnover and the wage structure. Although it does not directly
address the hypothesis we have advanced, this study could provide the basis for its empirical investigation. Furthermore, Steve
Davis has suggested that one useful empirical construct that could
be brought to bear on the hypothesis is the tenure distribution in
various disaggregated sectors of the economy. If sectors that were
exposed to the rolling stone gathers no moss effect of the type
discussed here also exhibited leftward shifts in the tenure distribu-
tions, especially of unskilled workers, then this would be consistent with the hypothesis and might constitute partial corroboration
of it.

A Rolling Stone Gathers No Moss Model

We can readily sketch the essential structure of the foregoing
argument in the 2×2 framework.[29] Let the economy be small —

[29] See also Dehejia (1992b). The model is set up to generate not merely the adverse
effect on the real wage of the unskilled, but also a widening differential between
the wages of the unskilled and the skilled. While we use the words 'skilled' and

that is, the terms of trade are given and invariant to its trade. Let two goods, X and Y, by produced according to standard neoclassical production functions with the use of two factors, skilled labour, H, and unskilled labour, L, which throughout are in fixed supply. Suppose as well that the terms of trade are such that this economy exports good X and that the economy remains within the Chipman–McKenzie diversification cone.

To capture the notion of volatility in terms of trade, suppose a two-period structure in which the terms of trade of the skilled labour-intensive good initially improve but then return to their original level. That is, suppose that the initial relative price of good X in terms of good Y is p, then it becomes p', $p' > p$, and finally returns to p.[30]

As regards the accumulation of human capital, this for simplicity is assumed to take place between periods — that is, between the period in which terms of trade p' and p prevail. Suppose that both types of labour, skilled and unskilled, acquire human capital through learning-by-doing, which is modelled as an augmentation of the effective stocks of the two types of labour, H and L. Crucially, skilled labour, H, augments at the same rate in either sector, X or Y. This augmentation is assumed to be unaffected by a shift of skilled labour between sectors.

Therefore, suppose that H augments at the end of the two periods to δH, $\delta > 1$, where δ is the gross rate of growth of the effective stock of H. By contrast, unskilled labour, L, augments if it remains in the same sector, but it is assumed not to augment if it moves between sectors. Therefore, total augmentation of the effective stock of unskilled labour, L, is $\delta(L - \Delta L) + \Delta L$, where ΔL is the amount of unskilled labour that moves between sectors X and Y in response to the initial terms of trade shift from p to p'.

'unskilled', Alan Deardorff has correctly noted that, since both types of labour can acquire skills but only differentially as assumed, it would be better to think of college and high school graduates, as earlier in this chapter.

[30] In more general form, we can envisage a stochastic progress for the terms of trade in which there are stationary disturbances around some trend growth-rate (which may be zero, in which case the terms of trade would be pure white noise). See also Dehejia (1992b).

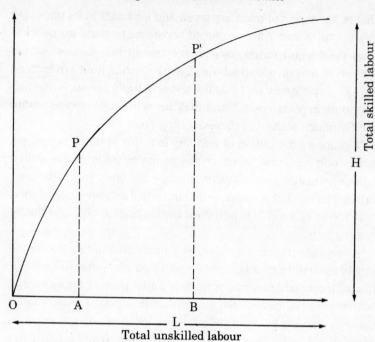

FIG. 23.5: Reallocation of Labour in Response to Terms of Trade Shock
SOURCE: Authors.

This is illustrated in Fig. 23.5 with the aid of the familiar
Edgeworth–Bowley box diagram. Let $OPP'O'$ be the contract
curve. At the initial terms of trade, the economy is at point P
on $OPP'O'$. The change in trade from p to p' induces a shift
in the equilibrium to a new point, P', along $OPP'O'$. Drop vertical
lines from P and P' to the horizontal axis and label the corresponding points A and B, respectively. The ΔL is equal to
the distance AB along the horizontal axis.

   In the final equilibrium, when the terms of trade have returned
to p, there is no change in the real wage per effective unit of
skilled or unskilled labour. The effective stocks per worker of the
two factors now differ, however, because of differential augmentation induced by the fluctuation of p to p' before its return to p.
The effective stock of skilled labour is now δH, whereas the
effective stock of unskilled labour is now $\delta(L - \Delta L) + \Delta L$.[31] This

---

[31] This model assumes that real wages will adjust immediately and fully to changes
in the terms of trade. But in reality there are often lags. Besides, we think of models

differential augmentation induces a Rybczynski (1955)-type real-location of resources from the unskilled labour-intensive sector, Y, to the skilled labour-intensive sector, X, but with no effect on the real wage per effective worker of either type since diversification is assumed.

Although real wages per effective worker are unchanged, however, the observed real wages per worker now differ. Recall that H and L represent total effective stocks of skilled and unskilled labour, respectively. Normalizing the populations of skilled and unskilled labour to unity for simplicity, H and L may thus be interpreted as the total stock of skilled labour per skilled labourer and the total stock of unskilled labour per unskilled labourer, respectively. Initially, the real wage of a skilled worker is $W_H H$ and that of an unskilled worker $W_H L$, where W_H and W_L are the respective real wages per effective worker.

At the end, real wages per effective worker, W_H and W_L, are unchanged, but real wages per worker have increased to $W_H \delta H$ and $W_L(\delta [L - \Delta L] + \Delta L)$, respectively.

Thus, while real wages per worker of both skilled and unskilled labour have increased because of on-the-job human capital accumulation, skilled labour becomes relatively better off (as compared with the initial situation) than unskilled labour. The real income of unskilled labour will thus be lower, as compared with having no terms of trade volatility in this model. This is caused not by the SS effect on real wages, as discussed in the FPE section above, but by the differential human capital accumulation that leaves unskilled labour relatively poorly endowed with human capital at the end. Skilled labour, conversely, by the model's assumption, is impervious to the volatility in terms of trade. It is evident that the real wage per unskilled labourer will be lower than if the rolling-stone effect were absent.

A multi-period version of this model has been analysed by Dehejia (1992b), combining the analytics of the 2×2 model of

---

of labour hiring and firing, their microeconomics suggests that, if terms of trade are expected to be volatile, firms will not adjust their employment to every change in the price of their output. Models that incorporate these ideas should nonetheless show that increased volatility of goods prices will be associated with increased volatility of factor prices.

trade theory with the twin new assumptions of the rolling-stone hypothesis on skills acquisition. The terms of trade of this small country evolve according to a pure, white-noise stochastic process. The terms of trade are assumed to have no trend, but rather to fluctuate noisily around some unspecified, long-run level, attributable to unspecified worldwide technology or taste shocks.

The simulation runs of the wage differentials (per worker)[32] that the model then generates, according to our hypothesis, attributable to the terms of trade fluctuations and the induced divergence of skills acquisition between the skilled and unskilled workers, do indeed show a rising time trend. Simulation runs by Dehejia on different values of the terms of trade noise parameter bear out the intuitive notion that the higher this parameter and hence the greater the volatility in terms of trade, the larger the wage-differential effect that is generated.[33]

Hysteresis – An Alternative Link between Kaleidoscopic Comparative Advantage and Wages

The modelling hitherto cited has simply embodied, in the otherwise-static framework, the rolling stone gathers no moss idea. There were no supply-side effects, in that each of the two types of labour followed its own skills-acquisition trajectory, as influenced critically by the kaleidoscopic comparative advantage implied volatility in the terms of trade.

But, of course, the two groups are not predetermined and non-intersecting over time. The unskilled (high school graduates and dropouts) can and do become skilled (college graduates and more) if the rewards are enticing. In the foregoing model, if the unskilled could costlessly become skilled, the relative supply of skilled labour would be infinitely elastic at a zero differential: that

[32] The wages per effective worker (that is, for given skill) remain constant in expected value terms by model specification of stationary white noise disturbances to the terms of trade. The trend change in a worker's real wage can in this model come only from the acquisition of greater skills.

[33] For details, see Dehejia (1992b). The simulations are necessary because an analytical solution to the model is not possible because of the inherent non-linearity in the key equation defining the time path of effective skilled to unskilled labour in the model.

is, any wage differential induced by terms of trade shifts would instantaneously disappear, which is obviously unrealistic.

But, to allow for costly fixed investment to enter the skilled group, we can realistically explore further the wage differential and wage effect of volatility in terms of trade. To do this, we must obviously introduce hysteresis into the analysis.[34] We now indicate how this might be done.

Take again as our starting point increased volatility in terms of trade, and introduce Dixit-style hysteresis in the following simple way. Thus, suppose that unskilled workers can transform themselves into skilled workers by incurring an irreversible fixed cost K.[35] Suppose next that the relative reward to being skilled versus being unskilled fluctuates stochastically (because of fluctuations in terms of trade) according to a geometric Brownian motion process (the continuous time analog of the random walk in discrete time). Under the critical assumption of a fixed cost of investment in an environment characterized by ongoing uncertainty, a band of inaction or hysteresis region will exist in which the wage differential (the excess return to being skilled versus being unskilled) will be positive, and in which there will be no supply response by unskilled workers to eliminate this differential.

It is important to note that hysteresis per se arises because of the existence of linear adjustment technology (that is, a fixed cost of retraining per worker), as opposed to neoclassical convex adjustment technology. Even in the absence of uncertainty, an inaction region will exist in which no retraining will take place. In a world without uncertainty, retraining will occur at the Marshallian investment trigger M, where M is defined by $M = \rho K$, where ρ is individuals' pure rate of time preference, which we can assume equals the interest rate. By assumption of the model, sufficient retraining will occur when the trigger is reached to ensure that the wage differential will never exceed ρK. Thus, for

---

[34] For a recent survey and synthesis of results in the investment and hysteresis literature, see Dixit (1992), on which we draw below.

[35] Formally, we must assume for analytical tractability in this simple model that the skilled can costlessly become unskilled. For professors who see how rapidly most students forget a subject once the examinations are over, this may well be the most realistic assumption in this chapter.

example, if it costs \$ 100,000 for an unskilled worker to 'upskill', so that $K = 100,000$, and if the interest rate is equal to 5 per cent, so that $\rho = 0.05$, then the maximum sustainable wage differential, which is equal to the Marshallian investment trigger M, is given by $(.05 \times 100,000)$, or \$ 5,000. The skilled job thus must pay \$ 5,000 more than the unskilled job to elicit a supply response. Furthermore, in this simple model, that is the maximum differential consistent with labour market equilibrium.[36]

The effect of uncertainty is essentially to *widen* the hysteresis region by increasing the investment trigger from M, given above, to H, where $H = \rho'K$, where the interest rate ρ must be replaced by an adjusted interest rate ρ', where $\rho' > \rho$. The precise definition of ρ' is furnished in Dixit (1992). It suffices for our purposes here to notice that the existence of uncertainty can make ρ' exceed ρ by an amount that is not trivial. Thus, sticking to the example in which $\rho = 0.05$, if we assume that σ, the coefficient of variation of the Brownian motion, is 0.2 – a magnitude of uncertainty by no means large, since the standard deviation is 20 per cent of the mean of the distribution – then ρ' is shown by Dixit to equal 0.093, or 9.3 per cent, giving a maximum wage differential of \$ 9,300.

Intuitively, in an inherently uncertain economic environment in which investment is costly and irreversible, in the sense that once an unskilled worker spends K to upskill he can never recover the investment, an unskilled worker will be reluctant to upskill because there is always the danger that the skill differential will drop after the costly investment is made. Of course, even in the presence of uncertainty, given a big enough wage differential, an unskilled worker will still be willing to upskill.

The existence of uncertainty essentially attaches a risk premium to the investment decision to upskill, which will raise the 'hurdle rate' on the investment. Furthermore, it is intuitively appealing (and is proved rigorously by Dixit) that this risk premium increases with the magnitude of uncertainty. Thus, in the numerical example above, if ρ remains at 5 per cent but σ is now set to 0.4, then ρ' jumps to 0.166, or 16.6 per cent – a very high hurdle rate indeed – that raises the maximum skill differential that the labour market will sustain to \$ 16,600.

[36] For details see Dixit (1992).

The connection between the Dixit-type hysteresis model and the assumption of terms of trade volatility made in this section thus becomes apparent. If indeed our assumption is correct that the 1980s have witnessed increased volatility in trade and hence induced volatility in the relative demand-driven wage differential, then the model suggests that in this increasingly uncertain economic environment, unskilled workers become increasingly reluctant to upskill. Hence, wage differentials that are larger than the historical norm will likely be observed.

Thus consider for illustration Fig. 23.6. Let H_0 be the investment trigger corresponding to an initial low level of uncertainty before the 1980s (σ_0), and let $H_1 > H_0$ be the new, higher investment trigger corresponding to a new, higher level of uncertainty in the 1980s (σ_1). Then the wage differential, which fluctuates stochastically in the smaller inaction band before the 1980s, breaks through its historical ceiling at date t', and rises above H_0, since now the new

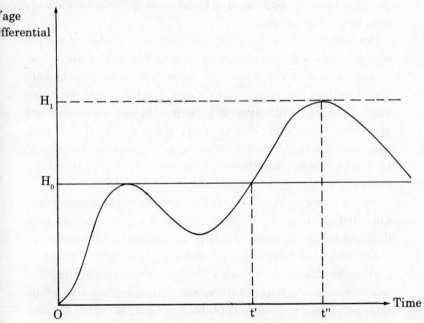

FIG. 23.6: Larger Wage Differential Induced by Greater Volatility of Terms of Trade

SOURCE: Authors.

trigger level H_1 is applicable. It is not until date t'' that the wage differential reaches its new ceiling, given by H_1, after which it cannot perforce rise any further. Thus, if t' is, say, 1980, and t'' is some indeterminate date in the future, then the time interval $[t', t'']$ would be characterized by a rising wage differential. This would seem puzzling to those accustomed to H_0 as the old maximum wage differential, presumably thought of as the historical norm, if H_0 had persisted for a long enough time. It makes sense, however, once it is understood that the level of uncertainty has increased.

Not only does this simple model build on the assumption of kaleidoscopic comparative advantage, and hence volatility of terms of trade, as did the rolling-stone model above; it is also ground firmly in individual choice-theoretic terms. This is its strength, and it helps to explain the puzzle first noted, it seems, by Jacob Mincer that the 1980s and early 1990s witnessed wage differentials well above historical norms. Relative supply responses have been muted compared to previous episodes of relatively high wage differentials.

An important corollary follows from this model. Since the action points are individually optimal in this model, and since, in the absence of any distortions in the system, those points are therefore also the social action points, it follows that the larger wage differentials observed in periods of higher uncertainty are also socially optimal. This corollary holds provided that such increased uncertainty is treated as truly exogenous and produced by kaleidoscopic comparative advantage in the highly globalized economy today.

In other words, in an inherently more uncertain environment, unskilled workers are doing the smart thing in delaying their decision to upskill. Hence the large wage differential we observe today should not be of policy concern. Government policy to narrow the differential by, say, subsidizing retraining by unskilled workers would be harmful in that some unskilled workers would be induced by the government subsidy scheme to retrain whereas they had previously optimally chosen to remain unskilled. The increment to their income gained from upskilling would not be large enough to warrant the investment.

Legitimate policy concerns about the incomes of the unskilled should therefore be met not by implementing retraining schemes but by direct *lump sum* income transfers to them. These transfers would accomplish the income distributional goals of policy without distorting incentives pertaining to the upskilling investment decision.

This conclusion, of course, presumes that the reduced real wages of the unskilled produced by other factors (such as the rolling stone effect) have not produced an imperfection in the credit market for borrowing for self-education. The effect of such a distortion in the context of the previous model is effectively to increase the private hurdle rate to some $\rho'' > \rho'$, whereas the social hurdle rate remains ρ'. The emergence of such distortions in the 1980s would provide an independent argument for subsidizing training and education to high school graduates and dropouts, the objective being to subsidize the unskilled workers to the extent that the gap $(\rho'' - \rho')$ is eliminated.

TRADE AND RENTS

We now turn to a more conventional, trade-related explanation that builds on the incorporation of imperfectly competitive *factor* markets into the picture. It is often claimed that international competition has led to the erosion of high-wage jobs, especially for automobiles and steel: either they have disappeared, or the wages on such 'good' jobs have been scaled down.

In the sense that the decline in the product prices of these sectors is putting downward pressure on labour that is specific to them or is intensively used in them, the resulting decline in the real wage of such labour is simply the SS phenomenon. But the aforementioned argument is rather than identical-quality labour is getting a higher wage (and hence a rent) in the import-competing sectors, and that this rent will be reduced in the new equilibrium, or that the number of people enjoying unchanged rents (that is, the number of good jobs) will be reduced, thanks to the import competition (that is, improved terms of trade).

Two questions must be asked before we consider this argument analytically: (1) is there any evidence that there are such rents? and (2) why do these rents exist?

The chief source of the current acceptance of the importance of rents in labour markets is the empirical work of Katz and Summers (1989) for US industries for 1984. They estimate the inter-industry dispersion of wages, controlling them for explanatory variables but finding that the standard deviation of the estimated wage differentials falls from 28 per cent without these controls to 15 per cent with them. This leaves a residual, which is then assigned to rents. The recent work of Jacob Mincer (1993), however, by adding better estimates of training and other variables and using different data sets, has succeeded in wiping out more than half of the Katz–Summers residual, leaving too emasculated a result on which to base serious explanations and policy conclusions.[37]

But assuming that the rents were significant, what could have caused them? The obvious answer is that the rents are obtained and protected by trade unions. This is surely true for the two major tradeable sectors that have faced import competition: automobiles and steel. In the more diffused analysis that Katz and Summers deploy, extended to aggregated groups of industries in the US, accounting for unions nonetheless leaves a residual to be explained by other factors. Katz and Summers then opt for an efficiency wage explanation of the type produced by Leibenstein and Mirrlees many years ago via the productivity effects of higher wages from better nourishment in developing countries and now extended to developed countries, in the shape of raising the cost of being fired and hence increasing efficiency in jobs where shirking is possible. As far as we can tell, Katz and Summers do not explore the technology of the industries where they do find significant non-union related rents to see if the hypothesis of shirking makes sense. It would appear that in sectors such as services, where a worker might be working on his own in relation to customers, shirking is easier than in manufacturing, where it may be difficult because he is on a tight assembly line with many others.

---

[37] This is not to say that the efficiency-wage models are not of great intellectual interest. Their relevance to the issue at hand is what we doubt.

Yet the rents seem to be higher in the latter than in the former. Then again, the rents seem to obtain in all jobs in an industry rather than in specific jobs in it; but it is hard to see why technology should be such that shirking obtains for all operations in an industry. Then again, Jacob Mincer's work shows that the average time spent in a queue for the higher-wage jobs is not longer than elsewhere, suggesting that the higher wages are for better people, whereas the 'rent' explanation would instead suggest longer wait-time.

For these reasons, we do not pursue the idea of modelling here the effect of import competition on rents in efficiency-wage models. Besides, a scanning of the Katz–Summers findings by industry does not suggest any relationship between rents in an industry and its status as a non-tradeable or tradeable and, if tradeable, as an exportable or an importable. We therefore confine ourselves to modelling the effect of import competition — that is, of fall in world prices on trade union-generated rents and jobs.

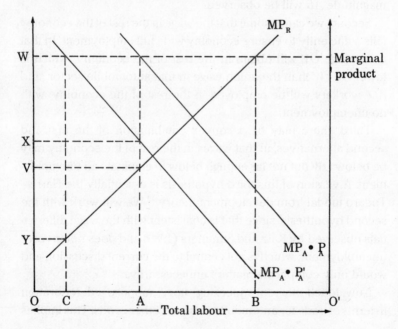

FIG. 23.7: Insider-Outsider Model of the Effect of Terms of Trade Shocks on Union Rents

SOURCE: Authors.

Consider then a simple general-equilibrium insider-outsider model, as in Fig. 23.7. Suppose that the economy consists of two sectors: A, automobiles, and R, the rest. Suppose that the workers in sector R are competitive, whereas the automobile workers are controlled by a union.[38] Suppose further that the union insiders are OA in number. OO' is the total labour force, P_A the relative price of automobiles, and MPs are the marginal product curves, measured for R from O' and for A from O as the origins. With OA insiders, whose full employment it will ensure, the automobile union will then bargain for (and we assume that the firms will accept) the wage rate OW.

There are at least three ways to close the model in terms of labour market behaviour in the rest of the economy:

First, we can assume that the union-determined wage has such widespread appeal that it perhaps becomes legislated into an economy-wide minimum wage of OW. In that case, employment in the rest of the economy will be $O'B$, and unemployment of magnitude AB will be observed.

Second, we can assume that the wage in the rest of the economy falls sufficiently to ensure economy-wide full employment. In that case, wage OV will obtain in the rest of the economy, which is lower by VW than the union wage in that automobile sector, and AO' workers will be employed in the rest of the economy, with no unemployment.

Third, there may be a convex combination of the first and second alternatives, in that wages in the rest of the economy may be below OW but not far enough below to eliminate all unemployment. A version of this third hypothesis is essentially the Harris–Todaro model from development theory.[39] We will work with the second hypothesis, since that is consistent with the wage differentials observed by Katz and Summers (1989) and does not involve unemployment, which is not central to the current discussion and would only complicate matters unnecessarily.

Now, to tell the 'rent-squeezing' story, suppose a deterioration in terms of trade for automobiles vis-à-vis other goods. This implies

---

[38] We make no Freudian slip in using the word 'controlled'. Substitute the word 'represented' if desired.

[39] Compare Harris and Todaro (1970) and Bhagwati and Srinivasan (1974).

an inward shift of the marginal product of labour schedule, MP_A, in proportion to the terms of trade change. If this change is anticipated by insiders, they will bargain for wage OX, which ensures full employment by insiders. Nominal wage will fall to OX, but notice that the real wage denominated in automobiles has remained constant, since nominal wages fall in proportion to the fall in terms of trade. Since by construction the numeraire is all other goods, the real wage will have fallen in terms of all other goods. Thus, insider automobile workers will typically perceive a fall in their real wages (unless they consume only automobiles for breakfast instead of cornflakes), but insider employment will be protected.[40]

Consider an alternative scenario in which the fall in trade was unexpected by the union. Then the union will bargain for and receive wage OW, but labour demand will fall short of MP_A. Thus the number of insiders will shrink to OC, with the disenfranchised insiders joining low-paid workers in the rest of the economy and earning the low wage OY. Now, what has happened to real wages? Since the nominal wage did not change, the real wage in terms of automobiles rises (since the price of automobiles fell). Since other goods are our numeraire, the real wage in terms of other goods stays constant. Thus, the real wage for the few insiders who are still employed will rise or stay roughly constant, but it will not fall. Good jobs will shrink, becoming even better jobs, and bad jobs will increase.

The two stories above at a very crude level might seem to fit the stylized facts of the US and European Community, respectively. In the US wages appear to be flexible downward, and thus insider employment levels in automobiles and steel are essentially unchanged. In the EC, by contrast, wages have been rigid and employment in automobiles and steel has been falling. If this simple insider-outsider model is correct, then either the US unions expected the shock and thus bargained for lower wages and European unions did not, or (stepping beyond the model) European unions stuck fast for high wages, as they were presumably

---

[40] The real wage of R-workers will however rise, because of cheaper automobiles, thus diluting the *total* reduction in the real wage of workers.

concerned about the 'super-insiders' *OC*, whereas US unions cared about *OA* and thus let wages fall.[41]

AGGREGATE PRODUCTION FUNCTION: THE ULTIMATE THREAT?

The models deployed in the foregoing analysis have been disaggregated (at least two sectors, exportables and importables) and in general equilibrium. But suppose we examine an aggregate production function for the entire economy.

This makes it analytically impossible to consider trade questions meaningfully. But it is perfectly compatible with thinking about the effects of accumulation and of technical change. (The real problem with it is that it can be quite misleading, since disaggregation shows, as trade theorists are aware, that effects such as diminishing returns, which seem natural and inevitable in the context of aggregate production functions can be eliminated by compositional effects. Thus, for example, if David Card's (1990) findings on the failure of the Mariel influx of Cubans into Miami are correct, and there was no effect of the substantial influx on real wages in Miami, that may well be because, as the Rybczynski (1955) theorem underlines, the added labour may have been absorbed at constant goods and factor prices by relative expansion of labour-intensive activities: a hypothesis that we suspect has not been examined.)

Using then the aggregate production function approach, suppose that we explicitly allow for three factors: capital K, skilled labour L_s and unskilled labour L_u. Then take a nested *CES* production function that captures the idea that K and L_s are relatively complementary, as compared with L_u.[42] In that case, the marginal

---

[41] Thea Lee has suggested that the effect of trade competition may simply be to weaken the unions' bargaining power generally. Thus, a shift from protecting insiders' wages to protecting their employment may soon yield to inability to be taken seriously and hence their eventual demise. If so, rents defining some jobs as better than others will obviously vanish with the unions.

[42] Such a production function is:

$$Y = \{ \delta \, [\alpha K^{-\rho 1} + (1 - \alpha) \, L_s^{-\rho 1}]^{\rho 2/\rho 1} + (1 - \delta) \, L_u^{-\rho 2} \}^{1/\rho 2},$$

product of L_u, and hence its real wage, will *fall* as capital accumulates. Technology is thus not kind to unskilled labour: the traditional engine for growth, Marx's primitive accumulation, hurts unskilled labour instead of improving its real wage. The same applies, of course, if we receive net inflows of foreign investment. Ross Perot gets to stand on his head!

Furthermore, technical change accentuates this phenomenon in the production function above,[43] as indeed in the real world, as the recent work on technical change confirms (for example, see Krueger 1993). Then, we have a real problem on our hands: *both* sources of growth, capital accumulation (including inward foreign investment) and technical change, will harm unskilled labour. That then becomes the *ultimate threat*. Marx is indeed striking again.

Once again, the analysis exaggerates and misleads. Compositional effects can kill the operation of the adverse effect within each industry. Then again, supply response by the unskilled to get skilled as the returns to skills rise will reduce ceteris paribus the supply of unskilled labour and increase that of the skilled. This effect will make the widened differential in rewards to the skilled relative to the unskilled a transitory phenomenon. The adjustment process whereby the unskilled become skilled, turning the differential back towards its original position, depends of course on the cost of such skill acquisition.[44]

We may conjecture here, however, that the adjustment may have become more costly, and hence the widening of the wage

---

where the condition that $\rho 1 > \rho 2$ guarantees that capital K and skilled labour L_s have a lower Hicks–Allen partial substitution elasticity than K and unskilled labour L_u, so that capital-skill complementarity holds in a relative sense. The production function is from Layard and Walters (1978). The original work on the three-factor production function, with the thesis that capital is more complementary with skilled labour, is due to Griliches (1969). More recent evidence is presented in Bartel and Lichtenberg (1987) and Berndt and Morrison (1991).

[43] This is easily verified by multiplying the production function in the preceding footnote with a technology shift parameter A, and then showing that the marginal product of unskilled labour (the partial derivative of Y with regard to L_u) is decreasing in A.

[44] The transition-path and the steady-state properties of such an adjustment process have been examined in Dehejia (1992a).

differential more persistent, in the 1980s. This could have been caused by the rise of lucrative alternatives such as drug-dealing, the fall in the quality of schools, and the collapse of the family and hence the fall in the motivation and aptitude for getting educated among those affected, particularly in inner cities.

CONCLUDING REMARK

Our review and analysis of alternative *theoretical* ways in which freer trade may affect real wages of the unskilled suggest several areas for further investigation.

But they also indicate that the *empirical* evidence to date fails to put the burden of the explanation for the observed decline in real wages of the unskilled on freer trade, leaving technology and technical change as the key culprits.

REFERENCES

Bartel, Ann P. and Frank R. Lichtenberg, 1987: 'The Comparative Advantage of Educated Workers in Implementing New Technology', *Review of Economics and Statistics*, vol. 69, pp. 343–59.

Baumol, William J., Sue Anne B. Blackman and Edward N. Wolff, 1989: *Productivity and American Leadership: The Long View* (Cambridge: Mass.: MIT Press).

Berndt, Earnst R. and Catherine Morrison, 1991: 'High-Tech Capital, Economic Performance, and Labor Composition in U.S. Manufacturing Industries: An Explanatory Analysis', mimeo. (Cambridge, Mass.: MIT).

Bhagwati, Jagdish N., 1959: 'Protection, Real Wages and Real Incomes', *Economic Journal*, vol. 69, pp. 733–48.

——, 1964: 'The Pure Theory of International Trade: A Survey', *Economic Journal*, vol. 74, pp. 1–94.

——, 1991 [1991a]: 'Free Traders and Free Immigrationists: Strangers or Friends?', Working Paper no. 20 (New York, N.Y.: Russell Sage Foundation).

——, 1991 [1991b]: 'Trade and Income Distribution', Paper presented at the Columbia University Conference, 'Deindustrialization', New York, N.Y., 15–16 Nov.

Bhagwati, Jagdish N., 1991 [1991c]: *The World Trading System at Risk* (Princeton, N.J.: Princeton University Press).

——, 1994 [1992]: 'Fair Trade, Reciprocity, and Harmonization: The New Challenge to the Theory and Policy of Free Trade', *in* A. Deardorff and R. Stern (eds), volume on GATT (Ann Arbor, Mich.: University of Michigan Press).

Bhagwati, Jagdish N. and M. Kosters (eds), 1994: *Trade and Wages* (Washington, DC: American Enterprise Institute).

Bhagwati, Jagdish N. and T.N. Srinivasan, 1974: 'On Reanalyzing the Harris–Todaro Model: Policy Rankings in the Case of Sector-Specific Sticky Wages', *American Economic Review*, vol. 64, pp. 502–8.

——, 1983: *Lectures on International Trade* (Cambridge, Mass.: MIT Press).

Blackburn, McKinley L., David E. Bloom and Richard B. Freeman, 1990: 'The Declining Economic Position of Less Skilled American Men', *in* G. Burtless (ed.), *A Future of Lousy Jobs?: The Changing Structure of U.S. Wages* (Washington, DC: Brookings Institution), pp. 31–67.

——, 1990: 'An Era of Falling Earnings and Rising Inequality?', *Brookings Review*, vol. 9, pp. 38–43.

Borjas, George J., Richard B. Freeman and Lawrence F. Katz, 1992: 'On the Labor Market Effects of Immigration and Trade', *in* G. Borjas and R. Freeman (eds), *The Economic Effects of Immigration in Source and Receiving Countries* (Chicago, Ill.: University of Chicago Press).

Bound, John and George Johnson, 1992: 'Changes in the Structure of Wages in the 1980s: An Evaluation of Alternative Explanations', *American Economic Review*, vol. 82, pp. 371–92.

Brown, Drusilla K., Alan V. Deardorff and Robert M. Stern, 1993: 'Protection and Real Wages: Old and New Trade Theories and their Empirical Counterparts', Paper presented the CEPR/CESPRI Conference, 'New Trade Theories: A Look at the Empirical Evidence', Bocconi University, Milan, 27–8 May.

Card, David, 1990: 'The Impact of the Mariel Boatlift on the Miami Labor Market', *Industrial and Labor Relations Review*, vol. 43, no. 2, pp. 245–57.

Cline, William R., 1990: *The Future of World Trade in Textiles and Apparel* (Washington, DC: Institute for International Economics).

Davis, Steven J. and John Haltiwanger, 1991: 'Wage Dispersion between and within U.S. Manufacturing Plants, 1963–86', *Brookings Papers on Economic Activity, Microeconomics* (Washington, DC: The Brookings Institution), pp. 115–80.

Deardorff, Alan V. and Dalia Hakura, 1994: 'Trade and Wages: What are the Questions?', *in* J.N. Bhagwati and M. Kosters (eds), *Trade and Wages* (Washington, DC: American Enterprise Institute), ch. 3.

Deardorff, Alan V. and John D. Haveman, 1991: 'The Effects of U.S. Trade Laws on Poverty in America', Discussion paper no. 285, Institute of Public Policy Studies (Ann Arbor, Mich.: University of Michigan).

Deardorff, Alan V. and Robert W. Staiger, 1988: 'An Interpretation of the Factor Content of Trade', *Journal of International Economics*, vol. 24, pp. 93–107.

Dehejia, Vivek H., 1992 [1992a]: 'Capital-Skill Complementarity and Endogenous Wage Structure', mimeo. (New York, N.Y.: Columbia University).

——, 1992 [1992b]: 'Kaleidoscopic Comparative Advantage and the Rising Skill Differential', mimeo. (New York, N.Y.: Columbia University).

Dixit, Avinash, 1992: 'Investment and Hysteresis', *Journal of Economic Perspectives*, vol. 6, pp. 107–32.

The Economist, 1993: 'Musical Chairs' (Economics Focus column), 17 July, p. 67.

Ethier, Wilfred J., 1984: 'Higher Dimensional Issues in Trade Theory', *in* R. Jones and P. Kenen (eds), *Handbook of International Economics*, vol. 1, International Trade (Amsterdam: North–Holland).

Findlay, Ronald and Harry Grubert, 1959: 'Factor Intensities, Technical Progress, and the Terms of Trade', *Oxford Economic Papers*, no. 11, pp. 111–21.

Freeman, Richard B., 1991: 'How Much Has De-Unionization Contributed to the Rise in Male Earnings Inequality?', NBER Working Paper Series, no. 3826, Cambridge, Mass.

Griliches, Zvi, 1969: 'Capital-Skill Complementarity', *Review of Economics and Statistics*, vol. 51, pp. 465–8.

Grossman, Gene M., 1986: 'Imports as a Cause of Injury: The Case of the U.S. Steel Industry', *Journal of International Economics*, vol. 20, pp. 201–23.

——, 1987: 'The Employment and Wage Effects of Import Competition in the United States', *Journal of International Economic Integration*, vol. 2, pp. 1–23.

Harris, John R. and Michael P. Todaro, 1970: 'Migration, Unemployment and Development: A Two-Sector Analysis', *American Economic Review*, vol. 60, pp. 126–42.

Helpman, Elhanan and Paul R. Krugman, 1985: *Market Structure and Foreign Trade* (Cambridge, Mass.: MIT Press).

Katz, Lawrence F. and Lawrence H. Summers, 1989: 'Can Interindustry

Wage Differentials Justify Strategic Trade Policy?', *in* R. Feenstra (ed.), *Trade Policies for International Competitiveness* (Chicago, Ill.: University of Chicago Press).

Krueger, Alan B., 1993: 'How Computers Have Changed the Wage Structure: Evidence and Implications', *Brookings Papers on Economic Activity, Microeconomics* (Washington, DC: The Brookings Institution), pp. 209–10.

Lawrence, Robert Z. and Matthew J. Slaughter, 1993: 'Trade and U.S. Wages: Great Sucking Sound or Small Hiccup?', Faculty Research Working Paper Series, John F. Kennedy School of Government, Harvard University.

Layard, P.R.G. and A.A. Walters, 1978: *Microeconomic Theory* (New York, N.Y.: McGraw–Hill).

Leamer, Edward E., 1992: 'Wage Effects of a U.S.–Mexico Free Trade Agreement', National Bureau of Economic Research Working Paper no. 3991 (Cambridge, Mass.: NBER).

Leontief, Wassily W., 1953: 'Domestic Production and Foreign Trade: The American Capital Position Re-examined', *Proceedings of the American Philosophical Society*, vol. 97, pp. 332–49.

Levinsohn, James, 1993: 'Testing the Imports-as-Market-Discipline Hypothesis', *Journal of International Economics*, vol. 35, pp. 1–22.

Levy, Frank and Richard J. Murnane, 1992: 'U.S. Earnings Inequality: A Review of Recent Trends and Proposed Explanations', *Journal of Economic Literature*, vol. 30, pp. 1333–81.

Lipsey, Robert E., 1992: 'Foreign Direct Investment in the United States: Changes over Three Decades', NBER Working Paper Series, no. 3581 (Cambridge, Mass.: NBER).

Mincer, Jacob, 1991: 'Human Capital, Technology, and the Wage Structure: What do Time Series Show?', NBER Working Paper Series, no. 3581 (Cambridge, Mass.: NBER).

——, 1993: 'Interindustry Wage Structure', mimeo. (New York, N.Y.: Columbia University).

——, 1993: *Studies in Human Capital: Collected Essays of Jacob Mincer* (Hampshire, England: Edward Elgar).

Mincer, Jacob and Yoshio Higuchi, 1988: 'Wage Structures and Labor Turnover in the United States and Japan', *Journal of the Japanese and International Economies*, vol. 2, pp. 97–133.

Minhas, B.S., 1962: 'The Homohypallagic Production Function, Factor Intensity Reversals, and the Heckscher–Ohlin Theorem', *Journal of Political Economy*, vol. 70, pp. 138–56.

Mitchell, Daniel J.B., 1989: 'Wage Pressures and Labor Shortages: The 1960s and 1980s', *Brookings Papers on Economic Activity*, no. 2 (Washington, DC: The Brookings Institution), pp. 191–232.

Murphy, Kevin M. and Finis Welch, 1991: 'The Role of International Trade in Wage Differentials', *in* M. Kosters (ed.), *Workers and their Wages* (Washington, DC: AEI Press).

Panagariya, Arvind, 1980: 'Variable Returns to Scale in General Equilibrium Theory Once Again', *Journal of International Economics*, vol. 10, pp. 499–526.

Passell, Peter, 1992: 'The Victim Has a Blue Collar, but Free Trade Has an Alibi', *New York Times*, sec. 4, p. 4, 16 Aug.

Perot, Ross and Pat Choate, 1993: *Save Your Job, Save Our Country: Why NAFTA Must Be Stopped — Now!* (New York, N.Y.: Hyperion).

Revenga, Ana L., 1992: 'Exporting Jobs: The Impact of Import Competition on Employment and Wages in U.S. Manufacturing', *Quarterly Journal of Economics*, vol. 107, pp. 255–84.

Rybczynski, T.M., 1955: 'Factor Endowment and Relative Commodity Prices', *Economica*, vol. 12, pp. 336–41.

Samuelson, Paul A., 1948: 'International Trade and the Equalisation of Factor Prices', *Economic Journal*, vol. 58, pp. 163–84.

——, 1949: 'International Factor-Price Equalisation Once Again', *Economic Journal*, vol. 59, pp. 181–97.

——, 1965: 'A Theory of Induced Innovation Along Kennedy–Weizsacker Lines', *Review of Economics and Statistics*, vol. 47, pp. 343–56.

——, 1992: 'A New Revolution at Century's End', mimeo. (Cambridge, Mass.: MIT Press).

Stolper, Wolfgang and Paul A. Samuelson, 1941: 'Protection and Real Wages', *Review of Economic Studies*, vol. 9, pp. 58–73.

24

Religion as DUP Activity[*]

CAN religion be rescued from the dark recesses of our souls and brought into the intellectual folds of the dismal discipline of economics?

Along with mortal suicide and divorce, divine Providence should be readily vulnerable to the desiccated diagnosis of conventional economics. At the same time, quiet contemplation of the social scene on Sundays in Christian countries, if not a pleasurable afternoon spent with G.K. Chesterson's entertaining Father Brown, immediately suggests that organized religion, where man must stand on the shoulders of other men to reach out to the heavens above, may be yet another DUP (directly unproductive, profit-seeking) activity whose implications can be analysed in the spirit of the unconventional public-choice-theoretic approach to economics.

Below, therefore, we proceed to centre our analysis on organized religion as indeed a DUP-theoretic phenomenon, revealing to our readers the Truth for their Enlightenment. In an appendix, we then consider the heresies of Dixit and Grossman (1984) who, in a contribution laced with frivolity and wit (which we seek to preserve here), have preceded us with an analysis of organized religion which they christened with characteristic inspiration as directly unproductive prophet-seeking activity.

1. THREE STATES OF NATURE:
ORGANIZED RELIGION AND COUNTERFACTUALS

1. To analyse organized religion (OR) and its consequences, we must construct an appropriate counterfactual.[1] There are really

---

[*] Written with T.N. Srinivasan. The knowledge embodied in this brief chapter was revealed to us, as were the Vedas to the ancient Hindus; no research support therefore needs to be acknowledged.

[1] The economist is paralyzed into inaction if a counterfactual is unavailable. As

two counterfactual states of nature that we could create. We have first simply the economists' conventional, godless world where religion is known not to rear its head at all. Then again, we can have a state of nature where religion does appear but *not* in an organized fashion: i.e. man communes with God but there are no intermediaries, simply the Lutheran directness or the quiet Hindu contemplation of the Infinite without the instrumentality of the Maharishi's Transcendental-Meditation mantra. The latter, we shall christen the 'unorganized religion' (*UR*) state of nature; the former, the 'godless' (*G*) state of nature.

Both these counterfactuals are interesting. The *UR* state of nature evidently implies, relative to *G*, that religion 'diverts' resources from worldly welfare. But, to suggest therefore that *UR* is a second-best situation and hence *UR* < *G*, we should *impose* the social planner's (and indeed the Marxist) view that the social weight to be assigned to heavenly welfare is zero. If we do not, and instead prefer individual valuation, then *UR* and *G* are simply characterized by different utility functions for the members of the population, and are each a non-comparable first-best, Pareto-optimal situation. In what follows later, we plan to take both points of view successively, to analyse the impact of the organized religion (*OR*) state of nature: for, each viewpoint leads to a different judgement on organized religion.

Next, we must consider the problem of an appropriate design of the *OR* state of nature. Organized religion does indeed pose intermediaries between man and God. In so doing, it turns religion into a DUP activity. But it simultaneously can affect the relative valuation of worldly and heavenly welfare (formally, a change in the utility function) and the perceived efficacy of prayer (formally, a change in the production function for brownie points in securing heavenly access). The earthly intermediaries of the God in heaven propagate doctrines that vary from a holistic rejection of worldly welfare to a wholesome Calvinistic compatibility of worldly and heavenly welfare; they also determine how many spins of the prayer wheel or rounds of rosary are necessary to secure access

---

the story goes, an economist, on being asked how his wife was, replies: 'Compared to what?' The counterpart of this for psychiatrists is the story where one runs into another and says: 'You are fine, how am I?'

to heaven.[2] These two elements must surely be considered necessary and intrinsic attributes of organized religion as we generally know it.

2. ORGANIZED RELIGION: CONSEQUENCES

An appropriate formalization of organized religion and its consequences should then contrast *OR* with *UR* and *G*, allowing the model specification to include the role of prayer, its perceived efficacy, and the relative valuation of worldly and heavenly welfare. We should distinguish between two contrasting approaches to religion: where the supplicant is sovereign and heavenly welfare cannot be disregarded from policy evaluation, and where heavenly welfare is regarded as illusion (like the *māyā* of Hindu metaphysical speculations) or equally as an opiate,[3] and hence assigned a social valuation of zero such that the three states of nature are ranked only on the scale of worldly welfare.

Case 1: Sovereign Supplicants: The High Road

In this case, we have already remarked that *UR* cannot generally be rank-ordered vis-à-vis *G*, since one state of nature introduces heavenly welfare whereas the other does not.

However, *UR* can indeed, under appropriate conditions, be rank-ordered vis-à-vis *OR*. The diversion of resources to the intermediaries that engage in DUP activity is evidently a loss since the resource-loss occurs from a first-best situation (Bhagwati 1982). On the other hand, these very intermediaries may increase the 'efficiency' of prayer, as would epicureans or churchmen who indulge in indulgences, such that one spin of the prayer wheel

[2] Organized religion may also serve to reduce, through assurance by the intermediaries, the uncertainty that may haunt the pious in the *UR* state of nature about their prospects for heavenly access. We leave this interesting aspect of organized religion to be modelled by those who doubtless will follow in our footsteps.

[3] The reader may want to ponder over the deep implications of the apocryphal Socratic exchange after China's conversion to communism, where the question. 'What is the opium of the Chinese masses', has the answer: 'opium'.

suffices where two were needed before.[4] If so, this is the equivalent of costless technical progress, albeit in producing the passes to heaven; and this is a welfare-improving effect. The net result could evidently be to give *OR* the edge over *UR*.[5] We thus draw the moral: *UR* and *G* are non-comparable; where comparable, $UR \lessgtr OR$.

Case 2: Valuing Only Worldly Welfare: The Low Road

But if heavenly welfare is wholly disregarded, the rules change and so can the outcome. *UR* now offends clearly vis-à-vis *G*: the use of any resources to pray is simply a wasteful, zero-output activity that must necessarily immiserize.

---

[4] A classic example of such 'technological innovation' by the Church is provided by Jacques Le Goff's (1984) fascinating intellectual analysis of the birth of Purgatory in the twelfth and thirteenth centuries. By creating a triad where the Purgatory was interjected between Heaven and Hell, and in tying the progress of the souls in the Purgatory to prayers of the living *provided* they were offered through the intermediation of the Church, the Church could be interpreted as innovating to its DUP-theoretic advantage. To quote from Goff (1984, pp. 11–12).

Purgatory is an intermediary other world in which the trial to be endured by the dead may be abridged by the intercessory prayers, the 'suffrages', of the living. . . . And for the Church, what a marvellous instrument of power! The souls in Purgatory were considered to be members of the Church militant. Hence, the Church argued, it ought to have (partial) jurisdiction over them, even though God was nominally the sovereign judge in the other world. Purgatory brought to the Church not only new spiritual power but also, to put it bluntly, considerable profit, as we shall see. Much of this profit went to the mendicant orders, ardent propagandists of the new doctrine. And finally, the 'infernal' system of indulgences found powerful support in the idea of Purgatory.

Again, it is interesting to note that the idea that the Church plays this critical intermediating role appears to have been supported and canvassed by none other than St Augustine. Goff (1984, p. 67) writes: 'Augustine is also explicit about who may offer up efficacious prayer for these souls capable of being saved: those affiliated in an institutional capacity with the Church, either the Church itself or "a few pious men" '. Lest the readers consider St Augustine's views to be wholly devoid of self-interest, they should heed Gordon Tullock's reminder that he was Bishop of Hippo.

[5] If the intermediaries were also to shift the relative weights between worldly and heavenly welfare, then we face again the dilemma that utility functions have changed, and the yardstick for making meaningful comparisons across different states of nature disappears.

On the other hand, *OR* cannot be ranked uniquely vis-à-vis *UR* even if the intermediaries (as in Dixit and Grossman 1984; see appendix) *merely* regulate heavenly access to their DUP-theoretic advantage. For, the DUP activity will divert resources from production of worldly goods and heavenly passes; but this diversion may, à la Rybczynski 'ultrabiased' effects, increase the production of worldly goods and reduce that of heavenly passes, so that worldly welfare rises and paradoxically results in *OR > UR*! The introduction of changes in the rates of substitution between worldly and heavenly welfare, and in the productivity of prayer, can again produce results in either direction. Generally, therefore, $OR \lessgtr UR < G$.

3. A Mathematical Offering and A Prayer

While these results are evident on slight reflection, we need not appeal to the faith of the faithful for their acceptance. We have developed them, in the conventional manner of our august discipline, in the form of a mathematical offering that is available from us for all those who seek complete knowledge. While the sacred scriptures of the Hindus assert that prayers to all gods must reach the same Supreme Being, just as all raindrops reach the same ocean,[6] all models need not yield the same answer. We have therefore two models, each yielding the lessons we have drawn above.[7] In lighting two candles, we also urge the Almighty to count one toward Dixit and Grossman's welfare, and pray that they be rewarded with heavenly access for their sparkling wit and their meritorious first steps without which our own would not have been possible.

[6] These syncretic and inclusive sentiments are repeatedly expressed in the Mahābhārata, the Indian epic, especially in the Vishnusāhasranāmam and the Celestial Song, the Bhagwad Gitā.

[7] Since we must consider the case where only worldly welfare is valued, this is done with simplicity and rigour by assuming in both models a social welfare function which is separable in worldly and heavenly welfare. The models differ however on their 'technological' dimensions: in particular, the DUP-theoretic diversion of resources to organized intermediaries is modelled in the 'tithes' model as a certain fraction of national income.

APPENDIX: A DISCOURSE ON DIXIT AND GROSSMAN

Dixit and Grossman (1984), hereafter DG, model organized religion differently from us, as a direct and immediate application of the Bhagwati–Srinivasan (1980) model of revenue-seeking.

In building their necessary counterfactual, DG assume that there is then no religious activity at all, that the production possibility set can therefore be defined properly and exclusively on worldly goods, and that 'places in heaven' (the rewards normally reserved for religious activity) are nonetheless present but are simply awarded randomly by an inscrutable omniscient Being with no perceived relationship to exertions and exhortations by the pious.[8] This bleak and brutal world of total determinism is christened, with dark humour, as Nirvana by DG.

Organized religion then intrudes on the scene as a DUP activity. It is assumed that there are only a limited number of places in heaven. The assumption of limited places is invoked by DG simply to generate a scarcity price or rent for heavenly access which then equals in worldly opportunity cost the value of worldly output that the average aspirant is willing to forgo in achieving heavenly access. Once this scarcity price $(\dot{P})$ of heaven here and now is so determined, organized religion leads to the Church cornering access to these pre-assigned heavenly slots $(\dot{N})$, such that the value of the resulting artificially constructed market rents on heavenly access is $\dot{P}\dot{N}$. With ministers and cathedrals, like Dennis Robertson's man and spade, moving into this lucrative market till they earn 'normal' profits in this DUP activity rather than in gainful employment elsewhere, the result is inevitable social waste. Organized religion has immiserized the population: Marx has triumphed, and the rejoicing of his flock must be sweeter still since the conquest is with neoclassical weapons! DG backtrack a trifle here, arguing that other *unrelated* imperfections may, apropos of Bhagwati and Srinivasan's (1980) discovery of the paradox of negative shadow factor prices, nonetheless make the diversion of resources to profiting from paradise-seeking of

[8] To quote them, 'the important point here is that the mechanism of awarding these places in heaven cannot be influenced by the population, and no resources need be spent in seeking activities' (1984, 1987).

the population socially profitable. But that religion, modelled as a DUP activity, creates primary waste and ultimate social loss remains the central message.[9]

In contrast to our analysis in the text, the DG model has two central features that are rather inappropriate: that there are limited places in heaven, and further that these are randomly awarded to the population without any religious activity on their part. DG have a heaven but no prayer! The exclusion of prayer distances the model from nearly all religious societies as we know them: for, there are few societies where, even in the presence of fatalism and determinism, prayer, and supplication aimed at earthly reward and heavenly access are absent.[10]

Equally unnatural is the assumption of limited places in heaven. Do not all modern religions assure every convert a place in heaven? Undoubtedly you have to be twice-born to do this in certain religions; and, in this respect, the Christians do it more efficiently than the Hindus since the Hindus generally must (and are indeed fated to) go through death to be reborn, whereas the Christian can do so instantaneously in this very life! But the notion that every soul cannot transcend to heaven, so long as certain necessary and sufficient conditions are fulfilled, appears to contradict the belief propagated by most religions. Religions simply do not seem to pattern their heavenly constructs after the game of musical chairs![11]

---

[9] In Bhagwati and Srinivasan (1980), and in Bhagwati (1982), the demonstration that DUP activities may be paradoxically welfare-improving is stricter: the second-best considerations are critically related to the DUP activities themselves, as when a distorting tariff itself triggers the revenue-seeking DUP activity.

[10] As discussed in the text, moreover, *OR* can influence the 'productivity' of prayer and thereby open up the paradoxical possibility of a welfare-improving organized religion.

[11] Alas, there are always exceptions to the most compelling generalizations. Jehova's Witnesses spring to our attention as being faithfully in the DG mould when they interpret, as some of them do, the sealing of the 144,000 members of the 12 Israeli tribes, in the Book of Revelations in the New Testament, as providing an upper bound to heavenly access. We are assured by our pastors, however, that even then it may be sensible to interpret this position as compatible with more places in heaven, with the élite places assigned to the 144,000 and the more proletarian ones open to all others. Evidently, the dual-markets characterization of heaven becomes then an intriguing research agenda!

REFERENCES

Secular Works Cited

Bhagwati, J.N., 1982: 'Directly-Unproductive Profit-Seeking Activities', *Journal of Political Economy* 90 (Oct.), pp. 988–1002.

Bhagwati, J.N. and T.N. Srinivasan, 1980: 'Revenue-Seeking: A Generalization of the Theory of Tariffs', *Journal of Political Economy* 88 (Dec.), pp. 1069–87.

Dixit, A. and G. Grossman, 1984: 'Directly-Unproductive Prophet-Seeking Activities', *American Economic Review* 74 (Dec.), pp. 1087–8.

Goff, Jacques Le, 1984: *The Birth of Purgatory*, trans. Arthur Goldhammer from the original *La naissance du Purgatoire* (1981, Editions Gallimard) (Chicago: University of Chicago Press).

Scriptures Mentioned

The Book of Revelations, The New Testament.
The Mahābhārata.

Patron Saints Invoked

Karl Marx, T.M. Rybczynski.

25

Democracy and Development: New Thoughts on an Old Question[*]

EARLIER, many subscribed to the view (for reasons that I shall presently discuss) that democracy definitely came at the expense of development, a choice having to be made between doing good and doing well. The new thinking is that this trade-off, or the 'cruel dilemma' as I called it nearly thirty years ago,[1] is by no means a compelling necessity; that it may be possible to eat one's cake and have it: either democracy does not handicap development or, in the best circumstances, even promotes it.

The pursuit of political and civil virtue, as the embrace of democracy implies, need not be at the expense of the drive for economic development. All good things may sometimes go together, just as we have discovered that literacy is good in itself and for development, and that female education emancipates women while restraining the growth of population and enhancing the possibility of greater economic prosperity for smaller numbers.

[*] This is the revised Feb. 1995 text of the Rajiv Gandhi Golden Jubilee Memorial Lecture, delivered in New Delhi on 22 Oct. 1994. It is the first of a set of four lectures on the occasion of the late Prime Minister Rajiv Gandhi's 50th Anniversary followed by those of Margaret Thatcher, Mikhail Gorbachev and John Kenneth Galbraith. Thanks are due to Bruce Akerman, Jon Elster, Karl–Goran Maler, Ed Mansfield, John Ruggle, Thomas Bernstein, Justice P.N. Bhagwati, Abid Hussain, Surjit Bhalla, Atul Kohli, K. Sundaram, Suresh Tendulkar and Stanislaw Wellisz for helpful conversations and suggestions. Earlier versions of the lecture have appeared in *The Indian Economic Review* (Jan.–June 1995), no. 1, vol. 30, pp. 1–18 and in the *Journal of Democracy* (Oct. 1995), no. 4, vol. 6, pp. 50–64.

[1] Cf. Jagdish Bhagwati, *The Economics of Underdeveloped Countries*, The World University Library Series (London: Weldenfeld & Nicolson, 1966). The Princeton political scientist, Atul Kohli, has thus christened this the 'cruel dilemma' thesis; see his 'Democracy and Development', *in* John Lewis and Valeriana Kallab (eds), *Development Strategies Reconsidered* (Washington, DC: Overseas Development Council, 1986).

ECHOES OF OLD THINKING

The new view represents of course a nuanced change. Few claim that democracy is necessarily, or even overwhelmingly, better for development, but only that democracy can be consonant with even the promotion of development. In doing so, they bear in mind the witticism, attributed to the Oxford social anthropologist Evans–Pritchard, that the only generalization in social sciences is that there is no generalization; or the Cambridge economist Joan Robinson's mischievous remark that, in economics, everything and its opposite are true (for you can almost always find evidence somewhere, for some historical period, in support of almost anything).

Indeed, if we eyeball the post-war performance on growth-rates and the prevalence of democracy in the developing countries, it is difficult to find a strong relationship between democracy or its absence in a country and its growth-rate. Democracy has broken out only in recent years across the developing world: in the past two decades, nearly forty countries have turned to democracy.[2] For the bulk of the post-war period, therefore, we had only India, Costa Rica and Sri Lanka as democracies over a sustained period. True, their growth-rates were far from compelling. But then the non-democratic countries had also an immense variety of performance, ranging from the spectacular in the Far East to disastrous in many nations of Africa. Looking only at the developing countries in the post-war period, therefore, it would be difficult to conclude that democracies have had less rapid developmental performance. Indeed, if the developed countries are considered instead, the democracies have done immensely better than the socialist dictatorships that have now happily vanished, at least for the present, from our midst.

To maintain therefore, as did the old view, that democracy necessarily handicaps development whereas authoritarianism aids it, is to argue a case that must explain away these facts by citing

[2] At the same time, Samuel Huntington has noted, since the early 1970s, only four or five of the new democracies have returned to authoritarian rule. Cf. 'The Ungovernability of Democracy', *The American Enterprise*, Nov.–Dec. 1993, p. 35.

other factors and cross-country differences that overwhelm the outcomes.[3] Indeed, democracy and authoritarianism are only one dimension on which countries and their developmental performances differ: and, to develop the more nuanced and new view that is favourable to democracy as compatible with, even conducive at times to, development, I shall address qualitatively and directly the ways in which, and the reasons why, such a happy symbiosis is the likely reality.

But it would be wrong for me to suggest that the old, dismal and deterministic view is necessarily dead. Echoes, amplified by non-democratic governments with successful developmental performance, can often be heard. It is not uncommon, for instance, to find Prime Minister Lee Kuan Yew talking continually on the theme of democracy's 'indisciplined' ways that his 'soft' authoritarian rule has prevented from debilitating Singapore and crippling her development. Thus, he has argued:[4]

I believe what a country needs to develop is discipline more than democracy. The exuberance of democracy leads to indiscipline and disorderly conduct which are inimical to development.

And indeed the phenomenal success of the Far Eastern economies — South Korea, Taiwan, Singapore and Hong Kong — none of them democracies in a substantive sense,[5] has created for some a sense that the old thinking was right after all, especially when these economic miracles are contrasted with India's poor economic performance over more than three decades within a democratic framework.

[3] A number of statistical and quasi-statistical studies, by economists such as John Helliwell and political scientists such as Atul Kohli, have argued that the evidence does not support the view that the relationship between democracy and growth-rates is negative, nor does it support the contrary view. These results are therefore more eclectic and enable us to raise the qualitative questions that are considered in the Lecture. Cf. Kohli, op. cit. and John Helliwell, 'Empirical Linkages between Democracy and Growth' (Cambridge, Mass.: National Bureau of Economic Research), Working Paper No. 4066.

[4] Cited in *The Economist*, 27 Aug. 1994, p. 15. Also, see Prime Minister Yew's nuanced and fascinating interview with Fareed Zakaria in *Foreign Affairs*, March–April 1994, pp. 109–26.

[5] Hong Kong, while not a democracy, has had more of its attributes than the other three countries.

Those who think thus, believing that authoritarianism facilitates more rapid growth (with other suitable policies such as market reforms in place, of course) have also argued that the optimal policy *sequencing* of markets and democracy in the developing countries, as also in the former socialist countries, must be to get markets first and democracy next. This conclusion is reinforced in their minds by the recent Russian descent from a superpower to a supine status when the sequence she chose was to put glasnost before perestroika while the Chinese, who clearly introduced markets before democracy, did immensely better. Does this not imply that perestroika must precede, not follow, glasnost? If so, this prescription rests on two legs:

First, it reflects the old view on democracy and development — that the two are at odds and authoritarianism must be tolerated to facilitate rapid growth.

Second, it invokes the notion, based both on historical experience and the recent evidence that democratic demands have arisen in South Korea and other economically successful countries, that growth will ultimately create an effective push for democracy. The historical experience is substantial and persuasive, starting from Ralf Dahrendorf's illuminating analysis of Germany[6] and Barrington Moore's classic demonstration that the rise of the bourgeoisie led to democracy.[7]

Yet, these proponents of the old view are now outnumbered by those who take the new view. The reason is not necessarily ideological: indeed, social scientists are not proof from the blinkers that blind us to facts that fail to support our beliefs, and it is indeed true that the new view has triumphed when democracy has become both a widespread value and reality, and dictatorship a devalued mode of governance, so that we may be seeing virtues in democracy the way a nomad in the desert finds water in a mirage. The fact rather is that the old view is now seen as having

[6] Cf. Ralf Dahrendorf, *Society and Democracy in Germany* (New York: Doubleday, 1966).

[7] Cf. Barrington Moore, *Social Origins of Dictatorship and Democracy* (Boston: Beacon Press, 1966). For those who work with regressions, a necessary caution is that a strong association between democracy and development may mean, not that democracy promotes development, but that development leads to democracy.

rested on premises that were false, and our thinking on the question has become more nuanced and acute.

THE OLD VIEW: THE 'CRUEL DILEMMA' THESIS

The old view reflected a particular way of looking at the developmental process, fashionable during the 1950s and 1960s. It was also grounded in a specific historical context which defined the constricting assumptions under which it gained credence.

The historical context was, of course, the contest between the two 'sleeping giants': China and India. China was totalitarian and India a democracy then; nothing has changed in that regard! In the intellectual eye, trained politically on the Cold War and the arena of the Third World, the developmental success of India, rather than of China, would set the correct example for the Third World nations: democracy would do better and totalitarianism worse, thus putting more nations in the Third World on a course that would favour the Western democracies in their struggle with the Soviet bloc.

The race was, in turn, between two nations that had committed themselves to economic development. This, of course, removed from the intellectual context the question that must be faced if democracy and authoritarian rule are to be contrasted fully: which system is more likely to seek development? The question rather was: once you are committed to development, which political regime, democracy or authoritarian rule, is likely to facilitate the fulfilment of that goal?

To answer that question, we must have a 'model' of the developmental process. Indeed, we always do, whether explicitly if an economist or implicitly if not. The model that nearly everyone actively planning for development in the early post-war decades happened to use was attributed to the British economist Sir Roy Harrod and the American economist Evsey Domar. It is called, quite properly, the Harrod–Domar model, even though Domar wrote independently about it only several years after Harrod, in contrast to the fiercely cruel practice in the natural sciences where, as James Watson reminded us in his vivid account of the

contest for the Nobel Prize in *The Double Helix*, if you beat your
rival to a discovery by an epsilon moment, you have reduced
her to the disappointment of oblivion. Contrary to their subject
matter which builds on man's basest, not his noblest, instincts
to show how the pursuit of private interest can be harnessed to
produce public good, economists can be quite generous indeed!

The Harrod–Domar model, much used then,[8] analysed development in terms of two parameters: the rate of investment and
the productivity of capital.[9] As it happened, for policy-making
purposes, the latter parameter was largely treated as 'given' as
a datum, so that the policy freedom was assigned only to the
former parameter, the investment rate.[10] The debate therefore
centred only on the question of how to promote investment. This
approach, favoured by mainstream economists, coincided with
the Marxist focus on 'primitive accumulation' as the mainspring
of industrialization and also with the cumbersome quasi-Marxist
models elaborated in the investment–allocation literature that
grew up around the Cambridge economist, Maurice Dobb.

[8] Perhaps the only other influential idea, to be formally modelled only forty years
later, was that of Paul Rosenstein–Rodan who, just at the end of the Second World
War, argued that several investments would have to be coordinated and simultaneously undertaken in a Big Push with the aid of state intervention to rescue a
developing country from a stagnant equilibrium. This idea provided the theoretical impetus for the planning approach to development and to the widespread
practice of Five Year Plans in several countries, even though the actual practice
went back to the Soviets.

[9] The idea is perfectly simple. The increment in income, which naturally deter-
mines the growth-rate of income, must obviously depend on how much you invest
and how much you get out of it. The two parameters in the text are precisely
what will tell you the magnitudes of these determinants of the growth-rate.

[10] Interestingly, some economists such as Gunnar Myrdal thought at the time that
the socialist countries would be able to grow faster than capitalist countries also
because they would be able to increase the productivity of investment, reducing
the capital required to produce output (and thus reducing the marginal capital–
output ratio in the denominator of the Harrod–Domar growth equation which can
be written to equate the growth-rate of income with the average savings ratio
divided by the marginal capital–output ratio), by technological innovation in
things like prefab housing. How wrong they were: for, as discussed in the text,
they failed altogether to consider the question of the incentives, in these regimes
that had neither markets nor democracy, to innovate and to produce efficiently.

But if the focus was on accumulation, with its productivity considered a datum, it was evident that democracies would be handicapped vis-à-vis authoritarian regimes, when both were similarly wedded to accelerating development. For, it seemed natural to assume that the authoritarian regimes would be able to extract a greater surplus from their populations through taxation and 'takings' and be able therefore to raise domestic savings and investment to higher levels than would democracies that had to woo voters to pay the necessary taxes and accept the sacrifices more willingly. The economist Richard Cooper of Harvard University has an amusing but telling analysis of the remarkable association between the fall of Finance Ministers and the fact that they had devalued their currencies: I have little doubt that the Finance Ministers who have wittingly or unwittingly crossed the line through tough taxation have fared no better, being scapegoated and sacrificed by their Prime Ministers or dumped by irate voters at the polls soon after. Hence I wrote in the mid-1960s of 'the cruel choice between rapid (self-sustained) expansion and democratic processes'.[11]

But this thesis was to be proven false for three reasons that have a bearing on the new view:

1. the argument that the state would generate the necessary savings through tax effort, to accelerate development, has simply not held true: public sector savings have not been one of the engines of growth since public sector profligacy and deficits, rather than fiscal prudence and budget surpluses, have been the norm;

2. savings rates have risen substantially in the private sector instead, when many thought that they would be relatively unimportant, suggesting that where *incentives* to invest have increased dramatically, so has the necessary savings to exploit those opportunities, in a virtuous circle that has taken savings and investments to higher levels in both democracies (including India) and authoritarian countries (such as the Far Eastern superperformers whose savings rates are higher than those of India); and

[11] Bhagwati, op. cit., 1966, p. 204. Also see Kohli, op. cit., p. 156.

3. the differential performance among different countries seems to have reflected, not so much differences in their investment rates as the productivity of these investments, and this in turn has surely reflected the efficiency of the policy framework within which these investments have been undertaken.

I would say that, by the 1980s, it was manifest that the policy framework, in its broadest sense, determining the productivity of investment (and possibly even increasing saving and investment themselves through incentive effects) was absolutely critical, and that winners and losers would be sorted out by the choices they made in this regard, and indeed quite differently from the way we thought in the 1950s.[12]

Incentives promoting development, not the ability to force the pace through draconian state action, became the objects of a key shift in focus. And here democracy was far from being the obvious loser; indeed, it seemed, at least at first blush, rather to be at an advantage for who could doubt that democracy would relate development to people and build on incentives rather than compulsions? Yet, this can only be the starting point for a fresh inquiry into the relationship between democracy and development, a question that is now seen to be more complex and difficult, and yielding an answer that is arguably more favourable to democracy than we thought earlier.

Indeed, reflection on the problem suggests three plausible and profound propositions that I will presently address:

1. for ideological and structural reasons, democracy may well dominate authoritarianism as a political system that produces economic development;

2. the quality of development can also generally be expected to be better under democracy; and the better the quality of the democracy itself, the greater is likely to be the quality of development; and

3. the dividends from political democracy are likely to be

[12] Cf. Bhagwati, 'Democracy and Development', *in* Larry Diamond and Marc Plattner (eds), *Capitalism, Socialism and Democracy Revisited* (Baltimore: The Johns Hopkins University Press, 1993), pp. 31–8.

greater if it is combined with economic markets: the combination of democracy and markets is likely to be a powerful engine of development.

These propositions are stated in terms of likelihoods rather than certainties because the argument must at times proceed in terms of the balance of contrary forces and a judgment of their relative importance. The apparent contradiction nonetheless between them and reality must also be resolved by observing that, in the real world, we cannot expect the factors that suggest the plausibility of these propositions to be proof from the invasion of other countervailing events. Thus, for instance, even if democracy were expected to generate greater development, initial conditions conducive to growth may be more favourable in an authoritarian country than in a democracy, leading to greater development in the former: as indeed may have been the case with the authoritarian super-performing Far Eastern economies that inherited both egalitarian land reforms and remarkably high rates of literacy: two factors that are widely considered by economists today to stimulate development.

DEMOCRACY AND DEVELOPMENT: BEDFELLOWS?

Democracy, considered to consist of the troika: the right to vote and turn out governments, an independent judiciary and a free press, defines both an ideology and a structure. The ideology is that of the process of governance: by consent. The structure consists of the institutions by which this ideology is implemented. Both the ideology and the institutions of a democracy can be argued to contribute to development, though there are also some downsides.[13]

(a) Ideology

The most plausible arguments in favour of democracy as being conducive to development on grounds of its ideological or

---

[13] I consider democracy broadly here, in contrast to authoritarianism, without

process-of-consent content are twofold. One, for which there is now substantial evidence, is that democracies rarely go to war against one another; the other, which is speculative, is that authoritarian regimes 'bottle up' problems while democracies permit catharsis; the apparent chaos of democracy in fact constituting a safety valve that strengthens, instead of undermining, the state and provides the ultimate stability that is conducive to development.

(1) *Democracies at Peace Among Themselves*

If democracies do not fight wars with one another, and they fight only with non-democratic nations that fight one another in turn, the probability of entering a war if a nation is democratic could well be less than if it was non-democratic.[14] That, in turn, could mean that democracies are more likely to both provide governance that is conducive to peace and hence prosperity, and to spend less on fighting wars and preparing for them.

As it happens, political scientists have now established that, over nearly two centuries, democracies 'have rarely clashed with one another in violent or potentially violent conflict and (by some reasonable criteria) have virtually never fought one another in a full-scale international war'.[15]

---

entering the added nuances that come from considering the quality of democracy, an issue taken up later.

[14] Take three countries. If there is one democracy and two dictatorships, the former will never fight a war, the latter can. If there are two democracies and one dictatorship, each of the former can fight only with the dictatorship, while the latter can fight with each democracy. Relying only on the data on *actual* wars to advance the foregoing argument is however not correct, for there may be many dictatorships which have not gone to war while every democracy has, so that the average tendency of a dictatorship to get into a war may be less than that of a democracy.

[15] Zeev Maoz and Bruce Russett, 'Normative and Structural Causes of Democratic Peace, 1946–1986', *American Political Science Review*, Sept. 1993, vol. 87 (3), p. 624. As always, there is extended debate among political scientists whether this observation is robust. Some have contended that the proposition is exaggerated by some fairly fast and loose characterization of selected countries in the data set, whereas others (e.g. Henry Farber and Joanne Gowa, 'Politics and Peace', *International Security*, no. 2, vol. 20, Fall 1995) have argued that the evidence for this

In his 'Perpetual Peace', published in 1795, the philosopher Immanuel Kant argued why democratic 'republics' would naturally pursue peace. The ingrained habit of 'respect' for others that such a republic would foster, as also the interests of the citizens whose welfare rather than that of absolute monarchs would be at stake, would both serve to promote peace rather than war.

Thus, Kant thought that the *ideology* of democracy, embodied in the idea of rule by consent, would mean that democracies, used to domestic governance by such consent, would naturally extend to other republics, similarly governed, accommodation by mutual discourse, dialogue and the resolution of disputes without war.[16]

But he also argued that the *structure* of democracy, or what we might call *interests*, would also inhibit wars because democratic leaders would find it more difficult to mobilize their citizens to fight wars. To quote him:[17]

If the consent of the citizens is required in order to decide that war should be declared (and in this constitution it cannot but be the case), nothing is more natural than that they would be very cautious in commencing such a poor game, decreeing for themselves all the calamities of war. Among the latter would be having to fight, having to pay the costs of war from their own resources, having painfully to repair the devastation war leaves behind, and, to fill up the measure of evils, load themselves with a heavy national debt that would embitter peace itself and that can never be liquidated on account of constant wars in the future. But, on the other hand, in a constitution which is not republican, and under which the subjects are not citizens, a declaration of war is the easiest thing in the world to decide upon, because war does not require of the ruler, who is the proprietor and not a member of the state, the least sacrifice of the pleasure of his table, the chase, his country houses, his court functions,

---

relationship between democracy and peace is less compelling before World War II and that, after World War II, the peace among democracies was due to shared political interests expressed in political alliances (a contention that itself may be rejected as a qualification since the alliances in turn may simply be reflecting a shared peaceability among the democracies).

[16] The most striking and original revival of Kant's argument is due to Michael Doyle, 'Kant, Liberal Legacies and Foreign Affairs, Part I', *Philosophy & Public Affairs*, Summer 1983, vol. 12 (3).

[17] Immanuel Kant, 'Perceptual Peace', in *The Enlightenment*, Peter Gay (ed.) (New York: Simon & Schuster, 1974), pp. 790–2; quoted in Doyle, ibid.

and the like. He may, therefore, resolve on war as on a pleasure party for the most trivial reasons, and with perfect indifference leave the justification which decency requires to the diplomatic corps who are ever ready to provide it.

It is not altogether clear whether the ideological or the structural argument should predominate as the explanation of democratic peace, even as both contribute to the outcome;[18] recent empirical tests suggest that the ideological one does.[19] This is perhaps what we should expect: the habits of mind, and patterns of practice and procedure, set by the 'norms' that a society works with domestically, will surely constrain and shape behaviour towards others beyond the nation state.

Thus, it is entirely in keeping with the Kantian argument that it is the liberal states in the Western world that maintain the rights of their own citizens to exit, who, despite the social and political strains posed by rising refugee flows and illegal immigration, have by and large worried about providing rights to such immigrants, not the states that have denied their own citizens the right to move away.[20]

[18] My former student, Manmohan Agarwal of Jawaharlal Nehru University, has suggested a quasi-Kantian reason that may prompt democracies at times to be peaceful in their disputes with other democracies. Consider cases where it is necessary to demonize the enemy before carrying the citizens of a country into a war. This may then be a lot more difficult if the enemy is a democracy that is open and accessible, and hence hard to paint in stark colours as a rogue nation than if the enemy were authoritarian and contacts with its subjects made it difficult to sustain the necessary propaganda. Of course, this is also a principal reason why totalitarian countries such as the Soviet Union have gone to great lengths to prevent contacts by their subjects with the citizens of the democracies such as the US that they were pitted against.

[19] Cf. Maoz and Russett, op. cit. Again, my political science colleague Ed Mansfield has reminded me that some political scientists have reservations about the Maoz–Russett tests and about the specific proxies used by them. Among the recent re-examinations of the issue, see in particular Christopher Layne, 'Kant or Cant: The Myth of the Democratic Peace', *International Security*, Fall 1994, no. 2, vol. 19, pp. 5–49; and David Spiro, 'The Insignificance of the Liberal Peace', *International Security*, Fall 1994, no. 2, vol. 19, pp. 50–86.

[20] I should also add that the Kantian argument, and the Russett–Moaz evidence in support of it, relate to democracy, not to the process of democratization. The latter raises the question as to how warlike the transition to democracy is likely

(2) 'Safety Valve' versus 'Bottling Up'

The 'respect' for others that Kant observed as the mark of republics as against monarchies, of democracies as against authoritarian rulers, also leads to dialogue and debate, at times vociferous and impassioned. This is often mistaken for crippling chaos: it is merely the robust clamour of a functioning democracy.

Its chief virtue is that where different groups, whether classes, tribes or castes, jostle for voice and representation, it provides a platform for the contest and an airing of the demands, yielding a catharsis if not the satisfaction that success brings and thus acting as a safety valve.

The instinct and the practice of authoritarian regimes, on the other hand, is to repress, to bottle up, these conflicts, building towards eventual eruption when the pressures have built up to an explosive level. I suspect that the success in some of the Far Eastern countries in maintaining an authoritarian structure over a long period owed in part to their initial equality of incomes that made class conflicts less to compelling, to the racial homogeneity of their populations (apart from Singapore) which ruled out inter-ethnic tensions, and to the absence of religious divisions. It is unlikely that they would have managed so well if these favourable conditions had not existed: the disadvantages of authoritarianism would probably have shown up in these regimes.

(b) Structure

The structure of democracy, with its institutions of voting rights, an independent judiciary that often requires judicial review and leads to judicial restraint on legislative and executive power, and a free press, also sets it apart from authoritarian rule. The restraint of arbitrary power can be a powerful source of development; but a functioning democracy can also lead to what Jonathan Rauch has called demosclerosis: the paralysis of gridlock afflicting a lobbying-infested democracy.

---

to be. Comparing no-change to such transition, Ed Mansfield and Jack Snyder have contended that the former is shown by some empirical evidence to be more peaceable. Cf. their 'Democratization, Nationalism, and War: The Evidence', *Foreign Affairs*, May–June 1995.

It may be argued that authoritarian governments might be prone to extravagance and waste, inhibiting development, because there is no restraining hand among the citizenry to hold them back and also because, as the late Nobel-laureate economist from St Lucia, Arthur Lewis, who had advised many governments in single-party authoritarian governments in Africa, remarked to me, the leaders in such governments manage to delude themselves that the monuments they build for themselves are really a gift to posterity, equating personal indulgence with social glory. Reflecting upon how the authoritarian governments of Latin America and the socialist bloc ran up impossibly large debts during the mid-1970s and much of 1980s, just before and after the debt crisis arrived on the world scene, it may well be concluded that, by and large, autocrats are likely to argue, with Keynes, that 'in the long run we are all dead', and then ignore posterity for immediate gain, whereas the democracies are likely to be characterized by leaders who see continuity of national interests beyond their own rule more naturally.

The economist Mancur Olson has produced a rather different argument that also militates in favour of democracy as an institution likely to produce development.[21] He argues that dictators are more likely to overshoot in the direction of 'takings' from their subjects than Kantian republicans, since they will attach less weight to their citizens' welfare than to their own. The effect will correspondingly be to leave citizens less secure in their property rights and hence to reduce their incentive to produce more income.[22] In effect, Olson suggests that the incentive to save and invest, and hence the growth of the economy, will be adversely affected under a dictatorship.

Not merely are authoritarian rulers more likely to be more self-regarding than democratic leaders. Their ability to be more

---

[21] Mancur Olson, 'Dictatorship, Democracy and Development', *American Political Science Review*, Sept. 1993.

[22] Theoretically, this argument can be invalidated if the dictator saves more than the citizens, implying that the dictator is future-regarding rather than simply self-indulgent. Olson must therefore be implicitly assuming that the dictator is extravagant rather than frugal, an assumption that must in turn be justified as I did earlier.

self-regarding also follows from the structure of democracy. For, democracy will lead to restraints on 'takings' from the citizens, in particular via the possibility of appeal to an independent judiciary that may well reverse such 'takings' as unconstitutional or unjustified, and the availability of a free press that can document and thus restrain the state's extravagance.

But the structure of democracy can, in other ways, also create waste, even paralysis of useful state action, through the lobbying activities of special interests. To see how lobbying can indirectly lead to waste as surely as directly wasting resources, conduct a mental experiment. Imagine that some revenue is to be spent. This may lead to conventional waste: the government may build tunnels that lead nowhere. But suppose now that the Minister for Trade is restricting imports and allocating licences for scarce imports which then fetch a hefty premium to those who are able to get the licences: economists call these premia 'windfall profits' or, more technically, 'rents' to scarcity. You and I will of course lobby to get these licences, for we can get rich by obtaining. The economist Anne Krueger, who highlighted this phenomenon, described the situation of people seeking to get these licences as 'rent-seeking' whereas I have called it unproductive profit-seeking.[23] Its effect is to have us spend resources trying to make money by lobbying to persuade politicians and bureaucrats to give these licences to us rather than to others, instead of using these resources to produce useful goods and services and make profits that way. Such rent-seeking wastes resources then as swiftly and surely as if our governments were directly wasting them by building white elephants.

The reality is that lobbies that inevitably indulge in rent-seeking, even in rent-creation where governments are persuaded to create by policy the scarcities that lead to the rents that are then collected by the lobbies, are an endemic and indeed a growing presence in democratic societies. The good that they produce, in creating for instance the different perspectives on policy that alone can lead to informed policy, can be outweighed by such costs. Economists are busy debating how large these

[23] Cf. Anne Krueger, 'The Political Economy of the Rent-seeking Society', *American Economic Review*, June 1974; and ch. 7 above.

costs are; but that they do obtain under democracies is indis-putable. And that such costs would be less under dictatorships is equally plausible even though there would be rent-seeking in the form of trying to become the brother-in-law of the dictator in order to obtain such licences (as they do in reality accrue to the families of most dictators)!

On the other hand, the other possible defect of democratic governance, the paralysis of government that a proliferation of lobbying can cause, is an outcome of lesser likelihood. It has however occurred to many shrewd observers who have con-templated the recent gridlock in the US Congress. Of course, the US has a form of democratic governance where the President must deal with a Congress whose members are not subject to the Party whip and instead regard themselves as autonomous agents with whom the President must bargain on each issue. David Broder, the perceptive political columnist of *The Washington Post* has remarked that the US has virtually 536 Presidents. In turn, these members of Congress are responsive to their constituents, hence to lobbies, to a degree that is unparalleled in other forms of democratic governance. As a wit has remarked, a US Congressman is virtually required to supply a missionary for breakfast if a cannibal constituent demands it!

But 'demosclerosis', the arteriosclerosis or clogging of arteries that afflicts the US democracy, is an acute product of a certain institutional structure of democracy, surely 'off the curve' and off the wall as far as other institutional forms of democracy (such as the British Parliamentary model) are concerned. It does not seem to me to be an affliction that democracy must inherently accept.

But if you do, then a benign or 'soft' authoritarianism sounds attractive as an alternative until you ask, as I have already, whether the authoritarian rulers will in fact have the incentives to deliver development to their subjects by making the 'right' choices. That a few did, as seems to have been the case in the Far East in the post-war period, when in fact countless others in the socialist world and in many nations in Africa and South America did not, is hardly proof that this would be the central tendency of authoritarian rulers. Indeed, the foregoing analysis and evidence strongly suggests otherwise.

THE QUALITY OF DEMOCRACY
AND THE QUALITY OF DEVELOPMENT

An analysis of democracy's impact on development must reflect, as I have already remarked, the fact that the institutional structure that democracy provides is critical. Indeed, Adam Smith's profound case for laissez-faire in economic matters[24] must be understood in light of the fact that democracy in his time was based on suffrage that was not universal but was confined to those with property, so that both he and the philosopher David Hume, two of the greatest minds of their century, could not vote. The government that such a democracy produced led to governance that, in economic matters, was one that Adam Smith castigated as inefficient and socially undesirable because it reflected oligarchic interests. Laissez-faire, if only adopted somehow in place of the economic governance produced by this form of democracy, would provide a superior organizing principle: but, to my knowledge, Adam Smith did not indicate how this could be effected![25]

So, what might be called the *quality of democracy* matters greatly. A defective oligarchic democracy may well distort economic choices in the inefficient direction, imperiling prosperity. But then it may also affect what might be called the *quality of development.*

Development is many-sided; it is not just the growth-rates of income. True social needs, such as public health, protection of the environment, and the elimination or relief of extreme poverty cannot be provided unless governments have the resources that only growth can generate. But the use of these resources for such public needs will not automatically follow unless the political

[24] Most economists are fully aware that Adam Smith did allow for governmental intervention, indeed asked for it, in matters such as education where he thought that, while the division of labour produced economic benefits, it would produce automatons turning the screw to the left or to the right every day, all the time, like Charlie Chaplin in *Modern Times*, so that education would have to be provided to restore them as human beings with texture and sensitivity. To regard Adam Smith as a strict proponent of abolition of all intervention by the state, as is often done by extreme conservatives and libertarians, is to misunderstand him.

[25] Adam Smith would thus have been an inadequate guide to economic reforms!

system permits, and provides the incentives, to mobilize and translate those needs into effective demands. I would say that democratic regimes that are characterized by structures and processes that provide effective access by the groups, often on the economic periphery, who are to profit most from these social programmes, are more likely to have such social needs translated into effective demands.

The central nature of this observation about the ability and the incentive to vote and to mobilize under democracy is seen best by examining the contention of economists such as Amartya Sen that democracy has promoted the control of famines in India because India's democracy implies a free press to provide us information about famines such as the Bihar famine, whereas the big Chinese famine under Mao was hidden from view by his iron rule.[26]

I believe that this contrast is a trifle too simplistic about the advantage of democracy in such matters. For one thing, information about the occurrence of a serious famine tends to diffuse and become widely available in one way or another within most countries; even authoritarian ones. There are several ways in which such information has traditionally spread among the people in even the most traditional societies: Indian sociologists have shown conclusively for example that the notion of the 'self-sufficient village' is a myth.[27] I have little doubt that this is equally true of China, and that serious research which may become possible with the political opening up of China will reveal that information on the Chinese famine was not confined wholly to where it occurred and must have diffused horizontally in traditional ways.

Of course, I can think of ways in which such horizontal diffusion of the information on the famine could have been handicapped in Mao's China. Thus, the extreme totalitarianism under Mao may have reduced such traditional diffusion of knowledge among his subjects because of severe restrictions on travel within China at the time.

Again, the horizontal diffusion of knowledge of the famine

[26] See, for example, Jean Drèze and Amartya Sen, *Hunger and Public Action* (Oxford: Clarendon Press, 1989).

[27] Cf. M.N. Srinivas and Arvind Shah, 'The Myth of the Self-Sufficiency of the Indian Village', *The Economic Weekly*, 12 (1960), pp. 1375–8.

may have been crippled due to 'denial'. Thus, we know from Nadezhda Mandelstam's poignant observation in her memoirs that the potential victims of Stalin's terror wished to assume that those who had been seized and destroyed were truly guilty of the crimes they were being charged with because, if they were not, then the reality of an individual's guiltlessness would not protect the person from a similar arbitrary fate at the hands of Stalin's police. Equally, China's peasantry may well have discounted reports of a catastrophic famine in China, unmet by corrective relief, so as to protect themselves psychologically from the prospects of a similar, cruel fate.

True, 'hard' authoritarian regimes make it easy for the rulers (as distinct from citizens) to be shielded from unpleasant news: the messenger is not protected in such regimes from the retribution that his disturbing message may provoke in an arbitrary regime. Thus, vertical diffusion of information could be impaired under totalitarian regimes simply because the incentive structure of such regimes makes it costly to those below.

However, whether the information on a serious famine is widely diffused horizontally or vertically, the key issue we must confront is that it *is* available for sure at the level where the famine occurs. The key question then is whether this information will translate better under democracy into pressures for a change in the regime's policies in the required direction.

And here we come to the real reasons why democracy would fare better than a dictatorship in addressing serious famines. Surely, a democratic regime is able to provide the *ability*, and the *incentive*, to translate the information on the famine on the ground into pressure on the government to change its policies as required. Mobilization by the citizens through meetings, marches, representations and petitions is surely difficult, if not impossible, in dictatorships. The incentive to do so would also be less because the probability of affecting a dictator's policies through such means is surely less (and the risks of retribu- tion for an individual's labours substantially greater)[28] than in a democracy.

---

[28] Thus, it is well-known that fear among the rural Party-government cadres was one of the most critical factors in the Chinese famine. The information certainly

Both the incentive and the ability to vote, to mobilize, and to be heard, are thus the key ways in which the quality of a democracy matters to the quality of development. A governance where the poor or the minorities (such as women until only recently in Switzerland) are effectively unable to vote, for example, is then simply not good enough. A judiciary that protects habeas corpus is not as good as one that also provides effective standing for the poor through public interest litigation (as in India). A free press is important but not as good as one that reflects broader interests than those of the élite.

IMPROVING DEMOCRACY: TECHNOLOGY AND NGOs

As it happens, not merely has democracy spread around the world; its quality has also improved. The diffusion of ideas and better democratic practices is swift today: public interest litigation is spreading from India; judicial review, originating in the US, is coming to the European nations.[29]

The two contributory factors of central importance in this steady progress of democracy and its quality, as also the quality

---

existed about the famine at the ground level, but the incentive to act on it by seeking immediate relief and action was missing because of the totalitarian structure of the Maoist government. Local officials in some of the famine-stricken areas assumed that Beijing would react to the famine by retribution against them because of failure to fulfil outlandish production targets, instead of reacting by procuring necessary food from, say, foreign countries via commercial or aid-financed imports as the Indian government did during the Bihar famine.

Hence, we must also ask whether totalitarian regimes will react to information, even when available, in a way that would address it meaningfully. The incentive for such regimes to address a serious famine is itself likely to be less compelling than for democracies.

On the Chinese famine, see the interesting article by Thomas Bernstein, 'Stalinism, Famine, and Chinese Peasants: Grain Procurements during the Great Leap Forward', *Theory and Society*, May 1984, no. 3, vol. 13, pp. 339–77.

[29] See Bruce Ackerman, 'What Kind of Democracy? The Political Case for Constitutional Courts', paper presented to the Nobel Symposium on *Democracy's Victory and Crisis*, Uppsala University, 27–30 Aug. 1994; also mimeo., Yale University Law School.

of development in consequence, are the revolutionary information technology today that makes the wilful rejection or suppres-
sion of the interests of the peripheral groups more difficult, and
equally makes the growth of non-governmental organizations that
represent these interests more effective in the political domain.

Ironically, the celebrated pessimists George Orwell and Aldous
Huxley, the authors of *1984* and *The Brave New World*, imagined
modern technology as the enemy of freedom and the unwitting
tool of totalitarianism: things however have turned out for the
better, not worse. Modern technology was supposed to make Big
Brother omnipotent, watching you into submission; instead it has
enabled us to watch Big Brother into impotence. Faxes, video
cassettes, CNN have plagued and paralyzed dictators and tyrants,
accelerating the disintegration of their rule.[30] As a wit has remarked, the PC (the personal computer) has been the death knell
of the CP (the communist party).[31]

Equally, modern technology has illuminated the obscure face
of poverty and pestilence, propelling us in the direction of better
development. Modern information technology thus produces the
extended empathy that can inform a democracy into better democracy. On the other hand, it also increasingly takes work into
homes where we work in isolation at our computer terminals,
linked only long-distance to others living and working elsewhere,
so that the economies from working under one roof, which the
Industrial Revolution ushered in and which Adam Smith theorized
about, and which led to factories in place of the earlier 'putting
out' system of production, are now receding. This can produce
less bonding and hence greater alienation that can coexist with
increase in extended empathy. Thus, we may well see both

[30] This observation also provides yet another critique of the emphasis on information within the country as the key difference that makes famine prevention
more likely under a democracy. It is not the information within the country that
is likely to be much different; it is the information that percolates out of the
country. Is there any doubt that even Mao would have found it difficult to ignore
the big famine in China if only the outside world had been able to see, through
CNN or other access to China, the deaths and pestilence?

[31] It may be conjectured what would have been the outcome of Mao's big famine
if only the *outside* world had had even a glimpse of it. As it happens, only the
journalist Alsop wrote about it at the time and no one quite believed him.

weakened bonds within communities and strengthened bonds between them.[32]

The recent rise of NGOs, cutting across countries but built around societal issues such as the protection of the environment and of labour rights, may be explained partly in terms of such extended empathy that produces common international causes and movements.[33] They certainly constitute a powerful new institutional phenomenon that serves to make the voice of the periphery within each nation more audible since it is exercised with other similar voices in unison.

It is also a remarkable fact that the hostility of governments in the developing countries to the activities of foreign institutions, among them NGOs, has reduced sharply today. This is a sea-change from the early post-war years when the developing countries jealously guarded their sovereignty and worried about neo-colonialism, embraced the West warily and, in place of the notion that such embrace would lead to mutual gain, feared instead a malign impact and even malign intent. Again, it is in keeping with Kantian reasoning that it is the democracies that have opened their doors wider in this way, not the authoritarian governments: witness again the contrast between India and China.

DEMOCRACY AND MARKETS

Evidently then the 'cruel dilemma' thesis, forcing us to choose between democracy and development, was too simple-minded; the relationship between the two is far more textured, and less unfavourable to democracy, than we thought then.

But we can say something more. Think of well-functioning markets as leading, ceteris paribus, to development: that seems to be quite plausible, both in the light of theory and empirical

[32] The former phenomenon seems to have arisen in the US for this and other reasons, as documented startlingly by the political scientist, Robert Putnam.

[33] Lester Salomon, in his article on 'The Rise of the Nonprofit Sector' in *Foreign Affairs*, July–Aug. 1994, has documented the rise of national and international NGOs, calling it the global 'associational revolution' and analysing several cultural and political aspects of this phenomenon.

evidence.[34] Since democracy and authoritarian rule are in reality combined with absence or prevalence of well-functioning markets, we may well ask whether experience suggests anything interesting in regard to the interaction among these two sets of institutions.

The post-war reality seems to divide into the following typologies on these two dimensions:

Democracy with Markets: By and large, these are the Western democracies; they have strong performance until the OPEC crisis; they also have generally good social indicators;

Democracy without Markets: India is the prime example; hers was a sorry economic performance and her social indicators are also unsatisfactory;

Authoritarian Rule with Markets: China in the last decade, and the Far Eastern countries since the 1960s, belong here; they had a rapid impact on poverty and their social indicators are not bad;

Authoritarian Rule without Markets: These are the former socialist countries; they are abysmal failures, both in terms of growth and social indicators.

What do we learn, if anything, from this typology? I should say: perhaps not much that is firm and compelling, in itself, since any typology on just the two dimensions of 'democracy' and 'markets', each in turn concealing variations in the 'quality' of democracy and of markets, leaves out too many complicating factors that effect specific outcomes. Nonetheless, the typology does suggest

[34] The economist Alice Amsden likes to say, in regard to Korean experience, that they did well by 'getting prices wrong', because the state used credit allocations, etc. to affect resource allocation. But surely this is conceptually confused or misleading: if they did the right things, then they were getting the social or 'shadow prices right and these were different from the market prices. In other words, market prices and social costs were unequal, requiring state taxes and/or subsidies to fix the market failure. So, the 'right prices' were different from the market prices, and the Korean authorities did well by using the 'right prices' rather than the inappropriate or 'wrong' market prices to guide allocation. Whether these interventions were in fact sensible is a different and difficult question, on which there is division of opinion.

three broad propositions that a reasonable analyst should be able
to defend without being summarily routed:

- where neither democracy nor markets function, the incentive
  structure for production and innovation will have weakened
  so much as to impair productivity and growth;
- markets can deliver growth, with or without democracy; and
- democracy without markets is unlikely to deliver significant
  growth.

The last proposition, which speaks naturally of India's experience in the post-war period until the current reforms, is
perhaps the most interesting to contemplate further.[35] Why should
the lack of well-functioning markets subtract from democracy's
possibly favourable effects on development?

The answer seems to cry out from Indian experience. Democracy, with its civil and political rights, including the ability to
travel,[36] work, and be able to learn and invent abroad, has
made the élite Indians, who had the advantage of access to
modern education over a century, extremely capable of absorbing, even building intellectually on, innovative ideas and technologies from everywhere. But the *ability* to translate those
ideas and know-how into effective innovation and productive
efficiency was seriously handicapped by the restrictions that
straitjacketed economic decisions at all levels. Thus, for instance,
even while Indian surgeons were right at the frontier in open
heart surgery, following the Massachusetts General Hospital's
feat shortly thereafter in Bombay, the inability to import medical
equipment without surmounting strict exchange controls, even

---

[35] India was of course not altogether without markets. But the vast overreach of
bureaucratic intervention in the economy meant that India came pretty close to
having few well-functioning markets in trade and in the modern economy.

[36] The Indian Supreme Court has arguably upheld this right more broadly than
even the US Supreme Court which has upheld restrictions on travel to Cuba, for
instance. Thus, in the well-known case, Mrs Maneka Gandhi *vs.* Union of India
and Another, decided on 25 January 1978, the leading judgment by Justice P.N.
Bhagwati treated the right to travel abroad as part of 'personal liberty' and the
impounding by the government of the passport of Mrs Maneka Gandhi under Sec.
10 of the Passports Act of 1967 was struck down as an infringement of Article 21
of the Constitution.

when gifts were at issue, prevented the effective diffusion of technology to India on a scale commensurate with her abilities. Equally, the *incentive* to produce and to innovate was seriously compromised because the returns to such activity could not be substantial when there were extensive restrictions on production, imports, and investment.[37]

By contrast, the Far Eastern economies, countries with markets despite authoritarianism, profited immensely from the far freer inward diffusion of technology that their substantially freer domestic and international markets permitted and facilitated. The economic interventions of the Indian government, after the early years of more satisfactory growth and promotional rather than restrictive interventions that jump-started the economy from its lower pre-Independence growth rates, degenerated quickly into a series of 'Don'ts', straitjacketing the economic decisions of the citizens. On the other hand, the Far Eastern economies worked with a series of 'Do's' that left open considerable room for freedom to produce and innovate (in shape, especially, of importing new-vintage and economically productive technologies).[38]

The chief lesson may then well be that democracy and markets are the twin pillars on which to build prosperity.[39]

[37] The deleterious effects of such restrictions on the Soviet economy's dismal performance have been extensively documented by Sovietologists such as Joseph Berliner, Abram Bergson and Padma Desai.

[38] The contrast between interventions in shape of 'Don'ts' and 'Do's' was made by me earlier in *Protectionism* (Cambridge: MIT Press, 1988).

[39] In this regard, I must also cite an ambitious statistical study by the economist Surjit Bhalla, 'Freedom and Economic Growth: A Virtuous Cycle?', paper presented to the Nobel Symposium on 'Democracy's Victory and Crisis', Uppsala University, 27–30 Aug. 1994. Bhalla works with 90 countries from 1973–90. His conclusions are broadly supportive of the propositions I have outlined here, while he concludes more strongly that the statistical evidence shows a favourable impact of 'political freedom' (i.e. democracy), when treated in a way that enables us to differentiate among different democracies in terms of how democratic they are on the different relevant dimensions. His definition of development also extends beyond growth-rates to include a couple of social variables: secondary school enrolment and decline in infant mortality. I might add that Bhalla's work is unique among several recent statistical studies in looking at both economic and political 'freedom' in exploring the connection between democracy and development.

26

Shock Treatment:
Poland and the Market Economy[*]

It is ironic that Jeffrey Sachs's celebratory account of economic 'shock therapy' in Poland arrives just as the same therapy seems to have foundered on the legendary shoals of Russia. After all, if Russia's failure was inspired by Poland's success, it may be that Poland has finally managed to repay Russia for all the trouble that Russia has visited upon Poland in the past. Now that the virtues of shock therapy are no longer taken for granted by all reasonable men and women, a real debate over its wisdom can begin. The stakes of this discussion are high: only a dispassionate analysis of what went wrong in Russia yesterday can illuminate the problems that await us there today.

As is often the case when great issues and articulate protagonists are involved, the analysis of shock therapy has been bedevilled by language. The proponents of shock therapy are masters of rhetoric; and they have often relied on attractive phrases and misleading analogies to advance their argument. The phrase itself suggests a drastic but necessary corrective to unmanageable disorder; and 'big bang' — another term in the shock therapists' lexicon — suggests nothing less than the creation of the universe. Both imply that we must push ahead at full speed: when there is chaos, and everything is a mess, surely that is the right thing to do. Gradualism, by contrast, suggests procrastination; a theory of lameness.

The debate over economic reform often becomes an angry exchange of analogies. One side claims that you can only cross a chasm in a single leap. The other side retorts that unless you are

* This is the text of a review of Jeffrey Sachs' *Poland's Leap to the Market Economy* (Cambridge, Mass.: MIT Press, 1993), published in the *New Republic*, 28 March 1994.

Indiana Jones, you drop a bridge. Then again, the shock therapists argue, if you want to cut a dog's tail, you do it with one slash of the knife, not bit by bit. And the gradualists reply that you train a dog by setting incrementally escalating heights for him to jump.

The shock therapists, who strike rather romantic figures on a dreary policy landscape, have succeeded in suggesting that economists who advocate gradualism are knaves or worse. But the truth is that the optimal speed of any reform is an issue of much controversy in theoretical research today, and there is no basis for the sweeping presumption that the more speed, the better. Indeed, gradualist thinking has a distinguished past in economics. Adam Smith, whose credentials on the subject of markets are naturally indisputable, wrote in *The Wealth of Nations:*

It may sometimes be a matter of deliberation, how far, or in what manner it is proper to restore the free importation of foreign goods . . . when particular manufacturers, by means of high duties or phohibitions upon all foreign goods which come into competition with them, have been so far extended as to employ a great multitude of hands. Humanity may in this case require that freedom of trade should be restored only by slow graduations, and with a good deal of reserve and circumspection.

And in a similar spirit, Keynes wrote in 1933 of the danger of haste, citing, ironically enough, the example of Russia moving toward socialism:

Paul Valery's aphorism is worth quoting — 'Political conflicts distort and disturb the people's sense of distinction between matters of importance and matters of urgency.' The economic transition of a society is a thing to be accomplished slowly. . . . We have a fearful example in Russia today of the evils of insane and unnecessary haste. The sacrifices and losses of transition will be vastly greater if the pace is forced. . . . For it is of the nature of economic processes to be rooted in time. A rapid transition will involve so much pure destruction of wealth that the new state of affairs will be, at first, far worse than the old, and the grand experiment will be discredited.

One thing is clear: the debate over shock therapy cannot be conducted with catchphrases and soundbites. It is only when these distractions are dismissed that the important issues come into view. The actual content of the reform strategy in Poland and Russia, and its contrasting fortunes in the two countries, are subjects that require serious investigation. Sachs has advised both the Polish and Russian governments, and so he is an invaluable guide through these dense thickets. His little book presents a protagonist's view with admirable clarity and conviction. The principal subject of his analysis is Poland, but he draws parallels between the 'failed' policies of Russia and Poland prior to shock therapy, and argues for the method's promise in Russia after its success in Poland.

Of course, Sachs's confident prescription for Russia contrasts sharply with Russia's sorry condition today. John Kenneth Galbraith once said wittily of an economist foe that his misfortune was to have his theories tried (and to have them fail); and Sachs's misfortune may be that his theories were so successful in Poland that they were tried again in Russia. What was bold in Poland turned out to be rash in Russia. Poland earned Sachs a place in history. But Russia overwhelmed him, laying waste, not for the first time, to a great ambition.

To understand what happened, it is necessary to trace the decline and disintegration of the Polish and Soviet economies before the introduction of shock therapy. Indeed, modern economic history would do well to distinguish among four historical phases: (1) the decline under socialism; (2) the deepening crisis as foreign borrowing without reforms led to excessive debt burdens; (3) the disintegration under 'market socialism', when market reforms were attempted within the Socialist framework; and (4) shock therapy, with its benign consequences in Poland and malign outcomes in Russia.

The economic decline under socialism has been well–documented. Scholars have long noted that the Eastern bloc's high rates of investment unfailingly produced few results. The blood, sweat and tears were to no avail: growth-rates plummeted; and efficiency and technical innovation, the twin sources of increased productivity from investment, were incompatible with a regime that decried initiative and ignored incentives.

Faced with the chilling prospect of economic decline, the Socialist regimes of Gorbachev in Moscow and Gierek in Warsaw passed through two phases of 'reform'. Initially, both leaders tried to preserve the inherited economic system. They urged workers to work harder, and they sought to improve technology and productivity with high levels of foreign borrowing. But the results were exactly what economists had earlier witnessed in the developing countries: huge foreign debts were contracted with little economic payoff. The influx of capital bought a little time, but it burdened the economy with interest and repayment bills that simply could not be met. Consider an impoverished peasant who borrows and invests with little return and then finds himself hopelessly indebted. For Poland and the Soviet Union, the results were much the same.

Thus began the phase of 'market socialism': market reforms carried out within the confines of continued state ownership. State-owned firms were now allowed to 'set wages, inputs and outputs (but typically, not prices)'. Sachs contends that these reforms were not merely incomplete and inadequate; because they were undertaken without privatization; he believes they contained the seeds of disaster.

Both Poland and Russia did indeed take nosedives under market socialism. But was the lack of privatization really to blame? Common sense suggests that privatization should yield greater gains by allowing greater play to the profit motive as market incentives are introduced. But losing these incremental gains is not the same thing as losing your shirt. Are we truly faced with the option of going all the way or going down the tubes? Not really.

Regardless of privatization, Poland's and Russia's reforms could not have been expected to produce significant results. A key problem, Sachs notes, was that the born-again reformers were still prisoners of the assumption that competition (which, in principle, is compatible with state-owned enterprises acting under new rules) did not matter. Restrictions on new enterprises, import controls, and a host of other interferences continued, and nipped competition in the bud. Reforms reinforce one another, one, without others, will not work.

But this does not explain the collapse of market socialism. To do so, Sachs follows a different line of argument, proposing that the liabilities of state ownership were exacerbated by the growth of democracy. In other words, glasnost helped to kill perestroika. This is a counter-intuitive and interesting thesis, because the normal presumption at the time was that democracy would bring immediate and palpable benefits to a people that had been starved of freedoms for too long. These benefits, it was thought, would buy Gorbachev the time to bring the economic reforms along in a gradual, measured way. But the general consensus today seems to be that Gorbachev's reforms and Gierek's economic reforms failed because the terror had died. Reforms freed gigantic state-owned enterprises from the 'command' system that communism worked with an iron fist. At the same time, the full play of the market and the invisible hand were not in place. Hence discipline broke down and so did the economy.

This view is not original with Sachs, but he states it well:

Under the old 'command economy', before the Gorbachev reforms, enterprise policies were controlled by central fiat, backed up by threat of force against workers and managers who tried to evade the commands. When the commands, and the threat of force, were (mercifully) removed in the enterprise reforms in the second half of the 1980s, managers and workers attempted, not surprisingly, to increase their incomes at the expense of the state by absorbing whatever income flow and whatever assets they could from state enterprises. They demanded higher wages and stripped assets through various means — either overt or covert.

This argument does not persuade me, at least in its general form. Sachs seems to think that wage explosions and asset stripping happened because 'when there are no capitalists, there is nobody to represent the interests of capital'. If state-owned enterprises had been replaced with private enterprise, he believes, these rude occurrences would have been avoided. But asset stripping, or 'looting', is also a fact of life in capitalist systems with private ownership. Thus the economists George Akerlof and Paul Romer have argued quite persuasively that our own S & L crisis was in no small measure the result of straightforward villainy, and not simply due to unwise financial deregulation. Nor are excessive wage demands a rare problem for capitalist societies.

Sachs also overlooks an important aspect of market socialism. Once economic decision-making was shifted to the state-owned enterprises, and there was less retribution from the state, it became a lot easier to direct supplies and outputs to more profitable uses. Indeed, as the Sovietologist Padma Desai noted several years ago, the breakdown of the command system did lead Soviet farms to ignore the state's procurement demands and to sell their products instead in open rural markets that fetched higher prices. As farmers' incomes rose, agricultural production increased. Meanwhile state-supplied urban shops began to run out of food as procurement flagged. One solution to this problem would have been to direct domestic effort and foreign financial and technical assistance to building a better transportation system so that profit-seeking entrepreneurs could shift their rural supplies to more profitable urban markets.

It's important to recognize that the ills of market socialism might have occurred even with privatization; and that some good did occur even without it. In short, it was not the absence of privatization that led to the implosion of Poland and Russia. And that is a good thing. If market reforms could not be pursued without privatization in place, we would be in deep and unmanageable trouble. Privatization takes time, just as building an effective population control policy or extending agricultural assistance programmes takes time. The critical problem was, rather, that neither Gierek nor Gorbachev had the instruments of social policy and of monetary and fiscal control in place as they experimented with market reforms.

If you shift to markets, you deserve to get micro-efficiency. But to reap the rewards in good measure, you have to use the social instruments that go with markets. A social safety net and adjustment assistance are necessary to reform, especially if you expect enterprises to respond to price signals and lay off workers when required. The shift from a society of entitlement to a society of opportunity, and hence from total security to total insecurity in working life, creates the kind of fear that Americans witnessed in their own country during the NAFTA debate. American workers, coming off a decade when real wages fell, were extraordinarily resistant to the administration's appeal for their support, because they knew that freer trade means greater flux and adds to insecurity.

A successful shift to a market economy requires the social instruments that capitalism has evolved over the last century. Unfortunately, these instruments were not readily available in Moscow and Warsaw for the simple reason that they had been unnecessary in a Socialist society. Ironically, monetary policy also slipped from government hands even though the monetarists were as much in charge under communism in its heyday as they were in Milton Friedman's utopias. The market Socialists might have tried to halt the wage explosion with tough monetary policies; but they failed to do so. In place of monetary restraint, Poland and Russia practised an accommodating monetary policy that indulged the wage explosion by printing the money necessary to pay for it.

This failure of macroeconomic policy had different causes in Poland and Russia. Gierek simply did not have the political legitimacy to enforce strict discipline on the workers. Under Gorbachev this legitimacy existed, at least for a time, but it did not help. When Yeltsin took control of Russian revenues, Gorbachev had to print money to pay for Soviet expenditures, and a profligate monetary policy inevitably resulted. Gorbachev had little choice in the matter.

Contrary to Sachs's conclusion, the absence of privatization was not the 'fatal flaw' that undermined Gorbachev's and Gierek's reforms. If there was a fatal flaw, it was the absence of the social and macroeconomic policy instruments that are essential to the effective functioning of market capitalism. In any case, market socialism did not work, and it became clear that a change of course was in order.

It may be that Sachs's apocalyptic view of market socialism predisposed him to drastic measures when he arrived in Poland in June 1989 at the invitation of Solidarity. It is also possible that Sachs was simply following orders; he writes that Solidarity instructed him to draw up 'a programme of rapid and comprehensive change'. In August 1989, the Mazowiecki government appointed as its deputy prime minister for the economy the now celebrated Leszek Balcerowicz to spearhead such a programme. It is hard to decide who led whom by the hand. It is certain, however, that they walked hand in hand.

The Balcerowicz plan that resulted must be clearly understood, for it is the essence of shock therapy. Sachs emphasizes the plan's dramatic and 'holistic' features.

[Poland had] to break decisively with the Communist system, *to end halfway reform* and . . . *to jump to the market economy* [my emphasis]. The goal was to create an economy 'in the style of Western Europe', based on private ownership, free markets and integration into world markets. The plan also combined long-term market reform with a short-run emergency stabilization programme to end the incipient hyper-inflation.

Like other economists, Sachs defines hyperinflation as a monthly rise in prices of 50 per cent or more. The phenomenon is a familiar one in South America, where it calls to mind the magical realist fiction of Garcia Marquez. But it is virtually unknown in the West or in India, where rates of inflation reaching even two digits lead to corrective action – an approach to macroeconomics more consonant with the tranquilly of the village of Malgudi in the fiction of R.K. Narayan. Americans can get a better feel for the phenom-enon from the advice to take a taxi instead of a bus under hyper-inflation, since you pay for a bus ride when it starts and for a taxi ride when it ends.

No macroeconomist will quarrel with the proposition that hyperinflation has to be attacked swiftly and surely. This requires a ruthless assault on the budget deficit, and on the printing of money that finances it. Fiscal and monetary policies must be geared toward the task of macroeconomic stabilization. And so in 1990 Poland initiated a drastic plan of action: food and other household subsidies were slashed or eliminated entirely; cheap credits to industry disappeared; and ceilings on borrowing were set.

The novelty of Sachs's plan, however, lay elsewhere. He insisted that reforms in the incentive structure of the Polish economy must be carried out with equal speed. Consider the convertibility of the zloty. The introduction of effective international competition is impossible, economists agree, without a convertible currency that enables traders to import cheaper foreign goods whenever do-mestic goods are particularly expensive. But Sachs rejected the conventional wisdom which held that a quick transition to con-vertibility for Poland was impossible since Western Europe had taken a decade after the Second World War to reach convertibility and most developing countries were still afflicted with inconvertible currencies. Instead, Sachs persuaded Poland to introduce convertibility practically overnight, setting the exchange rate at an attractively low level and backing it up with a stabilization fund that guarded against speculation. As a result, Poland maintained a stable exchange rate throughout 1990, even as its currency became convertible.

Shock therapy also mandated a full liberalization of prices. It was expected that prices would rise steeply once, and then they would stabilize as tough monetary and fiscal policies emptied the fuel tanks driving hyperinflation. At the same time, wage discipline was imposed through a tax on wage increases that exceeded a norm: the so-called 'popiwek' tax. It was expected that this curb on raises would limit unemployment and reduce the need for monetary restraint, since the government would not have to combat wage increases by refusing to print more money.

Sachs argues persuasively that this therapy produced dramatic results. Prices rose initially by 77 per cent in January, by 16 per cent in February, and then by less-than 4 per cent a month in the two following years. The exchange rate was stable. Foreign exchange reserves actually increased. Confidence in the currency rose, and Poles began exchanging dollars for zlotys. But the bad news, as feared by opponents of shock therapy, was that unemployment rose dramatically. It increased from an average of 3.5 per cent in 1990 to an average of 9.2 per cent in 1991, and to an average of 12.8 per cent in 1992. I suspect that the true rate of unemployment in Poland was even higher, since firms probably kept mostly idle workers on their rolls who shared work with each other in a makeshift way. The old gag from the years of communism was still good: asked where the unemployed had gone, a local wit replied that they were working.

Unemployment rates were of course high in Western Europe too, and were high in Eastern European countries that did not undergo shock therapy. But the increase in unemployment in Poland was surely not unrelated to shock therapy. And the increase was dramatic despite the 'popiwek' tax that a Solidarity-backed government had succeeded in imposing on Poland's workers. It is not surprising, then, that the social contract began to fray. In the parliamentary elections of September 1993, Polish voters gave less than 12 per cent of the vote to the pro-reform Suchoka government, while returning to the legislature former Communists and future fascists who added up to more than a third of the new Parliament. The many successes of the Balcerowicz reforms were overshadowed in the political marketplace by the pain attributed to the therapy.

This unfortunate turn of events should give us the clues we need as to why shock therapy failed in Russia. In Poland the political preconditions existed for shock therapy to be given a fair chance. In Russia the political preconditions appear not to have existed at all. In January 1992 Yegor Gaidar, Russia's deputy prime minister, announced a programme of reform that paralleled Poland's. Gaidar's plan, devised with Sachs's assistance, was to cut Russia's budget deficit from an officially estimated 17 per cent of gross domestic product all the way to zero in just four months. There was no consensus in support of this bold proposal. The Russian economist Yasin Yevgeni has said that the plan was conceived and announced 'Soviet-style'; no efforts were made to consult with Parliament or with the regional governments or with the people. At the same time, as in Poland, nearly all price controls were lifted, with the result that prices immediately rose by 300 per cent.

The price increases cut deeply into the population's cash savings, which were widely treasured because most other productive assets could not be legally held. Meanwhile the link between wages and prices was severed by the removal of wage indexation for state employees. These developments magnified the widespread, and understandable, fear that a rise in unemployment would follow from the proposed budget cuts.

In a country accustomed to full employment, in which full employment was not only a principle of economics but also a principle of culture, the fear of joblessness went very deep. For a Russian worker, the loss of employment raised a spectre of personal disaster that went beyond the loss of wages. Just as health insurance in the US is linked to employment by a strange quirk of wartime history, so much else is linked to an individual's employment in

Russia. Of course, no social safety net was yet in place: unemployment insurance was still being worked at. But even with a safety net, workers had little reason to assume that new jobs would become available to them. Meanwhile, a long tradition of paternalism toward workers, possibly reinforced the hostility of factory managers to economic change.

To be sure, many converts to shock therapy were aware of the pain that their policies would cause. But it was their expectation that large doses of foreign aid would ease that pain. Sachs himself was a party to the so-called 'Grand Bargain' or 'Harvard Plan', which proposed that foreign countries deliver as much as $ 30 billion per annum for five years. Though he later withdrew from its sponsorship, he did not abandon the numbers. An amusing story made the rounds at the time among Russian experts who were disconcerted by the fact that the Harvard plan had been put together by Americans who had little knowledge of Russia's history, institutions, or language. Someone asks an American reformer, 'How did you become an expert on Russia?' He responds, 'I have been there five times'. And the Russian replies, 'And if you have been to the bathroom five times, are you qualified to be a urologist?' But the real problem was not that the authors of the grandiose plan knew little about Russia; it was that they did not know enough about their own habitat. Numbers such as $ 30 billion were simply out of bounds. How could so much aid possibly have been mobilized?

The supporters of shock therapy in Russia were sadly miscalculating the aid they could get, confusing exhortations with expectations. Indeed, when shock therapy was announced in January 1992, Russia was not even a member of the IMF, and George Bush had not yet committed himself firmly to any aid at all. The complaint that the IMF did not deliver what it eventually promised is factually correct. But it is incorrect to imply, as Sachs has implied, that this was why the plan did not succeed. For shock therapy was already failing, and the system was returning to fiscal and monetary chaos, and so the IMF held up the release of funds until some fiscal discipline was restored. This is standard IMF policy everywhere in the world, and it surely has merit.

In the end, the Russian system simply could not accommodate the demands that shock therapy made upon it. And so shock therapy was reversed, returning the regime to large budget deficits and high rates of inflation. Political and economic realities on the ground drove the moderates in Parliament to join hands with the extremists. Meanwhile, the technocrats who were wedded to shock therapy branded all who opposed it as Communists, reactionaries, rejectionists, and worse. The eventual confrontation between the Russian Parliament and the Yeltsin government was a tragedy whose script had been written unwittingly by the shock therapists. The self-deluding world in which they lived was further in evidence when Anders Aslund, a former Swedish diplomat doubling with Sachs as an adviser to Gaidar, wrote in *The New York Times*, just before the disastrous election of 12 December, of the certain victory that awaited the reformers.

Would more modest efforts to cut the budget deficit and slow the inflation have been more acceptable to the country and more readily supported by foreign assistance? Such a course was feasible. Most analysts agree that Russia faced high inflation, not hyperinflation, at the time of the shift to shock therapy, and that this problem allowed a gradual assault. The gradualists contend that the shock therapists achieved too little in attempting too much. Of course, the gradualists have the advantage of having a theory that is only a counterfactual. The shock therapists, for their part, tried and failed.

APPENDIX I

Not So Dismal Science[*]

To the editors:

Jagdish Bhagwati's review of my book on Poland's economic reforms is irresponsible ('Shock Treatments', 28 March). Bhagwati

---

[*] Jeffrey Sachs' response to the review was published as a letter to the editor in the same edition.

is a trade economist with virtually no professional experience in Poland or Russia, or with problems of monetary stabilization in general. While he concedes Poland's successes (without revealing that he was a critic from the start), his main interest is to say that 'shock therapy' failed in Russia.

This is ludicrous. Any knowledgeable observer knows that Polish-style reforms were not carried out in Russia. To the extent that such reforms were partially implemented, they succeeded in heading off hyperinflation, ending shortages in the consumer markets and establishing private property rights for the first time in seventy-five years. After a few months in 1992, the strength of Russian monetary stabilization was hobbled by conservative opposition and the absence of timely Western assistance, as I have described in these pages (see 'Betrayal', 31 January). Perhaps Bhagwati does not realize that successful policies require years of persistence, not just a few months.

Bhagwati accuses me of naïveté for urging large-scale aid for Russia. I was told that such aid was impossible when I advocated debt reduction for developing countries in the 1980s; a stabilization fund for Poland in 1989; a cancellation of half of Poland's debts in 1990; and so on. In each case, the cynics said 'impossible' before the official community finally adopted these policies. Why doesn't Bhagwati instead chastise the G–7 governments for actually *promising* large sums to Russia $ 24 billion in 1992 and $ 28 billion in 1993, but then not delivering.

In Bhagwati's view, the false expectations that I raised concerning aid led Russia down the garden path to unnecessarily drastic measures. This bizarre assertion gets the economics exactly backwards. Russian reformers took drastic actions because Russia faced a financial calamity. Aid would have allowed *less* drastic budget cuts, and therefore more political sustainability.

No country in the region has come up with better alternatives than Polish-style stabilization. In countries other than Poland that have followed strong macroeconomic policies — such as the Czech Republic, Estonia, Latvia, Slovenia — economic recovery is underway. In countries that have eschewed such reforms — such as Romania and Ukraine — the result has been hyperinflation and collapse. If Bhagwati had familiarity with the region, he would know that his vaunted 'gradualist' stabilization strategy has been tried and has failed repeatedly.

If Russia does succeed, it won't be because of vague incantations of an illusory gradual path to monetary stability. It will be because Russia completes the policies that were started in 1992.

JEFFREY D. SACHS

Jagdish Bhagwati replies:

Jeffrey Sachs's letter is marred by false claims — that I was a critic of Poland's successes 'from the start': and that I accused him of 'naïveté for urging large-scale aid for Russia', when in fact I said that he was 'confusing exhortations with expectations'.

In asserting that I have no 'professional experience' on Poland and Russia, Sachs resorts to credentialism to discredit my review and also forgets that what he considers his great advantage was his fatal flaw. He got embroiled in local politics, allying himself with one group of politicians while denouncing in public as dishonest and knaves other politicians such as the centrist Viktor Chernomyrdin. Now the prime minister, Chernomyrdin predictably said that he had no use for Sachs, making the termination of his advisory role in Russia inevitable. Men of action are not necessarily wiser than men of reflection: Sachs wrongly confuses 'being there' with 'being correct'.

Sachs also indulges in the logical fallacy *ignoratio elenchi*, more popularly known as 'creating an Aunt Sally'. Sachs claims to have had success earlier in predicting debt relief and aid flows. But the fact that some predictions were correct does not prove that the one about aid to Russia was not incorrect! That the G–7 promised big aid flows that they did not deliver is again neither here nor there. There is a world of difference between executive promises and legislative outcomes.

The charge that more aid would have meant a less speedy cut in the budget deficit and that I have got the link backwards is also an inexcusable silliness. If aid were used only to delay the cutting of the deficit, aid would be counterproductive; the IMF conditionality that Sachs abhors would have properly prevented that. More aid would have meant more adjustment simply because the added costs of more adjustment would have been cushioned by the social safety net, labour-turnover programmes, imports of key consumer goods, etc., that would have been made possible.

The worst mistake of all is Sachs's failure to understand the distinction between shock therapy and gradualism. The question is not whether we want financial irresponsibility or not. The question is: At what speed do we eliminate it? I posed the question as clearly as anyone can, hoping that Sachs would tell us finally why gradualism would not have worked in Russia, instead of resorting to obfuscation, invective and bluster. Unfortunately, I miscalculated.

27

The Diminished Giant Syndrome: How Declinism Drives Trade Policy

THE perception, far exceeding the reality, of American decline is having subtly harmful consequences for US international economic policy. The curse of declinism, manifest from the mid-1980s but contained by the Bush administration, was indulged to excess by Bill Clinton's campaign. Its political success in ending Republican presidential reign adds a lethal edge to the prospect that US leadership will be sacrificed to the myopic and self-indulgent pursuit of 'what's in it for us' economic policies in the world arena.

The American mood parallels Great Britain's at the end of the nineteenth century. Germany and the US had emerged on the world economic scene as major players, threatening the end of the British Century. Today it is Japan that has emerged, threatening to open a Pacific Century. As was Great Britain at that time, America has been struck by a 'diminished giant syndrome' — reinforced by the slippage in the growth of its living standards in the 1980s. This affliction has caused a loss of confidence in America's inherited post-war trade policies.

When the syndrome hit Great Britain, unilateral free trade had been the received doctrine, with Germany and the US seen, correctly, as embracing tariffs to protect nascent industries. The ensuing debate was about renouncing British unilateralism, which had been practiced with a passion for nearly half a century. In the US a parallel view has grown — with presumably immense influence in the Clinton administration — that America too has disarmed itself unilaterally in trade while others compete 'unfairly', and that the time has come to shift from being patsies who turn the other cheek to becoming aggressive traders.

The British reality of asymmetrical trade barriers, that survived that nineteenth-century debate, is matched today only by America's perception of the same. This perception is grossly disproportionate to the reality, but it is driving Washington toward trade policies that could well endanger the post-war trading system that it has so assiduously nurtured for over forty years. It rests on a measure of self-serving exaggeration and distortion of facts, all a result of the panic and petulance that attend the diminished giant syndrome. Two examples should illustrate.

First, the belief is strong on Capitol Hill that, in the post-war period of nearly half a century, America gave away trade concessions and collected few in return. This was true in a few cases, as with developing countries and Europe right after the Second World War. But after the earliest rounds of multilateral negotiations, in every successive round America has sought and gained balanced concessions. Indeed, by most judgments the proposed 'Dunkel Draft' agreement for the Uruguay Round of the General Agreement on Tariffs and Trade (GATT) is heavily unbalanced in America's favour. Reciprocity, not unilateralism, has been America's motto in trade through nearly all its history. The contrary notion rests on a myth. But, held with conviction, it fuels the sense that America needs to switch from a multilateral exchange of concessions to unilateral demands for unrequited concessions by others. The earlier bargains were 'unfair'. Thus the new order should redress the imbalance that America's altruism spawned and which the aggrieved power can now ill afford.

Second, the notion that Japan is 'closed' is by now accepted among many as an article of faith. It continually leads to demands for managed trade in the shape of commitments by Tokyo for quantitative import targets and export concessions by Japanese industries. But these demands do not distinguish between 'openness' and 'penetrability'. The Japanese market is open to manufactured imports, largely as a result of the trade liberalizations of the early 1980s. The US market, on the other hand, is dominated by voluntary export restraints (on automobiles, among other items) and anti-dumping actions, from which Japan has abstained. But there remain many complaints of the difficulty of penetration resulting from Japanese institutions and practices that create witting and unwitting roadblocks to market access.

These cascading complaints are often a reflection of the fact

that the Japanese economy has different institutional features that are a consequence of its history. Japan's success in escaping colonization and its policy of selectively importing foreign technology and ideas — and even of keeping foreigners at a distance within Japan — have prevented the extensive acculturation that other countries such as China and India went through over a century ago. Japan has been exposed to this process only since its post-war occupation. By now, however, the nation is changing rapidly. The new pace of acculturation is reflected in the prominent Japanese novelist Junichiro Tanizaki's poignant essay, 'In Praise of Shadows', which laments the passing of the old Japan. But acculturation works not merely through the conventional diffusion of American culture. It also operates through the extensive presence abroad of Japanese multinationals, and hence Japanese executives and their families.

The perception that the Japanese market is open and substantial has finally led to an increased willingness to undertake the added fixed costs necessary to enter it. The complaints about Japan's impenetrability are a clear sign that Japan is, in fact, being penetrated effectively. The unfamiliarity of the terrain is generating unreasonable demands that the Japanese landscape be remade in America's own image. The results of this penetration are reflected in the unprecedented rise in the late 1980s in the ratio of manufactured imports to GNP and as a share of total imports. Demands for widespread changes in Japanese institutions and for managed trade, quite aside from their potential for damage to a rules-based world trading regime, thus reflect a panic that is not justified by the unfolding situation.

Japan's chronic payments surplus is not a sign of its 'closed' market or of predation by Japanese exporters in America's 'open' market. Balance of payments surpluses and deficits reflect macroeconomic factors, not trade barriers. Occasionally, concerned Congressional representatives will how to this economic logic. More often, however, they revert to what they think is surely 'obvious'. Thus many in Congress now seek to renew the Super 301 provision of the 1988 Omnibus Trade and Competitiveness Act, which would enable the Clinton administration to tag countries such as Japan as unfair traders — the criterion being that the competing nation accounts for more than 15 per cent of the US trade deficit. In her confirming testimony, even the president's chief economist, Laura D'Andrea Tyson, appeared to give a nod to this notion of a trade barrier-caused payments deficit.

The Japanese trade surplus has of course grown even as its trade barriers have come down. Nor should it be forgotten that, for a longer period than the 'chronic' Japanese surplus, there existed the dreaded 'dollar shortage' after the Second World War — and America would hardly accuse itself of being a closed or closing economy during those years of extensive trade liberalization. Nonetheless, the Japanese surplus creates an inexorable sense that this 'proves' that Japan is 'closed' and, in turn, it drives demands for foolish changes in US trade policy. The corrosive influence of these sentiments and misunderstandings is manifest in policy shifts that are already diluting the US commitment to multilateralism, even as the president offers occasional support for the Uruguay Round.

UNILATERALISM HURTS GATT

Support for aggressive unilateralism has grown. Threats of protectionist retaliation when others fail to meet either multilateral or bilateral treaty obligations is not the issue. It is only an issue when Washington uses its economic power to attempt to secure new concessions or changes in established trade practices that it unilaterally declares unfair or unacceptable. Such trade threats create the impression, now worldwide, that America believes in the law of the jungle rather than the rule of law — especially when these trade retaliations themselves are illegal under GATT.

The Clinton campaign unfortunately committed itself to reviving the lapsed Super 301 legislation in its manifesto, 'Putting People First'. This proposed legislation, alongside the attachment to the use of unilateralism, has added yet another objection to US acceptance of the Dunkel Draft to settle the Uruguay Round: Washington now seeks to make the use of 301-type trade retaliation legal under GATT. This demand is most unlikely to be met since, as GATT chief Arthur Dunkel is supposed to have remarked, the best thing that the US did for the GATT was to start down the 301 and Super 301 road, thus unifying an outraged and alarmed world behind the trading regime.

The problem with the embrace of aggressive unilateralism is that, in the end, other countries will not suffer it gladly. The use of Super 301 in 1989 did not work against India and Brazil, both refusing to bow to US demands. Japan responded tangentially and eventually settled with few concessions. Taiwan and South Korea made small concessions to avoid being named. The European Community (EC) was left unmolested, having made amply clear its intention not to be browbeaten.

The reaction in Japan to the prospect of reviving Super 301 is likely to be more spirited this time. The Matsushita Committee report and business groups have argued for Japan to arm itself with Super 301 legislation of its own; there has been similar talk in Europe. Undoubtedly some countries would take the US to the GATT dispute settlement process if it became clear that, unlike the Bush administration, which tended to moderate the use of such actions, the Clinton administration was enthusiastic for them.

Widespread use of Super 301-style tools would create an environment in which countries, even if not engaged in trade wars, would be charging each other unilaterally with unfair trade practices, psyching each other out with tough talk and threatened action. The atmospherics would become conducive to a breakdown of the trust and confidence necessary to maintaining an orderly, predictable trading system — precisely the climate in which protectionism may flourish. An excellent illustration is provided by the threatened use of the anti-dumping clause by Detroit's Big Three automobile makers. Once they thought that the Clinton administration favoured aggressive action against foreign competition they resorted to the 'unfair trade' mechanism to secure their ends, as would be expected. But once foreign firms are unilaterally characterized as predatory or as being unfairly assisted by their own governments, or once foreign governments are accused of protecting their home turf — as indeed the Clinton people are given to doing — the outbreak of real trade wars looms that much larger.

DANGER OF TRADE BLOCS

Declinist sentiments may push the United States dangerously close to regionalism. Again there is an interesting parallel with Britain. In nineteenth-century Britain those who wanted to resort to (reciprocal) protection often also favoured imperial preference, which would reserve British colonies for British goods, against Germany and America.

Today the enthusiasm for regional free trade areas is dressed up as a great free trade move. But it is evident that the principal motivation is protectionist: Mexico becomes America's preferential market, with Japan and the EC at a disadvantage. Surely the relatively lukewarm enthusiasm among most American business groups for the Uruguay Round – as compared to passionate support for the North American Free Trade Agreement – can be attributed in large part to the fact that any advantages America gains under GATT are equally doled out to rivals in the EC and Japan, while under NAFTA they flow asymmetrically to the US.

As long as the talk of 'head to head' confrontation with the EC and Japan drives US policy – with its zero-sum implication that their success means America's failure – Washington will move toward preferential trading arrangements. As it pushes yet further into South America, Washington will certainly provoke an Asian trading bloc. Unless the US stops NAFTA at Mexico and turns firmly toward GATT-based multilateralism, a likely consequence of its obsession with decline will be a fragmented world of four blocs: an augmented EC; NAFTA extending into the Americas; a Japan-centered Asian bloc; and a fourth 'bloc' of marginalized nations such as those of South Asia and Africa whose recent shift toward outward trade will be frustrated by preferential trade arrangements. That would be a tragedy.

Pessimism about America's ability to lead in the teeth of its diffidence and declinism is only accentuated when focusing on the prospects it faces in trade policy. Economists, whose science is soft rather than hard, are inordinately pleased when their predictions prove correct. Nonetheless, in the present instance my failure would please me all the more.

28

President Clinton versus Prime Minister Peel: The Obsession with Reciprocity

In 1846, Prime Minister Robert Peel, speaking in Parliament for a British policy of unilateral free trade, had argued eloquently:

I trust the Government . . . will not resume the policy which they and we have found most inconvenient, namely, the haggling with foreign countries about reciprocal concessions, instead of taking that independent course which we believe to be conducive to our own interests. Let us trust to the influence of public opinion in other countries — let us trust that our example, with the proof of practical benefits we derive from it, will at no remote period insure the adoption of the principles on which we have acted.

As US trade policy founders on the shoals of reciprocity, crippling the post-war leadership of that great nation on the world trading system, the 'proof of practical benefits' from her 'first mover's advantage' in unilateral deregulation and openness in modern sectors such as finance and telecommunications is indeed beginning to move other nations to follow the US course. President Clinton needs to ponder Prime Minister Peel's words, abandon the counsel of his current advisers, and change course.

Indeed, except when it aggressively seeks unrequited trade concessions from others under threat of sanctions, US trade policy has now become a prisoner of the doctrine of reciprocity, where no trade concession is made unless matched by the other nation's and access to the home market must be equal to that offered by others.

This was manifest in the withdrawal of the US from the WTO pact on banking and financial services because there were 'insufficient' reciprocal concessions by other countries and it wished to discriminate against these nations. Remarkably, leadership on the issue was seized by Sir Leon Brittan and the European Union; their efforts rescued the pact until 1997 with its non-discriminatory MFN feature intact.

The same exaggerated concern with reciprocity, reflecting the assertion that the Japanese markets are closed whereas the US markets are open, has prompted the Japan-baiting Section 301 tactics, with demands for instant gratification in the form of managed-trade targets such as on purchases of parts. It led to the thinly-disguised debacle at Geneva in the US–Japan car dispute. By threatening Japan with punitive tariffs which were bound and whose imposition would thus be manifestly WTO-illegal, and by demanding that Japanese firms in the US buy more US-made parts when in fact the TRIM agreement at the WTO forbids such domestic-content pressures, the US wound up with the predictable outcome of the Japanese government facing down these tactics and demands almost contemptuously. The US not merely lost face; it also lost the respect of the world community as a trade leader, mindful of rules and respectful of multilateralism.

But even as this obsession of the Clinton administration with reciprocity, carried well beyond that required by the political necessity that dictates that *some* element of reciprocity is inevitable when governments work on the twin assumptions that trade is good but imports are bad, economists have come to recognize that Peel's assertion of the virtues of unilateralism is coming into its own.

Thus, for some years now, many inward-looking developing countries, having learnt from the example of the success of the outward-oriented economies of the Far East, have been opting for 'autonomous' trade liberalizations outside of the reciprocity framework of the GATT negotiations.

Then again, cross-country studies of manufacturing firms by McKinsey & Company's Global Institute, as recently reported by the economists Martin Baily and Hans Gersbach in *Brookings Papers* (1995), have confirmed the obvious: that vigorous competition in open markets is a surefire recipe for the adoption of best-practice production methods that make firms truly competitive.

In the financial sector also, the openness and flexibility of

London and New York, maintained regardless of reciprocity to date, has clearly enabled them to attain and retain status as world class financial centres. By contrast, the excessive and counterproductive regulations of Tokyo have now created the serious prospect of Tokyo's loss of business to the more deregulated Singapore.

For these reasons, and not because of 301 pressures, there is visible considerable nervousness and a desire for deregulation and freeing of protected markets in Japan and, for that matter, in Europe and elsewhere. A country may be able to protect its own markets, developing what the Europeans call 'national champions'. But these champions will have puny muscles; they will not be able to compete against the lean and mean firms of the US which is ahead of the curve in openness and deregulation. This recognition is now manifest in Japan's famed MITI where visitors, including myself, have observed that old-style concerns with industry policy have now been replaced with concerns to ensure industry's foreign competitiveness by deregulation that would match that of the US. While *gaiatsu* (foreign pressure) exerted through 301 tactics has failed miserably in recent years, evidently the *gaiatsu* of external example is beginning to work well instead!

Unfortunately, the infatuation with reciprocity that grew to gargantuan size on the US scene in the late 1980s will not disappear easily. Declinism, the 'diminished giant syndrome' as I called it then, had partly prompted it, just as it had when many similarly urged reciprocity on unilateralist Britain at the end of the nineteenth century when Germany and the US emerged as rivals. Fortunately, declinism has disappeared with America's economic turnaround and Japan's economic difficulties.

But there is also the insidious legacy of both amateur and professional economic theorizing of the time. The amateur theorizing concerns the repeated claims that Japan's 'sanctuary' markets unfairly threaten the US firms. Behind their barriers, the Japanese firms are assumed to earn sizeable monopoly profits which are then used to compete their rivals into bankruptcy, thus lending force to US demands for reciprocal access. The problem with this contention is simply that it has no factual basis. Serious analysts agree that most of the Japanese industries are fiercely competitive; besides, their rates of return are generally low and below those of the US.

But the professional theorizing in favour of reciprocal access is more serious. It comes from my brilliant MIT student, Paul Krugman, who formalized the Silicon Valley entrepreneurs' reciprocitarian complaints. In essence they argued that, with their own markets closed while the US markets were open, the Japanese firms had two markets (and hence larger production) while the US firms had one. So, Japanese firms would have lower costs, reflecting the higher production levels because of learning by 'doing'.

Whatever the model's merits at the time, it can be seen now to be as ludicrous as its assumptions. Learning depends critically on the environment. A policy of openness and deregulation, especially in modern industries such as present-day finance and telecommunications, leads to the learning and efficiency that build competitiveness. The model, and the unfortunate support it provided for hypersensitivity to reciprocity, only serve to remind us of the witticism that illogic alone can protect the economist from the unfortunate consequences of making wrong assumptions.